HAMLET

The New Variorum Edition

In Two Volumes
Volume II

William Shakespeare

Edited by Horace Howard Furness

DOVER PUBLICATIONS, INC.
Mineola, New York

Published in Canada by General Publishing Company, Ltd., 30 Lesmill Road, Don Mills, Toronto, Ontario.

Bibliographical Note

This Dover edition, first published in 2000, is an unabridged republication of the tenth edition of the work originally published in 1877 by J. B. Lippincott & Company, Philadelphia, to which has been added a detailed Table of Contents.

Library of Congress Cataloging-in-Publication Data

Shakespeare, William, 1564–1616.
    Hamlet / William Shakespeare ; edited by Horace Howard Furness.
      p. cm.
    Originally published: 10th ed. Philadelphia : J.B. Lippincott, 1877, in series: A new variorum edition of Shakespeare ; v. 3–4.
    Includes bibliographical references and index.
    ISBN 0-486-41095-1 (v. 1) — ISBN 0-486-41156-7 (v. 2)
    1. Princes—Denmark—Drama. 2. Shakespeare, William, 1564–1616. Hamlet. I. Furness, Horace Howard, 1833–1912. II. Title.

PR2807.A2 F85 2000
822.3'3—dc21

00–020149

Manufactured in the United States of America
Dover Publications, Inc., 31 East 2nd Street, Mineola, N.Y. 11501

CONTENTS TO VOLUME II—APPENDIX

APPENDIX

APPENDIX

THE DATE, AND THE TEXT

THE year in which Shakespeare first wrote *Hamlet* has given rise to much discussion.

From fourteen to sixteen years before the date of the first edition that has come down to us of this tragedy, allusions to a Play apparently bearing the same title, and containing the same plot, are to be found in contemporary literature.

The question that still divides the Shakespearian world is, stated broadly, whether or not this older drama be one of Shakespeare's earliest works.

The earliest allusion to it was pointed out by DR FARMER, in his *Essay on the Learning of Shakespeare* (ed. ii, p. 85). The allusion is contained in an Epistle 'To the Gentlemen Students of both Universities,' written by Nash, and prefixed to Greene's *Menaphon*, or *Arcadia*, printed in 1589. Nash, referring to the makers of plays of that day, says: Ile turne backe to my first text, of studies of delight, and talke a little in friendship with a few of our triviall translators. It is a common practice now a daies amongst a sort of shifting companions, that runne through every arte and thrive by none to leave the trade of *Noverint* whereto they were borne, and busie themselves with the indevours of art, that could scarcelie latinize their necke-verse if they should have neede; yet English Seneca read by candle-light yeeldes manie good sentences, as *Blould is a begger*, and so foorth : and if you intreate him faire in a frostie morning, he will affoord you whole *Hamlets*, I should say Handfulls of tragical speaches.* But O grief! *Tempus edax rerum ;*—what is it that will last always? The sea exhaled by drops will in continuance be drie; and Seneca, let bloud line by line, and page by page, at length must needs die to our stage.'

MALONE (*Variorum*, 1821, vol. ii, p. 372), after quoting this passage, continues : Not having seen the first edition of this tract till a few years ago, I formerly doubted whether the foregoing passage referred to the tragedy of *Hamlet ;* but the word *Hamlets* being printed in the original copy in a different character from the rest, I have no longer any doubt upon the subject. It is manifest from this passage that some play on the story of *Hamlet* had been exhibited before the year 1589; but I am inclined to think that it was not Shakespeare's drama, but an elder performance, on which, with the aid of the old prose *Hystorie of Hamblet*, his tragedy was formed. The great number of pieces which we *know* he formed on the performances of preceding writers, renders it highly probable that some others also of his dramas were

---

* Thus far in this extract I have followed Staunton ; the rest is as Malone quotes it. ED.

5

constructed on plays that are now lost.   Perhaps the original *Hamlet* was written by Thomas Kyd; who was the author of one play (and probably of more) to which no name is affixed.   The only tragedy to which Kyd's name is affixed (*Cornelia*) is a professed *translation* from the French of Garnier, who, as well as his translator, imitated Seneca.   In Kyd's *Spanish Tragedy*, as in Shakespeare's *Hamlet*, there is, if I may say so, a play represented *within a play;* if the old play of *Hamlet* should ever be recovered, a similar interlude, I make no doubt, would be found there; and somewhat of the same contrivance may be traced in the old *Taming of a Shrew*, a comedy which perhaps had the same author as the other ancient pieces now enumerated.   Nash seems to point at some dramatic writer of that time who had originally been a scrivener or attorney, and instead of transcribing deeds and pleadings, had chosen to imitate Seneca's plays, of which a translation had been published many years before.   Shakespeare, however freely he may have borrowed from Plutarch or Holinshed, does not appear to be at all indebted to Seneca; and therefore I do not believe that he was the person in Nash's contemplation.'   Malone was inclined to believe at first that the person alluded to as having left the trade of *Noverint* (that is, of attorney, from the Latin formula with which deeds began : *Noverint Universi*, and of which our *Know all men* is a translation) could not have been Shakespeare; but afterwards, on a review of the numerous legal terms and phrases used by Shakespeare, he changed his opinion, and suspected that Shakespeare 'was early initiated in at least the forms of law; and was employed, while at Stratford, in the office of some country attorney who was at the same time a petty conveyancer, and perhaps also the Seneschal of some manor-court.'

In reference to the date of this *Epistle* of Nash's, DYCE in his edition of Greene's *Works* (vol. i, p. ciii), after citing the title of *Menaphon. Camillas alarum to slumbering Euphues, in his melancholie Cell at Silexedra,* &c., &c., 1589, 4to, adds : ' First printed 1587,' but gives no authority in the way of title or imprint.   This date of 1587 has been followed, on Dyce's authority, by Collier and one or two others, but KNIGHT thinks it is a mistake, and Dyce himself seems to have had a misgiving on the subject, for in his second edition of Shakespeare he gives the date of Greene's *Menaphon* as 1589 with ' [qy if first printed in 1587 ?] ' after it.   The surer date, therefore, is 1589.   This date is of importance; it makes Shakespeare twenty-five years old, instead of twenty-three, when Nash thus alluded to him,—no small gain for those who maintain that this older *Hamlet* was written by him.

C. A. BROWN (*Shakespeare's Autobiographical Poems*, p. 254) maintains emphatically that Shakespeare's tragedy was referred to in the phrase ' whole *Hamlets* of tragical speaches,' and that Shakespeare himself was alluded to as having left the trade of *Noverint;* and further, that his reason for assigning 1589 as the date of the composition of *Hamlet* is ' founded solely on this passage from Nash.   It is to be understood as regarding its original state before the alterations and enlargements had taken place.'   . . .   ' If there exists a description of that elder play, I do not hesitate in saying it is Shakespeare's and no other's, provided the Ghost appears in it. According to the old black-letter Quarto, whence the tragedy is derived, the killing of the Prince's father was public; consequently, no Ghost was employed to reveal it to the son.   Now the change from an open slaying, with some show of cause, to a secret murder, involving the necessity of the Ghost's appearance to seek revenge, is so important, so wonderful an invention for the dramatic effect of the story, that I cannot imagine it belonged to any but Shakespeare.   Should I be mistaken in this opinion, still I appeal to Nash's authority, published in 1589, that Shakespeare's

Hamlet had been played : the word in Italics, " *Hamlets,*" proving that *Hamlet* was then on the stage, and that it had been written by a " Noverint," or lawyer's clerk ; while the examples which I have given of Shakespeare's law-phrases, and which might be multiplied tenfold at least, if sought in all his works, prove that such must have been the employment of his early days.'

KNIGHT agrees with Brown, and sees nothing, on the score of Shakespeare's youth, ' extravagant in his [Brown's] belief,' adding : ' Let it be remembered that in that very year [1589], when Shakespeare was twenty-five, it has been distinctly proved by Collier that he was a sharer in the Blackfriars theatre with others, and some of note, below him in the list of sharers.'

In reference to this *Epistle* of Nash's, STAUNTON says : ' Here the " shifting companions, that runne through every arte," brings so distinctly to mind the epithet " an absolute *Johannes Factotum,*" which Nash's sworn brother, Greene, in his *Groats-worth of Wit,* &c., 1593, applied to Shakespeare ; and " the trade of *Noverint*" so well tallies with the received tradition of his having passed some time in the office of an attorney, that, *primâ facie,* the allusion to *Hamlet* would seem directly levelled at our author's tragedy. But then interposes a difficulty on the score of dates. Shakespeare, in 1589, was only twenty-three [*sic*] years old,—too young, it may be well objected, to have earned the distinction of being satirized by Nash as having " run through every art." It is asserted, too, on good authority that an edition of the *Menaphon* was published in 1587, and if that earlier copy contained Nash's *Epistle,* the probability of his referring to Shakespeare is considerably weakened.'

Just as Malone's edition of 1790 was issuing from the press, there was found at Dulwich College a large Folio MS volume, containing valuable information respecting theatrical affairs from the year 1591 to 1609. The volume is in the handwriting of Philip Henslowe, a proprietor, or joint lessee, of more than one theatre during that period, and contains, among others, his accounts of receipts and expenditures in connection with his theatrical management. Malone reprinted copious extracts from this MS in the first volume of his edition; but it was reprinted entire by the 'Shakespeare Society' in 1845, with a valuable Preface by Collier, from which the following extracts are given, which, although not strictly germane to the First Quarto of *Hamlet,* contain much important aid in estimating the value of the theories respecting it. But, first, a few words as to the *Diary* itself : ' Henslowe,' says Collier, ' was an ignorant man, even for the time in which he lived, and for the station he occupied ; he wrote a bad hand, adopted any orthography that suited his notions of the sound of words, especially of proper names (necessarily of most frequent occurrence), and he kept his book, as respects dates in particular, in the most disorderly, negligent, and confused manner. Sometimes, indeed, he observes a sort of system in his entries ; but often, when he wished to make a note, he seems to have opened his book at random, and to have written what he wanted in any space he found vacant. He generally used his own pen, but, as we have stated, in some places the hand of a scribe or clerk is visible ; and here and there the dramatists and actors themselves wrote the item in which they were concerned, for the sake, perhaps, of saving the old manager trouble ; thus, in various parts of the manuscript, we meet with the handwriting, not merely the signatures, of Drayton, Chapman, Dekker, Chettle, Porter, Wilson, Hathaway, Day, S. Rowley, Haughton, Rankins, and Wadeson ; but, although frequently mentioned, we have no specimen of the handwriting of Nash, Ben Jonson, Middleton, Webster, Marston, or Heywood.' Where the names of nearly all dramatic poets of the age are to be frequently found, we might certainly count on finding that of Shakespeare, but the shadow within which Shakespeare's earthly life was spent envelops him here, too, and 'his name,' as COLLIER says, 'is not met with in any part of the manuscript.' 'At various times and for uncertain periods, Henslowe was more or less interested in the receipts obtained by players acting under the names of the Queen, Lord Nottingham, Lord Strange, Lord Sussex, Lord Worcester, and the Lord Chamberlain. The latter was the company of which Shakespeare was a member, either as actor or author, from his first arrival in, until his final retirement from, London; which company, after the accession of James I. was allowed to assume the distinguishing title of *The King's Players.*'

So much for the general character of this interesting volume; the portion of the contents that is most important is the period which it covers from 3 June, 1594, to 18 July, 1596; during the whole of this time the *Lord Admiral's Players* were jointly occupying, or possibly playing in combination at, the theatre at Newington Butts with the *Lord Chamberlain's Players;* 'and here we find by Henslowe that no fewer than forty new plays were got up and acted. For about ten days of the two years the companies ceased to perform, on account, perhaps, of the heat of the weather, and the occurrence of Lent; so that two years are the utmost upon which a calculation can be made, and the result of it is, that the audiences of that day required a new play upon an average about every eighteen days, including Sundays. The rapidity with which plays must then have been written is most remarkable, and is testified beyond dispute by later portions of Henslowe's manuscript, where, among other charges, he registers the sums paid, the dates of payment, and the authors who received the money. Nothing was more common than for dramatists to unite their abilities and resources, and when a piece on any account was to be brought out with peculiar dispatch, three, four, five, and perhaps even six poets engaged themselves on different portions of it. Evidence of this dramatic combination will be found of such frequent occurrence that it is vain here to point out particular pages where it is to be met with.' The union of the two companies of players just referred to lasted a little more than two years. Possibly it may have been merely a joint occupation of the same theatre while the Globe was building, but at any rate it is singular that while it lasted, whatever may have been its character, 'most of the old plays which our great dramatist is supposed, more or less, to have employed, and of the stories of which he availed himself, are found in Henslowe's list of this period. Here we find a *Titus Andronicus*, a *Lear*, a *Hamlet*, a *Henry V*, and a *Henry VI*, a Buckingham, the old *Taming of a Shrew*, and several others. For aught we know, Shakespeare may have had originally some share in their authorship, or if he had not, as he probably acted in them, he may have felt himself authorised, as a member of the company, to use them to the extent that answered his purpose. . . . . No fact is more clearly made out, and very much by the evidence Henslowe furnishes, than that it was a very common practice for our early dramatists to avail themselves of the materials, whether of plot, character, or language, supplied by their immediate predecessors, and even by their actual contemporaries.'

Five lines before the entry in Henslowe's diary there is this memorandum: 'In the name of God Amen, beginninge at Newington, my Lord Admeralle and my Lorde chamberlen men, as foloweth. 1594.' (It is to be borne in mind that Shakespeare was one of the 'Lorde chamberlen men' at this date.')

The entry itself is as follows:

9 of June 1594, Rd at hamlet . . . .   viij^s

In a note MALONE says: 'In the *Essay on the Order of Shakespeare's Plays*, I have stated my opinion [quoted above], that there was a play on the subject of *Hamlet* prior to our author's, and here we have a full confirmation of that conjecture. It cannot be supposed that our poet's play should have been performed but once in the time of this account, and that Henslowe should have drawn from such a piece but the sum of eight shillings, when his share in several other plays came to three and sometimes four pounds. It is clear that not one of our author's plays was played at Newington Butts; if one had been performed, we should certainly have found more.'

COLLIER'S note (p. 35, ed. *Sh. Soc.*) is as follows: 'Malone contends, we think correctly, that this was the old *Hamlet*, and not Shakespeare's play. [If this be the case], our great dramatist might adopt the story, and feel that he had a better right to do so, because the old play had been acted by his friends and fellows, or perhaps with their assistance.'

Among other peculiarities of Henslowe's diary is the custom which he adopted of marking each *new* play with the abbreviation *ne*. The above entry has no such mark; it is therefore to be inferred that it was not a first performance.

The next trace that we find of the old tragedy is in Lodge's *Wits miserie*, which also was discovered by Dr FARMER (*Essay*, &c., p. 75, second edition, 1767), who, however, supposed that the allusion by Lodge referred to Shakespeare's own play, and not to any older tragedy. Aubrey having said that Shakespeare 'did act *exceedingly well*,' Farmer denies that we have any reason to suppose so, because 'Rowe tells us from the information of Betterton, who was inquisitive into this point, and had very early opportunities of inquiry from Sir W. Davenant, that he was no *extraordinary actor*, and that the top of his performance was the Ghost in his own *Hamlet*. Yet this *chef d'œuvre* did not please; I will give you an original stroke at it. Dr Lodge, who was for ever pestering the town with pamphlets, published in the year 1596, *Wits miserie, and the Worlds madnesse, discovering the Devils incarnat of this Age*. One of these Devils is *Hate-Virtue*, or *Sorrow for another mans good Success*, who, says the Doctor, is "*a foule lubber*, and looks as pale as the visard of yᵉ ghost, which cried so miserally [*sic*] at yᵉ theator, like an oisterwife, *Hamlet reuenge*."'

This phrase, 'Hamlet, revenge!' made a deep impression on the popular mind, and is referred to more than once before the present *Hamlet* appeared and obliterated the memory of it.

DYCE (*Preliminary Note to Hamlet*, p. 100): My own conviction is . . . . that the piece alluded to by Nash and Lodge, and acted at Newington, was an earlier tragedy on the same subject, which no longer exists, and which probably (like many other old dramas) never reached the press.

STAUNTON remarks: 'After duly weighing the evidence on either side, we incline to agree with Dyce, that the play alluded to by Lodge and Nash was an earlier production on the same subject; though we find no cause to conclude that the first sketch of Shakespeare's *Hamlet*, as published in 1603, was not the piece to which Henslowe refers in his entry, connected with the performance at Newington Butts.'

In the *Variorum* of 1773, STEEVENS says: 'I have hitherto met with no earlier edition of this play [*Hamlet*] than the one in the year 1605 [1604,— *Var.* 1778], tho' it must have been performed before that time, as I have seen a copy of Speght's edition of Chaucer, which formerly belonged to Dr Gabriel Harvey (the antagonist of Nash), who, in his own handwriting, has set down the play as a performance with which he was well acquainted, in the year 1598. His words are these : "The younger sort take much delight in Shakespeare's *Venus and Adonis*, but his *Lucrece* and his tragedy of *Hamlet Prince of Denmarke*, have it in them to please the wiser sort, 1598." '

In consequence of this note of Steevens, MALONE was induced to believe that Shakespeare's *Hamlet* was first published in 1596, but afterwards, in the *Variorum* of 1821 (ii, 369), he has the following note : ' In a former edition of this *Essay*, I was induced to suppose that *Hamlet* must have been written prior to 1598, from the loose manner in which Mr Steevens has mentioned a manuscript note by Gabriel Harvey, in a copy, which had belonged to him, of Speght's *Chaucer*, in which, we are told, he has set down *Hamlet* as a performance with which he was well acquainted in 1598. But I have been favored by the Bishop of Dromore [Dr Percy], the possessor of the book referred to, with an inspection of it, and, on an attentive examination, I have found reason to believe that the note in question may have been written in the latter end of the year 1600. Harvey doubtless purchased this volume in 1598, having, both at the beginning and end of it, written his name. But it by no means follows that all the intermediate remarks which are scattered throughout were put down at the same time. He speaks of *translated Tasso* in one passage ; and the first edition of Fairfax, which is doubtless alluded to, appeared in 1600.'

Wherefore, and in consequence of the allusion to the ' inhibition ' of the players spoken of in *Hamlet*, II, ii, 320, Malone supposed *Hamlet* to have appeared first in 1600

According to SINGER (*Preliminary Remarks to Hamlet*, p. 152, 1826), the *translated Tasso*, referred to by Malone, need not necessarily have been Fairfax's translation of 1600, but Harvey may have alluded to the version of the first five books of the *Jerusalem*, published by R. C[arew] in 1594. Singer therefore 'safely places the date of the first composition of *Hamlet* at least as early as 1597.'

KNIGHT : Not a tittle of distinct evidence exists to show that there was any other play of *Hamlet* but that of Shakspere ; and all the collateral evidence upon which it is inferred that an earlier play of *Hamlet* than Shakspere's did exist may, on the other hand, be taken to prove that Shakspere's original sketch of *Hamlet* was in repute at an earlier period than is commonly assigned to its date. . . . . In Henslowe's diary, the very next entry is ' at the taminge of a shrewe ;' and Malone, in a note, adds : ' the play which preceded Shakespeare's.' When Malone wrote this note he believed that Shakspere's *Taming of the Shrew* was a late production ; but in the second edition of his ' Chronological Order ' he is persuaded that it was one of his *very early* productions. ' There is nothing,' says Knight in conclusion, ' to prove that *both* these plays thus acted were not Shakspere's.'

MALONE, in his edition of 1790, finds another reference to this old tragedy in Jonson's *The Case is Altered*, which was written before the end of 1599. It is as follows : ' But first I'll play the ghost ; I'll call him out.' The allusion is so very doubtful that Malone did not refer to it in his subsequent editions. As Gifford says, we might as well find an allusion in ' the ghost of every play that has appeared since the days of Thespis.'

The last allusion to this old tragedy that we find before the publication of the First Quarto in 1603 is given by CAPELL (*Notes*, iii, 232), and bears witness to the distinguishing phrase before quoted : *'Asinius.* Wod I were hang'd if I can call you any names but Captaine and Tucca. *Tucca.* No. Fye'st; my name's Hamlet reuenge : thou hast been at Parris garden, hast not ?'—Dekker's *Satiro-mastix,* 1602.

This allusion by Dekker may be compared, says HALLIWELL, with another passage, in *Westward Hoe,* 1607,—' I, but when light wives make heavy husbands, let these husbands play mad *Hamlet;* and crie *revenge.'* So likewise in Rôwlands's *The Night Raven,* 1618,—' I will not cry *Hamlet Reuenge* my greeues, But I will call *Hang-man Reuenge* on theeues' [p. 27, ed. *Hunterian Club,* where the date of the first edition is given as 1620]. Halliwell adds : There is also reason to suppose that another passage in the old tragedy of *Hamlet* is alluded to in Armin's *Nest of Ninnies,* 1608,—' ther are, as Hamlet saies, things cald whips in store' [p. 55, ed *Sh. Soc.* But may not this refer to the ' whips and scorns of time ' in the later Hamlet ?].

DOUCE (ii, 265) : In a poem, written by Anthony Scoloker, a printer, entitled *Daiphantus, or The passions of love,* &c., 1604, there are the following allusions to *Hamlet :* '—or to come home to the vulgars *Element,* like *Friendly Shake-speare's Tragedies,* where the *Commedian* rides, where the *Tragedian* stands on Tip-toe : Faith it should please all, like Prince *Hamlet.* But in sadnesse, then it were to be feared he would runne mad.'

> ' *Calls players fooles,* the foole he judgeth wisest,
> *Will learne them action,* out of Chaucer's Pander. . . . .
> Puts off his cloathes, his shirt he only weares,
> Much like *mad-Hamlet;* thus his passion teares.'

In *Eastward Hoe,* by Chapman, Jonson, and Marston, 1605, says STEEVENS, there is a fling at the hero of this tragedy. A footman named Hamlet enters, and a tankard-bearer asks him : ' 'Sfoote, Hamlet, are you mad ?' MALONE says there was no satire intended. *Eastward Hoe* was acted at Shakespeare's own play-house (the Blackfriars), by the ' children of the revels.'

STEEVENS also cites from Dekker's *Bel-man's Night walkes,* 1612 :—' But if any mad Hamlet, hearing this, smell villainie, and rush in by violence,' &c.

DR LATHAM (*Two Dissertations on Hamlet,* &c. London, 1872, p. 87) says that we ' know the date' of this older *Hamlet* to be 1589, but gives no proofs for his assertion, and in the next sentence weakens our faith in his figures by stating that Shakespeare was then in his twenty-third year. We are still more puzzled by finding on page 91 a reference to the *Hamlet* of 1598. Under either date, I believe, Dr Latham denies that this older *Hamlet,* referred to by Nash, Lodge, and others, was written by Shakespeare, but maintains that ' it is wholly or partially preserved ' in the text of the *Bestrafte Brudermord.* See Note prefixed to a translation of this old German drama in this volume.

The foregoing are all the allusions, I believe, to a play of *Hamlet* which many critics believe preceded Shakespeare's tragedy. Some of these allusions that occur after 1602 probably refer to Shakespeare's tragedy, but I have given them all because they are mentioned by one or another of the editors, and because it is proper that in an edition for students, like this, every item of evidence should be set forth.

We now come to something more definitely connected with Shakespeare than anything thus far.

STEEVENS discovered the following entry in the *Stationers' Registers :*

[1602] xxvj ^{to} Julij

James Robertes   Entred for his Copie vnder the handes of master PASFEILD and
                  master waterson warden A booke called '*the Revenge of
                  HAMLETT Prince [of] Denmarke*' *as yt was latelie Acted
                  by the Lord Chamberleyne his servantes* . . . . . . vj^d

(I have exactly followed the transcript of the entry as given by ARBER.) Whether
or not the book, thus licensed, was printed in this year we cannot tell; no copy of it
has survived.   That it was Shakespeare's tragedy we can have but little doubt, since
it was acted by the company to which he belonged.   In the following spring, in 1603,
'The Lord Chamberlain's Servants' became 'The King's Players,' and the Quarto published in that year states that it had been acted 'by his Highness' servants.' 'Thus we
see,' says COLLIER, 'that in July, 1602, there was an intention to print and publish a
play called *The Revenge of Hamlet, Prince of Denmarke*, and this intention, we may
fairly conclude, arose out of the popularity of the piece, as it was then acted by "the
Lord Chamberlain's Servants," who, in May following, obtained the title of "the
King's Players."   The object of Roberts, in making the entry, was to secure it to
himself, being, no doubt, aware that other printers and booksellers would endeavor
to anticipate him.   It seems probable that he was unable to obtain such a copy of
Hamlet as he would put his name to; but some inferior and nameless printer, who
was not so scrupulous, having surreptitiously secured a manuscript of the play, however imperfect, which would answer the purpose, and gratify public curiosity, the
edition bearing date 1603 was published.'
    This edition of 1603 is reprinted in this volume; reference to the title-page will
show that although it is there stated to have been printed 'at London' 'for N. L.
[*i. e.* Nicholas Ling] and John Trundell,' no printer's name is mentioned.   Hence
COLLIER'S inference that the 'nameless printer' was some unscrupulous rival of
James Robertes.   But DYCE says (*Introduction to Hamlet*, p. 100, 1866), 'we have no
proof that Roberts was not the "nameless printer" of the Quarto of 1603; on the contrary, there is reason to suspect that he was, since we find that he printed the next Quarto
of 1604 for the same Nicholas Ling, who was one of the publishers of the Quarto
of 1603.'   The title-page of the Quarto published in 1604 states that it was printed
by J.[ames] R.[obertes] for N.[icholas] L.[ing]; wherefore Dyce's inference is
probably correct that James Roberts was also 'the printer of the Quarto of 1603,
or what we now call the First Quarto.'   COLLIER, in his second edition, in support
of his conjecture that Robertes did not print Q₁, calls attention to the fact that Q₂
'has Ling's device on the title-page, and that it was possibly from his types; the
edition of 1604 was printed for, not by, him;' be that as it may, it is a matter of
very small moment, and one thing is certain: that the edition, by whomsoever
printed, reflects but little credit on the printer; it gives a very inadequate idea of
the tragedy as it was acted, if not at the very time, certainly within a few months
afterwards.   Possibly, if Roberts was the printer, this consciousness withheld his
name from the title-page of a publication whose chief object appears to have been to
forestall the market until something better could be furnished.
    It will be noticed, by referring to the Reprint p. 37, that on the title-page of
the Quarto of 1603 it is stated that it had been acted 'in the two Vniuersities of
Cambridge and Oxford.'   'No evidence,' says CLARENDON, 'has yet been discovered of the occasion on which the play was acted at the two universities; but if we
might hazard a conjecture, it seems not improbable that it might have been at some

entertainment in honor of the king's accession, and it may have been selected as being connected with the native country of his queen.'

Of this edition of 1603 only two copies have survived, and both are imperfect; one lacks the title-page, and the other the last leaf. The Quarto of 1604 was the earliest copy known down to 1823, when a copy of the Quarto of 1603 was found by Sir Henry Bunbury, who gives the following account of it in his *Correspondence of Sir Thomas Hanmer*, London, 1838, p. 80 :—'[The only copy of the First Quarto] known to be in existence, was found by me in a closet at Barton, 1823. This curiosity (for a great curiosity it is, independently of its being an unique copy) is now in the possession of the Duke of Devonshire; it probably was picked up by my grandfather, Sir William Bunbury, who was an ardent collector of old dramas. For the satisfaction of bibliographers, I take this opportunity of recording the particulars of the little volume, which contained this *Hamlet* of 1603. It was a small quarto, barbarously cropped, and very ill-bound; its contents were as follows :— *Merchant of Venice*, 1600, complete; *Merry Wives of Windsor*, 1602, do.; *Much Ado about Nothing*, 1600, do.; *Midsummer Night's Dream*, 1600, do.; *Troilus and Cressida* (wanting the title-page); *Romeo and Juliet*, 1599, complete; *Hamlet*, 1603 (wanting the last page); *Second Part of Henry the Fourth*, 1600, complete; *First Part* of do., 1598, do.; *Henry the Fifth*, 1602, do.; *Richard the Third*, 1602, do.; *Two Noble Kinsmen*, 1634, with MS corrections of the text. I exchanged the volume with Messrs Payne and Foss, for books to the value of £180, and they sold it for £230 to the Duke of Devonshire.'

See also *The Athenæum*, 18 Oct. 1856, for a fuller account of this volume. There was a reprint of this copy made by Payne and Foss in 1825, which is said to be exceedingly accurate. It was lithographed in facsimile in 1858, under the supervision of COLLIER, at the expense of the Duke of Devonshire'. It was again reprinted in 1860 under the supervision of S. TIMMINS, esq., with the Quarto of 1604 printed on opposite pages,—a highly valuable edition. It takes its place also among the lithographic reprints by E. W. ASHBEE, under the supervision of HALLIWELL, and it is from this edition that the present reprint, in this volume, is made. It is also reprinted with extreme accuracy in the Cambridge Edition.

The CAMBRIDGE EDITORS state (I think without sufficient authority) that this copy 'belonged to Sir Thomas Hanmer, though he does not appear to have mentioned it in his notes to Shakespeare, or in his correspondence, and its existence was not known till his library came into the possession of Sir E. H. [*sic*] Bunbury in 1821.' Sir H. E. Bunbury, as we have seen, believed that its original owner was his grandfather, who was the nephew of Sir Thomas Hanmer.

In 1856 the second copy, lacking the title-page, was bought from a student of Trinity College, Dublin, by a Dublin book-dealer, for one shilling, and sold by him for £70; it was afterwards bought by Mr Halliwell for £120, and is now in the British Museum.

The next year after the First Quarto was issued the Second Quarto was published, with the following title-page :

THE | Tragicall Hiftorie of | HAMLET, | *Prince of Denmarke*. | By William Shakefpeare. | Newly imprinted and enlarged to almoft as much | againe as it was, according to the true and perfect | Coppie. | AT LONDON, | Printed by I. R. for N. L. and are to be fold at his | fhoppe vnder Saint Dunftons Church in | Fleetftreet. 1604.

Lowndes mentions an edition of 1604 as 'printed by J. R. for N. Landure,' but this is probably a mistake, which is repeated, however, in Halliwell's *Shakespeariana*. It has found its way into several editions,—Knight's, for instance, as well as Elze's and François-Victor Hugo's. ELZE called attention to it in *The Athenæum*, 11 Feb. 1860, and gave as his authority Halliwell's *Shakespeariana*. HALLIWELL replied in the same Journal, 25 Feb. 1860: 'I fear I have fallen into a blunder respecting the name of the publisher of the *Hamlet* of 1604. The initials are all that are given in the imprint, but the *fish* in the printer's device over the letters N. L. would seem clearly to show that *Ling*, not Landure, was the publisher.'

The statement that this edition is 'enlarged to almost as much again as it was' is correct enough for a bookseller's announcement,—there are about five hundred and sixty-seven lines lacking to make it exactly as much again. The First Quarto numbers two thousand one hundred and forty-three lines; the Second Quarto about three thousand seven hundred and nineteen.

This notable difference in quantity, coupled with a marked difference in words, phrases, and even in the order of the Scenes, together with a change in the names of some of the characters, has given rise to an interesting discussion, which probably will never be decided: it is whether, in the Quarto of 1603, we have the first draught of Shakespeare's tragedy, which the author afterwards remodelled and elaborated until it appears as we now have it substantially, in the Quarto of 1604, or is the First Quarto merely a maimed and distorted version ' of the true and perfect coppie' ?

COLLIER was, I think, the first to maintain, from a careful comparison of the two, that the copy of 1603 was printed from manuscript taken down in short-hand from the players' mouths. SINGER in his earlier edition in 1826, and in his later in 1856, suggests that it may have been 'printed from an imperfect manuscript of the prompt books, or the play-house copy, or stolen from the author's papers. It is next to impossible that it can have been taken down during the representation. . . . . The variations . . . . are too numerous and striking to admit of a doubt of the play having been subsequently revised, amplified, and altered by the poet.'

CALDECOTT (*Preface to Hamlet*, 1832, p. vi) : [This First Quarto exhibits] in that which was afterwards wrought into a splendid drama, the first conception, and comparatively feeble expression of a great mind.

The next and the chiefest advocate of this view is KNIGHT, and his arguments are here given almost in full; his extracts from Q₁ are omitted, and references to the lines of the Reprint in this edition are substituted. His remarks are to be found in the *Introductory Notice to Hamlet* in his edition of Shakespeare's Plays, p. 87; no difference has been observed between his first and last editions, twenty-four years apart.

In the reprint of the edition of 1603 [by Payne and Foss, 1825], it is stated to be the 'only known copy of this tragedy *as originally written by Shakespeare*, which he afterwards altered and enlarged.' We believe that this description is correct; that this remarkable copy gives us the play as originally written by Shakespeare. It may have been piratical, and we think it was so. It may, as Mr Collier says, have been 'published in haste from a short-hand copy taken from the mouths of the players.' But this process was not applied to the present *Hamlet;* the *Hamlet* of 1603 is a sketch of the perfect *Hamlet*, and probably a corrupt copy of that sketch. We agree with Caldecott, and we think, further, that this first conception was an early conception; that it was remodelled,—'enlarged to almost as much againe as it was,'—at the beginning of the seventeenth century; and that this original copy being then of comparatively little value was piratically published. . . . . The highest interest of this edition consists, as we believe, in the opportunity which it affords of studying the growth, not only of the great poet's command over language,—not only of his dramatic skill,—but of the higher qualities of his intellect,—his profound philosophy, his wonderful penetration into what is most hidden and obscure in men's characters and motives. We request the reader's indulgence whilst we attempt to point out some of the more important considerations which have suggested themselves to us, in a careful study of this original edition.

And, first, let us state that all the *action* of the amended *Hamlet* is to be found in the first sketch. The play opens with the Scene in which the Ghost appears to Horatio and Marcellus. The order of the dialogue is the same; but, in the Quarto of 1604, it is a little elaborated. The grand passage beginning: ' In the most high and palmy state of Rome,' is not found in this copy; and it is omitted in the Folio. The Second Scene introduces us, as at present, to the King, Queen, Hamlet, Polonius, and Laertes, but in this copy Polonius is called Corambis. The dialogue here is much extended in the perfect copy. We will give an example. [Compare lines 173–179 of Q₁ with I, ii, 77–86.]

We would ask if it is possible that such a careful working up of the first idea could have been any other work than that of the poet himself? Can the alterations be accounted for upon the principle that the first edition was an imperfect copy of the complete play, ' published in haste from a short-hand copy taken from the mouths of the players ? Could the players have transformed the line, ' But I have that within which passeth show,' into ' Him have I lost, I must of force forego.' The haste of short-hand does not account for what is truly the refinement of the poetical art. The same nice elaboration is to be found in Hamlet's soliloquy in the same scene. In the first copy we have not the passage so characteristic of Hamlet's mind: ' How weary, stale, flat, and unprofitable seem to me all the uses of this world.' Neither have we the noble comparison of ' Hyperion to a satyr.' The fine Shaksperian phrase, so deep in its metaphysical truth, ' a beast *that wants discourse of reason,*' is in the first copy, ' a beast *devoid of reason.*' Shakspere must have dropt verse from his mouth, as the fairy in the Arabian tales dropt pearls. It appears to have been no effort to him to have changed the whole arrangement of a poetical sentence, and to have inverted its different members; he did this as readily as if he were dealing with prose. In the first copy we have, ' as if increase Of appetite had grown by what it look'd on.' In the amended copy we have, ' by what it fed on.' Such changes are not the work of short-hand writers.

The interview of Horatio, Bernardo, and Marcellus with Hamlet succeeds as in the perfect copy, and the change here is very slight. The scene between Laertes and Ophelia in the same manner follows. Here again there is a great extension. The injunction of Laertes in the first copy is contained in these few lines. [See lines 331–339 of Q₁.]

Compare this with the splendid passage which we now have. Look especially at the four lines beginning, ' For nature, crescent,' &c. [I, iii, 11–14], in which we see the deep philosophic spirit of the mature Shakspere. Polonius and his few precepts next occur; and here again there is a slight difference. The lecture of the old courtier to his daughter is somewhat extended. . . . .

The character of Hamlet is fully conceived in the original play, whenever he is in action, as in this scene [where Hamlet encounters the Ghost]. It is the contemplative part of his nature which is elaborated in the perfect copy. This great scene, as it was first written, appeared to the poet to have been scarcely capable of improvement.

The character of Polonius, under the name of Corambis, presents itself in the original copy with little variation. We have extension, but not change. As we proceed we find that Shakspere, in the first copy, more emphatically marked the supposed madness of Hamlet than he thought fit to do in the amended copy. Thus Ophelia does not, as now, say,—' Alas, my lord, my lord, I have been so affrighted,' but she comes at once to proclaim Hamlet *mad*. [See lines 664–672 of Q_I.]

Again, in the next scene, when the King communicates his wishes to Rosencrantz and Guildenstern, he does not speak of Hamlet as merely put ' from the understanding of himself;' but in this first copy he says,—' Our dear cousin Hamlet Hath lost the very heart of all his sense.' In the description which Polonius, in the same scene, gives of Hamlet's madness for Ophelia's love, the symptoms are made much stronger in the original copy. [See Q_I, lines 788–792.]

It is curious that, in Burton's *Anatomy of Melancholy*, we have the stages of melancholy, madness, and frenzy indicated as described by Celsus; and Burton himself mentions frenzy as the worst stage of madness, ' clamorous, continual.' In the first copy, therefore, Hamlet, according to the description of Polonius, is not only the prey of melancholy and madness, but by ' continuance' of frenzy. In the amended copy the symptoms, according to the same description, are much milder,— a sadness—a fast—a watch—a weakness—a lightness,—and a madness. The reason of this change appears to us tolerably clear. Shakspere did not, either in his first sketch or his amended copy, intend his audience to believe that Hamlet was essentially mad; and he removed, therefore, the strong expressions which might encourage that belief.

Immediately after the scene of the original copy in which Polonius describes Hamlet's frenzy, Hamlet comes in and speaks the celebrated soliloquy. In the amended copy this passage, as well as the scene with Ophelia which follows it, is placed after Hamlet's interview with the Players. The soliloquy in the first copy is evidently given with great corruptions, and some of the lines appear transposed by the printer; on the contrary, the scene with Ophelia is very slightly altered. The scene with Polonius, now the Second Scene of the Second Act, follows that with Ophelia in the first copy. In the interview with Guildenstern and Rosencrantz the dialogue is greatly elaborated in the amended copy; we have the mere germ of the fine passage, ' This goodly frame,' &c.—prose with almost more than the music of poetry. In the first copy, instead of this noble piece of rhetoric, we have the somewhat tame passage:—' Yes, faith, this great world you see contents me not; no, nor the spangled heavens, nor earth, nor sea; no, nor man, that is so glorious a creature, contents not me; no, nor woman too, though you laugh.' . . . .

[Page 90.] Our readers, we think, will be pleased to compare the following passage of the first copy and the amended play, which offers us an example of the most surpassing skill in the elaboration of a first idea. [Compare Q_I, lines 1222–1231, with III, ii, 49–69.]

Schlegel observes that ' Shakspere has composed "the play" in *Hamlet* altogether in sententious rhymes, full of antitheses.' See the opening speech of the Player King [III, ii, 145–150]. Here is not only the antithesis, but the artificial elevation, that was to keep the language of the Interlude apart from that of the real drama. Shakspere has most skilfully managed the whole business of the Player King and

Queen upon this principle; but, as we think, when he wrote his first copy, his power as an artist was not so consummate. In that copy the first lines of the Player King are singularly flowing and musical; and their sacrifice shows us how inexorable was his judgement. [See Q , lines 1274-1279.]

The soliloquy of the King in the Third Act is greatly elaborated from the first copy; and so is the scene between Hamlet and his mother. In the Play, as we now have it, Shakspere has left it doubtful whether the Queen was privy to the murder of her husband; but in this scene, in the first copy, she says,—' But, as I have a soul, I swear by heaven, I never knew of this most horrid murder.' And Hamlet, upon this declaration, says,—' And, mother, but assist me in revenge, And in his death your infamy shall die.' The Queen, upon this, protests—' I will conceal, consent, and do my best, What stratagem soe'er thou shalt devise.' In the amended copy the Queen merely says,—' Be thou assured if words be made of breath, And breath of life, I have no life to breathe What thou hast said to me.'. . . .

The madness of Ophelia is beautifully elaborated in the amended copy, but all her snatches of songs are the same in both editions. What she sings, however, in the First Scene of the original copy is with great art transposed to the Second Scene of the amended one. The pathos of—' And will he not come again?' is doubled, as it now stands, by the presence of Laertes.

We are now arrived at a scene in the Quarto of 1603 altogether different from anything we find in the amended copy. It is a short scene between Horatio and the Queen, in which Horatio relates Hamlet's return to Denmark, and describes the treason which the King had plotted against him, as well as the mode by which he had evaded it by the sacrifice of Rosencrantz and Guildenstern. The Queen, with reference to the '—— subtle treason that the King had plotted,' says: ' Then I perceive there's treason in his looks,' &c. [See Q₂, lines 1756-1759.]

This is decisive as to Shakspere's original intentions with regard to the Queen, but the suppression of the scene in the amended copy is another instance of his admirable judgement. She does not redeem her guilt by entering into plots against her guilty husband; and it is far more characteristic of the irregular impulses of Hamlet's mind, and of his subjection to circumstances, that he should have no confidences with his mother, and form with her and Horatio no plans of revenge. The story of Rosencrantz and Guildenstern is told in six lines. [See Q₂, 1773-1778.] The expansion of this simple passage into the exquisite narrative of Hamlet to Horatio of the same circumstances presents, to our minds, a most remarkable example of the difference between the mature and the youthful intellect.

The scene of the Grave-digger, in the original copy, has all the great points of the present scene. The frenzy of Hamlet at the grave is also the same. Who but the poet himself could have worked up this line—' Anon, as mild and gentle as a dove,' into—' Anon, as patient as the female dove, When that her golden couplets are disclosed, His silence will sit drooping.'? The scene with Osric is greatly expanded in the amended copy. The catastrophe appears to be the same; but the last leaf of the copy of 1603 is wanting [*sic* in Knight's last edition]. . . . .

We must express our decided opinion, grounded upon an attentive comparison of the original sketch with the perfect play, that the original sketch was an early production of our poet. The copy of 1603 is no doubt piratical; it is unquestionably very imperfectly printed. But if the passage about the ' inhibition' of the players fixes the date of the perfect play as 1600, which we believe it does, the essential differences between the sketch and the perfect play,—differences which do not depend upon the corruption of a text,—can only be accounted for upon the belief that there was a considerable interval between the productions of the first and second copy, in which the author's power and judgement had become mature, and his peculiar habits of philosophical thought had been completely established. /This is a matter which does not admit of proof within our limited space, but the passages which we have already given from the original copy do something to prove it. . . . .

In proof that *Romeo and Juliet* is one of Shakspere's early plays, Hallam points out the 'want of that thoughtful philosophy which, when once it had germinated in Shakspere's mind, never ceased to display itself.' The *Hamlet* of 1604 is full of this 'thoughtfull philosophy.' But the original sketch, as given in Q₁, exhibits few traces of it in the form of didactic observations. Note the following passages which are *not there found:* 'For nature crescent,' &c., I, iii, 11; 'This heavy-headed revel,' &c., I, iv, 17; 'There is nothing, either good or bad, but thinking makes it so,' &c., II, ii, 244; 'I could be bounded in a nutshell,' &c., II, ii, 249; 'Bring me to the test,' &c., III, iv, 142; 'I see a cherub,' &c., IV, iii, 47; 'Nature is fine in love,' &c., IV, v, 157; 'There's a divinity,' &c., V, ii, 10. Further, the plays which belong to the beginning of the seventeenth century, as Hallam points out, indicate a censuring of mankind. If, then, this quality be not found in the original sketch of *Hamlet*, we may refer that sketch to an earlier period. It is remarkable that in this sketch the misanthropy, if so it may be called, of Hamlet can scarcely be traced; his feelings have altogether reference to his personal griefs and doubts. The first *Hamlet* was, we think, written when this 'bitter remembrance,' whatever it was, had no place in his heart. Note the following passages, which indicate these morbid feelings, which are wanting in Q₁: 'How weary, flat, stale, and unprofitable,' &c., I, ii, 133; 'Denmark's a prison,' &c., II, ii, 239; 'I have of late . . . . lost all my mirth,' &c., II, ii, 288. The soliloquy, 'To be, or not to be,' &c., where the outpourings of a wounded spirit are generalized in the Q₁, III, i, 56; 'Absent thee from felicity awhile,' &c., V, ii, 334, 335. These examples are sufficient, we think, to show that we have internal evidence that the original sketch and the augmented and perfect copy of *Hamlet* were written under different influences and habits of thought.

[The argument against the early composition of *Hamlet*, derived from the negative testimony of Francis Meres, who in 1598 mentioned twelve plays of Shakespeare's, among which *Hamlet* is not named, Knight (*Chronology of Shakespeare's Plays*) opposes by contending that Meres's list is not to be supposed to be complete. 'The expression which Meres uses, "for comedy *witness*," implies that he selects particular examples of excellence.']

Thus far Knight. No one, I think, can deny that his remarks are shrewd and forcible.

A writer in THE EDINBURGH REVIEW (April, 1845, vol. lxxxi, p. 378) maintains the same views, as follows:

The reason of the thing has long made it be admitted as probable that Shakespeare's activity as an original dramatist must have commenced much sooner than the dates commonly assigned to the oldest of his works in the received copies. . . . . In these circumstances we find that a play named *Hamlet*, and described by marks tending to establish (though not decisively establishing) its identity with a play of Shakespeare's is mentioned as existing in 1587, or the poet's twenty-fifth year [*sic*]; and that similar notices occur in 1594 and 1596. We are thus entitled to assume it as probable that *Hamlet* did exist, in one shape or another, from the oldest of those

dates.   If any of us still have difficulty in believing that this drama, as we possess
it in its complete form,—the most deeply contemplative of all its author's works,—
could have come into being as an effusion of his earliest manhood, there is now at
hand the hypothesis,—rendered plausible by what we know in regard to other works
of his,—that, as first composed, *Hamlet* may have been not inconsiderably unlike
what it is in the shape best known to us.   So far we are entitled to proceed without
knowing that any edition exists which throws more light on the question.

   When we open the Quarto of 1603, the conjectures previously formed become
certainties.   Though we had otherwise no reason to suspect that *Hamlet* had existed
in a different shape before its publication in 1604, we should at once perceive that it
had done so; and that the edition of 1603, notwithstanding the imperfections and
blunders which make it perhaps the very worst of all the badly printed plays of the
time, does yet present no unsatisfactory representation of the state and peculiarities
of the work in its earlier form.   Afterwards, taking again into account the external
circumstances, we find them to square, as exactly as could be expected, with the
internal evidence afforded by a comparison of the editions.   In short, we have no
difficulty in believing that Q_1 gives us, although with provoking imperfections and
corruptions, a form of the work older by a good many years than that in which we
have been accustomed to study it,—a form exhibiting such dissimilarities from the later
one, as indicate not obscurely the progress of the poet's mind, from the unripe fervor
of early manhood to the calmer and more philosophic inspiration of perfect maturity.

   [Page 380.]   In other words, the older Play evolves but partially either of the elements of the Prince's contemplative character,—the philosophic and the poetic,—those
deep and fine touches of a moody and cheerless yet noble philosophy,—those dazzling flashes of imaginative light which make all that is around them blaze up with
reflected splendor.   But it wants more of the philosophy than of the poetry.   Although the story, as Knight has appositely observed, does really, when we reflect
upon its accumulation of revolting and bloody incidents, present an aspect which
throws it back into the school of *Titus Andronicus;* although it is one which, perhaps, Shakespeare would not in later years have selected, in its full mass of horror
at least, as a fit subject for genuine tragedy; yet, even in the earliest form in which
we possess the drama, we perceive the theme to have been idealized by the high
working of a great poetic mind.   Thus, in the First Act, which puts in representation the most imaginative features of the idea, there is not in the most prominent
parts a material difference between the two editions.   The mighty conception had
arisen in the young poet's imagination with full and ripe distinctness; and that rich
strength of words and of illustrative images, that bright array of lights and shades
caught from external nature and reflected back upon the poetic heart, that early ease
and felicity which he had proved in his youthful lyrics and descriptive verses, here
enabled him to bestow on the induction of his drama a development to which subsequent changes in his own mind qualified him to add but little.   The Ghost scenes
receive only some additional polishing and a few additional strokes of imagery.   It
is in the minor scenes,—the scene at court, and the interview of Corambis (the Polonius of the old play) with his two children,—that the material changes occur.   In
them there is a remodelling of almost everything.   Even in the First Act, however,
there are not a few instances which would exemplify well the gradual progress by
which the character of Hamlet reached its full complement of representation.   His
first soliloquy, although glaringly misprinted in the older copy, is as apt an illustration as any.

In subsequent parts of the play, Shakespeare's views are perceived to have changed in many most important respects during the interval between the two copies. Much of this is seen in the elaboration of particular passages, of which specimens are given by Knight. Much of it will be seen, also, on an intelligent and patient analysis, in those transpositions which some critics would charge altogether to the account of the copyists. One of these may be noticed as illustrative of those broader conceptions of his art,—of that increase of gentleness and calmness, and of that addiction to gradual preparation for startling and violent scenes of passion,—which were taught to the poet by increased experience in thought and in dramatic composition.

A whole scene is transposed; the famous interview with Ophelia, where he madly reproaches and reviles her,—a scene whose harshness may not always be perceived in the closet, but from which, in acting, no skill has been able, unless by a gross violation of the text and meaning of the author, to remove an impression approaching to actual pain.

Let us recollect the place which this scene, so unharmonious in its palpable effect, holds in the drama. Let us recollect, also, how we are prepared for its approach.

In the play, as we have it in the newer edition, Hamlet's assumed madness is announced by degrees. First comes Ophelia to describe that pitiful act in which he had seemed to bid her an everlasting farewell. Then the King talks of Hamlet's 'transformation,' and sets the court-sponges to suck out the heart of his secret; and Polonius reasons wisely, like many other wise men, from false premises. After this, Hamlet himself enters, reading; and next ensues that most characteristic dialogue with Polonius, and afterwards with Rosencrantz and Guildenstern, in which there alternate deep scorn, wild and aimless taunting, majestic imagination, and philosophic thought,—and that unspeakably profound pathos, that hopeless sinking of the heart, which, recurring with increasing frequency as the drama proceeds, makes us feel more and more keenly that, after all, the Prince's madness was not wholly put on,—that the struggle of his intellect with his will had truly shaken the foundations upon which reason builds her seat. Afterwards come the Players; and when they have departed, the Prince bursts out into that terrific outbreak of passion, of self-reproach, of self-contempt, of grief, of hatred, and, finally, of determined revenge, which concentrates his whole history, and an abstract of his whole character, within the compass of less than a hundred lines. Thus, in the altered play, closes Act Second; and it is only at the opening of the Third that we find the scene with Ophelia.

But all this was originally managed by the poet in a different manner. The scene with Ophelia was inserted long before in all its harshness; nay, with an abruptness bringing it somewhat closer to the scene in the original Novel,—that coarse and mean model from which, for this as for much else, so very many things were borrowed. In the sketch the scene comes immediately after the wise reasonings of Polonius; and, introduced by the soliloquy, 'To be, or not to be,' it is Hamlet's first appearance since his interview with his father's spirit. The rough outline of the fine dialogue with Polonius and the two sponges immediately follows it. This was what Shakespeare planned when he first wrote the play; we know what he did when he came to revise it.

The change may be regarded in several lights. It may be thought of as bringing out the strong scene with Ophelia, after more gradual and complete preparation,—as thus at once softening the seeming sternness of the scene itself, and developing Hamlet's character, both as it was and as it seemed, with a more effective climax. Or it may be thought of in a higher view, as an expedient bearing upon the harmonious arrangement of the Play as a whole,—as enabling the imagination to contemplate the dramatic panorama more easily, and the sympathy to flow more quickly and smoothly with the current of the emotion. It may be thought of as infusing greater breadth and simplicity, and a stronger degree of contrast, into the masses into which the drama naturally falls. According to the old arrangement, there was in some measure a frittering away of strength,—a dividing of efforts which would have been better made in unison. The energetic passion of the scene with Ophelia breaks out suddenly and passes away without effect. The remainder of the Act is in a key far less passionate. And, again, when we come to the Third Act the vehemence of the play-scene breaks out with equal unexpectedness. Take the altered shape of the drama. How differently does everything now proceed! The Second Act is now an uninterrupted series of scenes, marked by repose; a broad mass of light on the picture, with heavy shadows on this side and on that. The mind of the Prince, the minds of all who stand about him, are for a time quiescent, brooding, expectant. And then, in the Third Act, of which the transposed scene is the opening, comes the convulsion, shock after shock;—the wild insults heaped upon Ophelia,—the suppressed suspicion which begins the play-scene,—the mad jubilee of revenge and hate which reigns in its close,—the vainly remorseful prayer of the murderer, with Hamlet's fiendish paroxysm of cool malice as he watches him on his knees (one of the most significant touches in the whole piece),—and, last of all, the fiery haste and terrible impressiveness of the scene in the Queen's chamber, which contains the slaughter of Polonius, the fearfully earnest reproof administered to the guilty mother, the apparition of the murdered father, awful and portentous.

The most eminent followers of Knight, although differing from him somewhat in minor details, are DELIUS, ELZE, STAUNTON, and DYCE, and their views will be set forth briefly before the arguments of the other side are given. It is well to remember the point under discussion: whether, making a full allowance for a certain percentage of typographical errors, the differences between Q_1 and Q_2 are due to a remodelling of the play by Shakespeare, or merely to the very imperfect transcript from which Q_1 was printed. KNIGHT may be considered as the chiefest advocate of the former theory, COLLIER the earliest of the latter.

DELIUS agrees with Knight in so far as that the variation between Q_1 and Q_2 is apparently too great to be wholly explained on Collier's hypothesis. After eliminating all the sources of corruption which Collier enumerates, there still remain differences between the two texts which can be attributed to the poet and to the poet alone, *e. g.* the change of names; the transposition of scenes; rhymed verses which no piratical printer would or could make; and, finally, the scene between the Queen and Horatio must have been Shakespeare's work. Knight does not seem to have given due weight to the corruption which Q_1 received at the unskilful hands of the printers. As Q_1 now stands, Shakespeare never wrote it, with all its omissions, abbreviations, and sophistications. If the old tragedy of which we have traces were not a youthful production of Shakespeare's, it is very possible that he drew largely from it for his own tragedy. Robertes was probably hindered from publishing the edition for which he took out a license by the unwillingness of the actors to permit the public to see the Play in any other way than on the stage. But as the interest of the

public in the Play continued, N. L. and John Trundell started the fraudulent speculation of offering for sale their version of the Play as though it were the same as that
which was holding the stage in 1603. [The omission to account for the way in which
N. L. and John Trundell obtained possession of a version while James Robertes could
not, is not to be laid to the desire for condensation on the part of the present ED.] This
imposture, and such impostures were not uncommon in those days, coupled with the
fear lest this spurious version should prove injurious to the acted Play, incited the
actors of Shakespeare's company to put their genuine version in press. The title-
page of Q_2 proves that its publication was due to the fraudulent edition of the preceding year. The words: ' *enlarged to almost as much againe as it was,*' possibly do
not refer to any remodelling of the Play by Shakespeare, but to Q_1, upon which the
object was to throw discredit in all respects, as an unauthorized and defective edition.
But, according to the usage in theatrical matters of those times, such antagonistic
competition among publishers applied only to a *new* drama; wherefore the version
of *Hamlet*, as set forth in the Qq, may be safely attributed to the beginning of the
seventeenth century, or about the middle of Shakespeare's productive career.

ELZE, (*Einleitung. Hamlet.* Leipzig, 1857, p. xix), after quoting the references
by Nash, Henslowe, Lodge, &c., to the old tragedy, says: All these allusions have
been referred to a *Hamlet* preceding Shakespeare's, because it is universally assumed
that Shakespeare arrived in London in 1586, and did not take the *Hamlet* in hand,
as it then existed, until 1597–1598. And the reason why this date is selected is because Francis Meres, in his *Palladis Tamia* of that year, did *not* enumerate *Hamlet*
among Shakespeare's other Plays. Now, from the connection in which this passage
occurs, it follows by no manner of means that Meres intended to give a complete
list of all Shakespeare's works that had appeared up to that time, but merely
vouchers sufficient to prove his assertion that Shakespeare was the Plautus and
Seneca among Englishmen; Meres mentioned as many comedies as tragedies, just
six of each kind, probably those that he held in highest esteem, and which would be
the most likely to carry the name of the poet down to posterity. For not only *Hamlet*, which assuredly did not exist at that time in the complete shape which has inspired
the wonder of succeeding ages, but *Pericles* also and *Henry VI*, are lacking in this
list of Meres's Plays, and they were undoubtedly written and had been acted before
1598. The assumption of the existence of an ante-Shakespearian *Hamlet* is a mere
make-shift to which recourse has been had through inability to reconcile the foregoing facts and allusions with Shakespeare's *Hamlet* as it was subsequently put forth.

[Page xxii.] There are two arguments which have hitherto escaped notice, by
means of which we can approximate to the date of the earliest sketch of *Hamlet*.
First: Shakespeare's ridicule of Euphuism, not only in the character of Osric, but
also of the Grave-digger, who is a Euphuist in his way. In the scene with the
latter Hamlet alludes to the 'three years' since the 'age has grown so picked.'
Now Lily's *Euphues* appeared, according to Malone and Collier, in 1579, according to Watts, in 1580, and according to Drake, in 1581; allowing some time for it
to permeate all classes of society, we have the year 1585 as about the time to which
Hamlet may allude. Secondly: in 1585, Shakespeare's son Hamnet was born,
one of twins. This unusual increase to his family must have added greatly to the
distress of Shakespeare's already straitened circumstances; and the youthful father
and poet was driven to London to seek his fortunes. It is perhaps not too much to
say that it was this little son that forced him to London. Is it not readily conceivable that at the very beginning of his career he should have chosen a subject for his

pen which bore the same name as his beloved boy, and that he should have recurred to it afterwards with undisguised preference? Hamnet died in 1596; and this blow, which must have fallen most heavily on the father, may possibly have led him to take up once more this spiritual child of the same name. Who can estimate the effect which grief for his only son may not have had in producing that deep-seated melancholy and distaste for the vanity of the world which have found in this tragedy their immortal expression?

[Page xxiv.] Further speculations are idle, as to how often or in what years Shakespeare remodelled *Hamlet;* it suffices to know that in Q_1 we have the next to the last version, and in Q_2 the last version. It must not be understood that the revision was made between these dates; on the contrary, the allusion to the 'inhibition' [see Notes, II, ii, 320] proves that it must have been between 1600 and 1602.

TIMMINS (*Preface to the Devonshire Hamlets*, p. ix): From allusions in literature at the close of the sixteenth century it is a reasonable assumption that this drama, bearing date 1603, may have been a recognized work of Shakespeare, publicly performed several years before that date and surreptitiously printed in that year. This would allow the further inference that the subject was a favorite one with Shakespeare, and that about the beginning of the seventeenth century he revised his early drama, and 'enlarged it to almost as much againe as it was.' . . . . My conviction is that in Q_1 we have a 'rough-hewn' draft of a noble drama (written probably 1587–1589), 'diverse times acted by His Highnesse servants' till 1602, when it was 'en tered' for publication, and soon afterwards 'enlarged,' and 'shaped,' as it appears in Q_2, by the divine bard's maturer mind.

STAUNTON: What really concerns us is to know whether, making large allowance for omissions and corruptions due to the negligence of those through whose hands the manuscript passed, the edition of 1603 exhibits the play as Shakespeare first wrote it and as it was 'diverse times acted.' We believe it does. The internal evidence is to our judgement convincing that in this wretchedly printed copy we have the poet's first conception (written probably at an early stage of his dramatic career) of that magnificent tragedy which, remodelled and augmented, was published in 1604.

DYCE (ed. 2, 1866): It seems certain that in Q_1 (as is the case with respect to the earliest Quartos of *The Merry Wives of Windsor* and *Romeo and Juliet*) we have Shakespeare's first conception of the Play, though with a text mangled and corrupted throughout, and perhaps formed on the notes of some short-hand writer, who had imperfectly taken it down during representation. Not to dwell on other particulars, the names borne by Polonius and Reynaldo in Q_1 are alone sufficient to show that the said Quarto exhibits a form of the tragedy very different from that which it afterwards assumed in Q_2 and F_1.

The following remarks of HUNTER'S belong to this side of the question, but are not inserted in chronological order because they do not attempt to discuss the point that is immediately at issue.

HUNTER (*New Illust.*, &c., ii, 204): The exact mode of the preparation of this tragedy will probably never be fully ascertained. Shakespeare seems to have worked upon it in a manner different from what was his usual practice. We collect from the newly-discovered copy, not only that large additions were made to the play after it had been presented at the theatres, but that very material changes were made in the distribution of the scenes and the order of events. This seems to show that there was no period when the poet sat down to his work having a settled project in his mind, and meaning to work out the design continuously from the opening to the catastrophe; and this may be, after all, the true reason of the difficulty, which has always been felt, of determining what the character really is in which the poet meant to invest the hero of the piece. It may account, also, for the introduction of scenes which appear to have been written for the sake of themselves alone; beautiful in themselves, but neither necessary for the maintenance of a general harmony in the whole, nor for carrying on the business of the story. To this want of continuity in the composition of the piece, and of having the mind steadily intent on one design, plan, and object, is also to be attributed the great falling off in the later portions, and the lame and impotent manner in which what ought to be the grand catastrophe is at last brought about.

It should perhaps be noticed that GERVINUS follows Knight.

Thus far the advocates of the theory that in Q_1 we have a reproduction, imperfect and garbled it is true, of the old *Hamlet*, alluded to by Nash and others, and written by Shakespeare in his youth, and revised by him in his maturer years.

On the other hand it is contended that Q_1 and Q_2 represent the same version, the difference between the two editions indicating not the growth of Shakespeare's mind, but the carelessness or incompetence of short-hand writers, transcribers, and printers.

COLLIER, as has been before stated, believes that Q_1 was put forth by some nameless and unscrupulous printer from an imperfect manuscript of a play surreptitiously obtained, and that but few copies were sold, as its worthlessness was soon discovered. As accurate reprints of this Quarto are accessible, Collier says: 'it will be unnecessary to go in detail into proofs to establish, as we could do without much difficulty, the following points:

' 1. That great part of the play, as it there stands, was taken down in short-hand.

' 2. That where mechanical skill failed the short-hand writer, he either filled up the blanks badly from memory, or employed an inferior writer to assist him.

' 3. That although some of the scenes were carelessly transposed, and others entirely omitted, in the edition of 1603, the drama, as it was acted while the short-hand writer was employed in taking it down, was, in all its main features, the same as the more perfect copy of the tragedy printed with the date of 1604. It is true that in the edition of 1603, Polonius is called Corambis, and his servant Montano, and we may not be able to determine why these changes were made in the immediately subsequent impression; but we may, perhaps, conjecture that they were names in the older play on the same story, or names which Shakespeare at first introduced and subsequently thought fit to reject. We know that Ben Jonson changed the whole *dramatis personæ* of his *Every Man in his Humour*. [DYCE, after quoting this last sentence, adds: ' Perhaps they were names which Shakespeare had originally retained from the earlier drama, and which, on revising and altering his tragedy, he changed to Polonius and Reynaldo.']

' But although we entirely reject Q_1 as an authentic *Hamlet*, it is of high value in enabling us to settle the text of various important passages. It proves, besides, that certain portions of the play as it appears in F_1, which do not form part of Q_2, were originally acted, and were not, as has been hitherto imagined, subsequent introductions.'

W. W. LLOYD (*Critical Essay on Hamlet*, contributed to SINGER's Second Edition, p. 345): I confess that the *Hamlet* of Q_1, marred and mangled as it is, does not give me the impression of one of Shakespeare's early works, and if some early allusions to a play of *Hamlet* are his, I should infer it must have been in yet another prior phase.

TYCHO MOMMSEN (*Athenæum*, 7 Feb. 1857): The discovery of the last leaf of the earliest *Hamlet* having some months ago excited great interest on both sides of the water, and again directed the public attention to that curious edition, you would, perhaps, allow me, though a foreigner, a column of your paper, in order to state the results of a careful examination of both this and of another First Quarto,—that of *Romeo and Juliet*, 1597,—which seem to be no first sketches, as some have imagined, but mere misrepresentations of the genuine text. This opinion is borne out by the following reasons:

1. There are in both editions very striking inconsistencies of the action, owing not only to omissions or transpositions, but also to certain alterations of the text, which cannot but have originated in foreign interpolation.

2. It seems improbable that a juvenile writer should have at first conceived and written his dramas in a shorter form. We might rather have expected the contrary, of which we have some instances in Schiller's *Don Carlos* and Goethe's *Goetz von Berlichingen*.

3. The deviations are less numerous and less considerable in the beginning of either play; this may be accounted for by the probability that the reviser's patience forsook him towards the end of his irksome task.

4. Very often the blunders of the mutilated *Hamlet* seem caused by abbreviations, eked out in the wrong way by an unskilful and ignorant reviser. Even the new names, which we find in the *Hamlet* of 1603,—Corambis for Polonius, and Montano for Reynaldo,—might be traced to the same source, if we think them pieced out from *Cor.* and *Mon.*, which might mean *Courtier* and *Man of Polonius*.

5. I apprehend that I discern two hands employed, one after the other, upon this *Hamlet*,—the one being probably that of an actor, who put down from memory a sketch of the original play as it was acted, and who wrote very illegibly; the other that of a bad poet, most probably ' a bookseller's hack,' who, without any personal intercourse with the writer of the notes, availed himself of them to make up his early copy of *Hamlet*. Numerous mistakes of the ear fall to the share of the former contributor, whereas much more numerous misconceptions of the eye and wrong out-piecings are to be attributed to the latter. The compositor may have added to these blunderings.

6. The earliest edition of *Romeo and Juliet*, though decidedly better, participates on a limited scale in the same errors.

7. Both copies concur in a great many vulgarisms; both often turn poetry into prose, and abound with every kind of shallow repetition,—now of set phrases, oaths, expletives, then (which is strongly indicative of interpolation) of certain lines and passages of peculiar energy, such as would impress themselves more literally upon the memory of the hearer. By these iterations the reviser endeavored to compensate for what was lost of the original.

8. Some of the characters in this *Hamlet* differ more from the authentic editions than others. This might be as easily explained upon the supposition of their being more imperfectly set forth in the notes, on account of certain peculiarities of the actors who personated them, or from the writer's being less acquainted with some scenes, as upon the supposition that Shakespeare afterwards retouched or remodelled them.

9. Out of these positions it would appear that there must be about the said copies a general tameness and prosaic languor, which leads us far away from everything that is peculiar to the well-known over-bold style of Shakespeare's juvenile productions.

10. This is chiefly observable in those scenes and passages which are entirely different from what we read in their stead in later copies. In those of the mutilated *Hamlet* there is an absolute want of that metaphorical language which was one of the fairy gifts of the poet from his cradle; while those of the spurious *Romeo and Juliet* read somewhat better, but are nevertheless far too bad for Shakespeare,—perhaps even some nice verses not excluded, which glare in the middle of other peculiarities of the interpolated copy as the *pannus purpureus* of Horace. Some of the additions in both copies are of a flat, sententious kind, not unfrequently out of keeping with the rest,—some are dull, coarse, nay, vulgar,—others are temporary allusions to theatrical affairs, which may very possibly have been of the players' making, even of the original ones belonging to Shakespeare's company.

11. Innumerable blunders with regard to scansion and metre are found only in these earliest editions, and in indissoluble connection with tautologous insertions, omissions, &c. Also, single alternate rhyme now and then balks the ear of the reader.

12. The above-mentioned coincidence of blunders is mainly to be met with in those lines and passages which serve to connect pieces of the genuine text (the ligatures).

13. The most curious misunderstandings of every kind are found on almost every page.

14. Such I take to be the genuine characteristics of all interpolations whatever; and it is by these means and no other that we endeavor to eliminate the spurious parts of the Homeric epics and of our own Nibelungen Lay.

15. But while we have every reason to set these editions down as thoroughly sophisticated, and no reason but mere speculation to deem even *part* of their peculiarities genuine, we must not forget that they are nevertheless of considerable practical value. Whenever the reading of such a copy, in some obscure passage, coincides with that of the better text, we can hardly think it corrupt; on the other hand, a various reading of the mutilated copy, though in itself without any authority, may lead us to discover typographical errors in the better edition. It is of some use, also, to have involved and difficult passages often rendered there with different words; it then aids us in the way of interpretation. But the greatest advantage, perhaps, is on the score of scenic effect; it is common to all the adulterated editions of Shakespeare that they explain much more of the stage business than the genuine ones; another proof that the foundation of such copies was that of actual performance.

16. Nevertheless, we ought to hesitate much before we adopt any of the peculiar readings of such editions into our text. [The language has been here and there very slightly modified where the meaning was obscure. ED.]

GRANT WHITE (*Introduction to Hamlet*, p. 10): The great difference in length between the texts of the first and the second edition has been generally regarded of late years as presumptive evidence that the play was revised and largely added to before the printing of the latter. And this opinion has been thought to derive very material support from the noteworthy announcement upon the title-page of the second edition; of which opinion that announcement, however (owing to what I regard as a misapprehension of its meaning), is rather the source. On this title-page the play is said to be ' Newly imprinted and enlarged to almost as much againe as it was, according to the true and perfect coppie,' which has been accepted on all hands as meaning that the play has been 'enlarged' by the author. But upon the very face of it, and especially under the circumstances, has it not clearly a very different purport? The previous edition is so corrupt, disconnected, and heterogeneous, that the least observant reader, even of that day when plays were printed so care-lessly, must have seen that as a whole it was but a maimed and mutilated version of the true text, and in some parts a mere travestie of it. It seems to be very plainly indicated that the enlargement announced on the title-page of Q_2 was the conse-quence of the procurement of a complete and authentic text, and was merely the work of the printer or publisher, and not of the author.

' A close examination of the text of Q_1 has convinced me that it is merely an im-perfect, garbled, and interpolated version of the completed play, and that its com-parative brevity is caused by sheer mutilation, consequent upon the haste and secrecy with which the copy for it was obtained and put in type. . . . . In III, i, the phrase, 'to a nunnery go,' is baldly repeated eight times within a few lines; showing that the reporter jotted down a memorandum of Hamlet's objurgation, but forgot to vary it as Shakespeare did,—a kind of evidence of the share that he had in the text of 1603, which he has left us on more than one occasion. The phrases 'for to,' ' when as,' and ' where as,' Shakespeare's avoidance of which has been noted in the *Essay on the Authorship of King Henry the Sixth*, occur in the earliest version several times; but in the Quarto of 1604 the two latter are not found at all, the former but once, and in the Folio it disappears entirely. [See III, i, 167.] . . . . It has been observed that many of the passages found in the later, but not in the earlier, ver-sion are distinguished by that blending of psychological insight with imagination and fancy, which is the highest manifestation of Shakespeare's genius, but we must remember that Q_1 was hastily printed to meet an urgent popular demand, and that the philosophical part of the play would be at once the most difficult to obtain by surreptitious means, and the least valued by the persons to supply whose cravings that edition was published. . . . . To minds undisciplined in thought, abstract truth is difficult of apprehension and of recollection; whereas, a mere child can remember a story. And in addition to this very important consideration, there is yet a more important fact, that some of the most profoundly thoughtful passages in the Play,— passages most indicative of maturity of intellect and wide observation of life,—are found essentially complete, although grossly and almost ludicrously corrupted, in the first imperfect version of the tragedy. Two of the most celebrated and most reflect-ive passages of the Play shall furnish us examples in point of the last remark, and also characteristic specimens of the kind of corruption to which the text of the Play was subjected in the preparation of Q_1.

' A comparison of [lines 195–215 of Q_1] with those of the perfect soliloquy [I, ii, 129] makes it apparent that these are but an imperfect representation of those. The latter are no expansion of the former. The thoughts are the same in both, with the exception of seven lines which were plainly omitted from the first version, not added to it in writing the second. The maimed and halting [lines 196, 197], which it is absurd to suppose that Shakespeare could have written at any period of his life, are the best that the person who furnished it could do to supply the place of the corresponding lines of the seven which follow them in the perfect soliloquy; the rest is all tangled and disordered, though but slightly defective, and shows in its very confusion of parts that it represents the perfect speech. Notice the misplacement of lines, such as the one containing the comparison to Hercules, and that about 'the shoes', and the 'unrighteous tears;' and see that 'Why, she would hang on him' is not only misplaced, but that 'him' is without an antecedent, owing to the omission of the allusion to Hamlet's father and his love for the Queen; yet see in this very derangement and in these defects the proof that the earlier version is merely mutilated, not a sketch; the latter, merely perfect, not elaborated. The evidence of the same relation of the two texts is perhaps yet stronger in the case of the second and more important soliloquy, which is printed thus in the first Quarto: [see lines 815–837]. This reads almost like intentional burlesque, so completely, yet absurdly, are all the thoughts of the genuine soliloquy represented in it. Like the shadow of a fair and stately building on the surface of a troubled river, it distorts outline, destroys symmetry, confuses parts, contracts some passages, expands others, robs color of its charm and light of its brilliancy, and presents but a dim, grotesque, and shapeless image of the beautiful original; while yet, with that original before us, we can see that it is a reflection of the whole structure, and not merely of its foundation, its framework, or its important parts. How ludicrously the well-known sentences, 'To sleep, perchance to dream,' and that, several lines below, about 'the dread of something after death,' are lumped together, and crushed into shapelessness in the lines [817–821]! That this soliloquy as it stands in Q_1 is merely a mutilated version of that which is found in Q_2 is as clear to my apprehension as that the latter was written by William Shakespeare.

'Another proof that Q_1 is but an accidentally imperfect representation of the completed Play is found in the fragment which it gives of the Fourth Scene of Act IV, in which Fortinbras enters at the head of the Norwegian forces. This consists only of the speech of Fortinbras. [See Q_1, lines 1614–1619.] This has the same distorted likeness to the genuine speech that the soliloquies just cited have to their prototypes in the true text. But,—to look farther,—with this speech the scene ends: we have '*exeunt all*,' and immediately, '*enter King and Queene*.' Now, will any one believe that Shakespeare brought Fortinbras at the head of an army upon the stage merely to speak these half dozen lines of commonplace? Plainly, the only object was to give Hamlet the opportunity for that great introspective soliloquy in which, with a psychological insight profounder than that which is exhibited in any other passage of the tragedy, the poet makes the Prince confess in whisper to himself the subtle modes and hidden causes of his vacillation. Considering the motive of the Play, the introduction of Fortinbras and his army without the subsequent dialogue and soliloquy is a moral impossibility which overrides all other arguments. Yet this one is not unsupported. For the speech of Fortinbras in the first version itself furnishes evidence that it was written out for the press by a person who had heard the dialogue which it introduces. The latter part of the line —'Tell him that Fortinbras, nephew to old Norway,'—has no counterpart in the genuine speech; but we detect in it an unmistakeable reminiscence of the following passage of the subsequent dialogue which is found in Q_2: '*Ham.* Who commands them, sir? *Cap. The Nephew to old Norway*, Fortenbrasse.' It is to be noted, too, that the absence of this dialogue and soliloquy from Q_1 is no proof whatever that they were not written when the copy for that edition was prepared; and this for the all-sufficient reason that they are also wanting in the Folio itself, which was printed twenty years afterwards. It seems almost certain that these passages were omitted in the representation, and struck out of the stage-copy from which the Folio was

printed, owing tc the great length of the Play and a lack of popular interest consequent upon their speculative character. And it is also safe to conclude that the
same considerations led the procurer of the copy for the surreptitious edition to
withhold even a garbled version of them, if, indeed, they were not already omitted
in the performance at the time when he did his work.

'And this brings us to another branch of the evidence in the case. There are
many important passages of the completed Play of which there is no vestige in the
Quarto of 1603, which would seem to favor the conclusion that that edition represents but an early sketch of Shakespeare's work, especially as some of them are reflective in character, and all indicate maturity of power. Of these I will mention
the lines about the ominous appearances in Rome ' ere the mightiest Julius fell,' I, i,
114; all that part of Hamlet's censure of Danish drunkenness, beginning, ' This
heavy-headed revel,' I, iv, 17; the reflection upon ' That monster custom,' III, iv,
161; the soliloquy just above alluded to, IV, iv, 32; the euphuistic passage between
Osric and Hamlet, beginning, ' Sir, here is newly come to court Laertes,' V, ii, 106;
and the Prince's brief colloquy with a Lord in the same scene. But the absence of
these passages from Q_1 is deprived of all bearing upon the question of the state of
the Play which that edition professed to represent by the fact that they are likewise
lacking in the Folio. On the other hand, there are passages in the Folio which are
not found in Q_2, enlarged though it was ' to almost as much againe ' as the Play had
been before, ' according to the true and perfect coppie;' and of these passages there
are traces at least in Q_1. Such is the passage about the company of child actors,—
' How comes it? Do they grow rusty?' and seven speeches afterwards, II, ii, 325,
—which, although entirely lacking in the Second Quarto, is thus represented in the
First : [See Q_1, 971–977].

'There are other vestiges in Q_1 of passages which do not appear in Q_2, but which
are found in the Folio; and, although they are of minor importance, they go to show
none the less that the surreptitious text of 1603 and the authentic text of twenty
years later had a common origin.

'In some parts of Q_1 the arrangement of the scenes is not the same as in that of
the subsequent editions, which might seem to favor the supposition that the Play was
re-cast after its first production. But the order of the earliest edition in these cases is
mere disorder, resulting from the inability of the person, who superintended the
preparation of the copy for the press, to arrange even the materials at hand in their
proper sequence. As evidence of this, it is only necessary to state that the soliloquy,
' To be, or not to be,' III, i, is introduced in Q_1 immediately after the proposal of
Polonius, II, ii, that Ophelia shall lure Hamlet into an exhibition of his madness.
It is immediately preceded by the command of her father: ' And here Ofelia, reade
you on this booke, And walke aloofe, the King shal be vnseene;' and, as in the
true and perfect copy, it closes with the entreaty, ' Lady in thy orizons be all my
sinnes remembred;' and yet, according to the imperfect, as well as the perfect, text,
Ophelia is not upon the stage! The circumstance that in two scenes Hamlet enters
just as the same personages (the King, the Queen, and Ophelia's father) leave the
stage, misled the purloiner of the text for the first edition into the supposition that
the old courtier's suggestion in the earlier scene was immediately followed.

'But the text of the First Quarto presents two features of difference from that of
any subsequent edition, which cannot be attributed to accident or haste. These are
the names of Ophelia's father and of his servant, and the existence of a scene which
(in form though not in substance) has no counterpart in the authentic text. The

scene in question is a brief one between Horatio and the Queen. It succeeds that of Ophelia's insanity; and in it Horatio informs Hamlet's mother of the manner in which her son escaped the plot laid by the King to have him put to death in England. [See Q₂, lines 1747–1782.] Here, at last, is no confusion or mutilation; all is coherent and complete; but, on the other hand, there is heaviness of form, empti ness of matter. Plainly Shakespeare never wrote this feeble stuff: it is an interpo- lation. What he did write, having the same purpose, the reader will find in the beginning of the Second Scene of Act V, and he will notice that the occurrences which Hamlet in that version relates to Horatio are exactly the same as those,—of which in this Horatio informs the Queen, even to the use of the dead king's seal,— to which there is no allusion in the old history. But it is to be observed that neither in Hamlet's letter to Horatio, nor in any other part of the authentic text, is there a hint of an appointed meeting between them 'on the east side of the city to-morrow morning.' From these circumstances it appears that the scene in the first edition does not represent a counterpart in Shakespeare's *Hamlet*, which the procurer of the copy for that edition had failed to obtain. It seems rather a remnant of a previous play on the same subject.

'Such I believe it and the names Corambis and Montano to be. We have seen, by Henslowe's *Diary*, that there was a *Hamlet* performed on the 9th of June, 1594. Henslowe heads the leaves upon which this memorandum is entered, 'In the name of God, Amen, beginning at newington, my lord admirell men and my lord cham- berlem men as followeth, 1594.' Here we have a *Hamlet* played, 1594, at a theatre where the company to which Shakespeare belonged was performing; in 1602 the same company still perform a *Hamlet;* and we know of no play of the same name performed at any other theatre. It seems at least most probable, then, that this tragedy belonged from the first to that 'cry of players; and I believe that when they shortened it (for the pruning was plainly their work, and not the poet's, as the case of the scene which opens with the entry of Fortinbras and his army makes manifest) they omitted Hamlet's long, discursive relation to Horatio of his stratagem against Rosencrantz and Guildenstern, and, as the story must be told, introduced the short scene between Horatio and the Queen from the old play, which, according to the stage practice of that time (and perhaps even of our day), they had a perfect right to do. As to two names from an older play, nothing is more probable than that Shakespeare himself should have retained them. But when in the height of his reputation as a poet and a dramatist, 1603, he saw a mutilated, and in some parts caricatured, version of his most thoughtful work surreptitiously published, nothing, also, is more probable than that he, and his fellow-players with him, should send immediately 'the true and perfect copy' to the press, and that from this, in case it had not been done before, he should eliminate even the slightest traces of the pre- vious drama, if they were but two names. I have hardly a doubt that this was done, and that the Quarto of 1604 was printed from a copy of the tragedy obtained with the consent of its author and the company to which it belonged.

'Shakespeare's tragedy was surely written between 1598, the date of Meres's *Pal- ladis Tamia*, and June, 1602, when Roberts made his entry in the *Registers of the Stationers' Company;* and yet a closer approximation to the exact date is afforded by the allusion to the 'inhibition' of the Players. We may, therefore, with some certainty attribute the production of Shakespeare's version of *Hamlet* to the year 1600.'

The CAMBRIDGE EDITORS (*Preface*, vol. viii, p viii): The manuscript for Q₂ may have been compiled in the first instance from short-hand notes taken during the representation, but there are many errors in the printed text which seem like errors of a copyist rather than of a hearer. Compare [lines 365, 366, of Q₁] with the corresponding lines of Q₂ [see I, iii, 73, 74, and notes, in this edition]. A few lines above, both Quartos give *courage* for 'comrade,' a mistake due undoubtedly to the eye, and not to the ear. We believe, then, that the defects of the manuscript from which Q₁ was printed had been in part at least supplemented by a reference to the authentic copy in the library of the theatre. Very probably the man employed for this purpose was some inferior actor or servant, who would necessarily work in haste and by stealth, and in any case would not be likely to work very conscientiously for the printer or bookseller, who was paying him to deceive his masters. . . . . The chief differences between Q₁ and Q₂ are only such as might be expected between a bona fide and a mala fide transcription.'

The Cambridge Editors modified their views of the origin of Q₁ before they published their next edition in the *Clarendon Press Series*, and suggested a solution of the mystery which will, I think, commend itself the more thoroughly it is understood, and the more closely the play is studied. HALLIWELL, in his folio edition of 1865, suggests what partly covers the same ground when he says, in the *Introduction* to *Hamlet*, 'there are small fragments peculiar to [Q₁], some of which may be attributed to the pen of the great dramatist.'

W. G. CLARK and W. A. WRIGHT (*Preface to Hamlet.* Clarendon Press Series, p. viii) : It is clear, upon a very slight examination, that Q₁ is printed from a copy which was hastily taken down and perhaps surreptitiously obtained, either from short-hand notes made during the representation, or privately from the actors themselves. These notes, when transcribed, would form the written copy which the printers had before them, and would account for the existence of errors which are errors of the copyist rather than of the hearer. But granting all this, we have yet to account for differences between the earlier and later forms of the Play which cannot be explained by the carelessness of short-hand writer, copyist, or printer. Knight, with great ingenuity, maintains that the Quarto of 1603 represents the original sketch of the Play, and that this was an early work of the poet. We differ from him in respect to this last conclusion, because we can see no evidence for Shakespeare's connection with the Play before 1602.

' First, there is the complete absence of any positive evidence on the point, and next, there is the very strong negative evidence that in the enumeration of Shakespeare's works by one who was an ardent admirer of his genius, Francis Meres, there is no mention whatever of *Hamlet*. That *Hamlet* should be omitted and *Titus Andronicus* inserted is utterly unintelligible, except upon the supposition that in 1598 the play bearing the former name had not in any way been connected with Shakespeare. Elze appeals to the omission of *Pericles* and *Henry VI* from the list as a parallel instance, but we submit that there is no reason at all for associating Shakespeare with *Pericles* at this period, and that his connection with the Three Parts of *Henry VI* is doubtful. In any case, the last-mentioned play would hardly be quoted by an admirer as a proof of his genius; whereas, if *Hamlet* had existed, even in the imperfect form in which it appears in Q₁, it would have supplied at least as good an instance of his tragic power as *Titus Andronicus* or *Richard III*. At some time, therefore, between 1598 and 1602 *Hamlet*, as retouched by Shakespeare, was put upon the stage. We are inclined to think that it was acted not very long before the date of Roberts's entry in the *Stationers' Registers*, namely, 26 July, 1602. Our reason for this opinion is that if the Play had been long a popular one, and had been frequently represented, the printer or publisher would have had many opportunities of procuring a more accurate copy than that from which the edition of 1603 was made. The errors of this edition, and the manifest haste with which it was printed, seem to show that the Play had been acted only a short time before, and that the publisher went to press with the first copy he could obtain, however imperfect. This supposition is favored by the expression in the *Stationers' Register*, 'as it was *lately* acted,' which would hardly have been used of a play which had long been popular. . . . .

'After a careful examination of Q_1, and a comparison of the Play as there exhibited with its later form, we have arrived at a conclusion which, inasmuch as it is conjectural, and based to a large extent upon subjective considerations, we state with some diffidence. It is this:—That there was an old play on the story of *Hamlet*, some portions of which are still preserved in Q_1; that about the year 1602 Shakespeare took this and began to remodel it for the stage, as he had done with other plays; that Q_1 represents the Play after it had been retouched by him to a certain extent, but before his alterations were complete; and that in Q_2 we have for the first time the *Hamlet* of Shakespeare. It is quite true, as Knight has remarked, that in the Quarto of 1603 we have the whole 'action' of the Play; that is to say, the events follow very much the same order, and the catastrophe is the same. There are, however, some important modifications even in this respect. The scene with Ophelia which in the modern Play occurs in III, i, is in the older form introduced in the middle of II, ii. Polonius is Corambis in the older Play, and Reynaldo is Montano. The madness of Hamlet is much more pronounced, and the Queen's innocence of her husband's murder much more explicitly stated, in the earlier than in the later Play. In fact, the earlier Play in these respects corresponds more closely with the original story. In the earlier form it appears to us that Shakespeare's modifications of the Play had not gone much beyond the Second Act. Certainly in the Third Act we find very great unlikeness and very great inferiority to the later Play. In fact, in the First, Third, and Fourth Scenes there is hardly a trace of Shakespeare, and in the Second, which is the scene where the Play is introduced, there are very remarkable differences. The Fourth Act, in language, has very little in common with its present form, and in the First Scene of the Fifth Act there are still some traces of the original Play. In the Second Scene of this Act the dialogue between Hamlet and Horatio is not found, and the interview with Osric in its old dress may fairly be put down to the earlier writer. The rest of the scene is much altered, and of course improved, and wherever these improvements come it strikes us with irresistible force that in comparing the later with the earlier form of the Play we are not comparing the work of Shakespeare at two different periods of his life, but the work of Shakespeare with that of a very inferior artist. If any one desires to be convinced of this, let him read the interview of Hamlet with his mother in the two Quartos of 1603 and 1604. Going backward, we come to the Second Act, and here the First Scene is so imperfectly given in Q_1 that it is impossible to say what it really represented. Here and there a line occurs as it now stands, but on the whole it is very defective, and appears to have been set down from memory. The opening of the Second Scene is changed, and in Q_1 seems to belong to the original Play; on the other hand, the speeches of Corambis (Polonius) and Voltemar (Voltimand) are nearly verbatim the same as the later edition. The rest of the scene is altered and much improved. The First Act is substantially the same in the two editions, allowing for the extremely imperfect and careless manner in which it is given in Q_1. The First Scene is fairly rendered; the speeches of Marcellus and Horatio being, so far as they go, almost word for word the same as in Q_2, where the dialogue is expanded. In the Second Scene the speeches are very imperfect, and it is difficult to say how far they represent the earlier or the later Play; Hamlet's soliloquy is sadly mutilated, as if written down in fragments from memory, but in the interview with Horatio the early Quarto agrees closely with the later. The Third and Fourth Scenes are badly reported, but otherwise contain the groundwork of the present Play; and Hamlet's address to the Ghost is given almost verbatim, as is the dialogue which follows. In the Fifth Scene the order of the dialogue is slightly altered, but not materially changed, and Hamlet's soliloquy after the Ghost's disappearance is very much mutilated. The interview with Marcellus and Horatio is but little altered. In conclusion, we venture to think that a close examination of Q_1 will convince any one that it contains some of Shakespeare's undoubted work, mixed with a great deal that is not his, and will confirm our theory that the text, imperfect as it is, represents an older play in a transition state, while it was undergoing a remodelling, but had not received more than the first rough touches of the great master's hand.'

So great was the popularity of this tragedy that in the year following the publication of Q_2 another edition was issued. This THIRD QUARTO is not, correctly speaking, a new edition. It is merely a reprint of the Second Quarto. The title-pages of the two editions are identical except in date. The CAMBRIDGE EDITORS say that it ' was printed from the same forms as Q_2, and differing from it no more than one copy of the same edition may differ from another.' In this assertion I think the range of books should be restricted to the Elizabethan printing-offices; the differences that are often found between two copies of the same edition issued in those early days are matters of common experience. But in modern times two copies of the same edition, ' printed from the same forms,' would hardly, perhaps, vary as much from each other as Q_3 varies from Q_2. For instance, I have found the following changes (be it remembered that I have collated Ashbee's Facsimiles, not the originals):

In I, i, 107,	Romadge	Q_2	Romeage	Q_3
IV, i, 31,	moft	Q_2	muft	Q_3
IV, vii, 78,	riband	Q_2	ribaud	Q_3
V, i, 286,	thirtie	Q_2	thereby	Q_3
V, ii, 9,	pall	Q_2	fall	Q_3
V, ii, 112,	dofie	Q_2	dazzie	Q_3
V, ii, 113,	yaw	Q_2	raw	Q_3
V, ii, 124,	too't	Q_2	doo't	Q_3
V, ii, 154,	it be	Q_2	it be might	Q_3
V, ii, 178,	A did fir	Q_2	A did fo fir	Q_3
V, ii, 259,	Vaice	Q_2	Onixe	Q_3
Signature on laf' page G 2		Q_2	O 2	Q_3

In V, ii, 154, the addition of ' might' in Q_3 ' drove over' a word in each succeeding line of the speech. The lines, in this passage, therefore, do not correspond in the two Quartos.

That eight out of twelve should occur in the last scene of the last Act is noteworthy. They are all trifling in quality, and may ' stand in numbers, yet in reck-

34 APPENDIX

oning none.' When it is considered that these twelve are all the variations to be found in more than two thousand lines, the quantity approximates the infinitely small, and may be neglected; practically, therefore, Q_3 is identical with Q_2, and if the work of collation for this edition were to be repeated Q_3 would be omitted from the list.

HALLIWELL says: If the initials I. R. [in the imprint of both Q_2 and Q_3] are those, as is most likely, of James Roberts, there must have been some friendly arrangement between him and Ling respecting the ownership of the copyright, which certainly now belonged to the latter, as appears from the following entry on the books of the Stationers' Company:

[1607.] 19 Novembris.

John Smythick Entred for his copies vnder th[e h]andes of the wardens. these bookes followinge Whiche dyd belonge to Nicholas Lynge [Nº] 6 A booke called *HAMLETT* . . . . . . vj^d

Accordingly, after this date all succeeding Quartos were published by John Smethwicke.

The FOURTH QUARTO appeared in 1611. On its title-page it is called 'The Tragedy of Hamlet,' instead of 'The Tragicall Hiftorie of Hamlet,' as the preceding Quartos have it. Otherwise, it is the same ('Coppie' is here spelled 'Coppy'), except the imprint, which reads: Printed for *Iohn Smethwicke*, and are to be fold at his fhoppe | in Saint *Dunftons* Church yeard in Fleetftreet. | Vnder the Diall. 1611.

It is, perhaps, worth while to note here some variations which occur in two different copies of this same edition:

III, iii, 57:	'corrupted'	Editor's Q_4.		*conrupted*	Q_4 Cam.	Ed.
III, iii, 70:	'fteele'	"	"	*steale*	"	"
III, iii, 73:	'but	"	"	*bot*	"	"
III, iii, 74:	'fo a goes'	"	"	*so goes*	"	"
III, iv, 22 and 23:	'hoe'	"	"	*how*	"	"
III, iv, 113:	'fighing'	"	"	*sighting*	"	"
III, iv, 135:	'liue'd'	"	"	*lives*	"	"

In every instance ASHBEE's facsimile agrees with the Editor's copy. The first four of these variations occur on the same page; and all add one more to the numberless proofs that in the old printing-offices the sheets were corrected while going through the press. The copy of the Cambridge Editors is therefore the older of the two it may be but by a few minutes. The unfortunate (or should we not say fortunate?) inference to be drawn from such facts as these points to the uselessness of minute collation.

The copy which has been used for the present edition formerly belonged to George Daniel, and was secured at the sale of Sir William Tite's library in 1875.

There is a FIFTH QUARTO, undated, whereof the title-page reads:

The | Tragedy | of | Hamlet | *Prince of Denmarke.* | Newly Imprinted and inlarged, according to the true | and perfect Copy laftly Printed. | By | William Shakefpeare. | London, | Printed by *W. S.* for *Iohn Smethwicke*, and are to be fold at his | Shop in Saint *Dunftans* Church-yard in Fleetftreet: | Vnder the Diall.

This edition MALONE (*Var.* 1821, ii, 652) believes was printed in 1607, because in that year the transfer to John Smethwicke was made in the *Stationers' Registers*, in the entry just quoted. For the same reason HALLIWELL thinks that it was ' possibly printed about 1609.' But the CAMBRIDGE EDITORS say : ' We are convinced, however, that the undated Quarto was printed from that of 1611,'—a conviction to which, I think, all will come who carefully examine the collation recorded in the first volume of this edition. The spelling of the undated Quarto constantly inclines to the more modern usage, *e. g. Sundayes* instead of Sondaies ; *thereunto* instead of there-vnto, &c. &c. Even the title-page is much more modern than that of Q$_4$, *e. g. Copy* instead of Coppy ; *London* instead of At London ; *Shop* instead of shoppe ; *Dunstan* instead of Dunston ; *Church-yard* instead of Church yeard.

These are all the Quartos that appeared during Shakespeare's lifetime, and before the publication of the First Folio ; consequently, they are all that possibly derived their texts from original sources. All subsequent Quartos are but reprints of these, with the spelling more and more modernized as years go on, with some manifest misprints in the earlier Quartos corrected, and with a natural percentage of errors of their own. They are generally called the 'Players' Quartos,' and their dates will be found in the Bibliography in this volume. The Quarto that immediately followed Q$_5$, or the undated Quarto, is the Quarto of 1637 ; the CAMBRIDGE EDITORS added this to their list of Quartos, whereof the variations are recorded in their notes, under the symbol Q$_6$.

A copy of this Quarto I have been unable to procure ; where, therefore, it is cited in the Textual Notes in vol. i, it is followed by an asterisk to indicate that it is taken at second-hand from the Cambridge Edition. The lack of this Quarto is the less to be regretted, since to judge by the Textual Notes of the Cambridge Edition only slight differences are to be perceived between it and my copy of the Quarto of 1676, which was evidently printed from it ; where the Cambridge Editors cite Q$_6$, I have generally had occasion to cite Q'76. I have just referred to ' my copy ' of 1676 ; I speak thus, because there are decided variations at times between it and the copy used by the Cambridge Editors. It is hardly worth while to occupy valuable space with a list of these *varias lectiones* in two unimportant editions. The list would be interesting only to those who possess copies of the edition, and it would be a pity to deprive such of the harmless pleasure of hunting these variations down, which can readily be done by comparing the Textual Notes in this edition with those of the Cambridge Editors ; and to all others the list would be weary, flat, stale, and unprofitable. Perhaps such discrepancies would never have been noted even by the present Editor were it not that in the dull monotony of collating, which becomes at times almost mechanical, such a trifling novelty as the detection of a difference between two copies of the same edition becomes by contrast wildly exciting. When Q'76 agrees with any of the other Qq, it is not noted.

THEOBALD, throughout his *Shakespeare Restored*, refers to an edition of 1703 by the ' accurate Mr John Hughs.' Of this edition the CAMBRIDGE EDITORS say that ' it is different from the Players' Quarto of 1703, and is not mentioned in Bohn's edition of *Lowndes's Bibliographers' Manual*. No copy of it exists in the British Museum, the Bodleian, the library of the Duke of Devonshire, the Capell collection, or any other to which we have had access.' Mr WINSOR, of the Boston Library, has noted that there are two editions of 1703, both with the same title, but one much less correctly printed than the other ; the test-word is ' Barnardo,' the last word on p. 1 ; in the inferior edition it reads *Bornardo*. Neither of these editions is that of the ' accurate Mr Hughs.' The test-word for his edition (which I have never seen) would be *faction* instead of ' fashion,' II, ii, 329, or else *Roaming* instead of ' Wrong ' of the Qq, in I, iii, 109. I mention this in the hope that it may some day lead to the discovery of a copy which at present certainly appears to be rarer than Q₁.

In the four Folios we have virtually one and the same text, and it is clearly a different one from the Quartos. COLLIER thinks that ' if the *Hamlet* in the First Folio were not composed from some now unknown Quarto, it was derived from a manuscript obtained by Heminge and Condell from the theatre. The Acts and Scenes are marked only in the First and Second Acts, after which no divisions of the kind are noticed, and where the Third Act commences is merely matter of modern conjecture. Some large portions of the Play appear to have been omitted for the sake of short ening the performance.' ' Certain portions are found in the Folio which are not in the Second and succeeding Quartos, but we have the evidence of the First Quarto that they were originally acted, and were not, as has been hitherto imagined, subsequent additions.'

In the Textual Notes I have not always recorded a typographical peculiarity of the Second Folio, which I do not remember ever to have seen noted : it is the fre· quent omission of the apostrophe in such cases of elision as ' wheres Polonius ;' ' whats the news ;' ' Happily hes the second time come to them ;' ' Ide fain know that ;' the apostrophe is almost invariably omitted before ' 'tis,' but not always; for instance, it is both present and absent in the line, ' That he is mad 'tis true : Tis true, tis pity.' I have looked in vain for any rule or system that may have guided the printer ; it was apparently spasmodic carelessness or indifference.

WHITE : The text of *Hamlet* is distinguished rather by a very few striking and important corruptions than by many of minor import. In fact, there is hardly a passage in the tragedy, excepting that in the First Scene about the ' stars with trains of fire and dews of blood,' that can give trouble to a reader intent only upon the enjoyment of his author, which, considering the style of the work, and the vicissitudes of the stage and the printing-office to which its text was subjected, is remarkable.

HALLIWELL : My sad and strong belief is that we have not the materials for the formation of a really perfect text; and that now at best we must be contented with a defective copy of what is in many respects the most noble of all the writings of Shakespeare. It is always asserted that the great dramatist was indifferent to literary fame, and that it is to this circumstance the lamentable state in which so much of his work has descended to us is to be attributed. Other views may, indeed, for a time have prevented a diligent attention to the publication of his writings; but there is nothing to show that he had not meditated a complete edition of them under his own superintendence while in his retirement at New Place. It would be a more reasonable supposition that the preparation of such an edition was prevented by his untimely death.

CAMBRIDGE EDITORS : In giving all the passages from both Folio and Quarto, we are reproducing, as near as may be, the work as it was originally written by Shakespeare, or rather as finally retouched by him after the spurious edition of 1603.

FLEAY (*Shakespeare Manual*, p. 41) : I should place the first draft in 1601, the complete play in 1603. I have little doubt that the early *Hamlet* of 1589 was written by Shakespeare and Marlowe in conjunction; and that portions of it can be traced in Q₁, as *Corambis*.

THE
Tragicall Hiftorie of
HAMLET

Prince of Denmarke

By William Shake-fpeare.

As it hath beene diuerfe times acted by his Highneffe fer-
uants in the Cittie of London : as alfo in the two V-
niuerfities of Cambridge and Oxford, and elfe-where

[*VIGNETTE.*]

At London printed for N.L. and Iohn Trundell.
1603.

The Tragicall Hiftorie of

H A M L E T

Prince of Denmarke.

Enter two Centinels.

1.   Tand : who is that?
2.   Tis I.
1.   O you come moft carefully vpon your watch,
2.   And if you meete *Marcellus* and *Horatio*,
The partners of my watch, bid them make hafte.   5
1.   I will : See who goes there.
         Enter Horatio and Marcellus.
Hor.   Friends to this ground.
Mar.   And leegemen to the Dane,
O farewell honeft fouldier, who hath releeued you?
1. *Barnardo* hath my place, giue you good night.   10
Mar.   Holla, *Barnardo.*
2.   Say, is *Horatio* there?
Hor.   A peece of him.
2.   Welcome *Horatio*, welcome good *Marcellus.*
Mar.   What hath this thing appear'd againe to night.   15
2.   I haue feene nothing.
Mar.   *Horatio* fayes tis but our fantafie,
And wil not let beliefe take hold of him,
Touching this dreaded fight twice feene by vs,
[I, i, 26.]   Therefore I haue intreated him a long with vs   20
To watch the minutes of this night,
That if againe this apparition come,
He may approoue our eyes,and fpeake to it.
     Hor.   Tut, t'will not appeare.
     2.   Sit downe I pray, and let vs once againe   25
Affaile your eares that are fo fortified,
What we haue two nights feene.

Hor.   Wel,fit we downe,and let vs heare *Bernardo* fpeake
of this.

   2.   Laft night of al,when yonder ftarre that's weft-   30
ward from the pole, had made his courfe to
Illumine that part of heauen.   Where now it burnes,
The bell then towling one.

Enter Ghoft.

Mar.   Breake off your talke, fee where it comes againe.
   2.   In the fame figure like the King that's dead,   35
Mar.   Thou art a fcholler, fpeake to it H*oratio.*
   2.   Lookes it not like the king?
Hor.   Moft like, it horrors mee with feare and wonder.
   2.   It would be fpoke to.

[I, i, 45.]   *Mar.*   Queftion it H*oratio.*   40
Hor.   What art thou that thus vfurps the ftate,in
Which the Maieftie of buried *Denmarke* did fometimes
Walke?By heauen I charge thee fpeake.
Mar.   It is offended.   *exit Ghoft.*
   2.   See, it ftalkes away.   45
Hor.   Stay, fpeake, fpeake, by heauen I charge thee
fpeake.
Mar.   Tis gone and makes no anfwer.
   2.   How now H*oratio,*you tremble and looke pale,
Is not this fomething more than fantafie ?   50
What thinke you on't?
Hor.   Afore my God, I might not this beleeue, without
the fenfible and true auouch of my owne eyes.
Mar.   Is it not like the King?
Hor.   As thou art to thy felfe,   55
Such was the very armor he had on,
When he the ambitious *Norway* combated.
So frownd he once,when in an angry parle
He fmot the fleaded pollax on the yce,

[I, i, 64.]   Tis ftrange.   60
Mar.   Thus twice before, and iump at this dead hower,
With Marfhall ftalke he paffed through our watch.
Hor.   In what particular to worke, I know not,
But in the thought and fcope of my opinion,
This bodes fome ftrange eruption to the ftate.   65
Mar.   Good,now fit downe, and tell me he that knowes
Why this fame ftrikt and moft obferuant watch,
So nightly toyles the fubiect of the land,
And why fuch dayly coft of brazen Cannon
And forraine marte, for implements of warre,   70
Why fuch impreffe of fhip-writes, whofe fore taske
Does not diuide the funday from the weeke:
What might be toward that this fweaty march
Doth make the night ioynt labourer with the day,

Who is't that can informe me? 75
   Hor. Mary that can I, at leaſt the whiſper goes ſo,
Our late King, who as you know was by Forten-
Braſſe of *Norway,*
Thereto prickt on by a moſt emulous cauſe, dared to
[I, i, 84.] The combate, in which our valiant H*amlet,* 80
For ſo this ſide of our knowne world eſteemed him,
Did ſlay this Fortenbraſſe,
Who by a ſeale compaɗ well ratified,by law
And heraldrie, did forfeit with his life all thoſe
His lands which he ſtoode ſeazed of by the conqueror, 85
Againſt the which a moity competent,
Was gaged by our King:
Now ſir, yong Fortenbraſſe,
Of inapproued mettle hot and full,
Hath in the skirts of *Norway* here and there, 90
Sharkt vp a ſight of lawleſſe Reſolutes
For food and diet tc ſome enterpriſe,
That hath a ſtomacke in't : and this (I take it) is the
Chiefe head and ground of this our watch.
Enter the Ghoſt.
But loe,behold,ſee where it comes againe, 95
Ile croſſe it,though it blaſt me : ſtay illuſion,
If there be any good thing to be done,
That may doe eaſe to thee,and grace to mee,
Speake to mee.
[I, i, 133.] If thou art priuy to thy countries fate, 100
Which happly foreknowing may preuent, O ſpeake to me,
Or if thou haſt extorted in thy life,
Or hoorded treaſure in the wombe of earth,
For which they ſay you Spirites oft walke in death, ſpeake
to mc, ſtay and ſpeake, ſpeake,ſtoppe it *Marcellus.* 105
   2. Tis heere.   *exit Ghoſt.*
   H*or.* Tis heere.
   Marc. Tis gone, O we doe it wrong, being so **maieſti-**
call, to offer it the ſhew of violence,
For it is as the ayre invelmorable, 110
And our vaine blowes malitious mockery.
   2. It was about to ſpeake when the Cocke crew.
   H*or.* And then it faded like a guilty thing,
Vpon a fearefull ſummons : I haue heard
The Cocke, that is the trumpet to the morning, 115
Doth with his earely and ſhrill crowing throate,
Awake the god of day, and at his ſound,
Whether in earth or ayre, in ſea or fire,
The ſtrauagant and erring ſpirite hies
[I, i, 155.] To his confines, and of the trueth heereof 120
This preſent obieɗ made probation.
   Marc. It faded on the crowing of the Cocke,

Some fay, that euer gainft that feafon comes,
Wherein our Sauiours birth is celebrated,
The bird of dawning fingeth all night long,   125
And then they fay, no fpirite dare walke abroade,
The nights are wholefome,then no planet frikes,
No Fairie takes, nor Witch hath powre to charme,
So gratious, and fo hallowed is that time.
     Hor. So haue I heard, and doe in parte beleeue it :   130
But fee the Sunne in ruffet mantle clad,
Walkes ore the deaw of yon hie mountaine top.
Breake we our watch vp, and by my aduife,
Let vs impart what we haue feene to night
Vnto yong H*amlet :* for vpon my life   135
This Spirite dumbe to vs will fpeake to him:
Do you confent,wee fhall acquaint him with it,
As needefull in our loue, fitting our duetie?
     Marc. Lets doo't I pray, and I this morning know,
[I, i, 175.] Where we fhall finde him moft conueniently.   140

     Enter King, Queene, Hamlet, Leartes, Corambis,
     and the two Ambaffadors, with Attendants.

[I, ii, 27.]   *King* Lordes,we here haue writ to *Fortenbraffe,*
Nephew to olde *Norway,* who impudent
And bed-rid, fcarcely heares of this his
Nephews purpofe : and Wee heere difpatch
Yong good *Cornelia,* and you *Voltemar*   145
For bearers of thefe greetings to olde
Norway, giuing to you no further perfonall power
To bufineffe with the King,
Then thofe related articles do fhew:
Farewell,and let your hafte commend your dutie.   150
     Gent. In this and all things will wee fhew our dutie.
     King. Wee doubt nothing, hartily farewel :
And now *Leartes* what's the newes with you?
You faid you had a fute what i'ft *Leartes?*
     Lea : My gratious Lord, your fauorable licence,   155
Now that the funerall rites are all performed,
I may haue leaue to go againe to *France,*
For though the fauour of your grace might ftay mee,
Yet fomething is there whifpers in my hart,
[I, ii, 56.] Which makes my minde and fpirits bend all for *France.*   160
     King Haue you your fathers leaue,*Leartes?*
     Cor. He hath, my lord,wrung from me a forced graunt,
And I befeech you grant your Highneffe leaue.
     Kiug With all our heart, *Leartes* fare thee well.
     Lear. I in all loue and dutie take my leaue.   165

153. Leartes] Leaites, B. Mus. copy.   153. newes] news B. Mus. copy.

King. And now princely Sonne *Hamlet,*   *Exit.*
What meanes thefe fad and melancholy moodes?
For your intent going to *Wittenberg,*
Wee hold it moft vnmeet and vnconuenient,
Being the Ioy and halfe heart of your mother.   170
Therefore let mee intreat you ftay in Court,
All *Denmarkes* hope our coofin and deareft Sonne.
    Ham. My lord, ti's not the fable fute I weare:
No nor the teares that ftill ftand in my eyes,
Nor the diftracted hauiour in the vifage,   175
Nor all together mixt with outward femblance,
Is equall to the forrow of my heart,
Him haue I loft I muft of force forgoe,
Thefe but the ornaments and futes of woe.

[I, ii, 87.]   *King* This fhewes a louing care in you,Sonne *Hamlet,*   180
But you muft thinke your father loft a father,
That father dead, loft his, and fo fhalbe vntill the
Generall ending. Therefore ceafe laments,
It is a fault gainft heauen, fault gainft the dead,
A fault gainft nature, and in reafons   185
Common courfe moft certaine,
None liues on earth, but hee is borne to die.
    Que. Let not thy mother loofe her praiers *Hamlet,*
Stay here with vs, go not to *Wittenberg.*
    Ham. I fhall in all my beft obay you madam.   190
    King Spoke like a kinde and a moft louing Sonne,
And there's no health the King fhall drinke to day,
But the great Canon to the clowdes fhall tell
The rowfe the King fhall drinke vnto Prince *Hamlet.*
       Exeunt all but Hamlet.

[I, ii, 129.]   *Ham.* O that this too much grieu'd and fallied flefh   195
Would melt to nothing, or that the vniuerfall
Globe of heauen would turne al to a Chaos!
O God within two moneths; no not two : maried,
Mine vncle: O let me not thinke of it,
My fathers brother: but no more like   200
My father, then I to *Hercules.*
Within two months, ere yet the falt of moft
Vnrighteous teates had left their flufhing
In her galled eyes : fhe married, O God, a beaft
Deuoyd of reafon would not haue made   205
Such fpeede : Frailtie, thy name is Woman,
Why fhe would hang on him, as if increafe
Of appetite had growne by what it looked on.
O wicked wicked fpeede, to make fuch
Dexteritie to inceftuous fheetes,   210

198. *God*] *God,* B. Mus. copy.   198. *maried*] *married* B. Mus. copy.
moneths] *months* B. Mus. copy.

Ere yet the fhooes were olde,
The which fhe followed my dead fathers corfe
Like *Nyobe,* all teares : married, well it is not,
Nor it cannot come to good:
But breake my heart, for I muft holde my tongue.   215
          Enter Horatio *and* Marcellus.

[I, ii, 160]   *Hor.*   Health to your Lordfhip.
          Ham.   I am very glad to fee you, (Horatio) or I much
forget my felfe.
          Hor.   The fame my Lord, and your poore feruant euer.
          Ham.   O my good friend, I change that name with you :   220
but what make you from *Wittenberg* Horatio?
Marcellus.
          Marc.   My good Lord.
          Ham.   I am very glad to fee you, good euen firs :
But what is your affaire in *Elfenoure?*   225
Weele teach you to drinke deepe ere you depart.
          Hor.   A trowant difpofition, my good Lord
          Ham.   Nor fhall you make mee trufter
Of your owne report againft your felfe:
Sir, I know you are no trowant: 230
But what is your affaire in *Elfenoure?*
          Hor.   My good Lord, I came to fee your fathers funerall.
          Ham.   O I pre thee do not mocke mee fellow ftudient,
I thinke it was to fee my mothers wedding.
          Hor.   Indeede my Lord, it followed hard vpon.   235
          Ham.   Thrift, thrift, H*oratio,* the funerall bak't meates
Did coldly furnifh forth the marriage tables,
Would I had met my deereft foe in heauen
Ere euer I had feene that day *Horatio*;
[I, ii, 184.]   O my father, my father, me thinks I fee my father,   240
          Hor.   Where my Lord?
          Ham.   Why, in my mindes eye H*oratio.*
          Hor.   I faw him once, he was a gallant King.
          Ham.   He was a man, take him for all in all,
I fhall not looke vpon his like againe.   245
          Hor.   My Lord, I thinke I faw him yefternight,
          Ham.   Saw, who?
          Hor.   My Lord, the King your father.
          Ham.   Ha, ha, the King my father ke you.
          Hor.   Ceafen your admiration for a while   250
With an attentiue eare, till I may deliuer,
Vpon the witneffe of thefe Gentlemen
This wonder to you.
          Ham.   For Gods loue let me heare it.
          Hor.   Two nights together had thefe Gentlemen,   255
Marcellus and *Bernardo,* on their watch,
In the dead vaft and middle of the night.
Beene thus incountered by a figure like your father,

Armed to poynt, exactly *Capapea*

[I, ii, 201.] Appeeres before them thrife, he walkes   260

Before their weake and feare oppreffed eies.

Within his tronchions length,

While they diftilled almoft to gelly.

With the act of feare ftands dumbe,

And fpeake not to him: this to mee   265

In dreadful fecrefie impart they did.

And I with them the third night kept the watch,

Where as they had deliuered forme of the thing.

Each part made true and good,

The Apparition comes : I knew your father,   270

Thefe handes are not more like.

    Ham. Tis very ftrange.

    Hor. As I do liue,my honord lord, tis true,

And wee did thinke it right done,

In our dutie to let you know it.   275

    Ham. Where was this?

    Mar. My Lord,vpon the platforme where we watched.

    Ham. Did you not fpeake to it?

    Hor. My Lord we did, but anfwere made it none,

[I, ii, 215.] Yet once me thought it was about to fpeake,   280

And lifted vp his head to motion,

Like as he would fpeake, but euen then

The morning cocke crew lowd, and in all hafte,

It fhruncke in hafte away,and vanifhed

Our fight.   285

    Ham. Indeed, indeed firs, but this troubles me:

Hold you the watch to night?

    All We do my Lord.

    Ham. Armed fay ye?

    All Armed my good Lord.   290

    Ham. From top to toe?

    All. My good Lord, from head to foote.

    Ham. Why then faw you not his face?

    Hor. O yes my Lord, he wore his beuer vp.

    Ham. How look't he, frowningly?   295

    Hor. A countenance more in forrow than in **anger**.

    Ham. Pale, or red?

    Hor. Nay, verie pal

    Ham. And fixt his eies vpon you.

[I, ii, 234.]   *Hor.* Moft conftantly.   300

    Ham. I would I had beene there,

    Hor. It would a much amazed you.

    Ham. Yea very like,very like,ftaid it long?

    Hor. While one with moderate pace

Might tell a hundred.   305

    Mar. O longer, longer.

    Ham. His beard was grifleld, nͬ.

Hor.   It was as I haue feene it in his life,
A fable filuer.

    Ham.   I wil watch to night, perchance t'wil walke againe.   310

    Hor.   I warrant it will.

    Ham.   If it affume my noble fathers perfon,
Ile fpeake to it, if hell it felfe fhould gape,
And bid me hold my peace, Gentlemen,
If you haue hither confealed this fight,   315
Let it be tenible in your filence ftill,
And whatfoeuer elfe fhall chance to night,
Giue it an vnderftanding,but no tongue,
I will requit your loues,fo fare you well,
Vpon the platforme, twixt eleuen and twelue,   320
Ile vifit you.

    All.   Our duties to your honor.   *exeunt.*

    Ham.   O your loues,your loues, as mine to you,
Farewell, my fathers fpirit in Armes,
Well, all's not well.   I doubt fome foule play,   325
Would the night were come,
Till then,fit ftill my foule, foule deeds will rife

[I. ii, 257.]   Though all the world orewhelme them to mens eies.   *Exit.*

           Enter Leartes and *Ofelia.*

[I, iii, 1.]   *Leart,*   My neceffaries are imbarkt, I muft aboord,
But ere I part, marke what I fay to thee: 330
I fee Prince *Hamlet* makes a fhew of loue
Beware *Ofelia*, do not truft his vowes,
Perhaps he loues you now, and now his tongue,
Speakes from his heart, but yet take heed my fifter,
The Charieft maide is prodigall enough,   335
If fhe vnmaske hir beautie to the Moone.
Vertue it felfe fcapes not calumnious thoughts,
Belieu't *Ofelia*,therefore keepe a loofe
Left that he trip thy honor and thy fame.

    Ofel.   Brother, to this I haue lent attentiue eare,   340
And doubt not but to keepe my honour firme,
But my deere brother,do not you
Like to a cunning Sophifter,
Teach me the path and ready way to heauen,
While you forgetting what is faid to me,   345
Your felfe, like to a careleffe libertine
Doth giue his heart, his appetite at ful,
And little recks how that his honour dies.

    Lear.   No, feare it not my deere *Ofelia*,

[I, iii, 52.]   Here comes my father, occafion fmiles vpon a fecond leaue.   350

           Enter Corambis.

    Cor.   Yet here *Leartes?* aboord,aboord,for fhame,
The winde fits in the fhoulder of your faile,
And you are ftaid for, there my bleffing with thee
And thefe few precepts in thy memory.

" Be thou familiar, but by no meanes vulgare;   355
" Thofe friends thou haft, and their adoptions tried,
" Graple them to thee with a hoope of fteele,
" But do not dull the palme with entertaine,
" Of euery new vnfleg'd courage,
" Beware of entrance into a quarrell;but being in,   360
" Beare it that the oppofed may beware of thee,
" Coftly thy apparrell, as thy purfe can buy.
" But not expreft in fafhion,
" For the apparell oft proclaimes the man.
And they of *France* of the chiefe rancke and ftation   365
Are of a moft felect and generall chiefe in that:
" This aboue all, to thy owne felfe be true,
And it muft follow as the night the day,
Thou canft not then be falfe to any one,

[I, iii, 81.]   Farewel, my bleffing with thee.   370
    Lear. I humbly take my leaue, farewell *Ofelia*,
And remember well what I haue faid to you.   *exit.*
    Ofel. It is already lock't within my hart,
And you your felfe fhall keepe the key of it.
    Cor. What i'ft *Ofelia* he hath faide to you?   375
    Ofel. Something touching the prince *Hamlet.*
    Cor. Mary wel thought on, t'is giuen me to vnderftand,
That you haue bin too prodigall of your maiden prefence
Vnto Prince Hamlet, if it be fo,
As fo tis giuen to mee, and that in waie of caution   380
I muft tell you; you do not vnderftand your felfe
So well as befits my honor, and your credite.
    Ofel. My lord, he hath made many tenders of his loue
to me.
    Cor. Tenders, I, I, tenders you may call them.
    Ofel. And withall,fuch earneft vowes.   385

[I, iii, 115.] *Cor.* Springes to catch woodcocks,
What, do I not know when the blood doth burne,
How prodigall the tongue lends the heart vowes,
In briefe, be more fcanter of your maiden prefence,
Or tendring thus you'l tender mee a foole.   390
    Ofel. I fhall obay my lord in all I may.
    Cor. *Ofelia*, receiue none of his letters,
" For louers lines are fnares to intrap the heart;
" Refufe his tokens, both of them are keyes
To vnlocke Chaftitie vnto Defire;   395
Come in *Ofelia*, fuch men often proue,
" Great in their wordes, but little in their loue.

[I, iii, 136.] *Ofel.* I will my lord.   *exeunt.*
        Enter Hamlet, Horatio, *and* Marcellus.

[I, iv, 1.]   *Ham.* The ayre bites fhrewd; it is an eager and
An nipping winde, what houre i'ft?   400
    Hor. I think it lacks of twelue,   *Sound Trumpets.*

Mar.   No, t'is ftrucke.

Hor.   Indeed I heard it not,what doth this mean my lord?

Ham.   O the king doth wake to night, & takes his rowfe,
Keepe waffel,and the fwaggering vp-fpring reeles,   405
And as he dreames, his draughts of renifh downe,
The kettle, drumme, and trumpet, thus bray out,
The triumphes of his pledge.

Hor.   Is it a cuftome here?

Ham.   I mary i'ft and though I am   410
Natiue here, and to the maner borne,
It is a cuftome, more honourd in the breach,
Then in the obferuance.

Enter the Ghoft.

[I, iv, 38.]   *Hor.*   Looke my Lord, it comes.

Ham.   Angels and Minifters of grace defend vs,   415
Be thou a fpirite of health, or goblin damn'd,
Bring with thee ayres from heauen, or blafts from hell :
Be thy intents wicked or charitable,
Thou commeft in fuch queftionable fhape,
That I will fpeake to thee,   420
Ile call thee *Hamlet*, King, Father, Royall Dane,
O anfwere mee, let mee not burft in ignorance,
But fay why thy canonizd bones hearfed in death
Haue burft their ceremonies:why thy Sepulcher,
In which wee faw thee quietly interr'd,   425
Hath burft his ponderous and marble Iawes,
To caft thee vp againe: what may this meane,
That thou, dead corfe,againe in compleate fteele,
Reuiffets thus the glimfes of the Moone,
Making night hideous,and we fooles of nature,   430
So horridely to fhake our difpofition,
With thoughts beyond the reaches of our foules?

[I, iv, 57.]   Say,fpeake,wherefore,what may this meane?

Hor.   It beckons you, as though it had fomething
To impart to you alone.   435

Mar.   Looke with what courteous action
It waues you to a more remoued ground,
But do not go with it.

Hor.   No, by no meanes my Lord.

Ham.   It will not fpeake, then will I follow it.   440

Hor.   What if it tempt you toward the flood my Lord.
That beckles ore his bace,into the fea,
And there affume some other horrible fhape,
Which might depriue your foueraigntie of reafon,
And drive you into madneffe : thinke of it.   445

Ham.   Still am I called, go on,ile follow thee.

Hor.   My Lord,you fhall not go.

[I, iv, 64.]   *Ham.*   Why what fhould be the feare?
I do not fet my life at a pinnes fee,

And for my foule,what can it do to that? 450
Being a thing immortall, like it felfe,
Go on, ile follow thee.
    Mar. My Lord be rulde, you fhall not goe.
    Ham. My fate cries out,and makes each pety Artiue
As hardy as the Nemeon Lyons nerue, 455
Still am I cald, vnhand me gentlemen;
By heauen ile make a ghoft of him that lets me,
Away I fay, go on, ile follow thee.
    Hor. He waxeth defperate with imagination.
    Mar. Something is rotten in the ftate of *Denmarke.* 460
    Hor. Haue after; to what iffue will this fort?

[I, iv, 88.]   *Mar.* Lets follow, tis not fit thus to obey him.   *exit.*
            Enter Ghoft and Hamlet.

[I, v, 1.]   *Ham.* Ile go no farther,whither wilt thou leade me?
    Ghoft Marke me.
    Ham. I will. 465
    Ghoft I am thy fathers fpirit, doomd for a time
To walke the night, and all the day
Confinde in flaming fire,
Till the foule crimes done in my dayes of Nature
Arepurged and burnt away. 470
    Ham. Alas poore Ghoft.
    Ghoft Nay pitty me not, but to my vnfolding
Lend thy liftning eare, but that I am forbid
To tell the fecrets of my prifon houfe
I would a tale vnfold, whofe lighteft word 475
Would harrow vp thy foule, freeze thy yong blood,
Make thy two eyes like ftars ftart from their fpheres,
Thy knotted and combined locks to part,
And each particular haire to ftand on end
Like quils vpon the fretfull Porpentine, 480
But this fame blazon muft not be,to eares of flefh and blood
Hamlet, if euer thou didft thy deere father loue.

[I, v, 24.]   *Ham.* O God.
    Gho. Reuenge his foule, and moft vnnaturall murder :
    Ham. Murder. 485
    Ghoft Yea, murder in the higheft degree,
As in the leaft tis bad,
But mine moft foule,beaftly,and vnnaturall.
    Ham. Hafte me to knowe it, that with wings as fwift as
meditation, or the thought of it,may fweepe to my reuenge. 490
    Ghoft O I finde thee apt, and duller fhouldst thou be
Then the fat weede which rootes it felfe in eafe
On *Lethe* wharffe : briefe let me be.
Tis giuen out, that fleeping in my orchard,
A Serpent ftung me; fo the whole eare of *Denmarke* 495
Is with a forged Proffes of my death rankely abufde :
But know thou noble Youth: he that did fting

Thy fathers heart, now weares his Crowne.

[I, v, 40.]   *Ham.*   O my prophetike foule, my vncle! my vncle!

    Ghoſt   Yea he, that inceſtuous wretch, wonne to his will   500
O wicked will,and gifts! that haue the power   (with gifts,
So to feduce my moſt feeming vertuous Queene,
But vertne, as it neuer will be moued,
Though Lewdneſſe court it in a ſhape of heauen,
So Luſt, though to a radiant angle linckt,   505
Would fate it felfe from a celeſtiall bedde,
And prey on garbage: but foft, me thinkes
I fent the mornings ayre, briefe let me be,
Sleeping within my Orchard, my cuſtome alwayes
In the after noone, vpon my fecure houre   510
Thy vncle came, with iuyce of Hebona
In a viall, and through the porches of my eares
Did powre the leaprous diſtilment,whofe effeƈt
Hold fuch an enmitie with blood of man,
That fwift as quickefilner, it poſteth through   515
The naturall gates and allies of the body,
And turnes the thinne and wholefome blood

[I, v, 69.] Like eager dropings into milke.
And all my fmoothe body, barked,and tettered ouer.
Thus was I fleeping by a brothers hand   520
Of Crowne,of Queene,of life,of dignitie
At once depriued, no reckoning made of,
But fent vnto my graue,
With all my accompts and finnes vpon my head,
O horrible, moſt horrible!   525
    Ham.   O God!
    ghoſt   If thou haft nature in thee, beare it not,
But howfoeuer, let not thy heart
Confpire againſt thy mother aught,
Leaue her to heauen,   530
And to the burthen that her confcience beares.
I muſt be gone, the Glo-worme ſhewes the Martin
To be neere, and gin's to pale his vneffectuall fire :
Hamlet adue,adue,adue : remember me.   *Exit*

[I, v, 92.]   *Ham.*   O all you hoſte of heauen! O earth,what elfe?   535
And ſhall I couple hell; remember thee?
Yes thou poore Ghoſt; from the tables
Of my memorie, ile wipe away all fawes of Bookes,
All triuiall fond conceites
That euer youth,or elfe obferuance noted,   540
And thy remembrance, all alone ſhall fit.
Yes, yes, by heauen, a damnd pernitious villaine,
Murderons, bawdy, fmiling damned villaine,
(My tables) meet it is I fet it downe,
That one may fmile, and fmile, and be a villayne;   545
At leaſt I am fure, it may be fo in *Denmarke.*

So vncle, there you are, there you are.

Now to the words; it is adue adue : remember me,

[I, v, 112.] Soe t'is enough I haue fworne. 550

    Hor. My lord,my lord.   *Enter. Horatio,*

    Mar. Lord Hamlet.   *and Marcellus.*

    Hor. Ill, lo,lo,ho,ho.

    Mar. Ill,lo,lo,fo,ho,fo,come boy, come.

    Hor. Heauens fecure him.

    Mar. How i'ft my noble lord? 555

    Hor. What news my lord?

    Ham. O wonderfull, wonderful.

    Hor. Good my lord tel it.

    Ham. No not I, you'l reueale it.

    Hor. Not I my Lord by heauen. 560

    Mar Nor I my Lord.

    Ham. How fay you then?would hart of man

Once thinke it? but you'l be fecret.

    Both. I by heauen,my lord.

    Ham. There's neuer a villaine dwelling in all *Denmarke*, 565

But hee's an arrant knaue.

[I, v, 125.] *Hor.* There need no Ghoft come from the graue to tell

you this.

    Ham. Right, you are in the right, and therefore

I holde it meet without more circumftance at all,

Wee fhake hands and part;you as your bufines 570

And defiers fhall leade you : for looke you,

Euery man hath bufines, and defires, fuch

As it is, and for my owne poore parte, ile go pray.

    Hor. Thefe are but wild and wherling words, my Lord.

    Ham. I am fory they offend you ;hartely,yes faith hartily. 575

    Hor. Ther's no offence my Lord.

    Ham. Yes by Saint *Patrike* but there is H*oratio*,

And much offence too, touching this vifion,

It is an honeft ghoft, that let mee tell you,

For your defires to know what is betweene vs, 580

Or'emaifter it as you may:

And now kind frends, as yon are frends,

Schollers and gentlmen,

Grant mee one poore requeft.

    Both. What i'ft my Lord? 585

[I, v, 144.] *Ham.* Neuer make known what you haue feene to night

    Both. My lord,we will not.

    Ham. Nay but fweare.

    Hor. In faith my Lord not I.

    Mar. Nor I my Lord in faith.

    Ham. Nay vpon my fword, indeed vpon my fword. 590

    Gho. Sweare.

            The Goft under the ftage.

    Ham Ha, ha, come you here, this fellow in the fellerige,

Here confent to fweare.

    Hor. Propofe the oth my Lord.   595

    Ham. Neuer to fpeake what you haue feene to night,

Sweare by my fword.

    Goft. Sweare.

    Ham. *Hic & vbique* ; nay then weele fhift our ground:

Come hither Gentlemen, and lay your handes   600

Againe vpon this fword, neuer to fpeake

Of that which you haue feene, fweare by my fword.

    Ghoft Sweare.

[I, v, 162.] *Ham.* Well faid old Mole, can'ft worke in the earth?

so faft, a worthy Pioner, once more remoue.   605

    Hor. Day and night,but this is wondrous ftrange.

    Ham. And therefore as a ftranger giue it welcome,

There are more things in heauen and earth *Horatio*,

Then are Dream't of, in your philofophie,

But come here,as before you neuer fhall   610

How ftrange or odde foere I beare my felfe,

As I perchance hereafter fhall thinke meet,

To put an Anticke difpofition on,

That you at fuch times feeing me, neuer fhall

[I, v, 174.] With Armes, incombred thus,or this head fhake,   615

Or by pronouncing fome vndoubtfull phrafe,

As well well, wee know, or wee could and if we would,

Or there be, and if they might, or fuch ambiguous.·

Giuing out to note, that you know aught of mee,

This not to doe, fo grace, and mercie   620

At your moft need helpe you, fweare.

    Ghoft. fweare.

    Ham. Reft, reft,perturbed fpirit: fo gentlemen,

In all my loue I do commend mee to you,

And what fo poore a man as *Hamlet* may,   625

To pleafure you, God willing fhall not want,

Nay come lett's go together,

But ftil your fingers on your lippes I pray,

The time is out of ioynt,O curfed fpite,

That euer I was borne to fet it right,   630

[I, v, 191.] Nay come lett's go together.   *Exeunt.*

          Enter Corambis, and Montano.

[II, 1, 1.]   *Cor.* *Montano*, here, thefe letters to my fonne,

And this fame mony with my bleffing to him,

And bid him ply his learning good *Montano*.

    Mon. Iwill my lord.   635

    Cor. You fhall do very well *Montano*, to fay thus,

I knew the gentleman, or know his father,

To inquire the manner of his life,

As thus; being amongft his acquaintance,

You may fay, you faw him at fuch a time, marke you mee,   640

At game,or drincking, fwearing, or drabbing,

You may go fo farre.

　　Mon.　My lord, that will impeach his reputation.

　　Cor.　I faith not a whit, no not a whit,

Now happely hee clofeth with you in the confequence,　　645

As you may bridle it not difparage him a iote.

What was I a bout to fay,

[II, i, 52.]　　*Mon.*　He clofeth with him in the confequence.

　　Cor.　I, you fay right, he clofeth with him thus,

This will hee fay, let mee fee what hee will fay,　　650

Mary this,I faw him yefterday, or tother day,

Or then, or at fuch a time, a dicing,

Or at Tennis, I or drincking drunke, or entring

Of a howfe of lightnes viz. brothell,

Thus fir do wee that know the world, being men of reach,　　655

By indirections, finde directions forth,

And fo fhall you my fonne; you ha me, ha you not?

　　Mon.　I haue my lord.

　　Cor.　Wel, fare you well,commend mee to him.

　　Mon.　I will my lord.　　660

[II, i, 73.]　　*Cor.*　And bid him ply his musicke

　　Mon.　My lord I wil.　　　　*exit.*

　　　　　　Enter, Ofelia.

　　Cor.　Farewel,how now *Ofelia*,what's the news with you?

　　Ofe.　O my deare father, fuch a change in nature,

So great an alteration in a Prince,　　665

So pitifull to him, fearefull to mee,

A maidens eye ne're looked on.

　　Cor.　Why what's the matter my *Ofelia?*

　　Of.　O yong Prince *Hamlet*, the only floure of *Denmark*,

Hee is bereft of all the wealth he had,　　670

The Iewell that ador'nd his feature moft

Is filcht and ftolne away, his wit's bereft him,

Hee found mee walking in the gallery all alone,

There comes hee to mee,with a diftracted looke,

[II, i, 80.]　His garters lagging downe, his fhoes vntide,　　675

And fixt his eyes fo ftedfaft on my face,

As if they had vow'd, this is their lateft obiect.

Small while he ftoode, but gripes me by the wrist,

And there he holdes my pulfe till with a figh

He doth vnclafpe his holde, and parts away　　680

Silent,as is the mid time of the night:

And as he went, his eie was ftill on mee,

For thus his head ouer his fhoulder looked,

He feemed to finde the way without his eies:

For out of doores he went without their helpe,　　685

And fo did leaue me.

　　Cor.　Madde for thy loue,

What haue you giuen him any croffe wordes of late?

[II, i, 109.]　*Ofelia*　I did repell his letters, deny his gifts,　　690

As you did charge me.
   Cor. Why that hath made him madde:
By heau'n t'is as proper for our age to caft
Beyond our felues, as t'is for the yonger fort
To leaue their wantonneffe. Well, I am fory   695
That I was fo rafh: but what remedy?
Lets to the King, this madneffe may prooue,
[II, 1, 120.]   Though wilde a while, yet more true to thy loue.   *exeunt.*
   Enter King and Queene, Roffencraft,and Gilderftone.
[II, ii, 1.]   *King* Right noble friends, that our deere cofin Hamlet
Hath loft the very heart of all his fence,   700
It is moft right, and we moft fory for him:
Therefore we doe defire, euen as you tender
Our care to him, and our great loue to you,
That you will labour but to wring from him
The caufe and ground of his diftemperancie.   705
Doe this, the king of *Denmarke* fhal be thankefull.
   Ros. My Lord, whatfoeuer lies within our power
Your maieftie may more commaund in wordes
Then vfe perfwafions to your liege men,bound
By loue, by duetie, and obedience.   710
   Guil. What we may doe for both your Maiefties
To know the griefe troubles the Prince your fonne,
We will indeuour all the beft we may,
So in all duetie doe we take our leaue.
[II, ii, 33.]   *King* Thankes Guilderftone, and gentle Roffencraft. 715
   Que. Thankes Roffencraft,and gentle Gilderftone.
       Enter Corambis and Ofelia.
   Cor. My Lord, the Ambaffadors are ioyfully
Return'd from *Norway.*
   King Thou ftill haft beene the father of good news.
   Cor. Haue I my Lord? I affure your grace,   720
I holde my duetie as I holde my life,
Both to my God, and to my foueraigne King:
And I beleeue, or elfe this braine of mine
Hunts not the traine of policie fo well
As it had wont to doe, but I haue found   725
The very depth of Hamlets lunacie.
   Queene God graunt he hath.
       Enter the Ambaffadors.
[II, ii, 59.]   *King* Now *Voltemar*,what from our brother *Norway?*
   Volt. Moft faire returnes of greetings and defires,
Vpon our firft he fent forth to fuppreffe   730
His nephews leuies, which to him appear'd
To be a preparation gainft the Polacke:
But better look't into, he truely found
It was againft your Highneffe,whereat grieued,
That fo his fickeneffe,age,and impotence,   735
Was falfely borne in hapd, fends out arrefts

On *Fortenbraffe*, which he in briefe obays,
Receiues rebuke from *Norway*:and in fine,
Makes vow before his vncle, neuer more
To giue the affay of Armes againft your Maieftie, 740
Whereon old *Norway* ouercome with ioy,

[II, ii, 73.] Giues him three thoufand crownes in annuall fee,
And his commiffion to employ thofe fouldiers,
So leuied as before, againft the Polacke,
With an intreaty heerein further fhewne, 745
That it would pleafe you to giue quiet paffe
Through your dominions, for that enterprife
On such regardes offafety and allowances
As therein are fet downe.

    King It likes vs well, and at fit time and leafure 750
Weele reade and anfwere thefe his Articles,
Meane time we thanke you for your well
Tooke labour : go to your reft,at night weele feaft togither:
Right welcome home.   *exeunt Ambaffadors.*

[II, ii, 85.] *Cor.* This bufines is very well difpatched. 755
Now my Lord,touching the yong Prince Hamlet,
Certaine it is that hee is madde: mad let vs grant him then:
Now to know the caufe of this effect,
Or elfe to fay the caufe of this defect;
For this effect defectiue comes by caufe. 760
    Queene Good my Lord be briefe.
    Cor. Madam I will: my Lord, I haue a daughter,
Haue while fhee's mine : for that we thinke
Is fureft, we often loofe:now to the Prince.
My lord, but note this letter, 765
The which my daughter in obedience
Delieuer'd to my handes.
    King Reade it my Lord.
    Cor. Marke my Lord.

[II, ii, 115.] Doubt that in earth is fire, 770
Doubt that the ftarres doe moue,
Doubt trueth to be a liar,
But doe not doubt I loue.
To the beautiful *Ofelia :*
Thine euer the moft vnhappy Prince *Hamlet.* 775
My Lord, what doe you thinke of me?
I, or what might you thinke when I fawe this?
    King As of a true friend and a moft louing fubiect.
    Cor. I would be glad to prooue fo.
Now when I faw this letter,thus I befpake my maiden: 780
Lord *Hamlet* is a Prince out of your ftarre,
And one that is vnequall for your loue:
Therefore I did commaund her refufe his letters,
Deny his tokens,and to abfent her felfe.
Shee as my childe obediently obey'd me. 785

Now fince which time, feeing his loue thus croff'd,
Which I tooke to be idle, and but fport,
He ftraitway grew into a melancholy,
From that vnto a faft, then vnto diftraction,
Then into a fadneffe, from that vnto a madneffe,   790
And fo by continuance,and weakeneffe of the braine
Into this frenfie, which now poffeffeth him:

[II, ii, 155.] And if this be not true, take this from this.
   King Thinke you t'is fo?
   Cor. How? fo my Lord, I would very faine know   795
That thing that I haue faide t'is fo, pofitiuely,
And it hath fallen out otherwife.
Nay, if circumftances leade me on,
Ile finde it out,if it were hid
As deepe as the centre of the earth.   800
   King. how fhould wee trie this fame?
   Cor. Mary my good lord thus,
The Princes walke is here in the galery,
There let *Ofelia*,walke vntill hee comes:
Your felfe and I will ftand clofe in the ftudy,   805
There fhall you heare the effect of all his hart,
And if it proue any otherwife then loue,
Then let my cenfure faile an other time.

[II, ii, 167.] *King.* fee where hee comes poring vppon a booke.
     Enter Hamlet.
   Cor. Madame, will it pleafe your grace   810
To leaue vs here?
   Que. With all my hart.   *exit.*

[III, i, 44.] *Cor.* And here *Ofelia*, reade you on this booke,
And walke aloofe, the King fhal be vnfeene.

[III, i, 56.] *Ham.* To be,or not to be, I there's the point,   815
To Die, to fleepe,is that all? I all:
No,to fleepe,to dreame, I mary there it goes,
For in that dreame of death, when wee awake,
And borne before an euerlafting Iudge,
From whence no paffenger euer retur'nd,   820
The vndifcouered country, at whofe fight
The happy fmile,and the accurfed damn'd.
But for this,the ioyfull hope of this,
Whol'd beare the fcornes and flattery of the world,
Scorned by the right rich,the rich curffed of the poore?   825
The widow being oppreffed,the orphan wrong'd,
The tafte of hunger, or a tirants raigne,
And thoufand more calamities befides,
To grunte and fweate vnder this weary life,
When that he may his full *Quietus* make,   830
With a bare bodkin, who would this indure,
But for a hope of fomething after death?
Which pufles the braine, and doth confound the fence,

Which makes vs rather beare thofe euilles we haue,
Than flie to others that we know not of.   835
I that,O this confcience makes cowardes of vs all,
[III, i, 90.] Lady in thy orizons, be all my finnes remembred.
   Ofel. My Lord, I haue fought opportunitie,which now
I haue,to redeliuer to your worthy handes, a fmall remem-
brance, fuch tokens which I haue receiued of you.   840
[III, i, 105.] *Ham.* Are you faire?
   Ofel. My Lord.
   Ham. Are you honeft?
   Ofel. What meanes my Lord?
   Ham. That if you be faire and honeft,   845
Your beauty fhould admit no difcourse to your honefty.
   Ofel. My Lord, can beauty haue better priuiledge than
with honefty?
   Ham. Yea mary may it; for Beauty may transforme
Honefty, from what fhe was into a bawd: 850
Then Honefty can transforue Beauty:
This was fometimes a Paradox,
But now the time giues it fcope.
[III, i, 96.] I neuer gaue you nothing.
   Ofel. My Lord, you know right well you did,
And with them fuch earneft vowes of loue,   855
As would haue moou'd the ftonieft breaft aliue,
But now too true I finde,
Rich giftes waxe poore, when giuers grow vnkinde.
   Ham. I neuer loued you.
   Ofel. You made me beleeue you did.   860
[III, i, 117.] *Ham.* O thou fhouldft not a beleeued me!
Go to a Nunnery goe, why fhouldft thou
Be a breeder of finners? I am my felfe indifferent honeft,
But I could accufe my felfe of fuch crimes
It had beene better my mother had ne're borne me,   865
O I am very prowde, ambitious,difdainefull,
With more finnes at my becke, then I haue thoughts
To put them in, what fhould fuch fellowes as I
Do, crawling between heauen and earth?
To a Nunnery goe, we are arrant knaues all,   870
Beleeue none of vs, to a Nunnery goe.
   Ofel. O heauens fecure him!
[III, i, 131.] *Ham.* Wher's thy father?
   Ofel. At home my lord.
   Ham. For Gods fake let the doores be fhut on him,   875
He may play the foole no where but in his
Owne houfe:to a Nunnery goe.
   Ofel. Help him good God.
   Ham. If thou doft marry, Ile giue thee
This plague to thy dowry: 880
Be thou as chafte as yce, as pure as fnowe,

Thou fhalt not fcape calumny,to a Nunnery goe.

Ofel. Alas, what change is this?

Ham. But if thou wilt needes marry,marry a foole,
For wifemen know well enough,   885
What monfters you make of them,to a Nunnery goe.

Ofel. Pray God reftore him.

[III, i, 142.] *Ham.* Nay, I haue heard of your paintings too,
God hath giuen you one face,
And you make your felues another,   890
You fig,and you amble, and you nickname Gods creatures,
Making your wantonneffe, your ignorance,
A pox, t'is fcuruy, Ile no more of it,
It hath made me madde : Ile no more marriages,
All that are married but one,fhall liue,   895
The reft fhall keepe as they are, to a Nunnery goe,

[III, i, 149.] To a Nunnery goe.   *exit.*

Ofe. Great God of heauen,what a quicke change is this?
The Courtier,Scholler,Souldier, all in him,
All dafht and fplintered thence, O woe is me,   900
To a feene what I haue feene,fee what I fee.   *exit.*

[III, i, 162.] *King* Loue? No,no, that's not the caufe,   *Enter King and*
Some deeper thing it is that troubles him.   *Corambis.*

Cor. Wel,fomething it is:my Lord,content you a while,
I will my felfe goe feele him:let me worke,   905
Ile try him euery way: fee where he comes,
Send you thofe Gentlemen, let me alone
To finde the depth of this,away,be gone.   *exit King.*

[II, ii, 172.] Now my good Lord,do you know me?   *Enter Hamlet.*

Ham. Yea very well,y'are a fifhmonger.   910

Cor. Not I my Lord.

Ham. Then fir, I would you were fo honeft a man,
For to be honeft,as this age goes,
Is one man to be pickt out of tenne thousand.

[II, ii, 190.] *Cor.* What doe you reade my Lord?   915

Ham. Wordes,wordes.

Cor. What's the matter my Lord?

Ham. Betweene who?

Cor. I meane the matter you reade my Lord.

Ham. Mary moft vile herefie: 920
For here the Satyricall Satyre writes,
That olde men haue hollow eyes,weake backes,
Grey beardes, pittifull weake hammes, gowty legges,
All which sir,I moft potently beleeue not:
For fir, your felfe fhalbe olde as I am,   925
If like a Crabbe, you could goe backeward.

[II, ii, 206.] *Cor.* How pregnant his replies are,and full of wit:
Yet at firft he tooke me for a fishmonger :
All this comes by loue,the vemencie of loue,
And when I was yong, I was very idle,   930

And fuffered much extafie in loue, very neere this:
[II, ii, 204.] Will you walke out of the airè my Lord?

    Ham. Into my graue.

    Cor. By the maffe that's out of the aire indeed,
Very fhrewd anfwers,   935
My lord I will take my leaue of you.

    Enter Gilderftone, and Roffencraft.

    Ham. You can take nothing from me fir,
I will more willingly part with all,
[II, ii, 216.] Olde doating foole.

    Cor, You feeke Prince Hamlet,fee,there he is. *exit.* 940

    Gil. Health to your Lordfhip.

    Ham. What, Gilderftone,and Roffencraft,
Welcome kinde Schoole-fellowes to *Elfanoure.*

    Gil. We thanke your Grace,and would be very glad
You were as when we were at *Wittenberg.* 945
[II, ii, 269.] *Ham.* I thanke you, but is this vifitation free of
Your felues, or were you not fent for?
Tell me true,come,I know the good King and Queene
Sent for you,there is a kinde of confeffion in your eye:
Come, I know you were fent for. 950

    Gil. What fay you?
[II, ii, 283.] *Ham.* Nay then I fee how the winde fits,
Come,you were fent for.

    Roff. My lord,we were, and willingly if we might,
Know the caufe and ground of your difcontent. 955

    Ham. Why I want preferment.

    Roff. I thinke not fo my lord.
[II, ii, 290.] *Ham.* Yes faith,this great world you fee contents me not,
No nor the fpangled heauens,nor earth,nor fea,
No nor Man that is fo glorious a creature, 960
Contents not me,no nor woman too,though you laugh.

    Gil. My lord, we laugh not at that.

    Ham. Why did you laugh then,
When I faid,Man did not content mee?

    Gil. My Lord, we laughed,when you faid, Man did not 965
content you.
What entertainement the Players fhall haue,
[II, ii, 307.] We boorded them a the way: they are comming to you.

    Ham. Players,what Players be they?

    Roff. My Lord,the Tragedians of the Citty,
Thofe that you tooke delight to fee fo often. (ftie? 970

    Ham. How comes it that they trauell? Do they grow re-

    Gil. No my Lord, their reputation holds as it was wont.

    Ham. How then?

    Gil. Yfaith my Lord, noueltie carries it away,
For the principall publike audience that 975
Came to them, are turned to priuate playes,
[II, ii, 327.] And to the humour of children.

      Ham. I doe not greatly wonder of it,

[II, ii, 347.] For thofe that would make mops and moes

      At my vncle, when my father liued,   980

      Now giue a hundred,two hundred pounds

      For his picture : but they fhall be welcome,

[II, ii, 309.] He that playes the King fhall haue tribute of me,

      The ventrous Knight fhall vse his foyle and target,

      The louer fhall figh gratis,   985

      The clowne fhall make them laugh   (for't,

      That are tickled in the lungs, or the blanke verfe shall halt

[II, ii, 314.] And the Lady fhall haue leaue to fpeake her minde freely.

        The Trumpets found, Enter Corambis.

[II, ii, 364.] Do you fee yonder great baby?

      He is not yet out of his fwadling clowts.   990

      Gil. That may be, for they fay an olde man

      Is twice a childe.   (Players,

      Ham. Ile prophecie to you, hee comes to tell mee a the

      You fay true, a monday laft, t'was fo indeede.

      Cor. My lord, I haue news to tell you.   995

      Ham. My Lord, I haue newes to tell you:

      When *Roffios* was an Actor in *Rome.*

      Cor. The Actors are come hither,my lord.

      Ham. Buz,buz.

      Cor. The beft Actors in Chriftendome,   1000

      Either for Comedy,Tragedy,Hiftorie,Paftorall,

      Paftorall,Hiftoricall,Hiftoricall,Comicall,

      Comicall hiftoricall, Paftorall,Tragedy hiftoricall:

      Seneca cannot be too heauy,nor *Plato* too light:

      For the law hath writ thofe are the onely men.   1005

[II, ii, 384.]   *Ha.* O *Iepha* Iudge of *Ifrael!* what a treafure hadft thou?

      Cor. Why what a treafure had he my lord?

      Ham. Why one faire daughter,and no more,

      The which he loued paffing well.

      Cor. A,ftil harping a my daughter!well my Lord,   1010

      If you call me *Iepha*, I hane a daughter that

      I loue paffing well.

      Ham. Nay that followes not.

      Cor. What followes then my Lord?

      Ham. Why by lot, or God wot,or as it came to paffe,   1015

      And fo it was, the firft verfe of me godly Ballet

      Wil tel you all:for look you where my abridgement comes:

[II, ii, 402.] Welcome maifters, welcome all,   *Enter players.*

      What my olde friend,thy face is vallanced

      Since I faw thee laft,com'ft thou to beard me in *Denmarke?*   1020

      My yong lady and miftris, burlady but your   (you were:

      Ladifhip is growne by the altitude of a chopine higher than

      Pray God fir your voyce, like a peece of vncurrant

      Golde, be not crack't in the ring: come on maifters,

      Weele euen too't, like French Falconers,   1025

Flie at any thing we fee, come, a tafte of your
Quallitie, a fpeech,a paffionate fpeech.
 Players What fpeech my good lord?
 Ham. I heard thee fpeake a fpeech once,
But it was neuer acted:or if it were,   1030
Neuer aboue twice, for as I remember,
It pleafed not the vulgar,it was cauiary
To the million : but to me
And others, that receiued it in the like kinde,
Cried in the toppe of their iudgements,an excellent play, 1035
Set downe with as great modeftie as cunning:
One faid there was no fallets in the lines to make the fauory,
But called it an honeft methode,as wholefome as fweete.
Come, a fpeech in it I chiefly remember
[II, ii, 425.] Was *Æneas* tale to *Dido*,   1040
And then efpecially where he talkes of Princes flaughter,
If it liue in thy memory beginne at this line,
Let me fee.
The rugged *Pyrrus*, like th'arganian beaft:
No 'tis not fo, it begins with *Pirrus:*   1045
O I haue it.
The rugged *Pirrus*,he whofe fable armes,
Black as his purpofe did the night refemble,
When he lay couched in the ominous horfe,
Hath now his blacke and grimme complexion fmeered 1050
With Heraldry more difmall, head to foote,
Now is he totall guife, horridely tricked
With blood of fathers,mothers,daughters,fonnes,
Back't and imparched in calagulate gore,
Rifted in earth and fire, olde grandfire *Pryam* feekes : 1055
So goe on.   (accent.
 Cor. Afore God, my Lord, well fpoke, and with good
[II, ii, 446.] *Play.* Anone he finds him ftriking too fhort at Greeks,
His antike fword rebellious to his Arme,
Lies where it falles, vnable to refift.   1060
Pyrrus at *Pryam* driues, but all in rage,
Strikes wide, but with the whiffe and winde
[II, ii, 452.] Of his fell fword, th'unnerued father falles.
[II, ii, 476.] *Cor.* Enough my friend,t'is too long.
 Ham. It fhall to the Barbers with your beard: 1065
A pox, hee's for a Iigge, or a tale of bawdry,
Or elfe he fleepes, come on to *Hecuba*,come.
 Play. But who,O who had feene the mobled Queene?
 Cor. Mobled Queene is good,faith very good.
 Play. All in the alarum and feare of death rofe vp, 1070
And o're her weake and all ore-teeming loynes,a blancket
And a kercher on that head,where late the diademe ftoode,
Who this had feene with tongue inuenom'd fpeech,

1073. *tongue inuenom'd*] The space between these words (if there be any at all) is of the very leaft.

Would treafon haue pronounced,
For if the gods themfelues had feene her then,   1075
When fhe faw *Pirrus* with malitious ftrokes,
Mincing her husbandes limbs,
It would haue made milch the burning eyes of heauen,
[II, ii, 496.] And paffion in the gods.
    Cor. Looke my lord if he hath not changde his colour,   1080
And hath teares in his eyes: no more good heart, no more.
    Ham. T'is well, t'is very well, I pray my lord,
Will you fee the Players well beftowed,
I tell you they are the Chronicles
And briefe abftracts of the time,   1085
After your death I can tell you,
You were better haue a bad Epiteeth,
Then their ill report while you liue.
    Cor. My lord, I will vfe them according to their deferts.
    Ham. O farre better man,vfe euery man after his deferts,   1090
Then who fhould fcape whipping?
Vfe them after your owne honor and dignitie,
The leffe they deferue, the greater credit's yours.
    Cor. Welcome my good fellowes.   *exit.*
[II, ii, 511.]   *Ham.* Come hither maifters, can you not play the mur- 1095
der of *Gonfago?*
    players Yes my Lord.
    Ham. And could'ft not thou for a neede ftudy me
Some dozen or fixteene lines,
Which I would fet downe and infert?   1100
    players Yes very eafily my good Lord.
    Ham. T'is well, I thanke you:follow that lord:
And doe you heare firs? take heede you mocke him not.
Gentlemen, for your kindnes I thanke you,
And for a time I would defire you leaue me.   1105
    Gil. Our loue and duetie is at your commaund.
          Exeunt all but Hamlet.
[II, ii, 523.]   *Ham.* Why what a dunghill idiote flaue am I?
Why thefe Players here draw water from eyes:
For Hecuba, why what is Hecuba to him,or he to Hecuba?
What would he do and if he had my loffe?   1110
His father murdred, and a Crowne bereft him,
He would turne all his teares to droppes of blood,
Amaze the ftanders by with his laments,
Strike more then wonder in the iudiciall eares,
Confound the ignorant, and make mute the wife,   1115
Indeede his paffion would be generall.
Yet I like to an affe and Iohn a Dreames,
Hauing my father murdred by a villaine,
Stand ftill,and let it paffe, why fure I am a coward:
Who pluckes me by the beard, or twites my nofe,   1120
[II, ii, 548.] Giue's me the lie i'th throate downe to the lungs,

Sure I fhould take it, or elfe I haue no gall,
Or by this I fhould a fatted all the region kites
With this flaues offell, this damned villaine,
Treacherous,bawdy,murderous villaine:
Why this is braue, that I the fonne of my deare father, 1125
Should like a fcalion, like a very drabbe
Thus raile in wordes.   About my braine,
I haue heard that guilty creatures fitting at a play,
Hath,by the very cunning of the fcene,confeft a murder 1130
Committed long before.
This fpirit that I haue feene may be the Diuell,
And out of my weakeneffe and my melancholy,
As he is very potent with fuch men,
Doth feeke to damne me, I will haue founder proofes, 1135
The play's the thing.

[II, ii, 581.] Wherein I'le catch the confcience of the King.   *exit.*

Enter the King, Queene, and Lordes.

[III, i, 1.]   *King*   Lordes, can you by no meanes finde
The caufe of our fonne Hamlets lunacie?
You being fo neere in loue, euen from his youth, 1140
Me thinkes fhould gaine more than a ftranger fhould.
    Gil.   My lord, we haue done all the beft we could,
To wring from him the caufe of all his griefe,
But ftill he puts vs off,and by no meanes
Would make an anfwere to that we expofde. 1145
    Roff.   Yet was he fomething more inclin'd to mirth
Before we left him, and I take it,
He hath giuen order for a play to night,
At which he craues your highneffe company.
    King   With all our heart, it likes vs very well: 1150
[III, i, 26.] Gentlemen, feeke ftill to increafe his mirth,
Spare for no coft, our coffers fhall be open,
And we vnto your felues will ftill be thankefull.
    Both   In all wee can, be fure you fhall commaund.
    Queene   Thankes gentlemen, and what the Queene of 1155
May pleafure you, be fure you fhall not want.   (*Denmarke*
    Gil.   Weele once againe vnto the noble Prince.
    King   Thanks to you both: Gertred you'l fee this play.
    Queene   My lord I will, and it ioyes me at the foule
He is inclin'd to any kinde of mirth. 1160
    Cor.   Madame, I pray be ruled by me:
And my good Soueraigne, giue me leaue to fpeake,
We cannot yet finde out the very ground
Of his diftemperance, therefore
I holde it meete, if fo it pleafe you, 1165
Elfe they fhall not meete,and thus it is.

King What i'ft *Corambis?*   (done.

[III, i, 181.]   *Cor.* Mary my good lord this,foone when the fports are
Madam, fend you in hafte to fpeake with him,
And I my felfe will ftand behind the Arras,   1170
There queftion you the caufe of all his griefe,
And then in loue and nature vnto you, hee'le tell you all:
My Lord,how thinke you on't?
   King It likes vs well, Gerterd, what fay you?
   Queene With all my heart, foone will I fend for him.   1175
   Cor. My felfe will be that happy meffenger,
Who hopes his griefe will be reueal'd to her.   *exeunt omnes*

Enter Hamlet and the Players.

[III, ii, 1.]   *Ham.* Pronounce me this fpeech trippingly a the tongue
as I taught thee,
Mary and you mouth it, as a many of your players do
I'de rather heare a towne bull bellow,   1180
Then fuch a fellow fpeake my lines.
Nor do not faw the aire thus with your hands,
But giue euery thing his action with temperance.   (fellow,
O it offends mee to the foule, to heare a rebuftious periwig
To teare a paffion in totters, into very ragges,   1185
To fplit the eares of the ignoraut,who for the   (noifes,
Moft parte are capable of nothing but dumbe fhewes and
I would haue fuch a fellow whipt,for ore doing, tarmagant
[III, ii, 13.]   It out,Herodes Herod.
[III, ii, 33.]   *players* My Lorde, wee haue indifferently reformed that   1190
among vs.
   Ham. The better, the better, mend it all together:
[III, ii, 26.]   There be fellowes that I haue feene play,
And heard others commend them,and that highly too,
That hauing neither the gate of Chriftian,Pagan,
Nor Turke,haue fo ftrutted and bellowed,   1195
That you would a thought, fome of Natures journeymen
Had made men,and not made them well,
They imitated humanitie,fo abhominable.
Take heede,auoyde it.
[III, ii, 14.]   *players* I warrant you my Lord.   1200
[III, ii, 35.]   *Ham.* And doe you heare? let not your Clowne fpeake
More then is fet downe, there be of them I can tell you
That will laugh themfelues, to fet on fome
Quantitie of barren fpectators to laugh with them,
Albeit there is fome neceffary point in the Play   1205
Then to be obferued:O t'is vile, and fhewes
A pittifull ambition in the foole that vfeth it.
And then you haue fome agen, that keepes one fute
Of ieafts, as a man is knowne by one fute of
Apparell, and Gentlemen quotes his ieafts downe   1210
In their tables, before they come to the play,as thus:

Cannot you ſtay till I eate my porrige? and,you owe me
A quarters wages:and, my coate wants a culliſon:
And,your beere is ſowre:and,blabbering with his lips,
And thus keeping in his cinkapaſe of ieaſts,   1215
When, God knows,the warme Clowne cannot make a ieſt
Vnleſſe by chance,as the blinde man catcheth a hare:
Maiſters tell him of it.

    players We will my Lord.
    Ham. Well, goe make you ready.   *exeunt players.*   1220
    Horatio. Heere my Lord.

[III, ii, 48.]   *Ham.* *Horatio,* thou art euen as iuſt a man,
As e're my conuerſation cop'd withall.
    Hor. O my lord!
    Ham. Nay why ſhould I flatter thee?   1225
Why ſhould the poore be flattered?
What gaine ſhould I receiue by flattering thee,
That nothing hath but thy good minde?
Let flattery ſit on thoſe time-pleaſing tongs,
To gloſe with them that loues to heare their praiſe,   1230
And not with ſuch as thou *Horatio.*

[III, ii, 70.] There is a play to night, wherein one Sceane they haue
Comes very neere the murder of my father,
When thou ſhalt ſee that Act afoote,
Marke thou the King, doe but obſerue his lookes,   1235
For I mine eies will riuet to his face:
And if he doe not bleach, and change at that,
It is a damned ghoſt that we haue ſeene,
Horatio, haue a care, obſerue him well.
    Hor. My lord, mine eies ſhall ſtill be on his face,   1240
And not the ſmalleſt alteration
That ſhall appeare in him, but I ſhall note it.
    Ham. Harke, they come.
    Enter King, Queene, Corambis, and other Lords. (a play?

[III, ii, 87.] *King* How now ſon *Hamlet,*how fare you,ſhall we haue
    Ham. Yfaith the Camelions diſh, not capon cramm'd,   1245
feede a the ayre.
I father: My lord, you playd in the Vniuerſitie.
    Cor. That I did my L: and I was counted a good actor.
    Ham. What did you enact there?
    Cor. My lord, I did act *Iulius Cæſar,* I was killed
in the Capitoll, *Brutus* killed me.   1250
    Ham. It was a brute parte of him,
To kill ſo capitall a calfe.
Come, be theſe Players ready?
    Queene Hamlet come ſit downe by me.
    Ham. No by my faith mother, heere's a mettle more at-   1255
Lady will you giue me leaue,and ſo forth: (tractiue:

1245. *feede] feed* Cam.

To lay my head in your lappe?

    Ofel. No my lord.   (trary matters?

[III, ii, 109.]   *Ham.* Vpon your lap,what do you thinke I meant con-

*Enter in a Dumbe Shew, the King and the Queene, he sits
downe in an Arbor, she leaues him : Then enters Lucianus with Poyson in a Viall, and powres it in his eares, and
goes away : Then the Queene commeth and findes him
dead : and goes away with the other.*

[III, ii, 128.]   *Ofel.* What meanes this my Lord?   *Enter the Prologue.*   1260

    Ham. This is myching Mallico, that meanes my chiefe.

    Ofel. What doth this meane my lord?

    Ham. you shall heare anone, this fellow will tell you all.

    Ofel. Will he tell vs what this shew meanes?

    Ham. I, or any shew you'le shew him,   1265

Be not afeard to shew, hee'le not be afeard to tell :

O these Players cannot keepe counsell, thei'le tell all.

    Prol. For vs, and for our Tragedie,

[III, ii, 139.] Heere stowpiug to your clemencie,

We begge your hearing patiently.   1270

    Ham. I'st a prologue, or a poesie for a ring?

    Ofel. T'is short my Lord.

    Ham. As womens loue.

         Enter the Duke and Dutchesse.

[III, ii, 145.] *Duke* Full fortie yeares are past, their date is gone,

Since happy time ioyn'd both our hearts as one: 1275

And now the blood that fill'd my youthfull veines,

Runnes weakely in their pipes, and all the straines

Of musicke, which whilome pleasde mine eare,

Is now a burthen that Age cannot beare:

And therefore sweete Nature must pay his due,   1280

To heauen must I, and leaue the earth with you.

    Dutchesse O say not so, lest that you kill my heart,

When death takes you, let life from me depart.

    Duke Content thy selfe, when ended is my date,

Thon maist (perchance) haue a more noble mate,   1285

More wise, more youthfull, and one.

    Dutchesse O speake no more, for then I am accurst,

[III, ii, 169.] None weds the second, but she kils the first:

[III, ii, 174.] A second time I kill my Lord that's dead,

When second husband kisses me in bed,   1290

    Ham. O wormewood, wormewood!

[III, ii, 176.] *Duke* I doe beleeue you sweete, what now you speake,

But what we doe determine oft we breake,

[III, ii, 202.] For our demises stil are ouerthrowne,

Our thoughts are ours, their end's none of our owne: 1295

So thinke you will no second husband wed,

But die thy thoughts, when thy first Lord is dead.

[III, ii, 212.] *Dutchesse* Both here and there pursue me lasting strife,

I once a widdow, euer I be wife

Ham. If fhe fhould breake now.   1300

Duke T'is deeply fworne,fweete leaue me heere a while,
My fpirites growe dull, and faine I would beguile the tedious time with fleepe.

Dutcheffe Sleepe rocke thy braine,
And neuer come mifchance betweene vs twaine.   *exit Lady*

    Ham. Madam, how do you like this play?   1305
    Queene The Lady protefts too much.
    Ham. O but fhee'le keepe her word.
    King Haue you heard the argument, is there no offence
in it?
    Ham. No offence in the world,poyfon in ieft,poifon in
    King What do you call the name of the play?   (ieft. 1310
    Ham. Moufe-trap:mary how trapically:this play is

[III, ii, 228.] The image of a murder done in *guyana, Albertus*
Was the Dukes name, his wife *Baptifta,*
Father,it is a knauifh peece a worke:but what
A that, it toucheth not vs, you and I that haue free   1315
Soules,let the galld iade wince, this is one
Lucianus nephew to the King.
    Ofel. Ya're as good as a *Chorus* my lord.
    Ham. I could interpret the loue you beare , if I fawe the
[III, ii, 236.] poopies dallying.
[III, ii, 114.]   *Ofel.* Y'are very pleafant my lord.   1320
    Ham. Who I, your onlie jig-maker, why what fhoulde
a man do but be merry? for looke how cheerefully my mo-
ther lookes, my father died within thefe two houres.
    Ofel. Nay, t'is twice two months,my Lord.
    Ham. Two months,nay then let the diuell weare blacke, 1325
For i'le haue a fute of Sables : Iefus, two months dead,
And not forgotten yet? nay then there's fome
Likelyhood, a gentlemans death may outliue memorie,
But by my faith hee muft build churches then,
Or els hee muft follow the olde Epitithe,   1330
[III, ii, 127.] With hoh, with ho, the hobi-horfe is forgot.
[III, ii, 237.]   *Ofel.* Your iefts are keene my Lord.
    Ham. It would coft you a groning to take them off.
    Ofel. Still better and worfe.
    Ham. So you muft take your husband, begin.   Murdred 1335
Begin, a poxe, leaue thy damnable faces and begin,
Come, the croking rauen doth bellow for reuenge.
    Murd. Thoughts blacke, hands apt, drugs fit, and time
Confederate feafon, elfe no creature feeing: (agreeing.
Thou mixture rancke,of midnight weedes collected,   1340
With *Hecates* bane thrife blafted, thrife infected,
Thy naturall magicke,and dire propertie,
One wholefome life vfurps immediately.   *exit.*

        1309. *in ieft*] *iniest* Cam.

[III, ii, 249.]   *Ham.* He poyfons him for his eftate.
           King Lights, I will to bed.   1345
           Cor. The king rifes,lights hoe.
                Exeunt King and Lordes.
           Ham. What, frighted with falfe fires?
[III, ii, 259.] Then let the stricken deere goe weepe,
           The Hart vngalled play,
           For fome muft laugh, while fome muft weepe,   1350
           Thus runnes the world away.
           Hor. The king is mooued my lord.
[III, ii, 274.]   *Hor.* I *Horatio*, i'le take the Ghofts word
           For more than all the coyne in *Denmarke.*

          Enter Roffencraft and Gilderftone.

           Roff. Now my lord,how i'ft with you?   1355
           Ham. And if the king like not the tragedy,
          Why then belike he likes it not perdy.
           Roff. We are very glad to fee your grace fo pleafant,
         My good lord, let vs againe intreate   (ture
         To know of you the ground and caufe of your diftempera- 1360
           Gil. My lord, your mother craues to fpeake with you.
[III, ii, 316.]   *Ham.* We fhall obey, were fhe ten times our mother.
           Roff. But my good Lord,fhall I intreate thus much?
[III, ii, 334.]   *Ham.* I pray will you play vpon this pipe?
           Roff. Alas my lord I cannot.   1365
           Ham. Pray will you.
           Gil. I haue no skill my Lord.
           Ham. why looke, it is a thing of nothing,
         T'is but ftopping of thefe holes,
         And with a little breath from your lips,   1370
         It will giue moft delicate mufick.
           Gil. But this cannot wee do my Lord.
           Ham. Pray now, pray hartily, I befeech you.
           Roff. My lord wee cannot.   (me?
           Ham. Why how vnworthy a thing would you make of 1375
         You would feeme to know my ftops, you would play vpon
         You would fearch the very inward part of my hart,   mee,
         And diue into the fecreet of my foule.
         Zownds do you thinke Iam eafier to be pla'yd
         On, then a pipe? call mee what Inftrument   1380
[III, ii, 354.] You will, though you can frett mee, yet you can not
[IV, ii, 12.] Play vpon mee, befides,to be demanded by a fpunge.
           Rof. How a fpunge my Lord?
           Ham. I fir,a fpunge, that fokes vp the kings
         Countenance, fauours, and rewardes, that makes   1385
         His liberalitie your ftore houfe : but fuch as you,
         Do the king,in the end, beft feruife ;
         For hee doth keep you as an Ape doth nuttes,

In the corner of his Iaw, firſt mouthes you,
Then ſwallowes you: ſo when hee hath need   1390
Of you, t'is but ſqueeſing of you,
[IV, ii, 20.] And ſpunge,you ſhall be dry againe,you ſhall.
 Roſ. Wel my Lord wee'le take our leaue.
 Ham Farewell, farewell, God bleſſe you.
  Exit Roſſencraft and Gilderſtone.

   Enter Corambis
[III, ii, 357.] *Cor.* My lord, the Queene would ſpeake with you. 1395
 Ham. Do you ſee yonder clowd in the ſhape of a camell?
 Cor. T'is like a camell in deed.
 Ham. Now me thinkes it's like a weaſel.
 Cor. T'is back't like a weaſell.
 Ham. Or like a whale.   1400
 Cor. Very like a whale. *exit Coram.*
 Ham. Why then tell my mother i'le come by and by.
Good night Horatio.
 Hor. Good night vnto your Lordſhip. *exit Horatio.*
 Ham. My mother ſhe hath ſent to ſpeake with me: 1405
O God, let ne're the heart of *Nero* enter
This ſoft boſome.
Let me be cruell, not vnnaturall.
I will ſpeake daggers, thoſe ſharpe wordes being ſpent,
[III, ii, 384.] To doe her wrong my ſoule ſhall ne're conſent. *exit.* 1410
   Enter the King.
 King O that this wet that falles vpon my face
[III, iii, 36.] Would waſh the crime cleere from my conſcience!
When I looke vp to heauen,I ſee my treſpaſſe,
The earth doth ſtill crie out vpon my faƈt,
Pay me the murder of a brother and a king, 1415
And the adulterous fault I haue committed:
O theſe are ſinnes that are vnpardonable:
Why ſay thy ſinnes were blacker than is ieat,
Yet may contrition make them as white as ſnowe:
I but ſtill to perſeuer in a ſinne,   1420
It is an aƈt gainſt the vniuerſall power,
Moſt wretched man,ſtoope,bend thee to thy prayer,
Aske grace of heauen to keepe thee from deſpaire.

   hee kneeles. *enters Hamlet*

 Ham. I ſo, come forth and worke thy laſt,
[III, iii, 75.] And thus hee dies: and ſo am I reuenged: 1425
No, not ſo: he tooke my father ſleeping, his ſins brim full,
And how his ſoule ſtoode to the ſtate of heauen
Who knowes, ſaue the immortall powres,
And ſhall I kill him now,
When he is purging of his ſoule?   1430

Making his way for heauen,this is a benefit,

[III, iii, 88.] And not reuenge:no, get thee vp agen,   (drunke,

When hee's at game fwaring, taking his carowfe, drinking

Or in the inceftuous pleafure of his bed,

Or at fome act that hath no relifh   1435

Of faluation in't, then trip him

That his heeles may kicke at heauen,

And fall as lowe as hel: my mother ftayes,

This phificke but prolongs thy weary dayes.   *exit Ham.*

[III, iii, 97.]   *King* My wordes fly vp,my finnes remaine below.   1440

No King on earth is fafe, if Gods his foe.   *exit King.*

Enter Queene and Corambis.

Cor. Madame,I heare yong Hamlet comming,

[III, iv, 4.] I'le fhrowde my felfe behinde the Arras.   *exit Cor.*

Queene Do fo my Lord.

Ham. Mother,mother, O are you here?

How i'ft with you mother?   1445

Queene How i'ft with you?

Ham, I'le tell you, but firft weele make all fafe.

Queene Hamlet, thou haft thy father much offended.

Ham. Mother, you haue my father much offended.   1450

Queene How now boy?

Ham. How now mother! come here,fit downe, for **you**

fhall heare me fpeake.

Queene What wilt thou doe? thou wilt not murder **me :**

Helpe hoe.   1455

Cor. Helpe for the Queene.

[III, iv, 24.]   *Ham.* I a Rat, dead for a Duckat.

Rafh intruding foole,farewell,

I tooke thee for thy better.

Queene Hamlet,what haft thou done?   1460

Ham. Not fo much harme, good mother,

As to kill a king,and marry with his brother.

Queene How! kill a king!

Ham. I a King:nay fit you downe, and ere **you part,**

If you be made of penitrable ftuffe,   1465

I'le make your eyes looke downe into your heart,

And fee how horride there and blacke it fhews.   (words?

Queene Hamlet, what mean'ft thou by thefe **killing**

[III, iv, 53.]   *Ham.* Why this I meane, fee here, behold this picture,

It is the portraiture,of your deceafed husband,   1470

See here a face, to outface *Mars* himfelfe,

An eye, at which his foes did tremble at,

A front wherin all vertues are fet downe

For to adorne a king, and guild his crowne,

Whofe heart went hand in hand euen with **that vow,**   1475

He made to you in marriage,and he is dead.

Murdred, damnably murdred, this was your husband,

Looke you now, here is your husband,

With a face like *Vulcan.*
A looke fit for a murder and a rape,   1480
A dull dead hanging looke, and a hell-bred cie,
To affright children and amaze the world:
And this fame haue you left to change with this.

[III, iv, 77.]   What Diuell thus hath cofoned you at hob-man blinde?
A! haue you eyes and can you looke on him   1485
That flew my father, and your deere hufband,
To liue in the inceftuous pleafure of his bed?
    Queene O Hamlet, fpeake no more.
    Ham. To leaue him that bare a Monarkes minde,
For a king of clowts, of very fhreads.   1490
    Queene Sweete Hamlet ceafe.
    Ham. Nay but ftill to persift and dwell in finne,
To fweate vnder the yoke of infamie,
To make increafe of fhame, to feale damnation.
    Queene Hamlet, no more.   1495
    Ham. Why appetite with you is in the waine,
Your blood runnes backeward now from whence it came,
Who'le chide hote blood within a Virgins heart,
When luft fhall dwell within a matrons breaft?

[III, iv, 156.]   *Queene* Hamlet,thou cleaues my heart in twaine.   1500
    Ham. O throw away the worfer part of it,and keepe the
better.

           Enter the ghoft in his night gowne.

[III, iv. 103.]   Saue me, faue me,you gratious
Powers aboue,and houer ouer mee,
With your celeftiall wings.
Doe you not come your tardy fonne to chide,   1505
That I thus long haue let reuenge flippe by?
O do not glare with lookes fo pittifull!
Left that my heart of ftone yeelde to compaffion,
And euery part that fhould affift reuenge,
Forgoe their proper powers, and fall to pitty.   1510
    Ghoft Hamlet, I once againe appeare to thee,
To put thee in remembrance of my death:
Do not negleft, nor long time put it off.
But I perceiue by thy diftracted lookes,
Thy mother's fearefull, and fhe ftands amazde: 1515
[III, iv, 115.]   Speake to her Hamlet, for her fex is weake,
Comfort thy mother, Hamlet, thinke on me.
    Ham. How i'ft with you Lady?
    Queene Nay, how i'ft with you
That thus you bend your eyes on vacancie,   1520
And holde difcourfe with nothing but with ayre?
    Ham. Why doe you nothing heare?
    Queene Not I.

Ham. Nor doe you nothing fee?

Queene No neither.   (habite 1525

Ham. No, why fee the king my father, my father, in the
As he liued, looke you how pale he lookes,
See how he fteales away out of the Portall,

[III, iv, 136.] Looke, there he goes.   *exit ghoft.*

Queene Alas, it is the weakneffe of thy braine,   1530
Which makes thy tongue to blazon thy hearts griefe:
But as I haue a foule,I fweare by heauen,
I neuer knew of this moft horride murder:
But Hamlet, this is onely fantafie,
And for my loue forget thefe idle fits.   1535

Ham. Idle, no mother, my pulfe doth beate like yours,

[III, iv, 141.] It is not madneffe that poffeffeth Hamlet.
O mother, if euer you did my deare father loue,

[III, iv, 165.] Forbeare the adulterous bed to night,
And win your felfe by little as you may,   1540
In time it may be you wil lothe him quite:
And mother, but affift me in reuenge,
And in his death your infamy fhall die.

Queene Hamlet, I vow by that maiefty,
That knowes our thoughts, and lookes into our hearts,   1545
I will conceale,confent,and doe my beft,
What ftratagem foe're thou fhalt deuife.

Ham. It is enough, mother good night:
Come fir, I'le prouide for you a graue,

[III, iv, 215.] Who was in life a foolifh prating knaue.   1550
Exit Hamlet with the dead body.

Enter the King and Lordes.

King Now Gertred, what fayes our fonne,how doe you
finde him?

[IV, i, 7.] *Queene* Alas my lord, as raging as the fea:
Whenas he came, I firft befpake him faire,
But then he throwes and toffes me about,
As one forgetting that I was his mother: 1555
At laft I call'd for help: and as I cried,*Corambis*
Call'd, which Hamlet no fooner heard,but whips me
Out his rapier,and cries,a Rat,a Rat, and in his rage
The good olde man he killes.

King Why this his madneffe will vndoe our ftate.   1560
Lordes goe to him, inquire the body out.

Gil. We will my lord.   *Exeunt Lordes.*

King Gertred, your fonne fhall prefently to England,

[IV, i, 29.] His fhipping is already furnifhed,
And we haue fent by *Roffencraft* and *Gilderftone,*   1565
Our letters to our deare brother of England,
For Hamlets welfare and his happineffe:

Happly the aire and climate of the Country
May pleafe him better than his natiue home:
Seewhere he comes.   **1570**

Enter Hamlet and the Lordes.

[IV, iii, 12.]   *Gil.* My lord, we can by no meanes
Know of him where the body is.
     King Now fonne Hamlet, where is this dead body?
[IV, iii, 20.]   *Ham.* At fupper, not where he is eating,but
Where he is eaten, a certaine company of politicke **wormes**   **1575**
are euen now at him.
Father,your fatte King,and your leane Beggar
Are but variable feruices, two difhes to one meffe:
Looke you, a man may fifh with that worme
That hath eaten of a King,   **1580**
And a Beggar eate that fifh,
Which that worme hath caught.
     King What of this?
     Ham. Nothing father, but to tell you,how a King
May go a progreffe through the guttes of a Beggar.   **1585**
     King But fonne *Hamlet*, where is this body?
     Ham. In heau'n, if you chance to miffe him there,
Father, you had beft looke in the other partes below
For him, aud if you cannot finde him there,
You may chance to nofe him as you go vp the lobby.   **1590**
     King Make hafte and finde him out.
     Ham. Nay do you heare? do not make too much **hafte,**
I'le warrant you hee'le ftay till you come.
     King Well fonne *Hamlet*, we in care of you:but fpecially
in tender preferuation of your health,   **1595**
The which we price euen as our proper felfe,
It is our minde you forthwith goe for *England,*
The winde fits faire, you fhall aboorde to night,
Lord *Roffencraft* and *Gilderftone* fhall goe along with **you.**
     Ham. O with all my heart:farewel mother.   **1600**
     King Your louing father,*Hamlet.*
     Ham. My mother I fay: you married my mother,
My mother is your wife, man and wife is one flefh,
[IV, iii, 51.] And fo(my mother)farewel:for England hoe.

exeunt all but the king.

     king Gertred, leaue me,   **1605**
And take your leaue of *Hamlet,*
To England is he gone, ne're to returne:
[IV, iii, 63.] Our Letters are vnto the King of England,
That on the fight of them,on his allegeance,
He prefently without demaunding why,   **1610**
That *Hamlet* loofe his head,for he muft die,
There's more in him than fhallow eyes can fee:

He once being dead, why then our ſtate is free.   *exit.*

Enter Fortenbraſſe, Drumme and Souldiers.

[IV, iv, 1.]   *Fort.*   Captaine, from vs goe greete
The king of Denmarke:
Tell him that *Fortenbraſſe* nephew to old *Norway*,   1615
Craues a free paſſe and conduct ouer his land,
According to the Articles agreed on:
You know our Randevous, goe march away.   *exeunt all.*

[IV, v.]   *enter King and Queene.*

King   *Hamlet* is ſhip't for England,fare him well,   1620
I hope to heare good newes from thence ere long,
If euery thing fall out to our content,
As I doe make no doubt but ſo it ſhall.
Queene   God grant it may,heau'ns keep my *Hamlet* ſafe:
But this miſchance of olde *Corambis* death,   1625
Hath pierſed ſo the yong *Ofeliaes* heart,
That ſhe, poore maide, is quite bereft her wittes.
King   Alas deere heart! And on the other ſide,
We vnderſtand her brother's come from *France*,
And he hath halfe the heart of all our Land,   1630
And hardly hee'le forget his father's death,
Vnleſſe by ſome meanes he be pacified.
Qu.   O ſee where the yong *Ofelia* is!

*Enter Ofelia playing on a Lute, and her haire
downe ſinging.*

[IV, v, 23.]   *Ofelia*   How ſhould I your true loue know
From another man?   1635
By his cockle hatte, and his ſtaffe,
And his ſandall ſhoone.
[IV, v, 34.]   White his ſhrowde as mountaine ſnowe,
Larded with ſweete flowers,
That bewept to the graue did not goe   1640
With true louers ſhowers:
[IV, v, 29.]   He is dead and gone Lady,he is dead and gone,
At his head a graſſe greene turffe,
At his heeles a ſtone.
king   How i'ſt with you ſweete *Ofelia?*   1645
Ofelia   Well God yeeld you,
It grieues me to ſee how they laid him in the cold ground,
[IV, v, 66.]   I could not chuſe but weepe:
[IV, v, 185.]   And will he not come againe?
And will he not come againe?   1650
No,no,hee's gone, and we caſt away mone,

And he neuer will come againe.
His beard as white as fnowe:
All flaxen was his pole,
He is dead, he is gone,   **1655**
And we caft away moane:
God a mercy on his foule.
And of all chriften foules I pray God.

[IV, v, 195.] God be with you Ladies,God be with you.   *exit Ofelia.*
　　　　　king A pretty wretch! this is a change indeede: **1660**
O Time, how fwiftly runnes our ioyes away?
Content on earth was neuer certaine bred,
To day we laugh and liue, to morrow dead.
How now, what noyfe is that?
　　　　　A noyfe within.　　　　*enter Leartes.*
　　　　　Lear. Stay there vntill I come,   **1665**

[IV, v, 111.] O thou vilde king,giue me my father:
Speake, fay, where's my father?
　　　　　king Dead.
　　　　　Lear. Who hath murdred him?fpeake, i'le not

[IV, v, 126.] Be juggled with, for he is murdred.   **1670**
　　　　　Queene True,but not by him.
　　　　　Lear. By whome, by heau'n I'le be refolued.
　　　　　king Let him goe *Gertred*,away, I feare him not,

[IV, v, 119.] There's fuch diuinitie doth wall a king,
That treafon dares not looke on.   **1675**
Let him goe *Gertred*, that your father is murdred,
T'is true, and we moft fory for it,
Being the chiefeft piller of our ftate:
Therefore will you like a moft defperate gamfter,
Swoop-ftake-like, draw at friend, and foe,and all?   **1680**

[IV, v, 141.] 　　*Lear.* To his good friends thus wide I'le ope mine arms,
And locke them in my hart,but to his foes,
I will no reconcilement but by bloud.
　　　　　king Why now you fpeake like a moft louing fonne:
And that in foule we forrow for for his death,   **1685**
Your felfe ere long fhall be a witneffe,
Meane while be patient, and content your felfe.
　　　　　Enter Ofelia as before.
　　　　　Lear. Who's this, *Ofelia?* O my deere fifter!
I'ft poffible a yong maides life,

[IV, v, 156.] Should be as mortall as an olde mans fawe?   **1690**
O heau'ns themfelues! how now *Ofelia?*
　　　　　Ofel. Wel God a mercy, I a bin gathering of floures:
Here, here is rew for you,

[IV, v, 177.] You may call it hearb a grace a Sundayes,
Heere's fome for me too : you muft weare your rew   **1695**
What a difference, there's a dazie.
Here Loue, there's rofemary for you
For remembrance: I pray Loue remember,

And there's panfey for thoughts.

 Lear. A document in madnes, thoughts, remembrance: **1700**
O God, O God!

 Ofelia There is fennell for you, I would a giu'n you
Some violets, but they all withered, when
My father died: alas, they fay the owle was

[IV, v, 40.] A Bakers daughter, we fee what we are, **1705**
But can not tell what we fhall be.

[IV, v, 182.] For bonny fweete Robin is all my ioy.

 Lear. Thoughts & afflictions, torments worfe than hell.

[IV, v, 44.] *Ofel.* Nay Loue, I pray you make no words of this now:

[IV, v, 166.] I pray now, you fhall fing a downe, **1710**
And you a downe a, t'is a the Kings daughter
And the falfe fteward, and if any body

[IV, v, 45.] Aske you of any thing, fay you this.
To morrow is faint Valentines day,
All in the morning betime, **1715**
And a maide at your window,
To be your Valentine:
The yong man rofe, and dan'd his clothes,
And dupt the chamber doore,
Let in the maide, that out a maide **1720**
Neuer departed more.
Nay I pray marke now,
By giffe, and by faint Charitie,
Away, and fie for fhame:
Yong men will doo't when they come too't: **1725**
By cocke they are too blame.
Quoth fhe, before you tumbled me,
You promifed me to wed.
So would I a done, by yonder Sunne,
If thou hadft not come to my bed. **1730**

[IV, v, 69.] So God be with you all, God bwy Ladies.
God bwy you Loue.   *exit Ofelia.*

 Lear. Griefe vpon griefe, my father murdered,
My fifter thus diftracted:
Curfed be his foule that wrought this wicked act. **1735**

 king Content you good Leartes for a time,
Although I know your griefe is as a floud,
Brimme full of forrow, but forbeare a while,
And thinke already the reuenge is done
On him that makes you fuch a hapleffe fonne. **1740**

 Lear. You haue preuail'd my Lord, a while I'le ftriue,
To bury griefe within a tombe of wrath,
Which once vnhearfed, then the world fhall heare
Leartes had a father he held deere.

 king No more of that, ere many dayes be done, **1745**

1707. *ioy*] *joy* Cam. ed.

You fhall heare that you do not dreame vpon.   *exeunt om.*
        Enter Horatio and the Queene.

  Hor. Madame, your.fonne is fafe arriv'de in *Denmarke,*
This letter I euen now receiv'd of him,
Whereas he writes how he efcap't the danger,
And fubtle treafon that the king had plotted,   1750
Being croffed by the contention of the windes,
He found the Packet fent to the king of *England,*
Wherein he faw himfelfe betray'd to death,
As at his next conuerfion with your grace,
He will relate the circumftance at full.   1755
    Queene Then I perceiue there's treafon in his lookes
That feem'd to fugar o're his villanie:
But I will foothe and pleafe him for a time,
For murderous mindes are alwayes jealous,
But know not you *Horatio* where he is?   1760
    Hor. Yes Madame,and he hath appoynted me
To meet him on the eaft fide of the Cittie
To morrow morning.
    Queene O faile not, good *Horatio* , and withall, com-
A mothers care to him, bid him a while   .mend me   1765
Be wary of his prefence, left that he
Faile in that he goes about.
    Hor. Madame, neuer make doubt of that:
I think by this the news be come to court:
He is arriv'de, obferue the king,and you fhall   1770
Quickely finde,*Hamlet* being here,
Things fell not to his minde.
    Queene But what became of *Gilderftone* and *Roffencraft?*
    Hor. He being fet afhore, they went for *England,*
And in the Packet there writ down that doome   1775
To be perform'd on them poynted for him:
And by great chance he had his fathers Seale,
So all was done without difcouerie.
    Queene Thankes be to heauen for bleffing of the prince,
Horatio once againe I take my leaue,   1780
With thowfand mothers bleffings to my fonne.
    Horat. Madam adue.

        Enter King and Leartes.

    King. Hamlet from *England!* is it poffible?
What chance is this? they are gone, and he come home.
    Lear. O he is welcome, by my foule he is: 1785
At it my iocund heart doth leape for ioy,
[IV, vii, 57.] That I fhall liue to tell him, thus he dies.
    king Leartes, content your felfe,be rulde by me,
And you fhall haue no let for your reuenge.
[IV, v, 133.]   *Lear.* My will, not all the world.   1790
    King Nay but Leartes,marke the plot I haue layde,

I haue heard him often with a greedy wifh,
Vpon fome praife that he hath heard of you
Touching your weapon, which with all his heart,
He might be once tasked for to try your cunning.   1795
   Lea. And how for this?
   King Mary Leartes thus: I'le lay a wager,
Shalbe on *Hamlets* fide, and you fhall giue the oddes,
The which will draw him with a more defire,
To try the maiftry, that in twelue venies   1800
You gaine not three of him : now this being granted,
When you are hot in midft of all your play,
Among the foyles fhall a keene rapier lie,
Steeped in a mixture of deadly poyfon,
That if it drawes but the leaft dramme of blood,   1805
In any part of him,he cannot liue:
This being done will free you from fufpition,
And not the deereft friend that *Hamlet* lov'de
Will euer haue Leartes in fufpect.
   Lear. My lord, I like it well: 1810
But fay lord *Hamlet* fhould refufe this match.
   King I'le warrant you,wee'le put on you
Such a report of fingularitie,
Will bring him on,although againft his will.
And left that all fhould miffe,   1815
I'le haue a potion that fhall ready ftand,
In all his heate when that he calles for drinke,
Shall be his period and our happineffe.
   Lear. T'is excellent, O would the time were come:
Here comes the Queene.   *enter the Queene.*   1820
   king How now Gertred,why looke you heauily?
   Queene O my Lord, the yong *Ofelia*
Hauing made a garland of fundry fortes of floures,
Sitting vpon a willow by a brooke,
[IV, vii, 175.] The enuious fprig broke, into the brooke fhe fell,   1825
And for a while her clothes fpread wide abroade,
Bore the yong Lady vp: and there fhe fate fmiling,
Euen Mermaide-like, twixt heauen and earth,
Chaunting olde fundry tunes vncapable
As it were of her diftreffe, but long it could not be,   1830
Till that her clothes, being heauy with their drinke
Dragg'd the fweete wretch to death.
   Lear. So,fhe is drownde:
[IV, vii, 187.] Too much of water haft thou *Ofelia*;
Therefore I will not drowne thee in my teares,   1835
Reuenge it is muft yield this heart releefe,
For woe begets woe,and griefe hangs on griefe.   *exeunt.*

     enter Clowne and an other.

[V, 1, 1.]   *Clowne* I fay no, fhe ought not to be buried

In chriftian buriall.

2. Why fir?   1840

Clowne Mary becaufe fhee's drownd.

2. But fhe did not drowne her felfe.

Clowne No, that's certaine,the water drown'd her.

2. Yea but it was againft her will.

Clowne No, I deny that, for looke you fir, I ftand here,   1845
If the water come to me, I drowne not my felfe :
But if I goe to the water, and am there drown'd,
Ergo I am guiltie of my owne death :
Y'are gone, goe y'are gone fir.

2. I but fee,fhe hath chriftian buriall,   1850
Becaufe fhe is a great woman.

Clowne Mary more's the pitty, that great folke
Should haue more authoritie to hang or drowne
Themfelues, more than other people :
Goe fetch me a ftope of drinke, but before thou   1855
Goeft, tell me one thing, who buildes ftrongeft,
Of a Mafon, a Shipwright, or a Carpenter?

2. Why a Mafon, for he buildes all of ftone,
And will indure long.

Clowne That's prety, too't agen, too't agen.   1860

2. Why then a Carpenter, for he buildes the gallowes,
And that brings many a one to his long home.

Clowne Prety agen, the gallowes doth well,mary howe
dooes it well? the gallowes dooes well to them that doe ill,
goe get thee gone :   1865
And if any one afke thee hereafter,fay,
A Graue-maker, for the houfes he buildes
[V, i, 58.] Laft till Doomef-day. Fetch me a ftope of beere, goe.

Enter Hamlet and Horatio.

[V, i, 89.] *Clowne* A picke-axe and a fpade,
A fpade for and a winding fheete,   1870
Moft fit it is, for t'will be made,   *he throwes vp a fhouel.*
For fuch a gheft moft meete.

Ham. Hath this fellow any feeling of himfelfe,
That is thus merry in making of a graue?
See how the flaue joles their heads againft the earth.   1875

[V, i, 65.] *Hor.* My lord, Cuftome hath made it in him feeme no-
Clowne A pick-axe and a fpade,a fpade,   (thing.
For and a winding fheete,
Moft fit it is for to be made,
For fuch a gheft moft meet.   1880

[V, i, 93.] *Ham.* Looke you, there's another *Horatio.*
Why mai't not be the fcull of fome Lawyer?
Me thinkes he fhould indite that fellow
Of an action of Batterie, for knocking

Him about the pate with's fhouel :now where is your   1885
Quirkes and quillets now,your vouchers and
Double vouchers, your leafes and free-holde,
And tenements? why that fame boxe there will fcarfe
Holde the conueiance of his land,and muft
The honor lie there? O pittifull transformance!   1890
Iprethee tell me *Horatio*,
Is parchment made of fheep-skinnes?
    Hor. I my Lorde,and of calues-skinnes too.
    Ham. Ifaith they prooue themfelues fheepe and calues

[V, i, 109.] That deale with them,or put their truft in them.   1895
There's another,why may not that be fuch a ones
[V, i, 81.] Scull, that praifed my Lord fuch a ones horfe,
When he meant to beg him? *Horatio*, I prethee
Lets queftion yonder fellow.
[V, i, 110.] Now my friend, whofe graue is this?   1900
    Clowne Mine fir.
    Ham. But who muft lie in it?   (fir.
    Clowne If I fhould fay, I fhould, I fhould lie in my throat
    Ham. What man muft be buried here?
    Clowne No man fir.   1905
    Ham. What woman?
    Clowne. No woman neither fir,but indeede
One that was a woman.
    Ham. An excellent fellow by the Lord *Horatio*,
[V, i, 131.] This feauen yeares haue I noted it : the toe of the pefant,   1910
Comes fo neere the heele of the courtier,
That hee gawles his kibe, I prethee tell mee one thing,
[V, i, 154.] How long will a man lie in the ground before hee rots?
    Clowne Ifaith fir, if hee be not rotten before
He be laide in, as we haue many pocky corfes,   1915
He will laft you, eight yeares, a tanner
Will laft you eight years full out, or nine.
    Ham. And why a tanner?
    Clowne Why his hide is fo tanned with his trade,
That it will holde out water, that's a parlous   1920
Deuourer of your dead body, a great foaker.
[V, i, 163.] Looke you, heres a fcull hath bin here this dozen yeare,
Let me fee, I euer fince our laft king *Hamlet*
[V, i, 136.] Slew *Fortenbraffe* in combat,yong *Hamlets* father,
Hee that's mad.   1925
    Ham. I mary, how came he madde?
[V, i, 150.]   *Clowne* Ifaith very ftrangely, by loofing of his wittes.
    Ham. Vpon what ground?
    Clowne A this ground, in *Denmarke*.
    Ham. Where is he now?   1930
    Clowne Why now they fent him to *England*.
    Ham. To *England!* wherefore?
    Clowne Why they fay he fhall haue his wittes there,

[V, i, 143.] Or if he haue not, t'is no great matter there,
It will not be feene there. 1935
    Ham. Why not there?
    Clowne Why there they fay the men are as mad as he.
    Ham. Whofe fcull was this?
[V, i, 168.]   *Clowne* This,a plague on him,a madde rogues it was,
He powred once a whole flagon of Rhenifh of my head, 1940
Why do not you know him? this was one *Yorickes* fcull.
[V, i, 173.]   *Ham.* Was this? I prethee let me fee it,alas poore *Yoricke*
I knew him *Horatio,*
A fellow of infinite mirth, he hath caried mee twenty times
vpon his backe, here hung thofe lippes that I haue Kiffed a 1945
hundred times,and to fee, now they abhorre me : Wheres
your iefts now *Yoricke?* your flafhes of meriment: now go
to my Ladies chamber, and bid her paint her felfe an inch
thicke, to this fhe muft come *Yoricke. Horatio,* I prethee
[V, i, 186.] tell me one thing, dooft thou thinke that *Alexander* looked 1950
thus?
    Hor. Euen fo my Lord.
    Ham. And fmelt thus?
    Hor. I my lord, no otherwife.
    Ham. No,why might not imagination worke, as thus of 1955
Alexander,Alexander died,*Alexander* was buried,*Alexander*
became earth, of earth we make clay, and *Alexander* being
but clay, why might not time bring to paffe, that he might
ftoppe the boung hole of a beere barrell?
Imperious *Cæfar* dead and turned to clay, 1960
[V, i, 202.] Might ftoppe a hole, to keepe the winde away.
    Enter King and Queene, Leartes,and other lordes,
        with a Prieft after the coffin.
    Ham. What funerall's this that all the Court laments?
[V, i, 209.] It fhews to be fome noble parentage:
Stand by a while.
    Lear. What ceremony elfe? say,what ceremony elfe? 1965
    Prieft My Lord, we haue done all that lies in vs,
And more than well the church can tolerate,
She hath had a Dirge fung for her maiden foule:
And but for fauour of the king,and you,
She had beene buried in the open fieldes, 1970
Where now fhe is allowed chriftian buriall.
    Lear. So, I tell thee churlifh Prieft, a miniftring **Angell**
fhall my fifter be, when thou lieft howling.
[V, i, 230.]   *Ham.* The faire *Ofelia* dead!
    Queene Sweetes to the fweete, farewell: 1975
I had thought to adorne thy bridale bed,faire maide,
And not to follow thee vnto thy graue.
    Lear. Forbeare the earth a while:fifter farewell:

      Leartes leapes into the graue.

82 *The Tragedie of Hamlet*

Now powre your earth on, *Olympus* hie,
And make a hill to o're top olde *Pellon*:   *Hamlet leapes*   1980
Whats he that coniures fo?   *in after* Leartes
   Ham. Beholde tis I, *Hamlet* the Dane.
   Lear. The diuell take thy foule.
   Ham. O thou praieft not well,
I prethee take thy hand from off my throate,   1985
For there is fomething in me dangerous,

[V, i, 251.] Which let thy wifedome feare, holde off thy hand:
[V, i, 257.] I lou'de *Ofelia* as deere as twenty brothers could:
Shew me what thou wilt doe for her:
Wilt fight, wilt faft, wilt pray,   1990

[V, i, 264.] Wilt drinke vp veffels, eate a crocadile? Ile doot:
Com'ft thou here to whine?
And where thou talk'ft of burying thee a liue,
Here let vs ftand: and let them throw on vs,
Whole hills of earth, till with the heighth therof,   1995
Make Oofell as a Wart.
   King. Forbeare *Leartes*, now is hee mad, as is the fea,
Anone as milde and gentle as a Doue:
Therfore a while giue his wilde humour fcope.
   Ham. What is the reafon fir that you wrong mee thus?   2000
I neuer gaue you caufe : but ftand away,

[V, i, 280.] A Cat will meaw, a Dog will haue a day.
     Exit Hamlet and Horatio.
   Queene. Alas, it is his madnes makes him thus,
And not his heart, *Leartes*.
   King. My lord, t'is fo : but wee'le no longer trifle,   2005
This very day fhall *Hamlet* drinke his laft,
For prefently we meane to fend to him,
Therfore *Leartes* be in readynes.
   Lear. My lord, till then my foule will not bee quiet.
   King. Come *Gertred*, wee'l haue *Leartes*, and our fonne,   2010
Made friends and Louers, as befittes them both,
Euen as they tender vs, and loue their countrie.
   Queene God grant they may.   *exeunt omnes.*
     Enter Hamlet and Horatio

[V, ii, 75.]   *Ham.* beleeue mee, it greeues mee much *Horatio,*
That to *Leartes* I forgot my felfe :   2015
For by my felfe me thinkes I feele his griefe,
Though there's a difference in each others wrong.
     Enter a Bragart Gentleman.

[V, ii, 82.]   *Horatio,*but marke yon water-flie,
The Court knowes him, but hee knowes not the Court.
   Gent. Now God faue thee, fweete prince *Hamlet*.   2020
   Ham. And you fir: foh, how the muske-cod fmels!
   Gen. I come with an embaffage from his maiefty to you
   Ham. I fhall fir giue you attention :

[V, ii, 93.] By my troth me thinkes t'is very colde.

    Gent. It is indeede very rawiſh colde.   2025

    Ham. T'is hot me thinkes.

    Gent. Very ſwoltery hote :

[V, ii, 140.] The King, ſweete Prince, hath layd a wager on your ſide,

Six Barbary horſe,againſt ſix french rapiers,

With all their acoutrements too,a the carriages: 2030

In good faith they are very curiouſly wrought.

    Ham. The cariages ſir,I do not know what you meane.

    Gent. The girdles, and hangers ſir, and ſuch like.

    Ham. The worde had beene more coſin german to the

phraſe, if he could haue carried the canon by his ſide,   2035

And howe's the wager? I vnderſtand you now.

[V, ii, 156.]   *Gent.* Mary ſir, that yong Leartes in twelue venies

At Rapier and Dagger do not get three oddes of you,

And on your ſide the King hath laide,

And deſires you to be in readineſſe.   2040

    Ham. Very well, if the King dare venture his wager,

I dare venture my skull:when muſt this be?

    Gent. My Lord, preſently, the king, and her maieſty,

With the reſt of the beſt iudgement in the Court,

Are comming downe into the outward pallace.   2045

    Ham. Goe tell his maieſtie, I wil attend him.

    Gent. I ſhall deliuer your moſt ſweet anſwer.   *exit.*

    Ham. You may ſir, none better, for y'are ſpiced,

Elſe he had a bad noſe could not ſmell a foole.

    Hor. He will diſcloſe himſelfe without inquirie.   2050

[V, ii, 199.]   *Ham.* Beleeue me *Horatio*, my hart is on the ſodaine

Very ſore, all here about.

    Hor. My lord,forbeare the challenge then.

    Ham. No *Horatio*, not I, if danger be now,

Why then it is not to come,there's a predeſtinate prouidence   2055

in the fall of a ſparrow : heere comes the King.

    Enter King, Queene, Leartes, Lordes.

    King Now ſonne *Hamlet*, we haue laid vpon your head,

And make no queſtion but to haue the beſt.

[V, ii, 248.]   *Ham.* Your maieſtie hath laide a the weaker ſide.

    King. We doubt it not,deliuer them the foiles.   2060

[V, ii, 213.]   *Ham.* Firſt Leartes, heere's my hand and loue,

Proteſting that I neuer wrongd *Leartes*.

If *Hamlet* in his madneſſe did amiſſe,

That was not *Hamlet*, but his madnes did it,

And all the wrong I e're did to *Leartes*,   2065

I here proclaime was madnes,therefore lets be at peace,

And thinke I haue ſhot mine arrow o're the houſe,

And hurt my brother.

    Lear. Sir I am satisfied in nature,

	But in termes of honor I'le ſtand aloofe,	2070
	And will no reconcilement,	
[V, ii, 235.]	Till by ſome elder maiſters of our time	
	I may be ſatisfied.	
[V, ii, 246.]	*King* Giue them tne foyles.	
[V, ii, 242.]	*Ham.* I'le be your foyle *Leartes*, theſe foyles,	2075
[V, ii, 252.]	Haue all a laught,come on ſir : *a hit.*	

        Lear. No none.   *Heere they play:*

[V, ii, 267.]   *Ham.* Iudgement.

        Gent. A hit, a moſt palpable hit.

        Lear. Well, come againe.   *They play againe.* 2080

        Ham. Another. Iudgement

        Lear. I, I grant, a tuch, a tuch.

        King Here *Hamlet*,the king doth drinke a health to thee

[V, ii, 275.]   *Queene* Here *Hamlet*,take my napkin,wipe thy face.

[V, ii, 270.]   *King* Giue him the wine.   2085

        Ham. Set it by, I'le haue another bowt firſt,

        I'le drinke anone.

[V, ii, 276.]   *Queene* Here *Hamlet*, thy mother drinkes to thee.

                       Shee drinkes.

        King Do not drinke *Gertred* : O t'is the poyſned cup!

[V, ii, 284.]   *Ham.* *Leartes* come, you dally with me,   2090

        I pray you paſſe with your moſt cunningſt play.

        Lear. I! ſay you ſo? haue at you,

        Ile hit you now my Lord:

        And yet it goes almoſt againſt my conſcience.

        Ham. Come on ſir.   2095

[V, ii, 289:]   *They catch one anothers Rapiers, and both are wounded,*
               Leartes falles downe, the Queene falles downe and dies.

        King Looke to the Queene.

        Queene O the drinke, the drinke, H*amlet*,the drinke.

        Ham. Treaſon,ho, keepe the gates.

        Lords How i'ſt my Lord *Leartes?*

[V, ii, 293.]   *Lear.* Euen as a coxcombe ſhould,   2100

        Fooliſhly ſlaine with my owne weapon:

[V, ii, 302.]   *Hamlet*, thou haſt not in thee halfe an houre of life,

        The fatall Inſtrument is in thy hand.

        Vnbated and invenomed : thy mother's poyſned

        That drinke was made for thee.   2105

        Ham. The poyſned Inſtrument within my hand?

[V, ii, 309.]   Then venome to thy venome,die damn'd villaine:

[V, ii, 313.]   Come drinke, here lies thy vnion here.   *The king dies.*

        Lear. O he is iuſtly ſerued:

        Hamlet, before I die, here take my hand,   2110

        And withall, my loue : I doe forgiue thee.   *Leartes dies.*

[V, ii, 325.]   *Ham.* And I thee, O I am dead *Horatio*,fare thee well.

        Hor. No, I am more an antike Roman,

        Then a Dane,here is ſome poiſon left.

Ham. Vpon my loue I charge thee let it goe,   2115
O fie *Horatio*, and if thou fhouldſt die,
What a ſcandale wouldſt thou leaue behinde?
What tongue ſhould tell the ſtory of our deaths,
If not from thee? O my heart ſinckes *Horatio*,
Mine eyes haue loſt their ſight, my tongue his vſe: 2120
Farewel *Horatio*,heauen receiue my ſoule.   *Ham. dies.*

Enter Voltemar and the Ambaſſadors from England.
enter Fortenbraſſe with his traine.

[V, ii, 349.]   *Fort.* Where is this bloudy ſight?
             Hor. If aught of woe or wonder you 'ld behold,
           Then looke vpon this tragicke ſpectacle.
[V, ii, 353.]   *Fort.* O imperious death! how many Princes   2125
           Haſt thou at one draft bloudily ſhot to death?   *(land,*
             Ambaſſ. Our ambaſſie that we haue brought from *Eng-*
           Where be theſe Princes that ſhould heare vs ſpeake?
           O moſt moſt vnlooked for time! vnhappy country.
             Hor. Content your ſelues, Ile ſhew to all, the ground, 2130
           The firſt beginning of this Tragedy :
[V, ii. 365.] Let there a ſcaffold be rearde vp in the market place,
           And let the State of the world be there :
           Where you ſhall heare ſuch a ſad ſtory tolde,
           That neuer mortall man could more vnfolde.   2135
             Fort. I haue ſome rights of memory to this kingdome,
           Which now to claime my leiſure doth inuite mee :
           Let foure of our chiefeſt Captaines
           Beare *Hamlet* like a ſouldier to his graue :
           For he was likely, had he liued,
           To a prou'd moſt royall.
           Take vp the bodie, ſuch a ſight as this
[V, ii, 389.] Becomes the fieldes, but here doth much amiſſe.   2143

Finis.

2142. *ſight*] *ſight* Cam

NOTE ON THE HYSTORIE OF HAMBLET

IN that chaotic mass of 'authentic Extracts from divers English Books that were in Print' in Shakespeare's time, CAPELL'S third volume of *Notes*, on p. 19, the title of *The Hystorie of Hamblet* is given, together with the contents merely of the eight chapters. To this Capell has added the following note: 'Upon the woman, who in Chapter ii, is set to tempt Hamlet is grounded Shakespeare's Ophelia; and his deliverance from this snare by a friend suggested his Horatio. The courtiers ['appointed to leade Hamblet into a solitary place,'—p. 96 of the Reprint] are likewise a shadow of Rosincrantz and Guildenstern. Amidst all this resemblance of persons and circumstances, it is rather strange that none of the relater's expressions have got into the play : and yet not one of them is to be found except in Chapter iii, where Hamlet kills the counsellor (who is described as of a greater reach than the rest, and is the poet's Polonius) behind the arras . . . . and is made to cry out: 'a rat, a rat. After which ensues Hamlet's harangue to his mother; and the manner in which she is affected by this harangue is better describ'd than any other thing in all the history, or, more properly, is the only good stroke in it. To speak the very truth, perhaps, the Geruthe of this picture is superior to Shakespeare's Gertrude in this one situation; allowance being made for the coloring, suiting the time 'twas done in. Shakespeare pursues the history no farther than to the death of the tyrant; and he brings this event to pass by means different from what are there related; yet it is easy to see that Hamlet's counterfeit funeral furnish'd him with the idea of Ophelia's true one; as his harangue to the Danes did the speech of Horatio. This history, as it is call'd, is an almost literal translation from the French of Belleforest; and is of much older date than the impression from which these extracts are made; perhaps but little later than it's original, which was written in 1570, and published soon after.'

In the *Introduction* to the first volume of his edition of Shakespeare, p. 52, Capell has the following additional remarks: About the middle of the sixteenth century Francis de Belleforest, a French gentleman, entertain'd his countrymen with a collection of novels, which he entitles *Histoires tragiques;* they are in part originals, part translations, and chiefly from Bandello. He began to publish them in the year 1564; and continued his publication successively in several tomes, how many I know not; the dedication to his fifth tome is dated six years after. In that tome the *troisième Histoire* has this title: *Avec quelle ruse Amleth, qui depuis fut roy de Dannemarch, vengea la mort de son pere Horvuendille, occis par Fengon son frere, & autre occurrence de son histoire.* Painter compil'd his *Palace of Pleasure* almost entirely from Belleforest, taking here and there a novel as pleas'd him, but he did not translate the whole : other novels, it is probable, were translated by different people, and publish'd singly; this, at least, that we are speaking of, was so, and is intitled '*The Hystorie of* Hamblet;' it is in Quarto, and black letter. There can be no doubt made, by persons who are acquainted with these things, that the translation is not much younger than the French original; though the only edition of it that is yet come to my knowledge is no earlier than 1608; that Shakespeare took his play from it there can likewise be very little doubt.

THEOBALD was the first to note that the plot of *Hamlet* is derived from Saxo Grammaticus. A brief extract of the story from *Historiæ Danicæ* is given by him on the first page of his edition of the tragedy.

SKOTTOWE (*Life of Shakespeare*, &c., 1824, ii, p. 1) analyses the *Hystorie* at greater length than any other commentator has thought worth the while, unless it be among the Germans. It is needless to repeat his remarks here; the curious student with the Reprint at hand can misspend what time he pleases, and make his own conclusions. Skottowe sums up: '*The Hystorie of Hamblet*, then, contributes much towards the illustration of a character deemed peculiarly difficult. It assigns rational motives for actions otherwise unintelligible, and lays the foundation for the necessary distinction that has been made between the natural and artificial character of Hamlet; a clue to the interpretations of his actions, which, carefully pursued, leaves little in his conduct dubious or obscure. Above all things, the reason for his deportment to Ophelia is explained.'

The copy of the black-letter Quarto owned by Capell is the only one that is known, and is preserved among his books at Cambridge. It was reprinted in 1841 by COLLIER in the first volume of his *Shakespeare's Library*, and of it Collier remarks: It was printed for Thomas Pavier, a well-known stationer of that time. There can be little doubt that it had come originally from the press considerably before the commencement of the seventeenth century, although the multiplicity of readers of productions of the kind, and the carelessness with which such books were regarded after perusal, has led to the destruction, as far as can now be ascertained, of every earlier copy. . . . . . It will be found that the tragedy varies in many important particulars from the novel, especially towards the conclusion; that nearly the whole conduct of the story is different; that the catastrophe is totally dissimilar, and that the character of the hero in the prose narrative is utterly degraded below the rank he is entitled to take in the commencement. The murder of Hamlet's father, the marriage of his mother with the murderer, Hamlet's pretended madness, his interview with his mother, and his voyage to England, are nearly the only points in common. We are thus able to see how far Shakespeare followed the *Hystorie;* but we shall probably never be able to ascertain to what extent he made use of the antecedent play [referred to by Nash, Lodge, and others]. The prose narrative of 1608 is a bald, literal, and, in many respects, uncouth translation from the *Histoires tragiques* of Belleforest, who was himself by no means an elegant writer for the time in which he lived: his story of *Amleth* was professedly copied from an earlier author, whom he does not name, but who was either Saxo Grammaticus or some writer who had intermediately borrowed the incidents and converted them to his own purposes. The English translator, especially in the descriptive portion of his work, has multiplied all the faults of Belleforest, including his lengthened and involved periods and his frequent confusion of persons. It may be suspected that one or two of the longer speeches, and particularly the oration of Hamlet, occupying nearly the whole of Chapter vi, was by another and a better hand, who had a more complete knowledge of French and a happier use of his own language.

'We must not have much hesitation in believing that the oldest copy (perhaps printed about the year 1585) was sufficiently corrupt in its readings; but the corruptions increased with the re-impressions, and a few portions of the edition of 1608 seem almost to defy correction. Some passages might be rendered more intelligi-

ble, such as, 'distill a field of tears' (page 112), instead of *distill a flood of tears;*
but it was thought best to present the curious relic, as nearly as it could be done, in
the shape and state in which it issued from the press not quite two centuries and a
half ago. For this reason it has not been considered right to make the orthography
of the name of the hero uniform; sometimes he is called Hamblet (as, no doubt, it
stood in the first impression), and at other times Hamlet, as we have every reason to
suppose it was altered in the old play, and as we find it in Shakespeare.'

ELZE contends that the translation from Belleforest is of a later date than the
drama. Prose versions are more likely to follow poetical versions than the reverse.
This is noticeable in the popular legends of both England and Germany. It is readily
conceivable that a poet should select from Belleforest the story of Hamlet's feigned
insanity and of his revenge, and cast it in a dramatic or poetic mould, but it is not
so conceivable that a mediocre translator should pick out this single story, unless he
were led to do so by the popularity of the poetic version. There are two points
or passages in the *Hystorie of Hamblet* which materially strengthen this view: as
has been before noticed, this *Hystorie* is a clumsy translation of Belleforest, adhering
throughout to the original with slavish fidelity, except in two places, which betray
the mark of a superior hand, and point very decisively to Shakespeare. In the *Histoires tragiques* the counsellor who acts the spy during Amleth's interview with his
mother conceals himself under the quilt (*stramentum*, according to Saxo; *loudier*
or *lodier*, according to Belleforest), and Amleth on entering the chamber *jumps* upon
this quilt (*sauta sur ce lodier*); whereas the English version converts the quilt into
a curtain or tapestry, and makes use of the very same terms employed by Shakespeare, viz.: 'hangings' and 'arras.' In the second place, it is still more striking that
the English translator makes Amleth exclaim in the very words of Shakespeare:
'A rat! a rat!' whereof not a trace is to be found in Belleforest. That this passage,
on the stage, made a deep impression on the audience is highly probable, and the
probability receives confirmation from the fact that Shirley in his *Traitor*, 1635,
imitated this scene almost word for word. What more likely, then, than that the
translator half unconsciously adopted an incident and phraseology which had caught
the popular fancy, and become almost proverbial? At any rate, we hold this explanation to be less forced than that which assumes that two such striking passages were
invented by a translator of a manifestly inferior stamp, and transferred from his work
to Shakespeare's. [Especially when, I think Elze might have added, they are the
only two points where the phraseology is common to both.] We by no means wish
to deny the possibility of the *Hystorie of Hamblet*'s having been published long
before 1608; perhaps, as Collier thinks, even as early as 1580. According to our
belief, the first sketch of *Hamlet* is to be set down at about 1585–86.

The above argument of ELZE's in favor of the existence of the drama before the
translation has not, I think, met with the acceptance it deserves. To my mind it is
convincing. Not that the early drama was by Shakespeare. That is not my belief.

Dr BELL (*Shakespeare's Puck*, ii, 231, and iii, 140) maintains that Shakespeare
passed three years of his life on the Continent, and while there became thoroughly
imbued with the German language and literature of the time, and that he took the
story of *Hamlet* from Hans Sachs, who wrote a version of it in 1558; and furthermore Dr Bell says that Shakespeare has followed his original 'religiously.' If the
present Editor could have perceived the lightest gossamer thread of connection between Hans Sachs's rude, uncouth doggerel and Shakespeare's tragedy, Hans Sachs's
bald version would have been reprinted in the present volume.

WHITE (*Introduction to Hamlet*, p. 7): Yet with all this dissimilarity between [*Hamlet* and the *Hystorie of Hamblet*], added to that which is the consequence of the addition of new characters and new incidents, there is remarkable resemblance in minute particulars. Thus, for instance, in the story as well as in the play, Hamlet, on detecting the hidden eavesdropper in his mother's closet, calls out, ' A rat, a rat!' and the purport and character of his subsequent reproaches to his mother are notably alike in both.

DYCE (Second Edition): Whether Shakespeare derived the incidents [which are common to both the tragedy and *The Hystorie*] from *The Hystorie*, or from the older drama on the same subject, we are left to guess.

There are several pages of Introductory matter, termed *Argument* and *Preface*, prefixed to the *Hystorie*, but as they contain no syllable in reference to Hamlet, and are very tedious besides, they are not reprinted here.

THE

HYSTORIE

OF HAMBLET.

LONDON:

Imprinted by *Richard Bradocke*, for *Thomas Pavier*, and are to be sold at his shop in Corne-hill, neere to the Royall Exchange.

1608.

CHAP. I.

How Horvendile and Fengon were made Governours of the Province of Ditmarse, and how Horvendile married Geruth, the daughter to Roderich, chief K. of Denmark, by whom he had Hamblet: and how after his marriage his brother Fengon slewe him trayterously, and married his brothers wife, and what followed.

You must understand, that long time before the kingdome of Denmark received the faith of Jesus Christ, and imbraced the doctrin of the Christians, that the common people in those dayes were barbarous and uncivill, and their princes cruell, without faith or loyaltie, seeking nothing but murther, and deposing (or at the least) offending each other, either in honours, goods, or lives; not caring to ransome such as they took prisoners, but rather sacrificing them to the cruell vengeance naturally imprinted in their hearts: in such sort, that if ther were sometime a good prince or king among them, who beeing adorned with the most perfect gifts of nature, would adict himselfe to vertue, and use courtesie, although the people held him in admiration (as vertue is admirable to the most wicked) yet the envie of his neighbors was so great, that they never ceased untill that vertuous man were dispatched out of the world. King Rodericke, as then raigning in Denmarke, after hee had appeased the troubles in the countrey, and driven the Sweathlanders and Slaveans from thence, he divided the kingdom into divers prov-

The Danes in times past barbarous and uncivill.

The crueltie of the Danes.

Rodericke king of Denmarke.

91

inces, placing governours therein; who after (as the like happened in France) bare
the names of Dukes, Marqueses, and Earls, giving the government of
Jutie (at this present called Ditmarsse) lying upon the conntrey of the
Cimbrians, in the straight or narrow part of land that sheweth like a
point or cape of ground upon the sea, which neithward bordereth upon
the countrey of Norway, two valiant and warlike lords Horvendile and Fengon,
sonnes to Gervendile, who likewise had beene governour of that province. Now
the greatest honor that men of noble birth could at that time win and obtaine, was
in exercising the art of piracie upon the seas, assayling their neighbours, and the
countries bordering upon them; and how much the more they used to rob, pill, and
spoyle other provinces, and ilands far adjacent, so much the more their
honours and reputation increased and augmented: wherin Horvendile
obtained the highest place in his time, beeing the most renowned pirate
that in those dayes seoured the seas and havens of the north parts: whose great
fame so mooved the heart of Collere, king of Norway, that he was
much grieved to heare that Horvendile surmounting him in feates of
armes, thereby obscuring the glorie by him alreadie obtained upon the
seas: (honor more than covetousnesse of richer (in those dayes) being the reason
that provoked those barbarian princes to overthrow and vanquish one the other, not
caring to be slaine by the handes of a victorious person).   This valiant and hardy
king having challenged Horvendile to fight with him body to body, the combate
was by him accepted, with conditions, that hee which should be vanquished should
loose all the riches he had in his ship, and that the vanquisher should cause the
body of the vanquished (that should bee slaine in the combate) to be honourably
buried, death being the prise and reward of him that should loose the battaile: and
to conclude, Collere, king of Norway (although a valiant, hardy, and
courageous prince) was in the end vanquished and slaine by Horvendile, who presently caused a tombe to be erected, and therein (with all
honorable obsequies fit for a prince) buried the body of king Collere, according to
their auncient manner and superstitions in these dayes, and the conditions of the
combate, bereaving the kings shippes of all their riches; and having slaine the
kings sister, a very brave and valiant warriour, and over runne all the coast of
Norway, and the Northern Ilands, returned home againe layden with much treasure,
sending the most parte thereof to his soveraigne, king Rodericke, thereby to procure his good liking, and so to be accounted one of the greatest favourites about his
majestie.

The king, allured by those presents, and esteeming himselfe happy to have so
valiant a subject, sought by a great favour and coutesie to make him become bounden
unto him perpetually, giving him Geruth his daughter to his wife, of
whom he knew Horvendile to bee already much inamored.   And the
more to honor him, determined himselfe in person to conduct her into
Jutie, where the marriage was celebrated according to the ancient manner: and to
be briefe, of this marriage proceeded Hamblet, of whom I intend to speake, and for
his cause have chosen to renew this present hystorie.

Fengon, brother to this prince Horvendile, who [not] onely fretting and despight-
ing in his heart at the great honor and reputation wonne by his brother
in warlike affaires, but solicited and provoked by a foolish jealousie to
see him honored with royall aliance, and fearing thereby to bee deposed
from his part of the government, or rather desiring to be onely gover-

Jutie at this time, called then Dit-marsse.

Horvendile a king and a pirate.

Collere king of Norway.

Horvendile slew Collere.

Hamlet sonne to Hor-vendile.

Fengon, his conspira-cie against his brother.

nour, thereby to obscure the memorie of the victories and conquests of his brother Horvendile, determined (whatsoever happened) to kill him; which hee effected in such sort, that no man once so much as suspected him, every man esteeming that from such and so firme a knot of alliance and consanguinitie there could proceed no other issue then the full effects of vertue and courtesie: but (as I sayd before) the desire of bearing soveraigne rule and authoritie respecteth neither blood nor amitie, nor caring for vertue, as being wholly without respect of lawes, or majestie devine; for it is not possible that hee which invadeth the countrey and taketh away the riches of an other man without cause or reason, should know or feare God. Was not this a craftie and subtile counsellor? but he might have thought that the mother, knowing her husbands case, would not cast her sonne into the danger of death. But Fengon, having secretly assembled certain men, and perceiving himself strong enough to execute his interprise, Horvendile his brother being at a banquet with his friends, sodainely set upon him, where he slewe him as traiterously, as cunningly he purged himselfe of so detestable a murther to his subjects; for that hee had any violent or bloody handes, or once committed parricide upon his brother, hee had incestuously abused his wife, whose honour hee ought as well to have sought and procured as traiterously he pursued and effected his destruction. And it is most certaine, that the man that abandoneth himselfe to any notorious and wicked action, whereby he becommeth a great sinner, he careth not to commit much more haynous and abhominable offences, and covered his boldnesse and wicked practise with so great subtiltie and policie, and under a vaile of meere simplicitie, that beeing favoured for the honest love that he bare to his sister in lawe, for whose sake, hee affirmed, he had in that sort murthered his brother, that his sinne found excuse among the common people, and of the nobilitie was esteemed for justice: for that Geruth, being as courteous a princesse as any then living in the north parts, and one that had never once so much as offended any of her subjects, either commons or courtyers, this adulterer and infamous murtherer, slaundered his dead brother, that hee would have slaine his wife, and that hee by chance finding him upon the point ready to do it, in defence of the lady had slaine him, bearing off the blows, which as then he strooke at the innocent princesse, without any other cause of malice whatsoever. Wherein hee wanted no false witnesses to approove his act, which deposed in like sort, as the wicked calumniator himselfe protested, being the same persons that had born him company, and were participants of his treason; so that insteed of pursuing him as a parricide and an incestuous person, al the courtyers admired and flattered him in his good fortune, making more account of false witnesses and detestable wicked reporters, and more honouring the calumniators, then they esteemed of those that seeking to call the matter in question, and admiring the vertues of the murthered prince, would have punished the massacrers and bereavers of his life. Which was the cause that Fengon, boldned and incouraged by such impunitie, durst venture to couple himselfe in marriage with her whom hee used as his concubine during good Horvendiles life, in that sort spotting his name with a double vice, and charging his conscience with abhominable guilt, and two-fold impietie, as incestuous adulterie and parricide murther: and that the unfortunate and wicked woman, that had received the honour to bee the wife of one of the valiantest and wiseth princes in the north, imbased her selfe in such vile sort, as to falsifie her faith unto him, and which is worse, to marrie him, that had bin the tyranous murtherer of her lawfull husband;

(marginal notes:)

Fengon killeth his brother.

Slanderers more honoured in court then vertuous persons.

The incestuous marriage of Fengon with his brothers wife.

which made divers men thinke that she had beene the causer of the murther, thereby to live in her adultery without controle. But where shall a man finde a more wicked and bold woman, then a great parsonage once having loosed the bands of honor and honestie? This princesse, who at the first, for her rare vertues and courtesses was honored of al men and beloved of her husband, as soone as she once gave eare to the tyrant Fengon, forgot both the ranke she helde among the greatest names, and the dutie of an honest wife on her behalfe. But I will not stand to gaze and mervaile at women, for that there are many which seeke to blase and set them foorth, in which their writings they spare not to blame them all for the faults of some one, or few women. But I say, that either nature ought to have bereaved man of that opinion to accompany with women, or els to endow them with such spirits, as that

If a man be deceived by a woman, it is his owne beastlinesse. they may easily support the crosses they endure, without complaining so often and so strangely, seeing it is their owne beastlinesse that overthrowes them. For if it be so, that a woman is so imperfect a creature as they make her to be, and that they know this beast to bee so hard to bee tamed as they affirme, why then are they so foolish to preserve them, and so dull and brutish as to trust their deceitfull and wanton imbraceings. But let us leave her in this extreamitie of laciviousnesse, and proceed to shewe you in what sort the yong prince Hamblet behaved himselfe, to escape the tyranny of his uncle.

CHAP. II.

How Hamblet counterfeited the mad man, to escape the tyrannie of his uncle, and how he was tempted by a woman (through his uncles procurement) who thereby thought to undermine the Prince, and by that meanes to finde out whether he counterfeited madnesse or not: and how Hamblet would by no meanes bee brought to consent unto her, and what followed.

GERUTH having (as I sayd before) so much forgotten herself, the prince Hamblet perceiving himself to bee in danger of his life, as beeing abandoned of his owne mother, and forsaken of all men, and assuring himselfe that Fengon would not detract the time to send him the same way his father Horvendile was gone, to beguile the tyrant in his subtilties (that esteemed him tb bee of such a minde that if he once attained to mans estate he wold not long delay the time to revenge the death of his father) counterfeiting the mad man with such craft and subtill practises, that hee made shewe as if hee had utterly lost his wittes: and under that vayle hee covered his pretence, and defended his life from the treasons and practises of the tyrant his uncle. And all though hee had beene at the schoole of the Romane Prince, who, because hee counterfeited himselfe to bee a foole, was called Brutus, yet hee imitated his fashions, and his wisedom. For every day beeing in the queenes palace, (who as then was more carefull to please her whoremaster, then ready to revenge the cruell death of her husband, or to restore her sonne to his inheritance), hee rent and tore his clothes, wallowing and lying in the durt and mire, his face all filthy and blacke, running through the streets like a man distraught, not speaking one worde, but such as seemed to proceede of madnesse and meere frenzie; all his actions and jestures beeing no other than the right countenances of a man wholly deprived of all reason and understanding, in such sort, that as then hee seemed fitte for nothing but to make sport to the pages and ruffling courtiers that attended in the court of his uncle and father-in-law. But the yong prince noted them well enough, minding one day to bee revenged in such manner, that the memorie thereof should remaine perpetually to the world.

Beholde, I pray you, a great point of a wise and brave spirite in a yong prince, by so great a shewe of imperfection in his person for advancement, and his owne imbasing and despising, to worke the meanes and to prepare the way for himselfe to bee one of the happiest kings in his age. In like sort, never any man was reputed by any of his actions more wise and prudent then Brutus, dissembling a great alteration in his minde, for that the occasion of such his devise of foolishnesse proceeded onely of a good and mature counsell and deliberation, not onely to preserve his goods, and shunne the rage of the proude tyrant, but also to open a large way to procure the banishment and utter ruine of wicked Tarquinius, and to infranchise the people (which were before oppressed) from the yoake of a great and miserable servitude. And so, not onely Brutus, but this man and worthy prince, to whom wee may also adde king David, that counterfeited the madde man among the petie kings of Palestina to preserve his life from the subtill practises of those kings. I shew this example unto such, as beeing offended with any great personage, have not sufficient means to prevaile in their intents, or revenge the injurie by them received. But when I speake of revenging any injury received upon a great personage or superior, it must be understood by such an one as is not our soveraigne, againste whome wee maie by no meanes resiste, nor once practise anie treason nor conspiracie against his life: and hee that will followe this course must speake and do all things whatsoever that are pleasing and acceptable to him whom hee meaneth to deceive, practise his actions, and esteeme him above all men, cleane contrarye to his owne intent and meaning; for that is rightly to playe and counterfeite the foole, when a man is constrained to dissemble and kisse his hand, whome in hearte hee could wishe an hundred foote depth under the earth, so hee mighte never see him more, if it were not a thing wholly to bee disliked in a christian, who by no meanes ought to have a bitter gall, or desires infected with revenge. Hamblet, in this sorte counterfeiting the madde man, many times did divers· actions of great and deepe consideration, and often made such and so fitte answeres, that a wise man would soone have judged from what spirite so fine an invention mighte proceede; for that standing by the fire and sharpning sticks like poynards and prickes, one in smiling manner asked him wherefore he made those little staves so sharpe at the points? I prepare (saith he) piersing dartes and sharpe arrowes to revenge my fathers death. Fooles, as I said before, esteemed those his words as nothing; but men of quicke spirits, and such as hadde a deeper reache began to suspect somewhat, esteeming that under that kinde of folly there lay hidden a greate and rare subtilty, such as one day might bee prejudiciall to their prince, saying, that under colour of such rudeness he shadowed a crafty pollicy, and by his devised simplicitye, he concealed a sharp and pregnant spirit: for which cause they counselled the king to try and know, if it were possible, how to discover the intent and meaning of the yong prince; and they could find no better nor more fit invention to intrap him, then to set some faire and beawtifull woman in a secret place, that with

Brutus esteemed wise, for counterfeiting the foole. Read Titus Livius and Halicarnassus.

David counterfeited the mad man before king Aches.

Rom, viii. 21.

A subtill answere of Prince Hamlet.

flattering speeches and all the craftiest meanes she could use, should purposely seek
to allure his mind to have his pleasure of her: for the nature of all young men,
(especially such as are brought up wantonlie) is so transported with
Nature cor-
rupted in man the desires of the flesh, and entreth so greedily into the pleasures
therof, that it is almost impossible to cover the foul affection, neither
yet to dissemble or hyde the same by art or industry, much lesse to shunne it. What
cunning or subtilty so ever they use to cloak theire pretence, seeing occasion offered,
and that in secret, especially in the most inticing sinne that rayneth in man, they
cannot chuse (being constrayned by voluptuousnesse) but fall to natu-
Subtilties
used to dis- rall effect and working. To this end certaine courtiers were appointed
cover Hamb- to leade Hamblet into a solitary place within the woods, whether they
lets madnes. brought the woman, inciting him to take their pleasures together, and
to imbrace one another, but the subtill practises used in these our daies, not to try
if men of great account bee extract out of their wits, but rather to de-
Corrupters
of yong gen- prive them of strength, vertue and wisedome, by meanes of such dev-
tlemen in ilish practitioners, and intefernall spirits, their domestical servants, and
princes courts
and great ministers of corruption. And surely the poore prince at this assault
houses. had him in great danger, if a gentleman (that in Horvendiles time had
been nourished with him) had not showne himselfe more affectioned to the bringing
up he had received with Hamblet, then desirous to please the tirant, who by all
meanes sought to intangle the sonne in the same nets wherein the father had ended
his dayes. This gentleman bare the courtyers (appointed as aforesaide of this
treason) company, more desiring to give the prince instruction what he should do,
then to intrap him, making full account that the least showe of perfect sence and
wisedome that Hamblet should make would be sufficient to cause him to loose his
life: and therefore by certain signes, he gave Hamblet intelligence in what danger
hee was like to fall, if by any meanes hee seemed to obaye, or once like the wanton
toyes and vicious provocations of the gentlewoman sent thither by his uncle. Which
much abashed the prince, as then wholy beeing in affection to the lady, but by her
he was likewise informed of the treason, as being one that from her infancy loved
and favoured him, and would have been exceeding sorrowfull for his misfortune, and
much more to leave his companie without injoying the pleasure of his body, whome
shee loved more than herselfe. The prince in this sort having both deceived the
courtiers, and the ladyes expectation, that affirmed and swore that hee never once
offered to have his pleasure of the woman, although in subtilty hee affirmed the
contrary, every man there upon assured themselves that without all doubt he was
distraught of his sences, that his braynes were as then wholly void of force, and
incapable of reasonable apprehension, so that as then Fengons practise took no
effect: but for al that he left not off, still seeking by al meanes to finde out Hamblet's subtilty, as in the next chapter you shall perceive.

CHAP. III.

How Fengon, uncle to Hamblet, a second time to intrap him in his politick madnes, caused one of his counsellors to be secretly hidden in the queenes chamber, behind the arras, to heare what speeches passed between Hamblet and the Queen; and how Hamblet killed him, and escaped that danger, and what followed.

AMONG the friends of Fengon, there was one that above al the rest doubted of Hamblets practises in counterfeiting the madman, who for that cause said, that it was impossible that so craftie a gallant as Hamblet, that counterfeited the foole, should be discovered with so common and unskilfull prac- Another subtilty used tises, which might easily bee perceived, and that to finde out his poli- to deceive tique pretence it were necessary to invent some subtill and crafty Hamblet. meanes, more attractive, whereby the gallant might not have the leysure to use his accustomed dissimulation; which to effect he said he knewe a fit waie, and a most convenient meane to effect the kings desire, and thereby to intrap Hamblet in his subtilties, and cause him of his owne accord to fall into the net prepared for him, and thereby evidently shewe his secret meaning. His devise was thus, that King Fengon should make as though he were to goe some long voyage concerning affaires of great importance, and that in the meane time Hamblet should be shut up alone in a chamber with his mother, wherein some other should secretly be hidden behind the hangings, unknowne either to him or his mother, there to stand and heere their speeches, and the complots by them to bee taken concerning the accomplishment of the dissembling fooles pretence; assuring the king that if there were any point of wisedome and perfect sence in the gallants spirit, that without all doubte he would easily discover it to his mother, as being devoid of all feare that she would utter or make knowne his secret intent, beeing the woman that had borne him in her bodie, and nourished him so carefully; and withall offered himselfe to be the man that should stand to harken and beare witnesse of Hamblets speeches with his mother, that hee might not be esteemed a counsellor in such a case wherein he refused to be the executioner for the behoofe and service of his prince. This invention pleased the king exceeding well, esteeming it as the onelie and soveraigne remedie to heale the prince of his lunacie; and to that ende making a long voyage, issued out of his pallace, and road to hunt in the forrest. Mean time the counsellor entred secretly into the queenes chamber, and there hid himselfe behind the arras, not long before the queene and Hamblet came thither, who beeing craftie Hamblets subtilty. and pollitique, as soone as hee was within the chamber, doubting some treason, and fearing if he should speake severely and wisely to his mother touching his secret practises he should be understood, and by that meanes intercepted, used his ordinary manner of dissimulation, and began to come like a cocke beating with his armes, (in such manner as cockes use to strike with their wings) upon the hangings of the chamber: whereby, feeling something stirring under them, he cried, A rat, a rat! and presently drawing his sworde thrust it into A cruell revenge taken the hangings, which done, pulled the counsellour (halfe dead) out by by Hamblet upon him that the heeles, made an end of killing him, and beeing slaine, cut his bodie would have in pieces, which he caused to be boyled, and then cast it into an open betraid him.

vaulte or privie, that so it mighte serve for foode to the hogges. By which meanes
having discovered the ambushe, and given the inventer thereof his just rewarde, hee
came againe to his mother, who in the meane time wepte and tormented her selfe to
see all her hopes frustrate, for that what fault soever she had committed, yet was
shee sore grieved to see her onely child made a meere mockery, every man reproach-
ing her with his folly, one point whereof she had as then seene before
her eyes, which was no small pricke to her conscience, esteeming that
the gods sent her that punishment for joyning incestuously in marriage

*Queene
Geruthes re-
pentance.*

with the tyrannous murtherer of her husband, who like wise ceased not to invent
all the means he could to bring his nephew to his ende, accusing his owne naturall
indiscretion, as beeing the ordinary guide of those that so much desire the pleasures
of the bodie, who shutting up the waie to all reason, respect not what maie ensue
of of their lightnes and great inconstancy, and how a pleasure of small moment is
sufficient to give them cause of repentance during their lives, and make them curse
the daye and time that ever any such apprehensions entred into theire mindes, or
that they closed their eies to reject the honestie requisite in ladies of her qualitie,
and to despise the holy institution of those dames that had gone before her, both in
nobilitie and vertue, calling to mind the great prayses and commendations given by
the danes to Rinde, daughter to king Rothere, the chastest lady in her
time, and withall so shamefast that she would never consent to marriage with any prince or knight whatsoever; surpassing in vertue all

*Rinde a
princes of an
admirable
chastitie.*

the ladyes of her time, as shee herselfe surmounted them in beawtie,
good behaviour, and comelines. And while in this sort she sate tormenting herselfe, Hamlet entred into the chamber, who having once againe searched every
corner of the same, distrusting his mother as well as the rest, and perceiving himselfe to bee alone, began in sober and discreet manner to speak unto her, saying,

What treason is this, O most infamous woman ! of all that ever prostrated themselves to the will of an abhominable whore monger, who, under the vail of a dissembling creature, covereth the most wicked and detestable crime that man could
ever imagine, or was committed. Now may I be assured to trust you, that like a
vile wanton adultresse, altogether impudent and given over to her pleasure, runnes
spreading forth her armes joyfully to imbrace the trayterous villanous tyrant that
murthered my father, and most incestuously receivest the villain into the lawfull bed
of your loyall spouse, imprudently entertaining him in steede of the deare father of
your miserable and discomforted soone, if the gods grant him not the grace speedilie
to escape from a captivity so unworthie the degree he holdeth, and the race and
nobie familie of his ancestors. Is this the part of a queene, and daughter to a king?
to live like a brute beast (and like a mare that yieldeth her bodie to the horse that
hath beaten hir companion awaye), to followe the pleasure of an abhominable king
that hath murthered a farre more honester and better man then himself in massacring
Horvendile, the honor and glory of the Danes, who are now esteemed of no force
nor valour at all, since the shining splendure of knighthood was brought to an end
by the most wickedest and cruellest villaine living upon earth. I, for my part, will
never account him for my kinsman, nor once knowe him for mine uncle, nor you
my deer mother, for not having respect to the blud that ought to have united us so
straightly together, and who neither with your honor nor without suspicion of consent to the death of your husband could ever have agreed to have marryed with his
cruell enemie. O, queene Geruthe, it is the part of a bitch to couple with many,
and desire acquaintance of divers mastiffes : it is licentiousnes only that hath made

you deface out of your minde the memory of the valor and vertues of the good king your husband and my father: it was an unbrideled desire that guided the daughter of Roderick to imbrace the tyrant Fengon, and not to remember Horvendile (unworthy of so strange intertainment), neither that he killed his brother traiterously, and that shee being his fathers wife betrayed him, although he so well favoured and loved her, that for her sake he utterly bereaved Norway of her riches and valiant souldiers to augment the treasures of Roderick, and make Geruthe wife to the hardyest prince in Europe: it is not the parte of a woman, much lesse of a princesse, in whome all modesty, curtesse, compassion, and love ought to abound, thus to leave her deare child to fortune in the bloody and murtherous hands of a villain and traytor. Bruite beasts do not so, for lyons, tygers, ounces and leopards fight for the safety and defence of their whelpes; and birds that have beakes, claws, and wings, resist such as would ravish them of their yong ones; but you, to the contrary, expose and deliver mee to death, whereas ye should defend me. Is not this as much as if you should betray me, when you knowing the perversenes of the tyrant and his intents, ful of deadly counsell as touching the race and image of his brother, have not once sought, nor desired to finde the meanes to save your child (and only son) by sending him into Swethland, Norway, or England, rather than to leave him as a pray to youre infamous adulterer? bee not offended, I praye you, Madame, if transported with dolour and griefe, I speake so boldely unto you, and that I respect you lesse then dutie requireth; for you, having forgotten mee, and wholy rejected the memorye of the deceased K. my father, must not bee abashed if I also surpasse the bounds and limits of due consideration. Beholde into what distresse I am now fallen, and to what mischiefe my fortune, and your over great lightnesse, and want of wisedome have induced mee, that I am constrained to playe the madde man to save my life, in steed of using and practising armes, following adventures, and seeking all meanes to make my selfe knowne to bee the true and undoubted heire of the valiant and vertuous king Horvendile. It was not without cause, and juste occasion, that my gestures, countenances, and words, seeme all to proceed from a madman, and that I desire to have all men esteeme mee wholly deprived of sence and reasonable understanding, bycause I am well assured, that he that hath made no conscience to kill his owne brother, (accustomed to murthers, and allured with desire of governement without controll in his treasons), will not spare, to save himselfe with the like crueltie, in the blood and flesh of the loyns of his brother by him massacred: and, therefore, it is better for me to fayne madnesse, then to use my right sences as nature hath bestowed them upon me: the bright shining clearnes therof I am forced to hide under this shadow of dissimulation, as the sun doth hir beams under some great cloud, when the wether in sommer time overcasteth. The face of a mad man serveth to cover my gallant countenance, and the gestures of a fool are fit for me, to the end that guiding my self wisely therein, I may preserve my life for the Danes, and the memory of my late deceased father; for the desire of revenging his death is so engraven in my heart, that if I dye not shortly, I hope to take such and so great vengeance, that these countryes shall for ever speake thereof. Neverthelesse, I must stay the time, meanes, and occasion, lest by making over great hast, I be now the cause of mine owne sodaine ruine and overthrow, and by that means end before I beginne to effect my hearts desire. Hee that hath to doe with a wicked, disloyall, cruell, and discourteous man must use craft and politike inventions, such as a fine witte can best imagine, not to discover his interprise; for seeing that by force I cannot effect my desire, reason

We must use subtiltie to a disloyall person.

alloweth me by dissimulation, subtiltie, and secret practises to proceed therein. To conclude, weepe not (madame) to see my folly, but rather sigh and lament your owne offence, tormenting your conscience in regard of the infamie that hath so defiled the ancient renowne and glorie that (in times past) honoured queene Geruth; for wee are not to sorrowe and grieve at other mens vices, but for our owne misdeedes, and great folloyes. Desiring you, for the surplus of my proceedings, above all things (as you love your owne life and welfare) that neither the king nor any other may by any meanes know mine intent; and let me alone with the rest, for I hope in the ende to bring my purpose to effect.

(margin: Wee must weepe for our owne faults and not for other mens.)

Although the queene perceived herselfe neerely touched, and that Hamlet mooved her to the quicke, where she felt herself interested, neverthelesse shee forgot all disdaine and wrath, which thereby she might as then have had, hearing her selfe so sharply chiden and reprooved, for the joy she then conceaved, to behold the gallant spirit of her sonne, and to thinke what she might hope, and the easier expect of his so great policie and wisdome. But on the one side she durst not lift up her eyes to beholde him, remembering her offence, and on the other side she would gladly have imbraced her son, in regard of the wise admonitions by him given unto her, which as then quenched the flames of unbridled desire that before had mooved her to affect K. Fengon, to ingraff in her heart the vertuous actions of her lawfull spouse, whom inwardly she much lamented, when she beheld the lively image and portraiture of his vertue and great wisedome in her childe, representing his fathers haughtie and valiant heart: and so, overcome and vanquished with this honest passion, and weeping most bitterly, having long time fixed her eyes upon Hamlet, as beeing ravished into some great and deepe contemplation, and as it were wholy amazed, at the last imbracing him in her armes (with the like love that a vertuous mother may or can use to kisse and entertaine her owne childe), shee spake unto him in this manner.

I know well (my sonne) that I have done thee great wrong in marrying with Fengon, the cruell tyrant and murtherer of thy father, and my loyall spouse: but when thou shalt consider the small meanes of resistance, and the treason of the palace, with the little cause of confidence we are to expect or hope for of the courtiers, all wrought to his will, as also the power hee made ready, if I should have refused to like of him, thou wouldest rather excuse then accuse me of lasciviousnes or inconstancy, much lesse offer me that wrong to suspect that ever thy mother Geruthe once consented to the death and murther of her husband: swearing unto thee (by the majestie of the Gods) that if it had layne in my power to have resisted the tyrant, although it had beene with the losse of my blood, yea and my life, I would surely have saved the life of my lord and husband, with as good a will and desire as, since that time, I have often beene a meanes to hinder and impeach the shortning of thy life, which being taken away, I will no lomger live here upon earth. For seeing that thy sences are whole and sound, I am in hope to see an easie meanes invented for the revenging of thy fathers death.   Neverthelesse, mine owne sweet soone, if thou hast pittie of thy selfe, or care of the memorie of thy father (although thou wilt do nothing for her that deserveth not the name of a mother in this respect), I pray thee, carie thine affayres wisely: bee not hastie, nor over furious in thy interprises, neither yet advance thy selfe more then reason shall moove thee to effect thy purpose.   Thou seest there is not almost any man wherein thou mayest put thy trust, nor any woman to whom I dare utter the least part of my secrets, that would not presently report it to thine adversarie, who, although in outward shew he dis

sembleth to love thee, the better to injoy his pleasures of me, yet hee distrusteth and
feareth mee for thy sake, and is not so simple as to be easily perswaded that thou
art a foole or mad; so that if thou chance to doe any thing that seemeth to proceed
of wisedome or policie (how secretly soever it be done) he will presently be informed
thereof, and I am greatly afraide that the devils have shewed him what hath past at
this present between us, (fortune so much pursueth and contrarieth our ease and
welfare) or that this murther that now thou hast committed be not the cause of both
our destructions, which I by no meanes will seeme to know, but will keepe secret
both thy wisedome and hardy interprise; beseeching the Gods (my good soone) that
they, guiding thy heart, directing thy counsels, and prospering thy interprise, I may
see thee possesse and injoy that which is thy right, and weare the crowne of Denmarke, by the tyrant taken from thee; that I may rejoyce in thy prosperitie, and
therewith content my self, seeing with what courage and boldnesse thou shalt take
vengeance upon the murtherer of thy father, as also upon all those that have assisted
and favoured him in his murtherous and bloody enterprise. Madame (sayd Hamlet)
I will put my trust in you, and from henceforth meane not to meddle further with
your affayres, beseeching you (as you love your owne flesh and blood) that you will
from hence foorth no more esteeme of the adulterer, mine enemie whom I wil surely
kill, or cause to be put to death, in despite of all the devils in hel: and have he
never so manie flattering courtezans to defend him, yet will I bring him to his death,
and they themselves also shall beare him company therein, as they have bin his per-
verse counsellors in the action of killing my father, and his companions in his
treason, massacre and cruell enterprise. And reason requireth that, even as trayterously they then caused their prince to bee put to death, that with the like (nay
well, much more) justice they should pay the interest of their fellonious actions.

You know (Madame) how Hother your grandfather, and father to
the good king Roderick, having vanquished Guimon, caused him to
be burnt, for that the cruell vilain had done the like to his lord Gevare,
whom he betrayed in the night time. And who knoweth not that
traytors and perjured persons deserve no faith nor loyaltie to be observed towardes
them, and that conditions made with murtherers ought to bee esteemed
as cobwebs, and accounted as if they were things never promised nor
agreed upon: but if I lay handes upon Fengon, it will neither be fellonie nor treason, hee being neither my king nor my lord, but I shall
justly punish him as my subject, that hath disloyaly behaved himselfe
against his lord and soveraigne prince. And seeing that glory is the
rewarde of the vertuous, and the honour and praise of those that do service to their
naturall prince, why should not blame and dishonour accompany traytors, and igno-
minious death al those that dare be so bold as to lay violent hands upon sacred
kings, that are friends and companions of the gods, as representing their majestie
and persons. To conclude, glorie is the crown of vertue, and the price of constancie; and seeing that it never accompanieth with infelicitie, but shunneth cow-
ardize and spirits of base and trayterous conditions, it must necessarily followe, that
either a glorious death will be mine ende, or with my sword in hand, (laden with
tryumph and victorie) I shall bereave them of their lives that made mine unfortunate, and darkened the beames of that vertue which I possessed from the blood and
famous memory of my predecessors. For why should men desire to live, when
shame and infamie are the executioners that torment their consciences, and villany
is the cause that withholdeth the heart from valiant interprises, and diverteth the

Hother, fa-
ther to Roder-
icke. Guimon
burnt his lord
Gevare.

We must
observe nei-
ther faithful-
nesse or
fidelitie to
traytors or
parricides.

minde from honest desire of glorie and commendation, which induieth for ever? I know it is foolishly done to gather fruit before it is ripe, and to seeke to enjcy a benefit, not knowing whither it belong to us of right; but I hope to effect it so well, and have so great confidence in my fortune (that hitherto hath guided the action of my life) that I shall not dye without revenging my selfe upon mine enemie, and that himselfe shall be the instrument of his owne decay, and to execute that which of my selfe I durst not have enterprised.

After this, Fengon (as if hee had beene out some long journey) came to the court againe, and asked for him that had received the charge to play the intilligencer, to entrap Hamlet in his dissembled wisedome, was abashed to heare neither newes nor tydings of him, and for that cause asked Hamlet what was become of him, naming the man. The prince that never used lying, and who in all the answers that ever he made (during his counterfeit madnesse) never strayed from the trueth (as a generous minde is a mortal enemie to untruth) answered and sayd, that the counsellor he sought for was gone downe through the privie, where being choaked by the filthy-nesse of the place, the hogs meeting him had filled their bellyes.

CHAP. IIII.

How Fengon the third time devised to send Hamblet to the king of England, with secret letters to have him put to death : and how Hamblet, when his companions slept, read the letters, and instead of them counterfeited others, willing the king of England to put the two messengers to death, and to marry his daughter to Hamblet, which was effected ; and how Hamblet escaped out of England.

A MAN would have judged any thing, rather then that Hamblet had committed that murther, nevertheless Fengon could not content himselfe, but still his minde gave him that the foole would play him some tricke of liegerdemaine, and willingly would have killed him, but he feared king Rodericke, his grandfather, and furthei durst not offend the queene, mother to the foole, whom she loved and much cher-ished, shewing great griefe and heavinesse to see him so transported out of his wits. And in that conceit, seeking to bee rid of him, determined to finde the meanes to doe it by the ayde of a stranger, making the king of England minister of his massa-creing resolution, choosing rather that his friende should defile his renowne with so great a wickednesse, then himselfe to fall into perpetuall infamie by an exploit of so great crueltie, to whom hee purposed to send him, and by letters desire him to put him to death.

Hamblet, understanding that he should be sent into England, presently doubted the occasion of his voyage, and for that cause speaking to the queene, desired her not to make any shew of sorrow or griefe for his departure, but rather counterfeit a gladnesse, as being rid of his presence; whom, although she loved, yet she dayly grieved to see him in so pittifull estate, deprived of all sence and reason: desiring her further, that she should hang the hall with tapestrie, and make it fast with nayles upon the walles, and keepe the brands for him which hee had sharpened at the points, then, when as he said he made arrowes to revenge the death of his father:

lastly, he counselled her, that the yeere after his departure being accomplished, she should celebrate his funerals; assuring her that at the same instant she should see him returne with great contentment and pleasure unto her for that his voyage. Now, to beare him company were assigned two of Fengons faithfull ministers, bearing letters ingraved in wood, that contained Hamlets death, in such sort as he had advertised the king of England. But the subtile Danish prince (beeing at sea) whilst his companions slept, having read the letters, and knowne his uncles great treason, with the wicked and villainous mindes of the two courtiers that led him to the slaughter, raced out the letters that concerned his death, and in stead thereof graved others, with commission to the king **Hamblets craft to save his life.** of England to hang his two companions; and not content to turne the death they had devised against him upon their owne neckes, wrote further, that king Fengon willed him to give his daughter to Hamlet in marriage. And so arriving in England, the messengers presented themselves to the king, giving him Fengons letters; who having read the contents, sayd nothing as then, but stayed convenient time to effect Fengons desire, meane time using the Danes familiarly, doing them that honour to sit at his table (for that kings as then were not so curiously, nor solemnely served as in these our dayes,) for in these dayes meane kings, and lords of small revenewe are as difficult and hard to bee seene, as in times past the monarches of Persia used to bee: or as it is reported of the great king of Aethyopia, who will not permit any man to see his face, which ordinarily hee covereth with a vaile. And as the messengers sate at the table with the king, subtile Hamlet was so far from being merry with them, that he would not taste one bit of meate, bread, nor cup of beare whatsoever, as then set upon the table, not without great wondering of the company, abashed to see a yong man and a stranger not to esteeme of the delicate meates and pleasant drinkes served at the banquet, rejecting them as things filthy, evill of tast, and worse prepared. The king, who for that time dissembled what he thought, caused his ghests to be conveyed into their chamber, willing one of his secret servantes to hide himselfe therein, and so to certifie him what speeches past among the Danes at their going to bed.

Now they were no sooner entred into the chamber, and those that were appointed to attend upon them gone out, but Hamlets companions asked him, why he refused to eate and drinke of that which hee found upon the table, not honouring the banquet of so great a king, that entertained them in friendly sort, with such honour and courtesie as it deserved? saying further, that hee did not well, but dishonoured him that sent him, as if he sent men into England that feared to bee poysoned by so great a king. The prince, that had done nothing without reason and prudent consideration, answered them, and sayd: What, think you, that I will eat bread dipt in humane blood, and defile my throate with the rust of yron, and use that meat that stinketh and savoureth of mans flesh, already putrified and corrupted, and that senteth like the savour of a dead carryon, long since cast into a valt? and how woulde you have mee to respect the king, that hath the countenance of a slave; and the queene, who in stead of great majestie, hath done three things more like a woman of base parentage, and fitter for a waiting gentlewoman then beseeming a lady of her qualitie and estate. And having sayd so, used many injurious and sharpe speeches as well against the king and queene, as others that had assisted at that banquet for the intertainment of the Danish ambassadors; and therein Hamblet said trueth, as hereafter you shall heare, for that in those dayes, the north parts of the worlde, living as then under Sathans lawes, were full of inchanters, so that there

was not any yong gentleman whatsoever that knew not something therein sufficient
to serve his turne, if need required: as yet in those dayes in Gothland and Biarmy,
there are many that knew not what the Christian religion permitteth, as by reading
the histories of Norway and Gothland, you maie easilie perceive: and so Hamlet,
while his father lived, had bin instructed in that devilish art, whereby the wicked
spirite abuseth mankind, and advertiseth him (as he can) of things past.

It toucheth not the matter herein to discover the parts of devination in man, and
whether this prince, by reason of his over great melancholy, had received those im
pressions, devining that, which never any but himselfe had before declared, like the
philosophers, who discoursing of divers deep points of philosophie, attribute the
force of those divinations to such as are saturnists by complection, who oftentimes
speake of things which, their fury ceasing, they then alreadye can hardly understand
who are the pronouncers; and for that cause Plato saith, many deviners and many
poets, after the force and vigour of their fier beginneth to lessen, do hardly understand what they have written, although intreating of such things, while the spirite
of devination continueth upon them, they doe in such sorte discourse thereof that
the authors and inventers of the arts themselves by them alledged, commend their
discourses and subtill disputations. Likewise I mean not to relate that which divers
men beleeve, that a reasonable soul becometh the habitation of a meaner sort of
devels, by whom men learn the secrets of things natural; and much lesse do I account of the supposed governors of the world fained by magitians, by whose means
they brag to effect mervailous things. It would seeme miraculous that Hamlet shold
divine in that sort, which after prooved so true (if as I said before) the devel had
not knowledg of things past, but to grant it he knoweth things to come I hope you
shall never finde me in so grose an error. You will compare and make equall derivation, and conjecture with those that are made by the spirit of God, and pronounced
by the holy prophets, that tasted of that marvelous science, to whome onely was declared the secrets and wondrous workes of the Almighty. Yet there are some im-
posturious companions that impute so much devinitie to the devell, the father of
lyes, that they attribute unto him the truth of the knowledge of thinges that shall
happen unto men, alledging the conference of Saul with the witch, although one
example out of the Holy Scriptures, specially set downe for the condemnation of
wicked man, is not of force to give a sufficient law to all the world; for they themselves confesse that they can devine, not according to the universal cause of things,
but by signes borrowed from such like causes, which are all waies alike, and by
those conjectures they can give judgement of thinges to come, but all this beeing
grounded upon a weake support, (which is a simple conjecture) and having so
slender a foundation, as some foolish or late experience the fictions being voluntarie.
It should be a great folly in a man of good judgement, specially one that imbraceth
the preaching of the gospell, and seeketh after no other but the trueth thereof, to
repose upon any of these likelihoods or writings full of deceipt.

As touching magical operations, I will grant them somewhat therein, finding
divers histories that write thereof, and that the Bible maketh mention, and forbid-
deth the use thereof: yea, the lawes of the gentiles and ordinances of emperors
have bin made against it in such sort, that Mahomet, the great hereticke and friend
of the devell, by whose subtiltyes hee abused most part of the east countries, hath
ordained great punishments for such as use and practise those unlawfull and damnable artes, which, for this time leaving of, let us returne to Hamlet, brought up in
these abuses, according to the manner of his country, whose companions hearing his

answere reproached him of folly, saying that hee could by no meanes show a greater point of indiscretion, then in despising that which is lawfull, and rejecting that which all men receaved as a necessary thing, and that hee had not grossely so forgotten himselfe as in that sorte to accuse such and so excellent a man as the king of England, and to slander the queene, being then as famous and wise a princes as any at that day raigning in the ilands thereabouts, to cause him to be punished according to his deserts; but he, continuing in his dissimulation, mocked him, saying that hee had not done any thing that was not good and most true. On the other side, the king being advertised thereof by him that stood to heare the discourse, judged presently that Hamlet, speaking so ambiguously, was either a perfect foole, or else one of the wisest princes in his time, answering so sodainly, and so much to the purpose upon the demaund by his companions made touching his behaviour; and the better to find the trueth, caused the babler to be sent for, of whome inquiring in what place the corn grew whereof he made bread for his table, and whether in that ground there were not some signes or newes of a battaile fought, whereby humaine blood had therein been shed? the babler answered that not far from thence there lay a field ful of dead mens bones, in times past slaine in a battaile, as by the greate heapes of wounded sculles mighte well appeare, and for that the ground in that parte was become fertiler then other grounds, by reason of the fatte and humours of the dead bodies, that every yeer the farmers used there to have in the best wheat they could finde to serve his majesties house. The king perceiving it to be true, according to the yong princes wordes, asked where the hogs had bin fed that were killed to be served at his table? and answere was made him, that those hogs getting out of the said fielde wherein they were kepte, had found the bodie of a thiefe that had beene hanged for his demerits, and had eaten thereof: whereat the king of England beeing abashed, would needs know with what water the beer he used to drinke of had been brued? which having knowne, he caused the river to bee digged somewhat deeper, and therin found great store of swords and rustie armours, that gave an ill savour to the drinke. It were good I should heere dilate somewhat of Merlins prophesies, which are said to be spoken of him before he was fully one yeere old; but if you consider wel what hath al reddy been spoken, it is no hard matter to divine of things past, although the minister of Sathan therein played his part, giving sodaine and prompt answeres to this yong prince, for that herein are nothing but natural things, such as were wel known to be true, and therefore not needfull to dreame of thinges to come. This knowne, the king, greatly moved with a certaine curiositie to knowe why the Danish prince saide that he had the countenance of a slave, suspecting thereby that he reproached the basenes of his blood, and that he wold affirme that never any prince had bin his sire, wherin to satisfie himselfe he went to his mother, and leading her into a secret chamber, which he shut as soone as they were entred, desired her of her honour to shewe him of whome he was ingendred in this world. The good lady, wel assured that never any man had bin acquainted with her love touching any other man then her husband, sware that the king her husband onely was the man that had enjoyed the pleasures of her body; but the king her sonne, alreadie with the truth of the Danish princes answers, threatned his mother to make her tell by force, if otherwise she would not confesse it, who for feare of death acknowledged that she had prostrated her body to a slave, and made him father to the king of England; whereat the king was abashed, and wholy ashamed. I give them leave to judge who esteeming themselves honester than theire neighbours, and supposing that there can be nothing amisse in their houses, make more enquirie then is requisite to know the which they would rather not have known.   Neverthelesse dissembling what he thought, and biting upon the bridle, rather then he would deprive himselfe by publishing the lasciviousnes of his mother, thought better to leave a great sin unpunished, then thereby to make himselfe contemptible to his subjects, who peradventure would have rejected him, as not desiring to have a bastard to raigne over so great a kingdome.

But as he was sorry to hear his mothers confession, on the otherside he tooke great pleasure in the subtilty and quick spirit of the yong prince, and for that cause went unto him to aske him, why he had reproved three things in his queene convenient for a slave, and savouring more of basenes then of royaltie, and far unfit for the majesty of a great prince?   The king, not content to have receaved a great displeasure by knowing him selfe to be a bastard, and to have heard with what injuries he charged her whom hee loved best in all the world, would not content himself untill he also understood that which displeased him, as much as his owne proper disgrace, which was that his queen was the daughter of a chambermaid, and with all noted certaine foolish countenances she made, which not onely shewed of what parentage she came, but also that hir humors savored of the basenes and low degree of hir parents, whose mother, he assured the king, was as then yet holden in servitude.   The king admiring the young prince, and behoulding in him some matter of greater respect then in the common sort of men, gave him his daughter in marriage, according to the counterfet letters by him devised, and the next day caused the two servants of Fengon to be executed, to satisfie, as he thought, the king's desire.   But Hamlet, although the sport plesed him wel, and that the king of England could not have done him a greater favour, made as though he had been much offended, threatning the king to be revenged, but the king, to appease him, gave him a great sum of gold, which Hamlet caused to be molten, and put into two staves, made hollow for the same purpose, to serve his tourne there with as neede should require ; for of all other the kings treasures he took nothing with him into Denmark but onely those two staves, and as soone as the yeere began to bee at an end, having somewhat before obtained licence of the king his father in law to depart, went for Denmarke ; then, with all the speed hee could to returne againe into England to marry his daughter, and so set sayle for Denmarke.

CHAP. V.

How Hamblet, having escaped out of England, arrived in Denmarke the same day that the Danes were celebrating his funerals, supposing him to be dead in England ; and how he revenged his fathers death upon his uncle and the rest of the courtiers ; and what followed.

HAMBLET in that sort sayling into Denmark, being arrived in the contry, entered into the pallace of his uncle the same day that they were celebrating his funeralls, and going into the hall, procured no small astonishment and wonder to them all, no man thinking other but that hee had beene deade : among the which many of them rejoyced not a little for the pleasure which they knew Fengon would conceave for so pleasant a losse, and some were sadde, as remembering the honourable king Horvendile, whose victories they could by no meanes forget, much lesse deface out of theire memories that which apperteined unto him, who as then greatly rejoyced to see a false report spread of Hamlets death, and that the tyrant had not as yet obtained his will of the heire of Jutie, but rather hoped God would restore him to his sences againe for the good and welfare of that province. Their amazement at the last beeing tourned into laughter, all that as then were assistant at the funerall banquet of him whome they esteemed dead, mocked each at other, for having beene so simply deceived, and wondering at the prince, that in his so long a voyage he had not recovered any of his sences, asked what was become of them that had borne him company into Greate Brittaine? to whome he made answere (shewing them the two hollow staves, wherein he had put his molten golde, that the King of England had given him to appease his fury, concerning the murther of his two companions), and said, Here they are both. Whereat many that already knew his humours, presently conjectured that hee had plaide some tricke of legerdemane, and to deliver himselfe out of danger, had throwne them into the pitte prepared for him: so that fearing to follow after them and light upon some evil adventure, they went presently out of the court. And it was well for them that they didde so, considering the tragedy acted by him the same daic, beeing accounted his funerall, but in trueth theire last daies, that as then rejoyced for their overthrow; for when every man busied himselfe to make good cheare, and Hamlets arivall provoked them more to drinke and carouse, the prince himselfe at that time played the butler and a gentleman attending on the tables, not suffering the pots nor goblets to bee empty, whereby hee gave the noble men such store of liquor, that all of them being ful laden with wine and gorged with meate, were constrained to lay themselves downe in the same place where they had supt, so much their sences were dulled, and overcome with the fire of over great drinking (a vice common and familiar among the Almaines, and other nations inhabiting the north parts of the world) which when Hamlet perceiving, and finding so good opportunitie to effect his purpose and bee revenged of his enemies, and by the means to abandon the actions, gestures, and apparel of a mad man, occasion so fitly finding his turn, and as it were effecting it selfe, failed not to take hold therof, and seeing those drunken bodies, filled with wine, lying like hogs upon the ground, some sleeping, others vomiting the over great abundance of wine which without measure they had swallowed up, made the hangings about the hall to fall downe and cover them all over; which he nailed to the ground, being boorded, and at the ends thereof he stuck the brands, whereof I spake before, by him sharpned, which served for prickes, binding and tying the hangings in such sort, that what force soever they used to loose themselves, it was unpossible to get from under them: and presently he set fire in the foure corners of the hal, in such sort, that all that were as then therein not one escaped away, but were forced to purge their sins by fire, and dry up the great abundance of liquor by them received into their bodies, all of them dying in the inevitable and mercilesse flames of the whot and burning fire: which the prince perceiving, became wise, and knowing that his uncle, before the end of the banquet, had withdrawn himselfe into his chamber, which stood apart from the place where the fire burnt, went thither, and entring into the chamber, layd hand upon the sword of his fathers murtherer, leaving his own in the place, which while he was at the banket some of the

[marginal note:] Drunkenes a vice over common in the north partes of the world.

[marginal note:] A strange revenge taken by Hamlet.

courtiers had nailed fast into the scaberd, and going to Fengon said : I wonder, disloyal king, how thou canst sleep heer at thine ease, and al thy pallace is burnt, the fire thereof having burnt the greatest part of thy courtiers and ministers of thy cruelty, and detestable tirannies; and which is more, I cannot imagin how thou sholdst wel assure thy self and thy estate, as now to take thy ease, seeing Hamlet so neer thee armed with the shafts by him prepared long since, and at this present is redy to revenge the traiterous injury by thee done to his lord and father.

A mocke but yet sharp and stinging, given by Hamlet to his uncle.

Fengon, as then knowing the truth of his nephews subtile practise, and hering him speak with stayed mind, and which is more, perceived a sword naked in his hand, which he already lifted up to deprive him of his life, leaped quickly out of the bed, taking holde of Hamlets sworde, that was nayled into the scaberd, which as hee sought to pull out. Hamlet gave him such a blowe upon the chine of the necke, that hee cut his head cleane from his shoulders, and as he fell to the ground sayd, This just and violent death is a just reward for such as thou art : now go thy wayes, and when thou commest in hell, see thou forget not to tell thy brother (whom thou trayterously slewest), that it was his sonne that sent thee thither with the message, to the ende that beeing comforted thereby, his soule may rest among the blessed spirits, and quit mee of the obligation that bound me to pursue his vengeance upon mine owne blood, that seeing it was by thee that I lost the chiefe thing that tyed me to this aliance and consanguinitie. A man (to say the trueth) hardie, couragious, and worthy of eternall comendation, who arming himself with a crafty, dissembling, and strange shew of beeing distract out of his wits, under that pretence deceived the wise, pollitike, and craftie, thereby not onely preserving his life from the treasons and wicked practises of the tyrant, but (which is more) by an new and unexpected kinde of punishment, revenged his fathers, death, many yeeres after the act committed : in no such sort that directing his courses with such prudence, and effecting his purposes with so great boldnes and constancie, he left a judgement to be decyded among men of wisdom, which was more commendable in him, his constancy or magnanimitie, or his wisdom in ordring his affaires, according to the premeditable determination he had conceaved.

Commendation of Hamlet for killing the tyrant.

If vengeance ever seemed to have any shew of justice, it is then, when pietie and affection constraineth us to remember our fathers unjustly murdered, as the things wherby we are dispensed withal, and which seeke the means not to leave treason and murther unpunished : seeing David a holy and just king, and of nature simple, courteous, and debonaire, yet when he dyed he charged his soone Salomon (that succeeded him in his throane) not to suffer certaine men that had done him injurie to escape unpunished. Not that this holy king (as then ready to dye, and to give account before God of all his actions) was carefull or desirous of revenge, but to leave this example unto us, that where the prince or countrey is interested, the desire of revenge cannot by any meanes (how small soever) beare the title of condemnation, but is rather commendable and worthy of praise : for otherwise the good kings of Juda, nor others had not pursued them to death, that had offended their predecessors, if God himself had not inspired and ingraven that desire within their hearts. Hereof the Athenian lawes beare witnesse, whose custome was to erect images in remembrance of those men that,

How just vengeance ought to be considered.

Davids intent in commanding Salomon to revenge him of some of his enemies.

revenging the injuries of the commonwealth, boldly massacred tyrants and such as troubled the peace and welfare of the citizens.

Hamblet, having in this manner revenged himselfe, durst not presently declare his action to the people, but to the contrary determined to worke by policie, so to give them intelligence, what he had done, and the reason that drewe him thereunto : so that beeing accompanied with such of his fathers friends that then were rising, he stayed to see what the people would doe when they shoulde heare of that sodaine and fearefull action. The next morning the townes bordering there aboutes, desiring to know from whence the flames of fire proceeded the night before they had seene, came thither, and perceiving the kings pallace burnt to ashes, and many bodyes (most part consumed) lying among the ruines of the house, all of them were much abashed, nothing being left of the palace but the foundation. But they were much more amased to beholde the body of the king all bloody, and his head cut off lying hard by him; whereat some began to threaten revenge, yet not knowing against whom; others beholding so lamentable a spectacle, armed themselves, the rest rejoycing, yet not daring to make any shewe thereof; some detesting the crueltie, others lamenting the death of their Prince, but the greatest part calling Horvendiles murther to remembrance, acknowledging a just judgement from above, that had throwne downe the pride of the tyrant. And in this sort, the diversities of opinions among that multitude of people being many, yet every man ignorant what would be the issue of that tragedie, none stirred from thence, neither yet attempted to move any tumult, every man fearing his owne skinne, and distrusting his neighbour, esteeming each other to bee consenting to the massacre.

CHAP. VI.

How Hamlet, having slaine his Uncle, and burnt his Palace, made an Oration to the Danes to shew them what he done ; and how they made him King of Denmark ; and what followed.

HAMLET then seeing the people to be so quiet, and most part of them using any words, all searching onely and simply the cause of this ruine and destruction, not minding to loose any time, but ayding himselfe with the commodotie thereof, entred among the multitude of people, and standing in the middle spake unto them as followeth.

If there be any among you (good people of Denmark) that as yet have fresh within your memories the wrong done to the valiant king Horvendile, let him not be mooved, nor thinke it strange to behold the confused, hydeous, and fearfull spectacle of this present calamitie : if there be any man that affecteth fidelitie, and alloweth of the love and dutie that man is bound to shewe his parents, and find it a just cause to call to remembrance the injuryes and wrongs that have been done to our progenitors, let him not be ashamed beholding this massacre, much lesse offended to see so fearfull a ruine both of men and of the bravest house in all this countrey : for the hand that hath done this justice could not effect it by any other meanes, neither yet was it lawfull for him to doe it otherwise, then by ruinating both sensible and unsensible things, thereby to preserve the memorie of so just a vengeance.

I see well (my good friends) and am very glad to know so good attention and devotion in you, that you are sorrie (before your eyes) to see Fengon so murthered, and without a head, which heeretofore you acknowledged for your commander; but I pray you remember this body is not the body of a king, but of an execrable tyrant, and a parricide most detestable. Oh Danes! the spectacle was much more hydeous when Horvendile your king was murthered by his brother. What should I say a brother? nay, rather by the most abhominable executioner that ever beheld the same. It was you that saw Horvendiles members massacred, and that with teares and lamentations accompanied him to the grave; his body disfigured, hurt in a thousand places, and misused in ten times as many fashions. And who doubteth (seeing experience hath taught you) that the tyrant (in massacring your lawfull king) sought onely to infringe the ancient liberties of the common people? and it was one hand onely, that murthering Horvendile, cruelly dispoyled him of life, and by the same meanes unjustly bereaved you of your ancient liberties, and delighted more in oppression then to embrace the plesant countenance of prosperous libertie without adventuring for the same. And what mad man is he that delighteth more in the tyrany of Fengon then in the clemencie and renewed courtesie of Horvendile? If it bee so, that by clemencie and affabilitie the hardest and stoutest hearts are molified and made tractable, and that evill and hard usage causeth subjects to be outragious and unruly, why behold you not the debonair cariage of the first, to compare it with the cruelties and insolencies of the second, in every respect as cruell and barbarous as his brother was gentle, meeke, and courteous? Remember, O you Danes, remember what love and amitie Horvendile shewed unto you; with what equitie and justice he swayed the great affaires of this kingdome, and with what humanitie and courtisie he defended and cherished you, and then I am assured that the simplest man among you will both remember and acknowledge that he had a most peaceable, just, and righteous king taken from him, to place in his throane a tyrant and murtherer of his brother: one that hath perverted all right, abolished the auncient lawes of our fathers, contaminated the memories of our ancestors, and by his wickednesse polluted the integritie of this kingdome, upon the necke thereof having placed the troublesome yoak of heavie servitude, abolishing that libertie wherein Horvendile used to maintaine you, and suffered you to live at your ease. And should you now bee sorrie to see the ende of your mischiefes, and that this miserable wretch, pressed downe with the burthen of his offences, at this present payeth the usury of the parricide committed upon the body of his brother, and would not himselfe be the revenger of the outrage done to me, whom he sought to deprive of mine inheritance, taking from Denmark a lawfull successor, to plant a wicked stranger, and bring into captivitie those that my father had infranchised and delivered out of misery and bondage? And what man is he, that having any sparke of wisdom, would esteem a good deed to be an injury, and account pleasures equal with wrongs and evident outrages? It were then great folly and temerity in princes and valiant commanders in the wars to expose themselves to perils and hazards of their lives for the welfare of the common people, if that for a recompence they should reape hatred and indignation of the multitude. To what end should Hother have punished Balder, if, in steed of recompence, the Danes and Swethlanders had banished him to receive and accept the successors of him that desired nought but his ruine and overthrowe? What is hee that hath so small feeling of reason and equitie, that would be grieved to see treason rewarded with the like, and that an evill act is punished with just demerit in the partie himselfe that was the occasion? who was ever sorrowfull to behold the murtherer of innocents brought to his end, or what man weepeth to see a just massacre done upon a tyrant, usurper, villaine, and bloody personage?

I perceive you are attentive, and abashed for not knowing the author of your deliverance, and sorry that you cannot tell to whom you should bee thankefull for such and so great a benefit as the destruction of a tyrant, and the overthrow of the place that was the storehouse of his villanies, and the true receptacle of all the theeves and traytors in this kingdome : but beholde (here in your presence) him that brought so good an enterprise to effect. It is I (my good friends), it is I, that confesse I have taken vengeance for the violence done unto my lord and father, and for the subjection and servitude that I perceived in this countrey, whereof I am the just and lawfull successor. It is I alone, that have done this piece of worke, whereunto you ought to have lent me your handes, and therein have ayded and assisted me. I have only accomplished that which all of you might justly have effected, by good reason, without falling into any point of treason or fellonie. It is true that I hope so much of your good willes towards the deceased king Horvendile, and that the remembrances of his vertues is yet so fresh within your memories, that if I had required your aide herein, you would not have denied it, specially to your naturall prince. But it liked mee best to doe it my selfe alone, thinking it a good thing to punish the wicked without hazarding the lives of my friends and loyall subjects, not desiring to burthen other mens shoulders with this weight; for that I made account to effect it well inough without exposing any man into danger, and by publishing the same should cleane have overthrowne the device, which at this present I have so happily brought to passe. I have burnt the bodyes of the courtiers to ashes, being companions in the mischiefs and treasons of the tyrant; but I have left Fengon whole, that you might punish his dead carkasse (seeing that when hee lived you durst not lay hands upon him), to accomplish the full punishment and vengeance due unto him, and so satisfie your choller upon the bones of him that filled his greedy hands and coffers with your riches, and shed the blood of your brethren and friends. Bee joyfull, then (my good friends); make ready the nosegay for this usurping king : burne his abhominable body, boyle his lascivious members, and cast the ashes of him that hath beene hurtfull to all the world into the ayre : drive from you the sparkes of pitie, to the end that neither silver, nor christall cup, nor sacred tombe may be the restfull habitation of the reliques and bones of so detestable a man : let not one trace of a parricide be seene, nor your countrey defiled with the presence of the least member of this tyrant without pity, that your neighbors may not smell the contagion, nor our land the polluted infection of a body condemned for his wickednes. I have done my part to present him to you in this sort; now it belongs to you to make an end of the worke, and put to the last hand of dutie whereunto your severall functions call you; for in this sort you must honor abhominable princes, and such ought to be the funerall of a tyrant, parricide, and usurper, both of the bed and patrimony that no way belonged unto him, who having bereaved his countrey of liberty, it is fit that the land refuse to give him a place for the eternal rest of his bones.

O my good friends, seeing you know the wrong that hath bin done unto mee, what my griefs are, and in what misery I have lived since the death of the king,

iny lcrd and father, and seeing that you have both known and tasted these things
then, when as I could not conceive the outrage that I felt, what neede I recite it
unto you? what benefit would it be to discover it before them that knowing it would
burst (as it were with despight) to heare of my hard chance, and curse Fortune for
so much imbasing a royall prince, as to deprive him of his majesty, although not
any of you durst so much as shew one sight of sorrow or sadnes? You know how
my father in law conspired my death, and sought by divers meanes to take away my
life; how I was forsaken of the queen my mother, mocked of my friends, and dis-
pised of mine own subjects: hetherto I have lived laden with griefe, and wholly
confounded in teares, my life still accompanied with fear and suspition, expecting
the houre when the sharp sword would make an end of my life and miserable an-
guishes. How many times, counterfeiting the mad man, have I heard you pitty my
distresse, and secretly lament to see me disinherited? and yet no man sought to
revenge the death of my father, nor to punish the treason of my incestuous uncle,
full of murthers and massacres. This charitie ministred comfort, and your affectionate complaints made me evidently see your good wills, that you had in memorie
the calamity of your prince, and within your harts ingraven the desire of vengeance
for the death of him that deserved a long life. And what heart can bee so hard
and untractable, or spirit so severe, cruel, and rigorous, that would not relent at the
remembrance of my extremities, and take pitty of an orphan child, so abandoned of
the world? What eyes were so voyd of moysture but would distill a field of tears,
to see a poore prince assaulted by his owne subjects, betrayed by his mother, pursued by his uncle, and so much oppressed that his friends durst not shew the effects
f their charitie and good affection? O (my good friends) shew pity to him whom
;ou have nourished, and let your harts take some compassion upon the memory of
my misfortunes! I speak to you that are innocent of al treason, and never defiled
your hands, spirits, nor desires with the blud of the greate and vertuous king Horvendile. Take pity upon the queen, sometime your soveraign lady, and my right
honorable mother, forced by the tyrant, and rejoyce to see the end and extinguishing
of the object of her dishonor, which constrained her to be lesse pitiful to her own
blood, so far as to imbrace the murtherer of her own dear spouse, charging her selfe
with a double burthen of infamy and incest, together wtth injuring and disannulling
of her house, and the ruine of her race. This hath bin the occasion that made me
counterfet folly, and cover my intents under a vaile of meer madnes, which hath
wisdom and pollicy therby to inclose the fruit of this vengeance, which, that it hath
attained to the ful point of efficacy and perfect accomplishment, you yourselves shall
bee judges; for touching this and other things concerning my profit, and the man-
aging of great affairs, I refer my self to your counsels, and therunto am fully determined to yeeld, as being those that trample under your feet the murtherers of my
father, and despise the ashes of him that hath polluted and violated the spouse of
his brother, by him massacred; that hath committed felony against his lord, traiterously assailed the majesty of his king, and odiously thralled his contry under servitude and bondage, and you his loyall subjects, from whom he, bereaving your
liberty, feared not to ad incest to parricide, detestable to al the world. To you also
it belongeth by dewty and reason commonly to defend and protect Hamlet, the
minister and executor of just vengeance, who being jealous of your honour and
your reputation, hath hazarded himself, hoping you will serve him for fathers, de-
fenders, and tutors, and regarding him in pity, restore him to his goods and in-
heritances. It is I that have taken away the infamy of my contry, and extinguished

the fire that imbraced your fortunes. I have washed the spots that defiled the reputation of the queen, overthrowing both the tirant and the tiranny, and beguiling the
subtilties of the craftiest deceiver in the world, and by that meanes brought his
wickednes and impostures to an end. I was grieved at the injurie committed both
to my father and my native country, and have slaine him that used more rigorous
commandements over you, hen was either just or convenient to be used unto men
that have commaunded the valiantest nations in the world. Seeing, then, he was
such a one to you, it is reason that you acknowledge the benefit, and thinke wel of
for the good I had done your posterity, and admiring my spirit and wisdome, chuse
me your king, if you think me worthy of the place. You see I am the author of
your preservation, heire of my fathers kingdome, not straying in any point from his
vertuous action, no murtherer, violent parricide, nor man that ever offended any of
you, but only the vitious. I am lawfull successor in the kingdom, and just revenger
of a crime above al others most grievous and punishable : it is to me that you owe
the benefit of your liberty receaved, and of the subversion of that tyranny that so
much afflicted you, that hath troden under feete the yoke of the tirant, and overwhelmed his throne, and taken the scepter out of the hands of him that abused a
holy and just authoritie; but it is you that are to recompence those that have well
deserved, you know what is the reward of so greate desert, and being in your hands
to distribute the same, it is of you that I demand the price of my vertue, and the
recompence of my victory.

This oration of the yong prince so mooved the harts of the Danes, and wan the
affections of the nobility, that some wept for pity, other for joy, to see the wisedome, and gallant spirit of Hamlet; and having made an end of their
sorrow, al with one consent proclaimed him king of Jutie and Cher- <small>Hamlet king of one</small>
sonnese, at this present the proper country of Denmarke. And having <small>part of Den-</small>
celebrated his coronation, and received the homages and fidelities of <small>mark.</small>
his subjects, he went into England to fetch his wife, and rejoyced with his father
in law touching his good fortune; but it wanted little that the king of England had
not accomplished that which Fengon with all his subtilties could never attaine.

[There remain two more chapters of *The Hystorie of Hamblet, Prince of Denmarke.* As the interest of the story ceases here, so far as Shakespeare's *Hamlet* is
concerned, the poet having made no use of it beyond this point, I subjoin merely
the titles of the last two chapters. ED.]

CHAP. VII.

*How Hamlet, after his coronation, went into England; and how the king of Eng-
land secretly would have put him to death ; and how he slew the king of England, and returned againe into Denmarke with two wives; and what followed.*

CHAP. VIII.

*How Hamblet, being in Denmarke, was assailed by Wiglerus his Uncle, and after
betrayed by his last wife, called Hermetrude, and was slaine : after whose death
she marryed his enemie, Wiglerus.*

NOTE ON 'FRATRICIDE PUNISHED'

TIECK, in the Preface to his *Alt-Englisches Theater* (Berlin, 1811, p. xii), was the first to call attention to the curious and almost inexplicable fact, that at the beginning of the seventeenth century companies of actors travelled through Germany, styling themselves ' English Comedians.' ' They performed,' says Tieck, ' chiefly in Dresden, and for the most part pieces imitated from Shakespeare's contemporaries, nay, even from Shakespeare himself; for instance, *Titus Andronicus*. Subsequently, they had their *Comedies* printed, and the first two parts contain nothing but old English Comedies.'

The fact thus announced by Tieck remained for many years a vague myth, so far lacking the elements of probability that its truth would have been incontinently .denied, except for the stubborn fact that the collection of ' English Comedies and Tragedies ' alluded to by Tieck stood recorded as printed in 1620. Within the last few years, however, the subject has received attention, not only in Germany, as is natural, but also in England, where it may be supposed to be a matter of some pride to have started a sister nation of poets and thinkers on its dramatic career.

It is not within the scope of this edition of *Hamlet* to give a history of the discussion to which this subject has given rise, however interesting and tempting such a history may be, but it is essential to know some of the facts, as proved by laborious and learned German scholars, before we can estimate justly the value of the old tragedy of *Fratricide Punished*, which is here translated; if a connection can be traced between itinerant English actors, strolling through Germany, and the stage of Shakespeare, such a tragedy as this, or as *Romio and Julietta*, or as *Tito Andronico*, acquires great interest.

In 1865 ALBERT COHN, of Berlin, published *Shakespeare in Germany*, a book admirable throughout and of indispensable value to the student of this subject. Shakespearian literature both in England and Germany is therein brought under contribution, and German libraries and town archives have yielded up their dusty records; in Cohn's exhaustive Preface no statement is made without authority, and we may safely accept his conclusions.

In Heywood's *Apology for Actors*, 1612 (printed by the *Shakespeare Society*), there is the following passage (p. 40, ed. *Sh. Soc.*) : ' At the entertainement of the Cardinall Alphonsus and the infant of Spaine in the Low-countryes, they were presented at Antwerpe with sundry pageants and playes : the King of Denmarke, father to him that now reigneth, entertained into his service a company of English comedians, commended unto him by the honourable the Earle of Leicester : the Duke of Brunswicke and the Landgrave of Hessen retaine in their courts certaine of ours of the same quality.'

COHN cites this extract, and shows that the King of Denmarke referred to is Frederick II, who died 1588; further, that of this company of English comedians five left the Danish service in 1586, and attached themselves to the household of the Elector of Saxony; and further still, which is most noteworthy, that two members of this small band were named Thomas Pope and George Bryan, men who subsequently, on their return to England, became fellow-actors in Shakespeare's company, and whose names appear in the list of actors in the First Folio.

This small company, however, did not enter the service of the Elector of Saxony as actors, although it is highly probable that they added acting to their other offices. In the decree appointing them to their post in the Elector's household they are termed 'Fiddlers and Instrumentalists,' and are required to 'perform music and feats of agility and other accomplishments which they have acquired, for the Elector's delectation.' It is enough for the present purpose that a connection be proved, and that a very close one, between Shakespeare's theatre and Germany.

However satisfactory the proof may be of the presence on the Continent of this single company of English actors, it is not alone sufficient to account for the frequent references in contemporary literature to 'English Comedians.'

Wherefore Cohn shows that towards the close of the sixteenth century no less than three companies of English comedians started on professional visits to the courts of various German princes. These comedians were, in truth, what their title implies, genuine Englishmen, and not, as Tieck conjectured, German amateurs, who had gone to London and returned with a stock of plays that they had there studied.

A twofold poverty took them from their homes: first, poverty of the purse; secondly, poverty of the German drama. The former is not difficult of belief; but it is hard to conceive the extent of the latter; it is only by knowing how wretched were the farces which passed at that time for dramas, that we can appreciate the welcome extended to strolling bands of actors, who, indifferent as they may have been in their quality on the London stage, nevertheless brought with them some whiff of the Shakespearian atmosphere, and at whom people could gaze, even though they barely understood what was said, with greater profit than at the indecent buffoonery of boorish clowns.

Sometimes the connection between Shakespeare and the German stage is of the closest. On page lxxxix Cohn shows that the *Merchant of Venice* was performed at Halle in 1611. A Landgrave of Germany in that year, in a letter to his nephew, describing some splendid banquets and theatrical performances with which he had been entertained at Halle, states that he had seen 'a German Comedy, *The Jew of Venice,* taken from the English.' No other *Jew of Venice* is known in England at that time but Shakespeare's, which was entered in the *Stationers' Registers,* 22 July, 1598, as 'the Marchaunt of Venyce or otherwise called the Jewe of Venyce.' Dekker's *Jew of Venice* was not entered until 1653. Here we have a translation of one of Shakespeare's plays performed in Germany during Shakespeare's lifetime.

In a diary kept by an officer of the court at Dresden in 1626 we have a list of the plays performed by 'the English actors,' and among them are *Romeo and Julietta, Julio Cesare, Hamlet a Prince in Dennemarck,* and *Lear, King in Engelandt.*

One more question should be answered which has doubtless occurred to every one at the first mention of English comedians in Germany : in what language were these Plays performed? Strange as it may seem, they were undoubtedly sometimes performed in English. Cohn (p. cxxxiv) cites the following entry from Röchell's *Chronicle of the City of Münster:* ' On the 26th of November (1599) there arrived here eleven Englishmen, all young and lively fellows, except one, a rather elderly man, who managed everything. They acted five successive days, in the Town-

hall, five different comedies in their English language. They had with them various instruments on which they played, such as lutes, citherns, fiddles, pipes, and the
like; they danced many new and strange dances (not common here in this country)
at the beginning and at the end of their comedies. They had with them a clown,
who, before each Act, when they had to change their costume, spoke much nonsense
in German, and played many pranks to make the people laugh. They were licensed
by the Town Council for six days only, after which they had to leave. During these
five days they got a great deal of money from those who wished to see and hear
them; for every one had to give them a shilling at their departure.' 'It is probable,' adds Cohn, 'that these English players all soon acquired a familiarity with
the German language, or that they associated themselves with Germans, and then
merely undertook the managing part of the performances. As early as 1600, Landgrave Maurice of Hesse stipulated in an agreement with his English players that
they should arrange such plays as he or they might wish to be acted. At a later
period, in 1659, we find that the English comedians at the Dresden Court had to
provide German translations of the plays they intended to act. . . . . It is most likely
that the clown was generally a German, and availed himself of his privilege to
interpret to the audience the foreign idiom of his fellow-players.'

ELZE (whom it is safe to follow in such matters) says, in the Preface to his edition
of Chapman's *Alphonsus*, that there is 'incontrovertible evidence that at first [the
English comedians] acted English,—particularly Shakespearian,—plays in their
own language. Afterwards, however, they associated with Germans.'

The foregoing pages have supplied us with sufficient evidence that the German
version of *Hamlet* is entitled to respectful consideration. After making due allowance for time, place, and actors, enough remains to show that we have here an old
drama of no ordinary interest to Shakespearian students.

BERNHARDY, in 1857, started the conjecture, which has been since then gradually
gaining acceptance, I think, with English scholars, that 'this German *Hamlet* is a
weak copy of the old tragedy which preceded the Quarto of 1603.'* 'What is
particularly striking is the contrast between the Prologue and the Play itself. The
latter presents us with little more than a mere skeleton of the Shakespearian piece,
while the Prologue, in spite of its coarseness, has many curious touches and expressions which remind us strongly of the turns of expression in Shakespeare and his
contemporaries.'

'It approaches,' says Cohn (p. cxx), 'most nearly to that form of Shakespeare's
Hamlet which we find in the Quarto of 1603.'

DYCE (ed. 2) also remarks that the German version 'approaches more nearly to
Q_1 than to that of the later editions; but as it gives certain passages which are
parallel to those of the received text of *Hamlet*, and of which there is no trace in Q_1,
the translator must have employed some other edition of the original besides that of
1603. . . . . The prologue is superior in composition to the play itself.'

COHN: There can be no doubt that there existed a far older version of this tragedy
than the one with which we are acquainted. . . . . About 1665 this piece was performed by the Veltheim company, but it is of a much older date than this; we find
it in the Dresden stage-library in 1626, and even then it was no new piece; there is

---

* *Shakespeare's Hamlet. Ein literar-historisch kritischer Versuch*, in the *Hamburger lite-
rarisch-kritische Blätter*, 1857. I regret that I have been unable to obtain a copy of this Essay. I
am indebted to Cohn for the above quotations. ED.

evҡ y reason to believe that it had been brought over to Germany by the English Players as early as 1603.

CLARK and WRIGHT, after quoting this statement of Cohn's, say: If this hypothesis be correct, it is probable that the German text even in its present diluted form may contain something of the older English Play upon which Shakespeare worked. . . . . It does not appear that the German playwright made use of Shakespeare's *Hamlet,* or even of the play as represented in Q₁. The theory that it may be derived from a still earlier source is therefore not improbable.

Unfortunately, the text, as we now have it, of this tragedy of *Fratricide Punished* can be traced no farther back than 1710. It is not given in the *English Comedies and Tragedies,* printed in 1620. The earliest copy is in manuscript, 'bearing date "Pretz, den 27 October, 1710," and had been at one time in the possession of Conrad Ekhof, the celebrated actor and manager of the Gotha Theatre, who was born in 1720, and died in 1778. After his death certain extracts were published in the *Theater-Kalender auf das Jahr 1779,* Gotha, under the care of its editor, H. A. O. Reichard, who afterwards gave the full text of the play in his Periodical: *Olla Potrida,* Berlin, 1781,' and this text has been reprinted by COHN, and translated in the present volume.

As we have seen, Cohn puts the date at which the tragedy was acted in Germany at 'about 1603,' but it is to be feared that his enthusiasm has 'outrun the pauser reason,' and the wish to put the tragedy as close to Q₁ as possible has been the father to the thought. Certain it is that the earliest authentic mention of this tragedy that I can find in Cohn's preface is where it was acted at Dresden in 1626, and we can only infer that the version then acted was substantially what we now have here. Under these circumstances it behoves us to search closely in the play itself for evidence of its date and of its English origin.

The Prologue of the old German *Hamlet* is spoken by mythological characters, and this fact, says BERNHARDY, 'as well as some turns of expression which forcibly remind us of English poets, and some harsh un-German constructions, appear to establish the foreign origin of the piece, and that it is a translation.' 'Single passages in the German piece show that an edition of the original must have been used which contained passages that are in the Folio, but not in the First Quarto, while other passages prove incontrovertibly that precisely this Quarto must have been the source employed by the translator. Thus, for instance, the Ghost says: " Hear me, Hamlet, for the time draws near when I must betake myself again to the place whence I have come," and concludes his speech with the words: " So was I of my kingdom, my wife, and my life robbed by this tyrant." The former is evidently taken from the words in our accepted text: " My hour is almost come," &c., I, v, 2; and in the latter the order of the words is the same [as in Q₁; see line 521].'

COHN: As the reader has the entire piece before him, it will not be necessary to call attention to the numerous passages, which, in spite of the dilution by unskilful hands, place its early origin beyond all doubt. In other places we can distinctly perceive the hand of the re-modeller, who kept in view the circumstances of the theatre of his own time, and which have given the tone to so many passages. His utter want of skill is sufficiently proved by his introduction of the comic characters, the peasant Jens and Phantasmo, the fool, both of whom are altogether out of place in the piece. The manner in which the scenes taken from Shakespeare's tragedy have been vulgarized, the coarse humour which has been mixed up with the serious

APPENDIX

incidents, the box on the ear which the Ghost gives the sentinel, and other absurdities must be laid to the account of the reviser, and not to the actors who first brought
the piece to Germany.

The 'pretty case' which Hamlet tells Horatio, p. 130, about the effect which the
cunning of the scene has upon guilty creatures sitting at a play, according to Cohn,
enables us to form a conclusion respecting the age of the piece. 'There can be no
doubt that this is the incident which, whether fact or fiction, is introduced in the
tragedy, *A Warning for fair women*, written a little before 1590.' Heywood gives
the same story as occurring in Norfolk, and also a similar one that happened in Amsterdam. 'It is not a little characteristic of the stage at that time,' adds Cohn, 'that
the actors who first performed the German *Hamlet* did not rest satisfied with the
mere allusion as they found it in Shakespeare, but related the incident itself. Whether the passage refers to the incident in Norfolk or in Amsterdam, it is a striking
evidence that *Hamlet* was transferred to the German stage at a very early period.
The later reviser transferred the scene to Strasburg, as more familiar to his audience.
It is probable that the company for which this new version was adapted had come
from Strasburg, where we have already seen that there were English Players in 1654.
We are inclined to believe that the first form of the version of the piece now come
us was made about that time, but that the form in which it is here presented to the
reader, and in which it has experienced many alterations and dilutions, is to be ascribed to a more modern hand.'

In 1872 Dr LATHAM subjected this old German *Hamlet* to a severer scrutiny than it
had before received; and his conclusion coincides, in the main, with that of Bernhardy,
Cohn, and Clark and Wright, viz.: that the old tragedy of *Hamlet* which preceded
Q_1 may be here preserved either wholly or partially in this translation into German.
The order in which the Dramatis Personæ are set down 'is more ancient than modern,
the males and females being mixed together, instead of the females being arranged by
themselves at the end of the list; and the order being less regulated by the rank of
the interlocutors than by the order in which they appear on the stage; though this
is not adhered to with the strictness of the classical drama.' In Sigrie Latham sees
a corruption of Signe—'the most famous Norse love-tale being that of Signe and
Hagbert, whose sad fate made their names household words to every youth and
maiden in the North.' . . . . 'The uncle's name is Eric. This has undoubtedly at
the first view as Scandinavian a look as Signe; but it is English as well. In the
tale of Argentile and Curan, a well-known episode in Warner's *Albion's England*,
the hero has a wicked uncle, and, just as in the present play, Eric is his name. But
in both romances from which the poem seems most especially to be taken no such
name is found; the usurper there being Godard. Without enlarging upon the extent to which this connects Warner's Curan with Shakespeare's Hamlet, we may
fairly infer that some lost tradition or some unknown record is the common foundation for the two names. Individually, I go further, and think either it may have had
a Latin title: *Gesta Erici* (or *Eorici*) *Regis;* or, that out of confusion both of title
and subject the actual *Chronicon Regis Erici* may have been so called. The assumed confusion, however, goes farther, until *Gesta Regis* ends in the *King's Jester*,
and *Eric* becomes *Yorick*. It is only, however, in Shakespeare that the Jester's
name appears: indeed, in the German *Hamlet* the whole scene of the Grave-diggers
is conspicuous for its absence.' [See note on V, i, 170.]

Latham finds three special points of detail, viz.: The blunder about Roscius, the
allusion to Juvenal, and the reference to Portugal,—of which the first two are more

against than in favor of Shakespeare's having been the author of the original of the German *Hamlet*, and the third is in favor of the date of the German *Hamlet* being about 1589.

' 1. The blunder about Roscius [see last line of p. 128]. In the original, *Marus Russig;* the latter word is doubtless meant for ' Roscius,' but what means *Marus ?* It is submitted that it means *Amerinus*. Now there were two *Roscii*, and Cicero delivered an oration in defence of both. One was Roscius the actor; the other *Sextus* Roscius *Amerinus*, who was no actor at all. This, however, is the Roscius of Corambus. Now this is a blunder that requires as much scholarship to commit as to avoid, being one that a learned man might make from inadvertency, whereas an unlearned one could not make it at all. It was certainly *not* made by Shakespeare. This we know from his text, where Roscius stands alone. It could scarcely have been made by the supposed adapters who came after him.

' 2. The allusion to Juvenal. This is in the same predicament with the preceding. It is more classical than the text of the supposed original. [Latham here cites V, ii, 94–100, and the corresponding passage in the German *Hamlet*, on p. 140, where Hamlet quizzes Phantasmo about the heat and coldness of the weather, and aftei comparing the two with Juvenal's *Satire*, iii, 100, adds : ' In the German text there is, to say the least, a similarity sufficient to suggest a comparison. The English text has never suggested anything, not even to Johnson, who had paraphrased the *Satire*.' This I do not understand. The English text suggested Juvenal's *Satire* to Theobald a hundred and forty years ago. See note on V, ii, 94. Verily, is not a *New Variorum* needed ? ED.]

' 3. The reference to Portugal. In the German *Hamlet* [p. 135, ninth line from the top], Hamlet says, "just send me off to Portugal, so that I may never come back again." ' In this reference to Portugal, Latham ingeniously finds an allusion to the unfortunate expedition to Portugal in 1589, in which eleven thousand soldiers perished out of twenty-one thousand, and of eleven hundred gentlemen who accompanied it only three hundred and fifty returned to their native country. And this, Latham thinks, fixes the date of the German *Hamlet*.

Dr LATHAM concludes as follows : In the first place, the dramatic exposition of an action or a situation is one thing : the mere statement that such an action or situation occurred, another. It is one thing to describe in a good business-like, prosaic manner the way in which the elder Hamlet was poisoned; it is another thing to describe the poisoning as Shakespeare does. The same applies to the situation of Hamlet with his drawn sword, and the wicked uncle at prayer. The idea of sparing the murderer until he is certain of eternal condemnation, though sufficiently devilish, is poetic or prosaic according to the mode of exhibiting it.

' Secondly : We must not only note what we find in the German play, but what we miss. Thus,—

' *a*. Of instances of realistic imagery, such as "not a mouse stirring," we find none.

' *b*. Of ironical bits of cynicism, such as " We would obey were she ten times our mother," not one.

' *c*. Of the soliloquies, not one.

' Of hypotheses by which the difference may be accounted for, I know but one, and to the notice of this I limit myself. It is, that the German Play is the Play of Shakespeare corrupted, attenuated, shorn of its great nobility, distorted, degraded, vulgarized. But was the German stage thus much below the English ? or even if it were so, how do we reconcile the recognition of the poetical element (such as it is), as shown by the Prologue, with the eschewal of it as manifested by the elimina. tion of the soliloquies?

' Again, it is not denied that what with the existence of imperfect texts, and what with " stuff " sometimes " foisted in," and sometimes omitted, by the players much may be achieved. But time is an element in such a process as this, and here we have something like tangible *data* to go by; or at any rate there are certain limits within which we must confine the effects of what we may call the wear-and-tear of time, and there are also criteria by which we may measure the inferiority (real or imaginary) of the German stage to the English. In neither case have we much latitude.'

It is probably needless to call attention to what must strike every one at the first glance, merely at the Dramatis Personæ of *Fratricide Punished,* and that is the name given to Polonius, which is, except in one letter, the same as that in Q_1. This is noted by all who have touched upon the subject of this German play. Again, the very name *Hamlet* shows that the adapter of the German play at least did not go to Belleforest for his tragedy. Furthermore, the allusion to Jephtha points so clearly to the old English ballad, that I think there can be little doubt that in *Fratricide Punished* we have a translation of an old English tragedy, and most probably the one which is the groundwork of the Quarto of 1603.

In conclusion, let me say a few words as to the following translation. I have endeavored to make it as literal as possible. The admirable translation by Miss GEORGINA ARCHER in Cohn's volume, while it is most felicitous in catching the turn of colloquial expressions, a highly difficult task, appeared to me, as it did to Dr Latham, to yield a little too much to the desire to reproduce Shakespeare's phraseology; if the translation be literal, the student will discover for himself these parallelisms as readily in the English as in the German. In one or two small matters I think I have discovered allusions or interpretations that have escaped my predecessors, *e.g. spanische Pfauentritte,* I suppose, is equivalent to *Pfauentanz,* and have therefore translated it by ' Spanish pavan;' again, in Phantasmo's swear-ings at Ophelia, I think *das elementische Mädchen* is not merely ' simpleton,' as Miss ARCHER translates it, nor ' that high-flying maiden,' as Dr LATHAM renders it, but that *elementische* is an adjective eliminated from *potz element,* and is intended to be comic. But these are the merest trifles, and scarcely worth a thought. By one phrase I confess I was completely gravelled,—as a phrase its meaning is clear enough, but its drift is puzzling: Phantasmo's last words, *dass euch die Klinge verlahme!* and I am by no means sure that Dr Latham's version is not nearer the genuine than mine: ' and may the blade hurt you.'

I have included in brackets words which seem to indicate the hand of the German translator, such as *harquebusirt, revange,* &c. Dr Latham has done it in many in-stances likewise.

As far as I know, attention was first directed in England to the subject of English actors in Germany by W. J. THOMS in the *New Monthly Magazine,* July, 1840, in an article which was afterwards reprinted in *Three Notelets on Shakespeare.*

TRAGŒDIA.

DER BESTRAFTE BRUDERMORD

ODER:

PRINZ HAMLET AUS DÆNNEMARK.

(FRATRICIDE PUNISHED

OR

PRINCE HAMLET OF DENMARK.)

DRAMATIS PERSONÆ.

I.—*In the Prologue.*

NIGHT, in a car covered with stars.
ALECTO.
THISIPHONE.
MÆGERA.

2.—*In the Tragedy.*

GHOST of the old King of Denmark.
ERICO, brother to the King.
HAMLET, Prince, son to the murdered King.
SIGRIE, the Queen, Hamlet's mother.
HORATIO, a noble friend to the Prince.
CORAMBUS, Royal Chamberlain.
LEONHARDUS, his son.
OPHELIA, his daughter.
PHANTASMO, the Court Fool.
FRANCISCO, Officer of the Guard.
JENS, a peasant.
CARL, the principal of the Actors.
Corporal of the Guard.
Two talking Banditti (*Zwei redende Banditen*).
Two Sentinels.
Life Guards,
Court Servants, } Mutes (*S'umme*).
Two Actors,

PROLOGUE.

Night [*from above*]. I am dark Night, which sends all things to sleep,
I am the wife of Morpheus, the time for vicious pleasure,
I am the guardian of thieves, and the protector of lovers;
I am dark Night, and have it in my might
To practice evil, to afflict mankind.
My mantle covers the shame and rest of the harlot.
Before Phœbus shall shine I will begin a game.
Ye children of my breast, and daughters of my lust,
Ye Furies, up, up! come forth and show yourselves!
Come, hearken attentively to what will soon take place.
    Alec. What says dark Night, the queen of quiet?
What new work does she propose? what is her wish and will?
    Mæg. From Acheron's dark pit come I, Mægera, hither,
From thee, thou mother of evil, to hear thy desire.
    This. And I, Thisiphone: what hast thou to the fore? Say on,
Thou black Hecate, whether I can serve thee.

    Night. Listen, ye Furies all three,—listen, ye children of darkness and mothers of all misfortune; listen to your poppy-crowned Queen of the Night, the patroness of thieves and robbers, the friend and light of the incendiary, the lover of stolen goods, the dearly loved goddess of unlawful love,—how often are my altars honored by it! During this night and the coming morrow must ye stand by me, for it is the King of this land who burns with love for the wife of his brother, whom for her sake he has murdered, that he may possess both her and the kingdom. Now is the hour at hand when they lie together. I will throw my mantle over them so that neither may see their sin. Therefore be ready to sow the seeds of disunion, mingle poison with their marriage, and put jealousy in their hearts. Kindle a fire of revenge, and let the sparks fly over the whole realm; entangle kinsmen in the net of crime, and give joy to hell, so that those who swim in the sea of murder may soon drown. Begone, hasten, and fulfil my command.

    This. I have already heard enough, and will soon perform
More than dark Night can of herself imagine.
    Mæg. Pluto himself shall not prompt me to so much
As shortly I shall be seen performing.
    Alec. I fan the sparks and make the fire burn;
Ere it dawns the second time, the whole game I'll shiver.
    Night. Then haste; while I ascend make good your work.

                               [*Ascends. Music*

ACT I.

Scene I.—*Two Soldiers.*

First Sentinel. Who's there?
Second Sentinel. A friend!
First Sent. What friend?
Sec. Sent. Sentinel!

First Sent. O ho, comrade!—if thou com'st to relieve me, I wish the time may not be so long to thee as it has been to me.

Sec. Sent. Eh! comrade, it is not so cold now.

First Sent. Cold or not, I've had a hell's sweat here.

Sec. Sent. Why so frightened?—that's not right in a soldier. He must fear neither friend nor foe; no, nor the devil himself.

First Sent. Yes, but just let him grab thee behind, and thou'lt soon learn to pray *Miserere Domine.*

Sec. Sent. But what is it that has particularly frightened thee?

First Sent. I'll tell thee. I've seen a ghost in the front of the castle, and he wanted twice to pitch me down from the bastion.

Sec. Sent. Then relieve guard, you fool! A dead dog doesn't bite. I'll see whether a ghost that has neither flesh nor blood can hurt me.

First Sent. Just look out, if he shows himself to thee again, what he does to thee. I'm off to the watch-house. Adieu!   [*Exit.*

Sec. Sent. Only be off; perhaps you were born on a Sunday: they say such folks can see all kinds of ghosts. I'll now mount guard. [*Healths proclaimed within, to the sound of trumpets.*] Our new King makes merry. They are drinking healths.

SCENE II.—*Ghost of the King approaches the Sentinel, and frightens him, and then exit.*

Sec. Sent. O holy Anthony of Padua, defend me! I see now what my comrade told me. O Saint Velten [*sic*]! if my first round were only over, I'd run away like any rogue. [*Sennet and drums within.*] If I only had a drink of wine from the king's table, to put out the fear and fire in my heart! [*Ghost from behind gives him a box on the ear, and makes him drop his musket, and exit.*] The devil himself is after me. Oh, I'm so frightened, I can't stir!

SCENE III.—*Horatio and Soldiers.*

Sec. Sent. Who's there?

Hor. The watch!

Sec. Sent. Which one?

Hor. The first!

Sec. Sent. Stand, watch! Corporal, forward, to arms!

[*Francisco and Watch come forward, and give the word from the other side.*

Hor. Sentinel, look well to thy post; the Prince himself may perhaps go the rounds. Be caught sleeping, and it may cost thee the best head thou'st got.

Sec. Sent. Ah! if the whole company were here, not a man of them would go to sleep; and I must be relieved, or I'll run away, though I be hanged to-morrow on the highest gallows.

Hor. What for?

Sec. Sent. Oh, your worship, there's a ghost here which appears every quarter of an hour; it set upon me so that I fancy myself a live man in purgatory.

Fran. Just what the sentinel last relieved told me.

Sec. Sent. Ay, ay; only just wait a bit. It won't keep away long.

[*Ghost goes across the stage.*

Hor. On my life it is a ghost, and looks just like the late king of Denmark.
Fran. He bears himself sadly, and seems as if he wanted to say something.
Hor. There is some mystery in this.

SCENE IV.—*Hamlet.*

Sec. Sent. Who's there?
Ham. Hush!
Sec. Sent. Who's there?
Ham. Hush!
Sec. Sent. Answer, or I'll teach thee better manners
Ham. A friend!
Sec. Sent. What friend?
Ham. Friend to the kingdom.
Fran. By my life, it is the Prince.
Hor. Your highness, is it you or not?
Ham. What! are you here, Horatio? What brings you here?
Hor. Your highness, I have gone [*visitirt*] the rounds to see that every one is at his post.
Ham. That's like an honest soldier, for on you rests the safety of the king and kingdom.
Hor. Your highness, a strange thing has happened: regularly every quarter of an hour a ghost appears; and, to my mind, he is very like the dead king, your father. He does much harm to the sentinels on this post.
Ham. I hope not; for the souls of the pious rest quietly till the time of their resurrection.
Hor. Yet so it is, your highness. I've seen it myself.
Fran. And he frightened me very much, your highness.
Sec. Sent. And he gave me a sound box on the ear.
Ham. What time is it?
Fran. It is just midnight.
Ham. Good!—just the time when ghosts, if they walk, show themselves. [*Healths again, and trumpets.*] Holloa! what is this?
Hor. I fancy that at court they are still jolly with their toasts.
Ham. Right, Horatio! My father and uncle makes himself bravely merry with his followers [*Adhærenten*]. Alas, Horatio! I know not why it is that since my father's death I am all the time so sick at heart, while my royal mother has so soon forgotten him, and this King still sooner, for while I was in Germany he had himself quickly crowned king in Denmark but with a show of right he has made over to me the crown of Norway, and appealed to the election of the states.

SCENE V.—*Ghost.*

Sec. Sent. Oh dear! here's the ghost again!
Hor. Does your highness see now?
Fran. Your highness, don't be frightened.
[*Ghost crosses the stage, and beckons to Hamlet.*
Ham. The Ghost beckons me. Gentlemen, stand aside a little.—Horatio, do not go too far away. I will follow the ghost, and see what he wants.   [*Exit.*

Hor. Gentlemen, let us follow him to see that he take no harm.   [*Exeunt.*
Ghost beckons Hamlet to the middle of the stage, and opens his jaws several times.
Ham. Tell who thou art, and say what thou desirest.
Ghost. Hamlet!
Ham. Sir!
Ghost. Hamlet!
Ham. What desirest thou?
Ghost. Hear me, Hamlet, for the time draws near when I must betake myself again to the place whence I have come; hear, and give heed to what I shall relate .o thee.
Ham. Speak, thou sacred shade of my royal father!
Ghost. Then hear, my son Hamlet, what I have to tell thee of thy father's unnatural death.
Ham. What? unnatural death?
Ghost. Ay, unnatural death! Know that I had the habit, to which nature had accustomed me, of walking in my royal pleasure-garden every day after my noontide meal, and there to enjoy an hour's rest. One day when I did this, behold, my brother came, thirsting for my crown, and had with him the subtile [*subtilen*] juice of so-called Hebenon [*Ebeno*]. This oil, or juice, has this effect: that as soon as a few drops of it mix with the blood of man, they at once clog the veins and destroy life. This juice he poured, while I was sleeping, into my ear, and as soon as it entered my head I had to die instantly; whereupon it was given out that I had had a violent apoplexy. So was I of my kingdom, my wife, and my life robbed by this tyrant.
Ham. Just Heaven! If this be true, I swear to revenge thee.
Ghost. I cannot rest until my unnatural murder be revenged.   [*Exit.*
Ham. I swear not to rest until I have revenged myself on this fratricide.

SCENE VI.—*Horatio. Hamlet. Francisco.*

Hor. How is it with your highness? Why so terror-stricken? Mayhap you have been hurt [*alterirt*].
Ham. Yes, verily, and indeed beyond measure.
Hor. Has your highness seen the Ghost?
Ham. Ay! truly have I seen it, and also spoken to it.
Hor. O Heaven! this bodes something strange.
Ham. He revealed to me a horrible thing; therefore I pray you, gentlemen, stand by me in a matter that calls for vengeance.
Hor. Of my fidelity you are surely convinced: only disclose it to me.
Fran. Your highness cannot doubt as to my help either.
Ham. Gentlemen, before I reveal the matter you must swear an oath on your honor and faith.
Fran. Your highness knows the great love I bear you. I will willingly risk my life if you wish to avenge yourself.
Hor. Only just propose the oath to us: we will stand by you faithfully.
Ham. Then lay your finger on my sword: We swear!
Hor. and Fran. We swear!
Ghost [*within*]. We swear!
Ham. Holla! what is this? Once more: We swear!

Hor. and Fran. We swear!

Ghost. We swear!

Ham. This must mean something strange. Come, once more, and let us go **to** the other side. We swear!

Hor. and Fran. We swear!

Ghost. We swear!

Ham. What is this? Is it an echo which sends back our own words? Come, we will go to another spot. We swear!

Ghost. We swear!

Ham. Oh! I hear now what this means. It seems that the Ghost of my father is displeased at my making the matter known. Gentlemen, I pray you, leave me; to-morrow I will tell you all.

Hor. and Fran. Your highness, farewell.   [*Exit Francisco.*

Ham. Horatio, come here.

Hor. What is your highness's will?

Ham. Has the other gone?

Hor. Yes, he has gone.

Ham. I know, Horatio, that thou hast been at all times true to me; to thee I will reveal what the Ghost told me,—namely, that my father died a violent death. My father,—he who is now my father,—murdered him.

Hor. O Heaven! what do I hear?

Ham. Thou knowest, O Horatio! that my departed father was wont every day after his noontide meal to sleep an hour in his pleasure-garden. The villain, knowing this, comes to my father and pours into his ear, whilst he is asleep, the juice of Hebenon, from which powerful poison my father at once gave up the ghost. This the accursed dog did in order to obtain the crown; but from this moment I will begin a feigned madness, and, thus feigning, so cunningly will I play my part that I shall find an opportunity to avenge my father's death.

Hor. If so it stands, I pledge myself to be true to your highness.

Ham. Horatio, I will so avenge myself on this ambitious man and adulterer and murderer that posterity shall talk of it for ever. I will now go, and, feigning madness, wait upon him until I find an opportunity to effect my revenge.   [*Exeunt.*

SCENE VII.—*King, Queen, Hamlet, Corambus, and Court.*

King. Although our brother's death is still fresh in the memory of us all, and it befits us to suspend all state-shows, we must nevertheless change our black mourning suits into crimson, purple, and scarlet, since my late departed brother's widow has now become our dearest consort. Let, then, every one show himself cheerful, and make himself a sharer of our pleasure But you, Prince Hamlet, do you be content. See here, how your lady mother is grieved and troubled at your melancholy. We have heard, too, that you have determined to go back to Wittenberg; do not do so for your mother's sake. Stay here, for we love you and like to see you, and would not that any harm should happen to you. Stay with us at court, or, if not, you can betake yourself to your kingdom, Norway.

Queen. Dearly-beloved son, Prince Hamlet, it greatly astonishes us that you have thought to go away from here, and to betake yourself to Wittenberg. You know well that your royal father has lately died, and if you leave us, the grief and melancholy which now oppress our hearts will only be the greater. Then, dearest son, stay here, and every pleasure and delight, if so it please you, shall be freely yours.

Ham. Your command I will obey with all my heart, and will here remain and not depart.

King. Do so, dearest Prince. But, Corambus, how is it with your son Leonhardo? Has he already set out for France?

Cor. Ay, gracious lord and King, he has gone already.

King. But is it with your consent [*Consens*]?

Cor. Ay, with over-consent, with middle-consent, and with under-consent. Oh, your majesty, he got an extraordinary, noble, excellent, and splendid consent from me.

King. As he has your consent, it may go well with him, and may the gods bring him safe back again. But we have it now in mind to hold a carouse [*Carisell*], whereby our dearest spouse may forget her melancholy. But you, Prince Hamlet, with the other nobles, must show yourself mirthful. For the present, however, we will make an end of our festivities, for the day is dawning to put to flight black night. You, however, dearest consort, I shall accompany to your bed-chamber.

Come, let us, arm in arm and hand in hand,
Enjoy the pledge that love and rest demand.

ACT II.

SCENE I.—*King. Queen.*

King. Dearest consort, how comes it that you are so sad? Tell, I pray you, the cause of your sadness. You are indeed our Queen. We love you, and all that the kingdom can afford is yours. What is it, then, that troubles you?

Queen. My King, I am greatly troubled at the melancholy of my son Hamlet, who is my only Prince; and this it is that pains me.

King. What! is he melancholy? We will gather together all the excellent doctors and physicians in our whole kingdom to relieve him.

SCENE II.—*Enter to them Corambus.*

Cor. News, gracious lord and King!

King. What news?

Cor. Prince Hamlet is mad—ay, as mad as the Greek madman ever was.

King. And why is he mad?

Cor. Because he has lost his wits.

King. Where, pray, has he lost his wits?

Cor. That I don't know. That he may know who has found them.

SCENE III.—*Ophelia.*

Oph. Alas, father! protect me!

Cor. What is it, my child?

Oph. Alas, father! Prince Hamlet plagues me. He lets me have no peace.

Cor. Make thyself easy, dear daughter. But he has not done anything else to thee?—Oh, now I know why Prince Hamlet is mad. He is certainly in love with my daughter.

King. Has love, then, such power as to make a man mad?

Cor. Gracious lord and King, love is certainly strong enough to make a man mad. I can still remember how it plagued me when I was young: it made me as mad as a March hare [*Märzhaasen*]. But now I do not mind it. I like better to sit by my fire and count my red pennies, and drink your majesty's health.

King. May not one see with one's own eyes his raving and madness?

Cor. Yes, your majesty. We will just step a little aside, and my daughter shall show him the jewel which he gave her, and then your majesty can see his madness.

[*They hide themselves.*

SCENE IV.—*Hamlet and Ophelia.*

Oph. I pray your highness to take back the jewel which you presented to me.

Ham. What, girl! wouldst thou have a husband? Get thee away from me; nay, come here. Hearken, girl, you young women do nothing but lead young fellows astray. Your beauty you buy of the apothecaries and peddlers. Listen, I will tell you a story. There was a cavalier in Anion [*sic*] who fell in love with a lady, who, to look at, was the goddess Venus. However, when bedtime came, the bride went first and began to undress herself. First, she took out an eye which had been set in very cunningly; then her front teeth, made of ivory, so cleverly that the like were not to be seen; then she washed herself, and off went all the paint with which she had smeared herself. At last, when the bridegroom came and thought to embrace her, the moment he saw her he started back, and thought it was a spectre. And thus it is that you deceive the young fellows; therefore listen to me. But stay, girl! No, go to a nunnery, but not to a nunnery where two pairs of slippers lie at the bedside. [*Exit.*

Cor. Is he not perfectly and veritably [*perfect und veritabel*] mad, gracious lord and King?

King. Corambus, leave us. When we have need of you we will send for you. [*Exit Corambus.*]—We have seen this madness and raving of the Prince's with great astonishment. But it seems to us that this is not genuine madness, but rather a feigned [*simulirte*] madness. We must contrive to have him removed from here, if not from life; otherwise some harm may come of it.

SCENE V.—*Hamlet. Horatio.*

Ham. My worthy friend Horatio, through this assumed madness I hope to get the opportunity of revenging my father's death. You know, however, that my father is always surrounded by many guards [*Trabanten*]; wherefore it may miscarry. Should you chance to find my dead body, let it be honorably buried; for at the first opportunity I will try my chance with him.

Hor. I entreat your highness to do no such thing; perhaps the Ghost has deceived you.

Ham. Oh no! his words were all too plainly spoken. I can, indeed, believe in him. But what news is the old fool bringing here?

SCENE VI.—*Corambus.*

Cor News, gracious lord! the comedians have come.

Ham. When Marus Russig [*sic*] was a comedian in Rome, what a fine time that was!

Cor. Ha! ha! ha! Your highness is always teasing [*vexiren*] me.

Ham. O Jeptha, Jeptha! what a fair daughter hast thou!

Cor. Your highness always will be bringing in my daughter.

Ham. Well, old man, let the master of the comedians come in.

Cor. It shall be so. [*Exit.*

Ham. These comedians come just in time. I will use them to test the Ghost, whether he has told the truth or not. I have seen a tragedy acted wherein one brother kills another in a garden, and this they shall now act. If the king change color, he has done what the Ghost has told me.

Scene VII.—*Actors.   Carl, the principal Actor.*

Carl. May the gods always bestow on your highness blessings, happiness, and health!

Ham. I thank you, my friend. What do you wish?

Carl. Your highness will graciously pardon us. We are foreign High-German actors, and our wish was to have had the privilege of acting at his majesty's wedding. But Fortune turned her back, and contrary winds their face, toward us. We therefore ask of your highness leave to act a story, so that our long journey shall not have been made in vain.

Ham. Were you not, a few years ago, at the University of Wittenberg? I think I saw you act [*agiren*] there.

Carl. Yes, your highness. We are the same actors.

Ham. Have you still got all of the same company?

Carl. We are not quite so strong, because some students took situations [*Condition*] in Hamburg. Still, we are strong enough for many merry comedies, and tragedies.

Ham. Could you give us a play to-night?

Carl. Yes, your highness: we are strong enough and in practice enough.

Ham. Have you still all three women with you? They acted very well.

Carl. No, only two. One remained with her husband at the court of Saxony.

Ham. When you were at Wittenberg you acted good comedies; but there were some fellows among you who had good clothes, but dirty shirts, and some who had boots, but no spurs.

Carl. Your highness, it is often a hard matter to have everything. Perhaps they thought they would not have to ride.

Ham. Still, it is better when everything is just right [*accurat*]. But listen a few minutes, and excuse me; you do not often hear directly what the spectators think of you. There were also some among you who had silk stockings and white shoes, but with black hats full of feathers on their heads, and with about as many feathers below as above. I think they must have gone to bed in them instead of nightcaps. That's bad, and is easily changed. You may, too, as well tell some of them that when they act a king or a princely personage, they should not leer so much when they pay a compliment to a lady, and not be always stepping a Spanish pavan [*spanische Pfauentritte*], nor putting on such braggadocio airs [*Fechtermienen*]. A man of rank laughs at such things. Natural ease is the best. He who plays a king must fancy that during the play he is a king, and a peasant must be a peasant.

Carl. Your highness, I accept this correction with humble respect, and we will try to do better for the future.

Ham. I am a great lover of your art, and mean well toward you; in a mirror one may see his own failings. Listen to me: you acted once at Wittenberg a piece about King Pir—, Pir—, Pir something or other.

Carl. Ah! perhaps it was one about the great King Pyrro [*sic*].

Ham. I think it was, but I am not quite sure.

Carl. If your highness could only name a character in it, or say what it was about.

Ham. It was about one brother murdering another in a garden.

Carl. That's the piece, I'm sure. Did not the king's brother pour poison into the king's ear?

Ham. Right, right! That's the very one. Can you play [*präsentiren*] that piece this evening?

Carl. Oh yes, easily enough: it requires only a few characters.

Ham. Well, then, go, get the stage ready in the great hall. If you want any timber, you can get it of the architect; if anything from the armory, or anything in the way of clothes, ask the Master of the Robes or the Steward. We wish you to be provided with everything.

Carl. I humbly thank your highness for these favors; we will set about it at once. Farewell.   [*Exit.*

Ham. These actors come most opportunely for me.—Horatio, give good heed to the King; if he turn pale or change color [*alterirt*], he has certainly done the deed; for these players with their fictions often produce the effect of truth. Listen, I'll tell thee a pretty tale. At Strasburg, in Germany, there was a pretty case [*Casus*]: a woman murdered her husband by stabbing him through the heart with a shoemaker's awl, and then, with the help of her paramour, she buried him under the threshold. Nine whole years did the deed remain concealed, until at last actors came that way and acted a tragedy containing a similar incident. The woman, who was with her husband [*sic*] at the play, was touched in her conscience, and began to cry aloud, and shrieked, 'Woe is me! that hits me; for so it was that I killed my innocent husband.' She tore her hair, ran out of the theatre to the judge, confessed of her own accord the murder; and as this was found to be true, she, in deep repentance for her sins, received the consolations of a priest, and in true contrition gave up her body to the executioner and commended her soul to Heaven. Oh, that my father and uncle might thus feel remorse if he has done this thing! Come, Horatio, we will go and await the King. Pray, however, observe [*observiren*] everything closely, for I shall dissemble [*simuliren*].

Hor. Your highness, I shall impose on my eyes a sharp lookout.   [*Exeunt.*

SCENE VIII.—*King. Queen. Hamlet. Horatio. Corambus. Ophelia. Courtiers.*

King. My dearest consort, I hope that now you will banish your melancholy, and let it give place to joy: there is to be, before supper, a comedy by the Germans, and after supper a ballet [*Ballet*] by our own people.

Queen. I shall be glad to see such mirth; I doubt much whether my heart will be at ease, for I know not what kind of an approaching misfortune disturbs our spirits.

King. Pray be content.—Prince Hamlet, we understand that some actors have arrived who are to act a comedy for us this evening. Tell us, is that so?

Ham. Yes, my father, it is. They applied to me, and I gave them permission. I hope your majesty will also approve.

King. What kind of a plot is it? There is nothing, I suppose, offensive in it or rude?

Ham. It is a good plot. We who have good consciences are not touched by it.

King. Where are they? Let them begin soon; for we would like to see what these Germans can do.

Ham. Marshal, see whether the actors are ready; tell them to begin.

Cor. Ye actors, where are ye? Ye must begin at once. Holla! they're coming.

Here enters the Play. The King with his consort. He wishes to lie down to sleep; the Queen begs him not to do so; he lies down, nevertheless; the Queen takes leave of him with a kiss, and exit. The King's brother comes with a phial and pours something into his ear, and exit.

Ham. That is King Pyrrus, who goes into the garden to sleep. The Queen begs him not to do so; however, he lies down. The poor little wife goes away; see, there comes the King's brother with the juice of Hebenon and pours it into his ear, which, as soon as it mixes with the blood of man, destroys the body.

King. Torches, lanterns, here! the play does not please us.

Cor. Pages, lackies [*Pagen, Lackeyen*], light the torches! The King wishes to leave. Quick, light up! The actors have made a mess of it.

[*Exeunt King, Queen, Corambus, and Courtiers.*

Ham. Torches here! the play does not please us.—Now thou seest that the Ghost has not deceived me.—Actors, go hence with this conclusion, that though you did not act the piece all through, and the King was displeased with it, yet it pleased us much, and in my behalf Horatio shall satisfy [*contentiren*] you.

Carl. We thank you, and beg you for a passport [*Reisepass*].

Ham. That you shall have. [*Exeunt Actors.*] Now, can I dare to go on boldly with my revenge.—Did you see how the King changed color when he saw the play?

Hor. Yes, your highness, the thing is certain.

Ham. Therefore my father was murdered just as you saw it in the play. But I will pay him off for his evil deed.

Scene IX.—*Corambus.*

Cor. The actors will get a poor reward, for their acting [*Action*] has sore displeased the King.

Ham. What sayest thou, old man: they will get a poor reward? The worse they are rewarded by the King, all the better will they be rewarded by Heaven.

Cor. Your highness, can actors get to heaven?

Ham. Dost thou suppose, old fool, that they won't find room there, too? Wherefore, begone, and treat [*tractiren*] these people well.

Cor. Ay, ay, I'll treat them as they deserve.

Ham. Treat them well, I say; for there is no greater praise to be got than through actors, for they travel far and wide. If they are treated well in one place, they cannot praise it enough in another; for their theatre [*Theatrum*] is a little world wherein they represent nearly all that happens in the great world. They revive the old forgotten histories, and set before us good and bad examples; they publish abroad the justice and praiseworthy government of princes; they punish vices, and exalt virtues; they praise the good, and show how tyranny is punished. Therefore you should reward them well.

Cor. Well, they shall have their reward, since they are such people.   Farewell, your highness.   [*Exit.*

Ham. Come, Horatio, I am going; and from this hour I shall endeavor to find the King alone, that I may take his life as he has taken my father's.

Hor. Pray, your highness, be very cautious, lest you yourself come to harm.

Verse.

Ham.   I shall, I must, I will, give this vile wretch his due.
            If stratagem should fail, with force I'll then break through.

ACT III.

SCENE I.—*Here is presented* [prasentirt sich] *an Altar in a Temple.*

King [*alone*]. Now begins my conscience to awaken, the sting of treachery to prick me sharply. It is time to turn to repentance, and to confess to Heaven the crime I have committed. I fear my crime is so great that they will never forgive me; nevertheless, I will pray to the gods from the bottom of my heart that they will forgive my grievous sins.   [*The King kneels before the altar.*

SCENE II.—*Hamlet with a drawn sword.*

Ham. Thus long have I followed the damned dog, until I have found him. Now is the time, when he is alone. I will slay him in the midst of his devotions. [*Is about to stab him.*] But no, I will first let him finish his prayer. But ah, when I think of it, he did not first give my father time for a prayer, but sent him to hell in his sleep and perhaps in his sins. Therefore will I send him after to the same place. [*Is again about to run him through from behind.*] But hold, Hamlet! why wouldst thou take his sins upon thyself? I will let him finish his prayer, and let him go this time, and give him his life; but another time I will fulfil my revenge.   [*Exit.*

King. My conscience is somewhat lightened; but the dog still lies gnawing at my heart. Now will I go, and with fastings, and alms, and fervent prayers appease the Highest. Ah, cursed ambition! to what hast thou brought me!   [*Exit*

SCENE III.—*Queen. Corambus.*

Queen. Corambus, say, how is it with our son, Prince Hamlet? Does his madness abate at all, or will not his raving cease?

Cor. Ah, no, your majesty; he is still just as mad as he was before.

SCENE IV.—*Horatio.*

Hor. Most gracious Queen, Prince Hamlet is in the antechamber, and craves a private audience [*Audienz*].

Queen. He is very dear to us; so let him come in at once.

Hor. It shall be done, your majesty.   [*Exit.*

Queen. Hide yourself, Corambus, behind the tapestry till we call you.

Cor. Ay, ay, I will hide myself a bit. [*Hides himself.*

SCENE V.—*Hamlet.*

Ham. Lady mother, did you really know your first husband.

Queen. Ah! remind me not of my former grief. I cannot restrain my tears when I think of him.

Ham. Do you weep? Ah, leave off; they are mere crocodile's tears. But see, there in that gallery hangs the counterfeit [*Conterfait*] of your first husband, and there hangs the counterfeit of your present. What think you now? Which of them is the comeliest? Is not the first a majestic lord?

Queen. He is indeed that.

Ham. How could you, then, so soon forget him? Fie, for shame! Almost on the same day you had the burial and the nuptials. But hush! are all the doors shut fast?

Queen. Why do you ask it? [*Corambus coughs behind the tapestry.*

Ham. Who is that listening to us? [*Stabs him.*

Cor. Woe is me, O Prince! What are you doing? I die!

Queen. O Heaven, my son! what are you doing? It is Corambus, the chamberlain.

SCENE VI.—*Ghost passes across the stage. It lightens.*

Ham. Ah, noble shade of my father, stay! Alas! alas! what wouldst thou? Dost thou demand vengeance? I will fulfil it at the right time.

Queen. What are you about? and to whom are you talking?

Ham. See you not the ghost of your departed husband? See, he beckons as if he would speak to you.

Queen. How? I see nothing at all.

Ham. I can readily believe that you see nothing, for you are no longer worthy to look on his form. Fie, for shame! Not another word will I speak to you.

[*Exit.*

Queen [*alone*]. O Heaven! how much madness this melancholy has brought upon the Prince! Alas! my only son has wholly lost his senses. Alas! alas! I am much to blame for it. Had I not wedded my brother-in-law, my first husband's brother, I had not robbed my son of the crown of Denmark. But when a thing is done, what can we do? Nothing. It must be as it is. If the pope had not allowed the marriage, it would never have taken place. I will go hence, and try my best to restore my son to his former sense and health. [*Exit.*

SCENE VII.—*Jens, alone.*

Jens. It is long since I have been to court and paid my taxes. I am afraid that, go where I may, I shall be put into jail [*ins Loch kriechen*]. If I could only find some good friend who would speak a good word for me, so that I might not be punished!

Scene VIII.—*Phantasmo.*

Phan. There are strange goings-on at court. Prince Hamlet is mad, Ophelia is mad too. In short [*in Summa*], things go on so very strangely that I am almost inclined to run away.

Jens. Potz tausend! I see my good friend Phantasmo. No better man could I hit upon. I will ask him to say a good word for me.—Good luck to you, Mr Phantasmo!

Phan. Many thanks! What do you want, Mr Clown?

Jens. Ah, Mr Phantasmo, 'tis a long time since I have been at court, and I owe a great deal. Therefore I beg that you will put in a good word for me; I will reward [*spendiren*] you with a good cheese.

Phan. What! dost thou think, churl, that at court I get nothing to eat?

Scene IX.—*Ophelia, mad.*

Oph. I run and race, but cannot find my sweetheart. He sent me word to come to him. We are to be married, and I am dressed for it already. But there is my love! See! art thou there, my lambkin? I have sought thee so; yes, have I sought thee. Alas! just think! the tailor has spoilt my cotton [*kattunen*] gown. See, there is a pretty floweret for thee, my heart!

Phan. Oh, the devil! I wish I could clear out. She thinks I am her sweetheart.

Oph. What sayest thou, my love? We will go to bed together. I will wash thee quite clean.

Phan. Ay, ay, I'll soap thee, and wash thee out, too.

Oph. Listen, my love: hast thou already put on thy new suit? Ay, that is beautifully made, just in the new fashion.

Phan. I know that well enough without—

Oph. Oh, Potz tausend! what I came near forgetting! The King has invited me to supper, and I must run fast. Look there! my little coach, my little coach!
                                                                                [*Exit.*

Phan. O Hecate, thou queen of witches, how glad I am that mad thing has cleared out! If she had stayed any longer, I should have been mad too. I must get away before the foolish thing comes back.

Jens. Oh, merciful Mr Phantasmo, I beg you not to forget me.

Phan. Come along, Brother Rogue. I'll see what I can do for thee with the tax-collector.   [*Exeunt.*

Scene X.—*King. Hamlet. Horatio. Two Attendants.*

King. Where is the corpse of Corambus? Has it not yet been removed?

Hor. He is still lying in the place where he was stabbed.

King. It grieves us that he has lost his life so suddenly. Go, let him be taken away. We wish to have him honorably buried.—Alas! Prince Hamlet! what have you done, to stab old, harmless Corambus! It grieves us to our heart, yet since it was done unwittingly, this murder is in some degree excusable; but I fear that when it gets known among the nobility, it will raise a riot among my subjects, and they may revenge his death on you. However, out of fatherly care we have devised a plan to avert this misfortune.

Ham. I am sorry for it, uncle and father. I wanted to say something in private to the Queen, but this spy lay in wait for us. I did not know, however, that it was this old fool. But what does your majesty intend as the best thing to be done [*procediren*] with me?

King. We have resolved to send you to England, because this crown is friendly to our own; there you can cool yourself off [*refrigiren*] for a while, since the air there is healthier, and may promote your recovery better than here. We will give you some of our attendants, who shall accompany you and serve you faithfully.

Ham. Ay, ay, King; just send me off to Portugal, so that I may never come back again. That's the best.

King. No, not to Portugal, but to England, and these two shall accompany you on the journey. But when you arrive in England you shall have more attendants.

Ham. Are those the lackeys [*Laquaien*]? They're nice fellows!

King. Listen, you two [*aside to the two Attendants*]. As soon as you get to England, do as I have ordered you. Take a dagger, or each one a pistol, and kill him. But should this attempt miscarry, take this letter and present it, along with the Prince, at the place which is written on it. There he will be so well looked to that he will never come back again from England. But on this point I warn you: reveal your business to no man. You shall receive your reward as soon as you return.

Ham. Well, your majesty, who are the right ones, then, that are to travel with me?

King. These two. Now, the gods be with you, that with a fair wind you may reach the place and spot!

Ham. Well, adieu [*Adieu*], lady mother!

King. How is this, my prince? why do you call us mother?

Ham. Surely, man and wife are one flesh. Father or mother—it is all the same to me.

King. Well, fare ye well. Heaven be with you! [*Exit.*

Ham. Now, you noble chaps [*noblen Quantchen*], are you to be my companions?

Attends. Ay, your highness.

Ham. Come, then, noble comrades [*taking each by the hand*], let us go, let us go to England; take your little message in your hands; thou art a brave chap. Let us go, let us go to England! [*Exeunt.*

SCENE XI.—*Phantasmo. Ophelia.*

Phan. Wherever I go or stay, that darned [*elementische*] girl, that Ophelia, runs after me out of every corner. I can get no peace along of her. She keeps saying that I am her lover, and it is not true. If I could only hide myself somewhere where she could not find me! Now, the plague is loose again! There she comes again!

Oph. Where can my sweetheart be? The rogue won't stay with me, but had rather run away.—But, see, there he is! Listen, my love: I have been at the priest's, and he will join us this very day. I have made all ready for the wedding, and bought chickens, hares, meat, butter, and cheese. There is nothing else wanting but the musicians to play us to bed.

Phan. I can only say, yes.—Come, then, let us go to bed together.

Oph. No, no, my poppet, we must first go to church together, and then we'll eat and drink, and then we'll dance. Ah, how merry we shall be!

Phan. Ay, it will be right merry,—three eating out of one dish.

Oph. What sayest thou? If thou wilt not have me, I'll not have thee [*strikes him*]. Look there! there is my love beckoning to me. See there! what fine clothes he has on! See, he is enticing me to him. He throws me a rose and a lily. He wants to take me in his arms. He beckons me: I am coming, I am coming.

[*Exit.*

Phan. Near to, she's not wise, but farther off, she's downright mad. I wish she were hanged, and then the carrion could not run after me so.   [*Exit.*

ACT IV.

Scene I.—*Hamlet. Two Banditti* [*Banditen*].

Ham. This is a pleasant spot, here on this island. Let us stay here a while, and dine. There's a pleasant wood, and there a cool stream of water. So fetch me the best from the ship; here we'll make right merry.

First Band. Gracious sir, this is no time for eating, for from this island you will never depart; for here is the spot which is chosen for your churchyard.

Ham. What sayest thou, thou scoundrel, thou slave [*Esclav*]? Knowest thou whom I am? Wouldst thou jest so with a royal prince? However, for this time, I forgive you.

Sec. Band. No, it is no jest, but downright earnest. Just prepare yourself for death.

Ham. Why so? What injury have I ever done you? For my part I can think of none. Therefore, speak out: why do you entertain such bad thoughts?

First Band. It is our orders from the King; as soon as we get your highness on this island we are to kill you.

Ham. Dear friends, spare my life! Say that you have done your work, and so long as I live I will never return to the King. Think well what good you gain by having your hands covered with the blood of an innocent prince! Will you stain your consciences with my sins? Alas! that most unfortunately I am unarmed! If I only had something in my hands! [*Snatches at a dagger.*]

Sec. Band. I say, comrade, take care of thy weapon.

First Band. I'll take care.—Now, Prince, get ready. We haven't much time.

Ham. Since it cannot be otherwise, and I must die at your hands at the bidding of the tyrannical King, I will submit without resistance, although I'm innocent. And you, bribed to the deed through poverty, I willingly forgive. My blood, however, must be answered for by the murderer of his brother and of my father at the great Day of Judgement.

First Band. What has that Day to do with us? We must do this day what we were told.

Sec. Band. That's true, brother.—Hurry up! there's no help for it.—Let us fire, —I on one side and thou on the other.

Ham. Hear me—one word more. Since the very worst of malefactors is not denied a time for repentance, I, an innocent prince, beg you to let me raise to my Maker a fervent prayer; after that I am ready to die. But I will give you a signal:

I will turn my hands toward heaven, and the moment I stretch out my arms, fire! Aim both pistols at my sides, and when I say ' Shoot !' give me as much as I need, and be sure to hit me so that I shall not be long in torture.

Sec. Band. Well, we can easily grant him this favor.—Therefore, go ahead.

Ham. [*spreading out his hands*]. Shoot! [*throwing himself forward on his face between the two, who shoot each other.*] O just Heaven! thanks be to thee for this angelic idea! I will praise for ever the guardian angel who through my own idea has saved my life. But these villains,—as was their work, so is their pay. The dogs are still stirring; they have shot [*harquebusirt*] each other. But out of revenge [*Revange*] I'll give them a death-blow to make sure, else one of the rogues might escape. [*Stabs them with their own swords.*] I'll search them, and see whether they have by chance any warrant of arrest about them. This one has nothing. Here on this murderer I find a letter; I will read it. This letter is written to an arch-murderer in England; should this attempt fail, they had only to hand me over to him, and he would soon enough blow out the light of my life. But the gods stand by the righteous. Now will I return to my father, to his horror. But I will not trust any longer to water; who knows but what the ship's captain is a villain too? I will go to the first town and take the post. The sailors I will order back to Denmark. These rascals I will throw into the water. [*Exit.*

SCENE II.—*King, with Attendants.*

King. We long to learn how matters have turned out with our son, Prince Hamlet, and whether the men whom we sent with him as his fellow-travellers have faithfully performed what we commanded.

SCENE III.—*Phantasmo. King.*

Phan. News, Monsieur [*sic*] King! The very latest news!

King. What is it, Phantasmo?

Phan. Leonhardus has come back home from France.

King. That pleases us; admit him to our presence.

SCENE IV.—*Leonhardus.*

Leon. Gracious lord and King, I demand of your majesty my father, or just vengeance for his lamentable murder. If this be not done, I shall forget that you are King, and revenge myself on him who has done the deed.

King. Leonhardus, be satisfied that we are guiltless of thy father's death. Prince Hamlet unawares ran him through, behind the hangings, but we will take care that he is punished for it.

Leon. Since your majesty is guiltless of my father's death, I therefore beg for pardon on my knees. Rage as well as filial affection so overcame me that I scarcely knew what I did.

King. Thou art forgiven. We can well believe that it goes to thy very heart to have lost thy father so miserably. But be satisfied, thou shalt have a father again in ourselves.

Leon. I thank you for this high royal favor.

SCENE V.—*Phantasmo.*

Phan. Uncle King, more news still!

King. What news dost thou bring again?

Phan. Prince Hamlet has come back.

King. The devil has come back, and not Prince Hamlet!

Phan. Prince Hamlet has come back, and not the devil.

King. Leonhardus, listen here. Now thou canst avenge thy father's death. The Prince has come home again; but thou must promise us on thy oath not to reveal it to any one.

Phan. Doubt me not, your majesty. What you reveal to me shall be as secret as if you had spoken to a stone.

King. We will arrange a match between thee and him, thus: you shall fence with rapiers [*Rapieren*], and the one who makes the first three hits shall win a white Neapolitan horse. But in the middle of this combat you must let your rapier drop, and instead of it you must have at hand a sharp-pointed sword, made exactly like the rapier, but the point thou must smear with strong poison: as soon, then, as thou shalt have wounded him with it, he will have to die. But thou wilt win the prize, and with it the King's favor.

Leon. Your majesty must pardon me. I dare not undertake this, because the Prince is a skilled swordsman, and he might easily practise all this on me.

King. Leonhardus, hesitate not, but do thy King this pleasure; to revenge thy father thou must do it. For know, as your father's murderer the Prince deserves such a death. But we cannot get justice upon him, because he has his lady mother to back him, and the subjects love him much. Hence, if we openly revenged ourselves on him, there might easily be a rebellion. But to shun him as our stepson and kinsman is only an act of sacred justice; for he is murderous and mad, and for the future we ourselves must be in fear of such a wicked man. If you do what we desire, you will relieve your King of his fears, and in a disguised way revenge your father's murder.

Leon. It is a hard matter, and one which I am scarcely equal to. For should it get abroad it would surely cost me my life.

King. Do not doubt! Should this fail, we have thought of another trick. We will have an oriental diamond pounded fine, and when he is heated present it to him, mixed with sugar, in a beaker full of wine. Thus shall he drink his death to our health.

Leon. Well, then, your majesty, under this safeguard I will do the deed.

SCENE VI.—*Queen.*

Queen. Gracious lord and King, dearest husband, I bring you bad news.

King. What is it, dearest soul?

Queen. My favorite attendant [*Staatsjungfer*], Ophelia, runs up and down, cries and screams; she eats and drinks nothing. They think she has quite lost her wits.

King. Alas! one hears nothing but downright sad and unhappy news!

SCENE VII.—*Ophelia, with flowers.*

Oph. See! there, thou hast a flower; thou too; thou too. [*Gives each a flower.*] But, potz tausend! what had I clean forgotten! I must run quick. I have forgotten my ornaments. Alas! my frontlet [*Fronte*]! I must go quickly to the court-jeweller, and ask what new fashions he has got. Sa, sa [*sic*], set the table quickly. I'll soon be back. [*Runs off.*

Leon. Am I, then, born to every misfortune? My father is dead, and my sister is robbed of her wits! My heart almost bursts with grief.

King. Leonhardus, be content, thou shalt live alone in our favor.—But do you, dearest wife, be pleased to walk within with us, for we have something secret to reveal to you.—Leonhardus, do not forget what we have said to you.

Leon. I shall be eager to do it.

Queen. My King, we must devise some means by which this unfortunate maiden may be restored to her senses.

King. Let the case be submitted to our own physician.—But do you, Leonhardus, follow us. [*Exeunt.*

ACT V.

SCENE I.—*Hamlet.*

Ham. Unfortunate Prince! how much longer must thou live without peace. How long dost thou delay, O righteous Nemesis! before thou whettest thy righteous sword of vengeance for my uncle, the fratricide? Hither have I come once more, but cannot attain to my revenge, because the fratricide is surrounded all the time by so many people. But I swear that, before the sun has finished his journey from east to west, I will revenge myself on him.

SCENE II.—*Horatio.*

Hor. Your highness, I am heartily glad to see you here again in good health, But, I pray you, tell me why you have returned so soon.

Ham. Ah, Horatio, thou hast nearly missed never seeing me again alive; for my life was already at stake, had not the Almighty power specially protected me.

Hor. How? What says your highness? How did it happen?

Ham. Thou knowest that the King gave me two fellow-travellers as servants to accompany me. Now it happened that one day we had contrary [*contrairen*] winds, and we anchored at an island not far from Dover. I went on shore with my two companions to get a little fresh air. Then came these cursed rascals, and would have taken my life, and said that the King had bribed them to it. I begged for my life, and promised to give them as great a reward, and that, if they reported me to the King as dead, I would never again go near the court. But there was no pity in them. At last the gods put something into my head; whereupon I begged them that, before my death, I might offer a prayer, and that when I cried 'Shoot!' they were to fire at me. But just as I gave the word I fell on the ground, and they shot each other. Thus have I this time escaped with my life. My arrival, however, will not be agreeable to the King.

Hor. Oh, unheard-of treachery!

SCENE III.—*Phantasmo.*

Ham. Look, Horatio, this fool is far dearer to the King than my person. Let us hear what he has to say.

Phan. Welcome home, Prince Hamlet! Do you know the news? The King has laid a wager on you and the young Leonhardus. You are to fight together with rapiers, and he who gives the other the first two [*sic*] hits is to win a white Neapolitan horse.

Ham. Is this certain what thou sayest?

Phan. Yes, it is precisely so.

Ham. Horatio, what can this mean? I and Leonhardus are to fight one another. I fancy they have been quizzing this fool, for you can make him believe what you choose.—See here, Signora [*sic*] Phantasmo, it is terribly cold.

Phan. Ay, ay, it is terribly cold.   [*His teeth chatter.*

Ham. It is not so cold now as it was.

Phan. Ay, ay, it is just the happy medium.

Ham. But now it is very hot.   [*Wipes his face.*

Phan. Oh, what a terrible heat!   [*Also wipes away the perspiration.*

Ham. And now it is neither really hot, nor really cold.

Phan. Yes, it is now just temperate [*temperirt*].

Ham. There, thou seest, Horatio, one can quiz him as much as one likes.—Phantasmo, go back to the King and say that I will shortly wait on him. [*Exit Phantasmo.*] Come now, Horatio, I will go at once and present myself to the King. But ah! what means this? Blood flows from my nose, and my whole body shakes. Oh, woe's me! what has happened?   [*Swoons.*

Hor. Most noble prince!—O Heaven! what means this?—Be yourself again, your highness. Most noble Prince, what's the matter? What ails you?

Ham. I know not, Horatio. When I thought of returning to the court, a sudden faintness came over me. What this may mean is known to the gods.

Hor. Ah, Heaven grant that this omen [*Omen*] portends nothing bad!

Ham. Be it what it may, I'll none the less go to the court, even though it cost me my life.   [*Exit.*

SCENE IV.—*King. Leonhardus. Phantasmo.*

King. Leonhardus, get thyself ready, for Prince Hamlet will soon be here too.

Leon. Your majesty, I am already prepared, and I will do my best.

King. Look well to it! Here comes the Prince—

SCENE V.—*Hamlet. Horatio.*

Ham. All happiness and health to your majesty!

King. We thank you, Prince   We are greatly rejoiced that melancholy has in some degree left you. Wherefore, we have arranged a friendly match between you and the young Leonhardus. You are to fight with rapiers, and the one who makes the first three [*sic*] hits shall win a white Neapolitan horse, with saddle and trappings.

Ham. Your majesty must pardon me, for I have had but little practice with rapiers. But Leonhardus has just come from France, where, doubtless, he has had good practice. Therefore you must excuse me.

King. Prince Hamlet, do it to gratify us, for we are desirous of knowing what sort of feints the Germans and French use.

SCENE VI.—*Queen.*

Queen. Gracious lord and King, I have to announce to you a great calamity!

King. Heaven forbid! What is it?

Queen. Ophelia went up a high hill, and threw herself down, and killed herself.

Leon. Alas! Unfortunate Leonhardus! thou hast lost within a short space of time both a father and a sister! Whither will misfortune lead thee? I could for grief wish myself dead.

King. Be comforted, Leonhardus. We are gracious to you; only begin the contest.—Phantasmo, bring the rapiers.—Horatio, you shall be umpire.

Phan. Here is the warm beer.

Ham. Well, then, Leonhardus, come on, and let us see which of us is to fit the other with the fool's cap and bells. Should I, however, make a mistake [*einen Exces begehen*], pray excuse [*excusiren*] me, for it is long since I have fought.

Leon. I am your highness's servant: you are only jesting.
[*During the first bout they fight fair. Leonhardus is hit.*

Ham. That was one, Leonhardus!

Leon. True, your highness! Now for revenge [*Allo Revange*]! [*He drops his rapier, and seizes the poisoned sword which lies ready* [parat], *and gives the Prince a thrust in carte* [die Quarte] *in the arm. Hamlet parries* [pariret] *on Leonhardus, so that they both drop their weapons. Each runs for his rapier. Hamlet gets the poisoned sword, and stabs Leonhardus mortally.*] Woe is me! I have a mortal thrust. I receive what I thought to pay another. Heaven have mercy on me!

Ham. What the devil is this, Leonhardus? Have I wounded you with the rapier? How does this happen?

King. Go quick, and bring my beaker with wine, so that the combatants may refresh themselves a little. Go, Phantasmo, and fetch it. [*Descends from the throne. Aside.*] I hope that when they both drink of the wine they will then die, and no one will know of this trick.

Ham. Tell me, Leonhardus! how has this come about?

Leon. Alas, Prince! I have been seduced into this misfortune by the King. See what you have in your hand! It is a poisoned sword.

Ham. O Heaven! what is this? Preserve me from it!

Leon. I was to have wounded you with it, for it is so strongly poisoned that who gets the least wound from it must straightway die.

King. Ho, gentlemen! rest yourselves a little and drink. [*While the King is rising from his chair and speaking these words, the Queen takes the cup out of Phantasmo's hand and drinks, the King cries out.*] Ho! what keeps the goblet?—Alas, dearest wife! what are you doing? This wine is mixed with deadly poison! Oh woe! what have you done?

Queen. Oh woe! I am dying! [*The King stands in front of the Queen.*

Ham. And thou, tyrant, shalt bear her company in death.
[*Hamlet stabs him from behind.*

King. Oh woe! I receive my evil reward!

Leon. Adieu [*sic*], Prince Hamlet!—Adieu, world! I am dying also.—Ah, for-give me, Prince!

Ham. May Heaven receive thy soul! for thou art guiltless. But this tyrant, I hope he may wash off his black sins in hell.—Ah, Horatio, now is my soul at rest, now that I have revenged myself on my enemies! 'Tis true I have also received a hit on my arm, but I hope it will signify nothing. I grieve that I have stabbed Leonhardus; but I know not how I got the accursed sword into my hand. But as is the labor, so is the reward; he has received his pay. Nothing afflicts me more than my lady mother. Still, she too has deserved this death for her sins. But tell me, who gave her the cup that has poisoned her?

Phan. I, Prince. I too brought the poisoned sword; but the poisoned wine was to be drunk by you alone.

Ham. Hast thou also been an instrument in this misery? Lo, there! thou also hast thy reward!   [*Stabs him dead.*

Phan. Stab away, till your sword is tired! [*dass euch die Klinge verlahme!*]

Ham. Alas, Horatio! I fear that my completed revenge will cost me my life, for I am sore wounded in the arm. I am growing very faint; my limbs grow weak; my legs will no longer stand; my voice fails me; I feel the poison in all my limbs. But I pray you, dear Horatio, carry the crown to Norway, to my cousin, the Duke Fortempras [*sic*], so that the kingdom may not fall into other hands. Alas! Oh woe! I die!

Hor. Alas, most noble Prince! still look for aid!—O Heaven! he is dying in my arms! Alas! what has not this kingdom suffered for ever so long from hard wars? Scarcely is there peace but internal disturbance, ambition, faction, and murder fill the land anew. In no age of the world could such a lamentable tragedy ever have happened as has now, alas! been enacted at this court. With the help of the faithful councillors I will make all preparations that these high personages shall be interred according to their rank. Then will I at once [*cito*] betake myself to Norway with the crown, and hand it over as this unfortunate Prince commanded.

> So is it when a King with guile usurps the throne,
> And afterward with treachery maintains it as his own.
> With mockery and scorn he ends his days abhorred,
> For as the labor is, so follows the reward.

ENGLISH CRITICISMS

ANTHONY, EARL OF SHAFTESBURY (1710)

(*Characteristics. Advice to an Author*,vol. i, p. 275. Fifth edition,1732.)—Besides some laudable Attempts which have been made with tolerable Success, of late years, towards a just manner of Writing, both in the heroick and familiar Style; we have older Proofs of a right Disposition in our People towards the moral and instructive Way. Our old dramatick Poet, SHAKESPEAR, may witness for our good Ear and manly Relish. Notwithstanding his natural Rudeness, his unpolish'd Style, his antiquated Phrase and Wit, his want of Method and Coherence, and his Deficiency in almost all the Graces and Ornaments of this kind of Writings; yet by the Justness of his MORAL, the Aptness of many of his *Descriptions*, and the plain and natural Turn of several of his *Characters*, he pleases his Audience, and often gains their Ear, without a single Bribe from Luxury or Vice.

That Piece of his, The Tragedy of HAMLET, which appears to have most affected *English* Hearts, and has perhaps been oftenest acted of any which have come upon our Stage, is almost one continu'd *Moral;* a Series of deep Reflections, drawn from *one* Mouth, upon the Subject of *one* single Accident and Calamity, naturally fitted to move Horror and Compassion. It may be properly said of this Play, if I mistake not, that it has only ONE *Character* or *principal Part.* It contains no Adoration or Flattery of *the Sex:* no ranting at *the Gods:* no blustring *Heroism:* nor any thing of that curious mixture of *the Fierce* and *Tender*, which makes the hinge of modern Tragedy, and nicely varies it between the Points of *Love* and *Honour*.

SIR THOMAS HANMER (1736)

(*Some Remarks on the Tragedy of Hamlet, Prince of Denmark.** London, 1736, p. 9.)—[The speech of Marcellus telling of Horatio's incredulity touching the dreaded sight] helps greatly to deceive us; for it shows one of the principal persons of the drama to be as incredulous in relation to the appearance of phantoms as we can be; but that at last he is convinced of his error by the help of his eyes. For it is a maxim entirely agreeable to truth, if we consider human nature, that whatever is supernatural or improbable is much more likely to gain credit with us, if it be in-

---

* In the Memoir of SIR THOMAS HANMER by SIR HENRY BUNBURY, p. 80, it is stated that ' there is reason to believe that he [Hanmer] was the author' of this anonymous work, and it is, I believe, generally ascribed to him. ED.

troduced as such by the persons of the drama, but at last proved to be true, though an extraordinary thing, than if it were brought in as a thing highly probable, and no one were made to boggle at the belief of it. The reason of this seems to be that we can for once, upon a very great occasion, allow such an incident as this to have happened, if it be brought in as a thing of great rarity; but we can by no means suspend our judgement and knowledge, or deceive our understandings as to grant that to be common and usual which we know to be entirely supernatural and improbable.

[Page 31.] Hamlet's light and even ludicrous expressions to his companions, his making them swear by his sword, &c., are all circumstances certainly inferior to the preceding part. But as we should be very cautious in finding fault with men of such an exalted genius as our author certainly was, lest we should blame them when in reality the fault lies in our own slow conception, we should well consider what could have been our author's view in such a conduct. I must confess I have turned this matter on every side, and all that can be said of it (as far as I am able to penetrate) is, that he makes the Prince put on this levity of behavior, that the gentlemen who were with him might not imagine that the Ghost had revealed some matter of great consequence to him, and that he might not be suspected of any deep designs.

. [Page 33.] Now I am come to mention Hamlet's madness, I must speak my opinion of our poet's conduct in this particular. To conform to the groundwork of his plot, Shakespeare makes the young Prince feign himself mad. I cannot but think this to be injudicious; for, so far from securing himself from any violence which he feared from the usurper, which was his design in so doing, it seems to have been the most likely way of getting himself confined, and consequently debarred from an opportunity of revenging his father's death. To speak truth, our poet, by keeping too close to the groundwork of his plot, has fallen into an absurdity; there appears no reason at all in nature why this young Prince did not put the usurper to death as soon as possible, especially as Hamlet is represented as a youth so brave and so careless of his own life. The case, indeed, is this: had Hamlet gone naturally to work, there would have been an end of our play. The poet, therefore, was obliged to delay his hero's revenge; but then he should have contrived some good reason for it. His beginning his scenes of madness by his behavior to Ophelia was judicious, because by this means he might be thought to be mad for her, and not that his brain was disturbed about state affairs, which would have been dangerous.

[Page 38.] I purposely omit taking notice of the famous speech: 'To be, or not to be,' &c. Every English reader knows its beauties.

[Page 39.] The scene represented by the Players is in wretched verse. This we may, without incurring the denomination of an ill-natured critic, venture to pronounce: that in almost every place where Shakespeare has attempted rhyme, either in the body of his plays, or at the ends of Acts or Scenes, he falls far short of the beauty and force of his blank verse. One would think they were written by two different persons. I believe we may justly take notice that rhyme never arrived at its true beauty, never came to its perfection, in England until long since Shakespeare's time.

[Page 42.] The Ghost's not being seen by the Queen was very proper; we could hardly suppose that a woman, and a guilty one especially, could be able to bear so terrible a sight without the loss of reason. Besides that, I believe, the poet had also some eye to a vulgar notion that spirits are only seen by those with whom their business is, let there be never so many persons in company. This compliance with these popular fancies, still gives an air of probability to the whole.

[Page 45.] Laertes's character is a very odd one; it is not easy to say whether it is good or bad; but his consenting to the villainous contrivance to murder Hamlet makes him much more a bad man than a good one. Surely, revenge for such an accidental murder as was that of his father's could never justify him in any treacherous practices. It is very nice conduct in the poet to make the usurper build his scheme upon the generous, unsuspicious temper of the person he intends to murder, and thus to raise the prince's character by the confession of his enemy, and to make the villain ten times more odious from his own mouth. The contrivance of the foil unbated is, methinks, too gross a deceit to go down even with a man of the most unsuspicious nature.

[Page 46.] It does not appear whether Ophelia's madness was chiefly for her father's death or for the loss of Hamlet. It is not often that young women run mad for the loss of their fathers. It is more natural to suppose that, like Chimene in the *Cid*, her great sorrow proceeded from her father being killed by the man she loved, and thereby making it indecent for her ever to marry him.

[Page 58.] As a proof of the bad taste of the multitude we find in this nation of ours, that a vile *Pantomime* piece, full of machinery, or a lewd, blasphemous Comedy, or a wretched Farce, or an empty, obscure, low Ballad Opera (in all which, to the scandal of our nation and age, we surpass all the world), shall draw together crowded audiences, when there is full elbow-room at a noble piece of Shakespeare's or Rowe's. [These foregoing extracts are given mainly for their historical value, as indicating the thoughtful appreciation,—not very profound, it must be confessed, but, still, true and genuine,—in which Sh. was held by eminent men (and Sir Thomas Hanmer was Speaker of the House of Commons) a little more than a hundred years after his death. It is also to be noted that Hanmer has anticipated much modern criticism, both English and German, which still continues to be put forth as novel or striking. ED.]

DR JOHNSON (1765)

(*The Plays of Shakespeare*, vol. viii, p. 311.)—If the dramas of Shakespeare were to be characterized, each by the particular excellence which distinguishes it from the rest, we must allow to the tragedy of *Hamlet* the praise of variety. The incidents are so numerous that the argument of the play would make a long tale. The scenes are interchangeably diversified with merriment and solemnity; with merriment that includes judicious and instructive observations; and solemnity not strained by poetical violence above the natural sentiments of man. New characters appear from time to time in continual succession, exhibiting various forms of life and particular modes of conversation. The pretended madness of Hamlet causes much mirth, the mournful distraction of Ophelia fills the heart with tenderness, and every personage produces the effect intended, from the Apparition, that in the First Act chills the blood with horror, to the Fop in the last, that exposes affectation to just contempt.

The conduct is perhaps not wholly secure against objections. The action is, indeed, for the most part, in continual progression, but there are some scenes which neither forward nor retard it. Of the feigned madness of Hamlet there appears no adequate cause, for he does nothing which he might not have done with the reputation of sanity. He plays the madman most when he treats Ophelia with so much rudeness, which seems to be useless and wanton cruelty.

Hamlet is, through the whole piece, rather an instrument than an agent. After he has, by the stratagem of the play, convicted the King, he makes no attempt to punish him; and his death is at last effected by an incident which Hamlet had no part in producing.

The catastrophe is not very happily produced; the exchange of weapons is rather an expedient of necessity than a stroke of art. A scheme might easily be formed to kill Hamlet with the dagger and Laertes with the bowl.

The poet is accused of having shown little regard to poetical justice, and may be charged with equal neglect of poetical probability. The apparition left the regions of the dead to little purpose; the revenge which he demands is not obtained but by the death of him that was required to take it; and the gratification which would arise from the destruction of an usurper and a murderer is abated by the untimely death of Oph., the young, the beautiful, the harmless, and the pious.

MRS MONTAGU (1769)

(*Essay on the Writings and Genius of Shakespear*, 1769, p. 163.)—The first propriety in dealing with preternatural beings seems to be that the ghost be intimately connected with the fable; that he increase the interest, add to the solemnity of it, and that his efficiency in bringing on the catastrophe be in some measure adequate to the violence done to the ordinary course of things in his visible interposition. To this end it is necessary that this being should be acknowledged and revered by the national superstition, and every operation that develops the attributes, which the vulgar opinion or nurse's legend taught us to ascribe to him, will augment our pleasure; whether we give the reins to imagination, and, as spectators, yield ourselves up to the pleasing delusion, or, as critics, examine the merit of the composition. In all these capital points Shakespeare has excelled. At the solemn midnight hour the scene opens, and Bernardo tells us that the ghost of the late monarch had appeared the night before ʻWhen yon same star, that westward from the pole, Had made his course t' illume that part of heaven, Where now it burns, The bell then beating one——.ʼ Here enters the Ghost, after you are thus prepared. There is something solemn and sublime in thus regulating the walking of the spirit by the course of the star. It intimates a connection and correspondence between things beyond our ken, *and above the visible diurnal sphere.* Horatio is affected with that kind of fear which such an appearance would naturally excite. He trembles and turns pale. When the violence of the emotion subsides, he reflects that probably this supernatural event portends some danger lurking in the State. This suggestion gives importance to the phenomenon, and engages our attention. Such appearances, says he, preceded the fall of the mightiest Julius, and the ruin of the great commonwealth. There is great art in this conduct. The true cause of the royal Dane's discontent could not be guessed at; it was a secret which could be revealed only by himself. In the mean time it was necessary to captivate our attention by demonstrating that the poet was not going to exhibit such idle and frivolous gambols as ghosts are by the vulgar often represented to perform. Horatio's address to the Ghost is, in its whole purport, in accordance with the popular conception of such matters. The vanishing of the Ghost at the crowing of the cock is another circumstance of established superstition.

STEEVENS (1778)

(*The Plays of William Shakspeare*, 1778, vol. x, p. 412.*)—Hamlet, at the command of his father's ghost, undertakes with seeming alacrity to revenge the murder; and declares he will banish all other thoughts from his mind. He makes, however, but one effort to keep his word, and that is when he mistakes Polonius for the King. On another occasion he defers his purpose till he can find an opportunity of taking his uncle when he is least prepared for death, that he may insure damnation to his soul. Though he assassinated Polonius by accident, yet he deliberately procures the execution of his school-fellows, Rosencrantz and Guildenstern, who appear not, [from any circumstances in this play,] to have been acquainted with the treacherous purposes of the mandate they were employed to carry. [To embitter their fate, and hazard their punishment beyond the grave, he denies them even the few moments necessary for a brief confession of their sins.] Their end (as he declares in a subsequent conversation with Horatio) gives him no concern, for they obtruded themselves into the service, and he thought he had a right to destroy them. From his brutal conduct towards Ophelia he is not less accountable for her distraction and death. He interrupts the funeral designed in honor of this lady, at which both the King and Queen were present; and, by such an outrage to decency, renders it still more necessary for the usurper to lay a second stratagem for his life, though the first had proved abortive. He insults the brother of the dead, and boasts of an affection for his sister, which, before, he had denied to her face, and yet at this very time must be considered as desirous of supporting the character of a madman, so that the openness of his confession is not to be imputed to him as a virtue. He apologizes to Horatio afterwards for the absurdity of his behavior, to which, he says, he was provoked by that nobleness of fraternal grief, which, indeed, he ought rather to have applauded than condemned. Dr Johnson has observed, that to bring about a reconciliation with Laertes he has availed himself of a dishonest fallacy; and to conclude, it is obvious to the most careless spectator or reader, that he kills the King at last to revenge himself, and not his father.

Hamlet cannot be said to have pursued his ends by very warrantable means; and if the poet, when he sacrificed him at last, meant to have enforced such a moral, it is not the worst that can be deduced from the play; for, as Maximus, in Beaumont and Fletcher's *Valentinian*, says :—

> ' Although his justice were as white as truth,
> His way was crooked to it; that condemns him.

The late Dr Akinside once observed to me, that the conduct of Hamlet was every way unnatural and indefensible, unless he were to be regarded as a young man whose intellects were in some degree impaired by his own misfortunes : by the death of his father, the loss of expected sovereignty, and a sense of shame resulting from the hasty and incestuous marriage of his mother.

I have dwelt the longer on this subject because Hamlet seems to have been hitherto regarded as a hero not undeserving the pity of the audience; and because no writer on Shakespeare has taken the pains to point out the immoral tendency of his character.

---

* These remarks Steevens changed somewhat in his edition of 1793. The changes are indicated by brackets. ED.

HENRY MACKENZIE (1780)

(*The Mirror*, No. 99, 18 April, 1780.)—Had Shakespeare made Hamlet pursue his vengeance with a steady determined purpose, had he led him through difficulties arising from accidental causes, and not from the doubts and hesitation of his own mind, the anxiety of the spectator might have been highly raised; but it would have been anxiety for the event, not for the person.

As it is, we feel not only the virtues, but the weaknesses, of Hamlet as our own; we see a man, who in other circumstances would have exercised all the moral and social virtues, placed in a situation in which even the amiable qualities of his mind serve but to aggravate his distress and to perplex his conduct. Our compassion for the first, and our anxiety for the latter, are excited in the strongest manner; and hence arises that indescribable charm in *Hamlet* which attracts every reader and every spectator, which the more perfect characters of other tragedies never dispose us to feel.

The Orestes of the Greek poet, who at his first appearance lays down a plan of vengeance which he resolutely pursues, interests us for the accomplishment of his purpose; but of him we think only as the instrument of that justice which we wish to overtake the murderers of Agamemnon. We feel with Orestes (or rather with Sophocles, for in such passages we always hear the poet in his hero), that 'it is fit that such gross infringements of the moral law should be punished with death in order to make wickedness less frequent;' but when Horatio exclaims, on the death of his friend: ' Now cracks a noble heart;' we forget the murder of the King, the villainy of Claudius, the guilt of Gertrude; our recollection dwells only on the memory of that ' sweet prince,' the delicacy of whose feelings a milder planet should have ruled, whose gentle virtues should have bloomed through a life of felicity and usefulness.

RITSON (1783)

(*Remarks*, &c., 1783, p. 217.)—Hamlet, the only child of the late king, upon whose death he became lawfully entitled to the crown, had, it seems, ever since that event been in a state of melancholy, owing to excessive grief for the suddenness with which it had taken place, and indignant horror at his mother's speedy and incestuous marriage. The spirit of the king, his father, appears, and makes him acquainted with the circumstances of his untimely fate, which he excites him to *revenge;* this Hamlet engages to do: an engagement it does not appear he ever forgot. It behoved him, however, to conduct hisself [*sic*] with the greatest prudence. The usurper was powerful, and had Hamlet carried his design into immediate execution, it could not but have been attended with the worst consequences to his own life and fame. No one knew what the Ghost had imparted to him, till he afterwards made Horatio acquainted with it; and though his interview with the spirit gave him certain proof and satisfactory reason to know and detest the usurper, it would scarcely, in the eye of the people, have justified his killing their king. To conceal, and, at a convenient time, to effect, his purpose, he counterfeits madness, and, for his greater assurance, puts the spirit's evidence and the usurper's guilt to the test of a play, by which the truth of each is manifested. . . .

[Page 221.] Hamlet's conversation with Laertes immediately before the fencing scene was at the Queen's earnest entreaty; and though Dr Johnson be pleased to give it the harsh name of 'a dishonest fallacy,' there are better, because more natural, judges who consider it as a most gentle and pathetic address; certainly Hamlet did not intend the death of Polonius; of consequence, unwittingly and by mere accident, injured Laertes, who declared that he was 'satisfied in nature,' and that he only delayed his perfect reconcilement till his honor was satisfied by elder masters, whom at the same time (for he has the instrument of death in his hand) he never meant to consult. Let the conduct and sentiments of Laertes in this interview and in his conversation with the usurper, together with his villainous design against the life of Hamlet, be examined and tried by any rules of gentility, honor, or humanity, natural or artificial, he must be considered as a treacherous, cowardly, diabolical wretch. . . . .

Dr Akinside was a very ingenious, sensible, and worthy man; but enough has been said to satisfy those who doubt, that the conduct of Hamlet is neither unnatural nor indefensible. That his intellects were really impaired by the circumstances enumerated by the above learned physician is very probable; and indeed Hamlet his self [*sic*], more than once, plainly insinuates it.

RICHARDSON (1784)

(*Essays on Some of Shakespeare's Dramatic Characters*, 1797, p. 75. Fifth edition.)—The mind of Hamlet, violently agitated and filled with displeasing and painful images, loses all sense of felicity. He even wishes for a change of being. The appearance is wonderful, and leads us to inquire into affections and opinions that could render him so despondent. The death of his father was a natural evil, and as such he endures it. That he is excluded from succeeding immediately to the royalty seems to affect him slightly; for to vehement and vain ambition he appears superior. He is moved by finer principles, by an exquisite sense of virtue, of moral beauty and turpitude. The impropriety of Gertrude's behavior, her ingratitude to the memory of her former husband, and the depravity she discovers in the choice of a successor, afflict his soul, and cast him into utter agony. Here, then, is the principle and spring of all his actions.

[Page 78.] To erase an established affection, and substitute aversion, or even indifference, does violence to our nature; our affliction will bear an exact proportion to our former tenderness. So delicate is your affection, and so refined your sense of moral excellence, when the moral faculty is softened into a tender attachment, that the sanctity and purity of the heart you love must appear without a stain. Such is the condition of Hamlet. Exquisitely sensible of moral beauty and deformity, he discerns turpitude in a parent. Surprise adds bitterness to his sorrow; and led, by the same moral principle, to admire and glory in the high desert of his father, even this admiration contributes to his uneasiness. Aversion to his uncle, arising from the same origin, augments his anguish. All these emotions are rendered still more violent, being exasperated by his recent interview [in I, ii] with the Queen. Overwhelmed with afflicting images, no exhilarating affection can have admission to his heart. He wishes for deliverance from his affliction by deliverance from a painful existence.

[Page 98.] The condition of Hamlet's mind becomes still more curious and interesting. His suspicions are confirmed. Conceiving designs of punishment, and sensible that he is already suspected by the King, he is thrown into violent perturbation.

Afraid at the same time lest his aspect or demeanor should betray him, his agitation is such as threatens the overthrow of his reason. He trembles, as it were, on the brink of madness; and is at times not altogether certain that he acts or speaks according to the dictates of a sound understanding. He partakes of such insanity as may arise in a mind of great sensibility, from excessive agitation of spirit, and much labor of thought; but which naturally subsides when the perturbation ceases. Yet he must act, and with prudence. He must even conceal his intentions,—his actual condition suggests a mode of concealment. Knowing that he must appear incoherent and inconsistent, he is not unwilling to have it believed that his reason is somewhat disarranged, and that the strangeness of his conduct admits of no other explanation. As it is of signal consequence to him to have the rumor of his madness believed and propagated, he endeavors to render the counterfeit specious. There is nothing that reconciles men more readily to believe in any extraordinary appearance than to have it accounted for. A reason of this kind is often more plausible and imposing than many forcible arguments, particularly if the theory be of our own invention. Accordingly, Hamlet, the more easily to deceive the King and his creatures, and to furnish them with an explication of his uncommon deportment, practises his artifice on Ophelia. There is no change in his attachment, unless in so far as other passions of a violent character have assumed a temporary influence. His affection is permanent. To confirm and publish the report that his understanding was disordered, he would act in direct opposition to his former conduct. Full of honor and affection, he would put on the semblance of rudeness. To Ophelia he would show dislike, because a change of this nature would be, of all others, the most remarkable, and because his affection for her was passionate and sincere.

[Page 102.] The tendency of indignation, and of furious and inflamed resentment, is to inflict punishment on the offender. But if resentment is ingrafted on the moral faculty and grows from it, its tenor and conduct will be different. In its first emotion it may breathe excessive and immediate vengeance; but sentiments of justice and propriety interposing will arrest and suspend its violence. An ingenuous mind, thus agitated by powerful and contending principles, exceedingly tortured and perplexed, will appear hesitating and undetermined. Thus the vehemence of the vindictive passion will, by delay, suffer abatement; by its own ardor it will be exhausted; and our natural and habituated propensities will resume their influence. These continue in possession of the heart until the mind reposes and recovers vigor; then if the conviction of injury still remains, and if our resentment seems justified by every amiable principle, by reason and the sentiments of mankind, it will return with power and authority. Should any unintended incident awaken our sensibility, and dispose us to a state of mind favorable to the influence and operation of ardent and impetuous passions, our resentment will revisit us at that precise period, and turn in its favor, and avail itself of every other sentiment and affection. The mind of Hamlet, weary and exhausted by violent agitation, continues doubtful and undecided till his sensibility, excited by a theatrical exhibition, restores to their authority his indignation and desire of vengeance. Still, however, his moral principles, the supreme and governing powers of his constitution, conducting those passions which they seem to justify and excite, determine him again to examine his evidence, or endeavor by additional circumstances to have it strengthened.

[Page 117.] On reviewing the analysis now given, a sense of virtue seems to be the ruling principle in the character of Hamlet. In other men it may appear with the ensigns of high authority; in Hamlet it possesses absolute power. United with amiable affections, with every graceful accomplishment, and every agreeable quality, it embellishes and exalts them. It rivets his attachment to his friends when he finds them deserving; it is a source of sorrow if they appear corrupted. It even sharpens his penetration; and, if unexpectedly he discerns turpitude or impropriety in any character, it inclines him to think more deeply of their transgression than if his sentiments were less refined. It thus induces him to scrutinize their conduct, and may lead him to the discovery of more enormous guilt. . . . . Yet with all this purity of moral sentiment, with the utmost rectitude of intention, and the most active zeal in the exercise of every duty, he is hated, persecuted, and destroyed. Nor is this so inconsistent with poetical justice as may at first sight be apprehended. The particular temper and state of Hamlet's mind is connected with weaknesses that embarrass, or may be somewhat incompatible with bold and persevering projects. His amiable hesitations and reluctant scruples lead him at one time to indecision; and then betray him, by the self-condemning consciousness of such apparent imbecility, into acts of rash and inconsiderate violence. Meantime, his adversaries, suffering no such internal conflict, persist with uniform determined vigor in the prosecution of unlawful schemes. Thus Hamlet, and persons of his constitution, contending with less virtuous opponents, can have little hope of success; and so the poet has not in the catastrophe been guilty of any departure from nature, or any infringement of poetical justice. We love, we almost revere, the character of Hamlet, and grieve for his sufferings. But we must at the same time confess, that his weaknesses, amiable weaknesses! are the cause of his disappointment and early death.

[Page 131.] The sentiments that Hamlet expresses when he finds Claudius at prayer are not, I will venture to affirm, his real ones. There is nothing in his whole character that justifies such savage enormity. We are therefore bound in justice and candor to look for some hypothesis that shall reconcile what he now delivers with his usual maxims and general deportment. I would ask, then, whether on many occasions we do not allege as the motives of our conduct those considerations which are not really our motives? Nay, is not this sometimes done almost without our knowledge? Is it not done when we have no intention to deceive others; but when by the influences of some present passion we deceive ourselves? When the profligate is accused of enormities he will have them pass for manly spirit, or love of society; and imposes this opinion not upon others, but upon himself. When the miser indulges his love of wealth, he says, and believes, that he follows the maxims of a laudable economy. So also, while the censorious and invidious slanderer gratifies his malignity, he boasts, and believes, that he obeys the dictates of justice. Apply this principle to the case of Hamlet; sense of supposed duty and a regard to character prompt him to slay his uncle; and he is withheld at that instant by the ascendant of a gentle disposition; by the scruples, and perhaps weakness, of extreme sensibility. But how can he answer to the world and to his sense of duty for missing this opportunity? The real motive cannot be urged. Instead of excusing, it would expose him, he thinks, to censure; perhaps to contempt. He looks about for a motive; and one better suited to the opinions of the multitude, and better calculated to lull resentment, is immediately suggested. He alleges, as direct causes of his delay, motives that could never influence his conduct; and thus exhibits a most exquisite picture of amiable self-deceit.

[Page 139.] Thinking himself incapable of happiness, he thinks he should be quite unconcerned with any human event. This is another effort of self-deceit, for in truth he is not unconcerned. He affects to regard serious and even important matters with a careless indifference. He would laugh; but his laughter is not that of mirth. Add to this, that in those moments when he fancies himself indifferent or unconcerned he endeavors to treat those actions, which would naturally excite indignation, with scorn or contempt. This on several occasions leads him to assume the appearance of an ironical, but melancholy, gayety.

[Page 141.] The character is consistent. Hamlet is exhibited with good dispositions, and struggling with untoward circumstances. The contest is interesting. As he endeavors to do right, we approve and esteem him. But his original constitution renders him unequal to the contest; he displays the weaknesses and imperfections to which his peculiar character is liable; he is unfortunate; his misfortunes are in some measure occasioned by his weakness; he thus becomes an object not of blame, but of genuine and tender regret.

COLERIDGE (1808)

(*Notes and Lectures upon Shakespeare*, New York, 1868, vol. iv, p. 144.)—I gave these lectures at the Royal Institution in the spring of the same year (1808) in which Sir Humphrey Davy, a fellow-lecturer, made his great revolutionary discoveries in chemistry. Even in detail, the coincidence of Schlegel with my lectures was so extraordinary that all who at a later period heard the same words, taken by me from my notes of the lectures at the Royal Institution, concluded a borrowing on my part from Schlegel. Mr Hazlitt replied to an assertion of my plagiarism from Schlegel in these words:—'That is a lie; for I myself heard the very same character of Hamlet from Coleridge before he went to Germany, and when he had neither read, nor could read, a page of German!' [COLLIER (*Introduction to Hamlet*, 1843, p. 193) also corroborates this by the assertion, that he had himself heard Coleridge 'broach these views some years before Schlegel's Lectures, *Ueber Dramatische Kunst und Literatur*, were published.' ED.] . . . .

I believe the character of Hamlet may be traced to Shakespeare's deep and accurate science in mental philosophy. Indeed, that this character must have some connection with the common fundamental laws of our nature may be assumed from the fact that Hamlet has been the darling of every country in which the literature of England has been fostered. In order to understand him, it is essential that we should reflect on the constitution of our own minds. Man is distinguished from the brute animals in proportion as thought prevails over sense; but in the healthy processes of the mind, a balance is constantly maintained between the impressions from outward objects and the inward operations of the intellect; for if there be an overbalance in the contemplative faculty, man thereby becomes the creature of mere meditation, and loses his natural power of action. Now, one of Shakespeare's modes of creating characters is to conceive any one intellectual or moral faculty in morbid excess, and then to place himself, Shakespeare, thus mutilated or diseased, under given circumstances. In Hamlet he seems to have wished to exemplify the moral necessity of a due balance between our attention to the objects of our senses and our meditation on the working of our minds,—an *equilibrium* between the real and the imaginary worlds. In Hamlet this balance is disturbed; his thoughts and the images of his fancy are far more vivid than his actual perceptions, and his very perceptions, instantly passing through the *medium* of his contemplations, acquire, as they pass, a form and a color not naturally their own. Hence we see a great, an almost enormous, intellectual activity, and a proportionate aversion to real action

consequent upon it, with all its symptoms and accompanying qualities. This character Shakespeare places in circumstances under which it is obliged to act on the spur
of the moment: Hamlet is brave and careless of death; but he vacillates from sensibility, and procrastinates from thought, and loses the power of action in the energy
of resolve. Thus it is that this tragedy presents a direct contrast to that of *Macbeth;*
the one proceeds with the utmost slowness, the other with a crowded and breathless
rapidity.

The effect of this overbalance of the imaginative power is beautifully illustrated
in the everlasting broodings and superfluous activities of Hamlet's mind, which,
unseated from its healthy relation, is constantly occupied with the world within, and
abstracted from the world without,—giving substance to shadows, and throwing a
mist over all commonplace actualities. It is the nature of thought to be indefinite;
—definiteness belongs to external imagery alone. Hence it is that the sense of sub-
limity arises, not from the sight of an outward subject, but from the beholder's reflection upon it;—not from the sensuous impression, but from the imaginative reflex.
Few have seen a celebrated waterfall without feeling something akin to disappointment; it is only subsequently that the image comes back full into the mind, and
brings with it a train of grand or beautiful associations. Hamlet feels this; his
senses are in a state of trance, and he looks upon external things as hieroglyphics.
His soliloquy: ' Oh! that this too, too solid flesh would melt,' &c., springs from that
craving after the indefinite,—for that which is not,—which most easily besets men of
genius; and the self-delusion common to this temper of mind is finely exemplified
in the character which Hamlet gives of himself:—

> ' It cannot be
> But I am pigeon-livered, and lack gall
> To make oppression bitter.'

He mistakes the seeing of his chains for the breaking of them, delays action till
action is of no use, and dies the victim of mere circumstance and accident.

With the single exception of *Cymbeline*, [the First Scenes of all of Shakespeare's
dramas] either place before us at one glance both the past and the future in some
effect, which implies the continuance and full agency of its cause, as in the feuds and
party-spirit of the Servants of the two houses in the first scene in *Romeo and
Juliet;* or in the degrading passion for shows and public spectacles, and the overwhelming attachment for the newest successful war-chief in the Roman people,
already become a populace, contrasted with the jealousy of the nobles, in *Julius
Cæsar;*—or they at once commence the action so as to excite a curiosity for the ex
planation in the following scenes, as in the storm of wind and waves, and the boat-
swain, in *The Tempest*, instead of anticipating our curiosity, as in most other First
Scenes, and in too many other First Acts;—or they act, by contrast of diction suited
to the characters, at once to heighten the effect, and yet to give a naturalness to the
language and rhythm of the principal personages, either as that of Prospero and Miranda by the appropriate lowness of the style,—or as in *King John*, by the equally
appropriate stateliness of official harangues or narratives, so that the after blank
verse seems to belong to the rank and quality of the speakers, and not to the poet;
—or they strike at once the key-note, and give the predominant spirit of the play, as
in *Twelfth Night* and in *Macbeth;*—or, finally, the First Scene comprises all these
advantages at once, as in *Hamlet*.

Compare the easy language of common life, in which this drama commences, with
the direful music and wild wayward rhythm and abrupt lyrics of the opening of

Macbeth. The tone is quite familiar;—there is no poetic description of night, no elaborate information conveyed by one speaker to another of what both had immediately before their senses (such as the first distich in Addison's *Cato*, which is a translation into poetry of ' Past four o'clock and a dark morning!') ;—and yet nothing bordering on the comic on the one hand, nor any striving of the intellect on the other. It is precisely the language of sensation among men who feared no charge of effeminacy for feeling what they had no want of resolution to bear. Yet the armor, the dead silence, the watchfulness that first interrupts it, the welcome relief of the guard, the cold, the broken expressions of compelled attention to bodily feelings still under control,—all excellently accord with, and prepare for, the after gradual rise into tragedy ;—but, above all, into a tragedy the interest of which is as eminently *ad et apud intra* as that of *Macbeth* is directly *ad extra*. [The rest of Coleridge's notes are incorporated in the commentary to the text. ED.]

COLERIDGE (1812)

(*Seven Lectures on Shakespeare and Milton*, London, 1856, p. 141.)—The first question we should ask ourselves is : What did Shakespeare mean when he drew the character of Hamlet ? He never wrote anything without design, and what was his design when he sat down to produce this tragedy ? My belief is, that he always regarded his story before he began to write much in the same light as a painter regards his canvas before he begins to paint : as a mere vehicle for his thoughts,—as a ground upon which he was to work. What, then, was the point to which Shakespeare directed himself in *Hamlet* ? He intended to portray a person in whose view the external world and all its incidents and objects were comparatively dim and of no interest in themselves, and which began to interest only when they were reflected in the mirror of his mind. Hamlet beheld external things in the same way that a man of vivid imagination, who shuts his eyes, sees what has previously made an impression on his organs. The poet places him in the most stimulating circumstances that a human being can be placed in. He is the heir-apparent of a throne : his father dies suspiciously ; his mother excludes her son from his throne by marrying his uncle. This is not enough ; but the Ghost of the murdered father is introduced to assure the son that he was put to death by his own brother. What is the effect upon the son ?—instant action and pursuit of revenge ? No : endless reasoning and hesitating, constant urging and solicitation of the mind to act, and as constant an escape from action ; ceaseless reproaches of himself for sloth and negligence, while the whole energy of his resolution evaporates in these reproaches. This, too, not from cowardice, for he is drawn as one of the bravest of his time,—not from want of forethought or slowness of apprehension, for he sees through the very souls of all who surround him, but merely from that aversion to action which prevails among such as have a world in themselves. . . . .

[Page 148.] Shakespeare wished to impress upon us the truth : that action is the chief end of existence,—that no faculties of intellect, however brilliant, can be considered valuable, or indeed otherwise than as misfortunes, if they withdraw us from, or render us repugnant to action, and lead us to think and think of doing, until the time has elapsed when we can do anything effectually. In enforcing this moral truth, Shakespeare has shown the fulness and force of his powers; all that is amiable and excellent in nature is combined in Hamlet, with the exception of one quality.

He is a man living in meditation, called upon to act by every motive human and divine, but the great object of his life is defeated by continually resolving to do, yet doing nothing but resolve.

HAZLITT (1817)

(*Characters of Shakespeare's Plays*, London, 1817, p. 104.)—Hamlet is a name: his speeches and sayings but the idle coinage of the poet's brain. What then, are they not real? They are as real as our own thoughts. Their reality is in the reader's mind. It is *we* who are Hamlet. This play has a prophetic truth, which is above that of history. Whoever has become thoughtful and melancholy through his own mishaps or those of others; whoever has borne about with him the clouded brow of reflection, and thought himself 'too much i' the sun;' whoever has seen the golden lamp of day dimmed by envious mists rising in his own breast, and could find in the world before him only a dull blank with nothing left remarkable in it; whoever has known 'the pangs of despised love, the insolence of office, or the spurns which patient merit of the unworthy takes;' he who has felt his mind sink within him, and sadness cling to his heart like a malady; who has had his hopes blighted and his youth staggered by the apparition of strange things; who cannot be well at ease while he sees evil hovering near him like a spectre; whose powers of action have been eaten up by thought,—he to whom the universe seems infinite, and himself nothing; whose bitterness of soul makes him careless of consequences, and who goes to a play as his best resource to shove off, to a second remove, the evils of life by a mock representation of them: this is the true Hamlet.

We have been so used to this tragedy that we hardly know how to criticise it any more than we should know how to describe our own faces. But we must make such observations as we can. It is the one of Shakespeare's plays that we think of oftenest, because it abounds most in striking reflections on human life, and because the distresses of Hamlet are transferred, by the turn of his mind, to the general account of humanity. Whatever happens to him we apply to ourselves, because he applies it so himself as a means of general reasoning. He is a great moraliser, and what makes him worth attending to is, that he moralises on his own feelings and experience. He is not a commonplace pedant. If *Lear* shows the greatest depth of passion, *Hamlet* is the most remarkable for the ingenuity, originality, and unstudied development of character. Shakespeare had more magnanimity than any other poet, and he has shown more of it in this play than in any other. There is no attempt to force an interest: everything is left for time and circumstance to unfold. The attention is excited without effort; the incidents succeed each other as matters of course; the characters think and speak and act just as they might do if left entirely to themselves. There is no set purpose, no straining at a point. The observations are suggested by the passing scene,—the gusts of passion come and go like sounds of music borne upon the wind. The whole play is an exact transcript of what might be supposed to have taken place at the court of Denmark at the remote period of time fixed upon, before the modern refinements in morals and manners were heard of. It would have been interesting enough to have been admitted as a bystander in such a scene, at such a time, to have heard and seen something of what was going on. But here we are more than spectators. We have not only 'the outward pageants and the signs of grief,' but 'we have that within that passes show.' We read the thoughts of the heart, we catch the passions living as they rise. Other dramatic writers give us very fine versions and paraphrases of nature; but Shakespeare, together with his own comments, gives us the original text, that we may judge for ourselves. This is a very great advantage.

The character of Hamlet is itself a pure effusion of genius. It is not a character marked by strength of will, or even of passion, but by refinement of thought and sentiment. Hamlet is as little of the hero as a man well can be; but he is a young and princely novice, full of high enthusiasm and quick sensibility,—the sport of circumstances, questioning with fortune and refining on his own feelings, and forced from the natural bias of his disposition by the strangeness of his situation. He seems incapable of deliberate action, and is only hurried into extremities on the spur of the occasion, when he has no time to reflect, as in the scene where he kills Polonius, and again, when he alters the letters which Rosencrantz and Guildenstern are taking with them to England, purporting his death. At other times, when he is most bound to act, he remains puzzled, undecided, skeptical, dallies with his purposes, till the occasion is lost, and always finds some pretence to relapse into indolence and thoughtfulness again. For this reason he refuses to kill the King when he is at his prayers. . . . .

He is the prince of philosophical speculators, and because he cannot have his revenge perfect, according to the most refined idea his wish can form, he misses it altogether. So he scruples to trust the suggestions of the Ghost, contrives the scene of the play to have surer proof of his uncle's guilt, and then rests satisfied with this confirmation of his suspicions, and the success of his experiment, instead of acting upon it. Yet he is sensible of his own weakness, taxes himself with it, and tries to reason himself out of it. Still, he does nothing; and this very speculation on his own infirmity only affords him another occasion for indulging it. It is not for any want of attachment to his father or abhorrence of his murder that Hamlet is thus dilatory, but it is more to his taste to indulge his imagination in reflecting upon the enormity of the crime, and refining on his schemes of vengeance, than to put them into immediate practice. His ruling passion is to think, not to act; and any vague pretence that flatters this propensity instantly diverts him from his previous purposes.

The moral perfection of this character has been called in question, we think, by those who did not understand it. It is more interesting than according to rules: amiable, though not faultless. The ethical delineations of ' that noble and liberal casuist' (as Shakespeare has been well called) do not exhibit the drab-colored Quakerism of morality. His plays are not copied either from *The Whole Duty of Man*, or from *The Academy of Compliments!* We confess we are a little shocked at the want of refinement in those who are shocked at the want of refinement in Hamlet. The want of punctilious exactness in his behavior either partakes of the ' license of the time,' or else belongs to the very excess of intellectual refinement in the character, which makes the common rules of life, as well as his own purposes, sit loose upon him. He may be said to be amenable only to the tribunal of his own thoughts, and is too much taken up with the airy world of contemplation to lay as much stress as he ought on the practical consequences of things. His habitual principles of action are unhinged and out of joint with the time. . . . .

Nothing can be more affecting or beautiful than the Queen's apostrophe to Ophelia on throwing flowers into the grave. Shakespeare was thoroughly a master of the mixed motives of human character, and he here shows us the Queen, who was so criminal in some respects, not without sensibility and affection in other relations of life. Ophelia is a character almost too exquisitely touching to be dwelt upon. Oh, rose of May! oh, flower too soon faded! Her love, her madness, her death, are described with the truest touches of tenderness and pathos. It is a character which nobody but Shakespeare could have drawn in the way that he has done, and to the conception of which there is not even the smallest approach, except in some of the old romantic ballads. Her brother, Laertes, is a character we do not like so well : he is too hot and choleric, and somewhat rhodomontade. Polonius is a perfect character in its kind; nor is there any foundation for the objections which have been made to the consistency of this part. It is said that he acts very foolishly and talks very sensibly. There is no inconsistency in that. Again, that he talks wisely at one time and foolishly at another; that his advice to Laertes is very sensible, and his advice to the King and Queen on the subject of Hamlet's madness is very ridiculous. But he gives the one as a father, and is sincere in it; he gives the other as a mere courtier, a busybody, and is accordingly officious, garrulous, and impertinent. In short, Shakespeare has been accused of inconsistency in this and other characters, only because he has kept up the distinction which there is in nature between the understandings and the moral habits of men, between the absurdity * of their ideas and the absurdity of their motives. Polonius is not a fool, but he makes himself so. His folly, whether in his actions or speeches, comes under the head of impropriety of intention.

We do not like to see our author's plays acted, and least of all, *Hamlet*. There is no play that suffers so much in being transferred to the stage. Hamlet himself seems hardly capable of being acted. Mr Kemble unavoidably fails in this character from a want of ease and variety. The character of Hamlet is made up of undulating lines; it has the yielding flexibility of ' a wave o' th' sea.' Mr Kemble plays it like a man in armor, with a determined inveteracy of purpose, in one undeviating straight line, which is as remote from the natural grace and refined susceptibility of the character as the sharp angles and abrupt starts which Mr Kean introduces into the part. Mr Kean's Hamlet is as much too splenetic and rash as Mr Kemble's is too deliberate and formal. His manner is too strong and pointed. He throws a severity approaching to virulence into the common observations and answers. There is nothing of this in Hamlet. He is, as it were, wrapped up in his reflections, and only *thinks aloud*. There should therefore be no attempt to impress what he says upon others by a studied exaggeration of emphasis or manner; no *talking at* his hearers. There should be as much of the gentleman and scholar as possible infused into the part, and as little of the actor. A pensive air of sadness should sit reluctantly upon his brow, but no appearance of fixed and sullen gloom. He is full of weakness and melancholy, but there is no harshness in his nature. He is the most amiable of misanthropes.

T. C. [THOMAS CAMPBELL?] (1818)

(*Letters on Shakespeare*, Blackwood's Magazine, February, 1818, p. 505.)—Shakespeare himself, had he even been as great a critic as a poet, could not have written a regular dissertation on Hamlet. So ideal, and yet so real an existence could have been shadowed out only in the colors of poetry. When a character deals solely or

---

* Is not this a misprint? Should it not be ' the *wisdom* of their ideas '? ED.

chiefly with this world and its events,—when it acts, and is acted upon, by objects that have a palpable existence, we see it distinctly, as if it were cast in a material mould,—as if it partook of the fixed and settled lineaments of the things on which it lavishes its sensibilities and its passions. We see in such cases, the vision of an individual soul, as we see the vision of an individual countenance. We can describe both, and can let a stranger into our knowledge. But how tell in words so pure, so fine, so ideal an abstraction as Hamlet? . . . .

When we know how unlike the action of Shakespeare's mind was to our own,—how deep and unboundedly various his beholdings of men's minds, and of all manifested existence,—how wonderful his celerity of thought, the dartings of his intellect, like the lightning glimpse, to all parts of his whole range of known being,—how can we tell that we have attained the purposes of his mind? We can reconcile what perhaps others cannot. How can we tell that he could not reconcile what we cannot? We build up carefully our conception of a character. He did not. He found springs of being in his man, and he unlocked them. How can we tell whither, to his conception, these flowings might tend? How can we know what he meant by so much in all Hamlet's discourse, in his madness, and everywhere else, that seems to us to have no direct meaning, no derivation from Hamlet's mind? It is most true, that they do not seem to agree with our ideal conception of Hamlet; but that is what we find in living men; and he would indeed be a sorry philosopher who should be startled by the exhibition of some feeling or passion in a character from which he had no reason to expect it, as if there were general laws unerringly to guide all the operations of 'that wild tumultuous thing, the heart of man.'

[Page 506.] Indeed, I have often thought that it is idle and absurd to try a poetical character on the stage, a creature existing in a Play, however like to real human nature it may be, precisely by the same rules which we apply to our living brethren of mankind in the substantial drama of life. No doubt a good Play is an imitation of life, as far as the actions, and events, and passions of a few hours can represent those of a whole lifetime. Yet, after all, it is but a segment of a circle that we can behold. Were the dramatist to confine himself to that narrow limit, how little could he achieve! He takes, therefore, for granted a knowledge, and a sympathy, and a passion in his spectators, that extends to, and permeates the existence of his characters long anterior to the short period which his art can embrace. He expects, and he expects reasonably, that we are not to look upon everything acted and said before us absolutely as it is said or acted. It is his business to make us comprehend the whole man from a part of his existence. But we are not to be passive spectators. It is our business to fill up and supply. It is our business to bring to the contemplation of an imaginary drama a knowledge of real life, and no more to cry out against apparent inconsistencies and violations of character, as we behold them in poetry, than as we every day behold them exemplified by living men. The pageants that move before us on the stage, however deeply they may interest us, are after all mere strangers. It is Shakespeare alone who can give to fleeting phantoms the definite interest of real personages. But we ought not to turn this glorious power against himself. We ought not to demand inexorably the same perfect, and universal, and embracing truth of character in an existence brought before us in a few hurried scenes (which is all a Play can be) that we sometimes may think we find in a real being, after long years of intimate knowledge, and which, did we know more, would perhaps seem to us to be truth no longer, but a chaos of the darkest and wildest inconsistencies.

[Page 508.] If there is anything disproportionate in [Hamlet's] mind, it seems to be this only,—that intellect is in excess. It is even ungovernable, and too subtle. His own description of perfect man, ending with ' In apprehension how like a god !' appears to me consonant with this character, and spoken in the high and overwrought consciousness of intellect. Much that requires explanation in the Play may perhaps be explained by this predominance and consciousness of great intellectual power. Is it not possible that the instantaneous idea of feigning himself mad belongs to this ? It is the power most present to his mind, and therefore in that, though in the denial of it, is his first thought to place his defence. So might we suppose a brave man of gigantic bodily strength counterfeiting cowardice and imbecility until there came a moment for the rousing up of vengeance. . . . .

Hamlet never gets farther, I believe, than one step,—that of self-protection in feigning himself mad. He sees no course clear enough to satisfy his understanding; and with all due deference to those critics in conduct who seem disposed to censure his dilatoriness, I should be glad if anybody would point out one. He is therefore by necessity irresolute ; but he feels that he is letting time pass ; and the consciousness of duty undone weighs down his soul. He thus comes to dread the clear knowledge of his own situation, and of the duties arising from it.

[Page 510.] Shakespeare never could have intended to represent [Hamlet's] love to Ophelia as very profound. If he did, how can we ever account for Hamlet's first exclamation, when in the churchyard he learns that he is standing by her grave, and beholds her coffin ? ' What, the fair Ophelia !' Was this all that Hamlet would have uttered, when struck into sudden conviction by the ghastliest terrors of death, that all he loved in human life had perished ? We can with difficulty reconcile such a tame ejaculation, even with extreme tenderness and sorrow. But had it been in the soul of Shakespeare to show Hamlet in the agony of hopeless despair, —and in hopeless despair he must at that moment have been, had Ophelia been all in all to him,—is there in all his writings so utter a failure in the attempt to give vent to overwhelming passion? When, afterwards, Hamlet leaps into the grave, do we see in that any power of love? I am sorry to confess that the whole of that scene is to me merely painful. It is anger with Laertes, not love for Ophelia, that makes Hamlet leap into the grave. Laertes's conduct, he afterwards tells us, puts him into a towering passion,—a state of mind which it is not easy to reconcile with almost any kind of sorrow for the dead Ophelia. Perhaps, in this, Shakespeare may have departed from nature. But had he been attempting to describe the behavior of an impassioned lover at the grave of his beloved, I should be compelled to feel that he had not merely departed from nature, but that he had offered her the most profane violation and insult.

Hamlet is afterwards made acquainted with the sad history of Ophelia,—he knows that to the death of Polonius, and his own imagined madness, is to be attributed her miserable catastrophe. Yet, after the burial-scene, he seems utterly to have forgotten that Ophelia ever existed ; nor is there, as far as I recollect, a single allusion to her throughout the rest of the drama. The only way of accounting for this seems to be that Shakespeare had himself forgotten her,—that with her last rites she vanished from the world of his memory. But this of itself shows that it was not his intention to represent Ophelia as the dearest of all earthly things or thoughts to Hamlet, or surely there would have been some melancholy, some miserable hauntings of her image. But, even as it is, it seems not a little unaccountable that Hamlet should have been so slightly affected by her death.

Of the character of Ophelia, and the situation she holds in the action of the play, I need say little. Everything about her is young, beautiful, artless, innocent, and touching. She comes before us in striking contrast to the Queen, who, fallen as she is, feels the influence of her simple and happy virgin purity. Amid the frivolity, flattery, fawning, and artifice of a corrupted court, she moves in all the unpolluted loveliness of nature. She is like an artless, gladsome, and spotless shepherdess, with the gracefulness of society hanging like a transparent veil over her natural beauty. But we feel, from the first, that her lot is to be mournful. The world in which she lives is not worthy of her. And soon, as we connect her destiny with Hamlet, we know that darkness is to overshadow her, and that sadness and sorrow will step in between her and the ghost-haunted avenger of his father's murder. Soon as our pity is excited for her, it continues gradually to deepen; and when she appears in her madness, we are not more prepared to weep over all its most pathetic movements than we afterwards are to hear of her death. Perhaps the description of that catastrophe by the Queen is poetical rather than dramatic; but its exquisite beauty prevails, and Ophelia, dying and dead, is still the same Ophelia that first won our love. Perhaps the very forgetfulness of her, throughout the remainder of the play, leaves the soul at full liberty to dream of the departed. She has passed away from the earth like a beautiful air,—a delightful dream. There would have been no place for her in the agitation and tempest of the final catastrophe.

MRS JAMESON (1832)

(*Characteristics of Women*, London, 1833. Second edition, vòl. i, p. 254.)—Ophelia, —poor Ophelia! Oh far too soft, too good, too fair to be cast among the briers of this working-day world, and fall and bleed upon the thorns of life! What shall be said of her? for eloquence is mute before her! Like a strain of sad, sweet music which comes floating by us on the wings of night and silence, and which we rather feel than hear,—like the exhalation of the violet dying even upon the sense it charms,—like the snow-flake dissolved in air before it has caught a stain of earth,— like the light surf severed from the billow, which a breath disperses,—such is the character of Ophelia; so exquisitely delicate, it seems as if a touch would profane it; so sanctified in our thoughts by the last and worst of human woes, that we scarcely dare to consider it too deeply. The love of Ophelia, which she never once confesses, is like a secret which we have stolen from her, and which ought to die upon our hearts as upon her own. Her sorrow asks not words, but tears; and her madness has precisely the same effect that would be produced by the spectacle of real insanity, if brought before us: we feel inclined to turn away, and veil our eyes in reverential pity and too painful sympathy.

[Page 259.] It is the helplessness of Ophelia, arising merely from her innocence, which melts us with such profound pity. She is so young that neither her mind nor her person have attained maturity; she is not aware of the nature of her own feelings; they are prematurely developed in their full force before she has strength to bear them; and love and grief together rend and shatter the frail texture of her existence, like the burning fluid poured into a crystal vase. She says very little, and what she does say seems rather intended to hide than to reveal the emotions of her heart; yet in those few words we are made as perfectly acquainted with her character, and with what is passing in her mind, as if she had thrown forth her soul with all the glowing eloquence of Juliet. Passion with Juliet seems innate, a part

of her being, 'as dwells the gathered lightning in a cloud;' and we never fancy her
but with the dark splendid eyes and Titian-like complexion of the South. While
in Ophelia we recognize as distinctly the pensive, fair-haired, blue-eyed daughter of
the North, whose heart seems to vibrate to the passion she has inspired, more conscious of being loved than of loving; and yet, alas! loving in the silent depths of
her young heart far more than she is loved.

[Page 262.] When her father catechises her, he extorts from her in short sentences, uttered with bashful reluctance, the confession of Hamlet's love for her, but
not a word of her love for him. The whole scene is managed with inexpressible
delicacy; it is one of those instances common in Shakespeare, in which we are
allowed to perceive what is passing in the mind of a person without any consciousness on their part. Only Ophelia herself is unaware that while she is admitting the
extent of Hamlet's courtship, she is also betraying how deep is the impression it has
made, how entire the love with which it is returned.

[Page 276.] Of her subsequent madness, what can be said? What an affecting,
what an astonishing, picture of a mind utterly, hopelessly wrecked! past hope, past
cure! There is the frenzy of excited passion,—there is the madness caused by
intense and continued thought,—there is the delirium of fevered nerves; but
Ophelia's madness is distinct from these: it is not the suspension, but the utter
destruction, of the reasoning powers; it is the total imbecility which, as medical
people well know, frequently follows some terrible shock to the spirits. Constance
is frantic; Lear is mad; Ophelia is *insane*. Her sweet mind lies in fragments
before us,—a pitiful spectacle! Her wild, rambling fancies; her aimless, broken
speeches; her quick transitions from gayety to sadness,—each equally purposeless
and causeless; her snatches of old ballads, such as perhaps her old nurse sang her
to sleep with in her infancy,—are all so true to the life, that we forget to wonder,
and can only weep. It belonged to Shakespeare alone so to temper such a picture
that we can endure to dwell upon it,—

> 'Thought and affliction, passion, hell itself,
> She turns to favour and to prettiness.'

That in her madness she should exchange her bashful silence for empty babbling,
her sweet maidenly demeanor for the impatient restlessness that spurns at straws,
and say and sing precisely what she never could or would have uttered had she
been in possession of her reason, is so far from being an impropriety, that it is an
additional stroke of nature. It is one of the symptoms in this species of insanity,
as we are assured by physicians. I have myself known one instance in the case of
a young Quaker girl, whose character resembled that of Ophelia, and whose malady
arose from a similar cause.

THOMAS CAMPBELL [?] (1833)

(*Blackwood's Magazine*, March, 1833, p. 407.*)—Neglected had [Ophelia] been by
one and all,—all but Horatio, that noble soul of unpretending worth, and he knew
not what ailed her till she was past all cure. He it is who feelingly, and poetically,
and truly describes the maniac; he it is who brings her in; he it is who follows her

---

* I infer that this article was written by Campbell, because in it the writer refers to himself as the
author of the *Letters on Shakespeare*, quoted on p. 157; and these *Letters* are signed T. C. ED.

away,—dumb all the while! And who with right soul but must have been speech-less amidst these gentle ravings? The adulterous and incestuous only it is that speak. 'How now, Ophelia?' 'Nay! but, Ophelia,' so minceth the Queen. 'How do you, pretty lady?' 'Pretty Ophelia!' so stuttereth the King. Faugh! the noisome and loathsome hypocrites! So that her poor lips were but mute, both would have fain seen them sealed up with the blue mould of the grave! But Laertes,—he with all his faults and sins has a noble heart,—his words are pathetic or passionate. Horatio says 'her speech is nothing.' It is nearly nothing. But the snatches of old songs, they are something,—as they come flowing in music from their once-hushed resting-places far within her memory, which they had entered in her days of careless child-hood, and they have a meaning now that gives them doleful utterance. It is Ham-let who is the maniac's Valentine. 'You are merry, my lord,' is all she said to him, as he lay with his head in her lap at the play. She would have died rather than sing to Hamlet that night the songs she sings now,—yet she had not sung them now had she not been crazed with love! 'Where is the beauteous majesty of Denmark?' She must mean Hamlet. 'He is dead and gone, lady,' &c. Means she her father? Perhaps,—but most likely not. Hamlet? It is probable. Mayhap but the dead man of the song. Enough that it is of death, and burial. Or to that verse, as haply to others too, she may attach no meaning at all. A sad key once struck, the melan-choly dirge may flow on of itself. Memory and Consciousness accompanying not one another in her insanity! 'They say the owl was a baker's daughter. Lord, we know what we are, but know not what we may be. God be at your table.' The King says, 'conceit upon her father.' Adulterous beast! it was no conceit on her father. The words refer to an old story often related to children to deter them from illiberal behavior to poor people. Ophelia had learnt the story in the nursery, and she who was always charitable thinks of it now,—God only knows why,—and Shake-speare, who had heard such dim humanities from the living lips of the deranged,—as many have done who are no Shakespeares,—gave them utterance from the lips of the sweetest phantom that ever wailed her woes in hearing of a poet's brain.

DR MAGINN (1836)

(*Shakespeare Papers*, London, 1860, p. 275.)—Shakespeare has written plays, and these plays were acted; and they succeeded; and by their popularity the author achieved a competency, on which he was enabled to retire from the turmoils of a theatrical life to the enjoyment of a friendly society and his own thoughts. Yet am I well convinced it is impossible that any one of Shakespeare's dramatic works,—and especially of his tragedies, touching one of which I mean to speak,—ever could be satisfactorily represented upon the stage. Laying aside all other reasons, it would be, in the first place, necessary to have a company such as was never yet assembled, and no money could at any time have procured,—a company, namely, in which every actor should be a man of mind and feeling; for in these dramas every part is a cha-racter fashioned by the touch of Genius; and therefore every part is important. But of no play is this more strictly true than it is of that strange, and subtle, and weird work, *Hamlet:* 'The heartache, And the thousand natural ills the flesh is heir to;' human infirmities, human afflictions, and supernatural agony are so blended,—ques-tions and considerations of Melancholy, of Pathology, Metaphysics, and Demonology are so intertangled,—the powers of man's Will, which are well-nigh almighty, and the dictates of inexorable Fate, are brought into such an appalling yet dim collision, that to wring a meaning from a work else inscrutable requires the exercise of every faculty, and renders it necessary that not an incident should escape the observation, that not a word should be passed over, without being scanned curiously.

Hamlet is, even more peculiarly than *Lear*, or *Macbeth*, or *Othello*, a play for the study. And not this alone; for it is, in good sooth, a work for the high student, who, through the earnestness of his Love, the intensity of his Thought, the pervading purity of his Reason, and the sweep and grasp of his Imagination, is, the while he reads, always thrilled by kindred inspirations,—sometimes visited by dreams, and not left unblessed by visions. To speak in other words, *Hamlet* is essentially a work for the student of Genius. And Genius, I consider with Coleridge, to be the action of Imagination and Reason,—the highest faculty of intellectual man, as contradistinguished from Understanding, that interprets for us the various phenomena of the world in which we live, giving to each its objectivity.

[Page 281.] Consider *Hamlet* in whatsoever light you will, it stands quite alone, most peculiarly apart, from every other play of Shakespeare's. A vast deal has been written upon the subject, and by a great number of commentators, by men born in different countries, educated after different fashions. ... We might hope to see a second Shakespeare, if the world had ever produced a commentator worthy of *Hamlet*. The qualities and faculties such a man should possess would be, indeed, ' rare in their separate excellence, wonderful in their combination.' Such a man as Shakespeare imagined in him to whom his hero bequeathed the task of ' Reporting him and his cause aright To the unsatisfied.'

[Page 325.] For this reason, also, *Hamlet* stands quite alone amongst Shakespeare's plays. The Spirit of Love is weakest in *Hamlet*, and therefore it commands but little human sympathy. Ophelia does love, and she dies. There is a majesty in her gentleness, which you worship with a gush of feeling in her earlier scenes of the play; the painful nature of her appearances, whilst mad, makes you feel that death is a release; and that release comes in an appropriate form,—the gentle, uncomplaining, sorrow-stricken lady dies gently, and without a murmur of bitterness or reproach,—the meek lady is no more, but the tragedy proceeds.

[Page 327.] I may here observe that, for a play so bloody for the English vulgar, and in itself so morally tragic for the scholar and the gentleman, *Hamlet* is for both, in its performance on the stage, strangely beholden to spectacle, and to its comic scenes or snatches of scenes: the visible show of the Ghost, the processions, funeral, squabble at Ophelia's grave, fencing-match, and at the last the ' quarry that cries on, havoc!' have much power over the common spectator. I doubt if he could abide it without these, and without having Polonius buffooned for him, and, to no small extent, Hamlet himself; as he always was whenever I saw the part played, and as the *great critic*, Dr Johnson, would seem to think he ought to be. For he says, ' the pretended madness of Hamlet *causes much mirth ! ! !*'

[Page 330.] In a word, *Hamlet*, to my mind, is essentially a psychological exercise and study. The hero, from whose acts and feelings everything in the drama takes its color and pursues its course, is doubtless insane. But the species of intellectual disturbance, the peculiar form of mental malady, under which he suffers, is of the subtlest character.

HALLAM (1837)

(*Introduction to the Literature of Europe*, vol. ii, p. 201, New York, 1868.)--—
There seems to have been a period of Shakespeare's life when his heart was ill at
ease, and ill content with the world or his own conscience; the memory of hours
misspent, the pang of affection misplaced or unrequited, the experience of man's
worser nature which intercourse with ill-chosen associates, by choice or circumstance, peculiarly teaches; these, as they sank down into the depths of his great
mind, seem not only to have inspired into it the conception of *Lear* and *Timon*, but
that of one primary character, the censurer of mankind. This type is first seen in
the philosophic melancholy of Jaques, gazing with an undiminished serenity, and
with a gayety of fancy, though not of manners, on the follies of the world. It assumes
a graver cast in the exiled Duke of the same play, and next one rather more severe
in the Duke of *Measure for Measure*. In all these, however, it is merely contemplative philosophy. In Hamlet this is mingled with the impulses of a perturbed
heart under the pressure of extraordinary circumstances; it shines no longer, as in
the former characters, with a steady light, but plays in fitful coruscations amid feigned
gayety and extravagance. In Lear it is the flash of sudden inspiration across the
incongruous imagery of madness; in Timon it is obscured by the exaggerations of
misanthropy. These plays all belong to nearly the same period: *As You Like It*
being usually referred to 1600, *Hamlet*, in its altered form, to about 1602, *Timon* to
the same year, *Measure for Measure* to 1603, and *Lear* to 1604. In the later plays
of Shakespeare, especially in *Macbeth* and *The Tempest*, much of moral speculation will be found, but he has never returned to this type of character in the personages.

JONES VERY (1839)

(*Essays and Poems. Hamlet*. Boston, 1839, p. 85.)—If Shakespeare's master-
passion then was, as we have seen it to be, the love of intellectual activity for its
own sake, his continual satisfaction with the simple pleasure of existence must have
made him more than commonly liable to the fear of death, or at least made that
change the great point of interest in his hours of reflection. Often and often must
he have thought, that to be or not to be forever was a question which must be settled; as it is the foundation, and the only foundation, upon which we feel that there
can rest one thought, one feeling, or one purpose worthy of a human soul. Here lie
the materials out of which this remarkable tragedy was built up. From the wrestling of his own soul with the great enemy, comes that depth and mystery which
startles us in Hamlet. It is to this condition that Hamlet has been reduced. . . . .
He fears nothing save the loss of existence. But this thought thunders at the very
base of the cliff on which, shipwrecked of every other hope, he had been thrown. . . . .
[Page 88.] This is the hinge on which his every endeavor turns. Such a thought
as this might well prove more than an equal counterpoise to any incentive to what
we call action. The obscurity that lies over these depths of Hamlet's character arises
from this unique position in which the poet exhibits him; a position which opens to
us the basis of Shakespeare's own being, and which, though dimly visible to all,
is yet familiar to but few. . . . .
[Page 91.] This view will account for Hamlet's indecision. With him the next

world, by the intense action of his thoughts, had become as real as the present; and, whenever this is the case, thought must always at first take precedence of action.

[Page 93.] Even the revenge which suggests itself to Hamlet is not of this world. To others it would assume a character of the most savage enormity, and one from which, of all men, the tender and conscientious prince would soonest shrink. But with him it is as natural as his most ordinary action. He has looked through the slight afflictions of this world, and his prophetic eye is fixed on the limitless extent beyond. Here, and here alone, will the fire of the King's incestuous lust burn unquenched, and the worm of remorse never die.

[Page 98.] We need not go further to show, what will now be apparent, the tendency of Shakespeare to overact this particular part of Hamlet, and thus give it an obscurity from too close a connection with his own mind,—a state so difficult to approach. It is plain that to him the thought of death, and the condition of being to which that change might subject him, would ever be his nearest thoughts; and that, wherever there exists the strong sense of life, these ideas must follow hard upon it. In the question of Hamlet the *thoughts*, as well as the words, have their natural order, when ' To be ' is followed by ' not to be.'

[Page 100.] The thoughts of this soliloquy are not found to belong to a particular part of this play, but to be the spirit of the whole. ' *To be, or not to be*,' is written over its every scene, from the entrance of the Ghost to the rude inscription over the gateway of the churchyard; and whenever we shall have built up in ourselves the true conception of this the greatest of the poets, ' To be, or not to be,' will be found to be chiselled in golden letters on the very keystone of that arch which tells us of his memory.

[Page 103.] In the height of emotion and mental conflict to which he is raised by these contemplations, he finds relief, as in the graveyard and after his first interview with the Ghost, in expressions which seem strangely at variance with each other, but which, in reality, are but natural alternations. So much does he dwell in the world of spirits, that there is a sort of ludicrous aspect upon which his mind seizes as often as it returns to this. ' There is something,' says Scott, ' in my deepest afflictions and most gloomy hours, that compels me to mix with my distresses strange snatches of mirth, which have no mirth in them.'

JOSEPH HUNTER (1845)

(*New Illustrations of the Life, Studies, and Writings of Shakespeare*, London, 1845, vol. ii, p. 205.)—Nothing in the dramatic art ever exceeded the skill with which the First Act is throughout constructed. It is in the highest style of tragic grandeur, making only this one reasonable claim upon our indulgence, that we must lay aside our modern philosophy, and look upon ourselves as belonging to a people who were firm believers in the reality of such spectral appearances. Now, even with all our skepticism, the poet has given to the scenes the spirit of reality. We have neither time nor inclination to doubt. There is the majestic spectre, and we seem to see and hear it. Had the poet proceeded continuously, according to what from this opening may be concluded to have been at first his design, as far as we have reason to believe that he had conceived a design, and shown us the young prince made acquainted with the manner of his father's death by the supernatural visitation, and at the same time engaged to avenge it on his uncle, not daring to do so openly, and thinking that the safest means of accomplishing his object was for a time to counterfeit lunacy, then seeking the opportunity, now opposed from without, now impeded by doubts of his uncle's guilt rising in his own mind, fearful of implicating his mother in the suspicions respecting his father's mode of death, but at length, in full satisfaction of his uncle's guilt, executing the Ghost's behest in some open and solemn manner :—this, with such an under-plot as is here wrought in, of his attachment to Ophelia, the effect of his assumed madness upon her, the impediments arising out of this attachment to the execution of the main purpose, would have formed the plot of as magnificent a tragedy as hath ever been conceived from the days when first the more awful passions were represented on the stage.

It would have afforded also scope for all that diversity of character and that variety of incident which we find in the play as it now is, even, if that were thought a suitable scene for such a drama, to the introduction of the play within the play, by which Hamlet seeks to convince himself of his uncle's guilt; scope also for all those striking scenes and speeches, to which, and not to that in which lies the chief and highest excellence of dramatic writing, *Hamlet* owes that high popularity it has so long maintained. No one can be insensible to the power of such a composition as this; and yet, of all the greater works, may not this be considered as that which is, on the whole, least honorable to him, showing us what he could do, and showing us also what a noble promise he has left unfulfilled?

To borrow an expression from the language of criticism in a sister art, the piece is *spotty*. The spots are beautiful when contemplated in themselves, still they are but spots.

There is also more by which the moral sense is offended in this play than in any other; offended, I mean, not with the characters, but with the author. The idea of a human being seeking to avenge a great and unpunished crime by the assassination of the criminal, even when we see that it involves parricide, however at variance it may be with Christian feeling, does not offend, because we see it to be essential to the very existence of such a story, and to belong to the history as it is found in the old chronicles of Denmark; but to make Hamlet forbear to execute his purpose when a favorable opportunity is presented, for the reason there given, is hideous, and more the affair of the poet than the historian. But the still greater offence is the introduction of Ophelia in a state of mind which, if ever it did exist in nature, ought to be screened from every human eye, nor should the sex be profaned by the remotest suspicion of its possible existence.

We have, also, here a pandering to the corrupt English taste in tragedy. 'An English audience at a tragedy love a clear stage;' and certainly in *Hamlet* they may be gratified. We start with the ghost of a murdered king; then there die the succeeding King, the Queen, Hamlet, Polonius and his two children Laertes and Ophelia, Rosencrantz, and Guildenstern. Of the conspicuous characters only Horatio is left alive. An acquaintance with the ancient tragedy would have taught him that this slaughter is committed under an erroneous impression of the requisites of tragedy for effect, and the true source of the pleasure we derive from it. Indeed, it is but too manifest that Shakespeare had a finer idea of comedy than of tragedy; great, however, in both.

The introduction of Osric and Fortinbras, new characters, towards the close of the play, is contrary to all rule; and though Shakespeare may be allowed to disregard the rules of dramatic art, and to be a law to himself, yet it may be submitted to the judgement of any one, whether it would not have been well for him to have conformed himself to the rule in this instance, especially in reference to the introduction of such a character as Osric. Fortinbras may be tolerated, as Horatio must have some one to listen to his summing up.

QUARTERLY REVIEW (1847)

(Vol. lxxix, 1847, p. 318.)—Every word which drops from the lips of Shakespeare's personages is the appropriate expression of their inward feelings; and owing to that characteristic we have mentioned of the mighty master,—that he will not stoop to be his own expositor in violation of nature,—we miss the spirit in which they speak unless we note accurately their position at the time. It is from the neglect of this precaution that the opening of *Hamlet*, which is alive with excitement, striking contrasts, and the most delicate touches of nature, seems to have been taken by the editors, old and new, for nothing more than an unimpassioned conversation between two sentinels. Twice had Bernardo been encountered on the platform by the Ghost of the King, and he is now for the third time advancing at midnight to the scene of the apparition, in the belief that he will again behold the dreaded spectre which had 'almost distilled him to jelly with the act of fear.' In this state of mind he would be startled at every sight and sound,—at the sighing of the wind, and the shadows cast by the moon. Thus alive to apprehension, he hears advancing footsteps; and the question, 'Who's there?' is, to our ear, the sudden, instinctive exclamation of uncontrollable alarm, and not the ordinary challenge between one sentinel and another. Fear, by concentrating the senses, endows them with a supernatural acuteness; and Shakespeare was not unmindful of the fact when he made the listening, breathless Bernardo to be first conscious of their mutual approach. Francisco, the sentinel on duty, not recognizing a comrade in the terrified voice which hails him, replies: '—— Nay, answer *me;* stand and unfold *yourself.*' But the moment Bernardo, reassured at hearing him speak, calls out the watchword, 'Long live the king!' in his habitual tones, the sentinel knows his fellow, and greets him by name. What follows is an exquisite specimen of Shakespeare's attention to the subtlest minutiæ. He shows us Bernardo eager with expectation, feverish to anticipate the appearance of the Ghost, and to keep the secret from extending further, by a circumstance that would be the certain consequence,—that he goes earlier than usual, and arrives at his post with unwonted punctuality. 'You come most carefully upon your hour,' says Francisco. And how nicely true to nature is the rejoinder of Bernardo, that it has already struck! He wishes to repel the notion that he is before his accustomed time, for, with a guilty feeling, he fears to be suspected. He then bids Francisco get to bed; and in the answer of Francisco we have another slight trait which strikingly exemplifies how careful Shakespeare was to preserve entire consistency in the conduct of his characters :—

> '*Fran.* For this relief much thanks. 'Tis bitter cold,
>   *And I am sick at heart.*'

And *because* he is sick at heart, absorbed in the contemplation of his individual griefs, he has not remarked the ill-concealed agitation of Bernardo. With a mind at ease, his attention would have been excited and his curiosity aroused. As he is going, Bernardo asks, with an off-hand air of assumed indifference, 'Have you had quiet guard?'—an inquiry he dares not make in a formal way, in direct conversation, lest he should betray his anxiety. The assurance he receives,—'Not a mouse stirring,'—in relieving him as to the hours past, fixes his thoughts the more exclusively on the coming moments. He has no wish to be left alone. He is impatien to be joined by his companions, and his parting word to Francisco is—

> ' Well, good night.
> If you do meet Horatio and Marcellus,
> The rivals of my watch, bid them make haste.'

Francisco has scarcely left Bernardo, when, hearing Horatio and Marcellus coming, he challenges them :—' Stand, ho ! Who is there ?' The few words which pass in the nex half-page, commonplace as they appear to the inattentive reader, are strokes of character the finest and the most expressive. Marcellus had been Bernardo's associate on the two preceding nights, and he shares Bernardo's solicitude. Horatio is skeptical about the Ghost, and maintains it to be a delusion. The difference of their emotions is seen in their replies to the interrogation of the sentinel. Horatio, light-hearted and disengaged, is the first to answer. He calls out quickly and buoyantly, ' Friends to this ground.' With slow solemnity, Marcellus adds, ' And liegemen to the Dane.' His mind is upon the mysterious phantom. He marvels what it forbodes. His vague suspicion that it portends some treason or misfortune to the State leads him to join to the careless exclamation of Horatio a protestation of their loyalty. Following the current of his thoughts, he is lost in meditation ; he is unconscious of the presence of Francisco, who has come up with them ; and when the latter says, ' Give you good night,' he exclaims, like one awakened from a trance, ' O ! farewell, honest soldier !' On any other supposition the ejaculation would be unmeaning, and it is conclusive to show what Shakespeare intended. The reverie of Marcellus once broken, he turns from fruitless speculation to the business of the night ; and, in the same breath in which he bids Francisco farewell, inquires who has relieved him, that he may be satisfied it is no other than his own partner, Bernardo. Francisco goes his way. Marcellus shouts, ' Holloa ! Bernardo !' ' Say,' returns Bernardo, without stopping to reply directly to the salutation. ' What ! is Horatio there ?' Horatio is the scholar that is to accost the Ghost ; he is the superior on whom both place their reliance, and Bernardo is all eagerness to learn that he has not failed in his appointment. Horatio speaks for himself, and continues to manifest his incredulity in his jocular rejoinder, ' A piece of him.' Bernardo, overjoyed to be relieved of his solitude, receives them with such rapturous warmth,— ' Welcome, Horatio ! welcome, good Marcellus !'—that Marcellus imagines from his excited manner that the Ghost has visited him already. ' What,' he says, not so much inquiringly as taking it for granted,—' What, has this thing appear'd again to-night ?' The answer of Bernardo, ' I have seen nothing,' brings Marcellus to Horatio's disbelief of the whole story : ' Horatio says 'tis but our fantasy,' &c.

The compression of the scene is wonderful, and there is, perhaps, no passage in any drama which exhibits equal variety in the same space. The fright of Bernardo, his suppressed emotion, his dislike to be by himself, the unconsciousness of Francisco, the levity of Horatio, the abstraction and highly wrought feelings of Marcellus, the intense excitement in the greeting with Bernardo, are all brought out clear and well defined in about twenty lines. Condensed and rapid as is the dialogue, it is complete. Nothing is omitted that was proper to the occasion. Nor is it the least remarkable part of the art that, in the midst of so much animation, and the play and conflict of so many passions, there is not a tinge of exaggeration. The soberness of reality is preserved throughout.

[Page 333.] The universality of Shakespeare's genius is in some sort reflected in Hamlet. He has a mind wise and witty, abstract and practical ; the utmost reach of philosophical contemplation is mingled with the most penetrating sagacity in the affairs of life; playful jest, biting satire, sparkling repartee, with the darkest and deepest thoughts that can agitate man. He exercises all his various faculties with surprising readiness. He passes without an effort 'from grave to gay, from lively to severe,'—from his everyday character to personated lunacy. He divines, with the rapidity of lightning, the nature and motives of those who are brought into contact with him; fits in a moment his bearing and retorts to their individual peculiarities; is equally at home whether he is mocking Polonius with hidden raillery, or dissipating Ophelia's dream of love, or crushing the sponges with sarcasm and invective, or talking euphuism with Osric, and satirising while he talks it; whether he is uttering wise maxims, or welcoming the players with facetious graciousness,—probing the inmost souls of others, or sounding the mysteries of his own. His philosophy stands out conspicuous among the brilliant faculties which contend for the mastery. It is the quality which gives weight and dignity to the rest. It intermingles with all his actions. He traces the most trifling incidents up to their general laws. His natural disposition is to lose himself in contemplation. He goes thinking out of the world. The commonest ideas that pass through his mind are invested with a wonderful freshness and originality. His meditations in the churchyard are on the trite notion that all ambition leads but to the grave. But what condensation, what variety, what picturesqueness, what intense, unmitigated gloom! It it is the finest sermon that was ever preached against the vanities of life.

So far, we imagine, all are agreed. But the motives which induce Hamlet to defer his revenge are still, and perhaps will ever remain, debateable ground. The favorite doctrine of late is that the thinking part of Hamlet predominated over the active,— that he was as weak and vacillating in performance as he was great in speculation. If this theory were borne out by his general conduct, it would no doubt amply account for his procrastination; but there is nothing to countenance, and much to refute, the idea. Shakespeare has endowed him with a vast energy of will. There could be no sterner resolve than to abandon every purpose of existence, that he might devote himself, unfettered, to his revenge; nor was ever resolution better observed. He breaks through his passion for Ophelia, and keeps it down, under the most trying circumstances, with such inflexible firmness, that an eloquent critic has seriously questioned whether his attachment was real. The determination of his character appears again at the death of Polonius. An indecisive mind would have been shocked, if not terrified, at the deed. Hamlet dismisses him with a few contemptuous words, as a man would brush away a fly. He talks with even greater indifference of Rosencrantz and Guildenstern, whom he sends 'to sudden death, not shriving-time allowed.' He has on these, and, indeed, on all occasions, a short and absolute way which only belongs to resolute souls. The features developed in his very hesitation to kill the King are inconsistent with the notion that his hand refuses to perform what his head contrives. He is always trying to persuade himself into a conviction that it is his duty, instead of seeking for evasions.* He is seized with a

---

* His reasons for not killing the King when he is praying have been held to be an excuse. But if Shakespeare had anticipated the criticism, he could not have guarded against it more effectually. Hamlet has just uttered the soliloquy:

'——Now could I drink hot blood,
And do such bitter business as the day
Would quake to look on.'

In this frame he passes his uncle's closet, and is for once, at least, equal to any emergency. His first

savage joy when the Play supplies him with indubitable proof of his uncle's guilt. His language, then, to Horatio is:

> '——is't not perfect conscience
> To quit him with this arm?'

He wants, it is clear, neither will nor nerve to strike the blow. There is, perhaps, one supposition that will satisfy all the phenomena, and it has, to us, the recommendation that we think it is the solution suggested by Shakespeare himself. Hamlet, in a soliloquy, charges the delay on,—

> ' Bestial oblivion, or some craven scruple
> Of thinking too precisely on th' event.'

The oblivion is merely the effect of the primary cause,—' the craven scruple,'—the conscience which renders him a coward. His uncle, after all, is King; he is the brother of his father, and the husband of his mother, and it was inevitable that he should shrink, in his cooler moments, from becoming his assassin. His hatred to his uncle, who has disgraced his family, and disappointed his ambition, gives him personal inducements to revenge, which further blunt his purpose by leading him to doubt the purity of his motives. The admonition of the Ghost to him is, not to taint his mind in the prosecution of his end; and no sooner has the Ghost vanished than Hamlet, invoking the aid of supernatural powers, exclaims:

> ' O all you host of heaven ! O earth ! what else?
> And shall I couple hell? O, fie !

But the hell, whose support he rejects, is for ever returning to his mind and startling his conscience. It is this that makes him wish for the confirmation of the Play, for evil spirits may have abused him. It is this which begets the apathy he terms oblivion, for inaction affords relief to doubt. It is this which produces his inconsistencies, for conscience calls him different ways; and when he obeys in one direction he is haunted by the feeling that he should have gone in the other. If he contemplated the performance of a deed which looks outwardly more like murder than judicial retribution, he trembles lest, after all, he should be perpetrating an unnatural crime; or if, on the other hand, he turns to view his uncle's misdeeds, he fancies there is more of cowardly scrupulosity than justice in his backwardness, and he abounds in self-reproaches at the weakness of his hesitation. And thus he might for ever have halted between two opinions if the King himself, by filling up the measure of his iniquities, had not swept away his scruples.

HUDSON (1848)

(*Lectures on Shakespeare*, New York, 1848. Second edition, vol. ii, p. 101.)— Properly speaking, therefore, Hamlet lacks not force of will, as some have argued, but only force of self-will; that is, his will is strictly subjected to his reason and conscience, and is of course powerless when it comes in conflict with them; where

---

thought is to kill him at his devotions; his second, that in that case Claudius will go to heaven. Instantly his father's sufferings rise into his mind; he contrasts the happy future of the criminal with the purgatory of the victim, and the contemplation exasperates him into a genuine desire for a fuller revenge. The threat relieves him from the reproach of inactivity, and he falls back into his former self.

they impede not his volitions he seems, as hath been said, all will. We are apt to estimate men's force of will according to what they do; but we ought often to estimate it according to what they do *not* do; for to hold still often requires much greater strength of will than to go ahead; and the peculiarity of this representation consists in the hero's being so placed that his will has its proper exercise, not so much in acting as in thinking. In this way the working of his whole mind is rendered as anomalous as his situation, which is just what the subject demands. Moreover, in the perfect harmony of the will and the reason, force of will would naturally disappear altogether; for, in that case, the will being entirely subject to the law, nothing but the law would be visible in our conduct; and yet to preserve or restore this harmony of will and reason is undoubtedly the greatest achievement in human power. Thus, the highest possible exercise of will is in renouncing itself and taking the law instead; so that, paradoxical as it may seem, he may be justly said to have most strength of will who has, or rather *shows*, none at all. Hamlet is equal to the performance of any duty, but not to the reconciliation of incompatible duties, and he cannot act for the simple reason that he has equal 'respect unto all' the duties of his situation. In a word, his inability is purely of a moral, not of a complexional kind, and this inability is only another name for the highest sort of power.

[Page 103.] Hamlet, it is true, is continually charging the fault of his situation on himself. Herein is involved one of the finest strokes in the whole delineation. True virtue never publishes itself; it does not even know itself: radiating from the heart through all the functions of life, its transpirations are so free and smooth and deep as to escape the ear of consciousness. Hence people are generally aware of their virtue in proportion as they have it *not*. We are apt to estimate the merit of our good deeds according to the struggles we make in doing them; whereas, the greater our virtue, the less we shall have to struggle in order to do them, and it is purely the weakness and imperfection of our virtue that makes it so hard for us to do well. Accordingly, we find that he who does no duty without being goaded up to it is conscious of much more virtue than he has; while he who does every duty as a thing of course, and a matter of delight, is unconscious of his virtue, simply because he has so much of it.

Moreover, in his conflict of duties, Hamlet naturally thinks he is taking the wrong one; for the calls of the claim he meets are hushed by satisfaction, while the calls of the claim he neglects are increased by disappointment. Thus the motives which he resists out-tongue those which he obeys, so that he hears nothing but the voice of the duty he omits. We are, of course, insensible of the current with which we move; but we are made sensible of the current against which we move by the very struggle it costs. In this way Hamlet comes to mistake his scruples of conscience for want of conscience, and from his very sensitiveness of principle tries to reason himself into a conviction of guilt. If, however, he were really guilty of what he accuses himself, he would be trying to find or make excuses wherewith to opiate his conscience. For the bad naturally try to hide their badness, the good their goodness, from themselves; for which cause the former seek narcotics, the latter stimulants, for their consciences. The good man is apt to think he has not conscience enough, because it does not trouble him; the bad man naturally thinks he has more conscience than he needs, because it troubles him all the while,—which accounts for the well-known readiness of bad men to supply their neighbors with conscience.

[Page 112.] The idea of Hamlet is conscious plenitude of intellect, united with exceeding fineness and fulness of sensibility, and guided by a predominant sentiment of moral rectitude.

STRACHEY (1848)

(*Shakespeare's Hamlet: An Attempt to find the Key to a great Moral Problem by Methodical Analysis of the Play.* London, 1848, p. 44.)—Observe how Hamlet's generalisations are really drawn from the excessive brooding over· his own character and circumstances, and only afterwards applied to the men and things about him. It is plainly he himself who is the original of this his description of the man in whom either nature or circumstances have unduly developed some one tendency of the character, to the injury of the proper and rational balance and harmony of the whole, and who, in consequence of this one defect, for which he is not responsible, and should be rather pitied than blamed, is looked on with disparagement by the world, however excellent all his other qualities may be. Coleridge has not noticed how exactly this description agrees with his own estimate and explanation of Hamlet's character, and the unobserved coincidence is a strong confirmation, if any can be needed, of the true insight of the great critic.

[Page 51.] The development of Hamlet's character is so rapid, that it cannot be considered as the mere ordinary opening out of the story and action of the play. The successive appearances of Hamlet on the stage are not (as in the case of other characters) merely the successive pages in a book, in which we read what has been written there long before; but the enormously quick growth, before our very eyes, of a plant subjected to the forcing action of tropical rain and sun. In all Shakespeare's varieties of characters there is none in which he has chosen to draw the *man of genius* so purely and adequately as in Hamlet; in Hamlet we see genius in itself, and not as it appears when its possessor is employing it in the accomplishment of some outward end; and this genius bursts forth with a sudden and prodigious expansion, into the regions of the pure intellect, as soon as its quiet course through its previous channel of the ordinary life of a brave, refined, and noble-minded prince-royal was violently stopped up by the circumstances with which we are familiar. Hamlet now shows himself in that character which is properly,—though not according to the popular appropriation of the word,—called *skeptical.* Partly because he is cut off from all legitimate practical outlet for his intellectual energies, partly from the instinctive desire to turn away from the harrowing contemplation of himself and his circumstances, he puts himself into the attitude of a bystander and *looker-on* (σκέπτικος) in the midst of the bustling world around him. And like other such skeptics he finds it more and more difficult to *act*, as his knowledge becomes more and more comprehensive and circular,—to take a *part* in the affairs of a world of which he seems to see the *whole;* and like them, too, he throws a satirical tone into his observations on men, who, however inferior to him in intellect, are always reminding him that he is dreaming while they are acting.

[Page 63.] I have endeavored already to point out that we can neither assert that Hamlet is mad, nor that his mind is perfectly healthy; much confusion and misapprehension about the character of Hamlet have arisen from thus attempting an impossible simplification of what is most complex. There are more things in heaven and earth than are dreamt of in the philosophy of the small critic who thinks he has only to rule two columns, with 'mad' at the top of one, and 'sane' at the top of the other, and then to put the name of Hamlet in one of the two. Hamlet, like all real men, and especially men such as he, has a character made up of many elements, ramifying themselves in many directions, some being healthy and some diseased, and intertwined now in harmony, now in contradiction with each other. And, accordingly, it presents different aspects to different observers, who look from opposite points of view, though each with considerable qualifications for judging rightly. We have just seen the view taken by Ophelia, whose deep love, and woman's tact and sentiment, can best appreciate the finer and more delicate features of Hamlet's character, though she, perhaps, exaggerates the extent of the untuning of his reason, from the influence of her own fears and of her father's declaration that he had gone mad. The shrewd, clear-headed King, with his wits sharpened by anxiety, considers the question from the side of its practical bearing on his own interests, and sees that as far as these are concerned Hamlet is not mad, but most dangerously sane.

[Page 77.] The speeches of the Ghost, and of the King and Queen in the Interlude, with the real Queen's behavior at the latter, give sufficient, though negative, evidence of her innocence of the murder; while Hamlet's whole conduct in the scene [with his mother] would be preposterous if he had any doubt of that innocence;—for how could he reprove the guilt of the second marriage, and pass over that of the murder, if the Queen had been a partaker in this? She must have known facts which might reasonably excite her suspicions after the event, and perhaps, from her neither pressing for an explanation, nor attempting a refutation of Hamlet's implied charge against her present husband, such suspicions may have passed through her mind. But nothing is more universal (though often nothing more puzzling) than that characteristic of the female mind which, even in grave and thoughtful women, and much more in the light and trifling, enables them to receive impressions, and make observations, without bringing them before their minds in distinct consciousness. Women feel and act with an intuitive wisdom far superior to that of men, but they have not the same power of reflecting on their feelings and acts, and translating them into the shape of *thoughts*. The Queen's want of any clear and distinct views and opinions on this occasion is in perfect keeping with her whole character, and at the same time it helps the action of the Play far better than her admission to a knowledge of Hamlet's designs, for it would have been madness for him to have trusted them with so weak a person, and one so much under the influence of the King.

[Page 84.] There is something very poetical in Ophelia sharing her Hamlet's destiny, even in the very form,—a mind diseased,—in which it has come upon him. Her pure and selfless love reflects even this state of her beloved; no cup is so bitter but that if it is poured out for him she will drink it with him. Nay, she, the gentle, unresisting woman, drains to the dregs that which his masculine hand can push aside (at least for a time) when he has but tasted it. United as their hearts were by love, this madness of Ophelia brings her closer to Hamlet than any prosperity could have done. So thoroughly feminine a being could never have *understood* the self-conscious wretchedness of Hamlet's gloomy moods, but now she is made to *feel* it in her own person. I do not, of course, mean that this would practically be an additional qualification for her as a wife to Hamlet, but that it heightens to the utmost the beauty of the tragic picture of a love which is to end, not in marriage, but in death. There is more to be felt than to be said in the study of Ophelia's character, just because she is a creation of such perfectly feminine proportions and beauty.

[Page 100.] Hamlet has come once more into the King's presence, not with any plan for the execution of his just vengeance, but with what is much better, the faith that an opportunity will present itself, and the resolution to seize it instantly. It does present itself, when he finds that he has in his hand a deadly weapon, unbated and envenomed by the King's own device, and when at the same moment he is spurred on by hearing that his mother and himself are already poisoned; he sees that the hour is come, recognizes the command he waited for, and strikes the blow.

If this be the true view of the closing act of Hamlet's career (and, as I have asked before, does any other explain all the circumstances equally well ?), we must not only utterly reject the notion that Hamlet kills the King at last to revenge himself and not his father,—though we may allow that the treachery to himself helped to point the spur which was necessary to urge him on to instant action,—but we must also come to the conclusion which I proposed to prove by this inquiry into the whole plot and purpose of the Play,—that Hamlet does *not*, as Coleridge and other great critics have asserted, ' delay action till action is of no use, and die the victim of mere circumstance and accident.' True it is that he delays action till it is of no use to himself, and has allowed his chains to hang on him till the time for *enjoying* liberty and life is past: and it is doubtless a part of the moral of the Play that we should recognize in this defect in Hamlet's character the origin of his tragic and untimely fate. He *ought* to have lived to enjoy his triumph, but surely he has triumphed, though only in death. If he had not triumphed, if he had not done his work before the night fell, but had been a mere idler and dreamer to the last, could we part from him with any feeling but that of the kind of pity which is half blame and contempt ? And is not our actual feeling, on the contrary, that of respect as well as sympathy ? Do we not heartily respond to Horatio's

> Now cracks a noble heart. Good night, sweet prince ;
> And flights of angels sing thee to thy rest !'

There is something so unpretending, and even homely (if I may apply the word to such a state of things) in the circumstances of Hamlet's death, that it does not strike us obviously that he dies for the cause to which he has been called to be the champion. Yet so it is.

REV. DR MOZLEY (1849)

(*The Christian Remembrancer*, vol. xvii, January, 1849, p. 174.*)—[After the revelation by the Ghost, Hamlet] has a vivid sense of a particular wrong which has been committed, and he vows, as a religious task, its punishment. But now comes in the philosophical element in him. It occurs to him that, after all, this dreadful act, carried out with such successful artifice and self-possession, is but a sample of a vast system of wrong and injustice in this visible state of things. The King and Queen represent to his mind a great evil power, or tyranny, resident in the system. The court of Denmark, the scene of their crime and prosperity, is the world; its business and festivity, in which his father's fate is forgotten, the world's stir and bustle burying thought, and covering up wrong as soon as done; its courtiers, the idle and careless mass of mankind who look on as spectators of injustice, and do not concern themselves with it. Now all things expand to his mind's eye, and no one

---

* For the admirable article from which these extracts are made I am indebted to my friend, D*r* INGLEBY. ED.

wrong deed retains him; he rises from the single to the generic, and from the concrete to the abstract; and he thinks of a system, and a wholesale scheme of things beneath the sun. He can think of nothing but he instantly thinks of the whole world. Denmark is a prison, and the world is a prison. If the world is grown honest, then is doomsday near.

> 'The time is out of joint;—O cursed spite
> That ever I was born to set it right.'

In all his soliloquies he deals in generals, and harps upon the discords and burdens in the order of things here as a whole. Upon this generalizing vein an unsettlement of will with respect to his task of vengeance immediately follows. For, after all (he seems to say), what is the good of it when it is done? This deed of violence is only one out of a thousand. You may adjust a particular case, but the wrong system goes on; it is out of your reach; do what you can you cannot touch it; and true evil, impalpable and ubiquitous, still mocks you like the air. To set one case right is only to commit yourself to do the same with respect to others, *ad infinitum*, and to enter upon an impossible task. Thus the work of vengeance lags; he takes it up and lays it down again, according to his humor; he plays with it, and, when he might easily execute it, puts it off for an absurd reason, which had he been practically earnest would not have weighed a feather with him. Upon the basis of the philosopher he erects the child again; an assumed volatility, waywardness, and indifference express the hopelessness which a large survey of things has produced in him. The lofty ruminator within exhibits himself as a jester and an oddity without; and, not content with levity, he assumes madness, as if to enable himself to enjoy a fantastic isolation from the world and human society altogether, and to live alone within himself. And when at last he does execute his work, he seems to do it by chance, and from the humor of the moment more than from any constancy of original purpose. Such appears the explanation of Hamlet's weakness and irresoluteness. So true is it that a mind may easily be too large for effectiveness, and energy suffer from an expansion of the field of view. . . . .

For success in action a certain narrowness and confinement of mind is indeed almost requisite. If a man is to do any work well, he must be possessed with the idea of that work's importance. He has this idea of necessity strongly so long as the particular scene in which he is is the whole world to him, and therefore, while he thinks this, he is effective; but once enlarge his vision, and show him that his field of labor is only the same with a thousand others, and that he himself is one of a class containing thousands; make him, that is to say, realize the world and its vastness, and he ceases to be absorbed in his task, and is tempted to unconcern and disrelish for it; and thus the class of what are called able men, in the departments of public business or trade, may be observed as a whole to have the idea of the immense importance of their several departments even to excess, and advantageously so,—a wise providence, securing, by the exclusive pretensions of each department of the world's business, a most effective pledge for the safe and careful administration of the whole, and converting the ignorance and narrowness of mankind individually to their great benefit as a body.

The stimulus of narrowness, then, being requisite for vigor in action, Hamlet wants vigor, because he is without it. His want of vigor does not proceed from a want of passion, for he has plenty of that, but from a disproportionate largeness of intellect. He has not too little feeling, but too much thought. He is never satisfied with, never rests in, feeling, however strong, but carries it up immediately into the intellectual sphere. The quickest impulse, by some twist of his mind, takes immediately the expansive form of some general contemplation. He is always thinking of the whole of things, and any one work seems nothing. As the air we breathe is not all air, and true courage has an ingredient of fear in it, the intellect should part with something of its own nature to qualify itself as proper human intellect. It should yoke itself contentedly with a wholesome narrowness in a compound, practical, and intellectual being. Its largeness tends, without such check, to feebleness. The mind of Hamlet lies all abroad, like the sea,—a universal reflector, but wanting the self-moving principle. Musing, reflection, and irony upon all the world supersede action, and a task evaporates in philosophy.

MRS LEWES (1860)

(*The Mill on the Floss*, Book VI, chapter vi, p. 355. New York, 1860.)—' Character,' says Novalis, in one of his questionable aphorisms—' character is destiny.' But not the whole of our destiny. Hamlet, Prince of Denmark, was speculative and irresolute, and we have a great tragedy in consequence. But if his father had lived to a good old age, and his uncle had died an early death, we can conceive Hamlet's having married Ophelia, and got through life with a reputation of sanity, notwithstanding many soliloquies, and some moody sarcasms towards the fair daughter of Polonius, to say nothing of the frankest incivility to his father-in-law.

KENNY (1864)

(*The Life and Genius of Shakespeare*, London, 1864, p. 379.)—We cannot help thinking that the perplexity to which we are thus exposed is founded on conditions which, from their very nature, are more or less irremovable. It has its origin, as it seems to us, in two sources. It is owing, in the first place, to the essential character of the work itself; and in the second place it arises, in no small degree, from the large license which the poet has allowed himself in dealing with his intrinsically obscure and disordered materials.

All Nature has its impenetrable secrets, and there seems to be no reason why the poet should not restore to us any of the accidental forms of this universal mysteriousness. The world of art, like the world of real life, may have its obscure recesses, its vague instincts, its undeveloped passions, its unknown motives, its half-formed judgements, its wild aberrations, its momentary caprices. The mood of Hamlet is necessarily an extraordinary and an unaccountable mood. In him exceptional influences agitate an exceptional temperament. He is wayward, fitful, excited, horror-stricken. The foundations of his being are unseated. His intellect and his will are ajar and unbalanced. He has become an exception to the common forms of humanity. The poet, in his turn struck with this strange figure, seems to have resolved on bringing its special peculiarities into special prominence, and the story which he dramatised afforded him the most ample opportunity of accomplishing this design. Hamlet is not only in reality agitated and bewildered, but he is led to adopt the disguise of a feigned madness, and he is thus perpetually intensifying and distorting the peculiarities of an already over-excited imagination. It was, we think, inevitable that a composition which attempted to follow the workings of so unusual an individuality should itself seem abrupt and capricious; and this natural effect of the scene is still further deepened, not only by the exceptionally large genius, but by the exceptionally negligent workmanship, of the poet. . . . .

We believe we can discover in the history of the drama a further reason why its details were not always perfectly harmonised. It was written under two different and somewhat conflicting influences. The poet throughout many portions of its composition had, no doubt, the old story which formed its groundwork directly present to his mind; but he did not apparently always clearly distinguish between the impressions in his memory and the creations of his imagination, and the result is, that some of his incidents now seem to his readers more or less inexplicable or discordant.

[Page 384.] *Hamlet* is, perhaps, of all the plays of Shakespeare the one which a great actor would find most difficult to embody in an ideally complete form. It would, we think, be a mistake to attempt to elaborate its multiform details into any distinctly harmonious unity. Its whole action is devious, violent, spasmodic. Its distempered, inconstant irritability is its very essence. Its only order is the mani-festation of a wholly disordered energy. It is a type of the endless perplexity with which man, stripped of the hopes and illusions of this life, harassed and oppressed by the immediate sense of his own helplessness and isolation, stands face to face with the silent and immovable world of destiny. In it the agony of an individual mind grows to the dimensions of the universe; and the genius of the poet himself, regardless of the passing and somewhat incongruous incidents with which it deals, rises before our astonished vision, apparently as illimitable and inexhaustible as the mystery which it unfolds.

It is manifest that *Hamlet* does not solve, or even attempt to solve, the riddle of life. It only serves to present the problem in its most vivid and most dramatic intensity. The poet reproduces Nature; he is in no way admitted into the secret of the mystery beyond Nature; he could not penetrate it; he only knew of the in-finite longings and the infinite misgivings with which its presence fills the human heart.

[Page 385.] *Hamlet* is, in some sense, Shakespeare's most typical work. In no other of his dramas does his highest personality seem to blend so closely with his highest genius. It is throughout informed with his skepticism, his melancholy, his ever-present sense of the shadowiness and the fleetingness of life. He has given us more artistically complete and harmonious creations. His absolute imagination is, perhaps, more distinctly displayed in the real madness of King Lear than in the feigned madness, or the fitful and disordered impulses, of the Danish Prince. But the very rapidity and extravagance of these moods help to produce their own pecu-liar dramatic effect. Wonder and mystery are the strongest and most abiding ele-ments in all human interest; and, under this universal condition of our nature, *Hamlet*, with its unexplained and inexplicable singularities, and even inconsistencies, will most probably for ever remain the most remarkable and the most enthralling of all the works of mortal hands.

HUDSON (1870)

(*Introduction to Hamlet*, Boston, 1870, p. 512.)—Hamlet himself has caused more of perplexity and discussion than any other character in the whole range of art. The charm of his mind and person amounts to an almost universal fascination; and he has been well described as 'a concentration of all the interests that belong to humanity.' I have learned by experience that one seems to understand him better after a little study than after a great deal; and that the less one sees into him the more apt one is to think he sees through him; in which respect he is indeed like Nature herself. One man considers Hamlet great, but wicked; another good, but weak; a third, that he lacks courage, and dare not act; a fourth, that he has too much intellect for his will, and so reflects away the time of action; some conclude his madness half genuine; others, that it is wholly feigned. Doubtless there are facts in the delineation which, considered by themselves, would sustain any one of these views; but none of them seems reconcilable with all the facts taken together. Yet, notwithstanding this diversity of opinions, all agree in thinking of Hamlet as an actual person. It is easy to invest with plausibility almost any theory respecting him, but very hard to make any theory comprehend the whole subject; and while all are impressed with the truth of the character, no one is satisfied with another's explanation of it. The question is, Why such unanimity as to his being a man, and at the same time such diversity as to what sort of a man he is?

(*Shakespeare : his Life, Art, and Characters.* Boston, 1872, vol. ii, p. 268.)— The Ghost calls for revenge, but specifies no particular mode of revenge. Hamlet naturally supposes the meaning to be payment in kind,—'an eye for an eye, and a tooth for a tooth.' Is this, from Hamlet's own moral point of view, right? It is nothing less than to kill at once his uncle, his mother's husband, and his king; and this, not in a judicial manner, but by assassination. How shall he justify such a deed to the world? how vindicate himself from the very crime which he must allege against another? For, as he cannot subpœna the Ghost, the evidence on which he is to act is available only in the court of his own conscience. To serve any good end, the deed must so stand in the public eye as it does in his own; else he will be in effect setting an example of murder, not of justice. And the crown will seem to be his real motive, duty but a pretence. Can a man of his 'large discourse, looking before and after,' be expected to act thus? His understanding seems indeed to be convinced, but yet I suspect he feels a diviner power in the shape of a 'still small voice' drawing the other way. He thinks he ought to do the thing, resolves that he will do it, blames himself for not doing it; still, an unspoken law, deeper and stronger than conviction, withholds him. And his not doing it he imputes to 'craven scruples,' or some ignoble weakness in himself; just as the best men sometimes charge themselves with acting only from a selfish fear of punishment, while their whole course of life shows them to be actuated by a disinterested love of virtue, and that they would rather be punished for doing right than rewarded for doing wrong.

[Page 271.] Will it be said that, if strength of conscience is what keeps him from killing the King, then the same strength should enable him to abandon the purpose altogether? I answer, that his mind is hedged off by similar scruples from that side also. Conscience urges him different ways, and whichever way he takes he is still haunted by the feeling that he ought to have taken the other. His will is indeed distracted between two opposing duties; so that his conscience is divided, not merely against his understanding, but against itself; while that very distraction operates as a stimulus to his intellect. Nor can I think it just to speak of his course as a failure. Morally, he succeeds, though, to be sure, at the cost of his own life. He falls, as many others have fallen, a martyr to his own rectitude and elevation of soul. It is a triumph of the noblest virtue, through the most trying struggles, and over temptation in the most imposing form. And it should be noted further, that whenever he sees or even thinks of the King his calmness instantly forsakes him, and a fury of madness takes possession of him, throwing his mind into the wildest exorbitancy. The best instance of this is in the horrid excuses which he raves out for sparing the King when he finds him praying; where it is plainly neither his moral reason nor his understanding, but simply his madness, that speaks, and this too in its fiercest strain.

[Page 276.] Horatio is one of the very noblest and most beautiful of Shakespeare's male characters : and there is not a single loose stitch in his make-up; he is at all times superbly self-contained; he feels deeply, but never gushes nor runs over; as true as a diamond, as modest as a virgin, and utterly unselfish; a most manly soul, full alike of strength, tenderness, and solidity. But he moves so quietly in the drama that his rare traits of character have hardly had justice done them. Should we undertake to go through the play without him, we might then feel how much of the best spirit and impression of the scenes is owing to his presence. He is the medium whereby many of the hero's finest and noblest qualities are conveyed to us, yet himself so clear and simple and transparent that he scarcely catches the attention. . . . . The great charm of Horatio's unselfishness is that he seems not to be himself in the least aware of it; 'as one, in suffering all, that suffers nothing.' His mild skepticism at first, 'touching this dreaded sight twice seen of us,' is exceedingly graceful and scholarly. And indeed all that comes from him marks the presence of a calm, clear head, keeping touch and time perfectly with a good heart.

REV. C. E. MOBERLY (1873)

(*Introduction to Hamlet.* Rugby edition.)—The main point to be noted in reference to the tone of reflection and sentiment which prevailed in Shakespeare's time, and the circumstances out of which it grew, is this: that there was in those times a conscious struggle in men's minds between cheerfulness and melancholy, more real, natural, and widely felt by far than that which we remember in our own days as springing from the conflict between the poetical principles of Byron and Wordsworth. On the one side, in these battles, stood the prodigious animal spirits and mental vigor of the time manifesting themselves in a thousand ways. It astonishes us in the wonderful cheerfulness with which men like Drake, Grenville, or Raleigh could bear the most awful trials in carrying on our undeclared naval war with Spain; in the fervid spirit which the commanders threw into the thankless and unremitting Irish struggle; in the personal devotion of her people to Elizabeth which made them cry, 'God save the Queen!' under the very mutilating knife of the executioner; perhaps, also, in the strenuous resistance to monopolies, and in the unsolicitous and cheerful persuasion of Elizabeth's ministers, that, in spite of all adverse appearances, she would always be safe against foreign aggression, because she could always hold the balance between France and Spain. And so in the field of literature we are amazed at the torrent-like flow of Lord Bacon's speeches, where image crowds on image, and thought on thought, with a rapidity beyond our conception; at the vigorous and unflagging optimism of Hooker; at the well-spring of independent speculation in Gilbert and Harvey; and at the creative power of the Elizabethan dramatists. But all this light and vigor had its reverse. It maintained itself only by battling unremittingly against the dark spirit of melancholy. We get glimpses of this

fact in the bitter laments of Elizabeth's great statesmen at the failure of their best
conceived projects through her wilfulness and vacillation, and in the sad end of the
great queen herself. But in literature it is patent to view. As if conscious of the
danger, Sir Henry Sidney writes to his son Sir Philip, expressly desiring him first to
lift up his mind to Almighty God by hearty prayer, then to give himself to be merry;
' for,' says the great statesman, 'you degenerate from your father, if you find not
yourself most able in wit and body to do anything when you are most merry.' We
see the same thing in the unbounded popularity of the tale of *Faustus*,—the Doctor
death-wearied with the unprofitableness of all study; and, in fact, in the general
taste for dramatic subjects in which the tragedy was partly mental, partly material.
Lastly, and above all, may the tendency be seen in the extraordinary *Anatomy of
Melancholy*, published by Robert Burton in 1620. In this strange work all the causes
and symptoms of melancholy are traced; not indeed with the intuitive truthfulness
of a genuine psychologist, but with an immensity of knowledge and learning; and
an attempt is made in it to discover and classify the remedies for every type of this
mental disease. It must be obvious to any one who reads this book, that attention
to the phenomena of melancholy must have been widespread and long continued in
England before any writer would have got together such a strangely combined mass
of materials on the subject, and attract to his work, when published, the singular
degree of esteem which Burton enjoyed.

Yet, as might be expected, Burton only dimly discerns what must have been the
real pervading cause for widespread melancholy at the end of the sixteenth century.
This was in reality the transition then in progress from an active out-of-door exist
ence to a sedentary student life. Those who studied did so without that physical
support against mental exertion which is derived from the habit of literary effort in the
generations immediately preceding. Just as at the present day it rarely happens that
the child of a laborer's family, whatever be his natural abilities, can stand the physi
cal exertion of much continued thought or study, so the men whose fathers and
grandfathers had been eternally on horseback, and engaged in quite other than
literary pursuits, could not, without suffering for it, give themselves up to study with
the devotion which they constantly displayed. Their only chance was to preserve a
due balance between the bodily exercises of their fathers and the studious habits
of their own time. Those who, like Sir Philip Sidney, succeeded in thus tempering
their occupations found life a well-spring of happiness. To them pre-eminently
belonged the ' mens sana in corpore sano.' Hard study supplied their minds profusely with objects of thought, while their energetic mode of life still absolutely
hindered them from losing practical ability and the force of action. But if this
balance was once disturbed, and bodily exercise gave way entirely to study, then
the aspect of life would alter to them at once. They would find, in George Her-
bert's words, that ' an English body and a student's body are pregnant with humors.'
And as the body, so also the mind would become incapable of discharging its functions rightly; it would lose itself in unpractical abstractions, in formulæ of the perfect, in aspirations for the impossible. When men had thus become incapable of
action, they would feel how bitter a thing the divorce between action and thought
really is; and the more so, as they would be affording almost the first instance in
the world's history of such a separation. Not yet awakened by experience to the
fact that thought produces its fruit only after many days, they must have imagined
that on their thoughts and studies there was laid the prophet's curse of a ' miscarry-
ing womb and dry breasts.' Hence must necessarily have come melancholy in the

truest sense of the word; the constant dwelling on the irremediable, on action and
duty undone, and now become impossible to be done; which is, as the poet says,
'like the sighs of the spendthrift for his squandered estate.'

If this melancholy was a tendency of the time, we might have assumed beforehand that it would find its place in Shakespeare's thoughts; and if the best spirits
of the time were battling against it, we might have ventured beforehand to assert
that traces of the conflict would be found in him. That such is emphatically the
case many of his works show; above all others, *As You Like It* and *Hamlet*. As
regards the former of these plays, Shakespeare, in imagining the character of Jaques,
wished to bring out to view the absurdity of an affected melancholy, and to compare
it with the genial light-heartedness of those whose soul is true and pure. This he
does with a repeated yet light touch of reproof, as if he was certain of his own victory over the fault reprehended. In *Hamlet* the note sounded is far deeper; the
melancholy is most entirely real, its effects most fully developed, both in the character of Hamlet and in the action of the play. In fact, the character and the events
act and re-act upon one another throughout, and the theme or ground-tone of the
whole is the effect of melancholy upon the active energies, and the misery felt by a
man of melancholy temper when a task is laid upon him which he can hardly bring
himself to do from want of heart. If we could have conceived a later dramatist com-
posing such a tragedy, he certainly would have called it the *Unwilling Avenger*,
or some such name, so as thus to give the key to its method and order. Shakespeare
did not do this; and hence arose a wonderful quantity of misunderstanding as to
the meaning of the piece, which is even now only partially dispelled as far as the
public is concerned. . . . .

Hamlet is introduced to us at the age of thirty years. . . . . Hamlet's grief is
increased by his mental habit of seeing all that goes on around him under the form
of reflection; no act appears to him incomplete, single, and unconnected. He
would argue from the one evil act of his mother, first, that her motive must have
been simple and unmixed evil; then that her whole nature must be homogeneous
with this motive; and, lastly, that all women must be as corrupt as she is. To this
we ought probably to add that he feels youth passing away from him; he is no
longer 'the glass of fashion and the mould of form.' Those youthful accomplishments, the vanishing of which would have seemed to him a trifle if he had been
engaged in ennobling and royal occupations, are sadly missed now that they are
passing, and have left nothing in their place. Finally, a cloud has come over his
hopes of being loved as he deserves. For Polonius, the father of the sweet Ophelia,
has taken, as we may safely conjecture from several indications, a most prominent
part in robbing Hamlet of his succession to the throne, and placing Claudius there
instead of him. The result is, that while Hamlet loves the daughter with the most
ardent passion, and has the kindest feelings to her brother Laertes, the sight of her
father fills him on every occasion with an angry contempt, which does not rise into
positive hostility only because the man is too old to be an adversary worthy of him.
. . . . He binds his friends to secrecy as to what they know, instead of calling on
them to assist him, and makes arrangements for assuming a feigned madness, such
as will disburthen him from the weight of silence and secrecy without any danger
of revealing his real purpose, as what he says will be considered only the raving of
a madman. He thus enables himself to escape from actions to mere words, as he
will always be able to say some cutting truth to every one whom he hates and despises, and so to relieve his soul from its burthen of hatred by means very far short

of those which he ought to adopt. . . . But above all other contrasts in the play stands out that which Hamlet himself expressly recognizes, the one between himself and Laertes; the latter is as purely worldly in his thoughts as Hamlet is the reverse. He is the man of Parisian training; no nurseling of grave and Protestant Wittenberg. Fencing and music are his studies. He is false and treacherous as one trained at the court of France in Shakespeare's time was likely to be; while Hamlet is most generous and void of suspicion. In all his utterances there is no single tinge of Hamlet's reflectiveness. But, in spite of all this, there is one quality in which he is immeasurably Hamlet's superior. This is that important one of instant energy and decision. When his father is slain, he does exactly what Hamlet longs in vain to be able to do,—he 'sweeps' home from France to his revenge. Nor is any need-less moment of time allowed to pass before he is bursting open the gates of the palace, with a crowd of partisans at his back, who are already proclaiming him king of Denmark,—a more apt one, perhaps, for those rough days than poor Hamlet would have been. Yet consider how different the real loss, when Hamlet's father, the noble and the majestic, was foully and treacherously murdered, from what was suffered when poor Polonius met the doom of a rat behind the arras where he had gone to spy; and how the difference between the sons is brought out by their oppo-site lines of conduct under trial, as it had been nurtured and gradually formed by their opposite courses of life.

D. J. SNIDER (1873)

(*The Journal of Speculative Philosophy*, St Louis, Jan. 1873, vol. vii, page 73.) —*Hamlet is never so mad as not to be responsible.* Hence, with any ordinary definition of insanity, he is not mad at all. He has undoubtedly weaknesses, so has every mortal; he possesses finite sides to his character and intelligence, other-wise he could hardly perish as the hero of a tragedy. A definition of insanity which includes Hamlet would sweep at least three-fourths of mankind into the mad-house. That he is lacking in the element of will, that he is melancholy in his feel-ings, that his reasoning is often unsound, and, in fact, so intended by Hamlet him-self, is all very true, but does not make out a case of insanity.

[Page 74.] He was the self-chosen instrument of a mighty design, which, however, for a time required concealment; concealment demanded cunning; cunning was the reversal of his entire rational nature; still, to carry out his end, he had to submit to the circumstances, and, hence, to assume the garb of the Irrational. How perfectly our poet has succeeded in portraying this disguise is shown by the fact that quite a number of modern critics have been deceived as badly as Polonius.

[Page 75.] Hence we cannot but regard those persons who believe in the madness of Hamlet as in the condition of Polonius in the play,—most completely befooled by Hamlet's disguise. If, too, the characters of the play are considered, but little will be found to justify the hypothesis of Hamlet's madness. Besides Polonius, only the two women, the Queen and Ophelia, neither of whom was strong enough to have an independent opinion, take Hamlet to be mad. The King knows better, and acts upon his conviction to the end; moreover, Horatio, the most intimate friend and chosen vindicator of Hamlet, does not seem to have the remotest notion of the insanity of Hamlet.

[Page 76.] First of all, the collision which constitutes the basis of the action of the entire play is between Hamlet and the King. They form the most wonderful contrast, yet both exhibit sides of the same great thought. Hamlet has morality without action, the King has action without morality. Hamlet cannot do his deed at the behest of duty, nor can the King undo,—that is, repent of,—his deed at the command of conscience. Hamlet represents the undone which should be done, the King represents the done which should be undone. Neither reaches the goal which reason so clearly sets before them, and both perish by the inherent contradiction of their lives. Each one seeks the death of the other, and, by the most rigid poetic justice, they die by the retribution of their deeds.

[Page 83.] But it is not our purpose to maintain that Hamlet is excluded from every species of action. On the contrary, there is only one kind of action from which he is wholly excluded, though his tendency to procrastination is always apparent. Just here occurs, perhaps, the greatest difficulty in comprehending Hamlet's character. He is wonderfully ready to do certain things; other things he will not do, and cannot bring himself to do. In fine, he acts and does not act. Hence different critics have given exactly opposite opinions of him; one class say he possesses no power of action, another class declare that he possesses a vast energy of Will. How can this contradiction be reconciled? Only by distinguishing the different kinds of action of which men are capable. Undoubtedly, Hamlet can do some things, but the great deed he cannot reach. We shall attempt a classification of the different forms of action, and point out what lies in the power of Hamlet.

1. Impulse has sway over Hamlet at times, as over every human being. This is the first and lowest form of action, unconscious, unreflecting, and belongs to the emotional nature of man, in which, as we have before seen, Hamlet is not wanting. Under its influence people act upon the spur of the moment, without thinking of consequences. Hence Hamlet's drawback,—reflection,—is not now present, and there is nothing to restrain him from action. But the moment there is delay sufficient to let his thoughts get a start, then farewell, deed; impulse possesses him no longer. . . . . .

2. Hamlet possesses what may be called negative action, the power of frustrating the designs of his enemies. He exhibits an infinite acuteness in seeing through their plans; in fact, this seems an exercise of intellectual subtlety in which he takes especial delight; he also possesses the practical strength to render futile all the attempts of the King against his person. He is prepared for everything; his confidence in himself in this direction is unlimited; he knows that he can ' delve one yard below their mines and blow them at the moon.' But here his power of action ends. . . . .

3. It is what we term Rational Action from which Hamlet is excluded. Here the individual seizes a true and justifiable end and carries it into execution. This end Intelligence knows as rational, for it alone can recognize the worth and validity of an end,—and the Will brings it to realization. Thus we have the highest union of Intelligence and Will, which gives the most exalted form of action. This unity Hamlet cannot reach; he grasps the end and comprehends it in its fullest significance, but there it remains caught in its own toils. . . . .

Hamlet's capture by the pirates is a most strange occurrence, and has always given great difficulty. Accident, contrary to the general rule of the poet, seems to determine the course of things in the most startling manner, and the whole poem to be made to rest upon a most improbable event. Hamlet is sent to England,—a pirate pursues his ship and grapples with it,—he boards the strange vessel, when it suddenly cuts loose with Hamlet alone, and afterwards puts him safely on shore. The whole proceeding is so suspicious that, were such an event to occur in real life, everybody would think at once of collusion. This impression is much strengthened by the confidence with which he speaks of his ability to foil all the machinations of the King in sending him to England :

> ' Let it work,
> For 'tis the sport to have the enginer
> Hoist with his own petar; and 't shall go hard
> But I will delve,' &c.

Indeed, he rejoices in the prospect :

> ' O, 'tis most sweet
> When in one line two crafts directly meet.'

Note how absolute his trust still is in his intelligence. Such confidence seems to be begotten of preparation. One is inclined, therefore, to explain the occurrence in this way : Hamlet hired the pretended pirate, and gave to its officers his instructions before he left port; indeed, he most probably had also some understanding with the officers of the royal ship which was to convey him. Yet this view, apparently so well founded, we must at once abandon when we read Hamlet's account of the affair (V, ii). In that he ascribes his action wholly to instinct; there was no premeditation, no planning at all. But, what is more astonishing, he has come to prefer unconscious impulse to deliberation; he has renounced intelligence as the guide of conduct. Yet before this event, how he delighted in his skill, in his counterplots, in his intellectual dexterity! Now, what is the cause of this great change in his character? In the first place, it ought to be observed that the expressions above quoted were uttered by him when there might be still some hope of being brought to action, before the last and strongest influence, the appearance of Fortinbras, revealed to him that his case was desperate. But the great cause of his conversion was this startling event, in which he saw that Accident, or some external power, was mistress over the best matured plans of men. Here is an element which had never been included in his calculations, upon which heretofore he had placed so great reliance; suddenly they are swept down by this unknown force. He sees that it is objectively valid in the world, but he knows that he himself is not, for he cannot do the deed; hence he must believe in it more than in himself. Hamlet thus becomes a convert from Intelligence to Fate, from self-determination to external determination. So must every person without will be, to a greater or less extent, a disbeliever in will, for his sole experience is that man is controlled from without. Thus it can be seen that the introduction of this accident is based upon the weightiest grounds, and is in the completest harmony with the development of the drama. Accident appears here in a manner which is legitimate in Art, not to cut a complicated knot, nor to create a sudden surprise, but to determine character.

W. MINTO (1874)

(*Characteristics of English Poets.* Edinburgh, 1874, p. 379.)—We must not allow the dazzling movement of lightnings in the atmosphere of Shakespeare's tragedies to blind us to the vast firmament that overhangs the whole, and displays itself in quiet grandeur when the hurly-burly of conflicting passions has stormed itself to rest. The poet recognizes an overruling Destiny above all the tumult. It is not a cold, remote power of marble majesty; it is estimated as being in intimate connection with human affairs—

> ' Reckoning Time, whose million'd accidents
> Creep in 'twixt vows, and change decrees of kings,
> Tan sacred beauty, blunt the sharp'st intents,
> Divert strong minds to the course of altering things.'—*Son.* 115.

Nothing is more remarkable in Shakespeare's plays, and nothing contributes more to make them a faithful image of life, than the prominence given to the influence of chance, of undesigned accidents. The most tragic events turn on the most trifling circumstances. . . . . But the predominance of chance over human designs is most powerfully brought home in Hamlet, whose fate turns on accident after accident. The passage just quoted from the *Sonnets* reads as a commentary on the fortunes of Hamlet, and should be printed at the beginning of all copies of the play, to in duce the lofty vein of reflection, designed by the poet as the main effect of the whole, and to undo the wretched criticism that would degrade it to the level of a sermon against procrastination. The poet leaves us in no doubt as to his intention, although one might easily have apprehended it from his treatment of slight turning-points and weak beginnings of things in other plays. [See V, ii, 6–11.] That is Shakespeare's poetical religion : a power variously denominated Destiny, Fate, Chance, Providence,—supreme over mortal affairs. The varied energies of the world, which no man has ever embodied with such force and subtlety of expression, are governed and shut in by great sublimities of time and space.

[Page 408.] Why does Hamlet still delay when he has received strong confirmation from the play ? He gets an opportunity ; he comes upon his uncle kneeling in prayer ; why does he withhold ? Not from fear ; not from irresolution ; but from cold, iron determination, sure of its victim, and resolved not to strike till the most favorable moment. He is tempted to the weakness of yielding to impulse ; but he holds back with inflexible strength. His words are instinct with the most iron energy of will (III, iii, 73). . . . . Hamlet still bides his time. Was this cowardice ? In his sharp self-questionings, he calls it so himself [IV, iv. 39–46].

His delay is inexplicable to Hamlet himself, though we are all so confident in explaining it for him. One might have pointed out to him, without seconding his own morbid and unjustifiable accusation of cowardice, that he had still no means of satis fying the people that he was a pious avenger, and not merely a mad or an ambitious murderer ; more particularly after he had incurred the accidental taint of the murder of Polonius, whom he was not to know that the King would inter in hugger-mugger. And the desire to be above suspicion, to have an unblemished reputation, was a strong motive with Hamlet, as we see from his dying injunction to Horatio. But I do not think that it was the dramatist's intention to represent this as the chief motive for Hamlet's delay, otherwise he would have brought it out more strongly. No ; the above passage, taken in conjunction with Hamlet's communication to Horatio in the beginning of the last Scene, supplies the real clue to the dramatist's intention in the concluding Acts. Hamlet does not know why he delays ; he is not afraid,— there is not the slightest trace of such a motive in his behavior from first to last,— but he restrains himself in a blind, inexplicable, vague trust that some supremely favorable moment will occur. Meantime, Destiny is ripening the harvest for him ; a Divinity is shaping his ends ; his indiscretions serve him when his deep plots do pall. . . . . The supreme moment comes without his contrivance, and is more comprehensive in its provisions for justice than any scheme that could have been devised by single wisdom, and executed by single power. Claudius is at last caught by vengeance in an act that has no relish of salvation in it, is surprised in an infamous plot, and sent to hell with a heavier load of guilt upon his back; and others, brought within the widening vortex of the original crime, are involved in the final ruin.

PROF. F. A. MARCH (1875)

At a meeting of The American Philological Association, held in July, 1875, Prof. F. A. MARCH, of Lafayette College, Easton, Pennsylvania, read an Essay on *The Immaturity of Shakespeare as shown in Hamlet*, of which the following abstract was published in the Society's *Transactions :*

An examination of the works of Shakespeare in the order of their composition shows that he rose very slowly to the heights of his power. He worked for years dramatizing popular tales with a comic vein, and then years more on patriotic parts of English history, before he tried the grand tragic style. After the love-story of *Romeo and Juliet, Hamlet* was his first tragedy, and it has some of the defects as well as the merits of such a work. It was probably long in hand. The following topics were discussed to exhibit traits of age or immaturity :

1. The metre. The formal metrical peculiarities of the early plays were pointed out, and the later changes. In *Hamlet*, it was said, the early rhymes and formal restraints have gone, but there is still care and finish, perfect art without the negligences of the latest period.

2. There are many things which are not natural utterances of the characters to carry out the thought of the play; but good things brought in to make hits :

Allusions to matters of the day, such as the talk about the children players, II, ii; the actor who played Hamlet, ' fat and scant of breath;' and, perhaps, allusions to Mary Queen of Scots.

Taking off the fashionable style of speech, as in Polonius's imitation of Euphues, and the ranting passage of the player in the style of Marlowe.

Good things from his own commonplace book, such as the advice to players, and large parts of the soliloquies, on the badness of the world in general, the effect of prayer, and the like.

3. The want of lively characterization of the subordinate characters. Many of them talk a good deal, but they leave no impression.

4. The youthful point of view from which the characters are seen. Ophelia is ripe in age; her sagacious father is a superannuated bore. Doubt is depth. Made-up minds seem superficial. Not so with Miranda and Prospero, or Perdita and Polyxenes.

5. Immature view of the problems of life and death. The writer is wrestling with them. By and by Shakespeare quietly gave them up, and was a cheerful believer that ' we are such stuff as dreams are made of, and our little life is rounded with a sleep.'

6. Immature treatment of the Ghost. In the later plays the ghosts are apparitions of unhinged minds; the *Hamlet* Ghost is the simple ghost of the story-books, visible to vulgar eyes, and what, with his poses and long-winded declamation on the stage, and his moveable subterranean noises, is a commonplace creation, a ' poor ghost.' Hamlet does not quite believe in him.

7. Immature treatment of insanity. Shakespeare had not so fully mastered this subject as to give the reins to his imagination, but made Hamlet and Ophelia speak by a theory. according to which the intolerable grossness of Hamlet was the neces-

sary utterances of madness n his circumstances. The writer f *Lear* would have felt that such grossness was no subject for art.

8. The general atmosphere of lechery.

9. The character of Hamlet is not brought to unity. Some passages seem to have been taken up from the old play, in which Hamlet has a different character from Shakespeare's prevailing thought of him. This, combined with the defective handling of his insanity, is the solution of the enigma of his character.

PROFESSOR DOWDEN (1875)

(*Shakespeare: A Critical Study of his Mind and Art*, London, 1875, p. 125.)— When *Hamlet* was written, Shakespeare had passed through his years of apprenticeship, and become a master-dramatist. In point of style the play stands midway between his early and his latest works. The studious superintendence of the poet over the development of his thought and imaginings, very apparent in Shakespeare's early writings, now conceals itself; but the action of imagination and thought has not yet become embarrassing in its swiftness and multiplicity of direction. Rapid dialogue in verse, admirable for its combination of verisimilitude with artistic metrical effects, occurs in the scene in which Hamlet questions his friends respecting the appearance of the Ghost; the soliloquies of Hamlet are excellent examples of the slow, dwelling verse which Shakespeare appropriates to the utterance of thought in solitude; and nowhere did Shakespeare write a nobler piece of prose than the speech in which Hamlet describes to Rosencrantz and Guildenstern his melancholy. But such particulars as these do not constitute the chief evidence which proves that the poet had now attained maturity. The mystery, the baffling, vital obscurity of the play, and in particular of the character of its chief person, make it evident that Shakespeare had left far behind him that early stage of development when an artist obtrudes his intentions, or, distrusting his own ability to keep sight of one uniform design, deliberately and with effort holds that design persistently before him. When Shakespeare completed *Hamlet*, he must have trusted himself and trusted his audience; he trusts himself to enter into relation with his subject, highly complex as that subject was, in a pure, emotional manner. *Hamlet* might have been so easily manufactured into an enigma, or a puzzle; and then the puzzle, if sufficient pains were bestowed, could be completely taken to pieces and explained. But Shakespeare created it a mystery, and therefore it is for ever suggestive; for ever suggestive, and never wholly explicable.

It must not be supposed, then, that any *idea*, any magic phrase, will solve the difficulties presented by the play, or suddenly illuminate everything in it which is obscure. The obscurity itself is a vital part of the work of art, which deals not with a problem, but with a life; and in that life, the history of a soul which moved through shadowy border-lands between the night and day, there is much (as in many a life that is real) to elude and baffle inquiry. . . . . The vital heart of the tragedy of *Hamlet* cannot be an idea; neither can it be a fragment of political philosophy. Out of Shakespeare's profound sympathy with an individual soul and a personal life the wonderful creation came into being.

[Page 132.] Hamlet is not merely or chiefly intellectual; the emotional side of his character is quite as important as the intellectual; his malady is as deep-seated in his sensibilities and in his heart as it is in his brain. If all his feelings translate themselves into thoughts, it is no less true that all his thoughts are impregnated with feeling. To represent Hamlet as a man of preponderating power of reflection, and to disregard his craving, sensitive heart, is to make the whole play incoherent and unintelligible. It is Hamlet's intellect, however, together with his abiding sense of the moral qualities of things, which distinguishes him, upon the glance of a moment, from the hero of Shakespeare's first tragedy, Romeo.

[Page 145.] Hamlet does not assume madness to conceal any plan of revenge. He possesses no such plan. And as far as his active powers are concerned, the assumed madness is a misfortune. Instead of assisting him to achieve anything, it is one of the causes which tend to retard his action. For now, instead of forcing himself upon the world, and compelling it to accept a mandate of his will, he can enjoy the delight of a mere observer and critic; an observer and critic both of him self and of others. He can understand and mock, whereas he ought to set himselt sternly to his piece of work. He utters himself henceforth at large, because he is unintelligible. He does not aim at producing any effect with his speech, except in the instance of his appeal to Gertrude's conscience. His words are not deeds. They are uttered self-indulgently to please the intellectual or artistic part of him, or to gratify his passing mood of melancholy, of irritation, or of scorn. He bewilders Polonius with mockery, which effects nothing, but which bitterly delights Hamlet by its subtlety and cleverness. He speaks with singular openness to his courtier-friends, because they, filled with thoughts of worldly advancement and ambition, read all his meanings upside down, and the heart of his mystery is absolutely inaccessible to their shallow wits. When he describes to them his melancholy, he is in truth speaking in solitude to himself. Nothing is easier than to throw them off the scent. 'A knavish speech sleeps in a foolish ear.' The exquisite cleverness of his mimetics and his mockery is some compensation to Hamlet for his inaction; this intellectual versatility, this agility, flatters his consciousness; and it is only on occasions that he is compelled to observe into what a swoon or syncope his will has fallen.

Yet it has been truly said that only one who feels Hamlet's strength should venture to speak of Hamlet's weakness. That, in spite of difficulties without and inward difficulties, he still clings to his terrible duty,—letting it go, indeed, for a time, but returning to it again, and in the end accomplishing it,—implies strength. He is not incapable of vigorous action,—if only he be allowed no chance of thinking the fact away into an idea. . . . . But all his action is sudden and fragmentary; it is not continuous and coherent. His violent excitability exhausts him; after the night of encounter with the Ghost, a fit of abject despondency, we may be certain, ensued, which had begun to set in when the words were uttered: 'The time is out of joint; O cursed spite, That ever I was born to set it right.' After he has slain Polonius, he weeps; after his struggle with Laertes in Ophelia's grave, a mood of depression ensues: 'Thus awhile the fit will work on him, Anon as patient as the the female dove,' &c. His feelings are not under control.

[Page 151. After speaking of Hamlet's interview with Ophelia in Act III, sc. i, and of his detecting the deceit that had placed Ophelia there as a decoy, Professor Dowden continues:] One of the deepest characteristics of Hamlet's nature is a longing for sincerity, for truth in mind and manners, an aversion from all that is false, affected, or exaggerated. Ophelia is joined with the rest of them; she is an impostor, a spy; incapable of truth, of honor, of love. Have they desired to observe an outbreak of his insanity? He will give it to them with a vengeance. With an almost savage zea., which underneath is nothing but bitter pain, he pounces upon Ophelia's deceit : ' Ha, ha ! are you honest ?' His cruelty is that of an idealist, who cannot precisely measure the effect of his words upon his hearer, but who requires to liberate his mind. . . . . And to complete the startling effect of this outburst of insanity, solicited by his persecutors, he sends a shaft after the Chamberlain and a shaft after the King :—

> '*Ham.* Where's your father?
> *Oph.* [*Coming out with her docile little lie*]. At home, my lord.
> *Ham.* Let the doors be shut upon him, that he may play the fool nowhere but in's own house.'

Hamlet bursts out of the lobby with a triumphant and yet bitter sense of having turned the tables upon his tormentors. Ophelia remains to weep. In the pauses of Hamlet's cruel invective she had uttered her piteous little appeals to heaven : ' Heavenly powers, restore him !' ' Oh help him, you sweet heavens !' When he abruptly departs, the poor girl's sorrow overflows. In her lament, Hamlet's noble reason, which is overthrown, somehow gets mixed up with the elegance of his costume, which has suffered equal ruin. He who was the ' glass of fashion,' noticed by every one, ' the observed of all observers,' is a hopeless lunatic. She has no bitter thought about her lover. All her emotion is helpless tenderness and sorrow. Her grief is as deep as her soul is deep. . . . . There is a touching devotion shown by Hamlet to Horatio in the meeting which follows the scene in the lobby with Ophelia ; a devotion which is the overflow of gratitude for the comfort and refuge he finds with his friend after the recent proof of the incapacity and want of integrity in the woman he had loved. Horatio's equanimity, his evenness of temper, are like solid land to Hamlet, after the tossings and tumult of his own heart.

[Page 157.] In the dawn of the following morning Hamlet is dispatched to England. From this time forward he acts, if not with continuity and with a plan, at least with energy. He is fallen in love with action ; but the action is sudden, convulsive, and interrupted. He is abandoning himself more than previously to his chances of achieving things ; and thinks less of forming any consistent scheme. The death of Polonius was accidental, and Hamlet recognized, or tried to recognize, in it (since in his own will the deed had no origin) the pleasure of Heaven [III, iv, 173-175]. When about to depart for England, Hamlet accepts the necessity with as resolute a spirit as may be, believing, or trying to believe, that he and his concerns are in the hands of God : ' I see a cherub that sees them.' That is, my times are in God's hand. Again, when he reflects that acting upon a sudden impulse, in which there was nothing voluntary (for the deed was accomplished before he had conceived what it was), he had sent his two school-fellows to death, Hamlet's thoughts go on to discover the divine purpose in the event [V, ii, 7-11]. Once more, when Horatio bids the prince yield to the secret misgiving which troubled his heart before he went to the trial of skill with Laertes, Hamlet puts aside his friend's advice with the words, ' We defy augury,' &c., V, ii, 207-210.

Does Shakespeare accept the interpretation of events which Hamlet is led to adopt? No ; the providence in which Shakespeare believed is a moral order which includes man's highest exercise of foresight, energy, and resolution. The disposition of Hamlet to reduce to a minimum the share which man's conscious will and foresight have in the disposing of events, and to enlarge the sphere of the action of powers outside the will, has a dramatic, not a theological, significance. Helena, who clearly sees what she resolves to do, and accomplishes neither less nor more than she has resolved, professes a different creed :—

> ' Our remedies oft in ourselves do lie
> Which we ascribe to heaven; the fated sky
> Gives us free scope, only doth backward pull
> Our slow designs when we ourselves are dull.'—*All's Well*, I, i, 231.

Horatio, a believer in the ' divinity that shapes our ends,' by his promised explanation of the events, delivers us from the transcendental optimism of Hamlet, and restores the purely human way of viewing things :—' let me speak to the yet unknowing world,' &c., V, ii, 366–373.

The arrival of Fortinbras contributes also to the restoration of a practical and positive feeling. With none of the rare qualities of the Danish Prince, he excels him in plain grasp of ordinary fact. Shakespeare knows that the success of these men, who are limited, definite, positive, will do no dishonor to the failure of the rarer natures, to whom the problem of living is more embarrassing, and for whom the tests of the world are stricter and more delicate. Shakespeare ' beats triumphant' marches, not for successful persons alone, but also for conquered and slain persons.

Does Hamlet finally attain deliverance from his disease of will? Shakespeare has left the answer to that question doubtful. Probably if anything could supply the link which was wanting between the purpose and the deed, it was the achievement of some supreme action. The last moments of Hamlet's life are well spent, and for energy and foresight are the noblest moments of his existence; he snatches the poisoned bowl from Horatio, and saves his friend; he gives his dying voice for Fortinbras, and saves his country. The rest is silence :—' Had I but time,—as this fell sergeant, death, Is strict in his arrest,—Oh, I could tell you.' But he has not told. Let us not too readily assume that we ' know the stops' of Hamlet, that we can ' pluck out the heart of his mystery.'

One thing, however, we *do* know,—that the man who wrote the play of *Hamlet* had obtained a thorough comprehension of Hamlet's malady. And assured as we are by abundant evidence, that Shakespeare transformed with energetic will his knowledge into fact, we may be confident that when *Hamlet* was written, Shakespeare had gained a further stage in his culture of self-control, and that he had become not only adult as an author, but had entered upon the full maturity of his manhood.

JOHN WEISS (1876)

(*Wit, Humor, and Shakespeare*, Boston, 1876, p. 156.)—After Hamlet's interviews with the Ghost, the ' antic disposition' which tints his behavior is ironical; his remarks keenly cut down to where our laugh lies, but scarcely let its blood. The mood does not throw open the great valves of the heart as the sun-burst of Humor does. We enjoy seeing with what superior insight he baffles all the spies, who cannot play upon a pipe, yet expect to play upon him. This gives to the scene the flavor of comedy. In the churchyard we taste the sub-acid of cynicism, so that Yorick's skull is quite emptied of its humor, and is only an ill-savored text to a chopfallen discourse upon mortality. . . . . No wonder [after his interview with the Ghost] that his wonted evenness of manner is shaken; and we hear him writing truisms in his tablet, in a flighty style, as for instance, that a man may smile and be a villain. But let us also make a note of that, as he did; it will interpret to us the tone of his subsequent demeanor, which everybody thought was madness. In the mean time we are upon this spectre-haunted platform, seeking with his friends to discover what news the Ghost brought. Hamlet trifles with them to put off their curiosity; but the scene soon rises to the solemnity of taking an oath, and one that is extorted by the experience of a vision, which comes to so few that mankind has only heard of such things. But just as the human voices are about to pledge them selves to a secrecy which they must feel all their lives, and shudder in feeling, to be reflected upon them from the glare and publicity of purgatorial fires, a voice comes, building this terrific chord of a nether world up to their purpose, that it may unalterably stand : ' Swear !' The deep craves it of them ; it has joined the company uninvited, but they feel convinced that it is a comrade fated to go with them to their graves. ' Swear !' it reiterates ; no change of place can remove them from this importunity. The centre of an unatoned murder is beneath every spot to which they shift their feet.

[Page 159.] Not the faintest streak of Humor appears in this tragedy to reconcile us with the drift of it. Polonius belongs to comedy, because he is an old counsellor who was once valuable, whose wits have grown seedy on purpose to delight us with his notion that he fathoms and circumvents the Prince. When a man's feeling of importance has outlived its value, so that his common sense trickles feebly over the lees of maxims, and his policies are absurd attempts to appear as shrewd as ever before persons who are in better preservation, he belongs to the comic side of life. We cannot help smiling at his most respectable recommendations ; for they are like hats lingering in fashion, but destitute of nap. He wears one of these, and goes about conceiting that his head mounts a gloss. There is not enough of Polonius left to tide him through this tragedy, unless it might have been in dumb show ; he must lurk behind an arras to get himself mistaken for a king ; and as he does this after sending a spy into France to watch his son's habits, we have not a tear to spare. And we only think how delightfully bewildered he will be if his ghost gets out of the body, escaping a politic convocation of worms, in time to help receive the other Ghost, and to understand then, if any wit is left over in him, that his king was murdered, and Hamlet is harping on something besides his daughter.

[Page 160.] The theories which undertake to explain the nature of the ' antic disposition,' which Hamlet hinted that he might assume, do not satisfy me that the heart of that mystery has been plucked out. But the key to it may be read engrossed upon his tablets. The subsequent behavior of Hamlet is the exact counterpart in Irony of the conviction that was so suddenly thrust upon him, and terribly emphasized by his father, that ' a man may smile, and be a villain.' In the first place, I notice that the behavior of Hamlet, which has the reputation of being feigned, is a genuine exercise of Irony, and consequently covers a feeling and purpose that are directly opposite to its tone of lightness ; but it results organically from Hamlet's new experience, and does not require to be premeditated as madness would be. We see his vigorous and subtle mind set open by the revelations of the Ghost ; but it is too well hung to be slamming to and fro in gusts of real madness, and its normal movement shuts out the need of feigning. When his father first tells that he has been murdered, we find that Hamlet thinks himself quite capable of decision ; there is no infirmity of purpose in that early mood to sweep to his revenge ' with wings as swift as meditation or the thoughts of love.' What is it that converts this mood into an irresoluteness which contrives the whole suspense, and, in fact, gives us the whole tragedy ? First partly, that his father tells Hamlet he was murdered by his own brother.

Then the question of revenge becomes more difficult to settle, especially as it involves widowing his mother; and it is noticeable that the father himself, who afterwards deplored Hamlet's irresolution, had previously made suggestions to him ['nor
let thy soul contrive Against thy mother aught'], which hampered his action by con-
straining him to feel how complicated the situation was.

[Page 165.] The oblique and enigmatic style into which Hamlet has fallen is not
a deliberate effort to sustain the character of a madman, because such a person as
Hamlet could find no motive in it; he could not need it to mask his desire to avenge
the Ghost, for he is prince, an inmate of the palace, and supernaturally elected to
be master of the situation.   He says he has ' cause and will and strength and means
to do't.' I conceive, then, that his mind, driven from its ordinary gravity, and the
channel of his favorite thoughts diverted, instinctively saves itself by this sustained
gesture of irony; and it appears to be madness only to those who do not know that
he is well informed of the event, and is struggling to set free from it a purpose.
And why should a man of such a well-conditioned brain, a noticer of nice distinctions, have selected for a simulation of madness a style which, nicely estimated, is
not mad? He could not calculate that everybody would interpret this difference
from his usual deportment into an unsettling of his wits; for the style shows unconsciousness and freedom from premeditation. If he wished to feign distraction, he
would have taken care to mar the appositeness of his ironical allusions, which are
always in place and always logical. And if he was half unhinged without knowing
it, his speech would have betrayed the same inconsequence. Nowhere is he so
abrupt, or delivers matter so remote from an immediate application, that he seems to
us to wander, because we, too, have been admitted to the confidences of the Ghost,
and share that advantage over the other characters.

[Page 168.] The other passage upon which the theory of premeditated madness
rests occurs in the great scene with his mother, during which she becomes convinced
that Hamlet is out of his senses by seeing him kill the good Polonius, and hearing
him rave as if he saw a spectre. She was the earliest of the critics and experts who
are profoundly convinced of his madness. At the close of the scene it occurs to
him to avail himself of her misapprehension to procure continued immunity from
any suspicion of design against the King. How shall he do this,—how contrive to
clinch her conviction of his madness, and send her reeking with it to inform the
King? His subtle intelligence does at this point invent the only simulation of madness that the play contains. He is just about to bid the Queen good-night: 'So
again, good-night.' Then the device occurs to him: 'One word more, good lady;'
and the Queen, turning, says: 'What shall I do?' [See III, iv, 181-188.]

This is the very craftiness of a madman, to try to convince people that, if he ever
seems to be insane, it is for a sane motive. Hamlet reckons that the Queen is so
deeply imbued with the idea of his insanity as to interpret this disclaimer of his into
the strongest confirmation. Hamlet, moreover, not only seems to be accounting for
symptoms of madness, but to be making a confidant of his mother; he begs her not
to betray the secret object of his strange behavior. This seems to her to be the
very quintessence of madness, to confess to her that he is feigning it out of craft,
and to suppose that she would not apprise her husband, who must be the special
object of that craft and most in danger from it. He must be, indeed, preposterously
mad; so, in parting, she pretends to receive his confidential disclosure :—' Be thou
assured, if words be made of breath, And breath of life, I have no life to breathe
What thou hast said to me.' She may safely promise that, when she means to repair

to the King with quite a different version of Hamlet's condition, the very one upon which he counts to keep the King deceived. . . . . She is the mother of the physio-logical criticism which issues from insane asylums to wonder why Hamlet is not an inmate; and Hamlet himself, by deceiving his mother, furnishes to psychological criticism the text that he was mad in craft. Between the lines of the genuine *Hamlet* you can read that Shakespeare belonged to neither school.

[Page 176.] In the churchyard scene we observe that Hamlet recurs uncon-sciously to his ordinary mental disposition, because he is alone there with Horatio, whose grave and silent friendship is congenial. It is the foil to Hamlet's restless specu-lation; it calls a truce to the civil war between his temper and his purpose. He is pacified in the society of Horatio, who gives him a chance to recur to his native mental habit. As he naïvely pours out his thoughts, how little does Horatio answer! as little as the ground beneath their feet, less laconic than the lawyer's skull. He is a continent upon which Hamlet finds that he can securely walk, the only domain in Denmark that is not honeycombed with pitfalls. Turning toward Horatio's loyal affection, he feels a response that is articulated without words. As little need the forest reply to her lover save in dumb show and in obscure reflex of feeling.

[Page 177.] It is by unconsciously remanding Hamlet to Irony that Shakespeare has expressed the effect of an apparition, and of the disenchanting news it brought, upon a mind of that firm yet subtle temper. Lear's noble mind tottered with age before grief struck it into the abyss of madness. Constance stands before us, like Niobe, all tears, or sits with sorrow; but she was a too finely-tempered woman to drip into craziness till health, hope, and life broke up. Shakespeare has not represented any of his mature and well-constructed natures as capable of being overthrown by passion the most exigent or events the most heart-rending. They preserve their sanity to suffer, as all great souls must do to make us worship them with tears. So Hamlet being incapable of madness, and lifted above the necessity of feigning it, gives to everything the complexion of the news which has revolted his moral sense, —that is, the King, his uncle, is not what he seems; his own mother's husband does not appear to be a murderer. The state of Denmark is rotten with this irony. No wonder that his brain took on the color of the leaf on which it fed. Oh, everything is not what it appears to be, but only an indication of its opposite, and must be phrased by contradiction! He is really in love with Ophelia, but this irony conceals it. With the mood into which he has been plunged, his own love is no more worth being seriously treated than is old Polonius, whom he knows excellent well,—he is a fish-monger; that is, not that he is a person sent to fish out his secrets, as Coleridge would explain it, but that he is a dealer in staleness, and yet not so honest as those who only vend stale fish.

If we return to a period in the play which follows closely upon the scene of the taking of the oath, Ophelia herself will discover for us the turning mood in Ham-let's character. The time and action of the piece allow us to suppose that he soon went from the oath-taking to visit Ophelia. Naturally, he turned from that bloodless and freezing visitation to see life heaving in a dear bosom, and reddening in lips which he had love's liberty to touch. The disclosures of the Ghost had worked upon him like a turbid freshet which comes down from the hills to choke the running of sweet streams, deface with stains of mud all natural beauties, and bury with the washings of sunless defiles the meadows spangled with forget-me-nots. His love for Ophelia was the most mastering impulse of his life; it stretched like a broad, rich domain, down to which he came from the shadowy places of his private thought to fling himself in the unchecked sunshine and revel in the limpid bath of feeling. How often, in hours which only over-curious brooding upon the problems of life had hitherto disquieted, had he gone to let her smile strip off the shadow of his thought, and expose him to untroubled nature! The moisture of her eyes refreshed his questioning; her phrases answered it beyond philosophy; a maidenly submission of her hand renewed his confidence; an unspoken sympathy of her reserve, that flowed into the slight hints and permissions of her body, nominated him as lover and disfranchised him as thinker; and a sun-shower seemed to pelt through him to drift his vapors off. But this open gladness has disappeared underneath the avalanche of murder which a ghostly hand had loosened. He ventures down to the place where he remembers that it used to expect him ; but we know that it has disappeared. His air and behavior announce it to us. The catastrophe seems to have swept even over his person, to dishevel the apparel upon that ' mould of form.' In this ruin of his life, Ophelia is the first one buried; for she was always more resident in his soul than maintained within a palace, and his soul is no longer habitable.

[Page 357.] [At the grave of Ophelia Hamlet] is forced into disgust at hearing a man vaunt love against his own. All scruples are shrivelled up in anger; and he instinctively assumes the tone he hears. The old ironical disgust for sham makes the imitation perfect. Afterwards he acknowledges that he forgot himself, that ' the bravery of his grief did put me Into a towering passion.' And this passion broke open his respect and prudence, and let loose the first cry of his love that had ever reached the ears of others. Else it would have lain buried with Ophelia in the silence of her lover's breast. . . . . But his bosom secret has escaped. He turns away, is followed by Horatio, to whom, before the next scene opens, we hear him (though no Folio nor Quarto ever lisped a syllable of it) pouring out the confidences of a fruitless passion to the only honest man of all the crowd, the still and trusty comrade. This Shakespeare would have us understand, I think, by giving Hamlet to say to Horatio as they enter the next scene together, ' So much for this, sir.' So much for what? we think. Then it dawns upon us that the only other interest of the moment must have been Ophelia's death. And we recollect that Horatio was absent at the time of her death, having gone to meet Hamlet. So both of them were ignorant of the occurrence. But now Horatio has been making inquiries during the time that elapses between the burial and the next scene. He picks up all the particulars, and has been detailing to the eager Hamlet all that we know. And Hamlet's entry upon the next scene is timed exactly when Horatio has ceased narrating. There is nothing more to tell. Hamlet enters, saying, ' So much for this, sir. Now you shall see the other.' That is, I will relate what has happened to me also, and how a divinity has shaped my ends to this return.

IS HAMLET'S INSANITY REAL OR FEIGNED?

[Dr Akinside was, I believe, the first to assert that Hamlet's insanity is real.
See Steevens's remarks, p. 147. Ed.]

MACKENZIE (1780)

(*The Mirror*, No. 100, 22 April, 1780.)—The distraction of Hamlet is clearly
affected through the whole play, always subject to the control of his reason, and
subservient to the accomplishment of his designs. At the grave of Ophelia, indeed,
it exhibits some temporary marks of a real disorder. . . . . Counterfeited madness,
in a person of the character I have ascribed to Hamlet, could not be so uniformly
kept up as not to allow the reigning impressions of his mind to show themselves in
the midst of his affected extravagance. It turned chiefly on his love to Ophelia,
which he meant to hold forth as its great subject; but it frequently glanced on the
wickedness of his uncle,—his knowledge of which it was certainly his business to
conceal.

In two of Shakespeare's tragedies are introduced at the same time instances of
counterfeit madness and of real distraction. In both plays the same distinction is
observed, and the false discriminated from the true by similar appearances. Lear's
imagination constantly runs on the ingratitude of his daughters and the resignation
of his crown; and Ophelia, after she has wasted the first ebullience of her distraction in some wild and incoherent sentences, fixes on the death of her father for the
subject of her song: 'They bore him bare-faced on the bier,' &c. But Edgar puts
on a semblance as opposite as may be to his real situation and his ruling thoughts.
He never ventures on any expression bordering on the subject of a father's cruelty
or a son's misfortune. Hamlet in the same manner, were he as firm in mind as
Edgar, would never hint anything in his affected disorder that might lead to a suspicion of his having discovered the villainy of his uncle; but his feeling, too powerful for his prudence, often breaks through that disguise which it seems to have
been his original, and ought to have continued his invariable, purpose to maintain,
till an opportunity should present itself of accomplishing the revenge which he
meditated.

DR FERRIAR (1813)

(*An Essay towards a Theory of Apparitions*, London, 1813, p. 114.)—The character of Hamlet can only be understood on this principle [of *Latent Lunacy*]. He
195

feigns madness for political purposes, while the poet means to represent his understanding as really (and unconsciously to himself) unhinged by the cruel circumstances in which he is placed. The horror of the communication made by his
father's spectre; the necessity of belying his attachment to an innocent and deserving
object; the certainty of his mother's guilt; and the supernatural impulse by which
he is goaded to an act of assassination abhorrent to his nature, are causes sufficient
to overwhelm and distract a mind previously disposed to 'weakness and to melancholy,' and originally full of tenderness and natural affection. By referring to the
book, it will be seen that his real insanity is only developed after the mock-play.
Then in place of a systematic conduct, conducive to his purposes, he becomes irresolute, inconsequent, and the plot appears to stand unaccountably still. Instead
of striking at his object, he resigns himself to the current of events, and sinks at
length ignobly under the stream.

DRAKE (1817)

(*Shakespeare and his Times,* London, 1817, vol. ii, p. 396.)—In th's play, as in
King Lear, we have madness under its real and its assumed aspect, and in both instances they are accurately discriminated. We find Lear and Ophelia constantly
recurring, either directly or indirectly, to the actual causes of their distress; but it
was the business of Edgar and of Hamlet to place their observers on a wrong scent,
and to divert their vigilance from the genuine sources of their grief and the objects
of their pursuit. This is done with undeviating firmness by Edgar; but Hamlet
occasionally suffers the poignancy of his feelings and the agitation of his mind to
break in upon his plan, when, heedless of what was to be the ostensible foundation
of his derangement, his love for Ophelia, he permits his indignation to point, and
on one occasion almost unmasked, towards the guilt of his uncle. In every other
instance he personates insanity with a skill which indicates the highest order of
genius, and imposes on all but the King, whose conscience, perpetually on the
watch, soon enables him to detect the inconsistencies and the drift of his nephew.

T. C. [THOMAS CAMPBELL?] (1818)

(*Letters on Shakespeare,* Blackwood's Maga., February, 1818, p. 509.)—Most certain it is that Hamlet's whole perfect being had received a shock that had unsettled
his faculties; that there was disorder in his soul none can doubt,—that is, a shaking
and unsettling of its powers from their due sources of action. But who can believe
for a moment that there was in his mind the least degree of that which, with physio-
logical meaning, we call disease? Such a supposition would at once destroy that
intellectual sovereignty in his being which in our eyes constitutes his exaltation.
Shakespeare never could intend that we should be allowed to feel pity for a mind to
which we were meant to bow; nor does it seem to me consistent with the nature of
his own imagination to have subjected one of his most ideal beings to such mournful
mortal infirmity. That the limits of disorder are not easily distinguishable in the representation is certain. How should they? The limits of disorder, in reality, lie in
the mysterious and inscrutable depths of nature. Neither surely could it be intended
by Shakespeare that Hamlet should for a moment cease to be a moral agent, as he
must then have been. Look on him upon all great occasions, when, had there been

madness in his mind, it would have been most remarkable; look on him in his mother's closet, or listen to his dying words, and then ask if there was any disease of madness in that soul.

BOSWELL (1821)

(*The Plays and Poems of William Shakspeare*, 1821, vol. vii, p. 536.)—That the madness of Hamlet is not altogether feigned is, I think, entirely without foundation. The sentiments which fall from him in his soliloquies, or in confidential communication with Horatio, evince not only a sound, but an acute and vigorous, understanding. His misfortunes, indeed, and a sense of shame for the hasty and incestuous marriage of his mother, have sunk him into a state of weakness and melancholy; but though his mind is enfeebled, it is by no means deranged. It would have been little in the manner of Shakespeare to introduce two persons in the same play whose intellects were disordered; but he has rather in this instance, as in *King Lear*, a second time effected what, as far as I can recollect, no other writer has even ventured to attempt,—the exhibition on the same scene of real and fictitious madness in contrast with each other. In carrying his design into execution, Hamlet feels no difficulty in imposing upon the King, whom he detests; or upon Polonius and his schoolfellows, whom he despises; but the case is very different, indeed, in his interviews with Ophelia: aware of the submissive mildness of her character, which leads her to be subject to the influence of her father and her brother, he cannot venture to entrust her with his secret. In her presence, therefore, he has not only to assume a disguise, but to restrain himself from those expressions of affection which a lover must find it most difficult to repress in the presence of his mistress. In this tumult of conflicting feelings he is led to overact his part from a fear of falling below it; and thus gives an appearance of rudeness and harshness to that which is in fact a painful struggle to conceal his tenderness.

HARTLEY COLERIDGE (*Blackwood's Maga.* 1828)

(*Essays and Marginalia*. London, 1851, vol. i, p. 153.)—Let us, for a moment, put Shakespeare out of the question, and consider Hamlet as a real person, a recently deceased acquaintance. In real life it is no unusual thing to meet with characters every whit as obscure as that of the Prince of Denmark,—men seemingly accomplished for the greatest actions, clear in thought, and dauntless in deed, still meditating mighty works, and urged by all motives and occasions to the performance,—whose existence is nevertheless an unperforming dream; men of noblest, warmest affections, who are perpetually wringing the hearts of those whom they love best; whose sense of rectitude is strong and wise enough to inform and govern a world, while their acts are the hapless issues of casualty and passion, and scarce to themselves appear their own. We cannot conclude that all such have seen ghosts; though the existence of ghost-seers is as certain as that of ghosts is problematical. But they will generally be found, either by a course of study and meditation too remote from the art and practice of life,—by designs too pure and perfect to be executed in earthly materials, or from imperfect glimpses of an intuition beyond the defined limits of communicable knowledge,—to have severed themselves from the common society of human feelings and opinions, and become, as it were, ghosts in the body. Such a man is Hamlet; an habitual dweller with his own thoughts.

[Page 162.] If it be asked, Is Hamlet really mad? or for what purpose does he assume madness? we reply that he assumes madness to conceal from himself and others his real distemper. Mad he certainly is not, in ꞏne sense that Lear and Ophelia are mad. Neither his sensitive organs nor the operations of his intellect are impaired. His mind is lord over itself, but it is not master of his will. The ebb and flow of his feelings are no longer obedient to calculable impulses,—he is like a star drawn by the approximation of a comet out of the range of solar influence. To be mad is not to be subject to the common laws whereby mankind are held together in community, and whatever part of man's nature is thus dissociated, is justly accounted insane. If a man see objects, or hear sounds, which others in the same situation cannot see or hear, and his mind and will assent to the illusion (for it is possible that the judgement may discredit the false intelligence which it receives from its spies), such man is properly said to be out of his senses, though his actions and conclusions, from his own peculiar perceptions, should be perfectly sane and rational. Hamlet's case is in some measure the reverse of this,—his actions and practical conclusions are not consistent with the premises in his mind and his senses. An overwhelming motive produces inertness,—he is blinded with excess of light.

[Page 166.] But for wringing the kind, fond heart of sweet Ophelia with words such as man should never speak to woman, what excuse, what explanation can be offered? Love, we know, is often tyrannous and rough, and too often tortures to death the affection it would rack into confession of itself; and men have been who would tear open the softest breast, for the satisfaction of finding their own names indelibly written on the heart within. But neither love nor any other infirmity that flesh is heir to can exempt the live dissection from the condemnation of inhumanity. Such experiments are more excusable in women, whose weakness, whose very virtue, requires suspicion and strong assurance; but in man they ever indicate a foul, a feeble, and unmanly mind. I never could forgive Posthumous for laying wagers on his wife's chastity. Of all Shakespeare's jealous husbands, he is the most disagreeable.

But, surely, the brave, the noble-minded, the philosophic Hamlet could never be guilty of such cruel meanness. Nor would Shakespeare, who reverenced womanhood, have needlessly exposed Ophelia to insult if some profound heart-truth were not developed in the exhibition. One truth at least it proves,—the fatal danger of acting madness. Stammering and squinting are often caught by mimicry, and he who wilfully distorts his mind, for whatever purpose, may stamp its lineaments with irrecoverable deformity. To play the madman is 'hypocrisy against the devil.' Hamlet, in fact, through the whole drama, is perpetually sliding from his assumed wildness into sincere distraction. But his best excuse is to be found in the words of a poet, whom it scarce beseems me to praise, and who needs no praise of mine :—

> ' For to be wroth with one we love
> Doth work like madness in the brain.'—*S. T. C.*

Hamlet loved Ophelia in his happy youth, when all his thoughts were fair and sweet as she. But his father's death, his mother's frailty, have wrought sad alteration in his soul, and made the very form of woman fearful and suspected. His best affections are blighted, and Ophelia's love, that young and tender flower, escapes not the general infection. Seemed not his mother kind, faithful, innocent? And was she not married to his uncle? But after the dread interview, the fatal injunction, he is a man among whose thoughts and purposes love cannot abide. He is a being severed from human hopes and joys,—vowed and dedicated to other work than courtship and dalliance. The spirit that ordained him an avenger, forbade him to be a lover. Yet, with an inconstancy as natural as it is unreasonable, he clings to what he has renounced, and sorely feels the reluctant repulse which Ophelia's obedience presents to his lingering addresses. Lovers, even if they have seen no ghosts, and have no uncles to slay, when circumstances oblige them to discontinue their suit, can ill endure to be anticipated in the breach. It is a sorrow that cannot bear the slightest show of unkindness. Hamlet, moreover, though a tardy, is an impatient nature, that would feel uneasy under the common process of maidenly delay. Thus perplexed and stung, he rushes into Ophelia's chamber, and, in amazed silence, makes her the confidant of his grief and distraction, the cause of which she must not know No wonder she concludes that he is mad for her love, and enters readily into what to her appears an innocent scheme to induce him to lighten his overcharged bosom, and ask of her the peace which unasked she may not offer. She steals upon his solitude, while, weary of his unexecuted task, he argues with himself the expediency of suicide. Surprised as with a sudden light, his first words are courteous and tender, till he begins to suspect that she, too, is set on to pluck out the heart of his mystery; and then, actually maddened by his self-imposed necessity of personating madness, he discharges upon her the bitterness of blasted love, the agony of a lover's anger, as if determined to extinguish in himself the last feeling that harmonized not with his fell purpose of revengeful justice. To me, this is the most terrifically affecting scene in Shakespeare. Neither Lear nor Othello are plunged so deep in the gulf of misery.

GEORGE FARREN (1829)

(*Observations on the Laws of Mortality and Disease*, &c. London, 1829, p. 12.) —It is not maintained in this essay that Hamlet was uniformly deranged, or that his malady disqualified him altogether for the exercise of his reason, but that he was liable to paroxysms of mental disorder. The death of his father, the marriage of his mother, and the consequent overthrow of his royal hopes, all these suddenly acting on a mind predisposed to gayety and to youthful follies, impart a tinge of melancholy to it, which speedily but imperceptibly produces an instability of intellect; and, by brooding over the Ghost's commandment, he nourishes a malady which at first he intended merely to feign. All Hamlet's words and actions before he resolves to feign insanity may be considered as those of a free agent, and it is by these that we are to decide whether or not he has from the start a perfectly healthy mind. Now, before he had any suspicion of his father's murder, and of course before he intends to feign insanity, we find him deliberating on suicide, and intolerant of life, —sure indications of mental disease. His mind was therefore affected from the first, and it is to be further noted, that whenever Hamlet is *alone* the true state of his mind reveals itself in melancholy soliloquies; furthermore, FARREN asks, whether the assumption of the rôle of a madman be not, under the circumstances, a clear act of insanity? So far from aiding his design, it was the very way to thwart it, as, in fact, it did. 'Madness,' says Claudius, 'in great ones must not unwatched go.' Hamlet's ' contumelious sarcasm ' in reference to the dead body of Polonius, and the ' language of defiance' that he ' hurls' at the King, ' must force the conclusion that he was a senseless and abandoned miscreant, if charity and a nicer estimate did not urge us to the commiseration of a masterless infirmity.' Again [p. 25]: ' If Hamlet be considered as *not* really mad, but merely feigning, his unmanly outrage on Laertes at the grave of Ophelia, and the despicable lie he utters by way of apology in the presence of the King, whom he detests, must stamp him as the most cruel, ser.seless, and cowardly miscreant that ever disgraced the human form.' FARREN cites Dr MASON GOOD'S *Study of Medicine*, where, in treating of *Ecphronia melancholia*, it is stated that: 'the disease shows itself sometimes suddenly, but more generally by slow and imperceptible degrees. *There is a desire of doing well, but the will is wayward and unsteady, and produces an inability of firmly pursuing any laudable exertion, or even purpose.* Melancholia Attonita, the *First Variety*, most commonly commences with this character, and creeps on so gradually that it is for some time *mistaken* for a mere attack of hypochondrism, or lowness of spirits, till the mental alienation is at length decided by the wildness of the patient's eyes, &c. *The first stage of this disease is thus admirably expressed by Hamlet :* " I have of late, but wherefore I know not, Lost all my mirth," &c. Grief (and particularly the loss of friends) have frequently produced it.' . . . . 'The unhappy individuals are at the same time not only sensible of what they do or say, but occasionally *sensible* of its being *wrong*, and will express their *sorrow* for it immediately *afterwards*, and say they will not do so again.'—Vol. iii, p. 86. ' Hamlet's momentary regret,' adds FARREN, ' for having killed Polonius, the expression of his sorrow that to Laertes he did forget himself, and his more explicit declaration of repentance before the King, are striking instances of the correctness of the medical opinions of Dr Good.' ' It may not be unimportant to point attention to the fact that *feigning madness* is a theory with many persons subject to mental aberrations.'

FARREN devotes much attention to the inconsistencies in Hamlet's character and expressions, and finds therein proofs of mental disease : How can that man be sane who is deterred from suicide by God's canon 'gainst self-slaughter, and yet shortly afterwards so forget this canon, ' which can only be that which says : " Thou shalt do no *murder*," ' as to meditate a murder of the most fiendish kind, where soul as well as body of the victim is to be killed? What sound mind would believe that the Almighty had fixed his canon 'gainst *self-slaughter* and not against *murder ?* ' Will it be believed that the studious and virtuous Prince, who in the First Act con sidered this world as an unweeded garden, and looked to other realms for a more blissful state of being, but was deterred from seeking them by his steady belief in the revelation which awards punishment for those who shall be guilty of self- slaughter, could be so entirely divested of his religious impressions, and, indeed, of his philosophy, as to utter, in the Third Act, a soliloquy in which his very *existence* in a future state is made a subject of doubt? Will it find belief, that in two Acts such a change in the mind of man could be wrought without supervening *malady* to *effect* the change ?' The belief is *forced* upon us ' that the poet *intended* to mark the growth of Hamlet's mental disorder ' by ' contrasting the states of his thoughts in the two soliloquies.' Not only is the defective logic which FARREN finds in the soliloquy, ' To be, or not to be,' an additional proof of Hamlet's insanity, but also the confusion of his metaphors : ' It certainly would be extremely difficult to paint as a metaphor on canvas :—Enterprises of pith, taking regard of the fear of a dream, and turning their currents awry.' In the First Act Hamlet is fully impressed with a belief in a future state, and is studious, religious, and virtuous. The inter· view with the Ghost unsettles his reason, and ' his mind takes a more horrid hent, but in the Third Act he endeavors *to recover his original train of thought,*—and to be, if possible, *his former self*. THIS IS A VERY COMMON EFFORT WITH THOSE WHO HAVE SUFFERED MENTAL ABERRATIONS ; and the result is the same in most cases, the sufferer either reasons *correctly* on *false* premises, or makes *erroneous deductions* from *correct* premises,—SO IT WAS WITH HAMLET.' Finally, FARREN finds it ' difficult to imagine how the poet's intention could ever have been mistaken; as, from the *first* scene to the *last*, he seizes every occasion to prepare his audience for a display of insanity by Hamlet, and when the mental eclipse has commenced, loses no opportunity in which he can fix their belief in the nature of his malady.'

SIR HENRY HALFORD (1829)

In an Essay on *Popular and Classical Illustrations of Insanity*, read in June, 1829, and published in a volume of *Essays*, &c., in 1833 (p. 47), Sir HENRY HALFORD adopted the same test for insanity proposed by Hamlet to his mother : ' bring me to the test And I the matter will re-word, which madness Would gambol from ' (III, iv, 142–144), and illustrated it by several striking examples which had occurred in his own practice, ' serving to prove the correctness ' of Shakespeare's discrimination. This volume of *Essays* was reviewed in an article in the Quarterly Review, from which the following extracts are taken.

QUARTERLY REVIEW (1833)

(*Review of Sir Henry Halford's Essays*, vol. xlix, p. 184.)—Hamlet's criterion of madness, however excellent as a mark for incoherence of intellect, will scarcely be used in detecting the more intricate forms of this Protean malady. The Prince's testimony in favor of his own perfect sanity is treated with as little ceremony by the commentators as similar words from the lips of a staring lunatic would be by the phalanx of modern mad-doctors. Some of them, however, are of opinion that the poet means to describe a mind disordered, and that the feigned madness is a part of the plot quite compatible with such a state of intellect; while others see nothing but the assumption of insanity in the inconsistencies of Hamlet. This discrepancy springs from the different notions included by different men in their definitions of madness. In fact, however, madness, like sense, admits of no adequate definition; no one set of words will include all its grades and varieties. Some of the existent definitions of insanity would let loose half the inmates of Bedlam, while others are wide enough to place nine-tenths of the world in strait-jackets. The vulgar error consists in believing the powers of the mind to be *destroyed* by the malady; but general disturbance of the intellect is only one form. The aberration may be confined to a few objects or trains of ideas; sometimes the feelings, passions, and even instincts of our nature may assume an undue ascendency over a mind not disjointed, but warped, urging it with resistless force to the commission of forbidden deeds, and to form the most consistent plans for their accomplishment.

[Page 186.] We have no doubt that Shakespeare intended to display in the character of Hamlet a species of mental malady, which is of daily occurrence in our own experience, and every variety of which we find accurately described by his contemporary, the author of the *Anatomie of Melancholy*. ' Suspicion and jealousy,' says Burton, ' are general symptoms. If two talk together, discourse, whisper, jest, he thinks presently they mean him,—*de se putat omnia*,—or, if they talk with him, he is ready to misconstrue every word they speak, and interpret it to the worst. Inconstant they are in all their actions; vertiginous, restless, unapt to resolve of any business; they will and they will not, persuaded to and from upon every occasion; yet, if once resolved, obstinate and hard to be reconciled. They do, and by and by repent them of what they have done; so that both ways they are disquieted of all hands; soon weary. They are of profound judgements in some things, excellent apprehensions, judicious, wise, and witty; for melancholy advanceth men's conceits more than any humor whatever. Fearful, suspicious of all, yet again many of them desperate hair-brains; rash, careless, fit to be assassinates, as being void of all ruth and sorrow. *Tædium vitæ* is a common symptom; they soon are tired with all things,—*sequitur nunc vivendi nunc moriendi cupido;* often tempted to make away with themselves,—*vivere nolunt, mori nesciunt;* they cannot die, they will not live; they complain, lament, weep, and think they lead a most melancholy life.' It would be difficult to find a criticism more applicable to the character of Hamlet than in this page of old Burton, who drew the picture as much from himself as from observation made on others. This form of madness (the *melancholia attonita* of nosologists) begins with lowness of spirits and a desire for solitude.

[Page 187.] Perhaps some may find it difficult to believe that Shakespeare observed these minute and almost technical distinctions of madness, which appear to belong rather to the province of the pathologist than that of the poet. But everything is still to be learned concerning this extraordinary man's habits of study and observation. The variety and individual clearness of his delineations of mental malady leave on our minds no doubt that he had made the subject his especial study, as both Crabbe and Scott certainly did after him, and with hardly inferior success. The various forms of the malady he has described,—the perfect keeping of each throughout the complications of dramatic action,—the exact adjustment of the peculiar kind of madness to the circumstances which induce it, and to the previous character of the 'sound man,' leave us lost in astonishment.

ᴕR MAGINN (*Fraser's Maga.* 1836)

(*Shakespeare Papers.* London, 1860, p. 330.)—In a word, *Hamlet*, to my mind, is essentially a psychological exercise and study. The hero, from whose acts and feelings everything in the drama takes its color and pursues its course, is doubtless insane, as I shall prove hereafter. But the species of intellectual disturbance, the peculiar form of mental malady, under which he suffers, is of the subtlest character. The hero of another of these dramas, *King Lear*, is also mad; and his malady is traced from the outbreak, when it became visible to all, down to the agony of his death. But we were prepared for this malady,—the predisposing cause existed always; it only wanted circumstance to call it forth. Shakespeare divined and wrote upon the knowledge of the fact which has since been proclaimed formally by the physician, that it is with the mind as with the body: there can be no local affection without a constitutional disturbance,—there can be no constitutional disturbance without a local affection. Thus there can be no constitutional disturbance of the mind without that which is analogous to a local affection of the body, namely, disease, or injury affecting the nervous system and the mental organs,—some previous irregularity in their functions or intellectual faculties, or in the operation of their affections and passions; and, again, general intellectual disturbance will always be accompanied by some particular affection. But I am using well-nigh the words of Esquirol. He says, 'Presque tous' (and by this qualification he only intends to exclude those in whom he had not the means of ascertaining the fact)—'Presque tous les alienés confiés à mes soins avoient offert quelques irregularités dans leur fonctions, dans leur facultés intellectuelles, dans leur affections, avant d'être malades, et souvent de la première enfance. Les uns avoient été d'un orgueil excessif, les autres très colérés; ceux-ci souvent tristes, ceux-là d'une gaiété ridicule; quelques-uns d'une instabilité désolante pour leur instruction, quelques autres d'une applica- tion opiniâtre à ce qu'ils entreprennoient, mais sans fixité; plusieurs vétilleux minu- tieux, craintifs, timides, irresolus; presque tous avoient eu une grande activité de facultés intellectuelles et morales qui avoient redoublés d'énergie quelque temps avant l'acces; la plupart avoient eu des maux des nerfs; les femmes avoient épreuves des convulsions ou de spasmes hystériques; les hommes avoient été sujets à des crampes, des palpitations, des paralysies. Avec ces dispositions primitives ou ac- quises, il ne manque plus qu'une affection morale pour déterminer l'explosion de la fureur ou l'accablement de la melancolie.'

Now, in all Shakespeare's insane characters, however slight may be the mental malady, with the exception only of Hamlet, we have accurately described to us the temperament on which madness is engrafted.

[Page 333.] But of Hamlet alone we have no account of any positive predis- posing cause to mania or faulty temperament; nor can we catch from the lips of any third person anything which might lead us to question his sanity before the com- mencement of the play. All is to his praise. He is the esteemed of Fortinbras, the friend of Horatio, the beloved of Ophelia. We are abruptly brought to con- template the noble nature warped, the lofty mind o'erthrown, the gentleman 'in his blown youth blasted with ecstasy.' To comprehend and account for this, we must study the drama with the same pervading sweep of thought that we would passages in human life occurring within our observation, from which we wished to wring a meaning, and by which we hoped to solve a mystery. There is nothing beyond to look to. We must judge Hamlet by what he said and did; I open the volume in which this is recorded.

BLACKWOOD'S MAGAZINE

(*On the Feigned Madness of Hamlet.* October, 1839, p. 452.)—One very mani- fest purpose of adopting the disguise of feigned madness was to obtain access to the King in some moment of unguarded privacy. . . . . The rambling of a maniac over all parts of the palace, and at all hours, would excite no suspicion; and thus an opportunity might be afforded of striking the fatal blow. . . . . The ordinary tone of social intercourse would be the last he would willingly or successfully support. This feint of madness offered a disguise to him more welcome, and which called for less constraint, than the labored support of an ordinary, unnoticeable demeanor. The mimicry of madness was but the excess of that levity and wildness which naturally sprang from his impatient and overwrought spirit. It afforded some scope to those disquieted feelings which it served to conceal. The feint of madness covered all,— even the sarcasm, and disgust, and turbulence, which it freed in some measure from an intolerable restraint. Nor was it a disguise ungrateful to a moody spirit, grown careless of the respect of men, and indifferent to all the ordinary projects and desires of life. The masquerade brought with it no sense of humiliation,—it pleased a misanthropic humor,—it gave him shelter and a sort of escape from society, and it

cost him little effort. That mingled bitterness and levity, which served for the repre
sentation of insanity, was often the most faithful expression of his feelings.

[Page 454.] It is not to be supposed that this state of mind, thus prompting to
the choice of this disguise, would be one of long continuance; and, accordingly,
we find, towards the close of the piece, that the feint of madness, which has never
in fact been very sedulously supported, is laid aside, and that without any seeming
embarrassment. As the excitement of his mind wears itself out, Hamlet assumes an
ordinary tone. He jests with Osric; and, from that time to the conclusion of the
drama, he presents to us the aspect of one exhausted by the violence and intensity
of his feelings. The Ghost might appear to him now, we think, and have been
seen without a start,—the tragedy of life was becoming as indifferent as its pleasures,
—and the secrets of another world would soon have been as little exciting as they
had previously made the interests of this. The bidding of his father's spirit is still
remembered; but we might almost doubt whether it would have been fulfilled if
the treachery of the King had not suddenly rekindled his wrath, and called upon
him to revenge his own as well as his father's death. . . . . A mind unhinged, vexed,
tortured, and bewildered, adopts as a scheme of action what, after all, is more impulse than policy.

KNIGHT (1841)

(*Introductory Notice to Hamlet*, p. 89.)—It is curious that in Burton's *Anatomy
of Melancholy* we have the stages of melancholy, madness, and frenzy indicated as
described by Celsus; and Burton himself mentions frenzy as the worst stage of madness ' clamorous, continual.' In Q_1, therefore, Hamlet, according to the description
of Polonius, is not only the prey of melancholy and madness, but ' by continuance ' of
frenzy. In Q_2 the symptoms, according to the same description, are much milder,—
a sadness—a fast—a watch—a weakness—a lightness,—and a madness. The reason
of this change appears to us tolerably clear. Shakspere did not, either in his first
sketch or his amended copy, intend his audience to believe that Hamlet was essentially mad; and he removed, therefore, the strong expressions which might encourage that belief.

DR RAY (1847)

[This article, from which the following extracts are taken, first appeared in *The
American Journal of Insanity*, April, 1847. It was afterwards reprinted in *Contributions to Mental Pathology*, Boston, 1873, p. 485.]—It is not to be supposed that
[Shakespeare] was guided solely by intuition. He unquestionably did observe the
insane, but he observed them as the great comparative anatomist of our age observed
the remains of extinct species of animals,—from one of the smallest bones recon-
structing the whole skeleton of the creature, re-investing it with flesh and blood,
and divining its manners and habits. By a similar kind of sagacity, Shakespeare,
from a single trait of mental disease that he did observe, was enabled to infer the
existence of many others that he did not observe, and from this profound insight
into the law of psychological relations he derived the light that special observation
had failed to supply.

[Page 506.] Hamlet's mental condition furnishes in abundance the characteristic
symptoms of insanity in wonderful harmony and consistency.

[Page 509.] On the supposition of his real insanity we have a satisfactory explanation of the difficulties which have received such various solutions. The integrity of every train of reason is marred by some intrusion of disease; the smooth, deep current of his feelings is turned into eddies and whirlpools under its influence, and his most solemn undertakings conducted to an abortive issue.

[Page 510.] With a skill founded on what would seem to be a professional knowledge of the subject, Shakespeare has selected for his purpose that form of the disease in which the individual is mad enough to satisfy the most superficial observer, while he still retains sufficient power of reflection and self-control to form and pursue if not to execute, a well-defined, well-settled purpose of revenge.

[Page 512.] The manner in which Hamlet speaks of and to the Ghost, while administering the oath of secrecy to his friends, is something more than the natural reaction of the mind after experiencing extraordinary emotions. It betrays the excitement of delirium,—the wandering of a mind reeling under the first stroke of disease.

[Page 513.] Although no single incident in his interview with Ophelia is incompatible with simulation, yet when we regard the whole picture which his appearance presented, his pallid face, his piteous look, his knees knocking each other, his hatless head and down-gyved stockings, his deliberate perusal of Ophelia's face, and the sigh, 'so piteous and profound as it did seem to shatter all his bulk,'—we feel as little disposed to believe all this to be a well-acted sham as we should the wail of a new-born infant, or the flush that glows on the cheek in the fever of consumption.

[Page 514.] In all Hamlet's interviews with Polonius the style of his discourse is indicative of the utmost contempt for the old courtier, and he exhibits it in a manner quite characteristic of the insane. . . . . Nothing is more so than a fondness of annoying those whom they dislike by ridicule, raillery, satire, vulgarity, and every other species of abuse. . . . . Had Hamlet been feigning insanity, it would have been hardly consistent with his character to have treated in such a style the father of one so dear to him as Ophelia.

[Page 515.] Towards his old friends, Rosencrantz and Guildenstern, his discourse and manner are suitable to his own character and to their ancient friendship. He treats them respectfully, if not cordially, discourses sensibly enough about the players and other indifferent subjects, occasionally losing his self-control and uttering a remark strongly savoring of mental unsoundness: 'O God, I could be bounded in a nutshell, and count myself a king of infinite space, were it not that I have bad dreams.' It is a well-observed fact, though not generally known, that in a large majority of cases the invasion of insanity is accompanied by more or less of sleeplessness and disagreeable dreams. I have not yet met with the case, however sudden the outbreak of the disease, in which this first symptom did not exist for some time before any suspicion of impending derangement was excited in the minds of the friends. Although strongly suspecting, if not knowing, that they are in the interest of the King, sent expressly for the purpose of observing his movements, he makes no attempt to impress them with a conviction of his madness, as might have been expected had he been acting a part. For certainly, if he had been anxious to spread the belief that he was really mad, he would not have neglected so favorable an opportunity.

[Page 517.] We next meet with Hamlet in his remarkable interview with Ophelia, —remarkable not more for his language and conduct than for the difficulties which it has presented to commentators, to whom it has proved a perfect *pons asinorum.* Some regard his treatment of Ophelia as unnecessarily harsh and unfeeling, even for the purposes of simulation, and in this instance, at least, can see no ' cause for mirth' in his pretended madness. If Homer sometimes nods, so may Shakespeare. Others think that Hamlet's love for Ophelia was but lukewarm after all, and there-fore he was justified in treating her in such a way as to lacerate her feelings and outrage her dignity. The most natural view of the subject,—that which is most readily and obviously suggested,—relieves us of all these difficulties, and reveals to us the same strong and earnest significance which appears in every other scene of this play. If Hamlet is really insane, as he presumptively is, and as we have much reason to believe that he is, then his conduct is what might have been naturally ex-pected. It discloses an interesting feature in mental pathology,—the change which insanity brings over the warmest affections of the heart, whereby the golden chains wrought by love and kindness are utterly dissolved, and the forsaken and desolate spirit, though it continues among men, is no longer of them. Such aberrations from the normal course of the affections were closely observed and studied by Shakespeare, who saw in them that kind of poetical interest which master-spirits like his are apt to discern in the highest truths of philosophy. The frequency with which he introduces insanity into his plays shows that it was with him a favorite subject of contemplation; and from the manner in which he deals with it, it is equally obvious that he regarded it as not only worth the attention of the philan-thropist and physician, but as full of instruction to the philosopher and the poet. . . . . If in this feature he differs from every other poet, it is not from that fondness for dwelling on the morbid anatomy of the mind which is the offspring of a corrupt and jaded taste, but from a hearty appreciation of all the works and ways of nature, and a ready sympathy with every movement of the human soul. In no instance are these views so strongly confirmed as in this remarkable scene.

[Page 523.] In this play, for the first and only time, Shakespeare has ventured on representing the two principal characters as insane. His wonderful success in man-aging such intractable materials the world has long acknowledged and admired. They are never in the way, and their insanity is never brought forward in order to enliven the interest by a display of that kind of energy and extravagance that flows from morbid mental excitement. On the contrary, it assists in the development of events, and bears its part in the great movement in which the actors are hurried along as if by an inevitable decree of fate. Herein lies the distinguishing of Shakespeare's delineations of insanity. While other poets have made use of it chiefly to diversify the action of the play, and to excite the vulgar curiosity by its strange and striking phenomena, he has made it the occasion of unfolding many a deep truth in mental science, of displaying those motley combinations of thought that are the offspring of disease, and of tracing those mysterious associations by which the ideas of the insane mind are connected. Few men, I apprehend, are so familiar with those diversities of mental character, that are in any degree the result of disease, as not to find the sphere of their ideas on this subject somewhat enlarged by the careful study of Shakespeare.

[Page 524.] Wisely has the poet abbreviated the duration of [Ophelia's] mad-ness. The prolonged exhibition of this afflictive disease in one so gentle and lovely would have distressed the mind of the beholder in a manner unfavorable to dramatic effect. We see enough to understand that she is no longer conscious of her suffer-ings; and after listening to the snatches of songs that flit through her memory, with the same kind of melancholy interest with which we hear the sighing of the autumnal breeze through the limbs and leaves of the trees, we are willing that the finisher of all earthly sorrows should come. There is no method in her madness; no quips and cranks of a morbidly active ingenuity surprise and gratify the curious beholder, and no bursts of passion such as madness alone can excite fall on his astonished ear. Like one who walks in his sleep, her mind is still busy, but the sources of its activity are within. Heedless of everything else, her mind wanders among the confused and broken recollections of the past, deserted by the glorious light of the Divinity that stirs within us, but which is soon to be rekindled with unquenchable brightness.

W. W. LLOYD (1856)

(*Critical Essay on Hamlet*, contributed to SINGER'S Second Edition. London, 1856, p. 332.)—Whether the boundaries of sanity are really over-passed by Hamlet, whether the very warning he gives of his purposed simulation may be but one of the cunningnesses of the truly insane, are questions that belong to a class most difficult to treat, whether in life or literature. I confess to be inclined to take the latter view, which by no means excludes the recognition of a main stream of sanity running through the action, and comprising very much that was really but the simulation of madness. But some such extremity of excitement seems to form part of the supernaturalism of the play; such an effect was ordinarily ascribed to apparitions, and in this sense Horatio alludes to it; and it is noteworthy that Hamlet's manner is already changed, and he has already given signs of an antic disposition without obvious motive, before he has given notice that at some time thereafter he should probably think meet to affect eccentricity as a disguise. His susceptibility of irritation has received a wrench, and although he professes to his mother with every appearance of conviction to be merely mad in craft, a suspicion of something more is intimated in his thought that possibly the Ghost may have been but diabolical abuse of weakness and melancholy,—ever subject to such ill influence; and when he excuses his injuries to Laertes on the ground of madness, distractions, it would be, I think, unworthy of him to suppose that his apology was a mere and conscious fabrication. Some palliation, moreover, must be borrowed hence for his treatment of Ophelia, which otherwise more than verges on the brutal.

[Page 333.] Whatever energy in action, therefore, is manifested by Hamlet is in the form of passionate outburst, or reply to sudden provocation, or the impulse of the moment, and his liability to such accesses of excitement appears to have been increased by the excitement of the apparition,—itself, from another point of view, a consequence of the excitability, till it carries his mind over the balance that gives fair claims to sane composure.

[Page 335.] Hamlet is ever reminded of the charge laid upon him by the Ghost, to recognize it with a pang, to find some excuse for deferring,—now mistrust of the Ghost, now inaptness of an opportunity,—to accuse himself of dullness and tardiness, even to declare a resolution, but immediately to diverge into the generalities of a philosophical deduction, and allow himself to be carried away from any definite design entirely. He has the means, the skill, the courage, and what should be sufficient motive, but the active stimulus is unequal to the contemplative inertia that opposes it, and never thoroughly masters and possesses his nature; it gains no permanent hold on his attention ; his spirit is soon wearied and oppressed by the incongenial intrusion, and he relapses into the vein more natural to him; it is cursed spite to be called upon to bring back to order an unhinged world,—we may believe from his manner that he finds no great hardship or disgrace either in having lost the chance of governing the kingdom, of the foreign affairs of which at least he has not cared to inform himself, and there is such entire absence of expressions of regret for his frustrate love that I am not sure he does not feel some relief in getting rid of an importunate and interrupting passion. Hamlet's mind is certainly unhinged, and I would prefer to say unsettled. He is two entirely different Hamlets in different scenes, and we see him in constant alternation of hurried and lucid intervals. If we could assume for a moment that his madness is entirely feigned, we should stumble over the inconsistency that it is so carried out as to answer no reasonable purpose, excites suspicion instead of diverting it, covers not, and is not fit to cover, any secondary design, and would amount at best to a weak and childish escapade of ill-humor and spleen. This is the really difficult aspect of Hamlet's character, and it is here,—perhaps we may say alone in the play,—that the poet has left us to our own resources, has placed the picture of nature before us, and called upon us to read and interpret it with no aid from him of marginal interpretation. It is here that the genius of a great Shakespearian actor, if ever such arise again, may be displayed, in so rendering these equivocal scenes as to blend them harmoniously with those portions that in themselves are perfectly illuminated and defined, and bring home enlightenment and conviction at once to the understanding and the heart.

[Page 339.] The players find nothing attractive in Fortinbras, and are too happy to retrench the character and extirpate all possible allusions to him, but there is a worse evil in this than the curtain falling on an unking'd stage, with four princely corpses, and Osric and Horatio only left alive ; these foreign incidents give range to the thought that relieves them in this longest of all the plays, that renders the voyage and return of Hamlet less abrupt and remote and exceptional, and the idea which they communicate of the Norwegian prince,—the young and tender leader of an adventurous expedition,—remains in the mind insensibly from essential congruity with the theme of the play, so that his appearance and mastery at last is satisfying as the closing in of a grand outlying circuit and the fulfilment of an expectation.

DR BUCKNILL (1859)

(*The Mad Folk of Shakespeare*, London, 1859. Second edition, 1867, p. 60.)— [' My tables! meet it is I set it down,' &c.] We regard this climax of the terrible in the trivial, this transition of mighty emotion into lowliness of action, as one of the finest psychological touches anywhere to be found in the poet.

[Page 61.] When the mind is wrought to an excessive pitch of emotion, the instinct of self-preservation indicates some lower mode of mental activity as the one thing needful. When Lear's passions are wrought to the utmost, he says : ' I'll *do !* I'll *do !* I'll *do !*' But he does nothing. Had he been able, like Hamlet, to have taken out his note-book, it would have been good for his mental health. Mark the effect of the restraint which Hamlet is thus able to put upon the tornado of his emotion. When the friends rejoin him, he is self-possessed enough swiftly to turn their curiosity aside.

[Page 67.] His conduct to Ophelia is a mixture of feigned madness, of the selfishness of passion blasted by the cursed blight of fate, of harshness which he assumes to protect himself from an affection which he feels hostile to the present purpose of his life, and of that degree of real unsoundness, his unfeigned 'weakness and melancholy,' which is the subsoil of his mind.

[Page 69.] Hamlet's letter to Ophelia is a silly enough rhapsody; of which, indeed, the writer appears conscious. It reads like an old letter antecedent to the events of the drama. The spirit it breathes is scarcely consistent with the intense life-weariness under which its author is first introduced to notice. The signature, however, is odd: 'Thine evermore, most dear lady, whilst this *machine* is to him;' and agrees with the spirit of Hamlet's materialist philosophy, which is so strongly expressed in various parts of the play, and which forms so strange a contrast with the revelations from the spirit-world of which he is made the recipient.

[Page 78.] Hamlet is not slow to confess his melancholy, and indeed it is the peculiarity of this mental state, that those suffering from it seldom or never attempt to conceal it. A man will conceal his delusions, will deny and veil the excitement of mania, but the melancholiac is almost always readily confidential on the subject of his feelings. In this he resembles the hypochondriac, though not perhaps from exactly the same motive. The hypochondriac seeks for sympathy and pity; the melancholiac frequently admits others to the sight of his mental wretchedness from mere despair of relief and contempt of pity.

[Page 90.] The true melancholy and the counterfeit madness are strangely com mingled in this scene [with Ophelia, III, i].

[Page 94.] When the crisis has come, and the King's guilt has been unkennelled, and Hamlet is again left alone with Horatio, before whom he would not feign, his real excitement borders so closely upon the wildest antics of the madness he has put on in craft, that there is little left to distinguish between the two.

[Page 105.] The ideas which almost exclude from Hamlet's thoughts the wrong he has done Polonius now become expressed with a vehemence inconsistent with a sound mind. . . . . Although he succeeds in his purpose of turning the Queen's eyes into her very soul, and showing black and grained spots there, it must be admitted that this excessive vehemence is not merely so much out of the belt of rule as might be justified by the circumstances, but that it indicates a morbid state of emotion; and never does Hamlet appear less sane than when he is declaring: 'That I essentially am not in madness, But mad in craft.'

[Page 111.] Hamlet, therefore, offers as tests of his sanity that his pulse is temperate, that his attention is under command, and his memory faithful; tests which we are bound to pronounce about as fallacious as could well be offered, and which could only apply to febrile delirium and mania. The pulse in mania averages about fifteen beats above that of health; that of the insane generally, including maniacs, only averages nine beats above the healthy standard; the pulse of melancholia and monomania is not above the average. That a maniac would gambol from reproducing in the same words any statement he had made is true enough in the acute forms of the disease; but it is not so in numberless instances of chronic mania, nor in melancholia or partial insanity. The dramatic representations which are in vogue in some asylums prove the power of attention and memory preserved by many patients; indeed, the possessor of the most brilliant memory we ever met with was a violent and mischievous maniac. He would quote page after page from the Greek, Latin, and French classics. The *Iliad*, and the best plays of Molière in particular, he seemed to have at his fingers' ends. In raving madness, however, the two symptoms referred to by Hamlet are as a rule present. The pulse is accelerated, and the attention is so distracted by thick-flowing fancies, that an account can scarcely be given of the same matter in the same words. It is, therefore, to this form alone that the test of verbal memory applies.

[Page 116.] Alas, for Hamlet! What with his material philosophy and his spiritual experiences, there was contention enough in that region of the intellect which abuts upon veneration to unhinge the soundest judgement,—let alone the grief and shame and just anger, of which his uncle's crimes and his mother's frailty were the more than sufficient cause in so sensitive a mind.

[Page 127.] Although we arrive at the conviction that Hamlet is morbidly melancholic, and that the degree to which he puts on a part is not very great; that, by eliminating a few hurling words, and the description which Ophelia gives of the state of his stockings, there is little either in his speech or conduct that is truly feigned; let us guard ourselves from conveying the erroneous impression that he is a veritable lunatic. He is a reasoning melancholiac, morbidly changed from his former state of thought, feeling, and conduct. He has 'foregone all custom of exercise,' and longs to commit suicide, but dares not. Yet, like the melancholiacs described by Burton, he is 'of profound judgement in some things, excellent apprehensions, judicious, wise, and witty; for melancholy advanceth men's conceits more than any humour whatever.' He is in a state which thousands pass through without becoming truly insane, but which in hundreds does pass into actual madness. It is the state of incubation of disease, 'in which his melancholy sits on brood,' and which, according to the turn of events or the constitution of the brain, may hatch insanity or terminate in restored health.

[Page 130.] Hamlet's character presents the contrast between his vivid intellectual activity and the inertness of his conduct. To say that this depends upon a want of the power of will to transmute thought into action is to do no more than to change one formula of words into another. There must be some better explanation for the unquestionable fact that one man of great intellectual vigor becomes a thinker only, and another a man of vehement action. That activity of intellect is in itself adverse to decisiveness of conduct is abundantly contradicted by biography. That activity of intellect may exist with the utmost powerlessness, or even perversity of conduct, is equally proved by the well-known biographies of many men, 'who never said a foolish thing, and never did a wise one.' The essential difference of men who are content to rest in thought, and those who transmute it into action, appears not to consist in the presence or absence of that incomprehensible function, that unknown quantity of the mind, the *will;* but in the presence or absence of clearly-defined and strongly-felt *desire*, and in that power of movement which can only be derived from the exercise of power, that is, from the habit of action. It is conceivable, as Sir James Mackintosh has well pointed out, that an intellectual being might exist examining all things, comparing all things, knowing all things, but desiring and doing nothing. It is equally conceivable that a being might exist with two strong desires, so equally poised that the result should be complete neutralization of each o her, and a state of inaction as if no emotional spring to conduct whatever existed. Hence, inaction may arise from want of desire, or from equipoise of desire.

DR CONOLLY (1863)

(*A Study of Hamlet*, London, 1863, p. 22.)—This first soliloquy seems distinctly to reveal both Hamlet's mental constitution and the already existing disturbance in his feelings, amounting to a predisposition to actual unsoundness.

[Page 23.] The circumstances are not such as would at once turn a healthy mind to the contemplation of suicide, the last resource of those whose reason has been overwhelmed by calamity and despair. . . . . . No thought of feigning melancholy can have entered his mind; but he is even now most heavily shaken and discomposed, indeed so violently that his reason, although not dethroned, is certainly well-nigh deranged.

[Page 43.] The balance of his mind is lost; the sovereignty of his reason is really gone, as Horatio feared it might, in the retired colloquy with the spirit of his father, so lately hearsed in death. He is left incapable of steady and defined purpose.

[Page 51.] It is generally overlooked that the interpretation [of Hamlet's eccentricity subsequent to the communication with the Ghost as mere acting] can scarcely extend to the eccentricity previously manifested, or explain his conduct or language before he had heard anything of the appearance of his father's ghost. Among his confused resolves, that of feigning madness seems suddenly to have suggested itself, either as subsidiary to some equally obscure plan of revenging his father's death, or merely to account for the wild words he had been uttering. The suggestion might have arisen in his mind in the short interval between the departure of the Ghost from his sight and his rejoining his friends. We shall find that it is never acted upon as a part of a consistent plan, but recurs to him now and then, and fitfully, and is at such times acted upon, not as a deliberately planned conduct, but as something lost sight of amidst the real tumult of a mind unfeignedly disordered.

[Page 53.] It certainly appears to me that the intention to feign was soon forgotten, or could not steadily be maintained, in consequence of a real mental infirmity; that it subsequently recurred to Hamlet's thoughts only in circumstances not productive of much emotion, but became quite unthought of in every scene in which his feelings were strongly acted upon, and that in such scenes a real and lamentable mental disorder swept all trivial considerations away.

[Page 54.] The very exhortations to secrecy, shown to be so important in Hamlet's imagination, are but illustrations of one part of his character, and must be recognisable as such by all physicians intimately acquainted with the beginnings of insanity. It is by no means unfrequent that when the disease is only incipient, and especially in men of exercised minds, that the patient has an uneasy consciousness of his own departure from a perfectly sound understanding. He becomes aware that, however he may refuse to acknowledge it, his command over his thoughts or his words is not steadily maintained, whilst at the same time he has not wholly lost control over either. He suspects that he is suspected, and anxiously and ingeniously accounts for his oddities. Sometimes he challenges inquiry, and courts various tests of his sanity, and sometimes he declares that in doing extravagant things he has only been pretending to be eccentric, in order to astonish the fools about him, and who he knew were watching him.

The young Hamlet has suddenly become a changed man. The curse of madness, —ever fatal to beauty, to order, to happiness,—has fallen upon him; deep vexation has undermined his reason, and thoughts beyond the reaches of his soul have agitated him beyond cure. His affections are in disorder, and the disorder will increase; so that he will become by turns suspicious and malicious, impulsive and reflective, pensive and facetious, and undergo all the transformations of the most afflicting of human maladies.

[Page 56.] From the time of the interview with the Ghost to the end of the play, Hamlet's conversation scarcely ever regains the composure and power of which it was previously capable. There is an appreciable change; often more brilliancy, but always less coherence; so that almost on all occasions his conversation is marred by flightiness, and by cynical disdain, both of himself and others, until nearly at the conclusion, when the agitations of life are ended, and he is dying. Then, indeed, in his brief and last conversation with Horatio, the consciousness of approaching death prevails over all temporal and minor influences, and his expressions are affectionate and noble.

[Page 74.] It [Hamlet's letter] was probably written before his abrupt visit to Ophelia in her chamber, and might have been the last she had received from him, written after his dreadful scene with the Ghost, and wrung from him as a kind of remonstrance, consequent on the doubt of his truth and honor implied by the repulsion of his letters following immediately after that shock. . . . . Except as the production of a disordered mind, there is no meaning in it; but it is perfectly consistent with what is observed in letters written every day by persons partially insane, both in and out of asylums, who labor under impulses to express in writing the sentiments occupying the imagination, but find the effort too much for them, and become bewildered, and unable to command words sufficiently emphatic to represent them.

In Hamlet's distraction, his thoughts have almost quitted the night-scene on the platform; and in his complicated distress they have turned chiefly to Ophelia. There is considerable risk of error in commenting on the precise application of many words used two centuries before our time, but even the accidental substitution of the word beautified, which Polonius condemns as a vile phrase, for the word beautiful, is not at all unlike the literal errors occurring often in madmen's letters; the writers aim at force, and are not satisfied with ordinary words. Altogether, the style of the letter has so singular a resemblance to that of insane persons of an intellectual character, but disturbed by insanity, as almost to justify the supposition that Shakespeare had met with some such letter in the curious case-books of his son-in-law, Dr Hall, of Stratford-upon-Avon.

[Page 77.] This garrulity (Polonius's) details to us the order of the symptoms already partly indicated in the action of the play, and might have been copied from the clinical notes of a student of medical disorders. We recognize all the phenomena of an attack of mental disorder consequent on a sudden and sorrowful shock; first, the loss of all habitual interest in surrounding things; then, indifference to food, incapacity for customary and natural sleep; and then a weaker stage of fitful tears and levity, the mirth so strangely mixed with ' extremest grief;' and then subsidence into a chronic state in which the faculties are generally deranged. These are occurrences often noticed in pathological experience, and even in the sequence mentioned.

[Page 85.] Hamlet knows, or suspects, that Rosencrantz and Guildenstern have been sent for to test the sanity of his understanding, and perhaps for ulterior objects which may concern him. He is not only desirous to ascertain the truth of this, but to impress them with a conviction that he has been acting a part. If he were feigning he would feign still; for if at first sight there was reason for feigning, the reason yet remains, and he would rather strive to send them back confirmed that his antic disposition was a real madness. But he is conscious that all is not well with him; he perceives that he is watched; perhaps he is apprehensive that this watching forebodes mischief to him, and he carefully endeavors to evade such an inconvenient consequence. This is an often-noticed tendency in cases of mental impairment, and this is not the only scene in which Hamlet manifests it.

[Page 88.] And even in this conversation with Rosencrantz and Guildenstern, whilst he exhibits the acuteness with which an insane man will for a short time discourse, he also shows the unfitness of an infirm mind for consecutive conversation or continued exertion. Every incidental trifle produces interruption, and drives thought from its proposed course. He now proceeds to tell his friends why they were sent for, but with a wish to prove to them that no valid reason existed for it. He confesses peculiarities which have lately crept upon him; some which he is conscious must have been observed, but also some which have only been experienced by himself. In thus imparting himself, his expressions take the unhappy character of an uneasy and oppressed mind, to which every ordinary source of pleasure has become indifferent or presents itself in a morbid and joyless form. This is so precisely the condition exemplified in the greater number of melancholy patients that we can scarcely imagine it merely copied from observation, and feel inclined to refer the eloquent description to some painful experience of the great poet himself.

[Page 110.] In his conversation with Ophelia his words and his conduct are simply those of a man distempered. For feigning such contempt and cruel disregard as he thus expresses, and towards one for whom he had professed and had really felt a lover's affection, there is no reason and no excuse except the sad excuse that he is not in his perfect mind. To suppose him feigning is impossible. No man, however resolved to act a cruel part, could be supposed to listen to words of trust sincerely spoken by a gentle woman, diffidently addressing him, and returning him the gifts he had in happier hours presented to her with honeyed vows, without casting away all predetermined simulation, and clasping her to his heart.

[Page 115.] The diffusion of the element of tenderness over the whole of Hamlet's character, however skilfully effected on the stage, is an unauthorized departure from the delineation of his character by Shakespeare.

[Page 123.] This advice to the Players includes directions so judicious and admirable as to seem to add to the difficulty of comprehending the real condition of Hamlet's mind. Such variations of mood and manner of discourse present nothing new to those whose painful duty it is to live with the insane. Hamlet has his days of calmness and his days of excitement, and the presence of different persons affects him differently, and sometimes excessively,—of some to contempt and anger, some to ridicule, and some to quieter reflection. In the first interview with the Players, Polonius is present, upon whom he exercises his customary jokes; the second interview is with the Players only, who know nothing of his suspected malady or of the designs he entertains, and to converse with them is agreeable to him, and even in some degree restorative of mental composure. . . . . For a time the Players make him almost forget the wretchedness, the thought of which has unsettled his reason.

[Page 126.] When the King and Queen, &c., enter with fleurishes of trumpet immediately after Hamlet's conversation with Horatio, it must be confessed that Hamlet instantly betrays, or appears at once to feign, an extravagance of manner and language at variance even with the deportment just maintained with Horatio.

The real promptings of malady seem at this particular time to be mingled with a wildness affected in order to bewilder the company or to deceive the King and the court; but the affected wildness is further stimulated by the ungovernable excitement of a brain too unfeignedly disordered to be made the subservient instrument of a wish merely to seem to be disordered. Part of the wild talk of the Prince seems to be only put on to tease or to insult the King or Polonius, but from this he soon passes on to expressions and conduct plainly dictated by a mind which, however cunning, he cannot control.

[Page 128.] Throughout the whole of the play-scene there is the same vein of craziness in Hamlet's language and deportment. Except his previous conduct to Ophelia, there is nothing more offensive in Hamlet's expressions than those which he indulges while speaking to her in this scene. Malady, and not feigning, has appeared to change the refined Prince into an indelicate mocker, who addresses a young lady in terms coarser than he would have employed if his controlling respect had not been obscured and his habitual courtesy gone from his mind. In this disordered state he has no apparent remembrance of his former repulse of her loving behavior, nor of his denial of having ever loved her, and he has equally forgotten his violent conduct and language, as insane persons alone do, and do so remarkably. Nor is what he says or does consistent with a rational anxiety, however intense, to watch the success of a device to which he attached, when shaping it, a great importance as the means of solving a serious question, and of dissipating a horrible suspicion, and thus determining his future course of action. All his actions and all his words are those of a distempered man, unmindful of the respects and proprieties of life. He never becomes composed; never recovers himself. He goes on jesting with Ophelia, as if incapable of deeper matter, and when the performance of the Players has affrighted the King and sent all the noble audience away, and he is left with Horatio alone, before whom he has no motive for maintaining an antic disposition, he still talks wildly. Since the sad night of his interview with his father's ghost he has, in some quieter hour, entrusted Horatio with the whole revelation made to him; but now, even with Horatio, he speaks as strangely as he formerly did with Horatio and Marcellus together, immediately after that unearthly discourse, and when he was surfeited with horrors. As no gravity then resulted from that interview, so no gravity now results from his conviction that the Ghost was a true ghost, the tale of the murder true, and his uncle the murderer. He takes no counsel with his friend. He exclaims that he will 'take the ghost's word for a thousand pounds,' just as recklessly as he had said, 'It is an honest ghost, that let me tell you.' His words are now, as they were then, wild and hurling. No resolution springs up in his mind; it is all disordered and unbalanced. He quotes doggerel verses, and calls for the recorders.

Just when he is in this unsettled humor, Rosencrantz and Guildenstern approach; they come to him, sent by the Queen. Their presence chafes him, and in the short conversation with them he assumes a contemptuous air, and baffles them with scoffing words, which amusingly and precisely resemble the expressions of certain persons partially insane, who delight in the power of exercising a cultivated intellect in bewildering plain people. This acuteness in putting their questioners out of countenance, and averting their unwelcome inquiries, is well known to those experienced in the ways of the insane, and, although not combined with consistent and reasonable actions, is often extremely embarrassing to the inexperienced.

[Page 139.] The speech of Hamlet upon finding the King praying is the speech of a man uttering maniacal exaggerations of feeling. Such exaggerations of anger or ferocity are occasionally recognized in the ravings of the mad,—of no other persons, however enraged or depraved. The speech, it is also to be observed, has no listeners; there is nobody by to feign to. The terrible words are the dictation of a mind so metamorphosed by disorder that all healthy and natural feelings, all goodness and mercy, have been forcibly driven out of it.

[Page 141.] The wild impulses of the night, in Hamlet's interview with his mother, are still acting on Hamlet's distempered brain, and exclude the natural sorrow and remorse with which he would, if sane, have been affected on finding that he had slain an innocent old man, once the friend and favorite of his father. Every feeling seems incontestably perverted by sheer madness. Nor does he at all recover himself all through his subsequent interview with the Queen. His self-command is so utterly gone that he puts into words the bitterest and coarsest thoughts that have passed through his mind in his previous reflections on her marriage,— thoughts natural in a mind angrily revolving what has strongly moved it, but of which a healthy mind would suppress or mitigate the expression. . . . . No sense of what he has done affects him; he turns fiercely on his mother, regardless of her natural horror at this wanton deed of blood. All through the interview with the Queen it is not a sorrowing, princely, respectful son earnestly and passionately remonstrating with his mother, but an impetuous madman forgetful of the proper object of his purposed revenge; forgetful of the admonition of that unearthly being, who, whilst exhorting him to revenge his murder, solemnly enjoined him not to contrive against his mother aught; and now so deprived of all self-control and healthful feeling as at the first to impress upon his mother's mind the idea that he has come to kill her; and then almost exclusively to abuse and insult her on the subject of her second marriage,—his first maddening grief.

[Page 143.] To the Queen's question, ' What have I done,' &c., her son's reply is but further reproach and insult on the subject, not of his father's murder, but of her second marriage. The terms of hatred which he employs show that morbid exaggeration on this subject which has so much to do with the explanation of his whole conduct. His personal abhorrence of his uncle is dwelt upon with revolting particularity, and as if his mother's acceptance of him was all that tortured his mind. His reproaches dwell most on her affections having been weaned from her late dignified lord, and even transferred, during his lifetime, to his more sensual brother.

[Page 146.] The figures he draws of his hated uncle provoke him still more; he forgets his mother as much as he has forgotten his father and his promise to his father's ghost, abandons himself to mere abuse of his uncle, and almost riots in a foul vocabulary.

[Page 155.] It is curious to observe that the arguments he adduces to disprove his mother's supposition. [that he is delirious] are precisely such as certain ingenious madmen delight to employ [Dr Conolly here confirms Dr Bucknill's assertion that this test which Hamlet proposes to his mother only applies to cases of acute mania. See p. 209.]

[Page 199.] If Hamlet is feigning here, our view of his character must become low indeed. In the open grave before him lies the body of the fair Ophelia, of her whom once he certainly loved, with whose death he has only just become acquainted; and which death, if he has been feigning, he must know was partly the result of his murder of her aged father, and partly of his unfeeling treatment of herself. Her distracted brother leaps into her grave, and if Hamlet feigns he insults the brother's distraction, mimics it, outdoes it. The surer reading must be that the whole scene, at once so unexpected and so agitating, has driven the Prince from his lately re-gained tranquillity, and, acting on a brain yet strongly disposed to excitement, has overcome his self-control. If, instead of this, we are to assume that he takes this opportunity, already so colored with calamity, again to put an antic disposition on, and act the madman, with no conceivable object but insulting death and grief, we must be forced to the conclusion that Hamlet's real character was insensible and contemptible. It is impossible to entertain the supposition that Shakespeare would have made so worthless a moral being the principal personage of one of his noblest compositions, and have wasted his genius to adorn such singular moral deformity.

And this is the last paroxysm by which the mind of the unhappy Prince is shaken. After this he shows no more madness; it has left him again, as madness does after a reign of terror, we often know not how or why; its invasion and departure being equally mysterious, originating in causes lying too deep to be discerned and ex-amined, among the equally hidden sources of feeling and thinking, and of sleep and waking, and of life and death. When in a subsequent interview with Laertes he makes a solemn apology to him, before their fatal fence commences, acknow-ledging that he has done him wrong, he ascribes what he did to 'a sore distraction,' even to a madness, which he affectingly alludes to as 'poor Hamlet's enemy.' This is the pitiable truth. To treat this serious avowal as a falsehood is what all our sympathies refuse us to permit.

DR KELLOGG (1860)

(*Shakespeare's Delineations of Insanity, Imbecility, and Suicide*, New York, 1866, p. 36.)—Shakespeare . . . . recognized what none of his critics, not conversant with medical psychology in its present advanced state, seem to have any conception of; namely, that there are cases of melancholic madness of a delicate shade, in which the reasoning faculties, the intellect proper, so far from being overcome, or even dis-ordered, may, on the other hand, be rendered more active and vigorous, while the will, the moral feelings, the sentiments and affections, are the faculties which seem alone to suffer from the stroke of disease. Such a case he has given us in the character of Hamlet, with a fidelity to nature which continues more and more to excite our wonder and astonishment as our knowledge of this intricate subject advances.

[Page 44.] After the disappearance of the Ghost, the first words Hamlet utters give the clew to his mental and physical state, and it is quite evident that the cord, which has been stretched to its utmost tension, here snaps suddenly, and the conse-quences are immediately apparent, and are evinced throughout his whole subsequent career. Here enters the pathological element into his mind and disposition, and the working of the leaven of disease is soon apparent, for it changes completely and for ever his whole character. Up to this time we see no weakness, no vacillation no want of energy, no infirmity of purpose. After this, all these characteristics are irrecoverably lost, and though some faculties of his great spirit seem comparatively untouched, others are completely paralyzed.

[Page 46.] The intimation that he conveys in this scene, that he may think it 'meet to put an antic disposition on,' and upon which the theory of feigned madness is mainly built, is quite natural, and quite as consistent with the theory of real as feigned madness, and may, in the commotion of his mind, have resulted as much from a vague consciousness of what was impending, as from any intention to act a part. This is quite clear to the expert, though he may not succeed in making it so to those critics who take an opposite view of it.

[Page 48.] Hamlet's mind, as we have seen, had been made to reel and stagger by the contending emotions excited in the former scene, but it has not been at any time so completely overthrown as to deprive him, even temporarily, of self-control, until it experiences the shock imparted to it by [Ophelia's] refusal to see him or receive his letters. This, however, together with what has preceded, is more than it can bear, and he becomes, for the time being, quite frantic. He rushes unbidden into her presence, quite regardless of his personal appearance.

[Page 49.] Ophelia could not, and, as it is quite evident, *did not*, mistake the import of all this, and if we are to regard it as a well-acted *sham*, then let us forever cease to draw a distinction between art and nature; the two are identical, one and the same.

[Page 50.] [Hamlet] appears to regard Polonius as all lovers, sane or insane, are apt to regard a fond and perhaps too judicious parent, who stands between them and their cherished idol, as a meddlesome old fool, over anxious as to consequences, and quite incapable of appreciating their motives and feelings.

[Page 50.] [Hamlet] seems to take a morbid delight in annoying the old man Polonius. Nothing is more natural than for the insane to fix upon some one individual, from whom they have, or imagine they have, received some slight or injury, and endeavor to tease him by every means their sane ingenuity can devise.

[Page 51.] 'O God! I could be bounded in a nutshell and count myself a king of infinite space, were it not that I have bad dreams.' Restlessness, imperfect sleep, and dreaming are peculiarly incident to the initiatory stages of most forms of mental disease, and this remark forms another link in the chain of evidence respecting the real state of his mind. He interrupts the short metaphysical disquisition on ambition which follows, with a remark which shows that he feels that his mind is not in a fit state to reason on certain things, and can only act as it is directed by the disturbed current of his feelings. 'By my fay, I cannot reason,' says he; yet in the direction these lead see how he can discourse: [see II, ii, 288–295.]

[Page 52.] Hamlet's well-known apostrophe to man, many no doubt will think, hardly contains the thoughts likely to emanate from a mind at all tinctured with insanity; but such have yet to learn that the peculiar form of madness delineated by Shakespeare in the character of Hamlet is quite compatible with occasional outbursts of grand poetical inspiration. Such will no doubt persist in believing him when he says, ' I am but mad north-north-west; when the wind is southerly, I know a hawk from a hand-saw.' Those, however, who are familiar with the halls of an asylum for the insane, and have repeatedly heard patients scout the idea of their insanity in language almost identical with the above, will persist in holding a contrary opinion.

[Page 54.] The successive steps in the progress of his disease now become more and more marked, and we next perceive an upheaving and overthrow of those deep moral feelings and affections so peculiar to his character before the invasion of the disease. And here let those who maintain the theory of feigned madness be careful to observe, that the very feelings and faculties of his soul which have been most intensely exercised are the very ones which first give way and become most completely upset by the diseased reaction which follows. This they may regard, if they choose, as a mere coincidence; it will, however, be somewhat difficult for them to show that it was more easy, natural, and convenient for Hamlet to assume this form of madness than a form more readily calculated to deceive others,—one more easily feigned to carry out his purpose of deception.

[Page 57.] Surely they must be blind to dramatic propriety who can perceive in all this [the scene with Ophelia] nothing more than a well-acted sham, in which the actor does violence to his own best feelings, and wounds and lacerates fearfully those of her whom he had loved so tenderly, when the deception which he is thereby supposed to attempt is attainable at so much less cost. Ophelia, certainly no incompetent judge under the circumstances, seems as before to have placed the proper estimate upon his conduct. The lynx-eyed vigilance of woman's love could not be deceived, and she has read correctly the riddle which has so perplexed all Shakespeare's critics down to the present time.

[Page 64.] The scene with the Grave-diggers is not merely rich in wit, humor, philosophy, and morality, but it possesses a profound psychological interest, and it is evident Hamlet acted very unnaturally under the circumstances, supposing him to be sane or feigning; or supposing him to be insane, acted in the true spirit of his disease very naturally. The latter supposition is the more reasonable.

[Page 65.] The wild manifestations of sorrow on the part of Laertes at the grave of his sister, which Hamlet has observed at a distance, very naturally excite in him a paroxysm of his malady, and his conduct here establishes beyond all question the existence of genuine madness. At times he could control himself completely, and act and talk rationally, yet ever since the interview with the Ghost, even during these intervals, we can detect the genuine manifestations of that disease, which is ready to burst out in marked paroxysms upon occasions of unusual excitement like this.

CARDINAL WISEMAN (1865)

(*William Shakespeare*, by His Eminence Cardinal Wiseman. London, 1865, p. 41.)—If a dramatist wished to represent one of his persons as feigning madness, that assumed condition would be naturally desired by the writer to be as like as possible to the real affliction. If the other persons associated with him could at once discover that the madness was put on, of course the entire action would be marred, and the object for which the pretended madness would be designed would be defeated by the discovery. How consummate must be the poet's art who can have so skilfully described, to the minutest symptoms, the mental malady of a great mind as to leave it uncertain to the present day, even among learned physicians versed in such maladies, whether Hamlet's madness was real òr assumed.

This controversy may be said to have been brought to a close by [Dr Conolly.]

[Page 43.] But let it be remembered that in those days mental phenomena were by no means accurately examined or generally known. There was but little attention paid to the peculiar forms of monomania, or to its treatment, beyond restraint and often cruelty. The poor idiot was allowed, if harmless, to wander about the village or the country to drivel or gibber amidst the teasing or ill-treatment of boys or rustics. The poor maniac was chained or tied in some wretched outhouse, at the mercy of some heartless guardian, with no protector but the constable. Shakespeare could not be supposed, in the little town of Stratford, nor indeed in London itself, to have had opportunities of studying the influence and the appearance of mental derangement of a high-minded and finely-cultivated prince. How, then, did Shakespeare contrive to paint so highly-finished and yet so complex an image? Simply by the exercise of that strong sympathetic will which enabled him to transport, or rather to transmute, himself into another personality. While this character was strongly before him, he changed himself into a maniac; he felt intuitively what would be his own thought, what his feelings, were he in that situation; he played with himself the part of a madman, with his own grand mind as the basis of its action; he grasped on every side the imagery which he felt would have come into his mind, beautiful even when dislorded, sublime even when it was grovelling, brilliant even when dulled, and clothed it in words of fire and tenderness, with a varied rapidity which partakes of wildness and of sense. He needed not to look for a model out of himself, for it cost him no effort to change the angle of his mirror, and sketch his own countenance awry. It was but little for him to pluck away the crown from reason, and contemplate it dethroned.

Before taking leave of Dr Conolly's most interesting monograph, I will allow myself to make only one remark. Having determined to represent Hamlet in this anomalous and perplexing condition, it was of the utmost importance to the course and end of this sublime drama that one principal incident should be most decisively separated from Hamlet's reverse of mind. Had it been possible to attribute the appearance of the Ghost, as the Queen, his mother, does attribute it in Act V, to the delusion of his bewildered phantasy, the whole groundwork of the drama would have crumbled beneath its superincumbent weight. Had the spectre been seen by Hamlet, or by him first, we should have been perpetually troubled with the doubt whether or not it was the hallucination of a distracted, or the invention of a deceitful, brain. But Shakespeare felt the necessity of making this apparition to be held for a reality, and therefore he makes it the very first incident in his tragedy, antecedent to the slightest symptom of either natural or affected derangement, and makes it first be seen by two witnesses together, and then conjointly by a third unbelieving and fearless witness. It is the testimony of these three which first brings to the knowledge of the incredulous Prince this extraordinary occurrence. One may doubt whether any other writer has ever made a ghost appear successively to those whom we may call the wrong persons before showing himself to the one whom alone he cared to visit. The extraordinary exigencies of Shakespeare's plot render necessary this unusual fiction. And it serves, moreover, to give the only color of justice to acts which otherwise must have appeared unqualified as mad freaks or frightful crimes.

DR ROSS (1867?)

(*Studies, Biographical and Literary*, London, n. d. p. 39.)—Filial love is the starting-point of Hamlet's action, and this drives him to courses which the mature men, who are his critics, deem puerile and inconsequential. So, indeed, they are; if they were otherwise, they would be incongruous with his character. With this inconsequence there is a subtlety of thought ever characteristic of the opening faculties of youth. The passion for metaphysical speculation, like filial love, is strongest in young minds, and quickens the powers into rapid development. Hundreds of men of genius have in their youth written quires of ingenious disquisition on the nature and destinies of man, which, when they have reached manhood, they have

discreetly burnt. Shakespeare is careful to tell that at the time the play opens
Hamlet wished to go ' back to school at Wittenberg.' . . . .

Hamlet was one of Shakespeare's early works; it was afterwards strengthened
and enlarged, but it still bears the marks of immaturity and inexperience.

[Page 41.] Was Hamlet really mad, or was he not? This question is answered
by himself in the negative, and requires no discussion.

[Page 43.] Hamlet, then, is not ' essentially' mad, but only ' mad in craft;' and
now it will be curious to inquire how Shakespeare has managed this ' craft' in his
hero. The assumption is very simple, and consists, in relation to external action,
of extravagant gestures, noddings of the head, tremblings of the limbs, and carelessness of attire. In this respect it is similar to the assumption of Edgar. Intellectually, it is evinced in the indulgence of a speculative train of thought always
natural to him, and in his serious moments exhibiting considerable ingenuity, and
bearing a relation to the difficulties of his position and the humiliating irresolution
of his character; but, in the passages of affected insanity, it is less sustained and
abstract, and is generally charged with satirical and insulting inferences applicable
to the conduct of those he dislikes or has a purpose of annoying   There is a savage
humor mingled with these speculations and argumentative qu.bbles which makes
them terribly scathing.   His soliloquy, ' To be, or not to be,' is delivered in his sane
character, and exhibits, with some infirmities as well as some marvellous beauties
of diction, a searching power of mental analysis and a pre-eminent faculty for consecutive argument.   In the interview with Ophelia, which immediately follows the
evolution of his inmost feelings, he lapses or rather forces himself into his lunatic
mood, and then he indulges in paradoxes and a cutting insolence of demeanor
which are characteristic of the assumption.   Shakespeare, who, in the spirit of a
true dramatic genius, is fond of drawing contrasts, has here contrasted in one character two antagonistic mental states,—Hamlet sane and Hamlet mad; and he has
put all his strength in the development of his masterly conception.

The question, yea or nay, of Hamlet's lunacy is connected with the prior question
of the necessity of feigning it. It has been said that the assumption was superfluous, inasmuch as it led to no consequences necessary to the development of the
plot. Most of the deaths occurred by accident, and the stabbing of the King resulted from an impulse of revenge. This is true. We may add, however, that the
necessity did not exist in the circumstances, but in the character; and this is a distinction that must be made when estimating his art, not only in this, but in all the
plays by our author. He cared not for other consistencies, if the characters were
consistent. Hamlet was agitated by a deep wrong; he was ' very proud, revengeful, and ambitious,' but he was also timid and irresolute. His philosophy had un-
nerved his will without tempering his passions. Although revengeful, he dared not
take his revenge; he wished murder done, but was too irresolute to do it; and being
unused in the ways of the world, his passions had not yet hardened into recklessness, nor his purposes matured into crime. Like most reflective and sensitive young
men, he was overawed by the presence of his elders, and, thrown back upon himself, he nursed his feelings in secret until they became morbid. He then sought
that relief in words which he dared not obtain from action. Such was his timidity,
however, that he feared even to utter in his proper character the bitter taunts his
heart meditated; he therefore affected insanity, that under its pretence he might
indulge, with comparative safety, a license in the use of cutting innuendoes and insolent retorts. Had he not affected lunacy, the development of the character in its

moral aspects would have been impracticable, because it would have been inconsistent. Shakespeare's aim was quite clear to himself, and he proves it by contrasting the promptitude of Laertes, who has suffered the same injury,—the murder of
nis father. . . . . He [Hamlet] was a youth of tongue, not a man of performance,
—a clever tongue, indeed, had he,—superlatively clever; but he was, at best, only
half-matured,—a giant in intellect, a dwarf in will, a wise idiot, a fool of nature,
who knew everything in the circle of being,—even himself, which is the highest
knowledge,—yet his very weakness mastered him, and made his wisdom the sport
of his imbecility.

RICHARD GRANT WHITE (1870)

(*The Case of Hamlet the Younger.* The Galaxy, April, 1870, p. 542.)—In the
consideration of Hamlet's case nothing should be kept more clearly in mind than
that from the time we hear of him until his death he was perfectly sane, and a man
of very clear and quick intellectual perceptions,—one perfectly responsible for his
every act and every word; that is, as responsible as a man can be who is constitution-
ally irresolute, purposeless, and procrastinating. They have done him wrong who
have called him undecided. His penetration was like light; his decision like the
Fates'; he merely left undone.

JAMES RUSSELL LOWELL (1870)

(*Among My Books. Shakespeare Once More.* Boston, 1870, p. 218.)—Another
striking quality in Hamlet's nature is his perpetual inclination to irony. I think this
has been generally passed over too lightly, as if it were something external and accidental, rather assumed as a mask than part of the real nature of the man. It
seems to me to go deeper, to be something innate, and not merely factitious. It is
nothing like the grave irony of Socrates, which was the weapon of a man thoroughly in earnest,—the *boomerang* of argument, which one throws in the opposite
direction of what he means to hit, and which seems to be flying away from the
adversary, who will presently find himself knocked down by it. It is not like the
irony of Timon, which is but the wilful refraction of a clear mind twisting awry
whatever enters it,—or of Iago, which is the slime that a nature essentially evil
loves to trail over all beauty and goodness to taint them with distrust: it is the half
jest, half earnest of an inactive temperament, that has not quite made up its mind
whether life is a reality or no, whether men were not made in jest, and which
amuses itself equally with finding a deep meaning in trivial things, and a trifling
one in the profoundest mysteries of being, because the want of earnestness in its
own essence infects everything else with its own indifference. If there be now and
then an unmannerly rudeness and bitterness in it, as in the scenes with Polonius and
Osric, we must remember that Hamlet was just in the condition which spurs men to
sallies of this kind; dissatisfied, at one neither with the world nor with himself, and
accordingly casting about for something out of himself to vent his spleen upon.
But even in these passages there is no hint of earnestness, of any purpose beyond
the moment; they are mere cat's-paws of vexation, and not the deep-raking ground-
swell of passion, as we see it in the sarcasm of Lear.
The question of Hamlet's madness has been much discussed and variously de-

cided. High medical authority has pronounced, as usual, on both sides of the question. But the induction has been drawn from too narrow premises, being based on a mere diagnosis of the *case*, and not on an appreciation of the character in its completeness. We have a case of pretended madness in the Edgar of *King Lear*: and it is certainly true that that is a charcoal sketch, coarsely outlined, compared with the delicate drawing, the lights, shades, and half-tints of the portraiture in Hamlet. But does this tend to prove that the madness of the latter, because truer to the recorded observation of experts, is real, and meant to be real, as the other to be fictitious? Not in the least, as it appears to me. Hamlet, among all the characters of Shakespeare, is the most eminently a metaphysician and psychologist. He is a close observer, continually analyzing his own nature and that of others, letting fall his little drops of acid irony on all who come near him, to make them show what they are made of. Even Ophelia is not too sacred, Osric not too contemptible for experiment. If such a man assumed madness, he would play his part perfectly. If Shakespeare himself, without going mad, could so observe and remember all the abnormal symptoms as to be able to reproduce them in Hamlet, why should it be beyond the power of Hamlet to reproduce them in himself? If you deprive Hamlet of reason, there is no truly tragic motive left. He would be a fit subject for Bedlam, but not for the stage. We might have pathology enough, but no pathos. Ajax first becomes tragic when he recovers his wits. If Hamlet is irresponsible, the whole play is a chaos. That he is not so might be proved by evidence enough were it not labor thrown away.

This feigned madness of Hamlet's is one of the few points in which Shakespeare has kept close to the old story on which he founded his play; and as he never decided without deliberation, so he never acted without unerring judgement. Hamlet *drifts* through the whole tragedy. He never keeps on one tack long enough to get steerage way, even if, in a nature like his, with those electric streamers of whim and fancy forever wavering across the vault of his brain, the needle of judgement would point in one direction long enough to strike a course by. The scheme of simulated insanity is precisely the one he would have been likely to hit upon, because it enabled him to follow his own bent, and to drift with an apparent purpose, postponing decisive action by the very means he adopts to arrive at its accomplishment, and satisfying himself with the show of doing something that he may escape so much the longer the dreaded necessity of really doing anything at all. It enables him to *play* with life and duty, instead of taking them by the rougher side, where alone any firm grip is possible,—to feel that he is on the way toward accomplishing somewhat when he is really paltering with his own irresolution. Nothing, I think, could be more finely imagined than this. Voltaire complains that he goes mad without any sufficient object or result. Perfectly true, and precisely what was most natural for him to do, and, accordingly, precisely what Shakespeare meant that he should do. It was delightful to him to indulge his imagination and humor, to prove his capacity for something by playing a part; the one thing he could not do was to bring himself to *act* unless when surprised by a sudden impulse of suspicion,—as where he kills Polonius, and there he could not see his victim. He discourses admirably of suicide, but does not kill himself; he talks daggers, but uses none. He puts by the chance to kill the King with the excuse that he will not do it while he is praying, lest his soul be saved thereby, though it is more than doubtful whether he believed it himself. He allows himself to be packed off to England without any motive, except that it would for the time take him farther from a present duty: the more disagreeable to a nature like his, because it *was* present, and not a mere matter for speculative consideration.   When Goethe made his famous comparison . . . . he seems to have considered the character too much from one side.   Had Hamlet actually killed himself to escape his too onerous commission, Goethe's conception of him would have been satisfactory enough.   But Hamlet was hardly a sentimentalist, like Werther; on the contrary, he saw things only too clearly in the dry north-light of the intellect.   It is chance that at last brings him to his end.   It would appear rather that Shakespeare intended to show us an imaginative temperament brought face to face with actualities, into any clear relation of sympathy with which it cannot bring itself.   The very means that Shakespeare makes use of to lay upon him the obligation of acting,—the Ghost,—really seems to make it all the harder for him to act; for the spectre but gives an additional excitement to his imagination and a fresh topic for his skepticism.

[Page 225.] If we must draw a moral from Hamlet, it would seem to be that Will is Fate, and that Will once abdicating, the inevitable successor in the regency is Chance.   Had Hamlet acted, instead of musing how good it would be to act, the King might have been the only victim.   As it is, all the main actors in the story are the fortuitous sacrifice of his irresolution.   We see how a single great vice of character at last draws to itself as allies and confederates all other weaknesses of the man, as in civil wars the timid and the selfish wait to throw themselves upon the stronger side.

DR STEARNS (1871)

(*The Shakespeare Treasury of Wit and Knowledge*, New York, 1871, p. 352.)— The majority of readers at the present day believe that Hamlet's madness was real. I therefore find myself in the minority; for I regard it as feigned. . . . . A madness so skilfully feigned, and in so moderate and exact a degree as to deceive not only those whom it was intended to deceive, but also to deceive alike spectators and readers, who are always privileged to know more of the action and the real characters in a play than do the personages themselves,—such a feigned madness serves to make the plot more ingenious and interesting than it would be if the hero's mental aberration had been made to appear unmistakably real.

[Page 357.] Any young man born and reared to large expectations with a like natural temperament, over-educated to a degree that has rather weakened than strengthened him for coping with great difficulties, and, moreover, prostrated under a heavy affliction, might feel a rush of emotions such as Hamlet gives vent to in his first soliloquy.   For the first time in his life he has just had a view of the worst side of the world, and of the people in it.   He could comprehend it, too, at sight, because he had read of it in his books, but had never before any personal experience of the reality.   The result that follows indicates that his mind had been rather unfitted for action by too much cultivation; like the bow of the fable, that was so weakened by ornamental carving, that it broke on the first severe trial.   But that Hamlet's faculties did not give way in like manner, I must try to prove.

Hamlet's passionate burst of feeling the first time we see him left alone, is not unlike that of Job in his distresses; for he would welcome death as a release from hopeless earthly trouble.   That speech, at the outset so full of gloomy thoughts, cannot therefore be considered as any proof of existing mental derangement, or as indicating that it was likely to follow.

[Page 359.] He comes away from that fearful conference both more composed and resolved than before, or is seen to be at any time after. He replies to his friends in a manner half serious, half jesting.

[Page 363.] I will not, therefore, attempt to gain any support for the theory of Hamlet's feigned madness by citing examples of his rare intellectual power, so superior to that of all others around him. For I doubt not that those who have made a study of the phenomena of insanity could demonstrate that the two were not incompatible.

[Page 366.] Moreover, it is to be remarked that this particular friend, Horatio, makes no reference to the Prince's insanity by any 'aside' and sorrowing expressions of regret and sympathy, as he most surely would do did he not know that his insanity was counterfeited, and for a special purpose.

[Page 368.] Hamlet's own protestation to his mother of his sanity would, I suppose, of itself be regarded as of little weight; as known lunatics very often make just such protestations, and support them, too, by the most cunning devices. Yet, on this point, there are two other circumstances to be remarked. The Prince had special reasons for wishing his mother might not continue to believe in his madness. For such a belief would act as 'a flattering unction' to the wounds he wished to make in her conscience by his severe reproof of her marriage with his uncle, which was criminal on her part and dishonoring to him.

Again, though real lunatics often try to disprove their lunacy, it must happen much more rarely that a real lunatic will beg that he may not be thought to be really insane, 'but only mad in craft.'

It is also to be remarked, that in this interview with his mother, the Prince's manner changes directly after the accidental killing of the old lord chamberlain, who was listening behind the arras; for then he knows that for this time he is freed from all spies and listeners. In direct contrast to this is that early scene with Ophelia, whom he has not met 'for this many a day,' and who was at that time specially 'let loose to him' as a decoy, while, as he very well knew, there were concealed listeners near by: so that his harshness to her on that occasion was intended to deceive her father and the eaves-dropping King. In direct contrast with this, again, is his friendly and confidential talk with Horatio, just before the performance of the court play begins, when he has managed to send away his spies and followers on a brief errand. Likewise, after the lord chamberlain is discovered and killed in his place of concealment, Hamlet knows that he is freed from further espionage for that time, and straightway he makes use of the unexpected opportunity not only to charge his mother with her disgraceful courses, but also proceeds to speak of other things with a plainness he would not have used unless he had felt certain that there were no more listeners about. . . . . What special use Hamlet intended to make of the King's betrayal of his guilt through the effect of the play upon his conscience, we can only now surmise. Perhaps he meant it to serve more as public evidence of the crime, than for the satisfying his own private judgement. But within an hour after that, he happened to kill the old lord chamberlain, and the next morning, by order of the King, he is far on his way to England. At this point, in the history or action of the piece, our inquest of his lunacy or sanity comes to an end. For, from the moment that Hamlet leaves for England, his vagaries of act and speech cease entirely; with the single exception, after his sudden return, of his strife with Laertes at Ophelia's grave; where, indeed, his conduct is hardly more extravagant than that of her brother.

Hamlet's after apology by a falsehood,—if his insanity was not real,—presents another difficulty in the conduct of so noble and brave a man. But as we know it was not prompted by cowardice or any selfish motive, but rather from a feeling of kindness towards a man who was himself under great bereavements, this falsehood should be judged of very lightly.

ARTHUR MEADOWS (1871)

(*Hamlet: An Essay*, Edinburgh, 1871, p. 10.)—But how this has ever come to be a matter for dispute we are at a loss to understand. Had Hamlet kept his intention to play the madman to himself, there would have been room for doubt; but after having taken Horatio and Marcellus into his confidence, by stating plainly his resolve to behave himself like a madman, it is inconceivable how any misconception of the proper reading should exist. It is no proof that his madness is real to say that the King, Queen, Polonius, and others, think and say he is mad; this only proves he imitated madness well when he succeeded in creating this belief. When David scrabbled on the doors of the gate at Gath, and let his spittle fall upon his beard, was he mad? Surely not. But Achish and others thought him mad. So it is in the present case; such proof is no proof, and is not entitled to a moment's considera-tion. There is not a whisper of Hamlet's madness up to the time when he warns his friends, in future, to take no heed of his acts,—not even from Polonius. The impression of his madness is created by his acts subsequent to this warning. In all his soliloquies, in his conversation with Horatio, in his instruction to the Players, in his interview with his mother, in his letter to Horatio, there is not the slightest trace of unreason, while his interviews with the King, Polonius, Ophelia, Rosencrantz and Guildenstern, are invariably and unmistakably associated with speech or actions resembling madness. Now, if Hamlet was really mad he never could have pre-served such an entire consistency throughout his behavior to so many people, only acting like a madman to those whom he wished to deceive. As a striking example of this fact, we would draw the attention of our readers to III, ii, and ask them to observe attentively his clear instructions to the Players, followed by his conversation with Horatio, and then note the remarkable change in his speech when answering the King. If he was mad, how is it his soliloquies are not interpolated with a mix-ture of irrelevant matter? Surely he must have betrayed himself at some time or other. There is ample scope for him to be caught tripping. We have the most secret thoughts of his heart placed before us. There is no attempt at concealment, to use the language of the conjurers. He who knew him best,—his schoolfellow, his dearest companion, the scholar Horatio,—does not think him mad. With Horatio, Hamlet spent most of his time, and was with him for days together, at the very time he was considered maddest. Horatio must have known well that Hamlet was thought mad by others, yet there is not a word from him. And why? Because he had sworn to take no notice of Hamlet's assumed madness. Either that or this, that Horatio failed to discover that he, whom he loved so well for his rare qualities of heart and mind, was mad. A supposition so preposterous,—that Horatio's bosom friend was mad, and Horatio knew it not,—is only worthy of a madman.

HUDSON (1872)

(*Shakespeare: His Life, Art and Characters*, Boston, 1872, vol. ii, p. 252.)—In my own view of the matter, as delivered more than twenty years ago, I used these words: 'After all, it must be confessed that there is a mystery about Hamlet which baffles the utmost efforts of criticism.' This was true then, but I think it is not so now. In plain terms, Hamlet is mad; deranged not indeed in all his faculties, nor perhaps in any of them continuously; that is, the derangement is partial and occasional; paroxysms of wildness and fury alternating with intervals of serenity and composure.

Now the reality of his madness is what the literary critics have been strangely and unwisely reluctant to admit; partly because they thought it discreditable to the hero's intellect, and partly because they did not understand the exceeding versatility and multiformity of that disease. And one natural effect of the disease, as we see it in him, is, that the several parts of his behavior have no apparent kindred or fellow-ship with each other: it makes him full of abrupt changes and contradictions; his action when the paroxysm is upon him being palpably inconsistent with his action when properly himself. Hence some have held him to be many varieties of character in one, so that different minds take very different impressions of him, and even the same mind at different times. And as the critics have supposed that amid all his changes there must be a constant principle, and as they could not discover that principle, they have therefore referred it to some 'unknown depth' in his being; whereas in madness the constant principle is either wholly paralyzed or else more or less subject to fits of paralysis; which latter is the case with Hamlet. Accordingly, insane people are commonly said to be, not themselves, but *beside themselves*.

And it is to be noted further, that in Hamlet the transpirations of character and those of disease interpenetrate and cross each other in a great many ways, so that it is often difficult and sometimes impossible to distinguish where they respectively end or begin. Rather say, his sanity and madness shade off imperceptibly into each other, so as to admit of no clear dividing line between them. This has been a further source of perplexity to the critics, who, because they could not see precisely when the malady comes in and goes out, have been fain to deny its existence altogether. Coleridge admits indeed, that 'Hamlet's wildness is but half false,' which seems to imply that it is but half true, or that he is not downright mad. And that his mind is full of unhealthy perturbation, thrown from its propriety and excited into irregular fevered action, was evident to me long ago; and I so stated it in my *Introduction* to the play, written as far back as 1855; but as I did not then understand either the fact or the possibility of a man's being himself and beside himself at the same time, or of his alternating so abruptly between the two, I was not prepared for a frank and clear admission of Hamlet's madness.

What was wanting in order to a just criticism of the delineation was a profound and comprehensive science of the nature and genesis of mental disease.

[Page 256.] I will now briefly advert to an authority very different indeed from that of scientific experts, but perhaps not less deserving of respect. It is well known that Shakespeare's persons, like those in real life, are continually misunderstanding each other, and misunderstanding themselves. It is also well known that on this point his women make the fewest mistakes. Their perceptions of character and of personal condition are apt to be quick and just, and in fact are seldom at fault. It is the fine tact, ' surer than Suspicion's hundred eyes,' of a pure, simple, ingenuous, disinterested mind; rather say, the wisdom of a good heart, which, indeed, is the divinest thing in human nature. Nor has any of them this wise and holy instinct in larger measure than the heroine of this play. Now Hamlet loves Ophelia with all his soul, and she knows it. She also loves him with all her soul, and he is him-self right well assured of the fact. We have her word for it, that he has impor-tun'd her with love in honorable fashion, and has given countenance to his suit with almost all the holy vows of Heaven. But, indeed, a language deeper and stronger than any spoken words has planted the mutual faith in them. And I must needs think that love, especially the love of an Ophelia, is a better judge in such matters than logic. It is to be noted, also, that when Ophelia speaks of ' that noble and most sovereign reason, like sweet bells jangled out of tune and harsh,' her meaning tallies exactly with the conclusion of Dr Ray. This concurring voice of womanly instinct and of scientific judgement might well suffice for closing the subject; and taking these, together with the belief of all the other persons in the play, except the King, whose doubts spring from his own guilt, and also with the solemn declaration of Hamlet himself to Laertes near the end, I must be excused for accepting them as decisive of the question. But then it must be remembered that a mind diseased is not necessarily a mind destroyed; and that it *may be* only a mind with some of its nobler faculties whirled into intemperate and irregular volubility, while others of them are more or less palsied.

[Page 259.] Thus all the forms of human greatness may be, and indeed seem to be, reciprocally transmutable. My own idea, then, is that the poet's design in Hamlet was to conceive a man great, perhaps equally so, in all the elements of character, mental, moral, and practical; and then to place him in such circum-stances, and bring such influences to work upon him, that all his greatness should be made to take on the form of thought. And with a swift intuitive perception of the laws of mind, which the ripest science can hardly overtake, he seems to have known just what kind and degree of mental disturbance or disease would naturally operate to produce such an irregular and exorbitant grandeur of intellectual mani-festation.

DR LATHAM (1872)

(*Two Dissertations on the Hamlet of Saxo Grammaticus and of Shakespeare*, London, 1872, p. 81.)—The more we isolate the narrative of Saxo, and limit our notions of his hero by the single account of him in the *Historia Danica*, the more freedom and latitude we allow both ourselves and the dramatist in the estimate of his character. The more, however, we recognize additional sources for his history, and the more we find that the evidence of these is uniform as to the nature of his mental ailment, the more we are constrained to treat him as a Dramatis Persona, whose character has come to us, to a certain extent, ready-made; and, as such, one which is not to be either tampered with or refined upon gratuitously. Common sense tells us this, and the old Horatian rule reminds us of it. We are not to make Medea mild; nor Ino cheerful; nor Ixion an honest man; nor Io domestic; nor Orestes jovial; neither must Achilles be' gentle and forgiving; but, on the con-trary, passionate, vindictive, and inexorable,—the moral of which is that we must think twice before, in the way of either will or intellect, we invest the madness of Hamlet with actual or even approximate reality. The pretendedness of Hamlet's malady is as genuine as the reality of that of Orestes; and .... I am inclined to think that long before it came under the cognizance of Shakespeare, his *dramatic* character [*i. e.* as one who feigned madness] was as strongly stamped and stereo typed as that of any one of the heroes or heroines in the Horatian list.

THOMAS TYLER (1874)

(*The Philosophy of Hamlet*, London, 1874, p. 7.)—'Polonius, after a remarkable display of Hamlet's "antic disposition," says: "though this be madness, yet there is method in't." Is it possible for us to discern this "method"? Can we discover any deeper meaning lying beneath what is outwardly so "odd" and "strange"?' [This 'deeper meaning,' and an explanation of Hamlet's assumed madness, TYLER, in common with DOERING and other Germans, finds in Hamlet's pessimittic phi- losophy. Thus, Hamlet's conduct to Ophelia, as described by her to her father, may be consistently explained on the supposition that Hamlet's pessimism had so jaundiced his vision that in his eyes all humanity was diseased, and even his dearly loved Ophelia, in that she was human, was diseased, and his treatment of her would in several particulars not inaptly represent the behavior of a person towards a dear friend in a hopeless condition from some fatal malady. Tyler goes even so far as to find corroboration in the phrase in Q_r: 'he holds my pulse.'] 'The reason why the poet omitted from the later text the holding of Ophelia's pulse may have been because, perhaps, he considered that such a circumstance, however suitable with respect to a physician, would not be equally appropriate in the case of a layman like Hamlet. I may add, that Hamlet's "going the length of all his arm" .... would seem to accord with the idea that her disease was repulsive or offensive.' Again, the emphasis given to 'the vile phrase "beautified"' seems clearly to show that Shakespeare used the word in its strict sense, appropriately representing the idea that 'Ophelia, though in reality, and beneath the surface, unsightly and re- pulsive, was yet rendered externally attractive and beautiful.'

[Page 12.] It must not be, however, for a moment supposed that it was Shake- speare's intention to depict Ophelia as singularly depraved, notwithstanding even that in her aberration she could sing verses of a somewhat questionable character,— a fact which Goethe has not inaptly explained. No; the idol of Hamlet's heart .... was not singularly depraved. Her disease was the disease of humanity. In- deed, it would appear to have been the poet's intention to represent Ophelia as dis- tinguished, in comparison with others, by a high degree of moral purity.

[Page 15.] What is meant by these 'bad dreams' which made the world a prison? This expression, as I take it, indicates those pessimistic views of nature which Hamlet had formed as the result of philosophic observation and reflection.

[Page 16.] Hamlet's pessimism reaches its climax in the dialogue with Ophelia which follows the soliloquy, 'To be, or not to be,' &c., ... and his excitement reaches its highest pitch when he contemplates the fact that women artificially stimulate men towards marriage, and towards that greatest of all abominations, to a consistently pessimistic philosophy, the perpetuation of the corrupt race of mankind. .... Hamlet's pessimism appears even before the commencement of his assumed mad- ness. See I, ii, 135.

[Page 21.] At Wittenberg, as we may reasonably suppose, much of Hamlet's attention had been given to philosophy. .... In the subtleties of such philosophy as we must suppose Hamlet had been studying, we may find in explanation of 'The body is with the King, but the King is not with the body,' &c., IV, ii. In this sentence, 'with' cannot denote nearness or contiguity. Probably the sense is to be given after this manner: 'The body is, like the King, a thing of nothing; therefore it is *with* the King in worthlessness.' But worthlessness is the only quality you can predicate of the body; for such material qualities as *weight* appear to be excluded. The body is not, as yet, offensive, though a month hence 'you shall nose him.' But the King possesses other qualities besides worthlessness; he possesses, for example, active malignity. But in these other qualities the King is not with the body; and so the King as a whole, being a congeries of qualities, 'the King is not with the body,' though at the same time, as already said, 'the body is with the King' in its one quality of worthlessness.

[Page 22.] There are several things in Hamlet's philosophy which may recall some of the opinions of the Stoics, and among them is the doctrine of an overmastering Fate or Destiny.

[Page 27.] During the interval before the soliloquy 'To be, or not to be,' we may suppose that Hamlet has reflected that his stratagem will probably be successful, and that then it will be for him to execute the command of the Ghost, and to put his uncle to death. At this juncture, as would appear probable, there arises in Hamlet's 'prophetic soul' a mysterious presentiment that the act of vengeance will be closely followed by his own death. If he takes arms against the 'sea of troubles,' opposes them, and, by opposing, ends them, he must die. This view appears to me preferable to the suggestion [see TIECK and FRIESEN. ED.] that Hamlet would be slain in the mêlée consequent on the King's death. But even this latter view is preferable to the interpretation that Hamlet contemplated suicide.

[Page 29.] Hamlet, though possessing both courage and energy, has nevertheless a peculiarly reflective disposition, a mind ever prone to turn inwardly on itself. A mind of such a nature, we may reasonably suppose, was regarded by the poet as especially susceptible of impression and suggestion from unseen and supernatural influence.

[Page 30.] We may then with probability conclude that we have in Hamlet a dramatic representation of the will of man governed by a Higher Will, a Will to which all actions and events are subordinate, and which, in a mysterious and incomprehensible manner, is ever tending to the accomplishment of inscrutable purposes.

[Page 32.] The philosophy of *Hamlet*, with regard to the state of things in the world, and especially with respect to the moral condition of mankind, is pessimistic. Still, notwithstanding the general depravity and the harsh and ungenial conditions of human life, all actions and all events are under the control of a superintending Providence. Man must execute the purpose of a Higher Power. But what is the nature of that purpose, what its intent, what its destined issue, is shrouded in mystery. Calamity and disaster fall upon men without regard to individual character. A retribution beyond death is possible; but the future destiny of mankind is obscure and doubtful. Now, if such is the philosophy of this great tragedy, we may easily see with what propriety it opens in the dark, cold, still midnight. I should think it, however, not quite impossible that there is a symbolical meaning in the fact that the darkness is not altogether complete, but that on the first night stars are shining, and on the second there are 'glimpses of the moon,' the sky being apparently for the most part concealed by clouds. Possibly we may look upon this mention of the 'moon' and 'stars' as intimating that the condition of the world is not altogether hopeless, notwithstanding the deep overhanging gloom.

GEORGE HENRY LEWES (1875)

(*On Actors and the Art of Acting*, London, 1875, p. 137.)—Much discussion has turned on the question of Hamlet's madness, whether it be real or assumed. It is not possible to settle this question. Arguments are strong on both sides. He may be really mad, and yet, with that terrible consciousness of the fact which often visits the insane, he may ' put an antic disposition on ' as a sort of relief to his feelings, or he may merely assume madness as a means of accounting for any extravagance of demeanor into which the knowledge of his father's murder may betray him. Shakespeare has committed the serious fault of not making this point clear; a modern writer who should commit such a fault would get no pardon. The actor is by no means called upon to settle such points. One thing, however, he is called upon to do, and that is, not to depart widely from the text, not to misrepresent what stands plainly written. Yet this the actors do in Hamlet. They may believe that Shakespeare never meant Hamlet to be really mad; but they cannot deny, and should not disregard the plain language of the text—namely, that Shakespeare meant Hamlet to be in a state of *intense cerebral excitement*, seeming like madness. His sorrowing nature has been suddenly ploughed to its depths by a horror so great as to make him recoil every moment from the belief in its reality. The shock, if it has not destroyed his sanity, has certainly *unsettled* him. Nothing can be plainer than this; every line speaks it. We see it in the rambling incoherence of his 'wild and whirling words' to his fellow-watchers and fellow-witnesses; but as this may be said to be assumed by him (although the motive for such an assumption is not clear, as he might have put them off, and yet retained his coherence), I will appeal to the impressive fact of the irreverence with which in this scene [I, v, 150–163] he speaks *of* his father and *to* his father,—language which Shakespeare surely never meant to be insignificant, and which the actors always *omit*.

[Page 141.] Now, why are these irreverent words omitted? Because the actors feel them to be irreverent, incongruous? If spoken as Shakespeare meant them to be,—as Hamlet in his excited and bewildered state must have uttered them,—they would be eminently significant. It is evading the difficulty to omit them; and it is a departure from Shakespeare's obvious intention. Let but the actor enter into the excitement of the situation, and make *visible* the hurrying agitation which prompts these wild and whirling words; he will then find them expressive, and will throw the audience into corresponding emotion.

But this scene is only the beginning. From the moment of the Ghost's departure, Hamlet is a *changed* man. All the subsequent scenes should be impregnated with vague horror, and an agitation compounded of feverish desire for vengeance with the perplexities of thwarting doubt as to the reality of the story which has been heard. This alternation of wrath and of doubt as to whether he has not been the victim of an hallucination, should be represented by the feverish agitation of an unquiet mind, visible even under all the outward calmness which it may be necessary to put on; whereas the Hamlets I have seen are perfectly calm and self-possessed when they are not in a tempest of rage, or not feigning madness to deceive the King.

It is part and parcel of this erroneous conception as to the state of Hamlet's mind (unless it be the mistake of substituting declamation for acting), which, as I believe, entirely misrepresents the purport of the famous soliloquy,—' To be, or not to be.' This is not a set speech to be declaimed to pit, boxes and gallery, nor is it a moral thesis debated by Hamlet in intellectual freedom; yet one or the other of these two mistakes is committed by all actors. Because it is a fine speech, pregnant with thought, it has been mistaken for an oratorical display; but I think Shakespeare's genius was too eminently dramatic to have committed so great an error as to substitute an oration for an exhibition of Hamlet's state of mind. The speech is passion‑ ate, not reflective, and it should be so spoken as if the thoughts were *wrung* from the agonies of a soul hankering after suicide as an escape from evils, yet terrified at the dim sense of greater evils after death. Not only would such a reading of the speech give it tenfold dramatic force, but it would be the fitting introduction to the wildness of the scene, which immediately succeeds, with Ophelia. This scene has also been much discussed. To render its strange violence intelligible, actors are wont to indicate, by their looking towards the door, that they suspect the King, or some one else, to be watching; and the wildness then takes its place among the *assumed* extravagances of Hamlet. Fechter also conceives it thus. I cannot find any warrant in Shakespeare for such a reading; and it is adopted solely to evade a difficulty which no longer exists when we consider Hamlet's state of feverish excite‑ ment I believe, therefore, that Hamlet is not disguising his real feelings in this scene, but is terribly in earnest. If his wildness seem unnatural, I would ask the actors what they make of the far *greater* extravagance with which he receives the confirmation of his doubts by the effect of the play upon the King? Here, it is to be observed, there is no pretext for assuming an extravagant demeanor; no one is watching now; he is alone with his dear friend and confidant, Horatio; and yet note his conduct [see III, ii, 259].

Of course the actors omit the most significant of these passages, because they are afraid of being comic; but, if given with the requisite wildness, these passages would be terrible in their grotesqueness. It is true that such wildness and grotesqueness would be out of keeping with any representation of Hamlet which made him calm, and only assuming madness at intervals. But is such a conception Shakespearian?

DR MAUDSLEY (1875)

(*Body and Mind*, &c., New York, 1875, p. 132. *Hamlet.* Westminster Review, No. 53.)—The direct occasion of Hamlet's rude and singular behavior in the pres‑ ence of Ophelia is, however, the inseparable blending of genuine affliction with his feigned extravagance; conscious dissimulation was almost overpowered by the un‑ conscious sincerity of real grief. In the moody exaggeration of his letter to her there is the evidence of true suffering; but he was compelled to dissimulate, because he could not trust even her with his plans. No design, therefore, could have been more skilful than that which he carried into execution; the strange guise which he purposely assumed was excellently well conceived to deceive the King and those about him, initiating, as it did with consummate ingenuity, the systematic feigning of madness. Nothing was so likely to make them believe in the reality of his mad ness as the conviction that they had discovered the cause of it. Flatter a man's in‑ tellectual acuteness, and he will be marvellously indulgent to your folly or your vice, stone‑blind to your palpable hypocrisy. Polonius fell headlong into the trap which had been set for him.

In truth, the character of Hamlet and the circumstances in which it is placed make destiny; and, from the relations of the two, to display the necessary law of the evolution of fate would seem to be the deepest aim of the drama.

This state of reflective indecision is a stage of development through which minds of a certain character pass before they consciously acquire by exercise a habit of willing. He who is passionately impulsive and has no hesitation at eighteen is, perhaps, reflective and doubtful at twenty-five, and in a few years more he may, if he develop rightly, be deliberately resolute. For the will is not innate, but is gradually built up by successive acts of volition: a character, as Novalis said, is a completely-fashioned will. Had Hamlet lived and developed beyond the melancholy stage of life-weariness in which he is represented, and through which men of a certain ability often pass, it may be supposed that he would have been affected very differently by a deed like that which was imposed upon him. Either it was a duty, and, according to his insight into its relations, practicable, and he would then lay down a definite plan of action; or it was not, according to his judgement, practicable, and he would then dismiss the idea of acting, and leave things to take their course. As years pass on, they bring surely home to the individual the lesson that life is too short for him to afflict himself about what he cannot help. There is a sufficiency of work in which every one may employ his energies, and things irremediable must be wisely left to take, unbewailed, their way. To rail at the events of Nature is nothing else but the expression of an extravagant self-consciousness; it is the vanity which springs from an excessive self-feeling that finds the world to be out of joint, and would undertake to set it right. He only would undertake the government of the universe who cannot govern his own mind. The wisely-cultivated man, conscious how insignificant a drop he is in the vast stream of life, learns his limitation, and accepts events with modesty and equanimity.

[Page 140.] He ruthlessly strips off the conventional delusions from things, and lays bare the realities; he utters the severest home-truths with the greatest satisfaction: 'These tedious old fools.' If any one in the full possession of his reasoning powers refuses to accept the delusions of life, and persists in exposing the realities beneath appearances, he is so much out of harmony with his surroundings that he will, to a certainty, be counted more or less insane. Strange, too, as it may seem, it is nevertheless true that such a one will commonly feign to be more eccentric or extravagant than he really is. Though intellectually he can contemplate objects and events in their extreme relations, his self-feeling incapacitates him from regarding himself objectively; and there is a certain gratification or vanity in acting extravagantly and in being thought singular or mad. Doubtless there was some solace to Hamlet's self-feeling in the mad pantomime by which he frightened and took leave of Ophelia; he was miserable, but there was conceit in his misery. He perceives the things of this world to be stale, flat, and unprofitable; but, by reason of his great self-feeling, he feels them much also. Had he recognized himself as a part of the stale, flat, and unprofitable things, he must have concluded that his individual feelings were of very little consequence to the universe, that there were many more woeful pageants than the scene wherein he played, and have thereupon attained to a healthier tone of mind.

[Page 143.] Let it not any longer escape attention that the deliberate feigning of insanity was an act in strict conformity with Hamlet's character; he was by nature something of a dissimulator,—that faculty having been born in him. Though it is not said that his mother, the Queen, was privy to the murder of her husband, yet from the words of the Ghost, who prefaces his revelations by stating how the uncle had ' won to his shameful lust the will of my most seeming virtuous queen,' it would appear that if she were not actual party to the crime, she was something almost as bad. . . . . But if Hamlet's character had received no taint from his mother, he was not altogether so fortunate on his father's side; for he was the nephew of the ' bloody, bawdy villain,'—the remorseless, lecherous, treacherous, kindless villain. We see, then, the signification which there was in his speech to Ophelia: ' You should not have believed me; for virtue cannot so inoculate our old stock but we shall relish of it.'

[Page 144.] As a heritage, then, Hamlet has that hatred of underhand cunning and treachery, that sincerity of nature, which justify Laertes in describing him as ' free from all contriving;' and as a heritage, also, he has that faculty for dissimulation which is evident in his character. . . . . Strange as it may seem, we not uncommonly observe the character of the mother, with her emotional impulses and subtle but scarce conscious shifts, in the individual when young, while the calm deliberation and conscious determination of the father come out more plainly as he grows older. Setting aside any necessity which Shakespeare might think himself under to follow the old play, it is in Hamlet's inherited disposition to dissimulation that we find the only explanation of his deliberately feigning madness, when, to all appearances, policy would have been much better served if he had not so feigned. But he has a love of the secret way for its own sake; to hoist the engineer with his own petard is to him a most attractive prospect; and he breaks out into positive exultation at the idea of outwitting Rosencrantz and Guildenstern, with whom he was to go to England.

[Page 161.] Struggle as earnestly and as constantly as he may, the reflecting mortal must feel at the end of all, that he is inevitably what he is; that his follies and his virtues are alike his fate; that there is ' a divinity which shapes his ends, rough-hew them as he may.' Hamlet, the man of thought, may brood over possibilities, speculate on events, analyze motives and purposely delay action; but in the end he is, equally with Macbeth, the man of energetic action whom the darkest hints of the witches arouse to desperate deeds, drawn on to the unavoidable issue. Mighty it must be allowed is the power of the human will; that which to him whose will is not developed is *fate*, is to him who has a well-fashioned will, *power;* so much has been conquered from necessity, so much has been taken from the devil's territory.

DR ONIMUS (1876)

(*Revue des Deux Mondes.* *La Psychologie de Shakspeare*, Paris, 1876, p. 12.)— For ourselves, we reluct at the idea that Hamlet is mad or within a step of becoming so. In the first place, Shakespeare would have shown us this tendency more decisively; it is his habit to indicate plainly what his personages are designed to be; but nowhere can we discover that it was his purpose to represent Hamlet as a morbidly affected and diseased person on the point of succumbing to insanity. Can it be affirmed that had he lived longer Hamlet would have become insane? There is no proof of it; on the contrary, at the close of the drama his mind appears to settle into a state of repose. There is no hallucination, no raving, no apparent premonitory symptom of insanity; he shows only a great exaltation of mind at the grave of Ophelia. On the other hand, if it is true that disease often begins with the predominance of the ideas which are found in Hamlet, it is impossible to consider these ideas as proofs of cerebral perturbations. They may exist in individuals who will never become insane, who will never give the least real sign of intellectual disturbance, but whose only peculiarity is that they are of a nature so sensitive and so impressionable, that they are greatly affected by the wrongs of the world. They cannot bear ' the whips and scorns of time, the oppressor's wrong,' &c. How many choice spirits there are who have shared these very thoughts, and in whom the spectacle of the world has led to disenchantment and disgust of life !

Physical organization doubtless contributes to aggravate this tendency, which consists in looking only at the dark side of things; and Shakespeare has taken care to show us Hamlet as ' fat and scant of breath.' In thus describing him, Shakespeare surely did not refer merely to the actor who filled the rôle, as some foolish critics have supposed. There are organizations less vigorous than that of Hamlet, morbid natures with nervous and lymphatic temperament, having, even in the bloom of life, none of the ardent and youthful qualities from which spring force and exuberant health, and which accompany heedless and lively spirits, eagerness for pleasure and for the work congenial to sanguine temperaments. Natures like Hamlet's are early thoughtful and suffering; they are all nerves, enthusiastic at one moment, depressed at another, according to circumstances; but notwithstanding their eccentricity, their originality and their conduct, oftentimes out of all ordinary rules, these persons never become crazed; as they were born, so they remain; they are misanthropes, kindly or morose, sympathetic or sneering, often rude and suspicious, but capable of fine repartees and keen hits. Consequently, we do not believe, with Drs Brierre de Boismont and Bucknill, that Hamlet was in one of those intermediary states between reason and madness which have been named the period of incubation, a period in which thousands succumb to disease, and from which hundreds are restored to health. In our opinion Hamlet would become never really mad, but only more rational. His is not an intermediary type, but a type real and complete in itself. If he has hallucinations, it is when his soul is overwhelmed by grief and by the greatness of the crime which he has caught sight of. His brain loses its balance, not from disease, but from excessive thought and suffering. It should be borne in mind that he has hardly had time to know where he stands, and to compare the world as it is with the world as, in his native goodness, he believed it to be,—that he is obliged, he so loving, so respectful, to turn away from the world from horror at the conduct of his mother !

There are children who are born musicians, whom a single false note irritates; from their earliest year they have the sense of harmony. Not a discord escapes them, and they cannot comprehend how there should be others differently organized, in whom the sense of harmony is wanting. Others again are born with an exquisite sense of color and form, and everything at variance with their art wounds and repels them. Hamlet is one of these artistic natures. He is an artist of the moral sense. Born with a feeling the most delicate for whatever is virtuous and noble, he is enamored with loyalty and truth, as the musician is with harmony and the sculptor with ideal forms; our vices and our weaknesses shock him; to him they are monstrosities.

With what loathing he endures the contact of flatterers and hypocrites, and how he loves to humiliate them ! It is with a secret pleasure that he torments the poor courtier Osric, to whom he presents the sight of his ridiculous meannesses and flatteries. He amuses himself by making Osric play in his own slime like some filthy animal. Here Hamlet recognises his natural enemy, who, in opposition to him, was born with a love of lying, and who 'did comply with his dug before he sucked it.' He hates the reprobates, or rather his heart revolts when they come in his way in the midst of the court of his uncle. It is the involuntary shrinking of terror and disgust which Marguerite feels in the presence of Mephistopheles. What joy is it, on the other hand, when he meets an honest man! His soul leaps to surrender itself to the ideal. With what pleasure does he grasp the frank and loyal hand of Horatio! Every time he finds himself with him, his heart is soothed, and humanity then appears to him less hateful.

NOTE

[On page 195, I have said that Dr AKINSIDE was probably the first to pronounce Hamlet's insanity real; since this was printed, I have noticed that DAVIES in his *Dramatic Miscellanies*, 1784, vol. iii, p. 85, says that: 'Aaron Hill, above forty years ago, in a paper called *The Prompter*, observed that besides Hamlet's assumed insanity, there was in him a melancholy, which bordered on madness, arising from his peculiar situation.'

Dr KELLOGG's Essay on Hamlet's insanity, from which extracts are given on p. 216, first appeared in the *Journal of Insanity* for April, 1860, as I have just been kindly informed by the author himself. These extracts, therefore, should follow those from Dr BUCKNILL, and precede those from Dr CONOLLY. The stereotype plates having been cast, the only change that could be made has been made in the date: 1860. ED.]

NAMES AND CHARACTERS

JAMES PLUMPTRE (1796)

IN 1796, JAMES PLUMPTRE, M. A., published some *Observations on Hamlet, &c.*, *being an attempt to prove that [Shakespeare] designed [this tragedy] as an indirect censure on Mary, Queen of Scots.* In this volume the author assumes, that since Shakespeare in 1592 did not hesitate, in the *Midsummer-Night's Dream*, to compliment Elizabeth at the expense of Mary, he would have no scruples in still further flattering his royal mistress in 1596 (the 'date when *Hamlet* was written') by adding his drop to the flood of calumny poured out over her rival. This hypothesis obliges him to maintain that the Queen in *Hamlet* was an accessory to her husband's death.

Plumptre adduces the following passages and allusions to show that Shakespeare had Mary, Queen of Scots, directly in mind when he wrote them: 'In second husband let me be accurst! None wed the second but who kill'd the first,' III, ii, 169; and 'The instances that second marriage move Are base respects of thrift, but none of love.'—*Ib.* 172. 'Which,' says the author, 'appear to be so strongly marked as almost of themselves to establish the hypothesis.' Next, Gertrude's *haste* to marry the murderer of her husband. Lord Darnley was murdered on the 10th of Feb. 1567, and Mary was married to Bothwell on the 14th of May following, a space of time but just exceeding *three* months. Lord Darnley was the handsomest young man in the kingdom, but of a weak mind; it is remarkable that in *Hamlet* no compliment is paid to the murdered king's intellectual qualities. Bothwell was twenty years older than Mary, and is represented as an ugly man by the historians. He was also noted for his debauchery and drinking, two circumstances which Shakespeare seems never to lose sight of in his character of Claudius. Ophelia's allusion to the '*beauteous* majesty of Denmark,' IV, v, Plumptre says is inapplicable to Gertrude, because 'she was past the prime of life, not to say, old,' whereas it applies most justly to Mary, who was only forty-five when she was beheaded, and very beautiful. In the beginning of *Hamlet* the hero is represented as very young, but in the grave-yard we are told that he was thirty years old; 'James was just *thirty* at the writing of this play.' Whereupon Plumptre remarks: 'Shakespeare seems to have been so blinded by the circumstances he wished to introduce that he has fallen into many improbabilities between his two plans.' Shakespeare mentions the King as having been taken off 'in the blossom of his sin,' 'which,' says Plumptre, 'is incompatible with the ideas we have of the King's *age* in the play, but most truly applicable to Lord Darnley.' In Hamlet's delay Shakespeare had in mind the backwardness of James to revenge his father's murder. 'Among other remarkable coincidences between the plot of *Hamlet* and the circumstances attendant on Mary and James, we may enumerate that of Dr Wotton being sent into Scotland by Elizabeth as a spy upon James, and who afterwards entered into a conspiracy to deliver him into her hands.' Here we have the part of Rosencrantz and Guilden stern. 'The incident of Polonius being murdered in the presence of the Queen in her closet bears a resemblance to the murder of Rizzio in Mary's apartment.' 'Bothwell had poisoned Mary's cup of happiness, and it was her marriage with him that was the cause of her sorrows and death.'

In 1797, Plumptre published an *Appendix*, in which additional parallelisms are given, and great stress is laid on the effects of poison on Darnley: Knox and Buchanan 'mention the black and putrid pustules which broke out all over his body;' this corresponds to the tetter which 'bark'd about, most lazar-like, with vile and loathsome crust, all the smooth body' of Hamlet's father. Hume's description of James (vol. i, p. 114, 4to ed.) is cited to show that the character of Hamlet is his character, 'but it is a flattering likeness; it is James drawn in the fairest colors; his harsh features softened and his deformities concealed.' Hamlet's love of the stage and patronage of the Players resembled James's. Finally, from travellers' accounts Plumptre infers that 'the shore on which Elsinor stands consists of ridges of sand, rising one above the other;' there could not, therefore, be any 'dreadful summit of a cliff that beetles o'er his base,' and 'looks so many fathoms down' amid such scenery; but this description suits Salisbury Crags and Holyrood Palace.

This theory of Plumptre's (who, by the way, apologizes in his Preface for any typographical errors to be found in the volume, on the ground of his excessive anxiety to publish his views before he could be anticipated and robbed of the glory of his discovery),—this theory was treated with silent indifference for nigh three-quarters of a century, until a few years ago it was revived in Germany, apparently without any suspicion that it was not novel. CARL SILBERSCHLAG, in the *Morgenblatt*, Nos. 46, 47, 1860, brought forward the same arguments with which we are familiar to prove that under Gertrude was veiled an allusion to Mary Stuart, that Hamlet was James, and Claudius, Bothwell. But the ingenious German scholar went farther, and found that other characters in the tragedy had their prototypes among James's contemporaries. The Laird of Gowrie had a father's murder to avenge, and had lived in Paris, and had a faithful servant named Rhynd, and met his death in an attempt by stratagem on the life of the king. All this prefigures Laertes and Reynaldo; unfortunately, an air of burlesque is cast over the theory by the argument, gravely uttered, that Laird is pronounced just like (*ganz so klingt*) Laertes! After the death of the Laird, his bride, Anna Douglas, became insane,— hence Ophelia. In the 'vicious mole,' I, iv, 24, Silberschlag finds cumulative evidence of the truth of his theory. See note *ad loc.* Vol. I.

MOBERLY noticed, though not in reference to this theory of Plumptre's, that the language with which Hamlet speaks of the dead body of Polonius is almost exactly the same as that used by the Porter at Holyrood in reference to the dead body of Rizzio. See III, iv, 215.

HUNTER (*New Illustrations*, &c., ii, 204) says that if the composition of *Hamlet* can really be carried back to a time before 1589, 'there may be some ground for the opinion of those who have thought that there were strokes in it levelled at the Queen of Scots, who was put to death in 1587.'

GEORGE RUSSELL FRENCH (1869)

(*Shakespeareana Genealogica*, London, 1869, p. 301.)—Bearing in mind that Belleforest's translation was published in 1560, and that the wonderful drama was written in 1596, we will proceed to the notice of the personages believed to be indicated by certain names in the play, who are nearly all in one way or other connected with the history of Sir Philip Sidney, who seems by common consent to stand for 'young Hamlet.' This is the key-note to the rest. His honored father, the wise and able Sir Henry Sidney, of Penshurst, is put down for the elder Hamlet, to whom the poet does not assign any other name, but to whom he ascribes so high a character, as when the son is looking on his portrait : ' See, what a grace was seated on his brow,' &c. Dr Zouch says, ' a more exalted character than that of Sir Henry Sidney can scarcely be found in the volume of history.' Of him, therefore, his son might say, as Hamlet of his father : 'I shall not look upon his like again.'

One of the parts supposed to have been filled by Shakespeare himself was that of ' The majesty of buried Denmark,' according to Rowe; and Shakespeare's only son, who died when under twelve years of age, was baptized Hamnet, which is considered synonymous with Hamlet; his godfather most probably being Hamnet or Hamlet Sadler, to whom the poet left a legacy of 'xxvj^s viij^d to buy him a ringe.'

It is worthy of remark that Sir Henry Sidney died (May 5, 1586) five months and twelve days before his accomplished son, and that very date is reckoned by commentators to have elapsed between the murder of the elder Hamlet and the final catastrophe in the play, young Hamlet's death.

The usurping Claudius of the drama has been regarded as a satire on the Lord Keeper, Sir Nicholas Bacon, not, of course, with reference to crime; nor has any one ever ventured to link the revered name of Sidney's mother, Lady Mary Dudley, with the guilty Queen Gertrude.

The next important personages in the play are the ' Lord Chamberlain,' Polonius; his son, Laertes; and daughter, Ophelia; and these are supposed to stand for Queen Elizabeth's celebrated Lord High Treasurer, Sir William Cecil, Lord Burleigh; his second son, Robert Cecil, and his daughter, Anne Cecil. Hamlet's bosom friend, Horatio, is said to be Hubert Languet (by Mr Julius Lloyd); Marcellus and Bernardo are allotted to Fulke Greville and Edward Dyer; ' Francisco may, perhaps, be intended for Harvey.'—(Lloyd.) Lamord, who is only alluded to in the play, IV, vii : ' he is the brooch, indeed, And gem of all the nation,' is meant for Raleigh; young Fortinbras, ' of unimproved mettle, hot and full,' for the brave but impetuous Robert Devereux, Earl of Essex, then in the height of his fame; ' Old Norway,' uncle to young Fortinbras, is ascribed to Sir Francis Knollys, whose daughter Lettice married Walter Devereux, first Earl of Essex, and their son was Robert, just noticed. ' Young Osric ' is a specimen of the foppish gallants of Queen Elizabeth's court, who affected the style of language called Euphuism, of which Sir Walter Scott has given an amusing example in the person of ' Sir Piercie Shafton,' in *The Monastery*.

With the exceptions of Horatio, Marcellus and Bernardo, the Compiler does not seek to disturb these appropriations. But first to examine into the history of the Cecils. It is well known that an alliance of marriage was proposed by their fathers to take place between Philip Sidney and Anne Cecil, the 'fair Ophelia' of the play: here is one link of resemblance in the story. Queen Gertrude says,—' I hop'd thou shouldst have been my Hamlet's wife.' Anne Cecil became the wife of Edward de Vere, seventeenth Earl of Oxford. This was not a happy marriage for the lady, and the only quarrel in which Philip Sidney ever engaged was with Oxford, who had behaved to him with great rudeness, and the challenge between them was only frustrated by the Queen's interference. Did our poet bear this quarrel in mind when he makes Hamlet leap into Ophelia's grave and grapple with Laertes? 'I will fight with him upon this theme.' In the drama, Polonius, on his son Laertes leaving him for foreign travel, gives him his blessing and advice, telling him, ' And these few precepts in thy memory Look thou character.' We have now come to a second link 'in the chain of evidence. When Robert Cecil was about to set out on his travels, his father (who lived till 1598) was careful to enjoin upon him ' ten precepts,' in allusion, as he explains, to the Decalogue, and in some of these the identity of the language with that of Polonius is so close, that Shakespeare could not have hit upon it unless he had been acquainted with Burleigh's parental advice to Robert Cecil, who was forty-six years old when the play was written.

[Page 304.] Among Lord Burleigh's ' ten precepts ' [occur the following:] Precept 4.—' Let thy kindred and allies be welcome to thy house and table. Grace them with thy countenance, and farther them in all honest actions. For by this means, thou shalt so double the band of nature, as thou shalt find them so many advocates to plead an apology for thee behind thy back; but shake off those glow-worms, I mean parasites and sycophants, who will feed and fawn upon thee in the summer of prosperitie, but in an adverse storme they will shelter thee no more than an arbour in winter. 5. Beware of suretyship for thy best friends. He that payeth another man's debts seeketh his own decay. But if thou canst not otherwise chose, rather lend thy money thyself upon good bonds, although thou borrow it. So shalt thou secure thyself, and pleasure thy friend. Neither borrow of a neighbour or of a friend, but of a stranger, whose paying for it thou shalt hear no more of it. 6. Undertake no suit against a poor man without receiving much wrong. 7. Be sure to make some great man thy friend. 8. Towards superiors be humble, yet generous. With thine equals familiar, yet respective. Towards thine inferiors show much humanity, and some familiarity. 9. Trust not any man with thy life, credit, or estate. 10. Be not scurrilous in conversation, or satirical in thy jests.' [See I, iii, 59.]

The Lord Treasurer Burleigh, was not over fond of actors and the drama, whereas Robert Dudley, the splendid Earl of Leicester, uncle to Philip Sidney, was the great friend of the players. In 1573, ' the Earl of Leicester's players' visited the town of Stratford-upon-Avon, when the future poet was nine years old. Burleigh was often in antagonism to Leicester, and prevented his obtaining the appointment of Lord Lieutenant of Ireland, and otherwise thwarted his ambitious views. Next to Leicester, the most able and bitter of Burleigh's adversaries was Sir Nicholas Throgmorton, father-in-law of Sir Walter Raleigh, and uncle of the wife of Edward Arden of Parkhall, Shakespeare's cousin on the mother's side, in whose condemnation the Lord Treasurer concurred. Moreover, Burleigh neglected Sir Francis Walsingham, whose daughter Frances became the wife, first of Sir Philip Sidney, and afterwards of the Earl of Essex. Hubert Languet on one occasion suggested to his pupil Philip Sidney to *affect* more attachment than he *felt* to Cecil. Shakespeare's inclinations would naturally take side with the great Warwickshire noble in remembering the political skirmishes between Leicester and Burle'gh, and his covert satire on the latter, under the guise of Polonius, would be well understood in his day, and probably relished by none more than by Queen Elizabeth herself, who could enjoy a jest, though at the expense of her wise and faithful William Cecil.

[Page 306.] When Philip Sidney, who was born in 1554, was on his 'grand tour,' in 1572, he fell in at Frankfort with the famous scholar, Hubert Languet, 'by whose advice he studied various authors, and shunned the seductions of popery' (Dr Zouch). The friendship between them was very strong, and many letters are preserved written in Latin from Languet to Sidney, which were first printed in 1639.

The writer of these remarks ventures to differ from those critics who assign Languet to Horatio, and in proposing Fulke Greville instead, he brings forward the following arguments to support the change. In the first place, Hubert Languet was at least thirty-six years older than Sidney. It is generally understood that Languet was sixty-three years old at his death in 1581. In the second place, their tone towards each other, in their correspondence, is rather that of master and pupil, or Mentor and Telemachus, than of bosom friends, equals in years. . . . .

Now to apply the test to Fulke Greville as Horatio. He was a kinsman of Philip Sidney; equally descended from the noble Beauchamps; born in the same year, 1554 educated with him at the same school, at Shrewsbury, which they entered on the same day; and they studied afterwards together at one, if not at both, of the Universities, Oxford and Cambridge; they were the dearest friends through life; fellow-travellers; comrades in the tilt-yard. They had prepared to accompany Sir Francis Drake in his expedition to the West Indies, but were forbidden to do so by Queen Elizabeth, who would not spare two such promising youths from her court.

Let us now examine Shakespeare's language. At their first interview, Hamlet recognizes his former comrade, Horatio,—' Sir, my good friend, I'll change that name with you;'—and again acknowledges their early association in school at Wittenberg,—' I pray thee, do not mock me, fellow-student.'

Next we have the expression of Hamlet's strong regard for Horatio, Act III, sc. ii, in the passage ending, ' Give me that man That is not passion's slave, and I will wear him In my heart's core, ay, in my heart of heart, As I do thee.' All these expressions, and the affectionate demeanor between the two friends throughout the play, point to a companion of the same age and station, as was Greville, rather than to one so much older than Sidney as was Hubert Languet. . . . .

One of Sir Philip Sidney's *Pastorals*, is addressed to his two most intimate friends (Sir) Edward Dyer, and (Sir) Fulke Greville, coupling their initials with his own. . . . . To these two cherished friends and congenial spirits, Sir Philip Sidney in his will left a precious legacy of regard; ' *Item*, I give and bequeath to my dear friends, Mr. Edward Dyer and Mr. Fulke Greville, all my books.' In the play Hamlet addresses Horatio and Marcellus, evidently as his chief intimates: 'And now good friends, As you are friends, scholars and soldiers, Give me one poor request.' With some fair reason, therefore, it is urged that Greville and Dyer were intended for Hamlet's friends, Horatio and Marcellus.

PROF. DR A. GERTH (1861)

(*Der Hamlet*, Leipzig, 1861, p. 223.)—This is the end and aim of the lesson which Hamlet teaches. Protestantism will never fulfil its calling so long as its adherents are content to oppose the inexhaustible strength and cunning of its ancient evil foe with the mere consciousness of their righteous cause; so long as they will·

learn to unite to the virtues of the Christian, the calm dispassionate prudence and consequent energy of the man; so long as they continue to waste in foolish infatuation the power and aid which lie in their own bosoms, instead of using them. Therefore, it is, that Shakespeare gave to this noble Prince, as a bosom friend, this *compatriot with a Roman name*, a man contented and thoughtful, honorable and learned, but who is silent and offers no counsel; and therefore, it is, also, that he represents Hamlet's *love*, Ophelia, ΩΦΕΛΕΙΑ, the symbol of the union of strength and help, as being destroyed by Hamlet *himself*.

RUSKIN (1872)

(*Munera Pulveris*, 1872, p. 126, foot-note.)—Shakespeare's names are curiously,— often barbarously,—much by Providence,—but assuredly not without Shakespeare's cunning purpose,—mixed out of the various traditions he confusedly adopted, and languages he imperfectly knew. . . . . Desdemona, δνσδαιμονία, *miserable fortune*, is plain enough. Othello is, I believe, *the careful;* all the calamity of the tragedy arising from the single flaw and error of his magnificently collected strength. Ophelia, *serviceableness*, the true lost wife of Hamlet, is marked as having a Greek name by that of her brother, Laertes; and its signification is once exquisitely alluded to in that brother's last word of her, where her gentle preciousness is opposed to the uselessness of the churlish clergy: 'a *ministering* angel shall my sister be when thou liest howling.' Hamlet is, I believe, connected in some way with *homely*, the entire event of the tragedy turning on the betrayal of home duty.

C. ELLIOT BROWNE (1876)

(*Notes on Shakespeare's Names*, The Athenæum, 29 July, 1876.)—Of the names of *Hamlet*, only two are afforded by the prose story of Belleforest,—that of Hamlet himself and his mother Geruthe, which Shakespeare has turned into Gertrude. Horatio is probably the Horatio of the *Spanish Tragedy*, where he plays the *rôle* of friend and best man to the hero. Andrea calls him, 'My other soul, my bosom, my heart's friend.'

The origin of the association is probably to be found in the legend of the Horatii. Marcellus, according to Camden, is a name 'martiall and warlike' from Mars, and therefore suitable for a military man. The names of Francisco and Bernardo, associated together in this play, had been previously associated in one of the greatest crimes of the sixteenth century. Bernardo Bandini and Francesco de' Pazzi were the assassins of Giuliano de' Medici in the cathedral of Florence. It is worth noting that in the original Italian cast of *Every Man in his Humour*, to which Shakespeare is said to have contributed, and in which he certainly performed, the principal personage was Lorenzo de' Pazzi,—no doubt chosen as a distinctively Florentine name. Fortinbras is evidently Fortebras or Strongarm of the family of Ferumbras of the romances, or may have come directly from Niccolo Fortebraccio, the famous leader of the *condòttieri*. Guildenstern and Rosencrantz were both historical names of Denmark: the first was borne by a chief actor in the melancholy history of Christian the Second, and therefore well suited by association to figure in *Hamlet;* the other, as Mr Thornbury has pointed out [anticipated by Steevens; see II, i, 1. Ed.], was the name of the ambassador sent to England at the accession of James the First.

Much ingenuity has been expended upon Ophelia. Miss Yonge, in her book upon *Christian Names*, hazards the conjecture that the word is a Greek rendering of an old Danske serpent-name like Ormilda. [Mr Ruskin's suggestion is here cited. ED.] The fact is, however, that Shakespeare, or the writer who is to be credited with the early *Hamlet*, probably adopted the name from the *Arcadia* of Sannazaro, where, in the form in which it appears in the first quarto edition, Ofelia, it is the name of one of the amorous shepherds of the ninth eclogue. This conjecture is greatly strengthened by the circumstance that Ofelia is introduced with Montano, another of the first-Hamlet names. It is probably only a modern form of the Roman Ofella, Horace's Ofellus.

Three characters in the first edition of *Hamlet* were re-named in the second impression. Corambis was altered to Polonius, his servant Montano to Reynaldo, and Albertus, the name of the murdered duke in the Play, became Gonzago. With the exception of Falstaff, these are the only instances in which Shakespeare is known to have made any changes in the names of his *dramatis personæ*. In the case of Corambis we may infer, perhaps, that when the poet's magic had transformed the low buffoon-courtier of the older drama into the highly-finished portrait of the Danish chancellor which we now possess, it became necessary to rid him of old associations by giving him a new name. Polonius is probably the typical Pole diplomatist and counsellor. The inhabitants of Poland at that time were known in England as Polonians, and the elective kingdom, with its elaborate system of assemblies and diets, was pre-eminently the land of policy and intrigue. The traditional Polonius, indeed, answers very nearly to the old marshals of Poland, who always carried the wand of office before the king. Corambis sounds like a pastoral name, derived, perhaps, from *Corymbus*. [See I, ii, 57. ED.]

Reynaldo, both here and in *All's Well*, is a servant or steward, and it is significant that the best known of the historical Rinaldos,—and several probably went to the composition of the Rinaldo of romance,—was high steward to Louis the Pious.

Albertus is clearly a more appropriate name for a duke of Austria (the scene is laid at Vienna) than Gonzago; but the story of the Play is certainly taken from the murder of the Duke of Urbano by Luigi *Gonzaga* in 1538, who was poisoned by means of a lotion poured into his ears. This new way of poisoning caused great horror throughout Europe, and we often meet with allusions to it. It is worth noting, also, that the wife of the duke was a Gonzaga. Some of the commentators have absurdly objected to Battista as a female Christian name. It was not only a common female name at this period, but especially connected with Mantua and the Gonzagas. [The remainder of these *Notes* will be found in connection with the appropriate characters in the text in Vol. I. There is an article in *The Cornhill Magazine* for February, 1876, on *Shakespeare's Greek Names*. ED.]

DURATION OF THE ACTION

HEUSSI (*Shakespeare's Hamlet*, Leipzig, 1872): The First Act embraces the first night, the following day, and the next night.

The Second Act begins some little time (from two to three months) after the close of the First; for in the First Act Laertes goes to Paris, and at the beginning of the Second, Polonius sends him money. The Second Act embraces one day.

The Third Act begins with the day following the close of the Second Act, and continues, as is to be inferred from the apparition of the Ghost, until the middle of the next night.

The Fourth Act ends with the death of Ophelia. The Fifth begins with the day of her burial, and two or three days might be supposed to intervene. But since the King reminds Laertes in the grave-yard of ' their *last night's* speech,' it follows that Ophelia was buried on the very day after her death; and the Fifth Act, therefore, begins on the day immediately following the conclusion of the Fourth. The duration of the events of the Fourth Act cannot be exactly computed. The first three Scenes take place on the day after Hamlet's interview with his mother. Not much time can elapse between the Third and Fourth Scene, because in the Fourth Scene Hamlet is on his way to England, which must have followed very close upon the King's command; the succeeding scenes continue without interruption. The Fourth Act, therefore, occupies two days at the most.

MISS KATE FIELD (*Fechter as Hamlet*. Atlantic Monthly, Boston, November, 1870, p. 558): After carefully scanning the play, we see that its entire action cannot cover more than ten days. In the First Act Laertes leaves for France, and Hamlet decides to ' put an antic disposition on.' The Second Act opens with Polonius sending Reynaldo to keep watch over Laertes, after which comes Ophelia's description of Lord Hamlet with his doublet all unbraced; this being the first symptom of Hamlet's madness, not more than a day is likely to have elapsed between the conception and execution of his plan. Concluding with the arrival of the Players and Hamlet's arrangement for the performance of *The Murder of Gonzago*, which he distinctly declares shall take place the following night,—' We'll have't to-morrow night,'—there can be no questioning as to the date of the Third Act. And the Fourth is like unto it. Hamlet kills Polonius in the Third Act. The Fourth Act opens with the Queen's narration of the bloody deed,—' Ah, my good lord, what have I seen to-night?' by which it is clear that the Fourth Act begins in point of time as quickly as the Third Act closes; that is, on the night of the third day. In the Third Scene Hamlet is brought in guarded, and replies to Claudius that ' you shall nose him (Polonius) as you go up the stairs into the lobby.' The time still remains the same, as proved by the King's immediately dispatching Hamlet to England: ' I'll have him hence to-night.' In Scene Fourth Hamlet appears upon a plain in Denmark, not yet having sailed. It may still be the night of the third day, although the meeting with Fortinbras and his forces would rather indicate day-light. If so, the fourth day has set in. Between this Scene and Scene Sixth four days must elapse, as it is then that Horatio receives Hamlet's letter, in which he says: ' Ere we were two days old at sea, a pirate of very warlike appointment gave

us chase. . . . . These good fellows will bring thee where I am.' Two days out
and two days returning to Denmark make four, and adding the previous four days,
we have eight in all. The next and last scene follows speedily, therein Hamlet's
letter to the King being delivered. Well, but how is it with Laertes, who reappears
in Scene Fifth, proclaiming revenge for the death of his father? How can he return from France in four days, especially if he be in Paris, where Polonius has sent
Reynaldo to seek him? Not leaving until the First Act, it is utterly impossible for
Laertes to have made very great progress in his journey, and travelling leisurely, as
would be likely, he is overtaken and brought back. Yes, but he sets sail for France,
and is it probable that, having such a start, he can be overtaken? Of course he sets
sail, Elsinore being on an island; but the route to Paris is far more direct by land
than by sea, and the time indicates that Laertes must have taken to horse on the
mainland, a mode of travelling in which he could be easily reached by forced post-
ing. Drowned at the close of the Fourth, Ophelia is buried in the last, Act, so that
but few days can intervene between the two events. How many one cannot assert;
although, as Hamlet in his letter to Claudius, in the Fourth Act, says, 'to-morrow
shall I beg leave to see your kingly eyes,' and the Fifth Act brings about this meeting, twenty-four hours need not have elapsed. European Catholics bury their dead
speedily. It is, therefore, safe to declare that the Fifth Act could transpire on the
ninth day, and cannot in reason be delayed beyond the tenth.

[See ECKARDT, II, i, 75. GEORGE B. WOODS (*Essays*, Boston, 1873, p. 104)
reaches the same conclusion with HEUSSI: that the 'time of the action occupies between two and three months, no more and no less,' and cites in proof Hamlet's
statement in the First Act, that his father had been dead 'not two months,' and
Ophelia's assertion in the Third Act, that he had been dead at that time 'twice two
months.'

See also I, i, 158, for the season of the year when the action is supposed to take
place. ED.]

GARRICK'S VERSION *

BOADEN (*Life of J. P. Kemble*, London, 1825, vol. i, p. 110): Having incident-
ally mentioned Garrick's strange alteration of the play of *Hamlet*, it may not be
improper to add here some account of it. In my youth I remember to have seen it
acted, and for many years I could not get the smallest information whether any copy
was preserved of this unlucky compliment to Voltaire. A strange story was in cir-
culation formerly, that it had been buried with the great actor; this, however, it was
said, was not upon the humane principle that a man's faults should die with him,
but as a sort of consecration of so critical a labor.

But Mr Kemble had in his library what I believe to have been the very copy of
the play upon which Mr Garrick's alterations were made. He probably received it
as a curiosity from Mrs Garrick. . . . .

[Garrick] cut out the voyage to England and the execution of Rosencrantz and

---

* In BOHN's *Bibliography* it is stated that this version was not printed. ED.

Guildenstern, 'who had made love to the employment, and marshalled his way to knavery.' He omitted the funeral of Ophelia, and all the wisdom of the Prince, and the rude jocularity of the Grave-diggers. Hamlet bursts in upon the King and his court, and Laertes reproaches him with his father's and his sister's deaths. The exasperation of both is at its height when the King interposes; he had commanded Hamlet to depart for England, and declares that he will no longer bear this rebellious conduct, but that his wrath shall at length fall heavy on the Prince. 'First,' exclaims Hamlet, 'feel you mine!' and he instantly stabs him. The Queen rushes out, imploring the attendants to save her from her son. Laertes, seeing treason and murder before him, attacks Hamlet to revenge his father, his sister, and his King. He wounds Hamlet mortally, and Horatio is on the point of making Laertes accompany him to the shades, when the Prince commands him to desist, assuring him that it was the hand of Heaven, which administered by Laertes 'that precious balm for all his wounds.' We then learn that the miserable mother had dropped in a trance ere she could reach her chamber door, and Hamlet implores for her 'an hour of penitence ere madness end her.' He then joins the hands of Laertes and Horatio, and commands them to unite their virtues (as a coalition of ministers) to 'calm the troubled land.' The old couplet as to the bodies concludes the play.

ACTORS' INTERPRETATIONS

GARRICK

FIELDING (*Tom Jones*, London, 1749, book xvi, chap. v.)—As soon as the play, which was *Hamlet, Prince of Denmark*, began, Partridge was all attention, nor did he break silence until the entrance of the Ghost; upon which he asked Jones, 'What man that was in the strange dress; something,' said he, 'like what I have seen in a picture. Sure it is not armour, is it?' Jones answered, 'That is the Ghost.' To which Partridge replied with a smile, 'Persuade me to that, sir, if you can. Though I cannot say I ever actually saw a ghost in my life, yet I am certain I should know one if I saw him, better than that comes to. No, no, sir, ghosts don't appear in such dresses as that, neither.' In this mistake, which caused much laughter in the neighborhood of Partridge, he was suffered to continue, 'till the scene between the Ghost and Hamlet, when Partridge gave that credit to Mr Garrick which he had denied to Jones, and fell into such a violent fit of trembling that his knees knocked against each other. Jones asked him what was the matter, and whether he was afraid of the warrior upon the stage? 'O la, sir,' said he, 'I perceive now it is what you told me. I am not afraid of anything; for I know it is but a play. And if it really was a ghost, it could do one no harm at such a distance, and in so much company; and yet if I was frightened, I am not the only person.' 'Why, who,' cries Jones, 'dost thou take to be such a coward here besides thyself?' 'Nay, you may call me a coward if you will; but if that little man there upon the stage is not frightened, I never saw any man frightened in my life. Ay, ay; "go along with you!" ay, to be sure! who's fool then! Will you? Lud have mercy upon such foolhardiness?

Whatever happens it is good enough for you. "Follow you!" I'd follow the devil as soon,—nay, perhaps it is the devil,—for they say he can put on what likeness he pleases. Oh! here he is again. "No farther!" No, you have gone far enough already; farther than I'd have gone for all the king's dominions.' Jones offered to speak, but Partridge cried, ' Hush, hush, dear sir, don't you hear him!' and during the whole speech of the Ghost he sat with his eyes fixed partly on the Ghost and partly on Hamlet, and with his mouth open; the same passions which succeeded in Hamlet, succeeding likewise in him.

When the scene was over, Jones said, ' Why, Partridge, you exceed my expecta-tions; you enjoy the play more than I conceived possible.' ' Nay, sir,' answered Partridge, ' if you are not afraid of the devil, I can't help it; but to be sure it is natural to be surprised at such things, though I know there is nothing in them; not that it was the Ghost which surprised me neither; for I should have known that to have been only a man in a strange dress; but when I saw the little man so fright-ened himself, it was that which took hold of me.' ' And dost thou imagine then, Partridge,' cries Jones, ' that he was really frightened?' ' Nay, sir,' said Partridge, ' did not you yourself observe afterwards, when he found it was his own father's spirit, and how he was murdered in the garden, how his fear forsook him by degrees, and he was struck dumb with sorrow, as it were, just as I should have been, had it been my own case. But hush! O la! what noise is that? There he is again. Well, to be certain, though I know there is nothing at all in it, I am glad I am not down yonder, where those men are.' Then turning his eyes again upon Hamlet, ' Ay, you may draw your sword; what signifies a sword against the power of the devil?'

During the Second Act, Partridge made very few remarks. He greatly admired the fineness of the dresses; nor could he help observing upon the King's counte-nance. ' Well,' said he, ' how people may be deceived by faces! *Nulla fides fronti* is, I find, a true saying. Who would think, by looking in the King's face, that he had ever committed a murder?' He then inquired after the Ghost; but Jones, who intended he should be surprised, gave him no other satisfaction, ' than that he might possibly see him again soon, and in a flash of fire.'

Partridge sat in fearful expectation of this; and now, when the Ghost made his next appearance, Partridge cried out: ' There, sir, now; what say you now? Is he frightened now or no? As much frightened as you think me, and, to be sure, no-body can help some fears, I would not be in so bad a condition as what's his name, 'Squire Hamlet, is there, for all the world. Bless me! what's become of the spirit? As I am a living soul, I thought I saw him sink into the earth.' ' Indeed, you saw right,' answered Jones. ' Well, well,' cries Partridge, ' I know it is only a play; and besides, if there was anything in all this, Madam Miller would not laugh so; for as to you, sir, you would not be afraid, I believe, if the devil was here in person. There, there,—ay, no wonder you are in such a passion; shake the vile, wicked wretch to pieces. If she was my own mother, I should serve her so. To be sure, all duty to a mother is forfeited by such wicked doings. Ay, go about your business; I hate the sight of you.'

Our critic was now pretty silent till the play which Hamlet introduced before the King. This he did not at first understand, till Jones explained it to him; but he no sooner entered into the spirit of it than he began to bless himself that he had never committed murder. Then, turning to Mrs Miller, he asked her, ' If she did not imagine the King looked as if he was touched; though he is,' said he, ' a good actor, and doth all he can to hide it. Well, I would not have so much to answe for as that wicked man there hath, to sit upon a much higher chair than he sits upon. No wonder he ran away; for your sake I'll never trust an innocent face again.'

The grave-digging scene* next engaged the attention of Partridge, who expressed much surprise at the number of skulls thrown upon the stage. To which Jones answered: 'That it was one of the most famous burial-places about town.' 'No wonder, then,' cries Partridge, 'that the place is haunted. But I never saw in my life a worse grave-digger. I had a sexton when I was a clerk that should have dug three graves while he is digging one. The fellow handles a spade as if it was the first time he had ever had one in his hands. Ay, ay, you may sing. You had rather sing than work, I believe.' Upon Hamlet's taking up the skull he cried out, 'Well, it is strange to see how fearless some men are; I never could bring myself to touch anything belonging to a dead man on any account. He seemed frightened enough, too, at the Ghost, I thought. *Nemo omnibus horis sapit.*'

Little more worth remembering occurred during the play; at the end of which Jones asked him which of the players he liked best. To this he answered, with some appearance of indignation at the question: 'The King, without doubt.' 'Indeed, Mr Partridge,' says Mrs Miller, 'you are not of the same opinion with the Town; for they are all agreed that Hamlet is acted by the best player who was ever on the stage.' 'He the best player!' cries Partridge, with a contemptuous sneer; 'why, I could act as well as he myself. I am sure if I had seen a ghost, I should have looked in the very same manner and done just as he did. And then, to be sure, in that scene, as you called it, between him and his mother, where you told me he acted so fine, why, Lord help me, any man, that is, any good man, that had such a mother would have done exactly the same. I know you are only joking with me; but, indeed, madam, though I was never at a play in London, yet I have seen acting before in the country; and the King for my money: he speaks all his words distinctly, half as loud again as the other. Anybody may see he is an actor.'

FRANCIS GENTLEMAN (*Dramatic Censor*, 1770, vol. i, p. 33.)—Where Hamlet says to his interposing friends: 'I say, away,'—then turning to the Ghost, 'Go on, I'll follow,' Garrick's variation from extreme passion to reverential awe is so forcibly expressed in eyes, features, attitude, and voice, that every heart must feel. Where the Queen says the Ghost is but 'the coinage of your brain,' his turning short from looking after the apparition with wildness of terror, and viewing his mother with pathetic concern, is most happily executed.

BETTERTON. GARRICK.

THOMAS DAVIES (*Dramatic Miscellanies*, vol. iii, p. 35.)—I have lately been told by a gentleman, who has frequently seen Betterton perform Hamlet, that he observed his countenance, which was naturally ruddy and sanguine, in the scene of the Third Act where his father's ghost appears, through the violent and sudden emotion of amazement and horror, turn instantly, on the sight of his father's spirit, as pale as his neckcloth; when his whole body seemed to be affected with a tremor inexpres-

---

* This is noteworthy as showing that Garrick does not always merit the reproach, which is constantly cast upon him, of excluding this scene in representation. ED.

sible, so that, had his father's ghost actually risen before him, he could not have been seized with more real agonies. And this was felt so strongly by the audience that the blood seemed to shudder in their veins likewise; and they in some measure partook of the astonishment and horror with which they saw this excellent actor affected. [See Vol. I, I, iv, 39, for an additional account of Betterton's acting. ED.]

[Page 55.] 'For some must laugh [*sic*], while some must weep [*sic*], Thus runs the world away.'—III, ii, 261. In the uttering of this line and a half it was Garrick's constant practice to pull out a white handkerchief, and walking about the stage to twirl it round with vehemence. This action can incur no just censure, except from its constant repetition. He, of all the players I ever saw, gave the greatest variety to action and deportment; nor could I help wondering that so great an artist should in this instance tie himself down to one particular mode, when his situation would admit of so many.

[Page 65.] At the appearance of the Ghost [in the closet scene with his mother], Hamlet immediately rises from his seat affrighted; at the same time he contrives to kick down his chair, which, by making a sudden noise, it was imagined would contribute to the perturbation and terror of the incident.

KEMBLE. GARRICK. HENDERSON.

BOADEN (*Life of John Philip Kemble*, London, 1825, vol. i, p. 94*): KEMBLE was instructed to say: ''Tis an *un*-weeded garden, that grows to seed.' But Kemble thought, and justly, that 'unweeded' was quite as intelligible with the usual and proper accent as the improper one; and besides, that the exquisite modulation of the poet's verse should not be jolted out of its music for the sake of giving a more pointed explanation of a word already sufficiently understood.

'Sir, my good FRIEND! I'll change *that* name with you.' Thus Kemble, upon Horatio's saying to Hamlet that he was his poor *servant* ever. Dr Johnson conceives it to mean, 'I'll be your servant, you shall be my friend.' In which case the emphasis would rest thus: 'Sir, my good FRIEND! I'll *change* that name with you.' Perhaps, it may be rather, 'Change the term servant into that of friend. Consider us, without regard to rank, as friends.' Henderson evidently so understood it, for he said, 'I'll change *that* name with YOU.'

It was, I think, a novelty when, after having recognized Horatio and Marcellus by name, Kemble turned courteously towards Bernardo, and applied the 'Good even, sir,' to him. The commentators were too busy in debating whether it should be evening or morning, to bestow a thought as to the *direction* of this gentle salutation.

It was observed how keenly Kemble inserted an insinuation of the King's intemperance, when he said to Horatio and the rest: 'We'll teach you to DRINK deep,— ere you depart.'

He restored, with the modern editors of Shakespeare, '*Dearest* foe,' and '*Beteeme*

---

* These extracts from Boaden's *Life of Kemble* were kindly made for this edition by my friend, Mr J. PARKER NORRIS, who in his search for stray interpretations of *Hamlet* has examined the following volumes: Campbell's *Life of Mrs Siddons;* Boaden's *Life of Mrs Siddons;* the *Life f Garrick* by Murphy; by Davies; by Fitzgerald; Macready's *Reminiscences;* and Hawkins's *life of Kean.* ED.

the winds of heaven,' and he was greatly censured for doing so, because, as the first term is unknown to the moderns in the sense of *most important*, or, as Johnson thought, *direst*, and the word *beteeme* not known at all, the critic said, it might show *reading* so to speak them, but did not show clear *meaning;* a thing of more moment to a popular assembly. This is a question, I am sensible, on which a great deal may be said; but let it be observed that it involves the *integrity of a poet's text.*

' My father,—methinks I see my father.' Professor Richardson terms this ' the most solemn and striking apostrophe that ever poet invented.' Kemble seemed so to consider it :—the image entirely possessed his imagination; and accordingly, after attempting to pronounce his panegyric, ' He was a man, take him for all in all,' a flood of tenderness came over him, and it was with tears he uttered: ' I shall not look upon his like again.' I know the almost stoical firmness with which others declaim this passage; and the political opposition affected, between the terms KING and MAN; but I must be excused, if I prefer the melting softness of Kemble, as more germane to ' the weakness and the melancholy' of Hamlet.

' Did YOU not speak to it ?' (*To Horatio.*) Not only personally put to Horatio, for this must certainly be done, with emphasis or without, (as the others had said they did not speak to the spectre, and had invited Horatio, that he might do so) but emphatically and tenderly, as inferring from the peculiar intimacy between them, that *he* surely had ventured to enquire the cause of so awful a visitation. Mr Steevens, from a pique which Kemble explained to me, thought fit to annoy him upon this in-novation, and, without naming the object of his sarcasm, has left it in the margin of his Shakespeare. [See Vol. I : I, ii, 214.] . . . . Kemble, however, told me that he had submitted this to Dr Johnson in one of those calls upon him which Boswell has mentioned, and that the doctor said to him : ' To be sure, sir,—YOU should be strongly marked. I told Garrick so, long since, but Davy never could see it.'

' And for my soul, what CAN it do to *that*, Being a thing immortal as itself ?' Gar-rick here, with great quickness, said: ' What can it do to THAT ?' There is, I think, more impression in Kemble's manner of putting it. In Garrick it was a truism as-serted; in Kemble not merely asserted, but *enjoyed*.

Having drawn his sword, to menace the friends who prevented him from following the Ghost, every Hamlet before Kemble presented the point to the phantom as he followed to the removed ground. Kemble, having drawn it on his friends, retained it in his right hand, but turned his left towards the spirit, and drooped the weapon after him,—a change both tasteful and judicious. As a defence against such a being it was ridiculous to present the point. To retain it unconsciously showed how com-pletely he was absorbed by the dreadful mystery he was exploring.

The *kneeling* at the descent of the Ghost was censured as a *trick*. I suppose merely because it had not been done before : but it suitably marked the filial rever-ence of Hamlet, and the solemnity of the engagement he had contracted. Henderson saw it, and adopted it immediately,—I remember he was applauded for doing so.

These two great actors agreed in the seeming intention of particular disclosure to Horatio : ' Yes, but there *is*, Horatio,—and much offence, too,' turned off upon the pressing forward of Marcellus to partake the communication. Kemble *only*, how-ever, prepared the way for this by the marked address to Horatio : ' Did YOU not speak to it ?'

In the scene with Polonius, where Hamlet is asked what is the matter which he reads, and he answers, ' Slanders, sir,' Kemble, to give the stronger impression of his wildness, tore the leaf out of the book. Even this was remarked, for he was of consequence enough, at first, to have everything he did minutely examined.

A critic observed that, in the scene with Rosencrantz and Guildenstern, he was not only familiar, but gay and smiling; and that he *should* be quite the reverse, because he tells them that he 'has lost all his mirth,' &c. This was pure mis-apprehension of the critic. The scene itself ever so slightly read would have set him right. Hamlet, from playing on Polonius, turns to receive gaily and with smiles his *excellent friends*, his *good lads*, who are neither the *button on Fortune's cap*, nor the *soles of her shoe*. And it is only when the conception crosses him that they were sent to sound him, that he changes his manner, puts his questions eagerly and importunately, and, having an eye upon them, gives that account of his disposition, which rendered it but a sleeveless errand which they came upon.

[Page 100.] 'The *mobled* queen.' Garrick repeated this after the Player, as in doubt; Kemble, as in sympathy. And accordingly Polonius echoes his approbation; and says, that the expression is good: '*Mobled* queen is good.'

'Perchance to *dream !*' Kemble pronounced the word 'dream' meditatingly. Just after, to Ophelia, he spoke the word *lisp* with one—lithp. A refinement below him.

Henderson and he concurred, in saying to Horatio: 'Ay, in my heart *of* heart, as I do thee.' Garrick gave it differently: 'heart of *heart*.' But I think would have attained his purpose better by changing his emphasis to '*heart* of heart,' as I remember somewhere, I think in Thomson: 'And all the *life* of life is gone;' that is, I cherish thee in the divinest particle of the heart, which is to that organ itself what the heart is to the body.

[Page 102.] Kemble gave the argument of the [court-play] in the finest manner possible: 'They do but *jest :* POISON in jest,' in *tone* and *observation* at the time, beyond all praise.

The reference to Rosencrantz, after Guildenstern, with the pipe, 'I do beseech YOU,' is an innovation. It involves both persons in the disgrace; but, if allowed at all, it can only be permitted as a felicity of *action* in the performance. At all events, the stately *march* from Guildenstern to Rosencrantz always seemed to me a *poor* thing, and indeed chilling what was to follow: too formal, in a word, for the condition of Hamlet's mind.

In the chamber of the queen, 'Is it the king ?' was addressed to the million. Hamlet's nature is so little vindictive ! In this scene it was doubted whether, in 'speaking daggers' to the Queen, they were *drawn* and *sharp* enough. . . . . Kemble *knelt* in the fine adjuration to his mother. . . . . [Kemble thus read the following lines :] 'And when you are desirous to *be* blest, I'll blessing *beg* of you.' Henderson read them differently : 'And when you are desirous to be *blest*, I'll blessing beg of YOU.' In the grave-yard scene [Kemble] never entirely satisfied himself; he was too studiously graceful; and, under his difficulties, seemingly too much at his ease. The exclamation ['What ! the fair Ophelia !'] had not the pathos of Henderson's; who seemed here struck to the very soul. The tone yet vibrates in my ear with which he uttered it.

[For an admirable description of some points in GARRICK'S acting, see LICHTEN-BERG, in *German Criticisms* in this Volume. ED.]

KEAN. HACKETT. YOUNG. MACREADY.

J. H. HACKETT * (*Notes, Criticisms, &c.*, New York, 1863, p. 49.)—Edmund Kean, as Hamlet, after concluding his words to Ophelia, ' To a nunnery, go !' and departing abruptly out of sight of his audience, used to come on the stage again, and approach slowly the amazed Ophelia still remaining in the centre; take her hand gently, and, after gazing steadily and earnestly in her face for a few seconds, and with a marked expression of tenderness on his own countenance, appeared to be choked in his efforts to say something, smothered her hand with passionate kisses, and rushed wildly and finally from her presence. [EDWIN BOOTH does the same thing. J. C.] [See III, i, 149. ED.]

[Page 79.] In my youth I had read the work called *Wilhelm Meister's Appren-ticeship*, and been struck with and remembered Goethe's idea of causing, in repre-sentation, Hamlet's description and comparison of his father's and his uncle's respec-tive persons to be painted as full-length portraits, and suspended in the Queen's closet. With the aid of Mr Thomas Barry (a most capital stage-director, as well as good and sound actor), I determined to *try* such an effect. Mr Barry, who acted the Ghost, consented to change the costume (*armour*) worn when it was seen upon the *platform*, and which, as it would seem, was designed to suggest surprise, and increase Hamlet's wonder (' My father's spirit—*in arms !* all is not well !'), and to adopt one similar to *that* worn by ' My father in his *habit as he lived*,' and *painted* for the portrait. The canvas was so constructed, by Mr Barry's direction, and split, but backed with a spring made from whalebone, which rendered its prac-ticability unperceived by the audience, that it enabled him at the proper juncture, as the *Ghost* behind, to step apparently *out* of it upon the stage; the rent through which the figure had passed was closed up again, and the canvas, with a light behind it, then looked *blank* and illuminated; but the instant after the departure of the spirit from sight of the audience, the light was removed, and the *painting* appeared as before. The whole effect proved wonderful and surprising, and was vehemently applauded.

[Page 133. Speaking of CHARLES MAYNE YOUNG, Mr Hackett says :] His con-ception of the character of Hamlet seemed pretty just in the main, though I am bound to take particular exception to Mr Young's marked hauteur in receiving the Players, and to his dictatorial bearing while conversing with them; his utterance especially of, ' Com'st thou to beard me in Denmark ?' was characterized by a tone of rebuke instead of that of a jocose and condescending familiarity, such as Hamlet would be likely to use in welcoming ' the tragedians of the city, in whom he was wont to take such delight, and who had come expressly to offer him their service.'

[Page 144.] Hackett takes exceptions to MACREADY's rendering of the Prince's question, ' Arm'd, say you ?' He thinks Macready hurried through the dialogue too rapidly, making no pause before ' Arm'd, say you ?' so that the audience might be misled into supposing that Hamlet meant to inquire connectedly whether those who should hold the watch would be *armed :* ' whereas, if after addressing the two soldiers then on his *right* hand with, " Hold you the watch to-night ?" he had made a short *pause*, and with the fixed eye of abstract and profound consideration turned his face

---

* These extracts from Hackett's volume were kindly selected for this edition by my friend, Mr JOSEPH CROSBY. ED.

from them towards Horatio standing at his *left,* and sinking his voice into a musing and an undertone inquired of Horatio particularly, " Arm'd, say you?" no one could have been misled from this special reference to the Ghost.'

In the *First Folio,* and in the early *Quarto* editions, the *answers* to Hamlet's particular inquiries are printed differently; being in one copy ascribed to ' *both,*' and in another to ' *all*'; but whether these answers properly belong to the *two officers* only, or to *all three who were witnesses,* is quite immaterial; because in the *acting* of the scene it is right and proper to use the most obvious method to convey to an audience the dramatist's meaning. . . . . And Hackett recommends the actor of Hamlet to confine his questions concerning the Ghost t ' Horatio, for various good reasons.

[Page 148.] 'His beard was grizzled? No?' Mr Macready after 'grizzled,' allowed the witnesses not a moment for reflection, but impatiently and rather comically stammered, ' N'—n'—no ?'

'*Pol.* Will you walk out of the air, my lord? *Ham.* Into my grave!' Mr Macready uttered Hamlet's reply *interrogatively,* which was new to my ear upon the stage; but, though it is the punctuation of the Folio 1623, I would prefer that it should be given as an *exclamation.*

Mr Macready's style wanted the philosophic sententiousness requisite for an harmonious delivery of the analysis of ' man;' besides which he adopted the late John Kemble's omission of the indefinite article ' *a*' before ' *man*'; an omission not warranted by any of the original and authentic editions : the true text is, when Hamlet would analyze God's animated machine, 'What a piece of work is a man!' The article ' a' prefixed to the word ' man' is essential here, because Hamlet descants particularly upon the male sex and their attributes as constituting the ' paragon of animals,' and in contradistinction to the female portion of human kind, enumerates the peculiar and highest order of *men's* intellectual gifts combined with a perfection of personal formation, and when he has summed them all up, he adds, 'Man delights not me!' The courtier then smiles, and he rebukes him with, ' Nor *woman* neither,' &c. Now had Hamlet begun with ' What a piece of work is *man*?' such a general term, *man,* in his premises would have signified the *genus Homo,* and been understood by the courtier as comprehending *woman* also, and thus the point of Hamlet's rebuke at this imagined impertinence been lost.

[Page 149.] Mr Macready's emphasis and intonation of the word ' *southerly,*' ' I am but mad north, northwest; when the wind is southerly I know a hawk from a handsaw,' were such as to imply to a listener that when the wind may be from the south the atmosphere is clearer than when from the north, northwest; whereas the very reverse, according to Shakespeare elsewhere, is the fact; for example, see *As You Like It,* III, v : 'You foolish shepherd, wherefore do you follow her, Like *foggy south,* puffing with wind and rain.' Hamlet, as I understand the passage, means to reflect gently upon the conceited cleverness of those clumsy spies, Rosencrantz and Guildenstern, whose ill-concealed designs are transparent to him, by intimating to them that their employers are deceived in respect to the point or direction of his madness; that, figuratively, his brain is disordered only upon one of the clearest points of the compass, to wit, north, northwest; but that even when the wind is *southerly,* and his intellectual atmosphere in consequence most befogged and impenetrable, his observation is not so mad or erratic as to be unable to distinguish between two such dissimilar objects, for example, as ' *a hawk and a handsaw,*' &c.

[Page 151.] In the sentence ' To die? to sleep,—No more!' Mr Macready to my

surprise, but not satisfaction, punctuated by his tone of voice the words ' no more '
(?) as an interrogatory, and as though they involved the *continuity* of a question, instead of that denoting an emphatic and responsive exclamation (!) of a *conclusive
reflection* upon his own preceding answer to his self-inquiry.

[Page 159.] ' *Guil.* The king, sir, is in his retirement, marvellously distempered.
Ham. With drink, sir?' Mr Macready, instead of as an interrogation, utter'ed the
words rapidly and in a tone of exclamation, denoting an *unquestionable conclusion.*
It was good and not objectionable, for the reason that the sneer at the habits of ' the
bloat king' is practically conveyed to the listener by either punctuation.

[Page 168.] ' That skull had a tongue in it and could sing once.' Mr Macready,
like every other actor seen by me, by his emphasis rendered ' tongue' and ' sing '
antithetical, which fails to point to the listener the *moral* intended. Hamlet begins
moralizing to Horatio as they enter the graveyard, upon the grave-digger's habit of
singing whilst engaged in so melancholy an employment; when they have approached
him more nearly the grave-digger sings a *second* verse, and with his spade at the
same time throws up a *skull;* Hamlet then remarks, ' That SKULL had a tongue in
it and could sing ONCE!' to convey the idea that the *skull* now so mute, and knocked
about by the rude clown, ONCE had a tongue in it, and could do that which he (the
grave-digger), is *then* doing, namely SINGING; this *moral*-painting of Hamlet's reflection can be most clearly conveyed to an auditor's comprehension by special emphasis and intonation, rendering the words, ' SKULL' and ' *once,*' strongly emphatical
as *antitheses,* thus, ' That SKULL, had a tongue in it and could sing ONCE.'

[Mr Barry Sullivan, when playing Hamlet during his recent tour of the United
States, uniformly rendered the passage ' When the wind is southerly I know a hawk
from a handsaw,' thus, ' When the wind is *southerly* I know a hawk from a *heron.
Pshaw !*'

I have heard the late Charles Kean, and other actors, emphasize the following
passage thus, ' *Hor.* I saw him once; he was a goodly *king. Ham.* He was a MAN!
Take him for all in all,' &c. J. C.]

FECHTER

MISS KATE FIELD (*Fechter as Hamlet.* Atlantic Monthly, November, 1870):
' I'll cross it though it blast me.' Heretofore Horatios have senselessly *crossed the
Ghost's path,* as if such a step would stay its progress. Not so with Fechter, whose
Horatio makes the sign of the cross, at which the Ghost stops, as a Catholic ghost
should. . . . .

He is gloomy enough, is Fechter's Hamlet, as he sits beside his mother, starting
when the King addresses him as ' our *son,*' yet gently exclaiming, while kissing the
Queen's hand with courtly grace, and giving by an almost imperceptible accent a
key to the estimate in which he holds his uncle-father: ' I shall in all my best obey
you, madam.' Left to himself, he gazes fondly at his father's portrait, worn about
his neck, and illustrates his beautiful apostrophe by reference to it. . . . .

Fechter, meditating on the startling intelligence that the apparition wore *his
beaver up,* murmurs: ' Very like,' as if the sentence read: ' Very like — my
father! . . . .

When Horatio calls without, ' Heaven secure him,'—meaning Hamlet,—Fechter,
intent upon the Ghost, prayerfully adds, ' So be it.' . . . .

'Conception is a blessing; but as your daughter may conceive,—friend, look to't. It is a mad laugh that follows 'friend.' Hamlet points to his open book as he mutters 'look to't,' and Polonius, literal in all things, runs his eye over the page to learn the 'cause of this defect.'

Hamlet's reception of Rosencrantz and Guildenstern is most cordial until he sees his uncle's portrait around the neck of the latter; then the expression and manner change. . . . . Hamlet's rejoinder, 'And those that would make mouths at him while my father lived give twenty, forty, fifty, an hundred ducats apiece for his picture in little,' is illustrated by his taking up the picture pendent from Guildenstern's neck. Upon dropping it, he crosses to the right, and makes an 'aside' of the succeeding sentence, 'There is something in this,' &c. . . . .

Fechter points the moral of the soliloquy, 'To be, or not to be,' by bringing on an unsheathed sword, as if he had again been contemplating the suicide that would free him from his oath. . . . .

[When the Players enter, Fechter] was the first to introduce a boy with chopins, in lieu of a woman actress [*sic*] . . . .

[Hamlet] never forgets to spare Polonius in the presence of others. . . . . 'It was a brute part of him,' Hamlet replies; and then, walking away, *adds as an aside*, 'to kill so capital a calf there!' . . . .

'That's wormwood' is addressed to Horatio.

Before the sobbing Queen retires, she once more turns to her son, exclaiming, 'Hamlet!'—this is Fechter's introduction,—and stretches out her hands for a filial embrace. Hamlet holds up his father's picture, the sight of which speaks volumes to the wretched woman, who staggers from the stage. Kissing this picture, Hamlet murmurs sadly, 'I must be cruel only to be kind;' then, taking light in hand and raising the arras, gazes at Polonius, exclaiming: 'Thus bad begins, and worse remains behind.'

When Fechter produces *Hamlet* in his own theatre, the time of the churchyard scene is that of a brilliant sunset, making a fine contrast between the thoughtless joy of Nature and the grief of humanity. . . . .

'What, the fair *Ophelia?*' and, overwhelmed with agony, Hamlet falls on his knees beside a tomb, and buries his head in his hands. In the controversy between Hamlet and Laertes, Macready and Kemble leaped into the grave, and there went through the grappling in true Punch and Judy fashion. The illustrious example [see the stage-direction in the First Quarto. ED.] has been often followed; but Fechter wisely abstains from the absurdity, hot approaching the grave until his last word is spoken, when, gazing in agony at the gaping void and at Ophelia's corse, he is dragged off the stage by Horatio.

Fechter's arrangement of the stage [in the last scene] is admirable. In the background runs a gallery, to which a short flight of stairs leads on each side of the stage, and by which all exits and entrances are made. To the left stands the throne where sits the King. The moment Hamlet exclaims, 'Ho! let the door be locked; Treachery! seek it out,' the King exhibits signs of fear, and, while Laertes makes his terrible confession, he steals to the opposite stairs, shielding himself from Hamlet's observation behind the group of courtiers, who, paralyzed with horror, fail to remark the action. Laertes no sooner utters the words, 'The king's to blame,' than Hamlet turns suddenly to the throne in search of his victim; discovering the ruse, he rushes up the left-hand stairs, meets the King in the centre of the gallery, and stabs him. . . . . Descending, the potent poison steals upon Hamlet, who, murmuring, 'The rest is silence,' falls dead on the corpse of Laertes, thus showing his forgiveness of treachery and remembrance of Ophelia.

MACREADY

(*The Hamlets of the Stage.* Atlantic Monthly, August, 1869.)—In the scene before the [court-play,] where the Prince says to Horatio, 'They are coming to the play; I must be idle,' all other Hamlets had taken 'idle' in the sense of being listless and unoccupied. Macready gave it a much more liberal construction [see III, ii, 85, and note. ED.], counterfeiting a foolish youth, skipping across the stage in front of the footlights, and switching his handkerchief, which he held by one corner, over his right and left shoulder alternately, until the King asked after his health.

EDWIN FORREST *

In the line, 'I shall in all my best obey you, madam,' Mr Forrest has the good taste not to emphasize 'you.'

'Niobe' was pronounced Niobe, not Neeobe.

The line, 'Thrift, thrift, Horatio,' was read so as to convey the idea of haste, not the motive of economy which the word seems to imply, in making 'funeral-baked meats furnish forth the marriage-tables.'

The line, 'Then saw you not his face?' was given as a soliloquy.

By Forrest's instruction, no doubt, the Ghost read: 'So art thou to revenge when thou shalt hear I am thy father's spirit,' no pause being made after the word 'hear.'

In the line, 'Than are dreamt of in your philosophy,' the last word was emphasized, not 'your.'

'Sea of troubles' was read 'siege of troubles.'

The line to Ophelia, 'Nymph, in thy orisons Be all my sins remembered,' was read as a tender question: 'Be all my sins remembered?'

The instructions to the Player, 'Speak the speech,' &c., were made a great point by Forrest. It was subdued and wholly conversational. After speaking a few sentences he turned his back on the Player, and walked toward a chair. He then faced him, and again approached, again retired and seated himself, delivering the greater part of the speech in this attitude.

In the interview with the Queen large pictures on the wall were used, instead of miniatures.

The line to Polonius, 'Do you see yonder cloud?' was addressed to him at the wing, the wand pointing off the side scene, as through a window

EDWIN BOOTH

(*Atlantic Monthly*, May, 1866.)—Where a burlier tragedian must elaborately pose himself for the youth he would assume, this actor so easily and constantly falls into beautiful attitudes and movements, that he seems to go about, as we heard a humor-

---

* This extract is from an old newspaper cutting, from which all indication of its date or title has been cut away. ED.

ist say, 'making statues all-over the stage.' No picture can equal the scene where Horatio and Marcellus swear by his sword, he holding the crossed hilt upright between the two, his head thrown back and lit with high resolve.

LUCIA GILBERT CALHOUN (*The Galaxy*, Jan. 1869) : 'O that this too too solid flesh would melt,' was given moving from side to side of the stage, or half flung down upon his chair in an attitude of utter abandonment. The story of the appearance of the Ghost he hears with feverish eagerness, but with extreme quiet.

In the scene with the Ghost, Hamlet is turned away, when Horatio suddenly exclaims, 'Look, my lord, it comes!' He catches sight of the vision, staggers toward Horatio, falls against him, gasping, 'Angels and ministers of grace, defend us!' It is not terror of the supernatural alone. It is the appalling confirmation of his fears. It is the presence of his father hovering on some awful border-land, which is not life nor death, but wherein is seen the horrible image of both. His voice is husky and far away. He shivers as if the cold of the grave were upon him. Then reverence for the majestical presence banishes fear. His voice gathers power and sweetness as the words struggle forth. When he utters the one word *father*, his love seems to overflow it, and expand it into volumes of tenderest speech as he falls on his knees and stretches out eager hands to the solemn shade. [See I, iv, 45. ED.] The 'Oh, answer me!' was incredibly imploring and persuasive.

In the Third Act, the scene is handsomely set as an audience-chamber. A stately double staircase leads to a gallery, from which small doors open on the corridors without. In a deep embayed window Ophelia kneels. From a low arched door beneath the stairway glides the Prince, his head bent, his hands clasped before him, his step slow and uncertain. He steadies himself by the balustrade, moves on again mechanically, is stopped by a chair, sinks into it,—still silent, utterly absorbed. In another moment the 'To be, or not to be,' is uttered in a voice at first almost inaudible. . . . . Rising suddenly and crossing toward the window, he sees Ophelia. His whole face changes. A lovely tenderness suffuses it. Sweetness fills his tones as he addresses her. When, with exquisite softness of manner, he draws nearer to her, he catches a glimpse of the 'lawful espials' in the gallery above. . . . . When he says suddenly, 'Where's your father?' he lays his hand on Ophelia's head, and turns her face up to his as he stands above her. She answers, looking straight into the eyes that love her, 'At home, my lord.' No accusation, no reproach, could be so terrible as the sudden plucking away of his hand, and the pain of his face as he turns from her. The whole scene he plays like one distract. He is never still. He strides up and down the stage, in and out at the door, speaking outside with the same rapidity and vehemence. The speech 'I have heard of your paintings, too, well enough, he begins in the outer room, and the contemptuous words hiss as they fall. 'It hath made me mad,' was uttered with a flutter of the hand about the head more expressive than words. As he turned toward Ophelia for the last time, all the bitterness, all the reckless violence seemed to die out of him; his voice was full of unutterable love, of appealing tenderness, of irrevocable doom, as he uttered the last 'To a nunnery go!' and tottered from the room as one who could not see for tears.

During the court-play, Hamlet lies at Ophelia's feet, watching the guilty King with ever fiercer regard. As the action proceeds he creeps toward him, and, as the mimic murder is accomplished, he springs up with a cry like an avenging spirit. It seems to drive the frightened court before it. In an instant he is alone with Horatio, and, staggering forward, he falls on his neck with the long, loud, mirthless laugh of a madman. When he lifts his face it is one over which ten years have passed, yet with a fierce gladness on it as of a man to whom a blocked way is open, though it lead through blood. Rosencrantz and Guildenstern, coming suddenly upon him while in this mood, are received no longer with the courtly kindness of the friend, but with the haughty courtesy of the King's successor. . . . . The greeting in this scene to Polonius, 'God bless you, sir,' is one of the finest single lines. There is such utter weariness, there is such scorn of this miserable, dishonest, luxurious court, there is such despair of a noble nature set upon by ignoble natures, there is such impatience of this last crafty, unscrupulous, lying courtier, that the grace of speech is more bitter than a curse.

The wild hope of the cry ' *Is* it the King ?' as he stands with the lamp he has snatched up flickering above his head and his hand on the parted arras, makes the air shudder. . . . . Looking down at the old man, he utters ' Thou wretched, rash, intruding fool, farewell,' with accumulating emphasis of bitterness, not more repenting the blow bestowed than deploring the failure of the blow intended.

The whole stage is open for the graveyard scene. From the shadow of the gloomy trees in the distance Hamlet and Horatio come slowly forward; Hamlet sits down to rest on a low knoll, and talks with the Clown. Here, again, the grace and delicate breeding of the Prince are finely shown. From the lighted chapel wails a funeral dirge; the sad procession enters; the two friends withdraw and stand uncovered in the shadow of a tall monument. When Laertes says, ' A ministering angel shall my sister be,' Hamlet starts back, muffles his face in his mantle, and falls on Horatio's neck with a despairing cry, in which all words are lost. In the scene that follows there is the agony of a wounded soul, but no artificial frenzy; there is the wrestle with Laertes, but no pothouse wrangling ; there is the sad appeal to the old affection and the memory which should make them friends, but it is the appeal of a proud and clear soul, not of a weak nor sullied one.

(*The New York Tribune*, 21 November, 1876) : If we were to pause upon special points in Booth's interpretation of Hamlet, we should indicate the subtlety with which, almost from the first, the sense of being haunted is conveyed to the imagination; the perfection with which the weird and awful atmosphere of the ghost-scenes is preserved by what may well be called the actor's transfiguration into supernatural suspense and horror; the human tenderness and heart-breaking pathos of the scene with Ophelia; the shrill, terrific cry and fate-like swiftness and fury that electrify the moment of killing Polonius; and desolate calmness of despairing surrender to bleak and cruel fate, with which Hamlet, as he stands beside the grave of his love, is made so pitiable an object that no man with a heart in his bosom can see him without tears. . . . . Nor does it detract from the loveliness of the ideal that it is cursed with incipient and fitful insanity. . . . . The insanity is a cloud only, and only now and then present,—as with many sane men whom thought, passion, and suffering urge at times into the border-land between reason and madness. This lurid gleam is first conspicuously evident in Mr Booth's Hamlet after the first apparition of the Ghost, and again after the climax of the play-scene; but, flowing out of an art-instinct too spontaneous always to have direct intention, it plays intermittently along the whole line of the personation, and adds weight, and weirdness, and pathos to that immedicable misery which we feel can find no relief this side of the grave.

[In the fencing-scene, the wounding of **Laertes** with his own weapon is thus skilfully managed by Mr Booth : Hamlet secures Laertes's foil by a powerful parry of his thrust in *carte*, by which Hamlet disarms him; catching his foil as it leaves his grasp with the left hand, Hamlet uses it as a dagger, being too close to him for a free use of his own weapon. Should a stickler for the ' code ' object to this ' pass of practice,' it may be urged that the men are ' incensed,' and excitement must excuse it, and Laertes is estopped from demanding fair play, since his own has been foul from the start. ED.]

HENRY IRVING

FREDERIC WEDMORE (*The Academy*, 12 Dec. 1874) : Notice the half-indulgent, yet half-jeering sigh of relief which follows Hamlet's hearing Polonius's praise of the little speech which he delivers as an example to the Players. Here and elsewhere, Irving suggests to you, that among all great troubles, there is always this nagging little one, of the ' tedious old fool's ' presence and commendation. Many things weigh upon Hamlet, one thing worries him,—to be praised by Polonius. . . . . Probably Irving is right in treating Polonius's death quite lightly at first. Hamlet is pre-occupied, he hardly understands it; he is foiled in his task. . . . . Then comes, with great significance, the after reference to it. After bidding his mother goodnight, he steps back, stops a moment with an after-thought,—the dead Polonius. And with a now regretful gravity :—' For this same lord, I *do* repent.'

EDWARD R. RUSSELL (*Irving as Hamlet*, London, 1875, p. 13) : Irving has noticed that Hamlet is not merely simple-minded, frankly susceptible, and naturally self-contemplative, but has a trick,—not at all uncommon in persons whose most real life is an inner one,—*of fostering and aggravating his own excitements*. This discovery of Irving is a stroke of high genius, and will identify his Hamlet as long as the memory of it endures. . . . . The vivid, flashing, half-foolish, half-inspired hysterical power of Irving in the passages where it is developed is a triumph of idiosyncrasy. . . . . For factitious mystery, Irving substitutes natural susceptibilities.

Upon the entrance of Horatio with Bernardo and Marcellus, it is at once seen that Irving has chosen the right tone for his intercourse with the courtiers. This is of immense importance. . . . . It is rather difficult to hit the medium between the beetle-browed ' distance ' of the ordinary leading tragedian and the back-slapping, rib-poking sort of familiarity of [other actors]; but Irving, like Edwin Booth, has accomplished the feat to a nicety, to a glance, to a tone, to a gesture, with incalculable benefit to the reality and domestic interest of the play.

When Horatio tells him that he thinks he saw his father yesternight, Hamlet does not start. He has enough to think of, and cannot quite keep his mind on chit-chat. ' Saw ! who ?' he says, almost casually, barely following the discourse. Then, with a perfect and most artistic truth to nature, he hears the story of the apparition. He has not anticipated it, but the misgivings of his mind and the intensity of his distress have prepared him for anything. . . . . *He* will watch to-night, not announcing his resolve in a thunderous voice with the practised *aplomb* of a veteran tragedian, but in tones full of rapt, nervous excitement.

The extreme and plaintive beseechingness of Irving's address to the Ghost is the distinctive novelty of his reading. It has been complained that Irving does not look so frightened as a man would who saw a ghost; but this is in reality a fine and true touch of character. To Hamlet this is not *a* ghost, but *the* Ghost.

[Page 30.] Does Irving discard the tablets? By no means. But he makes the use of them lifelike and probable. His snatching them from his pocket, and writing on them, is the climax of an outburst hardly distinguishable from hysteria. Hamlet is evidently one of those who, though capable of any amount of acting and reticence in company, finds in solitude a license and a cue for excitement, and who, when alone and under the influence of strong feelings, will abandon themselves to their fancies.

At the words, 'With arms encumbered thus,' it is usual for Hamlets to fold their arms and look mysterious. Irving takes the arm of one of his companions, as he supposes they may take each other's hereafter, and assumes a confidential air, as if the two were comparing their past recollections.

[Page 35.] A silly practice has prevailed amongst Hamlets of uttering the words, 'The play's the thing Wherein I'll catch the conscience of the king,' as if the idea had just struck them. Irving makes them partly the culmination of a line of thought, and partly the natural accompaniment of a most striking action. With an exuberance exactly corresponding in another groove of feeling with the quasi-hysterical use of his tablets in the First Act, he rushes to a pillar, and, placing his notebook against it, begins, as the Act-drop descends, to scribble hints for the speech he means to write.

In Hamlet's interview with Ophelia in the Third Act, we learn that there are circumstances which may bring out, even when he is not alone, the strange ecstasy which it is Hamlet's nature, as Irving reads it, to expatiate. When he begins to talk with Ophelia, he is on his guard. An instinct warns him to shun the distractions and wooings of the passion. Yet the fair Ophelia is before him, and the love of forty thousand brothers is in his heart. He has no shield, no disguise, but his 'antic disposition;' and he puts it on. The rule with modern Hamlets is to pretend to be mad later, when they have perceived the 'lawful espials.' This is not Irving's idea. It is in the coolness of the opening conversation that he affects the forgetfulness, the eccentricity, the insensibility of derangement. . . . . The excitement, however, as it mounts is evidently too much for him. . . . . Then suddenly he sees Polonius and the King, and the climax comes. But not in the shape of pretended madness. Rather does his lunacy become all but real and pronounced. . . . . 'Let the doors be shut on him,' &c.—these are the last words he can say with any degree of sanity. His first sudden 'farewell' is a frantic ebullition of all-encompassing, all-racking pain. What was till now histrionic, passes, as the histrionic phase of highly-strung natures easily does, into real frenzy. His words come faster and wilder. His eyes flash with a more sinister lightning as he gives Ophelia the plague of inevitable calumny for her dowry. Again, 'farewell;' and now he rushes forth, but only to return laden, as it were, with a new armful of hastily-gathered missiles of contumely. He is getting now to the very leavings of his mind. He has nothing to hurl at his love but the commonplaces of men against women. . . . . A flash of frenzy, and he has quitted the scene.

The key [to Irving's conduct during the quiet parts of the court-play] is in the remark made to Horatio before it begins: 'I must be idle.' Irving is idle. Before the spectators enter, his demeanor is not subtle and contriving, but anxious, and his looks are haggard. He has set more than his life upon the cast. But when the King and Queen and courtiers enter, he becomes gay and *insouciant*. Ophelia's fan, with which he plays, is of peacock's feathers, and as he lies at her feet, patting his breast with it, at the words, ' Your majesty, and we that have free souls,' the feathers themselves are not lighter than his spirits seem. In his double-meaning replies to the King there is none of that malignant significance with which it is the custom for Hamlets to discount the coming victory. His ' no offence i' the world ' is said drily, and that is all. His watching of the King is not conspicuous. He does not crawl prematurely towards him or seize his robe. Even up to the crisis, though his excitement rises, his spirits bear him almost sportively through. But when once the King and Queen start from their chairs, Hamlet springs from the ground, darts with a shrill scream to the seats from which they vanished like ghosts, flings himself,—a happy thought,—into the chair which the King had vacated, his body swaying the while from side to side in irrepressible excitement, and recites there,—though the roar of applause into which the audience is surprised renders it barely audible,—the well-known stanza : ' Why, let the stricken deer go limp ' [*sic*]. A still greater, because wild and bizarre, effect follows as Hamlet leaves the chair, and in a sort of jaunty nonsense rhythm chants the seldom-used lines :

> ' For thou dost know, O Damon dear,
> This realm dismantled was
> Of Jove himself, and now reigns here
> A very, very—peacock.'

At the last word, said suddenly after a pause, he looks at Ophelia's fan, which he has kept till now, and throws it away, as if it had suggested a word and was done with.   There is infinite significance in the apparent inconsequence of this last boyish burst, and it is very suggestive of the force and truth of Irving's conception, that the audience receive it with as much enthusiasm as if it were a perfectly logical and intelligible climax.   The doggerel has only the faintest, if any, connection with the event, but it is evidently introduced by Shakespeare as another example of Hamlet's constitutional exuberance, and upon this Irving has worked.

———————

[In DOWNES'S *Roscius Anglicanus*, reprinted in WALDRON'S *Literary Museum*, on p. 29 it is stated that *Hamlet* was the third play acted at Sir William Davenant's new theatre in Lincoln's-Inn-Fields after the Restoration, in the spring of 1662, and Downes adds : ' No succeeding tragedy for several years got more reputation or money to the company than this.' ED.]

COSTUME

BOADEN (*Life of J. P. Kemble*, London, 1825, vol. i, p. 104): We have been accustomed for so many years to see Hamlet dressed in the Vandyke costume, that it may be material to state that Kemble played the part in a modern court-dress of rich black velvet, with a star on the breast, the garter and pendent ribbon of an order,—mourning sword and buckles, with deep ruffles; the hair in powder, which, in the scenes of feigned distraction, flowed dishevelled in front and over the shoulders.

As to the expression of the face, perhaps the powdered hair, from contrast, had a superior effect to the short curled wig at present worn. The eyes seemed to possess more brilliancy. With regard to costume, correctness in either case is out of the question, only that the Vandyke habit is preferable, as it removes a positive anachronism and inconsistency. The ghost of Hamlet's father appears in *armor;* a dress certainly suited to a warrior, but to one of other times. Now this was not at all incompatible with the dress called after Vandyke, in whose time armor was undoubtedly worn, as he has shown in a great variety of portraits. But a completely *modern* suit upon young Hamlet, with his father in armor, throws the two characters into different and even remote periods.

KNIGHT: It has been conjectured, and with sufficient reason, by Strutt and other writers on the subject of costume, that the dress of the Danes during the tenth and eleventh centuries differed little, if anything, in shape from that of the Anglo-Saxons; and although from several scattered passages in the works of the Welsh bards and in the old Danish ballads we gather that black was a favorite color, we are expressly told by Arnold of Lubeck, that at the time he wrote (circa 1127) they had become 'wearers of scarlet, purple, and fine linen;' and by Wallingford, who died in 1214, that 'the Danes were effeminately gay in their dress, combed their hair once a day, bathed once a week, and often changed their attire.' Of their pride in their long hair, and of the care they took of it, several anecdotes have been preserved. . . . . A young Danish warrior going to be beheaded begged of an executioner that his hair might not be touched by a slave, or stained with his blood.*

In a MS register of Hide Abbey, written in the time of Canute, that monarch is represented in a tunic and mantle, the latter fastened with cords or ribands, and tassels. He wears shoes and stockings reaching nearly to the knees, with embroidered tops, or it may be chausses or pantaloons, with an embroidered band beneath the knee; for the drawing being uncolored leaves the matter in doubt. When Canute's body was examined at Winchester in 1766, it was adorned with several gold and silver bands, and a wreath or circlet was round the head. A jewelled ring was upon one finger, and in one of his hands a silver penny.† Bracelets of massive gold were worn by all persons of rank, and their most sacred oath before their conversion to Christianity was by their 'holy bracelet;' a sacred ornament of this kind being kept on the altars of their gods or worn round the arm of the priest. Scarlet was the color originally worn by the kings, queens, and princes of Denmark. In

---

* Jomswinkinga Saga in Bartholinus   † Archæologia, vol. iii.

the ballad of Childe Axelvold we find that as soon as the young man discovered himself to be of royal race, he ' put on the scarlet red,'—the word red being used [in this and other instances] to distinguish the peculiar sort of scarlets, as in those times scarlet, like purple, was used to express any gradation of color formed by red and blue, from indigo to crimson.   It thus happens, curiously enough, that the objections of the Queen and Claudius to the appearance of Hamlet in black are authorized, not only by the well-known custom of the early Danes, never to mourn for their nearest and dearest relatives or friends, but also by the fact that although black was at least their favorite,* if not, indeed, their national color, Hamlet, as a prince of the blood, should have been attired in the royal scarlet.   Of the armour of the Danes at the close of the tenth century we have several verbal descriptions. By the laws of Gula, said to have been established by Hacon the Good. who died in 963, it is ordered that every possessor of six marks should furnish himself with a red shield of two boards in thickness, a spear, an axe, or a sword.   He who was worth twelve marks, in addition to the above was ordered to procure a steel cap; whilst he who had eighteen marks was obliged to have also a coat of mail, or a tunic of quilted linen or cloth, and all usual military weapons, amongst which the bipennis, or double-bladed axe, was the most national.   The Danish helmet, like the Saxon, had the nasal, which in Scandinavia is called nef-biòrg (nose-guard), and to which the collar of the mail-hood, which covered the chin, was frequently hooked up, so as to leave little of the face unguarded except the eyes.

E. W. GODWIN (*The Architecture and Costume of Shakespere's Plays.*   The Architect, 31 October, 1874.) [From the reference in the First Scene of the Third Act to the 'neglected tribute,' the author of this essay infers that the date of the play should be about the year 1012, when England paid tribute to the Danes ; to be *historically* correct, therefore, the architecture and costume. of this play should conform to that period] : The play itself gives us no references to Elizabethan architecture, for ' the sepulchre's ponderous and marble jaws ' might apply to any time from this back to the age of cromlechs.   The stage-directions give us:

1. A platform before the royal castle, Elsinore.
2. Platform further removed.
3. A room of state in Elsinore Castle, with a lobby or arcade to it at a highei level.
4. A hall in the same.
5. The Queen's closet.
6. The hall in Polonius's house.

With ' the plain ' and ' the churchyard,' architecture need not interfere, unless, indeed, we give to the first a background among sea and cliff of the ramparts and towers of Elsinore, and to the last a church of wood quaintly carved, with shingled roof and turret.   There are really only eight scenes wanted for the play in its completed form, and these may be reduced, for the platform can be the same in both cases if the back cloth, or scene, is changed to one showing a more distant view of the castle.   Nor can I see why the ' room of state ' should not be the same as ' the hall,' and why the Second Scene of Act Third should not be continuous of the First. The Queen's closet in 1012 was simply the bed-chamber where the chief dignitaries of the court were received.

* Black bordered with red is to this day common amongst the Northern peasantry.

We have then external views of Elsinore Castle from the platform, and two plain and internal views of its hall (or room of state) and its bed-chamber; besides these two rooms, a king's house in 1012 would have a kitchen, a larder, a sewery, a cellar, and a chapel. Into these Shakespeare does not conduct us, so that we have only to think of them in picturing the external views. Before the year 1000, as most of us know, there was a prevailing belief that that year was to be the last in this world's history. Building (for there was more done in this way than heaping together thatch and mud) had come to be looked on as a vain employment, and except to gain the common necessaries of life, men's strength failed them for lack of hope. When, however, the awful year had passed, and nothing unusual had occurred, an unwonted activity succeeded to the former laggard state, and everywhere masons, carpenters, and other craftsmen were loudly called for. It is improbable that the royal castle of Elsinore would have remained unchanged from 1000 to 1012, and we may there-fore conclude that what was not stone before was now rebuilt in the strongest masonry then known in Denmark. Now, among the features of the buildings of that day which we may note as architectural are:

1. Pyramidal-shaped roofs and plain gable roofs covered with wood, shingle, or tile of stone or clay, the overlapping part being shaped triangularly or curvilinearly, having the appearance of fish-scales.

2. Tall, thin pilasters, with capitals and bases of rude structure, occurring at the angles of walls, sometimes covering the entire wall-space, and sometimes united by arches forming continuous arcades.

3. Enclosing walls or ramparts with crenellations, or, as more commonly called, battlements.

4. Elaborate carving, especially on the wood-work,—flat intertwining of foliage and dragons.

5. Large open pinnacles inside as well as outside the hall.

6. Florid iron-work on the doors.

7. Windows had square heads, semicircular or triangular, and if grouped were divided by shafts with swelling mouldings, from which we derive the name baluster shaft.

8. Broad string courses and angle pilasters, or courses of long and short stones, were used when the walls were of rubble or flint, as was commonly the case.

9. Loopholes for arrows are distinctly shown in the illuminated MSS of the period.

10. Doors are of rare occurrence; they are generally folding, and the common doorways are usually closed by a curtain looped back on a hook.

11. Curtains across arches in the hall, and dividing the aisles from the centre, were usual. These served the purpose of modern partitions, and cut up the large hall into numerous apartments, for we must remember that almost every one slept in the hall,—the principal lords in the centre, round about the hearth, and the re-tainers and others in the aisles, curtained off from the nobility and gentry.

It is fortunate that we possess a manuscript copiously illustrated, and produced within a few years of 1000; it is the MS of Cædmon, preserved in the Bodleian Library, and published by the Society of Antiquaries. Of course, the drawings are crude, very crude, but in the hands of a fairly-educated antiquary they can be turned to immense practical use. In these illuminations we see the walled town and the crenellated castle, the floriated hinges, the arcaded hall, the shingled roofs, the plat-forms before the castle, the rich carving of pillar and lintel, the curtains, the seats, the beds, the harp, the tools of the laborer, and the weapons of the soldier. From this source and from the tombs of Vikings and Danes that have been hitherto explored, we find that their instruments of warfare were spears, bows, and arrows for the common men,—Francisco, for instance,—and for their officers and nobles swords of large size with cross-hilts often inlaid with gold, daggers, and heavy double axes. For defence, conical helmets with nasal pieces, shirts or coats of mail sewn on leather, quilted cloth or linen, and shields were worn by the chiefs. The common folk were both bare-legged and bare-armed, and in battle wore pieces of hide sewn on their coarse frieze clothing. The shields were of two forms, one completely round, and the other what would have been round if two curved segments, equal to one-half the circumference, had not been cut out of it. These shields were made of wood, strengthened with an iron boss and sometimes with iron margins, the surface often ornamented with interlaced carved patterns, and painted red as a rule. One other defence they had was a spiral iron armlet or bracelet, about a foot long, which they wore upon the arm. The colors of the hose, the tunic, &c., were originally black, except for members of the blood royal, who wore red. Indeed, red, white, and black were for a long time their favorite colors, although in 1012, when Christianity and a degree of civilization had toned down these sea-robbers to something more inviting, the black was given up,—except among the lower orders, where, I believe, it is still retained, decorated more or less with red, and in its place all sorts of gay colors were adopted, as both in England and France. Their long, wavy hair, of which they were so prodigiously proud, was another Danish fashion; but it gave way in Canute's time, when already the fashions were governed by France, and was worn very much as we wear it at the present time. A small triangular banner, fringed, bearing a black raven on a blood-red field, was the war-flag at this time, and was known and written of as 'The Raven.'

Such, then, are some of the generalities of the architecture and costume of the Danes in 1012. To go further, we know that the Roman manner of building was that which France, Germany, Denmark, and England endeavored to follow as well as they could. We see it in the MSS of Hamlet's time, and we see it, moreover, in the buildings which have been spared us. So that about the architecture in this play of *Hamlet* there can be no more doubt than about the architecture in *King John*.

Of the costume, on the other hand, we have only two sources of information, both of which are sometimes questionable,—I mean the descriptions in the poems, or sagas, and the drawings in the MSS. Of implements of warfare, and of metal-work generally, we meet occasionally with unimpeachable evidence in exhuming the remains contained in Danish and English tombs. The conclusion to which we arrive from these discoveries is, that the spear, shield, with knife and sometimes javelin, were common to the people generally; that the large-headed spear belonged to the minor officers; and that the sword was so honorable as to be entrusted only to the very highest nobles, who as landowners served in the cavalry, a form of service which was absolutely necessary for the use of this long, broad, heavy weapon. The blades of these swords were from thirty to thirty-seven inches long, and double-edged; the guard was curved away from the handle; the pommel was large, and these last were inlaid sometimes with copper, silver, or gold, and sometimes with all three. This conclusion is supported by the laws and by the illuminations in the MSS. Of the shape and quality of the destructible material of dress, we learn from the illuminations the first, and from the sagas, &c., the second. Thus, royal and ecclesiastical robes were often of silk embroidered with gold, and even enriched with pearls. Shoes were always worn by the better classes, and were made to fit the feet, laced up from the toe to the ankle. The stockings reached to just below the knee, had sometimes bordered and embroidered tops, and were sometimes strained over the leg and sometimes in folds or wrinkles, the long fillets bound cross-wise over the leg having become *outré* in the best society of 1012. A linen shirt was worn next the skin; over this came a tunic, very full in the skirt, high up in the shoulders, and reaching to the knees. It was cut down in the middle of the neck to give room to put it over the head, and this, with the neck-piece, was not uncommonly enriched by a border. The waist was girded in by a broad sash-like belt, usually of the same material as the tunic, and the sleeves were ruffled or wrinkled up from the wrist nearly to the elbow. Over the tunic was worn (for battle) the coat-of-mail, and for State occasions the mantle or cloak, fastened by a fibula on the right shoulder, and not reaching much lower than the tunic. The female dress had full sleeves; the skirt, trailing a little on the ground, was girdled as in the male costume, and over the head and shoulders, in plenitude of fold, was worn the hood and cape. The very highest class wore golden bracelets or armlets, and bands of gold encircling their hair. The crowns were merely hoops of gold, with a few ornaments placed crestwise on them. The Phrygian cap and the simple fillet were the only other apparel for the head in times of peace, and these were by no means commonly worn. For the ornaments and patterns of the time we have abundant evidence, but the most common were the spiral, the chevron, the dot, and the interlaced pattern, which stretches across Denmark to the farthest shores of Scotland and Ireland.

WAS THE QUEEN AN ACCESSORY BEFORE THE FACT?

ANONYMOUS (1856)

(*Hamlet. An Attempt to Ascertain whether the Queen were an Accessory, before the Fact, in the Murder of her First Husband.* London, 1856.)—For the purposes of discussion the author of this very able essay reserves to the close the direct testimony furnished by Q_1 as to the Queen's innocence (see lines 1532, 1533 of the Reprint in this volume), and discussing the question as it is presented in the received text, virtually decides it in the negative; even if he leaves it still a question. For in this case we are bound to give the Queen the benefit of the doubt. But I think the conclusion, drawn solely from the received text, to which the writer comes is decisive, and leaves unquestionable the Queen's innocence of the murder of her first husband.

Eleven facts and passages, 'heads of accusation,'—all that can be alleged against the Queen as an accomplice of the King in that crime,—are thoroughly examined in this *Attempt*, and shown to be without positive or cumulative weight. The charge against his mother which Hamlet dwells upon is her second and 'incestuous' marriage. The Ghost ascribes his death exclusively to Claudius. The King never treats the Queen as a sharer with him in the guilt of that murder. Nor, unlike the

King, does the Queen betray any consciousness of having acted that part. If she was the accomplice of Claudius, then her self-command proves her to be the strongest character in the play, while everything else shows her to be the weakest.

' If I had to narrate in prose,' says the author of the *Attempt*, ' the argument of the play, so far as it affects the subject of my paper, I should do it in the following manner:

' Before it opens, Claudius and the Queen have been guilty of adultery, and Claudius alone of murder.

' The Queen's uneasiness and anxiety are sufficiently accounted for by her remembiance that she had sinned most grievously against her former husband during his lifetime, and was insulting his memory, when dead, by her incestuous marriage with his brother.

' Her uneasiness about the changed state of Hamlet proceeds from her belief that it was occasioned in part by her " o'erhasty marriage," coupled with her recollection that he had l een the most frequently a witness of her expressed great love for his deceased father, as he has told us in the words: " Why, she would hang on him As if increase of appetite had grown By what it fed on." Also, from her reflection that she had bastardized and injured Hamlet as far as a mother who is subsequently faithless to her husband can do; and, moreover, that Claudius was keeping him from the crown. Also, from her great natural fondness for Hamlet, and the consequent conflict in her mind in attempting to reconcile her grief at his changed state with her desire to continue in her incestuous union with Claudius, and her wish that the latter should retain his crown and kingdom.

' Seeing her own sin of fickleness mirrored in the play-scene, and her consequent infidelity suggested, she might naturally conclude that, as she recognized that part of the representation, Claudius, as the cause of his visible alarm, might have recognized his part in the poisoning scene; which suspicion would be strengthened by her remembrance of the very sudden death of her late husband.

' Thus, " in great amazement and admiration," as Rosencrantz and Guildenstern describe her directly after the play-scene,—amazed at the dreadful fear suggested to her by the play-scene; for if one part were true, why not the other?—amazed at the fear that her husband had been murdered, and that she had linked herself to the murderer, Hamlet comes and confirms to her this awful suspicion, and leaves in her mind no doubt of its truth.

' Upon this, for the first time, she revolts from Claudius and sides with Hamlet.

' Upon this, " To her sick soul, as sin's true nature is, Each toy seems prologue to some great amiss." Claudius, now fearing her discovery, and evidently suspecting it, treats her with even less confidence than before; plans to murder her son; and, when the poison mixed for Hamlet is swallowed ly her, cares nothing about it, and hopes yet to live himself: " Oh, yet defend me, friends; I am but hurt!" doubtless not sorry that she, whom he suspects to be now informed of his crime, is removed by death.

' And finally tastes of his own venom; and " The rest is—silence." '

GERMAN CRITICISMS

LESSING

(*Hamburgische Dramaturgie, Den 5ten Junius*, 1767, Leipsic, 1841.)—[Voltaire's *Semiramis* having been performed at Schroeder's theatre, Lessing, who was the dramatic critic to the theatre, and whose masterly criticisms created a revolution in taste throughout Germany, and elevated the Hamburg stage to the highest position for a while in dramatic culture, has thereupon the following remarks :]

The appearance of a ghost [of *Ninus*] in a French tragedy is so bold a novelty, and the poet, who ventures it, defends it upon such peculiar grounds, that it is worth while to pause over them for a moment.

'People cry out on all sides,' says M. Voltaire, 'that ghosts are no longer believed in, and that the apparition of the dead in a drama must be regarded as childish by an enlightened nation. Why so?' he replies. 'All antiquity believed in this miracle, and should it be forbidden to follow antiquity? Our religion has consecrated such extraordinary visitations of Providence, and must it be ridiculous to repeat them?'

These appeals, it seems to me, are more rhetorical than rational. Above all things, I could wish that religion had been left out of view. In matters of taste and criticism, arguments drawn from religion serve very well to silence one's opponents, but they are not equally effective in convincing them. Religion as religion can here decide nothing; only as a sort of tradition from antiquity has its testimony any weight, and it has no more and no less weight than other ancient testimonies. And therefore it is only with antiquity that we have here to do.

Very well; all antiquity believed in ghosts. Then the dramatic poets of antiquity were right in availing themselves of this belief; when in their works we find apparitions introduced, it is unreasonable to judge them by our better views. But has the modern dramatic poet, who shares in these our better views, the same right? Certainly not. How if he lays his history back in those superstitious times? Then, too, not. For the dramatic poet is not an historian. He represents not what was formerly believed to have happened, but he lets what happened happen again before our eyes, and lets it happen again, not for the sake of mere historical truth, but with another and higher view; historical truth is not his aim, but only the means to

267

his end; he sets an illusion before us, and through the illusion moves us. If it is true, then, that we now no longer believe in ghosts, if this unbelief must necessarily prevent the illusion, if without the illusion our sympathy cannot be awakened, then the dramatic poet defeats himself in dressing up for us such incredible tales; all the art he expends upon them is lost.

Consequently? Consequently, is it not permitted to bring ghosts and apparitions on the stage? Consequently, is this source of the terrible and the pathetic dried up for us? No, it were too great a loss for poetry; and has it not in its favor examples which show how genius defies all our philosophy, and knows how to make things, which cold reason ridicules, fearful to the imagination? Hence the consequence must be otherwise, and the supposition is simply false. Do we no longer believe in ghosts? Who says so? Or rather what does this mean? Does it mean so much as this—namely, that we have reached such a point of enlightenment that we can demonstrate that such things are impossible; that certain indisputable truths, in direct opposition to the belief in ghosts, having become so universally known, so ever-present to the commonest man, that even to him whatever contradicts those truths must necessarily appear ridiculous and absurd? This cannot be meant. That we now do not believe in ghosts means only so much as this, that upon this question, upon which almost as much may be said for as against—a question which is not and cannot be decided, and upon which the present prevailing mode of thinking has given the preponderance to the arguments for the negative—some few really disbelieve in ghosts, and the many would fain disbelieve in them, and the latter it is whose voices are heard and who set the fashion. They are silent and indifferent, and think now in this way, now in that, laugh at ghosts by day, and shudder at ghost-stories at night.

The dramatic poet is therefore not prevented by our unbelief in ghosts, thus understood, from making use of them. The seeds of faith in them are in us all, and most frequently in those for whom the poet writes. It is the part of his art to make these seeds germinate. If he is able to do this, we may in every-day life believe what we will; in the theatre we must believe what he wills.

Such a poet is Shakespeare, and Shakespeare almost singly and alone. Before his ghost in *Hamlet* the hair stands on end, whether it cover a believing or an unbelieving brain. M. Voltaire is not wise in referring to this ghost; it only makes him and his ghost of Ninus laughable.

Shakespeare's ghost comes really from the other world. It comes in the solemn, shuddering stillness of night, with the full accompaniment of all the gloomy, mysterious accidents, with which, and at the very hour when, we were taught by our nurses to think of and expect ghosts. But Voltaire's ghost is not even so much as a bugaboo to frighten babes withal: it is nothing but an actor disguised, who has nothing, says nothing, does nothing that can make it probable that he is what he gives himself out to be; all the circumstances under which he appears disturb the illusion, and betray the work of a cold poet who is trying to delude and frighten us, but does not know how. Just consider this one thing: in broad day, in the midst of the assembled dignities of the realm, announced by a clap of thunder, Voltaire's ghost comes forth from his grave. Where has Voltaire ever heard that ghosts are so bold? What old woman could not have told him that ghosts shun the sunlight, and will not visit large companies? Voltaire must certainly have known that; but he was too timid, too fastidious to make use of these vulgar circumstances; he would show us a ghost, but it must be a ghost of a genteel kind, and by this gentility he ruined all. The ghost that behaves contrary to the customs and good manners among ghosts seems to me to be no true ghost; and what does not help the illusion destroys the illusion.

If Voltaire had for a moment thought wherein a pantomime consists, he would have felt the awkwardness of making a ghost appear before the eyes of a multitude of persons. At the first sight of the ghost, all to whom it appears have to express fear and horror; they must express these emotions in different ways, if the spectacle is not to have the frosty symmetry of a ballet. Suppose a number of stupid mutes should be properly arranged, it is evident that the diversity of expression must distract the attention from the chief characters. If these are to make the right impression, we must see them not only alone, but we should see nothing else. In Shakespeare, Hamlet is the only person to whom the Ghost speaks; in the scene with Hamlet's mother, his mother neither hears nor sees the Ghost. Our whole attention is fixed upon Hamlet, and the more signs we observe in him of a mind excited by horror, so much the more ready are we to hold the apparition that has this effect upon him for what it really is. The Ghost affects us more through Hamlet than by itself. The impression which it makes upon him is communicated to us, and the effect is too instantaneous and too powerful to permit us to doubt the extraordinary cause which produces it. How little Voltaire understands this art! His ghost frightens many, but not much. Semiramis cries, ' Heavens! I die!' and the rest make no more ado about the apparition than one would if a friend, supposed to be far away, should suddenly appear before us.

G. C. LICHTENBERG (1775)

(*Briefe aus England, London, October*, 1775. Works, vol. iii, p. 214, ed. 1867.)—[In this letter Lichtenberg describes to a friend Garrick's performance of Hamlet.]

Hamlet appears in black. Horatio and Marcellus are with him, in uniform; they are expecting the Ghost. Hamlet's arms are folded, and his hat overshadows his eyes : the theatre is darkened, and the whole audience of some thousands is as still and all faces are as immovable as if they were painted on the walls; one might hear a pin drop in the remotest part of the theatre. Suddenly, as Hamlet retires somewhat farther from the front to the left, turning his back upon the audience, Horatio starts, exclaiming, ' Look, my lord, it comes !' pointing to the right, where, without the spectators being aware of its coming, the Ghost is seen standing motionless. At these words Garrick turns suddenly about, at the same instant starting with trembling knees two or three steps backward; his hat falls off; his arms, especially the left, are extended straight out, the left hand as high as his head, the right arm is more bent, and the hand lower, the fingers are spread far apart; and the mouth open; thus he stands, one foot far advanced before the other, in a graceful attitude, as if petrified, supported by his friends, who, from having seen the apparition before, are less unprepared for it, and who fear that he will fall to the ground; so expressive of horror is his mien that a shudder seized me again and again even before he began to speak; the almost fearful stillness of the audience which preceded this scene, and made one feel that he was hardly sure of himself, contributed, I suppose, not a little to the effect. At last Hamlet exclaims, not at the beginning, but at the end of an expiration, and with an agitated voice : ' Angels and ministers of grace, defend us !'—words which complete all that this scene could want to render it one of the greatest and most terrible. His eyes are fixed upon the Ghost even while he speaks with his friends, from whom he struggles to free himself. But at last, as they will not let him go, he turns his face to them, tears himself violently from them, and with a quickness which makes one shudder draws his sword upon them: 'I'll make a ghost of him that lets me,' he exclaims. That is enough for them. He then extends his sword towards the Ghost: 'Go on, I'll follow thee.' The Ghost leads the way. Hamlet, with the sword still held before him, stands motionless in order to gain a wider interval. At last, when the Ghost is no longer visible to the spectators, he begins slowly to follow it, pausing, and then advancing, with the sword still extended, his eyes fixed upon the Ghost, his hair all disordered, and still breathless, until he disappears behind the scenes. In the soliloquy, 'O that this too too solid flesh,' &c., the tears of most righteous sorrow for a virtuous father, for whom a light-minded mother not only wears no mourning, but feels no grief,—of all tears the hardest, perhaps, to be kept back, as they are the sole solace of a true man in such a conflict of duties,— these tears completely overpower Garrick. Of the words, 'So excellent a king,' the last is uttered inaudibly; it is caught only from the movement of the lips, which close upon the word firmly and with a quiver, in order to suppress an expression of grief which might seem unmanly. Tears of this kind, revealing the whole weight of grief and the manly soul suffering beneath it, fell without cessation through the soliloquy. At the close, righteous indignation mingled with the sorrow, and once as his arm fell forcibly, as if giving a blow, in order to emphasize a word expressive of his indignation, this word, unexpectedly to the hearers, is choked by tears and is uttered only after some moments, with the tears at the same time flowing.

In the celebrated soliloquy, 'To be or not to be,' Hamlet, having already begun to assume the madman, appears with hair all in disorder, locks of it hanging down over one shoulder, one of his black stockings has fallen down, allowing the white understocking to be visible, and a loop of his red garter hangs down midway of the calf of his leg. Thus he slowly comes to the front, wrapt in thought, his chin resting on his right hand, and the elbow of the right arm in the left hand: his looks are bent, with great dignity, sideways to the ground. Taking his right hand from his chin, but holding the arm still supported by his left hand, he utters the words, 'To be or not to be,' &c., softly, but, on account of the profound stillness, audible all over the house.

Before the soliloquy begins which follows the Ghost's disclosure to Hamlet, Garrick stands as if he were Hamlet himself, stupefied almost to utter ruin, and when at last the stupor gradually ceases, into which yawning graves, horror without compare, and the cry of a father's blood, have cast the noble soul, and when, his pained, stupefied sensibilities awakening to thought and speech, Hamlet collects himself for secret resolves, Shakespeare has taken care that every thought and word shall bear witness to the depth and the tumult from which they burst forth, and Garrick also takes care that every gesture shall tell, even to a deaf spectator, of the earnestness and weight of the accompanying words. One only line excepted, which, according to my feeling as it was then spoken by Garrick, could not have satisfied either the dumb or the blind. He uttered the physiognomical remark, which he also noted down in his tablets, 'That one may smile, and smile, and be a villain,' with a look and tone of petty mimicry as if he would represent the man who always smiled, and smiled, and yet was a villain. Upon the second representation, however, he pronounced these words entirely in accordance with my idea of them—namely, *with*

the tone of a well-considered note for immediate use. The smile of the villain, to
which Hamlet alludes, was in his case too serious on the one side and too horrible
on the other to permit him to relieve himself in a soliloquy with a mimicking mockery; the lips which had so smiled must be taught seriousness by death at Hamlet's
hands, and by death only, and the sooner the better.

[P. 235.] I think I have told you that Garrick acts the part of Hamlet dressed in
modern French fashion. It certainly appears odd. I have often heard him blamed
for it, never, however, between the acts, nor upon the way home from the playhouse,
nor at supper afterwards, but always after the first impression was worn off, and when
the brain was cool again, in calm conversation, in which, as you know, the erudite is
given and received for the true, and what is strikingly said passes for evidence of
acuteness. I must confess I have never been disposed to give into this fault-
finding. You may judge whether it was very hard to withhold one's assent to it.

I knew that Garrick is a very sharp-witted man, who keeps the exactest register
of the taste of his countrymen, doing nothing on the stage without reason, and
having a house full of antique properties—a man, moreover, with whom daily experience results not in an excessive indulgence of mere talk, but in silently adapt-
ing to the proper places the harmonious products of a healthy brain. And should
not such a man be capable of perceiving what every London macaroni fancies he
knows how to seize by the handle?—he who stood thirty years ago at a point to
which most of these carping critics have now barely begged their way. Instead,
therefore, of agreeing with them, I began to query what it was that moved him to
dress as he does. I thought long about it simply to satisfy myself. At the second
representation of *Hamlet* I fancied I caught Garrick's feeling on this point, just at the
moment when he drew his sword against Horatio. According to my system, not only
is he excused, but he would have lost in my opinion had he been otherwise dressed.
I grant every one his liberty, *damus petimusque*. I know very well that in such
things one is too often led at last, by over-refining, into the same error into which
another falls by a more convenient overhaste. But let every one think as he pleases,
I must needs give you my reasons, which, although they may not be Garrick's, may
yet lead intelligent actors, here and there, to something better.

It occurs to me that antique costumes on the stage are to us, if we are not too
learned, a sort of masquerade habit, which indeed, if it is handsome, gives us pleasure, but a pleasure so small that it can hardly add to the sum of all else that goes
to increase the effect of the piece. It is to me like German books printed in Roman
characters: I regard them always as a sort of translation. The moment which I
employ in translating these characters into my old Darmstadt 𝕬 𝕭 𝕮 is unfavorable
to the impression. An epigram would lose, to my mind, all the force of the first
effect, if, for example, I had to spell it out in a book upside down. Of the subtle
threads upon which our pleasures hang here below, it is a sin to sever one without
necessity. I should think then, when our modern dress in a play does not offend
the sensitive dignity of our scholastic learning, we ought by all means to retain it.
Our French dress-coats have long since attained to the dignity of a skin, and their
folds have the significance of personal traits and expressions, and all the wrestling
and bending and fighting and falling in a strange costume we may understand, but
we do not feel. The falling off of a hat in a combat I feel completely, but the same
accident to a helmet I feel far less,—it might happen from the awkwardness of the
actor, and look ridiculous. I do not know how firmly a helmet ought to set on the
head. When Garrick in the above-mentioned scene partly turned his back to the

spectators, and I saw in his attitude the well-known diagonal fold from the shoulder to the opposite hip, I for one was ready twice over to give up a sight of his countenance. In the inky cloak of which Hamlet speaks, I should not have seen what I then saw. An actor with a good physique (and such all actors should have who undertake this tragedy) always loses in a dress too far removed from that which to every one in life, earlier or later, is not the least of our wants and the sweetest satisfaction of youthful vanity, and in which the eye knows how to give the too much and too little to things not the breadth of a straw. Understand me, I am not saying that Cæsar and the Henries and Richards of England should appear on the stage in the uniform of the guard, with epaulettes and gorgets. To feel and resent these and similar departures from a universal custom, every one has got sufficient knowledge and antiquarian pride, got at school and from engravings, coins and stoveplates. I only mean that when the antiquarian still slumbers in the heads of the public in regard to a certain article, the actor ought not to be the first to awaken him. The little episodical pleasure, if I may so speak, which the poor pomp of a masquerade habit gives me does not atone for the injury which the piece suffers on the other side. The spectators all feel the injury, only they do not know the cause of it. But herein is the taste of a gifted actor, who knows the strength and the weakness of the eyes before which he appears. London is in the condition which I suppose, in relation to the Danish Hamlet, and is it necessary that Garrick should make them wiser at the cost of both parties? On the one hand, Garrick denied himself a little bit of reputation for learning, while on the other hearts by the thousand became his.

GOETHE (1795)

(*Wilhelm Meister*, Book v.)—[Carlyle's Trans.; slightly varied. Vol. i, p. 261, Boston, 1851.]

I sought for every indication of what the character of Hamlet was before the death of his father; I took note of all that this interesting youth had been, independently of that sad event, independently of the subsequent terrible occurrences, and I imagined what he might have been without them.

Tender and nobly descended, this royal flower grew up under the direct influences of majesty; the idea of the right and of princely dignity, the feeling for the good and the graceful, with the consciousness of his high birth, were unfolded in him together. He was a prince, a born prince. Pleasing in figure, polished by nature, courteous from the heart, he was to be the model of youth and the delight of the world.

Without any supreme passion, his love for Ophelia was a presentiment of sweet needs. His zeal for knightly exercises was not entirely his own, not altogether natural to him; it had rather to be quickened and inflamed by praise bestowed upon another. Pure in sentiment, he knew the honorable-minded, and could prize the repose which an upright spirit enjoys, resting on the frank bosom of a friend. To a certain degree he had learned to discern and value the good and the beautiful in arts and sciences; the vulgar was offensive to him; and if hatred could take root in his tender soul, it was only so far as to make him despise the false and fickle courtiers, and scornfully to play with them. He was calm in his temper, simple in his behaviour, neither content in idleness, nor yet too eager for employment. An academic routine he seemed to continue even at court. He possessed more mirth or numor than of heart; he was a good companion, compliant, modest, discreet, and could forget and forgive an injury; yet never able to unite himself with one who overstept the limits of the right, the good, and the becoming.

[Page 294.] Figure to yourselves this youth, this son of princes, conceive him vividly, bring his condition before your eyes, and then observe him when he learns that his father's spirit walks; stand by him in the terrible night when the venerable Ghost itself appears before him. A horrid shudder seizes him; he speaks to the mysterious form; he sees it beckon him; he follows it and hearkens. The fearful accusation of his uncle rings in his ears; the summons to revenge and the piercing reiterated prayer: 'Remember me!'

And when the Ghost has vanished, whom is it we see standing before us? A young hero panting for vengeance? A born prince, feeling himself favored in being summoned to punish the usurper of his crown? No! Amazement and sorrow over-whelm the solitary young man; he becomes bitter against smiling villains, swears never to forget the departed, and concludes with the significant ejaculation: 'The time is out of joint: O cursed spite, That ever I was born to set it right!'

In these words, I imagine, is the key to Hamlet's whole procedure, and to me it is clear that Shakespeare sought to depict a great deed laid upon a soul unequal to the performance of it. In this view I find the piece composed throughout. Here is an oak tree planted in a costly vase, which should have received into its bosom only lovely flowers; the roots spread out, the vase is shivered to pieces.

A beautiful, pure, noble, and most moral nature, without the strength of nerve which makes the hero, sinks beneath a burden which it can neither bear nor throw off; every duty is holy to him,—this too hard. The impossible is required of him,—not the impossible in itself, but the impossible to him. How he winds, turns, ago-nizes, advances, and recoils, ever reminded, ever reminding himself, and at last almost loses his purpose from his thoughts, without ever again recovering his peace of mind.

[Page 296.] Of Ophelia there cannot much be said, for a few master-strokes com-plete her character. Her whole being floats in sweet, ripe passion. Her inclination to the prince, to whose hand she may aspire, flows so spontaneously, the good heart obeys its impulses so unresistingly, that both father and brother are in fear,—both warn her directly and harshly. Decorum, like the thin lawn upon her bosom, cannot hide the movement of her heart: it is rather the betrayer of this light movement. Her fancy is touched, her still modesty breathes an amiable longing, and should the accommodating goddess Opportunity shake the tree, the fruit would at once fall. And then, when she sees herself forsaken, cast off, and despised, when in the soul of her crazed lover the highest has changed to the lowest, and instead of the sweet cup of love, he offers her the bitter cup of woe, her heart breaks, the whole structure of her being is loosened from its joinings, her father's death breaks fiercely in, and the beautiful edifice falls into a ruin.

[Page 304.] It pleases, it flatters us greatly to see a hero who acts of himself, who loves and hates as his heart prompts, undertaking and executing, thrusting aside all hindrances, and accomplishing a great purpose. Historians and poets would fain persuade us that so proud a lot may fall to man. In *Hamlet* we are taught other-wise: the hero has no plan, but the piece is full of plan. Here is no villain upon whom vengeance is inflicted according to a certain scheme, rigidly and in a peculiar manner carried out. No, a horrid deed occurs; it sweeps on in its consequences, dragging the guiltless along with it; the perpetrator appears as if he would avoid the abyss to which he is destined, and he plunges in, just then when he thinks happily to fulfil his career. For it is the property of a deed of horror that the evil spreads itself out over the innocent, as it is of a good action to extend its benefits to the undeserving, while frequently the author of one or of the other is neither punished nor rewarded. Here in this play of ours, how strange! Purgatory sends its spirit and demands revenge; but in vain! All circumstances combine and hurry to revenge; in vain! Neither earthly nor infernal thing may bring about what is reserved for Fate alone. The hour of judgement comes. The bad falls with the good. One race is mowed away, and another springs up.

[Page 305.] Should not the poet have furnished Ophelia, the insane maiden, with another sort of songs? Could not one select out of melancholy ballads? What have double meanings and lascivious insipidities to do in the mouth of this noble maiden? In these singularities, in this apparent impropriety, there lies a deep sense. Do we not know from the very first what the mind of the good child was busy with? Silently she lived within herself, scarcely concealing, however, her longing, her wishes. Secretly the tones of desire were ringing in her soul, and how often may she have endeavored, like an unwise nurse, to sing her senses to sleep with songs which only kept them more wide awake? At last, when all command of herself is taken from her, when her heart hovers upon her tongue, her tongue turns traitress, and in the innocence of insanity she solaces herself, before king and queen, with the echo of beloved, loose songs.

[Page 353.] In the composition of this play, after the most exact investigation and the most mature reflection, I distinguish two classes of objects. The first are the grand internal relations of the persons and events, the powerful effects which arise from the characters and proceedings of the main figures; these, I hold, are severally excellent, and the order in which they are presented cannot be improved. Through no kind of treatment can they be destroyed or essentially changed in form. These are the things which stamp themselves deep in the soul, which every one desires to see, which no one ventures to meddle with, and which, I hear, have been almost all retained upon the German stage. But our countrymen have erred, in my opinion, with regard to the second class of objects, which are observable in this piece; I allude to the external relations of the persons, whereby they are taken from one place to another, or connected together in one way or another, by certain accidental incidents; they have been regarded as quite unimportant, have been mentioned only in passing, or left out altogether. It is true these threads are slender and loose, yet they run through the whole piece, and hold together what otherwise would fall apart and does actually fall apart when you cut them away, and think you have done enough in leaving the ends hanging.

Among these external relations I include the disturbances in Norway, the war with young Fortinbras, the embassy to his old uncle, the settling of that feud, the march of young Fortinbras to Poland and his coming back at the end; of the same sort are Horatio's return from Wittenberg, Hamlet's wish to go thither, the journey of Laertes to France, his return, the despatch of Hamlet into England, his capture by pirates, the death of the two courtiers by the letter which they carried. All these circumstances and events would be very fit for expanding a novel, but they injure exceedingly the unity of the piece, especially as the hero has no plan, and are extremely faulty. These errors are like temporary props of an edifice; they must not be removed till we have built a firm wall in their stead.

[Page 357. To the suggestion that Rosencrantz and Guildenstern might be compressed into one, Goethe replies :] What these two persons are and do, it is impossible to represent by one. In such small matters we discover Shakespeare's greatness. This lightly stepping approach, this smirking and bowing, this assenting, wheedling, flattering, this whisking agility, this wagging of the tail, this allness and empti ness, this legal knavery, this ineptitude and insipidity,—how can they be expressed by a single man? There ought to be a dozen of these people, if they could be had; for it is only in society that they are anything : they are society itself; and Shakespeare showed no little wisdom and discernment in bringing in a pair of them. Besides, they are needed as a couple that may be contrasted with the single, noble, excellent Horatio.

[Page 361.] Shakespeare introduced the travelling players with a double purpose. The player who recites the death of Priam with such feeling, in the *first* place, makes a deep impression on the prince himself; he sharpens the conscience of the wavering youth; and accordingly the scene becomes a prelude to that other, where, in the *second* place, the little play produces such effect upon the king. Hamlet sees himself reproved and put to shame by the player, who feels so deep a sympathy in foreign and fictitious woes; and the thought of making an experiment upon the conscience of his stepfather is in consequence suggested to him. What a royal monologue is that which ends the second act: ' O what a rogue and peasant slave am I !' &c.

[Page 364.] The repose and security of this old gentleman [Polonius], his emptiness and his significance, his exterior agreeableness and his essential tastelessness, his freedom and his sycophancy, his sincere roguery and pretended truth, should be represented in due elegance and proportions. This genuine, gray-haired, enduring, time-serving half knave should be shown in the most courtly style, which will be greatly helped by our author's somewhat coarse and rough strokes. He should speak like a book when prepared beforehand, and like a fool when in good humor,—insipid in order to chime in with every one, and always so conceited as not to observe when people are laughing at him.

[Page 365.] Although it is not especially expressed, but by comparison of passages I think it incontestable that Hamlet, as a Dane, as a Northman, is fair-haired and blue-eyed. The fencing tires him; the sweat is running from his brow; and the Queen remarks : ' He's fat and scant of breath.' Can you conceive him to be otherwise than plump and fair-haired? Brown-complexioned people, in their youth, are seldom plump. And does not his wavering melancholy, his soft lamenting, his irresolute activity, accord with such a figure? From a dark-haired young man one would look for more decision and impetuosity.

[Page 367.] Hamlet is endowed more properly with sentiment than with a character; it is events alone that push him on; and accordingly the piece has somewhat the amplification of a novel. But as it is Fate that draws the plan, as the piece proceeds from a deed of terror, and the hero is steadily driven on to a deed of terror, the work is tragic in the highest sense, and admits of no other than a tragic end.

CHRISTIAN GARVE (1796)

(*Ueber die Rollen der Wahnwitzigen in Shakespeares Schauspielen*, &c., in *Versuche*, &c. Breslau, 1796, vol. ii, p. 433.)—In this thoughtful essay the author discusses the reason why Shakespeare is so fond of introducing in his dramas characters who

are either mad or touched in their wits. This he finds arises from two causes; first: Shakespeare liked to deal, like Michael Angelo, in grand effects that verge on the monstrous; the passions he depicts are always in extreme: Lear's rage, Othello's jealousy, Macbeth's ambition, Hamlet's thirst for revenge, &c.; thus the way is prepared for a very gradual, almost imperceptible, lapse from sanity to insanity, and expressions that would be deemed exaggerated and unnatural become eminently befitting when uttered under such conditions. Secondly: Shakespeare gained, in depicting madmen and fools, this great advantage, that he could put into their mouths his own philosophy, clad in an elevated and poetic garb. A man of sound understanding keeps back much of what he thinks, and utters no more than will serve the occasion, moderating his fancy and eschewing poetic flights. The insane man, on the contrary, loses himself in his ideas; he is always as though he were alone and talking with himself. His fancy is always on the alert, and he speaks in pictures. His speeches are a series of riddles, from which we can decipher more of the circumstances of his life than the mere words alone would give. Hence it is that when we discern the signs of truth or observation in such a character, it makes a deeper impression. The wise remarks of a fool are like lightning in the collied night. Thus it is that Shakespeare, the greatest philosophical poet that ever lived, and in whose philosophy is found the greatest originality, delights in portraying characters that hover betwixt sanity and insanity.

Too much use, however, must not be made, in a single play, of this effect, produced by insanity. Two insane characters, like Hamlet and Ophelia, would be inadmissible where the circle of dramatis personæ is so small. Now we know that Ophelia was certainly insane; Hamlet therefore was not. Moreover, when insanity is introduced in a tragedy, there must always be given a sufficient cause therefor, either in the past or the present. In Hamlet's case no sufficient cause is given.

There can be no question that the source from which Shakespeare drew his plot represented Hamlet as feigning insanity; and there can be no doubt that Hamlet feigns insanity in the present play. At the same time it is equally undoubted that he speaks and conducts himself on several occasions as he alone would, whose mind was already more or less shattered: for instance, in the first monologue, where he dwells on suicide; again, in his behavior to Ophelia, in III, i, &c.

Garve asserts that a man really insane cannot feign insanity; to assume insanity as a mask demands complete presence of mind and a high degree of mastery over one's self. 'When, therefore, sanity and insanity are mingled in Hamlet's case, I cannot avoid the conclusion that there is a departure from nature and truth.'

HERDER (1800)

(*Literatur und Kunst*, 12.*)—After learning the cause of his father's death, why does not Hamlet instantly go and murder the murderer? He is not wanting in will, and certainly not in strength, as his thrust at Polonius, his fight with Laertes, and his soliloquies show. But his killing the king would have served neither the poet nor his tragedy, which is to lead us **into** the very soul of Hamlet; for from the moral nature and the opinions of a man springs his character.

Hamlet is as tender as he is reflective: from Wittenberg he comes home a scholar.

---

* For this extract from Herder I am indebted to Hackh, page xxiv of the Preface to his translation of *Hamlet*. Ed.

The death of his father, the marriage of his mother, have sickened him with the world, with man and woman; then comes the apparition of his father, and lifts the gates of his soul, as it were, quite off their hinges; so that the young metaphysician now hovers between two worlds. Do we not know, from many instances, how some strange, extraordinary incident, either happy or unhappy, bereaves sensitive souls of calm self-possession, so that they recover it again late or never? Hamlet now looks, as from another world, at everything in this, even at his Ophelia. The future, and indeed the whole spectacle of humanity, hangs confused and mournful before him. Hence is it that, besides being given to study, he now feels himself only a guest in his orphaned paternal home. What an influence the academic enthusiasm for metaphysics has upon young men of Hamlet's character is well known. The Queen thinks he has become melancholy in Wittenberg, and entreats him not to return thither. In this mood he belongs now most assuredly more to the *speculative* than the *active* portion of mankind,—happy idea which the poet takes from our Wittenberg, from the German fondness for metaphysics! To it we owe the metaphysical strain running through the whole piece, and also the celebrated soliloquy, 'To be or not to be.' From France, Hamlet's friend, Laertes, brings a livelier character. In this metaphysical mood even the apparition of his father becomes, as Hamlet reflects, a matter of suspicion: 'The spirit that I have seen may be a devil.' The testing piece is played; Hamlet, with due caution, calls an observing friend to his assistance. It was not base cowardice, then, which delayed his revenge, but, as Hamlet himself often says, a *metaphysical* and *conscientious scruple.* This the thoughtful Orestes [in the Introd. to this *Essay*, Herder styles Hamlet, Shakespeare's Orestes] resolves to dispose of *before* the deed, that it may not torment him *after* it. The plot succeeds; the black conscience of the King rises to the light at the theatrical representation of his crime; the mouse-trap falls; and now may Hamlet sing, 'Why, let the stricken deer go weep,' &c. Relieved of his doubts, he finds the King,—but at prayer. To send the criminal praying out of the world, the *intellectual* feeling of Hamlet does not permit, still less the *tender* feeling of the poet, who watches over this darling of his, this noble spirit, the courtier's eye, the soldier's sword, the scholar's tongue, the expectancy and the rose of a fair state. He goes quickly to his mother, burning with the fire of his just wrath; even from purgatory must his father's ghost come and seek the chamber of his false wife, and step between mother and son. Wound her, but only with words; leave her 'to the thorns that in her bosom lodge.' How stand ye in this scene, Orestes, Electra, Clytemnestra! The criminal anticipates Hamlet, and politely banishes him,—politely sends him to death in a foreign land. *Fate steps in the way.* It rescues him and drives him back to expiate a deed, vengeance for which had fallen, in Polonius, on an innocent head. This guiltless act he must himself first atone for with the bitterest pain: his Ophelia is dead. After delivering a lecture (*Collegium*) in the churchyard upon a skull, he finds himself in the grave over her coffin, with her brother, his friend, in a rivalry of love, which the cunning of the criminal, Claudius, changes into a duel that shall prove fatal to Hamlet. Then *Fate decides.* Weapons and cups are exchanged; Hamlet's mother drinks of the poison; the criminal must drink the rest. Thus is his father's murder *guiltlessly* avenged by *this* Orestes.

But all, criminal, wife, and son,—all are dragged down together. *Destiny* has done the work of vengeance by the unstained hands of him to whom the work was committed. The criminal himself fills the measure of his crime, according to *his* character, and becomes the instrument of vengeance. Even the ghost of his father, notwithstanding all that had gone before, could not drive the good Hamlet from being true to his character.

Hamlet was at first written by Shakespeare as a brief sketch; slowly, by degrees, it was amplified. With what love the poet did this, the work itself shows: it contains reflections upon life, the dreams of youth, partly philosophical, partly melancholy, such as Shakespeare himself (rank and situation put out of view) may have had. Every still soul loves to look into this calm sea in which is mirrored the universe of humanity, of time and eternity. The only piece, perhaps, which the pure *sensus humanitatis* has written, and yet a tragedy of Destiny, of dark, awful Fate.

F. W. ZIEGLER (1803)

ACTOR TO THE ROYAL AND IMPERIAL COURT

(*Hamlet's Character*, &c., Wien, 1803.)—Physically speaking, Hamlet's temperament is melancholic. Oldenholm [Polonius] in Hamlet's eyes had committed, first, a crime, in that he helped Claudius to the throne, and, second, a folly, in that he attempted to be a chop-logic; but he had one merit, he was Ophelia's father. . . . . The mere announcement to Hamlet in Wittenberg that his father had died *suddenly* implied that he had been murdered; such a phrase applied to a king's death in those days always meant murder. . . . . After the Ghost had vanished, having told Hamlet that Claudius was the murderer, Hamlet was athirst for revenge; which at that instant was impossible. The King was surrounded by his guards. But as this thirst for revenge must be gratified in some way, Hamlet relieves his feelings by hanging his uncle in his tables *in effigie*. This touch is true to nature and beautiful, although it is highly improbable that one could write at night in his tables. . . . If Hamlet were only at the head of an army in the field, he would go to work quickly enough and with no delay.

[Page 75.] Hamlet's soliloquy, ' To be or not to be,' follows just after he has instructed the player how to speak his dozen or sixteen lines [ZIEGLER adopts Schroeder's arrangement of scenes. ED.], and he is reflecting on the effect these lines will have on the King, and on the consequences to himself that may, nay, must follow. If the King's occulted guilt unkennel itself, Hamlet's sword must be plunged in the murderer's heart. If the royal bodyguards do not instantly cut him down, which is to be expected, he will certainly have to justify the assassination of the King before a legally constituted court; and even though Gustav [Horatio] and Barnfield [Marcellus] can testify that they had seen the Ghost, and heard the ' Swear !' from under their feet, yet this would constitute no legal ground for Hamlet's acquittal. He puts his mother, whom his father had commanded him to spare, in a frightful position,—she must accuse herself if she wishes to acquit her son, and he has everything to fear should she attempt to screen herself. . . . . The issue of the court play in all its frightful proportions is before his soul,—he sees the quick glittering swords of the bodyguard, or else the cold array of judges condemning the slayer of the King. . . . . Thus surrounded by peril, he utters his despairing reflections on life and death,—not on taking his own life, but on meeting death in the attempt on the King. [This extract is remarkable in that it anticipates TIECK, and KLEIN, and WERDER. In the interview between Hamlet and Ophelia, in III, i,

ZIEGLER finds a sufficing cause for Hamlet's contemptuous treatment of the poor maiden, in her privately visiting him unattended by a *chaperone*. Hamlet's exclamation of ' A mouse!' [sic] when he kills Oldenholm [Polonius] is, according to this author, an instance of great presence of mind. On the trial for the murder the Queen could testify that her son had no intention of killing a human being. ED.]

A. W. SCHLEGEL (1809)

(*Lectures on Art and Dramatic Literature*, trans. by John Black. London, 1015, vol. ii, p. 192.)—*Hamlet* is single in its kind: a tragedy of thought inspired by continual and never-satisfied meditation on human destiny and the dark perplexity of the events of this world, and calculated to call forth the very same meditation in the minds of the spectators. This enigmatical work resembles those irrational equations, in which a fraction of unknown magnitude always remains, that will in no manner admit of solution.

[Page 193.] The only circumstance in which this piece might be found less fitted for representation than other tragedies of Shakespeare is, that in the last scenes the main action either stands still or appears to retrograde. This, however, was inevitable, and lies in the nature of the thing. The whole is intended to show that a consideration, which would exhaust all the relations and possible consequences of a deed to the very limits of human foresight, cripples the power of acting; as Hamlet expresses it: ' And thus the native hue of resolution,' &c.

Respecting Hamlet's character, I cannot, according to the views of the poet as I understand them, pronounce altogether so favorable a sentence as Goethe's. He is, it is true, a mind of high cultivation, a prince of royal manners, endowed with the finest sense of propriety, susceptible of noble ambition, and open in the highest degree to enthusiasm for the foreign excellence in which he is deficient. He acts the part of madness with inimitable superiority; while he convinces the persons who are sent to examine him of his loss of reason, merely because he tells them unwelcome truths, and rallies them with the most caustic wit. But in the resolutions which he so often embraces and always leaves unexecuted, the weakness of his volition is evident: he does himself only justice when he says there is no greater dissimilarity than between himself and Hercules. He is not solely impelled by necessity to artifice and dissimulation; he has a natural inclination to go crooked ways; he is a hypocrite towards himself; his far-fetched scruples are often mere pretexts to cover his want of resolution: thoughts, as he says on a different occasion, which have but one part wisdom and ever three parts coward. He has been chiefly condemned for his harshness in repulsing the love of Ophelia, to which he himself gave rise, and for his unfeelingness at her death. But he is too much overwhelmed with his own sorrow to have any compassion to spare for others: his indifference gives us by no means the measure of his internal perturbation. On the other hand, we evidently perceive in him a malicious joy when he has succeeded in getting rid of his enemies more through necessity and accident, which are alone able to impel him to quick and decisive measures, than from the merit of his courage; for so he expresses himself after the murder of Polonius, and respecting Rosencrantz and Guildenstern. Hamlet has no firm belief either in himself or in anything else: from expressions of religious confidence he passes over to skeptical doubts; he believes in the ghost of his father when he sees it, and as soon as it has disappeared, it appears to him almost in the light of a deception. He has even got so far as to say, 'There is nothing either good or bad but thinking makes it so;' the poet loses himself with his hero in the labyrinths of thought, in which we neither find end nor beginning. The stars themselves, from the course of events, afford no answer to the questions so urgently proposed to them. A voice, commissioned as it would appear by Heaven from another world, demands vengeance for a monstrous enormity, and the demand remains without effect; the criminals are at last punished, but, as it were, by an accidental blow, and not in a manner requisite to announce with solemnity a warning example of justice to the world; irresolute foresight, cunning treachery, and impetuous rage are hurried on to the same destruction; the less guilty or the innocent are equally involved in the general destruction. The destiny of humanity is there exhibited as a gigantic sphinx, which threatens to precipitate into the abyss of skepticism whoever is unable to solve her dreadful enigma.

[Page 197.] This speech [of the Player about Pyrrhus] must not be judged of by itself, but in connection with the place where it is introduced. To distinguish it as dramatic poetry in the play itself, it was necessary that it should rise above its dignified poetry in the same proportion that the theatrical elevation does above simple nature. Hence Shakespeare has composed the play in *Hamlet* altogether in sententious rhymes full of antitheses. But this solemn and measured tone did not suit a speech in which violent emotion ought to prevail, and the poet had no other expedient than the one of which he made choice: overcharging the pathos. The language of the speech in question is certainly falsely emphatical; but yet this fault is so mixed up with true grandeur, that a player practiced in calling forth in himself artificially the emotions which he imitates may certainly be carried away by it. Besides, it will hardly be believed that Shakespeare knew so little of his art as not to be aware that a tragedy, in which Æneas has to make a lengthened epic relation of a transaction that happened so long before as the destruction of Troy, could neither be dramatical nor theatrical.

C. A. H. CLODIUS (1820)

(*Ueber Shakespeare's Philosophie besonders im Hamlet*, Urania, Leipzig, 1820, p. 297.)—Grant that Hamlet's insanity, as it is revealed in his speeches, is occasionally assumed, it eventually becomes a habit; the appalling apparition of his father's spirit, which suddenly broke in upon his somewhat soft and gloomy nature, made him really melancholy and insane. His father's ghost whimpering for revenge becomes a *fixed idea* in his brain, to which everything else is baser matter. . . . .

[Page 301.] Hamlet's spiritual pride, mingled with philosophical pride, pride of rank, and of genius, and of ambition, is hurried on by the appearance of his father's spirit to the most violent thirst for revenge, and then to insanity, which, though it was at first assumed, becomes afterwards real, almost by way of punishment, and which prompts his imagination to ridicule everything, and distort every natural aspect and all harmony of proportiı n. Herein we may find the true tragedy in the piece.

FRANZ HORN (1823)

(*Shakespeare Erläutert*, Leipzig, 1823, vol. ii, p. 20.)—It is commonly understood that Hamlet and Horatio were friends in the higher sense of the word, but such is not the idea of the poet.   Horatio is an honest, loyal subject, very modest, contented in the humblest sphere, without any great elevation of mind, without indeed any uncommon degree of intellect, yet using well all he has learned.

But why has not Shakespeare made Horatio a person of high intellectual ability? Because it would have distorted the whole piece.   Were Horatio a strong, able man, he would either have had an undue influence over his friend, or he would have acted for him, and all would then have been different.   But as it is, he does not help the prince to act; in many respects, in acuteness, wit, imagination, eloquence, he stands below the prince, although he excels him in his way of thinking, morally considered.   It is, moreover, very tragic that the poor prince, among all around him, finds no greater friend than this Horatio, and must cling to him, as no other is at hand.   Horatio is, however, at least an honest man, which is certainly *very much;* but Hamlet has to console and content himself with Horatio's intellectual mediocrity.   Perfect love and reverence he has had for one only, his father, whose loss can never be supplied.

[Page 30.] 'As I, perchance, hereafter shall think meet To put an antic disposition on,' I, v.   What a plan, or rather what a half-plan! for the word 'perchance' is not to be overlooked.   It seems as if Hamlet himself had an idea that nothing special would be gained in this way, and as if it only flitted as a vague dream before his eyes that thus he would be able to watch his uncle.

[Page 54.] We see the King busy with the arrangements for the departure of Hamlet for the country where he is to meet his death.   The King's instruments, Rosencrantz and Guildenstern, manifest special zeal in this service, and it is noteworthy that Rosencrantz, whom Hamlet pronounces a fool [IV, ii, 25], holds forth in a manner almost inspired in behalf of the King's safety.   His speech really contains excellent things, but in reference to Claudius it sounds like the most fearful irony.   But this is just one of the most characteristic features of the whole piece, that often the best things are said by officious flatterers seeking favor of the criminal. The poet has an eye to this, and makes use of this tragic irony only to refine the passion of the spectator.

[Page 58.] This moment [the death of Polonius] forms a tragic *epigram*, the deepest, perhaps, which a poet ever conceived.   One would willingly have granted years or a score of years to the poor, half-honest, half-wise, witty fool of a man, who would so gladly live on in his happy and ornamental fashion; and now he must be suddenly hurried off, so entirely without preparation, as it were, in the intoxication of his clumsy intrigue, caught in the pitiful attitude of an eaves-dropper, which he had just volunteered to take, in order to win a new word of praise from a king rich only in phrases.   But not merely for poor Polonius's sake do we speak of the tragically epigrammatic point of this moment; it is far more so on account of Hamlet, whose best opportunity is now *lost*, since he effects nothing but that wretched thrust, a crime that begets nothing but new misery.   He would hurl the terrible usurper from the throne, and now when he might do so, for he has (perhaps for the first time) collected all his strength for the blow, Fate plays a bitter jest with the unfortunate temporizer, who applies the whole fulness of his power to the killing of a fly, that he might just as well have brushed away with his handkerchief.

[Page 62.] That with the fourth act the piece begins to drag has, I believe, often been remarked; but it has not been observed that it *could not* be otherwise. The hero has not merely let slip the moment for putting forth the highest power of which he was capable, in that very moment he has done a pitiable and criminal act; and although he tries again and again to deceive himself, and in a harsh fashion to be witty about it, such a mood cannot suffice. He gradually comes to see what he has done; after this moment he withdraws so deeply into himself as almost to give up the possibility of ever acting at all. Hence the fourth and fifth acts proceed almost wholly after the manner of an epic or a romance; we see hardly anything else but incidents, situations, glimpses of character, profound observation, and things done without or even against the will; and in this awful work, in which nearly all the persons are *sick*, there appears the Gravedigger, as a *Choragus*, sound, healthy, and odd, with very delightful witticisms upon kings' crowns and graves, making jests of the gallows and of madness, of genteel and not gentle suicides, of dead court-jesters, and living, unhappy princes.

[Page 63.] The first thing which we cannot but a little wonder at in the begin-ning of the fourth act is the almost wholly unchanged relation of Gertrude to the King; but on further consideration all wonder vanishes. Only in thorough re-pentance can a change of character, or new birth, be possible; half-repentance renders men only worse,—it disables them; and the horrible tedium which Gertrude carries with her causes her at last to give up *all* repentance. This, Shakespeare, who one might say knew everything, well knew. We think of the great scene, so fully presented, in which Hamlet, summoning all his power, crushes the heart of his guilty mother, and how she, overwhelmed and agonized, promises amendment. What impression does Hamlet's eloquence and his mother's half-repentance leave? When we see her again she is on as good terms as ever with the King; yes, even on better. She is only more firmly fixed in the delusion that she no longer has the power to amend; the great difficulties in the way of a thorough amendment terrify and deter her; she pursues her course as before,—indeed, she is worse than before, for she has coquetted with the thought of amendment, and then thrown it aside as not the proper thing. From now on there is only one step to the conclusion (in the silence of her own mind, at least), that all amendment would be a prepos-terous extravagance, and we do not err in believing that this step she would have taken had not an unlooked-for death suddenly come in her way.

[Page 67.] But it is time for another and a higher person to appear, for without him the piece were surely at an end. To quiet us, there comes forward a blooming young hero, beautiful and sound to the core—Fortinbras, Prince of Norway. We see him now upon his march against the Poles, availing himself of the permission to pass through Denmark. Superficial readers may say, ' Does he come in here merely as a *deus ex machinâ ?*' To which the only answer is, that every intelligent reader must have recognized him as such long before. The wise poet lets him pass before our imagination in the first scene, and indeed in the story of Horatio, imme· diately after the first appearance of the Ghost. He comes still nearer to us in the audience-scene with the King, in the going to and fro of Voltimand and Cornelius, until in IV, iv, he actually appears in person, and in a few words announces him-self, and his captain adds all that is necessary. Indeed, should we omit all these historic references, and let the prince appear only at the conclusion, he would be nothing more than a puppet, who can neither bury the dead nor pretend to live. But why is this young hero represented so sparing of words, almost monosyllabic? I think there was a most excellent reason for it. Upon a closer study of this inexhaustible drama, almost all the persons in it appear to suffer from a plethora of words, and for this reason the spoken word loses for them its healing efficacy. If the State is to be saved and a new life begun, all this must be changed, and the simple word, accompanied by fit action, must regain its power. We are to be made aware that such a time will soon appear; all in the *last* scene that we see of Fortinbras points to it.

[Page 79.] The gravedigging scene has always highly delighted thousands upon thousands. Who can fail to be diverted by this philosophical thinker, laughing at philosophy,—this witty fellow, throwing out his wit as his shovel throws out the earth. Only one must not merely enjoy his wit; there is underneath it all a deeply tragical idea. To my thinking, it is as if at the close of the fourth act the whole soil, upon which this great drama is acted, were about to yawn and crumble; it quakes at every step, and naphtha-flames already burst out, the instant a heavy foot steps on it. Hence it is that Hamlet's words, 'The time is out of joint,' become realized, and there is no one there who is able to set the time right, Fortinbras excepted, who, however, is on his expedition against the Poles. The miserable usurper is in partnership with the no less miserable Laertes in a new poison-mixing; they have both shown very special talents in the practice, on a large scale, of this horrible art. A country in which such things can be is most assuredly without a king and without a government, and is stiff and stark for decay. What now can follow? It seems to me one can look for nothing else or other than a churchyard, and the appearance among all these persons, diseased through and through, of a man thoroughly sound and healthy, at whose hyper-originality we take no offence, and all whose fantastic impertinences we forgive in the lump, because he is so genuine and harmless, and has the courage to jest over the grave and all the world as well. In the scene with his underling, and afterwards with Hamlet and Horatio, this vigorous old Gravedigger seems like one who is bold enough to incline to be king himself. In fact, he tries at least to bear himself like one. He settles things for all time, upon what principles self-murder is to be judged, pronounces himself and his office the noblest things in the world, treats his man as if he were his body-servant with a jest, expresses himself very freely as to Hamlet's madness, and still more freely about the people living in England, which in his arrogant view lies, as it were, at his feet; all which the merry, insolent fellow presumes to do, because, among so many sick, he is the only sound one. He has, indeed, to retreat when the bedizened King appears in the funeral train; but through three scenes he is very king, and, although with no right, yet with better right than Claudius, who stole the crown from the shelf and put it in his pocket.

It may well be asked, what does Hamlet want in the churchyard? And how comes he there,—that the funeral of his beloved is to take place he is ignorant,—he who appears to trouble himself no longer about what is going on? But such questions embarrass neither the poet nor the critics. Hamlet is intent upon only one thing, the punishment of the King; but, fully conscious of his own weakness, he appears to give over the execution of vengeance entirely to fate, or rather to accident,—he, who has never really been alive, is now more than half dead, and so he finds himself best among graves and in the midst of the dead. With a true pleasure he riots in thoughts of death and dissolution, yet even here his particular individual

interest is never forgotten in his meditations, as is seen by his allusion to the jaw
bone of Cain, the first fratricide.

[Page 85.] This courtier, who is never otherwise named than as the 'young'
Osric, as if this pleasant word were his nickname, is painted by the poet with special
love and truth. Consider the situation : ruin is striding triumphantly on; the ground
under our feet does not merely tremble, it is already sinking; one fancies he hears
the subterranean muttering that precedes the earthquake: it is as if we heard the
rushing wings of Fate. The King and the Queen, Hamlet and Laertes, already,
like the doomed, wear the mark of near death upon their foreheads; but the young
Osric, naturally enough, perceives *nothing* of all this, and cannot therefore share in
the tragical mood of the reader or spectator ; he knows nothing of any overruling
Fate, lives in the common order of the day, rejoices in the honor of serving the
King, appears before the prince jaunty and dainty and fulsome. This young Osric,
whose fatality it is never to be simple in his speech, never to be able to stick to the
unvarnished truth, serves to give the spectator great comfort; for we see with joy
how this strange stripling succeeds in drawing from the gloomy prince the last spasm
of wit, humor, and scorn.

TIECK (1824)

(*Dramaturgische Blätter*, 1824. Kritische Schriften, iii, 248. Leipzig, 1852.)—
Claudius, descended from an heroic line, has many great and excellent qualities,
heavily overbalanced, however, by as many bad and degrading traits. In one respect he is through and through regal; his bearing is always dignified; evil and
depraved he may be, but never little. Treachery is his nature ; duplicity and faith-
lessness his very being; but a lofty, winning deportment clothes all these detestable
vices. He is a strong, large, and handsome man; the Ghost, even in his vehement denunciation of him, styles him seductive; Hamlet, behind his back, depicts
him as altogether hateful and base, but, in his presence, is always constrained and
embarrassed, quite unable to make good a word of the contempt which he pours
upon him in his soliloquies. The usurper is not altogether as bad, nor the murdered
king quite as excellent, as the son, in his excitement, in that extraordinary scene
with his mother, describes them.

[Page 251.] While waiting for the play to commence, the King is friendly
towards Hamlet; he jests with the Queen or with other ladies and persons of the
court; he is so absorbed in merry talk that he does not observe the dumb show
by which, after the fashion of the old English theatre, the plot is foretold; Hamlet's
repeated hints and the accents of Hamlet's voice at last arrest the King's notice.
As Hamlet is no longer able to control himself, the King must needs become aware
that something peculiar, something concerning himself, is going on. Then when the
poisoner appears and murders the sleeper, as Claudius had murdered his brother,
the King observes it, and is forced at last to perceive that his sin is no longer a
secret; his conscience breaks through all his hypocrisy; he retreats, horror-struck,
as before a ghost. The development, the preparation for this event, its suddenness,
all truly represented, must needs be of the greatest interest, and make the King
unquestionably the chief figure in this scene. In order to give the scene its fullest
effect, it were well if the scenery could be arranged as it was in Shakespeare's
theatre.

[Page 255.] Although (as neither Shakespeare nor his contemporaries paid any attention to the elucidation of their dramas, which were simply acted, and not easily to be read by any one who had seen them played only once)—although, as has already been remarked, these stage-directions have no weight, yet this oldest one (*Laertes wounds Hamlet, then in scuffling they change weapons, and Hamlet wounds Laertes*), which the actors found it necessary to write down, deserves some consideration. According to the present mode of speech, *to scuffle* is *to tussle.* Even Shakespeare himself uses it thus; but its primitive derivation is from *to shuffle:* it is one with this word. In *scuffling* or shuffling then, in tussling one with the other, in the clash, they exchange rapiers. Why must the *they* refer to Hamlet and Laertes? Is it not much more intelligible that one of the judges of the combat, at the bidding of the King, changes the weapons? or the King himself? or a page at a hint from the King? It must be had in mind that after each essay at arms there came a pause, when the combatants walked up and down to rest, their weapons being laid aside together in one place, and at the last pause the weapons were thus changed by the direction of the King, that Hamlet might kill Laertes. [This shrewd but erroneous explanation of the exchange of rapiers was probably devised before the discovery of Q$_1$, but it was not printed until just after. In a footnote, TIECK refers to the stage direction in Q$_1$, 'They catch one another's rapiers, and both are wounded,' and adds that the word 'catch' does not in the least disturb his explanation. By stretching a point this might be granted, but no stretching will force 'one another's' to bear out this theory; which I have inserted because it has been, not infrequently, accepted by German commentators. ED.]

[Page 257.] I see in Polonius a real statesman. Discreet, politic, keen-sighted, ready at the council board, cunning upon occasions, he had been valued by the deceased King, and is now indispensable to his successor. How much he suspected as to the death of the former king, or how sincerely he accepted that event, the poet does not tell us.

When Polonius speaks to Ophelia of her relations to Hamlet, he pretends ignorance; he has only heard through others that his daughter talks with the prince, and often and confidentially. Here the cunning courtier shows himself, for the visits of the prince to his house could not have been unknown to him. But these visits were made in the time of the late king, and afterwards in the interregnum before the new ruler ascended the throne. The election was doubtful; Hamlet, as we know, had the first right, and the prospect of becoming father-in-law to the king was tempting. But Hamlet, who had no faculty for availing himself of circumstances, or even for maintaining his rights, allowed himself to be set aside, and Polonius saw, even when the great assembly was held, that Hamlet's position at court was Hamlet's own fault. Consequently, for double reasons, Polonius forbids his daughter to have any intercourse with the prince; first, because the prince was a cypher, and then again, because the King might become suspicious if he learned that such intercourse existed.

Ophelia calms her father with the report of the madness of the prince, who was cruel enough to begin the rôle with her, but she innocently imagines that it is her withdrawing herself from him which is the cause of his unhappy disease. Polonius is beside himself: 'Come, go with me; I will go seek the King,' he cries; for he fears that Hamlet in his insanity will betray his passion, and that thus the matter can no longer be kept secret. He explains for us his real opinion: 'I am sorry that with better heed and judgement I had not quoted him,' &c., II, i, 111. Hamlet is nothing: it is a matter of indifference should the prince be offended; but he dares not keep silence to the King; it might have serious consequences.

In this state of mind he goes to his majesty; on the way, however, the difficulty of the affair which he is to manage becomes more apparent. The cause of Hamlet's madness is his love for the daughter of the minister, of the King's confidential servant. The father then must have permitted, nay, encouraged, the prince's addresses, which have been kept from the knowledge of the King until they can no longer be concealed. What appearance would the old courtier make in the affair? Since a shadow of suspicion must fall upon the father of Ophelia, the disclosure must be made to the King when his majesty is in a good humor. Fortunately, the ambassadors have returned with good tidings from Norway; this is the feast which Polonius prepares for the King,—the explanation is to be the dessert. As he cares little for the Queen, he ventures to represent the prince in a ridiculous light,— the prince's jesting allusions exposing his weakness, while Polonius himself acts the part of a true-hearted, unsuspecting character, so that, after all these preliminaries, the King shall be put in the happy humor in which he may be told how the case stands. 'But how hath she received his love?' is the first question which the King gravely asks. The King wants instant satisfaction upon the point which alone is of interest to him. And then out of half truth and prevarication the old man is to spin a lie, that shall set himself in the most blameless light, but which, however, does not satisfy the King. Conscious that he has not been innocent of ambitious designs, and anxious to set himself fully right, Polonius, all too eagerly, proposes that his daughter and the prince be brought together, while he himself and the King listen, concealed, to what passes between the two.

How much of fine observation is there in what is said of Ophelia in Goethe's *Wilhelm Meister* ! But if I do not entirely misunderstand Shakespeare, the poet has meant to intimate throughout the piece that the poor girl, in the ardor of her passion for the fair prince, has yielded all to him. The hints and warnings of Laertes come too late. It is tender and worthy of the great poet to leave the relation of Hamlet and Ophelia, like much else in the piece, a riddle; but it is from this point of view alone that Hamlet's behavior, his bitterness, and Ophelia's suffering and madness, find connection and consistency; and we perceive why it is that all in this young creature, hell itself, as Laertes says, is turned to favor and to prettiness. While the riddle is thus solved, the representation of this character on the stage is rendered all the more difficult.

When she first appears with Laertes, who tells her that Hamlet's love-making is only a violet in the youth of primy nature, conscious that it was a great deal more, she naïvely and smilingly asks, 'No more but so?' After the speech of her brother, she answers: 'But, good my brother, Do not as some ungracious pastors do,' &c., I, iii, 46–51. I do not understand how an innocent girl could thus answer,—an answer wide of that warning. But she believed she knew her brother; she felt deeply how contemptible it was that these lessons should never have been addressed to her until after her acquaintance with the prince had been permitted or ignored. Towards her father she has already been reserved; she takes care not to say too much; she contents herself with a few general expressions, and is painfully aware that, all of a sudden, as a stern parent, he treats the prince with contempt.

Terrified, deeply moved, well nigh distraught, she mentions the visit of the prince. Here we are made prophetically to see upon what a dizzy height her whole being totters. This scene is always represented too coldly and thoughtfully.

In this condition she suffers herself to be used that her mad lover may be overheard. An actress in this character must employ all her skill, in order to show how painful to Ophelia this unworthy part is; to know that, in this interview with her lover, her father and the King are listening to every word; that she is to see him no more, when she had so much to say to him; and to feel herself forced to show herself to him in this strange, unnatural attitude, compelled to bear all his reproaches, his bitterness, bordering on brutality, and not daring to breathe a word in vindication of herself, until at last, when she is no longer observed, she breaks out into lamentation. Certainly, a most involved task for the artist! Instead of this, one commonly sees on the stage, in Ophelia, a maiden taking everything very quietly, while the prince is suffering, complaining, and sentimental, and thus the poet is completely misrepresented.

[Page 266.] At the acting of the play before the court, Ophelia has to endure all sorts of coarseness from Hamlet before all the courtiers; he treats her without that respect which she appears to him to have long before forfeited. The prince is sent away, her father has been killed by him, and her anguish, long pent up, her deserted state, the remembrance of happy hours,—all overwhelm her and overpower her tottering understanding.

Of Laertes less is to be said. It is enough that the actor does not allow himself to be misled into representing him as a noble and affectionate son and brother. In the beginning he appears merely as a gallant of those days. He warns Ophelia in beautiful set phrases, in which he loves to hear himself speak, as indeed is the case with all the persons of the drama.

[Page 270.] The Ghost must have been one of Schroeder's most artistic and impressive representations. I am convinced of it, although I never saw him in this part. But what has since passed on the German stage for an imitation of this great artist is certainly not to be commended. I mean that slow, dull, monotonous recitation, accompanied by hardly a gesture, whereby the scene drags, and the illusion is greatly disturbed. The old Hamlet no longer has flesh and blood; but he has all human passions, anger, revenge, jealousy. Although modified, his utterance should be felt to be pathetic. He must express himself in intonation and by gestures. In both theatres in London the Ghost was simply ridiculous, stalking up and down, without grace or dignity, and speaking his part as if it were a cold-blooded lecture.

Is it necessary to consider this soliloquy ['To be or not to be,' &c.] as having reference to suicide? Did Shakespeare really mean it so? It could not have been so understood in Shakespeare's time, although we have no evidence bearing on the point. As often as Hamlet was acted by the poet's contemporaries, this character and this soliloquy were made subjects of criticism and ridicule. [The course of Hamlet's feelings is here traced by TIECK, from the beginning of the tragedy until it reaches the intense dissatisfaction with himself, expressed in the monologue after the Player had recited the passage about the 'rugged Pyrrhus;' this dissatisfaction, however, is soothed by the prospect of the play wherein the conscience of the King is to be caught; this relief lasts only for a moment, and Hamlet begins to ask himself why it is that he cannot carry out his revenge; and it is in this self-searching mood that we next see him. TIECK finds fault with the present division into Acts. The Second Act, he says, should end with what is now III, i, whereby the two monologues should be brought into closer connection. He then proceeds to give the following explanation of 'To be or not to be,' &c.; an explanation that I believe has never found favor with any one, except TIECK's warm personal friend and admirer, Freih. v. FRIESEN, who acknowledges that TIECK was anticipated by ZIEGLER. See p. 315. ED.]

[Page 282.] It comes to this, he says to himself (the spectator is understood to keep in mind all that precedes, and to follow this apparent leap in Hamlet's thoughts): the only point is whether a man live or do not live, *i. e.* more than life I cannot risk and lose, so that the only thing is life, whether I set all upon that. This consideration is altogether just; it has often been expressed, who fears not Death need fear nothing else. But, he continues after a pause, it may be the greatest magnanimity calmly to bear the worst, to practice that patience which is commended as Christian, and which requires as much strength and greatness of soul as positive resistance: ' Or to take arms against a sea of troubles, And, by opposing, end *them*,' *i. e.* these troubles: but how? By suicide? What then is meant by this ' opposing,' this positive resistance? Would *taking* arms, then, be fitting, if the arms were to be directed against him who took them up? No, it is these troubles that I seek to annihilate; it is my opponent that I am to put an end to. This must I accomplish, in case my patience does not suffice, if I do not possess strength enough, to keep from valuing my own life too highly; for that may be imperilled; but I dare to meet this peril the more readily, as dying is only a release from all earthly burthens.

[Page 288.] By forcing the meaning somewhat, the common interpretation of the soliloquy may be justified, until we come to: ' And enterprises of great pith and moment With this regard,' &c. Here, if one goes candidly to work, is a passage difficult, if not impossible, to be reconciled with the idea that self-murder is the one great topic of the soliloquy. Is self-murder an enterprise of great pith and moment? And could Hamlet deceive himself so egregiously as to give such honorable names to the miserable cowardice that prompted him to destroy himself, in order to escape the heavy task imposed upon him? He is no hero; he shows, as he confesses to Ophelia, weaknesses of all sorts; almost everything good and bad in man has been contended for in his character. But it is sinking altogether too low to think seriously of destroying himself, and this out of base fear. I wonder that his friends and admirers can allow him to be thus degraded without turning away with disgust.

A certain disposition to suicide and to a contempt for life, which existed for a while, is partly, perhaps, the cause why this soliloquy has been misunderstood and so excessively admired. But now looking back from its conclusion to all that goes before, and reading it once more according to my understanding of it, we find that all is natural, significant, and fitting. Enterprises of great pith and moment, *e. g.* to hurl an usurper from the throne, to avenge a murdered father, to take the position of a king, to which birth and the law of the land entitled him, to gain over the army, the nobles, and the people to this revolution,—and these, like all similar great undertakings, are turned awry, and die in the intention, because he who attempts them hesitates, because it is not a matter of indifference to him whether or not he himself perishes in the contest.

PROF. J. F. PRIES (1825)

(*Ueber Shakespeare's Hamlet*. Rostock, 1825, p. 54.)—Fault has been found with Hamlet's conversation with Ophelia before the court-play begins, and very properly, if it is read without reference to what precedes and what follows. There is one explanation which fully justifies it, although it is true Shakespeare gives no intimation thereof. Hamlet is now, as never before, acting *at* the King. Claudius has attained to his present good fortune through woman's love. Surrounded by court beauties, would he have neglected the chance of casting the lustful eye of an old fop at the fairest of them all; indeed, such a course on the part of her husband would have proved an additional stimulus to the love of such a woman as Gertrude. Hamlet may have suspected it; for he observes keenly. Woe be it, if the uncle succeeds to the thousandth degree in the case of the son as he has been altogether successful in the case of the father. Distracted by such jealous thoughts, Hamlet utters his coarse jests.

K. H. HERMES (1827)

(*Ueber Shakespeare's Hamlet und Seine Beurtheiler, Goethe, A. W. Schlegel, und Tieck.* Stuttgart, 1827, p. 20.)—' I see a cherub,' &c., IV, iii, 50. In these words is the key to Hamlet's character. He is not precipitate, because, conscious of his worth, he does not despair of the result. He does not overestimate himself, and attribute this result to himself, but he confides in a higher guidance,—without knowing that he has it in his own breast,—he trusts to the hand of the Highest, by which that will happen that must. Only in moments of depression, when the flame of passion blazes wildly up in him, does his revenge seem to lag, only then does he reproach himself that his thoughts are not bloody enough. But is this hesitation, dodging, skulking? Does he on this account ever lose sight of his purpose?

L. BOERNE (1829)

(*Gesammelte Schriften, Dram. Blätter,* 2d Abth., p. 172. Hamburg, 1829.)— Among the plays of the British poet, the scenes of which are laid neither in history nor fable, *Hamlet* is the only one that has a Northern soil and a Northern heaven. Shakespeare, in his sympathy with Nature, well understood what atmosphere best harmonized with his various characters. To lively wit, to light-winged joy, to quick passion, to the clear, decisive deed, he gave the blue sunny South, where night is only day asleep; the melancholy, brooding, dreamy Hamlet he places in a land of clouds and long nights, under a gray sky, where the day is only a sleepless night. This tragedy holds us imprisoned in the North, the damp dungeon of Nature, and we are cheered, as by a sunbeam penetrating the darkness through a fissure in the wall, when, of a sudden, we hear the glowing word, *Rome,* and the bright word, *France.*

The most exact admirers, as well as the warmest friends, of the poet have declared *Hamlet* his masterpiece. We must define this estimate. *Hamlet* is not the most admirable of Shakespeare's works; but Shakespeare is most admirable in *Hamlet.* That is, an extraordinary force astonishes us, not when its activity begins, but when it ceases; only the endurance of a force testifies of its greatness. So here. We wander along the brilliant path of the poet, and as our wonder, having reached the end, turns, wearied, around, we are affronted by Hamlet, whom we had not expected, on our way back. To create him, Shakespeare had to double himself, had to step out of himself; herein he has surpassed himself. But this is not said in the rhetorical language of eulogy, but in the sober terms of description. The play of *Hamlet* is a colony of Shakespeare's genius, lying under another zone; it has another nature, and obeys other laws than the motherland.

Before the painting hangs a curtain. Let us draw it aside, to examine the painting more narrowly; but the curtain itself is a picture. The nearness of the eye must compensate for the feebleness of the light. First, we cast a look upon the surroundings of our hero, the hero of suffering. Hamlet is not the central point, we have to *make* him that; we first form his circle, and then place him in it. But, above all things, we must arm ourselves manfully against the error which so often conquers in life as well as on the stage. In life we judge men by their repute; on the stage we believe, without examination, what the virtuous people in the play say and think of the persons represented. This is not the right way; we must ourselves observe and try them. Hamlet is by no means so noble and amiable as he appears to Ophelia; the King is not by far so worthless as Hamlet describes him. Indeed, we must take care lest we prefer the bad uncle to the good nephew.

[Page 178.] When the King suddenly leaves Hamlet's play, it is not because he cannot master his emotion; if that be the reason, he would have left just after the pantomime, which must have taken him by surprise the more, as it was the first thing to startle him. He withdraws simply to save himself, fearing that the play might end seriously, and execution follow upon Hamlet's condemning sentence. Herein he mistook Hamlet; he did not reflect that a strong man, who has once determined upon an act, never threatens beforehand.

[Page 179.] The Queen is a weak thing; she is Hamlet's mother. Her share in the crime remains doubtful; she is a receiver of stolen goods, buys stolen things cheap, and never asks if a theft had been committed. The King's masculine art overpowers her; her son's lamp of conscience, not lighted till midnight, burns only until morning, and she awakes with the sins of the day before.

[Page 182.] Hamlet had seduced Ophelia, and she saw not what she had lost until, by the murder of her father, the loss became irreparable. Happily for her virtue, the etiquette of piety, the policy of morality came to her aid. She loses both her wits and her life, and knows not why.

Is the Ghost really as lofty a personage as he has so often been described? He enters in armor, but, as it seems to me, only his hull is mailed, his soul is soft and bare. The family likeness between him and his son Hamlet is not to be mistaken. He is a weak, philosophic, winged Ghost, whose home is in the air. Beings of this sort sing like the birds, whose utterance has no word for its body. Hamlet's father speaks fluently, says much and says it rhetorically; we may easily imagine that we are listening to a glorified play-actor. The time permitted to him to walk is so very short, and yet he lets it pass unused. Instead of beginning with the business on hand, his murder, he tells first of his torments in hell, and manifests the greatest pleasure in giving a great poetical picture thereof. He is bent upon making a regular climax, and ending with the greatest horror, his murder by a brother. But this is a fault. The terrible thing about a ghost is, that it appears and speaks; what it does and says, were it never so horrible, is childish in comparison.* The Ghost, moreover, in that other world does not appear to have improved his knowledge of men; if he had, he would have chosen any other than Hamlet to avenge him. Perhaps that was not

---

* The description which the Ghost gives of the world whence he came, and which precedes the important communication,—is it not a proof of Shakespeare's art? The Ghost could not be made to look like a *real* ghost on the stage; if he could have been, he would have so startled the spectators that his bare appearance and three or four words would have sufficed. As it was, the Ghost had to tell what he was, and where he came from, in order to supply what was wanting and produce the full effect of a ghost.—TRANSLATOR.

at all the intention of his appearance. He wanders forth into the upper air, seeking some one to be his avenger, but unfortunately in all the court Hamlet was the only one who could communicate with spirits, a Sunday-born child. The Ghost must have Horatic and the other witnesses swear that they would not talk of what they had seen; but he lingers, which was much the more important, to enjoin silence upon his son. His son prates and babbles, and thereby baulks his father's wish and his own purpose. It is true the King is killed at last, yet he is not condemned as the murderer of his brother, but as the murderer of his nephew. The old mole was blind.

[Page 186.] Hamlet is a philosopher of death, a scholar of the night. If the nights are dark, he stands there irresolute, immovable. If they are clear, is it only a *moon-dial* that shows him the shadow of the hour, he acts unseasonably, and goes about distracted in the deceptive light. Life is to him a grave, the world a church-yard. Therefore the churchyard is his world, his kingdom,—there he is lord. How amiable he appears there! Everywhere else melancholy, there he is cheerful; everywhere gloomy, there he is serene; everywhere else distraught, there he is com-posed! How excellent, how bright and witty, does he show himself there! Every-where else depressed by his thoughts on death, among graves he gives us ghostly comfort. While he sneers at life as a dream, he sneers at death as nothing. There is he not weak,—who is strong in the presence of death? There ends all force, all worth, all calculation, all esteem, all contempt, all difference. There Hamlet may, unreproved, forget his father's command. There he need not avenge his father's death. Shall he drag to the scaffold a criminal lying in the last pains of disease? How cruel! To kill in the presence of death, how ridiculous! what childish impatience! It is as if a snail were to affront the coming wind.

[Page 192.] Does Hamlet *feign* himself mad? He *is* so. He thinks he is play-ing with his madness, and it is his madness that plays with him.

[Page 198.] Had a German written *Hamlet*, I should not have wondered at the work. A German needs but a fair, legible hand. He makes a copy of himself, and *Hamlet* is done.*

EDUARD GANS (1834)

(*Vermischte Schriften.* Berlin, 1834, vol. ii, p. 270.)—If Shakespeare's *Hamlet* is to be characterized in a word, it is the tragedy of the *Nothingness of Reflection,* or, as even this phrase may be varied, it is the tragedy of the Intellect. The tragic element of the intellect lies herein, that the intellect appears to be the true, and yet it is the untrue; that it is neither the substantial nor does it tolerate the substan-tial, but that it is only the disintegrating force before whose onslaughts the world would go down, were it not that reason converts this negative power to her service, and makes it organs of true completeness. But, on the other hand, the intellect is the highest, strongest, and greatest power, that which makes man, man; man's jewel and his crown; and therefore the contest between the intellect and the sub-stantial and reasonable is the sphere in which everything true succumbs, and every-thing true is born again. Hence it is that, next to *Faust, Hamlet* is the profoundest, boldest, most characteristic tragedy that has ever been written, because its hero suc-cumbs not through that which otherwise is well named human weakness, but through that which one must perforce call human strength, [&c. &c.]

---

* Dr Döring says that this was written in 1816. Ed.

[Page 274.] Hamlet has no confidant, and dares not have one. Had he a confidant, the whole action would be, on the side of Hamlet, withdrawn from the sphere of pure subjectivity; that which ought to have lodged in Hamlet's breast alone would have taken external shape. Horatio is his confidant only as he offers a vent to Hamlet's humor, and no further. Hamlet never asks counsel of Horatio, who is only a bystander, so far intimate with the prince that the latter is not always compelled to think aloud in soliloquy.

[Page 279.] It is certainly one of the profoundest characteristics of this piece, that Hamlet resolves that he will have certainty through confession, by means of the play, which, while it is the pretext to save Hamlet in his own eyes, it at the same time elevates to truth and certainty what is wholly uncertain.

[Page 330.] Polonius is certainly a shrewd, intelligent man; but many a fool is that. The King knows perfectly well what he has to look for from Hamlet, but Polonius does not know. This ignorance, this beating about the bush, must make him appear a comic personage to those who know how the case stands, and to this class belongs the public. For the comic consists partly in missing the right, when one is confident that he has hit it.

F. MARQUARD (1839)

(*Ueber den Begriff des Hamlet*, 1839, p. 15.)—The explanation of the piece is apparent, if we keep in mind the ghostly background. Hamlet, like Macbeth, is encompassed by a ghostly world, only it is not so glaringly so in Hamlet's case; the catastrophe is hence brought about by ghostly agency. The notorious exchange of rapiers, by which Hamlet is forced, just before his death, to fulfil his work, appears to be the work of spirits; the punishing and, at the same time, guiding hand is thrust in to bring on the end, as in the planetary system the force of physical law rules with an iron necessity, although the event is accomplished, apparently, by accident.

[Page 26.] The second scene of the fifth act is almost abominable. Hamlet shows himself in a naturalness most repugnant. We look into a soul which seems not to hesitate, but rather to act from an inborn baseness; and Horatio, who at the last has degenerated into a *supe*, is in this scene ridiculous: he does nothing but open his mouth and cry out, 'Why, what a king is this!' It is very fine and interesting that Hamlet, so young, amiable, and innocent, has to share in expiating the sins of his house, only he need not on that account be made a Gurli of.

DR HERMANN ULRICI (1839)

(*Shakespeare's Dramatische Kunst*, Halle, 1839. Translated by Rev. A. J. W. Morrison, London, 1846, p. 215.)—Hamlet does not lack courage nor energy, nor does he lack *will* or *resolution :* it is only in having the will guided by the *judge ment* that he is slow to act and backward in resolve. He is by nature a philosophi cal spirit, having the desire and power to accomplish great things, but it must be in obedience to the dictates of his *own thoughts and by his own independent, original, and creative energy*. On this account it goes against his disposition to execute a deed whose springs are external to himself, and which was *enjoined* on him by outward circumstances, even though the execution of it be by no means beyond his powers.

[Page 218.] The backwardness to give immediate credence to the word of the Ghost would perhaps look like skepticism, were it not that the whole fabric, as expressly intimated in the first scene, is based on the religious ideas and moral doctrines of *Christianity*. According to *these* ideas, it cannot be a pure and heavenly spirit that wanders on earth to stimulate his son to avenge his murder. Even when Hamlet has assured himself of the King's guilt by the device of the play, he still hesitates, and forms no resolve; he is still beset with doubts and scruples,—but pre-eminently *moral* doubts and *moral* scruples! Most justly. Even though the King were trebly a fratricide, in a *Christian* sense it would still be a sin to put him to death with one's own hand, without a trial and without justice. In Hamlet, therefore, we behold the Christian struggling with the natural man, and its demand for revenge in a tone rendered still louder and deeper by the hereditary prejudices of the Teutonic nations. The natural man spurs him on to immediate action, and charges his doubts with cowardice and irresolution; the Christian spirit,—though, indeed, as a feeling rather than as a conviction,—draws him back, though still resisting. He hesitates, and delays, and tortures himself with a vain attempt to reconcile these conflicting impulses, and between them to preserve his own liberty of will and action.

[Page 221.] The mind of Hamlet,—not more noble and beautiful than it is strong and earnest, and as great as human greatness can reach to,—is throughout struggling to retain the mastery which the judgement ought invariably to hold over the will, shaping and guiding the whole course of life. This aim he nevertheless misses. *For in spite of all its grandeur and excellence, his mind is engrossed with this earthly existence; nay, more, the ignorantly cherished and presumptuous wish, to be able, by the creative energy and perfection of thought, to rule and shape at pleasure the general course of things bears on its very face the foul taint of sin,* for it is nothing less than the desire to reject the guiding hand of God, and to make of man's will an absolute law,—to be a very god. Accordingly, whenever Hamlet does act, it is not upon the suggestion of his deliberate judgement, but hurried away rather by the heat of passion or by a momentary impulse.

[Page 223.] Horatio alone is without any ends of his own; he does not aim at making any profit of life for himself, but devotes himself entirely and unreservedly to his friend. And for this disinterested conduct he gains that which all the others lose. It is clear that Fortinbras, young and unacquainted with the circumstances of his new kingdom, will select Horatio,—the friend of Hamlet, and named by the dying heir to the throne to be his exculpator and the defender of his fair fame,—for the high but responsible office of restoring peace and order to the racked and disjointed kingdom.

[Page 226.] Why, in the last act, a noble and powerful race of kings is given up *entirely* to destruction ought to have its reason, its intrinsic necessity; and so it has. Fortinbras, in whose favor Hamlet gives his dying voice, possesses an ancient claim and hereditary right to the throne of Denmark. Some deed of violence or injustice, by which his family were dispossessed of their just claims, hung in the dark background over the head of that royal house which has now become extinct. Of this crime its last successors have now paid the penalty. And thus, in this closing scene, that idea of the overruling justice of God, which pervades all the other tragedies of Shakespeare, impresses on the whole play its seal of historical significance.

DR H. T. ROETSCHER (1844)

(*Cyclus Dramatischer Charaktere*, Berlin, 1844, p. 103.)—Hamlet, outraged in his better feeling by his mother's conduct, has come to look with bitterness upon the whole female sex. This is an important point; it reveals to us the moral basis upon which Hamlet stands: the filial relation has been cherished by him in its greatest purity. Accustomed to look up to his mother with the profoundest respect, the levity which she has manifested affects him most painfully.

[Page 104.] The Ghost only makes that an absolute certainty which already existed as a strong suspicion. The Ghost can communicate only with Hamlet, because Hamlet alone is capable of believing in the certainty that a crime had been committed. The Ghost can appear also to those who have kept themselves free from moral blight, who deplore the condition of Denmark, and who have thus naturally become the adherents of the prince.

[Page 105.] Hamlet is a great specific character. For in him is individualised nothing less than *the fault of the theorising consciousness*, which is unable to resolve upon acting, unable to pass from the broad expanse of thought to the narrow and self-confining path of action, because it is lost in the boundlessness of reflection, and only wills to act when thought has become entirely clear, *i. e.* when it is assured of the absolute purity of its action and of all the consequences thereof. It is thus doomed to inaction.

[Page 106.] The character of Hamlet is, from its truth, an eternal one, continually repeated in the world. In him, Shakespeare has, like a prophet, seized the nature of the German character in its deepest significance. Hamlet's strength and weakness are the strength and weakness of the German people. Like Hamlet, it stands high among all the nations through its profoundly reflective, ideal nature. It has investigated, more deeply than any other, the nature of the mind; it has descended into the abyss of self-consciousness, and measured its depth; it has thrown itself into the conflict of theoretic contradictions, and made itself their master; it has delivered itself from the power of ecclesiastical authority, and shivered into ruin religious institutions; through the universality of its intellect, it has made the treasures of all nations its own; although high toned, and a foe to all that is base in word and deed, it yet has not the spirit and the strength to conform actual reality to the picture, which it carries in itself, of the greatness and grandeur of freedom. It cannot fill up the chasm which separates its knowledge from the real world; like Hamlet, it would fain act; it would, like him, accomplish what is necessary, but it cannot break through the network of considerations that separate it from action, [&c. &c. &c.]

MORIZ RAPP (1846)

(*Amleth der Däne. Shakespeare's Werke.* Stuttgart, 1846, vol. vi, Einleitung, p 7.) [A critical comparison of the first and second Quarto results, according to RAPP, greatly in favor of the earlier edition, on the score of dramatic power; its movement is not buried under a mass of reflections; and there is more harmony between its action and its plot; it is therefore more complete, more effective dramatically, than Q₂, which was enlarged by its author in consequence of the immense applause with which Q₁ was received.]

It is by no means a paradox, 1 or will the reader misunderstand me, when, after what has been said, I hazard the opinion, that while of all the poet's works, and indeed of all works in the world, *Hamlet* appears to me to be the richest in thought and the profoundest, yet regarded in a dramatic light it is the most unsatisfactory, indeed the very worst. For through the whole piece there runs a discord most painful to the mind and feelings. Poetry has never fashioned anything grander than the beginning of this drama. From the first word on the platform before the castle the hearer, be he who he may, is riveted. The supernatural is the most popular motive which modern tragedy can employ; even our over-cultivation, even our tough rationalism, cannot resist the appeal so powerfully made in this scene to faith in the supernatural; or if there is any one who can withstand it, let him quietly turn his back upon all poetry; for him poetry is not. The mystery of the supernatural goes deepening on more and more powerfully through the whole first act. But after the Ghost appears and speaks, the piece no longer advances in interest, and with the first act ends also all effective power. It is therefore in reality the first act to an impossible drama, and if it is permitted to judge of a work piecemeal, the height of the poetry of Shakespeare is here reached. The faults, which become visible from the second act on, are the following. The tragic centre of the whole action lies behind us, and what elsewhere in Shakespeare's works is wont to affect us so irresistibly, instead of growing upon us, is here rather presupposed. The dramatic knot of the piece is the murdered father of the hero. After the Ghost has related the fearful story, nothing more remains for the stage.

[Page 8.] In Act II, as soon as Polonius produces the mad love-letter, the reader, still under the influence of Act I, feels as much puzzled about Hamlet as the latter is afterwards about himself, and we see, instead of the youthful chivalric prince, bound to avenge his father, nothing more than a hypochondriacal misanthrope,—nay, to say it boldly in one word, but yet not too strongly, nothing but a life-wearied stage-manager. For that from now on the poet entirely forgets the hero of his fable, and, with all the bitterness at his command, entertains us with his own personal trials, who can for a moment doubt? That the complete transformation and destruction of the first plan of the piece made a different and yet powerful impression upon his public is readily understood: there is nothing here but the contest of the hour against all his antagonists,—against the actors who reduced him to despair, against the poets who were jealous of him, against the public who neglected his works and ran after a troop of children and dancers,—in fine, against everything which could make such a sensitive and poetic nature miserable.

Comparing the piece as it now stands with the first Quarto, we come to the conclusion that the scheme of the work was from the beginning wrongly contrived—*i.e.* undramatically; but only upon repeated amplifications did the ill adjustments of the parts become really visible; the poet then indulged himself in elaborating with his rich genius single scenes, which took weight and energy from the coloring given them, standing in no relation to the lightly-planned dramatic motives of the piece; but these last he left as they were. The power with which details are carried out overpowers the hearer so entirely that he finds himself more and more caught in the magic circle of the poem, and comes at last to find pleasure in the purely impossible.

L. KLEIN (1846)

(*Berliner Modenspiegel*, 1846.*)—There is no drama, as all the world knows, upon which so much has been written as Shakespeare's *Hamlet.* Quick-witted heads (Herr Rötscher's excepted) have all had their say about it. After all sorts of fashions, lofty, profound, radical, superficial, polished, crude, desultory (Herr Rötscher's lucubrations not excepted), it has been æstheticised about, romanced about, dogmatized about, bemastered, berated, cut up, quibbled at, be-Hegeled, and be-Rötschered. A critical tower of Babel of amazing height and breadth has been reared, and for the same purpose as in the Scripture: to scale celestial heights, and, as people see, with the same result. The celestial heights remain unscaled. A glib little sophomore (*Schulfuchs*) clambering up over the shoulders of Goethe, Gans, Tieck, and others, has reached the loftiest pinnacle of the tower, and there he is waving high in the air a school-programme with the device, '*The Nothingness of Reflection*,' but showing only the nothingness of his own reflection; for his motto assumes that the all-powerful imagination of Shakespeare was impregnated by a miserable scholastic abstraction that has not virility enough to engender anything. It assumes that it was Shakespeare's design to portray in Hamlet a German half-professor, all tongue and no hand, for ever cackling, and hatching nothing, like a dog wagging his tail at the sound of his own barking, whom one would fain help out of his dream, like Polonius, with a 'Less art and more matter!' It assumes that Shakespeare had in mind a pedant who perchance likes to scrawl flourishes and arabesque abstractions in the school-room dust, but who is found at heart to be good for nothing when summoned to action, to the business of life, instantly losing all presence of mind, darting now here and now there, bobbing now to the right and now to the left, instead of doing, trying how not to do, running from cook to tapster, from shop to shop, hoping thus, with the devil's aid, to make his hobby go,—in the end, however, bringing nothing to pass, but at the last, as at the first, hanging, silly dunce that he is, tangled in 'the nothingness of reflection' of his own brain. In the place of the prolific genius of the most original of poets, there is foisted upon us that dogmatic art-criticism which ignores life and history alike, the mere shell of a great system, but barren and impotent; an empty scholastic formula, a stereotyped phrase. The Fortunatus cap of the latest metaphysic is drawn so completely over Shakespeare's ears that the poet is hidden under it, and becomes invisible. His conceptions are covered all up with a web of metaphysical phrases of the Hegelian stamp, with very modern fringes and facings of the livery of the school; so furious is the rage against all modern notions of poetry. Does Aristotle's *Art of Poetry* wear philosophism pinned on its sleeve? Does Lessing's *Dramaturgie* deal in metaphysical scholastics, or in solid coin rather? But a birch-rod rider, tricked out with scrappy abstractions, fashions Hamlet right scientifically, and makes him show himself to be the schoolmaster, the turner out of formulas, befooled by phrases, a Do-nothing, a ruminating theorist, a moral weakling, whose tragic end it is to die of an undigested Hegelian catchword. It is proved also, from the Hegelian Bible, that Shakespeare was a right orthodox Hegelian, who created Hamlet in strict accordance with the orthodox doctrine of identity. It was the split between thought and action, that, according to the Hegelian idea, Shakespeare had in mind

---

* I am indebted to Mr Albert Cohn, of Berlin, for a MS copy of this extract. Ed.

in Hamlet! According to a ready-made category of Hegel's stamping, Hamlet was fashioned! But let the stamp go! How about the split? How? Why, does not every word in the play speak of this split? Does not the essence of the tragic lie in this hunting down of thought and act, this hide and seek of willing and doing, self-stinging at one moment, and then limp, languishing away into lazy melancholy? O strange, strange, supremely strange! The tragic? The comic, you mean! . . . .

[In thus inserting the above extract, I have broken my rule of admitting no criticism on fellow-critics. The temptation was too strong for me. The fun is too sparkling to be lost; even those against whom it is directed cannot feel hurt, I imagine, but will be ready to join the laugh. Besides, this extract is introductory to the position which is taken in the next extract, wherein is found the germ of that re-markable theory which has been lately very fully developed by WERDER. Lastly, it is with no slight pleasure that I am able to give so good a specimen of the brilliant style of a writer too little known here and in England, whose forthcoming volume on the *English Drama* is eagerly looked for. ED.]

The tragic root of this deepest of all tragedies is secret guilt. Over fratricide, with which history introduces its horrors, there rests here in this drama a heavier and more impenetrable veil than over the primeval crime. There the blood of a brother, murdered without any witness of the deed, visibly streaming, cries to Heaven for vengeance. Here the brother in sleep, far from all witnesses or the possible knowledge of any one, is stolen upon and murdered. And how mur-dered? ' With juice of cursed hebenon in a vial, and in the porches of my ears did pour the leperous distilment.' Murder most secret, murder, as it were, in its most primitive shape, murder invisibly committed; the most refined privy murder, the most subtle regicide; a thief-like murder, such as they only commit who steal a crown. The victim himself is all unconscious. He slumbers in unsuspecting repose; upon his securest hour murder steals. And as the eye of the murdered king is for ever closed, so is the eye of discovery sunk in the sleep of death. In the ear were poured some drops of poison, and with the ear of the murdered man the ear of the world is deadened. For this deed of blood there is no human eye, no human ear. The horror of this crime is its security; the horror of this murder is that it murders discovery. This globe of earth has rolled over it. The murdered man is the grave of the murder. ' O horrible, O horrible, most horrible!' Over the first fratricide the blood of the slain cries for vengeance. This murdered brother, dispatched without a trace, has no blood to cry woe! over him, except his blood in the ideal sense, his son. But ' Oh, cruel spite!' the blood of the murdered father cries in the son, and only in the son. This Cain's deed is known to no one but the mur-derer, and to Him who witnesses the murderer's secret remorse. The son has no other certainty of the unwitnessed murder than the suspicion generated by his ardent filial love, the prophecy of his bleeding heart, ' O my prophetic soul!'—no other con-viction but the inner psychological conviction of his acute mind; no other power of proving it but that which results from the strength of his strong, horror-struck under-standing, highly and philosophically cultivated by reflection and education; no other testimony than the voice of his own soul inflamed and penetrated by his filial affection; no other light upon the black crime hidden in the bosom of the murderer than the clear insight of his own soul. Vengeance is impossible, for its aim hovers in an ideal sphere. It falters, it shrinks back from itself, and it must do so, for it lacks the sure basis, the tangible hilt; it lacks what alone can justify it before God and the world, material proof. The act being unprovable has shattered the power to act. In this tragedy the centre of gravity in the conscience is displaced. It lies in the soul of him who is to punish the crime, not, as in the other tragedies of Shakespeare, in the soul of him who has committed the deed. This change of the 'spectrum' is the ghostly point of the tragedy, and one of the most terrible consequences of the assassination, indeed the most terrible; the all-ruinous crime destroys even the punishment; like the sword of Pyrrhus in the speech of the player, it 'seemed i' the air to stick, And like a neutral,' between power and will, it does nothing. The nature of the crime has, as it were, paralyzed vengeance, which grows not to execution, because, in collision with the unprovable deed of blood, it is shattered to pieces, —its wings are broken. The soundless, silent deed has blasted vengeance itself and struck it dumb. The vengeance of the son,—O horrible!—must thus be the seal of the murder of the father. His power to act festers in contact with the secret ulcer of the crime, and the poison, which with sudden effect wrought upon the pure blood of the father, works on in the son, and corrodes the sinews of his resolution.

But how then? Is the subjective, moral conviction which, for the popular sense, is reflected from without by the poet in the Ghost,—is not this motive sufficient to give wings to the revenge of the son? Is not this inner conviction the catchword, 'the cue to passion,' which must spur him on to take public vengeance upon a crime which no one suspects but himself? No! if Hamlet is not to be pronounced by all the world to be what he feigns, stark mad. No! if he is not to appear to all Denmark, with all its dignitaries and nobles at its head, otherwise than a crazy homicide; not though he appeals ten times over to the 'Ghost' that appears to him; not unless he would appear to be that which he undertakes to punish, a parricide! No! if he would not appear in his own eyes as a black-hearted John-a-dreams, as a visionary, a crazy ghost-seer; he the free-thinking, knightly prince, with his powerful understanding. In the nature of the crime, I repeat, the solution of the riddle is to be sought. The assassination, for which there is no evidence to satisfy the popular mind, is the veil of the tragedy. The quality of the deed necessitates the apparent inaction of Hamlet and his subtle self-tormenting; they come not from cowardice nor any native weakness of character, not from an idle fondness for reflection.

It is the only one of all Shakespeare's tragedies in which the crime to be avenged lies outside of or beyond its sphere. In *Hamlet*, Shakespeare has illustrated his great historical theorem by modes of proof different from those employed in his other tragedies : that punishment is only guilt developed, the necessary consequence of a guilt voluntarily incurred. As the genius possessing the profoundest insight into human history, it was incumbent on him to set the truth of this dogma above all doubt in a case in which no outward sensible sign appeared against a deed of blood. The dogma, that 'Foul deeds will rise though all the earth o'erwhelm them to men's eyes,' is proved here with fearful import. By this fundamental idea is *Hamlet* to be explained. This it is that renders the portraiture clear. The tragic action is here the hot conflict of the divining mind with an invisible fact. Hamlet's apparent inaction is a prodigious logic (*Dialektik*). His supposed weakness has in reality the character of the heroic pathos of the antique tragedies, for here as there this weakness is a stormy struggle against the overwhelming pressure of an imposed expiation; the athleticism of a bitter agony every moment at its utmost tension, and this is the real action, the movement in the tragedy, but which our prating critics have not learned, who are in criticism just such shovellers as the Gravedigger, and know nothing more of what action consists in than that it is action at work, action dispatching business. Argal, in Hamlet nothing less is personified than 'the fault

of the theorising consciousness,' which is unable to act, even were it run through
with a spit (*gespiesst*).

HOFFMANN (1848)

(*Studien zu Shakespeare's Hamlet.* Archiv für das Studium der neueren Sprachen,
1848, p. 394.)—To each form of the query, whether Hamlet's madness were real or
pretended, one may say yes and no. If by madness be understood the want of
consciousness, Hamlet was by no means insane. His self-consciousness is rather
increased and made more keen. It might be said that he had become all consciousness. The particular becomes to him the universal; while he analyzes life,
he takes in view only what is peculiar, and then flings it into the abyss of despair,
in which his own life perishes. But if madness be the want of freedom, the ruin
or the restriction of the active powers, then may the prince be said to be insane.
He himself sees that he has no power over his actions; on this ground he explains
to Laertes the death of Polonius. A lie in this case would have been as mean as it
was inconsistent with his whole character. All who have had occasion to observe
the insane know that such a fettering of the will may easily co-exist with great
uprightness and a morbid keenness of insight and judgement. Only, indeed, there
is usually observable that obstruction to freedom of action which is called a fixed
idea. In Hamlet there is certainly nothing of this kind. Its place is supplied by
his deep melancholy, which, like a heavy veil, lies over all things, and deadens
their natural colors.

[Page 412.] In the business with the players, the shattered soul of Hamlet has
its longest respite from the torments which continually beset it, and the introduction
of the court-play is the only thing in which, during the whole piece, Hamlet shows
some degree of interest. This act alone, contradicting all the rules of prudence,
appears in a moment to decide the fate which, all resistance notwithstanding, leads
the royal house to destruction. It increases the remorse of the King almost to
distraction.

Into the scenes with the players, Shakespeare, it seems to me, has put his whole
soul. How small, how mean does the theatre in all its exterior conditions appear,—
a plaything of the great, an amusement of fops, subject to the fickle humors of the
ignorant rabble! And then again, how mighty in its effects, how great in its aim,
from the speech of the player, who is so deeply moved by the imaginary griefs of
Hecuba that his emotion communicates itself to his whole body, and with silent re
proaches punishes Hamlet for being so quiet under the greatest real injuries, to those
deeply significant words upon the nature of Art!

How noble and how strong must have been the soul which, under all these exterior
and apparently vulgar circumstances, kept so lofty an aim immovably in view, and,
in pursuing the same, solaced himself over the riddles and contradictions of life
which, as this work especially shows, no one felt so deeply as himself.

DR G. G. GERVINUS (1849)

(*Shakespeare Commentaries*, 1849; trans. by Miss Bunnett, 1863, ii, 126.)—When,
surprised by the tidings of Ophelia's death, Hamlet hears Laertes's ostentatious
lament over her grave, a storm of passion rises within him, and finds vent in a burst
of exaggerated language. By this excess of excitement Hamlet blunts the edge of

purpose and action, which the habitual tardiness of his nature renders dull; he alternately touches the chords of the two different moral themes of the drama: namely, that intentions, conceived in passion, vanish with the emotion; and that human will changes, and is influenced and enfeebled by delays.

[Page 134.] We become acquainted with Hamlet as the friend and judge of acting, as a poet and a player. He has seen the players before, and has had closer intercourse with them; he inserts a passage in the piece they are playing; he declaims before them; he gives them instructions. His praise of the fragment of Pyrrhus, sustained in the old Seneca-like style, is perfectly serious; it distinguishes him from Polonius, whom a jig pleases better. This, as well as his instructions to the players, exhibits him as a man of cultivated mind and taste, as the judge whose single appreciation is worth more than that of all the rest of the theatre. It is, therefore, natural that the idea should occur to him of 'catching' the King's conscience in a play; he seeks, as it were, an ingenious revenge, and to accomplish this under the touching effect of the presence of his conscience-stricken mother had evidently a kind of theatrical charm for him. When this trial of the King by means of the play succeeds, it is extremely characteristic that it is not the fearful evidence of the crime which occupies him at first, but the pleasure in his skill as actor or poet; not the result so much, as his art which has effected it. 'Would not this,' are his first words, 'get me a fellowship in any cry of players?' This question, still more than the performance itself, would certainly appear to mark his aptitude for the position. It is from this same inclination of Hamlet's, as much as from his character, that he adopts the strangely indirect course of feigning himself mad; and that he is able to sustain his part naturally and ingeniously. He had the power of disguising himself artfully and artistically, and of skilfully remaining his own master behind the mask, averse as he is to dissimulation in life.

Immediately after the departure of the Ghost, still agitated by the apparition, he receives his friends with a falcon-call, as if in the most joyful mood, and knows how to conceal his emotion at first as well as his secret at last. To imagine himself in the position of the player, and on all occasions to study 'the word,' is a natural trait, resulting from his intellectual life and pursuits. He goes with a kind of joyful preparation to rouse his mother's conscience by a moral lecture and a flood of impressive eloquence, to speak daggers rather than to use them, whilst he neglects the deed of vengeance, which would of itself have gained his object. When Laertes bursts forth in the bombastic outpouring of his brotherly grief, he receives it as a challenge for a war of words. Hamlet is aware of the fault in himself; he recognizes it as a hindrance to his active emotion, and blames it in himself with the same vehemence as he declaims against the conscientiousness of his cowardice and the cowardice of his conscience.

[Page 144.] He appears to us as an idealist, unequal to the real world, who, repelled by it, not only laments in elegiac strains over its deficiencies and defects, but grows embittered and sickly about it, even to the injury of his naturally noble character. If Hamlet on the side of his sensibility is an anticipation of the feeble generation of the former century, on the side of this bitterness of feeling he is a type of our German race at the present day. And this it is which has made *Hamlet* the most known of all Shakespeare's plays, and the most discussed among us for now nearly a hundred years; because the conditions of the soul, which are here depicted, seem to us the most expressive and the most living. We feel and see our own selves in him, and, in love with our own deficiencies, we have long seen only the bright side of this character, until of late we have had a glimpse of its shadows also. We look upon the mirror of our present state as if this work had first been written in our own day; the poet, like a living man, works for us and in us in the same way as he intended to do for his own age.

[Page 151.] The conversation between Hamlet and Ophelia, in III, i, affords the actor scope sufficient to intimate *indirectly* the nature of Hamlet's feelings for Ophelia. It is the farewell of an unhappy heart to a connection broken by fate; it is the serious advice of a self-interested lover, who sends his beloved to a convent because he grudges her to another, and sees the path of his own future lie in hope less darkness.

[Page 152.] At Hamlet's first advances, Ophelia, inexperienced and unsuspicious, has given him her heart; she has been free in her audience with him, so that neighbors perceiving it have warned the family, and the family have warned her; his conversation with her is equivocal, and not as either Romeo, Bassanio, or even Proteus, have spoken with their beloved ones. This has affected her imagination with sensual images, and inspired her in her quiet modesty with amorous passions; this is seen in the songs which she sings in her madness, and in the significant flowers which she distributes, as clearly as anything so hidden in its nature can and may be unveiled.

DR L. ECKARDT (1853)

(*Vorlesungen über Shakespeare's Hamlet.* Aarau, 1853, p. 8.)—Faust *is the great poem upon the opposition and reconciliation of the divine and human natures. . . . .* Hamlet *is the great poem upon the opposition and reconciliation of necessity and human freedom.*

Thus Faust and Hamlet are the *modern* Titans, who, at war with the Christian heaven, pile up each his colossus of thought, and at last perish on the ruins of these presumptuous structures. They teach *humanity, renunciation.*

[Page 41.] Hamlet is a character of the North, where all life is more earnest and intense; where man has to rise out of a deeper soul, in order to get into contact with the outer world; where, consequently, the danger is far more imminent of sinking one's self in the objects one sees around him, and all the more, as in scant sunlight and under cloudy skies all things are perceived in a gloomier aërial perspective. The South leads us out of ourselves; the North fosters subjectivity, separates us more from Nature, withdraws us from external impressions, causes us to grow up in a one-sided way, too much engrossed with ourselves. The flute is an instrument of the North, which in sweet solitude breathes its soul into it; it therefore does not surprise us to find the flute in the hands of Hamlet. He certainly knew how to make it speak. He who prefers this instrument shows a thoughtful spirit and a self-contented imagination. It is not pain which the flute expresses, but a sigh for love, a sweet earthly desire, a longing such as may steal over the happiest. But a happy, inner life it was that blest the young Hamlet [&c. &c.].

DR EDUARD VEHSE (1854)

(*Shakespeare als Protestant, Politiker, Psycholog.* Hamburg, 1854, vol. i, p. 293.) —*Hamlet* is the poesy and tragedy of the melancholic temperament just as *Lear* is of the choleric. *Hamlet* is the drama that utters the most startling, the most touching, the saddest truths over this deep riddle, this fearful sphinx, called life,—a drama that reveals to us what a heavy burden this life is when a profound sorrow has robbed it of all charm.

[Vol. ii, 141.] In Hamlet's character the melancholic temperament is the natural pedestal whereon his moral figure rests. It is not to be denied that phlegm must be reckoned as an element of this melancholic temperament. Hamlet is a phlegmatic Northman. His sadness, 'his weakness and his melancholy,' for which he upbraids himself, are the essential elements of his activity, or rather of his very decided inactivity. His phlegm is a recurring product of his melancholy, and he constantly recurs to his melancholy over this phlegm. However deep may be the philosophy which his meditating soul evolves while watching the compass of the times, and discerning something rotten in the state of Denmark, his melancholy temperament for ever keeps him from letting his sails fill with the powerful wind of passion.

F. KREYSSIG (1858)

(*Vorlesungen über Shakespeare*, 1858. Berlin, 1862, vol. ii, p. 235.)—From the rich troop of his heroes, Shakespeare has chosen Hamlet as the exponent, to the spectators and to posterity, of all that lay nearest to his own heart. It is Hamlet to whom Shakespeare has confided his confession of faith as an artist. Through him the opponents of the Globe Theatre get their lecture, the boys of St. Paul's, 'little eyases, who cry out on the top of question, and are most tyrannically clapped for 't.'

The public also is made to know how by its bad taste it encourages falsehood, how it delights in scandal, in passages in which poet and actor maul their opponents. In his talk with the players, Shakespeare makes Hamlet utter his own deepest convictions. He puts in Hamlet's mouth the finest, most striking, in all simplicity the wisest, things, that have ever yet perhaps been said upon the actor's art.

[Page 239.] The whole interest is concentrated, so to speak, on the interior of the drama, on the soul's life of the hero. In opposition to most of Shakespeare's tragedies, it is the conflict of duties in its labyrinthine windings, which engrosses us, far more than the pathology of passion lifting existence from its foundations. When it is considered that Shakespeare was about to write *Hamlet* when the opposite solution of a similar conflict in *Julius Cæsar* was still fresh in his mind, and at the very time when, in the comedy *As You Like It*, he poured forth the whole rich humor of a soul in full harmony with itself and with life, one must needs be amazed at an objectivity, at a sovereign command of creative force, which appears to pass the natural boundaries of human power.

[Page 250.] According to my view, wrong is done to the poet in dignifying Hamlet's relation to Ophelia by the sweet and honorable name of love. It were more like an Iago, than like the highly-gifted, tender prince, thus to treat one who had formerly been an object of genuine deep devotion; there must have been some cause which in times past was sufficient to convert love into hate. And in Ophelia, as well as in Hamlet, hardly a trace is to be discerned of that which would indicate a tragic love. Even that love-letter which the obedient daughter handed over to papa is anything but a passionate outburst of love from a man as tender and refined and warm-hearted as Hamlet. Every doubt on the subject is set at rest by that tête-à-tête before the court-play begins. How could a man of Hamlet's scope and culture, even in private, so behave towards a girl whom he had once really and deeply loved, and whose holiest feelings he thus purposely outraged? Only Jove turned to hate is capable of such refined cruelty, not love merely grown cold under alien influences.

[Page 263.] The horrible harvest of death in the fifth act shows that aimless weakness, even though clad in the finest garb of intellectual keenness, spreads around far more misery than the most inconsiderate violence.

D. B. STORFFRICH.*

(*Psychologische Aufschlüsse über ·Shakespeare's Hamlet*. Bremen, 1859.)—[This author examines the tragedy on psychological principles, and finds that although Hamlet's spiritual organization is the centre around which the drama revolves, yet the range of this spiritual organization includes not Hamlet alone, but all the other characters, so that the whole drama presents a group of sharply-defined psychical figures. The psychological traits which characterize this group have their origin in the false moral atmosphere of the Danish court, clothing each one's inner nature with a false, sham character, or, as Shakespeare expresses it, 'a frock or livery that aptly is put on.' Everywhere throughout the drama we find clear references to this hollow life: 'That one may smile, and smile, and be a villain;' 'My most seeming virtuous queen;' 'You call your ignorance your wantonness,' &c. Except in monologues, in asides, in extreme excitement, in madness, where the true character is displayed, in feigned madness behind which Hamlet masks himself,—nowhere are words the direct outpourings of the soul. The only exceptions are Horatio and Fortinbras. The key to Hamlet's character, Storffrich, in common with many English critics, finds in 'the vicious mole of nature,' I, iv, 36, and also in 'the dram of eale,' which apparently does not present the same difficulties to the German as to the English mind.

Storffrich thinks that when Polonius undertakes to read to the King and Queen Hamlet's letter to Ophelia, he adroitly interpolates the words, 'in her excellent white bosom these.' The Queen, instantly detecting the deceit, asks, 'Came this from Hamlet to her?' Polonius, disconcerted at being detected, replies, 'Good madam, stay awhile; I will be *faithful*,'—and then reads the genuine letter.]

[Page 101.] Had the court-play been, even in Hamlet's own eyes, a means to a predetermined goal, a circuit, no matter how roundabout, leading to some action, it would have served Shakespeare to show how unpractical such a mode of proceeding was; had there been any course decided upon by Hamlet, which had to follow in case the play was successful, then the task which was before him would have stood revealed like a mountain overtopping all others. But the play was no more the result of a well-concerted plan than was the feigned insanity; there is no syllable of an intimation whither it would lead Hamlet. It was a mere pretext to get the very absolutest last (*allerletzt-letzten*) degree of certainty about his uncle's guilt. It was the only way he knew to have that spoken by another which he dare not speak himself. He wanted to make himself believe that he was going to do something.

[Page 109.] Here [where Hamlet kills Polonius], in the middle point of the drama, Shakespeare offers us the key to it. Why is it that Hamlet, a man so rarely gifted, at home in the highest realms of knowledge, so eloquent in his soliloquies, should have been elsewhere so mute? What is it that thus palsies the arm of a

---

* This is said to be a pseudonym for G. D. Barnstorff, who is immortalized by his conjecture that the 'Mr. W. H.,' to whom the *Sonnets* are dedicated, is 'Mr. William Himself.' Ed.

man thus desperately thirsting for revenge? *It is the ban which those near him lay upon him, the psychic-physical ban under which the personal presence of others holds him.* Had not Polonius been behind the arras, or had Hamlet, on turning round at the cry of 'Help!' caught sight of Polonius or the King, his arm would have absolutely failed him. To Polonius he would merely have thrown a sarcastic remark. To the King he would have behaved precisely as he did when they next met.

CARL ROHRBACH (1859)

(*Shakespeare's Hamlet erläutert.* Berlin, 1859, p. 11.)—When the Ghost actually appears, Hamlet's whole being gathers itself up, and he not only fearlessly addresses the apparition, he is even ready to follow it, and he actually does follow it in spite of the opposition, even the active opposition, of his friends. But how does this consist with his previous lack of resolution? Perfectly well. Had there been any serious thing to be done on the terrace, a battle to be fought, Hamlet would probably not have gone there, and he would have been 'ill about his heart,' as before the fight with Laertes. But it was only a Ghost that was to be conjured, and that did not require in him so very much courage, especially as he saw at once that the officers and his friends had stood face to face with the Ghost and suffered no harm, and as he knew, moreover, that they would be at hand. So his following the Ghost is explained. That his courage does not fail him when he stands before the Ghost is natural; like all weak men, he is obstinate; the opposition of his friends only makes him more and more set in his purpose.

[Page 13.] Upon the arrival of his friends Hamlet plays the madman, full of merriment and jests. Thus quickly does his humor change, or, better, thus quickly is he able to represent himself other than he is. He was a good actor, for his conduct with his friends is a play, and he continues it subsequently before everybody. He feigns to be crazy. What a pity he was born to a throne! He would have made his fortune on the stage, and Polonius's praises of his speech to the players are certainly just. Even the prince knows this perfectly well, and he is proud of it. He understands such matters better than the performance of the smallest act. Had he reached the throne, he would have been a crowned play-actor, and at his death he might with justice have said with Augustus, 'Clap, friends, for the play is over.'

But where does he begin his making believe insane? We should think that he would begin and end it with his uncle, and at all events with his mother. By no means! He begins it with the innocent Ophelia, who is not at all within the range of his revenge. There, farthest off, he begins. His aim is for the east, but he steers warily westward. And why? out of cowardice!

[Page 15.] Observe how the hardness of his behavior towards Ophelia increases in the different scenes. In spite of all this, he indulges in the most inflated phrases over her coffin. This is heroic with a witness! And what else is it? It is cheap, and costs nothing but a little breath. And, so far as words go, Hamlet knows how to act with distinction, as he boasts, at the grave, against Laertes.

[Page 16.] The celebrated soliloquy, 'To be or not to be,' to which much too much value is commonly ascribed, as it is superior to the others [II, ii, 575, and IV, iv, 31] in nothing save that it is altogether general, without anything personal in it, gives us a new insight into his character. Hamlet fears death, or rather what comes after death, —the unknown! One is amazed at the clearness and depth of his thoughts, and the knowledge he shows of his own situation. He justifies himself, and then weakens his justification by declaring it only a cover for cowardice. This soliloquy is often called the point of the drama, probably because it is so purely philosophical, or because it gives at the close the key-note of Hamlet's character. But, as has been said, altogether too much importance has been ascribed to it, and why? Because it begins so like a conundrum: 'To be or not to be!' That sounds very interesting! People are peculiar, and have their fancies. Many do not know even what these words specially mean, and think of the murder of the old Hamlet. When on the stage this soliloquy is reached, it is observable that the audience instantly set themselves to listen very attentively to see how it is delivered. It has become a tradition to consider this as the most important passage, and everybody knows the passage, that is, the beginning of it. The interest taken in it decreases greatly towards the end; there are no conundrums there. . . . . .

As to his feigned madness, prudent it certainly is not, for it draws upon him the attention of the whole court. But still more strange is it, and a shot beyond the mark, that he tells his three friends that he means to represent himself as crazed. What was the use of that? They might think him really crazy! What harm would that do him? Was it not enough that they had vowed to him not to blab about the Ghost? Why let them into his secret? But he always talks more than is necessary: the very opposite of Claudius. Besides, his madness would help to excuse him in case he should kill his uncle. At all events, he can under this mask give free play to his tongue, and that, and not the use of his hands, suits him above all things. Were he a whole man and no weakling, and if he would go wisely to work, why does he not at least keep his mouth shut? 'Meditation and the thoughts of love' are not only quick, but also still and silent. There is an inexhaustible consistency in this work of Shakespeare's.

[Page 18.] Immediately after the play and Polonius's murder, the King, learning from these events what was in Hamlet's mind, gives orders for Hamlet's execution. He does not wait two months and a half, as Hamlet does after the appearance of the Ghost,—not like a cat, that just for play lets the mouse run to and fro between her claws, to see it escape in the end,—but his first clutch is death.

[Page 20.] Immediately [after killing Polonius] Hamlet turns to his favorite business, a thing for which he always has time and means,—namely, making a speech! This time to his mother. He neglects his own special duty,—for so he regards it,—perpetrates a murder, and then sets himself to read his mother a lecture upon the sixth commandment. In so doing he falls, as always, to reviling his uncle, and when the Ghost again appears to him, he can do nothing else but come down on his marrowbones. And his cause, which would animate stones, can draw from him nothing, at the best, but 'tears.' He does not see, or is not able to see, that his fate reminds him by this apparition that it is the *very* time for action. As he knows that his departure is fixed for the next day, he has not a minute to lose. But, instead of acting, he preaches to his mother. He should have been, if not a play-actor, a preacher, as this scene bears witness, for his sermon has hands and feet, and could not be better.

[Page 21.] On his way to the haven yet one last warning is sent him by Fate. Fortinbras passes by on his march to gain honor by the conquest of a Polish village. That ought to have startled the dreamy prince from his slumber, but nothing has any effect upon him. As the second appearance of the Ghost is as unavailing as the first, so this powerful warning, which he recognizes as such perfectly well, is of no use; he still makes believe, still makes it plain in an ingenious soliloquy, which is distinguished by its perfect repose, that he is a special coward; recollects that for the sake of both his parents he must stride on to revenge; and then he goes,—not back to the court sword in hand, but,—on board ship for England, cheered on in his *thoughts*, to seek for blood. As if he had no arms to his body wherewith at last to make an assault! Always his head, and only the head of him, is active. It is a pitiable spectacle to see him so steadily plunging himself and others into destruction, but the picture is, alas! only too exactly taken from life. Hamlets there are by the legion on this earth,—rare in North America, but in Germany more numerous. And it is evident why so many people are unwilling to grant that Shakespeare meant to portray in Hamlet a *sickly talking hero*, and are for regarding the prince, with Ophelia for witness, as a model of manly virtue: they fight for their own skin! Hence they style Fortinbras the gloomy heathenish barbarian, Hamlet the accomplished Christian. If Master William could hear them, he would probably open his own work, and, pointing to it with his finger, ask, ' Have you eyes?'

[Page 26.] In concluding all that has been said of the chief person of the piece, it is necessary briefly to recapitulate. Hamlet philosophises well, knows how to speak, knows himself, can control himself (but does not always do it), has no self-confidence and no courage; from anything to be done shrinks back, especially if it is to be done in the light of day. He loves night and its privacy. He is without gratitude and love towards Ophelia, and shows this to coarseness. He is cruel and vindictive, as seen in his murder of Rosencrantz and Guildenstern. He is childishly silly at the grave of Ophelia, in that he does not tolerate Laertes's emphasis, which does not concern him, as he was there unseen. He is a weakling. When he says, ' Frailty, thy name is woman,' he might have used his own name here. He is the worthy son of his wordy father and weak mother. Ambitious he is not, or he would not have allowed the crown to slip from him to his uncle. Neither was he by nature desirous of glory, yet he was envious of the renown of others, as the King twice intimates (IV, vii).

[Page 27.] Two opinions of his character may be adduced from the piece as appearing to contradict all this,—the judgment of Ophelia and that of Fortinbras. Let us look into them. Ophelia strews rich praises over the loved one, and this is natural. All that she says may be granted, and Hamlet remain the same. For she does not speak of his defects; she leaves out *the heart*. She praises his eye, good! his tongue, ay, indeed! his arm, which is really skilful, only the driving force is wanting! When she calls him 'the flower of the state,' there is nothing to be said against that. If it is not youthful admiration merely that renders her praise extravagant, why, then perhaps Denmark had not at that time anything better to show. At least the piece shows none (Fortinbras is a Norwegian), and Hamlet might thus be the best, 'the flower of the state.' In a field of stinging nettles a solitary thistle is really a distinguished sight. Everything on earth is relative; and, moreover, in all countries and at all times *complete* men are a great rarity. Just look around. When the most are only *tolerable*, we must be content. Thus it is with the persons of the drama. Ophelia says nothing of his courage, and therefore she is entirely right, and Hamlet is, in spite of her praises, a weakling.

It stands otherwise with the judgment of Fortinbras. It rather pains me to refer to this, because I would almost rather submit to the objection that the Norwegian's opinion condemns as erroneous that which I have expressed above. But let it be so. I must here lift a veil, and I know not but that Shakespeare would be angry, were he here to perceive that in so doing I am giving my readers a sight of his cards. But it is a truth which ought to see the light, and as I have gone so far as to say what I have said, in order to animate and enliven the right feeling for Hamlet, I may as well go on. Whoever does not know what I am about to say will laugh at this long introduction to a brief word, the worth of which, moreover, may seem to be very small. For things of this sort have value, for the most part, in the eyes of the finder and not in those of the buyer. Be it so. Fortinbras concludes the whole with, 'Let four captains bear Hamlet, like a soldier, to the stage; for he was likely, had he been put on, to have proved most royally.' Here lies the pearl. (Whoever perceives it may skip what follows.) First, observe that Fortinbras pronounces no judgment; he only makes a supposition. But let it be that it is a judgment. He says, therefore: 'Bear the prince to the stage, in order to exhibit the corpse to the people, for were he alive and crowned, he would probably have proved most royally.' This is the Norwegian's plain opinion; he thinks nothing but good of the prince, and now that he is dead, is all the more disposed to think so. I look somewhat closer into the eyes of the youth; he turns aside and lifts his helmet, as if he were hot. I see he has a mask, and, as he thinks no one sees him, he lifts that also. Whom do I now see?—*Shakespeare!* He looks at me with a waggish smile, and suddenly mask and helmet are again in their places. But this look says infinitely much. Ought I put it into words? 'Let four captains bear Hamlet, like a soldier, to the stage, for he was likely, had he been put on, to have proved most royally.' Bear Hamlet, *like* a soldier (not *as* a soldier), to the *stage;* for had he been placed there, had Fate called him to the stage instead of the throne, he would have proved most royally. For that was he created. Such was the meaning of the smile of the poet behind the mask,—and when? At the *conclusion of the whole!* It is as a seal set thereon. But, enough; Fortinbras knows nothing of it, and we would fain seem to know nothing of it also. D'ye understand?

[Page 92.] In obedience to the repeated urging of his friend, Horatio speaks to the apparition. The apparition is offended. Why? Because they do not take him for a real ghost, but for a piece of mummery. The two Hamlets, father and son, have their peculiar humors. The son is offended because in his presence another, who does not, however, see him, talks big and vaunts himself, when he (Hamlet, Jr.) can, as he thinks, do that sort of thing so much better; and Hamlet, Sr., is offended because they won't believe he is a ghost when he is one. People, he thinks, ought to have penetration enough, in spite of their studying at Wittenberg, to see that he is a genuine ghost from the other world. It is a point of honor with him to pass for nothing else. Perhaps, also, his royal blood is up at the idea of being taken for a common man under a mask. And so when he is thus addressed, he is not going to answer. When, however, Horatio calls him 'Ghost,' and speaks of the fate of *his* country, then he observes that he is held to be a 'king' and 'a ghost,' and he raises his head and is about to speak. What a pity it is that just at that moment the cock crows, and he has no time! He should have come to the point sooner. Like father, like son; always too late! On this occasion it is wounded vanity that causes the loss of time. Shakespeare has here portrayed character with a minuteness that is hardly to be described.

[Page 98.] Hamlet's first soliloquy, in I, ii, ends with, 'But break, my heart; for I must hold my tongue,'—thus concluding, as with a prophecy which exactly fulfils itself, the sad utterances of his pain. Indeed, at his death we hear these self-same words, which refer back to this early scene and to his first appearance. After Hamlet has *talked* much too much the whole drama through, he concludes, as after this monologue, 'The rest is *silence;*' whereupon Horatio says, 'There *breaks* a noble *heart!*' Thus at the close sounds literally on the ear the echo from the beginning. As in a good opera the last chord is the same as the first.

[Page 104.] Hamlet comes with Horatio to await the Ghost. He is not in a good humor. He complains of the eager air and the nipping cold. It is, however, right comfortable and warm and stirring where the King is, who honors Hamlet's complaisance with a feast, the mention whereof by Hamlet sharpens our sense of the still, weird darkness that surrounds Hamlet himself. The uncle is enjoying full draughts of the pleasures of this world; the nephew is anxiously waiting for intelligence from the torments of the next.

[Page 107.] '*I find thee apt.*' The iron was warm, but the old Hamlet was a poor smith. Just think only of his long, useless introduction, his call to his son, four times repeated, to hearken to him. He keeps so long mixing with the glowing metal the ill-flavored fluid of wailing and emotion, that it runs cold and gray. He tells of his torments, and if any one is disposed to doubt whether or not he be a genuine ghost, the doubt will be set at rest by the botanical observation from the nether world. Only an eye-witness can speak of the vegetation of the Lethean wharf.

[Page 108.] Hamlet's railing expressions, after the Ghost has vanished, signify nothing. They are a fire of straw, soon burnt out. For how otherwise could he be so childish as to write down in his pocket-book what he is resolved not to forget, —namely, that his uncle, in spite of his smile, is a villain? He has only just said that he will write down the command of the Ghost in the book of his brain, and wipe out and forget everything else. Why then set down a general philosophical remark in his pocket-book? If, after such startling communications, one has composure enough to make general remarks and write them down in his pocket-book, just as an insect-collector catches and keeps a beetle that happens to come droning by, the aforesaid communications cannot have made much of an impression. This peculiarity of Hamlet's to bring out, under such circumstances, what he has learned at college, he possesses in common with Horatio,—they both got it at Wittenberg,—who has also learned, as we have remarked, that ghosts dread the crowing of the cock. These Wittenberg students are a cold-blooded, phlegmatic folk, eager for learning. When the house is burning over their heads, they consult the thermometer to ascertain the degree of heat, or make observations on the consuming effect of the fire.

[Page 140.] There is here, moreover, a new little bit of art. Polonius acts the spy upon his son with the help of his servant; the King and Queen are spies upon Hamlet with the help of Rosencrantz and Guildenstern; the King and Polonius are eavesdroppers to the prince with the help of Ophelia; then Hamlet and his mother are spied upon in like manner; Hamlet is a spy upon the King with the help of Horatio. It is the design of the poet. The people at the Danish court all resemble one another. The Hamletian art is visible everywhere. It is a genuine race of molelike pioneers.

[Page 158.] Hamlet, who has thus far always hesitated, now draws his sword for the first time against the fratricide: 'Now or never!' might his good angel have said to him; and his father's ghost appears once more just after; why not five minutes sooner, behind the praying Claudius? But that would have been just at the right time, and the Hamlets are always *too late!* Shakespeare is fine in the web he weaves: it is delightful to follow him.

[Page 162.] The King stands up, and has not really prayed; he still clings to the world and its joys. Hamlet's scruples, therefore, were ill timed.

DR FRIEDR. THEOD. VISCHER (1861)

(*Kritische Gänge*, Stuttgart, 1861. Zweites Heft, p. xvi.)—Hamlet's fault lies in that twilight, into which every true tragic poet throws the fault of his hero. Though we are angry at Hamlet, yet we must pity him, and we know not which we must feel the more; we must gaze into that dark abyss where responsible freedom and the insuperable natural barriers of character are secretly confounded.

[Page xx.] I agree with Kreyssig and Gans in ascribing Hamlet's procrastination to an excess in him of a reflective, meditative habit of mind: it is only necessary that this point should be set forth more fully than has yet been done. By the way, Kreyssig's analysis confirms me in the conviction, that I have done well to take the part of the much-abused hero, and to show how Fate, while it condemns him, justifies him also; for how wretchedly is the poor, hesitating youth represented,—as sophisticated all over, a courtier without conscience, a frivolous prince, a bloated, intellectual aristocrat! No, this is not Hamlet! In every stage of his distracted condition the true Hamlet is always great, genuine, noble, one of those chastened and chosen ones of the Lord, above whom we are to learn not to exalt ourselves, and who are too good and too unfortunate for the world to appreciate.

[Page 73.] Hamlet lives in a world surpassingly bad; court-vermin, false show, eye-service, lip-service, surround him on every side, and he sees the refinement of a hollow culture allied to rude barbarous customs. . . . . He was right in despising such a world, and because it was *his* world, we can understand and pardon him when he extends too widely his impression of loathing, and embraces the whole world in his field of vision.

[Page 89.] Shakespeare has ventured to make, as the central figure of a drama, a hero who is for ever hesitating and delaying. The success of this bold attempt is commonly ascribed to the fact that the more the hero hangs back, the more does his environment press him on, until at last, while it crushes him, it drives him, nevertheless, to the goal. This is certainly the one great crisis whereby a tragedy with such a hero becomes possible. It is, as it were, a huge screw, ever turning closer and closer in, and compelling the passive hero at last to such reaction that both the screw and its victim, all are crushed and shivered into atoms together. It is a horrible machine, in which the cog-wheels, running in opposite directions, catch in one another, and steadily and straightly work out the course of fate. But this is not all; in this view a hero, always shrinking back, would still be undramatic. Shakespeare has taken still another way to make a drama out of such unusual materials. He has given to his hero all the fire and force consistent with his keeping to his dilatory gait. Look more closely at the man, and you discern a nature passionate, violent, relieving itself in fierce ebullitions, stern, occasionally, even in its frenzy, malicious. Hamlet is a volcano, only, as we may indeed see, his violence is inward, not outward; outwardly he emits merely many-colored, tantalizing lights, sparkles of wit, even sharp lightning-flashes, and from time to time the deadly lava-stream bursts forth with fatal effect, while the inner rumble and roar is always heard, telling us that the pent-up force can find no outbreak.

[Page 98.] I see a tender violet, a sincere, modest German maiden, a thoroughly Northern woman's nature, poor in words, shut up in herself, unable to bring the deep rich heart to the lips; she is kindred to Cordelia and Desdemona, and in these three I behold the veiled beauty of the soul. The life ineloquent enhances their

grace, their hidden wealth; the concealed treasure is brought to light only by suffering, for they know not and speak not of it,—one must read between the lines. Still
waters are deep is true of Ophelia, and: no fire, no coal, so hotly glows, as the secret
love of which nobody knows. Thoroughly German, old German, is she in her
household relations. Her obedience as a daughter is implicit; only to her brother,
who warns her, does she reply with that dry coolness which belongs to true natures,
and which is also apparent, in the first scenes, in Cordelia and Desdemona. We
know not what it costs her when she promises obedience to her father's stricter and
weightier authority. 'I will obey, sir;' further she says nothing. What is passing
within her a good actress must tell us by a tone that reveals to us that under this
obedience her heart is breaking, when she says, 'With almost all the holy vows of
Heaven.' In this patriarchal submission to her father, in this touching defenceless-
ness, this inability of resistance, which characterizes natures that are boundlessly
good and created only for love, she allows herself without demur to be used, when
she is sent in Hamlet's way, that they may talk together, while her father and the
King privily listen; Hamlet, under the mask of madness, treats her rudely; the
pure nobleness of her true, unstained tenderness speaks in the sorrowful words with
which the return of his gifts is accompanied; unsuspicious, she believes in his feigned
madness; and then her pain breaks out into a lament that points to an abyss from
which comes no speech. The deepest tone of the heart, of which a voice is capable,
is demanded in this soliloquy; there are few tragic passages sadder or more moving
than, 'And I, of ladies most deject and wretched, That suck'd the honey of his
music vows.' If it ever can be said of a poetical creation that it has a fragrancy in
it, it is this picture of the crazed Ophelia, and the inmost secret of this bewitching
fragrancy is innocence. Nothing deforms her; not the lack of sense in her sense,
not the rude naïveté of those snatches of song: a soft mist, a twilight is drawn
around her, veiling the rough reality of insanity, and in this sweet veil, this dissolving
melancholy, the story of her death is also told.

[Page 109.] Thinking alone never leads to action; there is no bridge from it to
the fulfilment of the thought. Thinking goes on in an endless line. When all is
thought out in regard to the deed to be done, all that remains is to seize the right
moment. There comes a moment which appears to be the fit one. But who will
say that a succeeding moment may not be a fitter? The idea of fitness is relative;
thought seeks an *absolutely* fit moment, and there is none, it never comes. To him
whose inmost nature is given to thinking, the *Now* is formidable. In a decisive,
bold deed, what we specially admire is, that the man who ventures it has seized the
Now, taken his stand upon the knife-like edge of the Instant. The transition from
thinking to acting is irrational; it is a leap, a jerk, a breaking off of an endless
chain. How does this leap become possible? Through another force than thought,
but a force that must be connected with thought,—a force that is *blind* face to face
with thought, and which works unconsciously. This force *no longer asks*, whether
the moment may not be so favorable that a more favorable one may not be thought
of. Enough, it is favorable; seize it then by the forelock, and up and away! Have
I deceived myself? does the act miscarry? I cannot have any regrets, for I say to
myself, that under the circumstances, so far as human discernment reaches, I was
bound to regard that moment as the right one. It is only this venturous force that
gives resolution, expansion, so that the door at last flies open, and what is within
breaks forth as action, and becomes real. . . . .

The absence of this force Hamlet calls dullness, beastly oblivion, and in a preceding soliloquy he says, 'I am pigeon-livered, and lack gall.' It is not true that he lacks gall, but the gall does not flow out at the right moment upon the point where it lifts the arm to strike, for that too much thinking of his is in the way, his rage is not discharged with a duly measured thought into the act. After all that is necessary has been thought out, his thinking is not, as it were, quenched in that other force which is to actualize the thought.

[Page 111.] That other force, into which thought should be lifted, we call instinct; we call it passion, or the native force of the mind: it is ultimately nature in the mind. Passion, specially considered, Hamlet does not lack, but it is force in the core of his being that is wanting. It accompanies thought in the organism of our nature in endless forms; an act arises only when the two meet at the right moment, and thought is lost in an impulse of native force. . . . .

Only just when the supreme interest, the one great object of his life, is concerned, does Hamlet's nature waste away, caught in the net of thought, confined within the charmed circle of reflection; a proof, indeed, that the incongruity of thought and instinct in him,—the fact that they never hit together—lies deeply seated in his inmost organization.

[Page 131.] We have now found the positive reason why he resolves to wear the inappropriate mask of madness, and thus is completed what we have said above. As a means to his end it is wrong, but, in fact, it is not a means, but an object of his own. It is Hamlet's taste to play the part of a fool; it is a pleasure to him in itself. First of all, because he delights in the theatre, in acting. He goes among play-actors, he understands their art; he has doubtless often had the pleasure of acting himself. This is so perfectly human in him that nothing more need be said of it. But the main thing is, that under this mask he can draw out the vermin of the court, give free play to his wit,—that is his glory, and it is a still greater glory that he can thus lash out freely, and parody the consciousness of his own madness. The earlier English critics, with a narrowness in dialectic questions peculiar to the nation, seriously entertained the query, whether Hamlet really were crazy. He is just as insane as all men of genius are, who do not find that everything is so perfectly clear to them as it is to ordinary heads; just as insane as all deep natures are, in whom particular faculties are developed in such strength that the harmony of their being is disturbed, and Hamlet knows that, and yet cannot make it otherwise; that is, as he himself says, enough to drive one mad; but he is not, therefore, mad in the medical sense of the word; he knows infinitely more about himself than many a critic who seeks to analyze him to his very heart and reins. In this sense, then, it may be said of him, that he plays the fool because he is one.

[Page 136.] Justice to Hamlet demands that it should be clearly seen how easy it is to say that the right is the higher union of the thinking and active powers, and how hard it is to accomplish this union. One must take care what he is about in demanding the higher unities. A man without depth may easily seize the right moment, and act right off; when the depth reaches a certain degree, then the good fortune of this lightmindedness ceases. Men with brains have in their weakness a strength which should well save them from ridicule; we pity them, but in their misfortunes there is a tragic greatness, which mingles reverence with our pity. In Hamlet there has justly been found the type of the German character; the Frenchman, the modern Englishman, laugh at us for our irresoluteness. The former is more lightminded, more versatile in his organization, and the latter narrower and harder; and both, while they ridicule us, have a dim suspicion that there is something in us for which they have no plummet. Moreover, nations are not individuals. The Hamlet, who is a people, will survive the ridicule, and there will come, perhaps, a time when we may say, ' He laughs the longest who laughs last.' Briefly, a genuine Hamlet-irresolution has exposed us to the laughter and contempt of the nations; but when the Laertes, France, makes a lunge at us with the poisoned dagger, then will the Hamlet, Germany, survive both the thrust and the counter-thrust.*

[Page 155.] The question has been asked, whether modern poetry can have a tragedy of Fate after the false form of it, the imitation of the Antique, has been entirely overcome. Here, without doubt, is such a tragedy, and a genuine one; that is, such a tragedy of the kind as is, at the same time, a true tragedy of character also. All is *motived* from within, from the actors and especially from the hero. All teaches us that circumstances are stronger than man, the whole infinitely greater than the individual, and yet that the whole of the circumstances is developed only from individual men. Therefore it is, on account of the depth of this involution of man and fate, that Shakespeare's most wonderful creation is his *Hamlet*.

PROF. DR A. GERTH (1861)

(*Der Hamlet von Shakespeare*. Leipzig, 1861, p. 60.)—When Hamlet calls Polonius a ' fishmonger,' he refers to the English proverb, ' Fishes and guests smell when they are three days old,' and means thereby to say that, since Polonius has found out that a prince, without expectations and yet dangerous, is in love with his daughter, he will probably barter her away as quickly as possible, with no more honorable motives than a genuine fishmonger disposing of his wares.

[Page 74.] People now begin to talk. They suspect, they put things together, they whisper, they tell of hints of fearful things; the old king was a Hercules, hale and hearty,—such a man does not die from merely sleeping in the garden (for nobody believes the story of his being bitten by a serpent),—*and, since he thus lives in all hearts, the excited people now see him ; his ghost walks !* But the people, that is, the watch, the friends of Hamlet, tell him of it. Thus the prince receives the idea of the Ghost at secondhand, but the nearer he was to it, in the fever-heat of his own suspicions, the more powerfully does it seize hold of him and possess him. Thus it comes to him from without, and yet it is within, in his own mind. To others it has appeared and vanished in silence eight times; to him alone it speaks. Why? because, while the others are moved only by *grief* and *love*, he has thoughts of *vengeance*.

[Page 77.] The poet thus gives us the voice of the Ghost, by no means as a voice speaking with *divine authority*, but rather presents the whole apparition, as an illusion of the mind of his hero, rendered vivid to him by reports from without.

[Page 99.] This word 'slings' ['the slings and arrows of outrageous fortune'] signifies the strong *cables* or *chains* which are bound round the *buoys*, commonly *barrels*, that float upon the surface of the water, holding fast the anchors to which they are attached. They serve, first, when a ship has let slip her anchor, to mark the place where she may find it again, and, secondly, to mark shoals or reefs. Imagine such a buoy afloat, tossing on the water, and you will perceive how well the poet indicates Hamlet's constrained situation in the midst of his stormy passions. The picture

---

* When the date of the above is noted, it has a ring of prophecy. ED.

is continued in the line following: 'To arm oneself against a *sea* of troubles.' The *arrows* are consequently the missiles which, like the vultures of Prometheus, all the more painfully lacerate the hero fast bound with *slings*.

[Page 106.] Hamlet's coarse sarcasms, addressed to Ophelia in the presence of the King and Queen, are nothing more than an intentional parody of the 'wicked wit' with which Claudius inflamed the amorous Queen.

DR L. SCHIPPER (1862)

(*Shakespeare's Hamlet*. Münster, 1862, p. 58.)—The morally reflective character of Hamlet, looking at things on all sides, the character which the poet has kept always before us and portrayed with the greatest care in every word and deed, would be departed from at the very point of accomplishing the one great task of 'setting right a world out of joint,' had Hamlet thought only of assassinating Claudius, and not of a purely moral expiation of the crime. Had Shakespeare re-garded the murder of the murderer as the sole business of Hamlet, had he wished to show in what a hesitating, irresolute, tortuous manner Hamlet proceeded to ac-complish it,—had such been the poet's purpose, why is it that, throughout the whole tragedy, only *one* single opportunity appears, and that only for one moment, favor-able for the commission of the deed,—an opportunity which, moreover, for *good reasons*, and not for lack of resolution, Hamlet lets pass unused? Several oppor-tunities might easily have been introduced, of which Hamlet might have been rep-resented as refusing, without sufficient reasons, to avail himself, and which would have shown him to be an incorrigible and vacillating procrastinator. This simple fact, that Shakespeare has not introduced a single opportunity of the kind, may well satisfy us that it is not the design of the piece to show that Hamlet's delay proceeded from want of resolution. [On the contrary, incidents are introduced, showing with what promptness and energy Hamlet could act. TRANS.] A satisfactory solution of this point is found in the supposition that the poet intended, as the task imposed upon Hamlet, something *more* than a *simple* assassination. The punishment which Claudius in full measure merited, and which poetic justice demanded, was that for his wickedness and hypocrisy he should, so to speak, be publicly put in the pillory, and that, finally, for seduction he must be deprived of the love of her whom he had seduced, and for murder and usurpation must lose both crown and life, all that he had sought to secure.

[Page 67.] Thus while in the course of the action of the piece, there is no evi-dence of indecision or hesitation on the part of Hamlet, neither does the final accomplishment of his aim furnish any proof of the kind. The task is 'to set the world right,' *i. e.* to punish the hypocritical seducer and murderer; and the whole course of the piece shows incontestably that this task is fully executed, and that it is not left unfulfilled through any moral imbecility.

[Page 69.] Consequently, neither during the course of the action, nor in the com-pletion of his task, with its attendant results, do we come upon any circum-stance which justifies casting the slightest reproach upon Hamlet, on the score of indecision in the punishment of the criminal. It may, indeed, be affirmed, if one insists upon it, that the drama shows delay and hesitation; but it is Claudius, most obviously, who manifests this weakness. From the very beginning Claudius be-lieves, and naturally too, that Hamlet alone is the sole obstacle in his way, and that Hamlet alone is dangerous. Although his attempts to find out what Hamlet means often fail, and although he has already stained his hands with blood, yet he hesitates for a long time to make any attempts upon Hamlet's life. This is the punishment of wickedness, that it is blind and insensible to the nearest and most decisive opportunities, as experience often shows.

[Page 79.] Thus, in accordance with real life, our tragedy shows *how the hypocritical seducer, and secret murderer, and plunderer of a crown, in consequence of circumstances, comes to be suspected, and how he is completely unmasked and destroyed by the retributive justice which never rests, and this mainly by the means which iniquity plans and uses for its own security.*

PROF. DR J. L. F. FLATHE (1863)

(*Shakespeare in seiner Wirklichkeit.* Leipzig, 1863, vol. i, p. 28.)—Hamlet is no sensualist. Of a decidedly opposite character does he appear to be.

[Page 31.] As we find no weak or cowardly Hamlet, neither is there here before us a Hamlet so morbidly conscientious that he torments himself with moral considerations, and is unable to free himself from them.

[Page 37.] The relation between Hamlet and Polonius is emphatically the most important point in the tragedy. . . . . Claudio [*sic*] and his crime with its consequences, and the vengeance which Hamlet seems resolved to inflict, stand in the background in comparison with Polonius. This readily appears from the fact, that long passages of the piece occur in which there is not a single mention of Claudio's affair. Especially is this the case in Act II. There, Hamlet has forgotten the matter, and it would scarcely have recurred to him had not an event in his outward world recalled it.

[Page 42.] When once we begin to regard mankind and human life as an empty nothing, a mere vapor without any connection with a higher world, it will not be long before we come to look upon all thinking and doing in like manner, as without use or purpose, whatever direction they take, whether to heaven or to hell. Lies will run in the same line with truth, guilt rank with innocence, the one having no more worth than the other, both being bound together by a common worthlessness. And this is Hamlet's case, and must needs be so. And therefore it is that he declares that nothing is good or evil in itself,—that it is only our thinking that makes it so.

[Page 47.] The family of Polonius have not thrown themselves on the side which in the Danish court seeks only pleasure. They are ambitious of splendor and greatness. What they aim at stands perfectly clear before them. It is royal power and majesty which they strive for. First of all, the love of Hamlet for Ofelia [*sic*] is to be used for this purpose. For the wise, moreover, everything that life and circumstances afford exists only to be taken advantage of. The family of Polonius [*the Polonii ?* TRANS.] see Hamlet's sorrow over his father's early and sudden death. It does not trouble them in the least, and they even hasten to prepare another sorrow for him, which they have found out, as they imagine, to be necessary in order to establish the daughter of the house in the king's palace. Their hearts are cased in ice ; they care not for human sorrows ; their sole object is to succeed in their machinations.

But the old Polonius and his Ofelia have to pay dearly. Their sins break upon their own heads, and, through the very madness which they thought to have turned to their advantage, they must go down into the darkness of the grave, where they receive a stern answer to their question as to their dreams of earthly greatness.

[Page 68.] The whole course of the tragedy shows as clearly as light that Polonius could sooner doubt the existence of the world than Hamlet's love for Ofelia. This conviction, upon which hang all his royal hopes, is fixed firm as a rock in his heart. Even when proof to the contrary storms upon him, he still clings convulsively to this faith until he himself draws into his breast the fatal sword.

[Page 70.] The Polonius people speculate in Hamlet's suffering. From the pain of a human being they would fain extract the splendor of their house. . . . . The one purpose is to wring out of life, success. With useless sensibilities they have nothing to do. Even Ofelia cares not for the grief of the youth whom she calls her lover. On the contrary, she soon catches the aim and purpose of her father's talk, and feels hat, in truth, it involves no great danger. On this account she does not complain over the destruction of her royal hopes, but, dry and hard, she promises her father her obedience. . . . . The men of the family, so far as decency permits, make their half-satanic calculations *vivâ voce.* Ofelia observes silence, and in silence carries them out.

[Page 86.] As Raynaldo [*sic*] retires, Ofelia appears, terrified, as she herself says. In no other part of the piece is it so plain as here that Ofelia is a traitress to the sanctity of true love. She does not love Hamlet; she only speculates in him, aims through him at the throne. Had she loved him ever so lightly, she could not stand there, frosty, cold, beholding his pain and even his madness. When in England Ofelia has been regarded as a maiden as tender and sweet as if she had been made up of rose-perfume and lily-dust, it is simply ridiculous. Ofelia is a frail creature with a tragic fate.

[Page 151.] The reason is obvious enough why Ofelia became insane. The death of her father by the hand of Hamlet put the finishing stroke to her ambitious hopes.

[Page 173.] Before the Queen dies, Laertes had thrust the poisoned sword-point into Hamlet's breast. But the evil deed made his hand tremble, and he had to let his sword drop. Hamlet let his sword fall, also, as he received his deathblow. . . . . Hastily seizing at the fallen swords, Hamlet caught hold not of his own, but of the poisoned one, and Laertes received from Hamlet's hand the deadly blow in his booby (*bübische*) breast.

HERMANN FREIHERR VON FRIESEN (1864)

(*Briefe über Shakespeare's Hamlet.* Leipzig, 1864.)—[In this admirable volûme, of over three hundred pages, will be found a thorough discussion of various topics of interest pertaining to *Hamlet*, the sources of the plot, the state and corruptions of the text, the theatrical representations in England and Germany, German criticism, an analysis of the characters, &c. &c. I know nowhere any single volume, not an edition of the play itself, that contains more valuable matter relating to this tragedy. To a German student it must be simply invaluable. I have already mentioned (p. 288) that v. FRIESEN adopts TIECK's and ZIEGLER's theory, that the soliloquy, 'To be or not to be,' refers not to suicide, but to the hazard of an attempt on the life of the King; and on this interpretation v. FRIESEN lays great stress: 'Because,' as he says on p. 236, 'if we suppose Hamlet to be here asking himself in all earnestness, whether or not he is brave enough to meet his death in a perilous undertaking, we shall have a very different idea of his character than we should have if we believe him to be merely discussing the idea of suicide, in order to escape by a blow his all-tormenting doubts.' ED.]

[Page 264.] But while we contemplate Hamlet in the church-yard, and hear him exchanging keen queries with the gravediggers, and making ironical remarks upon the skull of the court-jester, Yorick, and at last pondering over the change of all human greatness into dust,—where is the philosophic insight which so many admire? where the flight of those thoughts which would soar into the infinite? where the great heart that bleeds for rage at the shame of his mother and the crime of the King? After all that has been said of this scene, I have never contemplated it otherwise than with a feeling of the deepest sadness over the ruin in Hamlet's soul of all that is great, and noble, and elevated, and this feeling becomes only the more intense as I recognize in the captious criticisms of the clown the idle aberrations of the human understanding; it is to me as if Shakespeare meant to say, ' Take from what Hamlet says the varnish with which education, and rank, and skill in speech have overlaid it, and you will find that it has no higher worth than the talk of the clowns, to which you have scarcely listened.' It is, in a word, the beginning of the catastrophe approaching us here with overwhelming power. I do not mean that there is a peculiarity in this great tragedy in this respect, as if I saw in it an exception to the method which Shakespeare usually follows in his tragedies. In all his great tragic works you may observe this same preparation for the final blow. It would lead me too far should I undertake to show you in *Lear, Coriolanus, Anthony & Cleopatra*, or in *Macbeth* and *Julius Cæsar*, the very moment when this feeling is awakened in us of ruined greatness, with the mysterious power of utter hopelessness. Only here in *Hamlet* this transition is veiled in such a wondrous form that we are liable to overlook its significance.

[Page 284.] Old servants, like Polonius, are always in possession of the secrets of the family. Even though they are not the most intimate friends of the prince and his household, it is nevertheless impossible that things, which do not reach the ear of the world, should be concealed from them. Claudius and the Queen, as the Ghost intimates, have long lived in criminal intercourse. This could have been no impenetrable secret to Polonius, and Claudius was unquestionably too cunning to flatter himself that it was unknown to Polonius. Has Polonius, perhaps, at earlier periods, in order to find out some secret, made use of the very means which he recommends to the King, or has he before now crept behind the very tapestry where he finally meets his death?

[Page 285.] We must not forget that Polonius is convinced of the insanity of Hamlet, and hence he takes no offence at the insulting speeches of the latter, as he would have done under other circumstances. . . . . Such a man as Polonius could hardly have stood very high with the old king. It is at least quite credible that Hamlet would have put some restraint upon himself had he known, as he must have known had it been the case, that Polonius was esteemed and honored by his father.

[Page 323.] The essential indication of what is tragic in Hamlet's nature, I find in the fact that Hamlet, under the stress of his destiny, assumes the rôle of a madman. I reject the idea that real insanity is to be supposed. By supposing Hamlet really insane, we most directly contradict what Shakespeare's genius conceived and represented; in other words, the essential demands of tragedy. Two instances, outside of this piece, are before us, in which Shakespeare represents real derangement of the mind,—King Lear and Lady Macbeth. But in these two, insanity is the consequence of a tragical event which has passed before our eyes, and which took from the persons their native freedom and led to that catastrophe. And Ophelia? With her, as with them, madness ensues at the end of her career, and is a means to the catastrophe that overtakes her; in other words, madness comes when her freedom is overthrown in conflict with passion. But in *Hamlet* the career is yet to be begun, and accordingly it is inconceivable that Shakespeare has put the hero of the drama in a condition which destroys that freedom of action, and with it all soundness of mind. Indeed, the essentially tragic character of the whole would then be destroyed. . . . . The longer and the more attentively we consider this repulsive idea of assuming the rôle of a madman, the more difficult and embarrassing is the question that presses upon us: how was it possible that a finely-cultured man, the same man whose incomparable advantages we have just been considering, an honored prince, the offspring of an heroic king, a member of the regal court, could take upon himself the shame of a disordered brain? Here there certainly lies before us a riddle, which we strive in vain fully to solve, the secret of a soul into whose abyss only the greatest of poets was able to look. But what the soul of Hamlet must have suffered, what agonies it must have undergone, before it came to this fatal conclusion, at least no understanding, however keen, will be able to fathom. Every attempt, I conceive, to find an explanation in any parallel drawn from ordinary life, or by any analysis of the several faculties, be it ever so ingenious, must appear useless. We have before us an individuality, standing high above common life, and yet connected with our human nature by innumerable and most tender ties. And what forever fascinates the heart anew is, that, as we glance into this depth, all the great and elevated qualities of Hamlet, so far from being lost to sight, erased by madness, or maimed and mutilated by a morbid excitement, fashion themselves into a picture in which passion holds the reins, and our sympathy, stirred to the deepest, hears forever sounding the tones of a noble soul, notwithstanding they are jangled, out of tune, and harsh.

[Page 327.] The certainty that Hamlet is not what it is his purpose to appear; the positive certainty that he is not mad, and that he obeys his highly-endowed nature in defiance of a power which seems the more formidable because, although working similarly to madness, it does not destroy the means by which it could be mastered:—this is the ground upon which the profoundest tragical effect rests. There is carried on here before our eyes a combat, in which all that is most noble and most elevated in this finite human existence of ours is ranged in opposition to the decrees of an infinite power; and the combatant unceasingly hastens to his defeat, because, erring in the means chosen, by every step which ought to lead to victory his downfall is only the more accelerated. What word can be spoken in such a case but in sympathy and fear?

[Page 331.] Let us now, in conclusion, once more consider that, however our weak words may attempt to elucidate the great mystery of these world-wide complications (*Weltgeschichten*), we must nevertheless bow down before its depth and unfathomableness. What is here felt and wrought out and contemplated,—the unconscious germ of it all dwells in the still breast of universal humanity, and therefore this tragedy strikes with equal power the coarse strings of the least sensitive, as well as the finer and more tender sympathies of the more susceptible. It carries both alike too far away into the realm of the most mysterious of our feelings to leave them the power of ever expressing them. The mysterious power of a great crime, which stalks through the world like a fearful apparition, and in the vengeance which visits it involves whole generations,—*that* has been felt by many who have given themselves to the study of life and the world; but that a single human mind should be able, with the power of a prophetic enchanter, to produce this feeling in us by a dramatic creation,—this is the great mystery, which is here before our eyes, and which takes captive our senses in wonder, reverence, and admiration.

PROF. C. HEBLER (1864)

(*Aufsätze über Shakespeare.* Bern, 1864, p. 83.)—There would not be such a difference of opinion about this tragedy, and especially about the hero of it, were it only borne in mind that it is a tragedy written simply for the stage. But how has the poor prince been taken to task the last ten years! He could not help it that things went all askew in Germany in 1848. 'Hamlet is Germany' in a most indubitable sense, in that the German attempts at elucidating *Hamlet* are the contemporaneous history of the German mind in miniature. It has long ago been evident that it is an error to run into æsthetics when the matters in hand are State affairs; and for a long time we have been talking politics, when the thing we have sought to understand was a work for the playhouse. But this fault must be avoided, and we must render to the State the things that are the State's, and to Hamlet the things that are Hamlet's. Only thus can Hamlet come to be understood, for where politics are mixed up with æsthetics, there will always be the danger that æsthetics will be mixed up with politics,—the very thing that is objected to in Hamlet so strongly. That our hero should have his share in this mingle, we have recently had set off against the political Hamlet a religious and Protestant Hamlet, and, for example, the words: 'The time is out of joint;—O cursed spite, That ever I was born to set it right!'—are explained to have this significance, namely, 'It never should have become necessary for a party to break off from the Romish Church.' Hamlet represents the principle of Protestantism. The shame were for the Church, the sorrow for him.* No; the sorrow is for the purchaser of a ticket. The opposite of this interpretation is afforded us by that romanticist, who, on the other hand, finds in the words, 'You cannot speak of reason to the Dane' [I, ii], a blow at Protestantism, and a proof that Shakespeare was a Catholic. In opposition to these judgments, that Hamlet is Germany, or Hamlet is Protestantism, there is a third, which, little as it enlightens us, appears to me to possess an undeniable advantage: Hamlet is Hamlet.

[Page 125.] When Hamlet accuses himself of timidity, or even of cowardice, he does not deserve the least credence, in view of such facts as the killing of Polonius, or the boarding of the pirate, but he merely exposes himself to the suspicion that he occasionally inclines to the opposite extreme. But, forsooth, why does energy desert him at the very moment when it can be best displayed? Or not to put it too strongly, why does it reveal itself so late? No more favorable moment could be hoped for than that immediately after the court-play; Claudius had as good as confessed his crime by the involuntary and improvised rôle that he had there enacted. . . . . Why did not Hamlet force him to repeat in words the confession that he had just made by his actions? When Claudius calls for lights, why did not Hamlet volunteer to light him home? Hamlet is not to be reproached with thinking too

---

*This allusion can be appreciated only by reference to the German translation of these lines: 'Die Zeit ist aus den Fugen: *Schmach* und *Gram*, Dass ich zur Welt, sie einzurichten, kam.' ED.

nuch here, but rather with letting his 'reason fust in him unused.' Even more favorable for this view is the second opportunity, when Hamlet comes upon the criminal all ready for the death-blow, but withholds his hand at the thought that death to a man at prayer is hire and salary, not punishment. What does it concern the judge, forsooth, how a criminal stands with heaven? Furthermore, why does not he who reflects so much also reflect that there is a difference between salvation and praying, and between praying and kneeling? Meanwhile, we have presented to us what is undoubtedly a positive, but at the same time a perverted, habit of reflection, which might even be styled transcendental, since it transcends the sphere of every reasonable, practical consideration. That Hamlet should here deliberate is not to be censured,—for, after all, the opportunity is favorable chiefly in a physical sense; neither are we to blame the result of his reflecting, which holds back his sword, but rather must we blame the grounds of his inaction, which cut off all hope that he will act in the future any more practically than he acts here and now, because he does not put the question to himself thus : 'Shall I with any probability find another opportunity more favorable than this ?' The chance was offered awhile ago before a large assembly, when the King was driven to an unequivocal confession,— it is offered here again, in solitary, silent prayer. Both situations embrace, and to a certain extent represent, all possible favorable chances; Hamlet was prepared for neither. At one time 'cowardice and bestial oblivion,' the next time 'a thinking too precisely on the event ;' both times 'a thinking' that led to nothing, but wherein the former is to be fairly inferred from the latter, and demands none the less a reference to the passionate element in the hero.

[Page 132.] No one who does not know Hamlet's strength has a right to talk about his weaknesses. Let it be that, judged by an ordinary standard, he is nothing, yet this nothing is 'more than something.' His critics forget that a very extraordinary task is imposed upon him, that he is in an extremely peculiar situation, and therefore he is not to be unceremoniously classed with people who have never seen a ghost, nor had a royal father to avenge. He stands, indeed, surrounded by the Danish court, almost as a human being in a circle of beasts (one or two persons excepted); it is not accidental that he repeatedly commends the peculiarly human gift, the most human thing in man, distinguishing him sharply from the brute—namely, the capacity for a disinterested devotion to an object, without which there is not merely no scientific and no artistic work, but no sound practical activity possible; this capacity it is which Hamlet possesses in an exceptional degree. In the midst of the masculine villainy of the King, the senile cunning of Polonius, the base eye-service of the court-rabble, and the boyish blustering of Laertes, there is Fortinbras alone, following only the call of honor, who could have served Hamlet in any practical sense as a model; and Fortinbras, at the close, bids him be buried like a soldier, and bears a testimony to our hero which richly indemnifies him for all our modern rough treatment.

[Page 137.] From the way Hamlet receives the commands of the Ghost, and is affected by the apparition, we should suppose that his uncle will never again see the sun. But the hero first contents himself with tying a knot in his handkerchief, *i. e.* makes a memorandum in his pocket-book of what has happened; for what one has down in black and white, one is comfortably sure of carrying home with him,—this he learned in his Wittenberg. Truly he could not worse travestie the 'Remember me' of the Ghost, or more quickly encoffin his purpose. The only fault was that he did not ask the Ghost for his address, or hand him a little leaf from his note-book. One may try to find an answer to the question, whether the poet has not here suffered his hero to speak out his (the poet's) opinion of him too decisively and too early, as it has been objected to Shakespeare, with or without reason, that he does with his villains. He lets the prince perpetrate such sillinesses, but elsewhere only among and towards others. The actual writing in his note-book had not, to the taste of those days, the singularity which it has for us. Elsewhere Shakespeare makes use of an outward action, when a poet now-a-days would content himself with words. Thus, Richard II upon his dethronement asks for a looking-glass, to see what a countenance he has when deprived of majesty; Bolingbroke directs one to be brought,—certainly not in ridicule, but to gratify the king who makes use of it. But a little littleness the poet intends to delineate in both cases, and in the case before us it is to be considered, in connection with the disturbed state of Hamlet's mind at the time, as a dim, colorless counterfeit of the previous frenzy, and even as such is it to be justified. At the same time the poet designs, by the odd form which he gives to this folly, to intimate beforehand, in a very intelligible way, that his hero is a man with whom memory will occasionally take the place of action, and wear the appearance of a mere memorandum.

DR AUGUST DOERING (1865)

(*Shakespeare's Hamlet seinem Grundgedanken und Inhalte nach erläutert.* Hamm, 1865, p. 34.)—In this first soliloquy we undoubtedly have the germ of Hamlet's fault (*Verschuldung*), which may be termed the perversion of an undeceived idealism into an embittered and passionate pessimism. The first inciting cause of this perversion was the marriage of the Queen, the second was Ophelia's treatment of him.

[Page 49.] When Hamlet comes before Ophelia, as she was sewing in her closet, there is no attempt on his part to feign insanity. He comes in fearful excitement, forced by his anguish to assure himself whether or not her exquisitely chiselled features proclaim a noble, free soul, and in her dumb embarrassment, unrelieved by a single heart-throb of sympathy, he reads the confirmation of his fears. With that sigh that seemed to shatter all his bulk he parted from his love, and thereafter felt for Ophelia only bitter scorn.

[Page 64.] Hamlet's call for music and the recorders, after the King has fled discomfited from the court-play, is the joy which every habitual pessimist feels over a fresh confirmation that the world is really as bad and that men are really as depraved as he maintains. This perverted idealism has its origin not so much in the objective side of human nature, in the intellect, as in the subjective side of excessive sentiment. His pessimism is not a conviction, but a mood; it is not the result of a universal observation, but only of a few lively impressions. Nevertheless, this mood places him in antagonism to all human kind; he shares none of their interests, but is separated by a high barrier from all their ends and aims. *His* sole interest is to find food for this scornful feeling, and to live in this perverted world only as long as he absolutely must. And can he mingle in the affairs of this world, where everything is bad? Can he feel tempted to avenge outwitted virtue, when there is no such thing as virtue? Shall he feel impelled to restore an interrupted moral order, when he does not recognize the continuance of any such?

[Page 68.] When Hamlet finds Claudius at prayer, his passion knows no bounds, and he longs not for a human, but for a devilish, revenge. While the most ruthless criminal code of past ages always treated its victims with tenderest reference to their

Hereafter, Hamlet wished to make his revenge eternal. In order to perceive how naturally this train of thought springs from Hamlet's disposition, we need but remember how prominent was the share that the Hereafter took in all his reflec tions, and furthermore, that death itself was far from being abhorrent to him, but on the contrary was vehemently longed for.

[Page 70.] His passion leads him to reproach his mother with killing her husband, a reproach which could have been meant as only so far true as, by her yielding to the seducer, she had, without her wish or will, inspired his impulse to commit the murder. . . . . The appearance of the Ghost in the midst of the interview is to be explained by the fact that the midnight hour was past, during which the spirit, freed from purgatorial fires, hovers around the appointed executor of revenge. He had seen how Hamlet had suffered the praying King to escape, and he comes to whet his almost blunted purpose.

[Page 72.] The Queen remains true to her promise, and gives a distorted account to the King of Hamlet's killing Polonius. She says that he was mad as the raging sea (against her better knowledge she here implies genuine insanity); and then that he heard not a human voice, but *something* stir behind the arras; so that, according to her report, Hamlet might readily be supposed to nave made a pass at a rat. She naturally keeps back that Hamlet had supposed that he had killed the King, and she further adds, falsely, that he weeps for what he has done, &c. But the King is not deceived : ' It had been so with us had we been there.'

[Page 87.] The faith in Providence, with which Hamlet dared to comfort himself in recounting to Horatio his treatment of Rosencrantz and Guildenstern, is by no means a symptom of a healthy tone of mind; in the whole tragedy there is no trace in Hamlet of any want of faith in the fundamental truths of religion. Rather is the appeal to this faith in this connection a proof of weakness, which finds comfort in the belief of a wonderful interposition of a higher power in cases where daring is required, and where the issue is uncertain, and where, therefore, the interposition of Providence, so far as it can be affirmed to exist at all, may just as well favor the opposite party. . . . . Rosencrantz and Guildenstern are the only persons in this tragedy who die an innocent death.

[Page 91.] The change of rapiers is to be thus explained. The same thrust with which Laertes gives Hamlet his mortal wound also disarms him,—that is, jerks Hamlet's weapon out of his hand. The courtesy of a contest merely for exercise, or as a trial of skill, obliges him who disarms his opponent to pick up the fallen weapon, and then offer both weapons to his antagonist to take which he pleases Through this accident, on which Laertes had not counted, he was caught in his own springe, for the semblance of a trial of skill had still to be kept up. Hamlet chooses the envenomed rapier, and in the following fourth bout Nemesis overtakes Laertes.

DR E. W. SIEVERS (1866)

(*William Shakespeare. Sein Leiben und Dichten.* Gotha, 1866, p. 441.)—Goethe did not, in his later years, rest satisfied with his explanation. When, in the year 1828, he was looking over Retsch's ' Gallery of Shakespeare's Dramatic Works,' and came to *Hamlet :* ' After all is said,' he remarked, ' *that* weighs upon one's soul as a gloomy problem.' And it must be confessed that Goethe did *not* solve ' the gloomy problem,' although he came nearer to the solution than any one else. The gift of

poetic intuition which he carried with him into this domain of criticism, at first
foreign to him, enabled him to apprehend correctly the ground-tone of Hamlet's
character, and thus the beautiful figure by which he illustrates it may, with a slight
change, be retained.   Hamlet is indeed a costly vase full of lovely flowers, for he is
a pure human being, penetrated by enthusiasm for the Great and the Beautiful, living
wholly in the Ideal, and, above all things, full of faith in man; and the vase is shivered into atoms from within,—this and just this Goethe truly felt,—but what causes
the ruin of the vase is not that the great deed of avenging a father's murder exceeds
its strength, but it is the discovery of the falseness of man, the discovery of the
contradiction between the ideal world and the actual, which suddenly confronts him
as a picture of man: it is, in fact, what he gradually finds in himself as the true
portrait of the human nature which he once deified,—in short, Hamlet perishes because the gloomy background of life is suddenly unrolled before him, because the
sight of this robs him of his *faith* in life and in good, and because he now *cannot* act.
Only that man can act, act for others and for all, who is inwardly sound; and Hamlet's mind is ʻout of joint,' after he has been robbed of his earlier faith.   This it is
that Goethe correctly felt, and it is just this ʻruin of the costly vase' which more
recent critics have entirely disregarded, giving their attention to that point alone,
where Goethe's idea of Hamlet is erroneous or inadequate,—namely, to the ʻgreat
deed,' to which Hamlet is alleged to be unequal.   The drama is emptied of all its
rich, purely human contents, if Hamlet be reduced to a bloodless shadow, ʻthe
hero of reflection,' who, from mere abstract reflection *upon* the deed, never arrives
at the deed.

[Page 442.] Let us first look a little more closely at Hamlet's way of viewing
things, at his ideal nature.   While Romeo and Juliet find their ideal, each in the
other, and keep the world with all that it morally imports at a distance, Hamlet's
aspirations, on the other hand, are intimately connected with the world; he seeks
the ideal directly in life, in the moral relations of man to man, in the supremacy of
the spirit, and, above all, in the moral sense of individuals.   He goes directly to the
world, and demands that it shall show him his ideal actualized.   He would find
in the world a warrant for his deepest consciousness, for his faith in man and in
goodness; there must be *harmony* between spirit and life, and such a necessity of his
nature is it that it is the very condition of his existence.   In short, Hamlet is the
representative of *the spirit in man, conscious of its divine capacity.*   In this consciousness he dares to set himself above the world, and apply to it his subjective
standard; he is the champion of the highest moral demands which the human mind
makes upon life, and is far removed from everything weak, sentimental, sickly; he
is through and through a brave, truehearted man, and by the preponderance of the
spiritual element he is a radically *energetic* person, and the declaration which Shakespeare at the close puts into the mouth of Fortinbras, who stood outside the circle
of the opposing parties: ʻHe was likely, had he been put on, to have proved most
royally,'—this declaration gives us Shakespeare's own opinion, and is confirmed by
Hamlet's tragic end.   Indeed, we Germans have a special interest in not admitting
the representation of Hamlet as a person originally of a morbid character, defective
at the core; for, turn and twist as we may, we must confess that it is the *German
mind* that presents itself to us in Hamlet; the saying of Freiligrath, ʻGermany is
Hamlet,' which, in reference to Hamlet's dread of action, is repeated *ad nauseam*,
and is yet only half true, is wholly true in respect of the *intellectual* principle represented in Hamlet, the self-conscious, subjective intellect, which here, for the

first time, independently opposes the world, and subjects it to its own standard. That Shakespeare makes his Hamlet study in Wittenberg has often been attributed to the fact that the Reformation originated there, and we ourselves trust in the sequel to prove that this drama is intended to represent the peculiar, fundamental principle of Protestantism,—although we are of opinion that Shakespeare, when he placed his hero in connection with the city of Luther, was influenced rather by Marlowe's Faust than by the historical significance of Wittenberg; he meant, we think, to set in contrast with Marlowe's Faust another purely intellectual Faust. But be this as it may, it is certain that Shakespeare's Hamlet, like no other of his characters in this first period of the poet's genius, is created in a thoroughly German spirit; he is a spiritual brother of Werther and, most emphatically, of Goethe's Faust.

[Page 445.] When Hamlet first appears, before he has seen, or even heard of the Ghost, he stands on the brink of despair. We note this fact particularly, because it alone suffices to show how inadequate is the common representation of Hamlet, according to which it is the 'great deed' that lies heavy upon his soul. Shakespeare here most explicitly assigns the marriage of Hamlet's mother as the one cause of the melancholy of his hero, which drives him to wish that 'the Eternal had not fixed his canon against self-slaughter.' And how it is that the marriage of his mother has affected him so deeply plainly appears: it has destroyed his faith in his mother; he perceives what it is that has impelled her to a second marriage,—that it was not *love*, nor any pure motive, but base sensual desire; and now the world is to him 'an unweeded garden that grows to seed; things rank and gross in nature possess it merely.' He cries fie! fie! upon it: *it is the first look into the actual world of men which Hamlet takes*, and what a spectacle is it that is presented before him! He stands before nothing less than an utter contradiction in the being of man, before an abortion, by which his whole previous view of things is inverted, and it is rendered impossible for him ever after to have faith in the moral nature of man.

[Page 454.] The solution of the riddle of this powerful tragedy, which may be described as the peculiarly classic work expressive of the Protestant aspect of the world (*Weltanschauung*), is as follows: What the poet here represents is the torture and weakness of a nature that has fallen out with the world, and *lost its hold;* it is the *break of the consciousness* which robs the soul of *faith*, and renders it incapable of all self-forgetting devotion, of all elevation above self. *The great Protestant idea of man's need of faith*, of faith as the condition of his peace, and of the fulfilment of his mission as a moral being,—*this* it is to which this profoundest and most moving of all the works of Shakespeare's genius owes its origin. Hamlet is the human being who seeks his hold, his resting-place, in the interior nature of man. Shakespeare lets him go to destruction because he has *nothing* to hold to after his purely idealistic faith in *man* is shivered into atoms. This is the vivifying motive in Shakespeare, which has passed from his soul into his work, and thus is it clear what is the idea upon which is based his representation of humanity, as he unfolds it in the King and Queen: against the idealistic way of looking at things and the *deification* of man, he has sought to set the *sinfulness* of the human being, which first appears in history in Protestantism; accordingly, out of the rude Hamlet of the legend, he has fashioned a being who represents, in fact, the Incarnation of Idealism, and for the same purpose he contrasts him with the characters which, in the King and Queen, are the actual personifications of the essential corruption of human nature. But in the foreground is represented the internal instability of the soul when not rooted in God as the only sure source of life, and the weakness and suffering to which it is in consequence given over.

GUSTAV RÜMELIN (1866)

(*Shakespearestudien.* Stuttgart, 1866, p. 75.)—The truth of the matter is this: Hamlet's conduct is confused, and his actions are inadequate to the end proposed; he chooses strange and unintelligible means to gain his point. But the reason is not that the poet *intended* so to represent him; conduct of this sort belongs only to comedy, not to tragedy. The unmistakable inadequacy of Hamlet's practical methods is characteristic, not so much of Hamlet as of Shakespeare. It could not possibly have been the design of the poet to depict a mere incapacity of rightly and intelligently carrying out a purpose. Aristotle long ago mentioned among the examples of dramatic action those, as the most useless for the poet, in which the tragic hero has an object in view which he never attains.

But if Shakespeare ever had attempted this problem, he would have been compelled to solve it in a very different fashion. Shakespeare is by no means one of those poets who draw in lines all too fine and uncertain; his faults are rather on the side of excess than of deficiency. But where are we to find the clear proofs of Hamlet's irresolution? Retarding moments are as indispensable in a tragedy as the escapement in a watch. Had Hamlet, immediately after the appearance of the Ghost, executed the act of vengeance, the drama would have ended with the second scene. But, in fact, Hamlet is acting uninterruptedly throughout; his feigned madness is an act, and a very strong and intensive act, too. That he repeatedly reproaches himself, that he finds examples that condemn him,—in the player who weeps for Hecuba, and in young Fortinbras,—only shows how completely he is filled with the thought of his task. . . . . With how much plainer colors would Shakespeare have painted, had he intended to depict an incapacity for decisive action made morbid by too much thinking!

May it be permitted briefly to contribute to the numerous interpretations of Hamlet yet another, which appears to elucidate much, although not all, but which cannot, however, be acceptable to the æsthetic ideologists?

In the old legend of Hamlet, which directly calls to mind Livy's story of the elder Brutus, one thing appears as the essential and specific point. In order to lull the usurper and murderer of his father into security, and to draw upon himself no suspicion, Hamlet feigns to be insane, but in this pretended insanity there is evidence of great intelligence, which, according to the northern legend, is shown by an uncommon acuteness of mind, by an instinctive suspicion of the concealed connections of events. To put deep sense and hidden wisdom into speeches and actions, which are apparently insane, was for him who sought to treat this subject dramatically the one special task, and while it was difficult enough to deter all mediocre talent from attempting it, it would naturally charm and attract a great and highly gifted poet.

But for Shakespeare this problem had something more than the charm of affording him an opportunity to let his light shine, and his mind and wit disport themselves in new forms. Before he undertook it, he had grown from youth to manhood, and through manifold errors and conflicts without and within gathered a treasure of

serious experience, to which he was moved to give poetical expression. It occurred
to him to make the legend of Hamlet the vessel from which to draw the wisdom of
his own experience, hidden under the wild utterances of insanity, and to produce
his own moods and thought before the public in a strange and unsuspected form.
The idea of thus using the subject of Hamlet lay not so far from a poet of so prolific a faculty as may at first sight appear.

As the young prince of Denmark, returning home, unsuspicious of evil, from the
German high-school, hears the startling news,—that his noble father has miserably
perished, that he himself has been cheated out of the crown, that his mother has
given her hand to the fratricide, and that the court and the people had consented to
this new order of things,—as he himself is now to live and work and avenge himself
in this base world, and as all this works in him a sudden change of his whole view
of life, a change reaching to the very borders of insanity, so also the poet himself,
perhaps, had passed, unsuspiciously and with ideal aspirations, from a fair dream-
world into the actual world, and there had opened before him an abyss of degen·
eracy, weakness, and iniquity, from which he could not withdraw, in which he was
summoned to live, and work, and contend with malignant opponents. To him, too,
a stupid and prejudiced present refused a throne, the poet's throne to which he was
the born, rightful heir. From this experience, also, his soul was filled with melancholy, a sharp and bitter contempt of the world, a humor of despair, which sought
to vent itself in utterances unintelligible to the multitude, and to all appearances only
the ravings of a maniac.

Other characters he had sent forth as fugitive apparitions from his rich dream-
world; this figure he nourished with his heart's blood, and caused it to throb with
the warmest pulsations of his own bosom. Do we not hear his very self, the melan·
choly poet of the *Sonnets*, when Hamlet says: 'I have of late (but wherefore, I
know not) lost all my mirth,' &c. [II, ii, 288-301]? How manifest, moreover, is
the accord, with Hamlet's well-known soliloquy, of the 66th Sonnet: 'Tired with
all these, for restful death I cry,' &c.

[Page 81.] But if we find it easy to admit that in a dramatic treatment of the legend,
the main thing appears to be, under cover of pretended madness, to conceal a deep
wisdom, and that the poet used the occasion to give, in an unwonted guise, poetical
expression to his passing mood and to his own views of life, while we freely grant that
this peculiar view of the poet's purpose renders his *Hamlet* the most interesting, the
most intellectual and profound of his dramatic works, we nevertheless must not fail
to see that this use of the legend enters into the dramatic subject and into the course
of the action as a somewhat foreign and disturbing element; we must perceive that
the legend, whose essential features the piece still keeps, is in itself little fitted for
the interpolation of an element so subjective and so modern; that the poet has taken
no special pains, or, at all events, has not succeeded, in setting aside the inconve-
niences necessarily resulting from his peculiar use of the legend; and that, finally,
on this account, the piece, in respect of the consistency of the characters, and on the
pragmatic side, in the course and arrangement of the action, presents the greatest
discrepancies; nay, it is from precisely this point of view that it must be numbered
among the most imperfect of the poet's works.

The same Hamlet, to whom the poet gives the tender sensibility, the melancholy,
the spirit, and the wit of his own soul, is no longer suited to be the Northern hero,
a bloody avenger of a bloody deed, a fivefold murderer. When the poet sought to
introduce the elements of modern culture and feeling into the old legend, he should

have done as Goethe has done in his *Iphigenia,* fashioned the subject humanly and symbolically. When Shakespeare adopts from the old legend the killing of the courtier listening behind the tapestry, the cunning treachery towards the companions of Hamlet on the voyage to England, when the same tender nature, that feels so deeply for the moral weakness of others and for the degeneracy of the world, takes the lives of three innocent persons, and this, too, as if it were nothing strange, about the same impression is made upon us as would be made if Goethe had represented Iphigenia as, between the acts, slaughtering a couple of prisoners on the altar of Diana.

The most striking instance in point is the scene with the Queen. With what moral nobleness and fire, in what stirring and dagger-like words, does Hamlet arouse the conscience of his mother, and yet the sword-blade of this wise preacher of repentance is smoking at the time with the fresh blood of an old man,—the father of his beloved,—who had done him no harm. He excuses himself therefor pretty much as one would apologize for treading on another's foot. Where has the noblest language of moral indignation ever been introduced in a more unfitting situation, or put into the mouth of a more unsuitable Father Confessor! This very scene with the Queen, which the poet has painted with such evident art and care, and wrought up so powerfully, is at the same time an evidence of how easily, while seeking to exhaust to the very bottom the poetical contents of single situations, it happened to him to transcend the mark. The reproaches Hamlet addresses to his mother prove altogether too much,—that her crime was not only inexcusable, but that it was inconceivable. If the contrast between Hamlet's father and Claudius, in personal beauty, in mind and character, was so infinite that only a downright madman could, in any one respect, give the preference to the latter, if, from the age of the Queen, the mother of a son thirty years old, sensual passion were out of the question, if her first husband loved her so that he would not beteem the winds of heaven visit her too roughly, what was it then that drove her to violate her marriage vows and to an incestuous marriage? An action for which we can see no conceivable motive evaporates and loses all reality. It is only from the Ghost, in the first act, that we gather some hints towards an understanding of the case; but of these Hamlet makes no use.

It is by a comparison of the piece with the Hamlet of the legend that its realistic defects are brought out into full light.

In the old legend all hangs together. Hamlet there feigns to be, not crazy, but, like Junius Brutus, stupid and weak-minded; he does it in order to appear harmless to the King. It is there understood that Hamlet's object is not by a sudden blow to execute vengeance upon the King, but, in the presence of the army and of the people, to prove himself the competent and true heir to the crown. This is accomplished by the covert proofs which he gives of his intelligence and cunning, as well as by his heroic behavior in the war in England. In Shakespeare no good reason appears why Hamlet pretended madness. He is not threatened; rather is the King afraid of him; and his conduct as a madman was far more fitted to excite suspicion than to lull the King into security. The effect upon the people and the army is not at all considered, and if one puts himself in the place of an intelligent citizen of Elsinore, he must surely say that it is fortunate for Denmark that the crown of the old Hamlet had fallen to his brother Claudius, and not to this foolish, crack-brained prince, whose behavior one can make nothing of, who kills a faithful old servant as he

would kill a rat, to whose daughter he makes love, and then, without any apparent
reason, deserts her, and drives her to madness and suicide. . . . .

[Page 86.] If he had killed the King, what was to be done next? How is he
to justify the act before the people? Can he refer to the communications made to
him by a ghostly apparition? or to the looks and conduct of the King at the play?
And why does he suffer himself to be sent off to England? The Hamlet of the
legend goes thither with an army, gains it to his side, and returns at its head as a
claimant to the crown and an avenger of blood. This is intelligible, but Shakespeare's Hamlet suffers himself to be sent away from the theatre of his work, and
returns only by a series of the strangest accidents. His modes of proceeding are
throughout incalculable, and irrational from beginning to end, and no one has yet
been able to discover any reasonable connection between his object and his means.

We are by no means disposed to maintain that our hypothesis of an unsatisfactory
interlacing of an episodical, modern, subjective element with the old Northern
legend is a sufficient key to the solution of these difficulties. We must admit that
in many a scene the poet has, at least, so woven the two together that we cannot discover the seam. His imagination was prolific enough to accomplish in the task of
combination what was apparently impossible. In introducing the players into the
piece, the primary aim evidently was to bring out those allusions to the condition of the London theatricals and to his own stage experiences, and we may
easily picture to ourselves what a jubilee and what a stirring effect upon the stage
as it then existed, this scene must have produced. But the question arose,—how
could players be interpolated into the old legend? There occurred to the poet the
plausible idea of testing the veracity of the Ghost by the effect upon the King of a
play, in which his alleged crime should be represented, so that now the interviews
of Hamlet and the actors appear only as a secondary matter, a mere episode. It
could not escape the poet that the acute and witty dialogue of the subjective Hamlet
being allowed so much space, the retarding moments in the action were all too
strong. The legendary Hamlet had from time to time to accuse himself of delay
and inactivity, and thus the representation of an intellectual, irresolute dreamer came
in as a means of reconciling inconsistent elements,—a representation which then,
here and there, and especially by the contrast with the resolute Laertes, gave the
appearance as if the whole had been devised at one stroke, an appearance which
upon further reflection by no means holds good.*

---

* Even the celebrated soliloquy, 'To be or not to be,' we reckon among the episodes introduced,
and as one of the proofs of the double character of Hamlet. It stands in no necessary connection
with what succeeds or what goes before. The poet himself signifies as much, since he makes Hamlet
come in reading in a book. There runs through the soliloquy a religious vein quite different from
that of the rest of the piece. The rest of the piece stands upon the ground of a very massive popular
faith. The old Hamlet wanders at night after death until the cock crows, and then spends the day-
time in purgatory. Hamlet will not kill the King at prayer because his soul may fly to heaven. How
is it to be reconciled that the same person, who has such solid views upon things invisible, and whose
faith has been accredited by the apparition of a departed spirit, at the same time treats as unsolved
problems the questions, whether to be or not to be, and whether in the sleep of death dreams may
not come? How can he talk about the undiscovered country from whose bourne no traveller returns,
when the night before he had been and spoken with such a traveller, and has received from him the
most important intelligence concerning the Hereafter? Who does not see that there are here two
independent trains of thought having no relation to each other? Evidently in the soliloquy and in
the graveyard it is the poet who is speaking, and who contemplates death as it appears to the natural
man without any dogmatic coloring. The course of thought in the soliloquy has something, moreover, quite peculiar. From the two premises: that the evils of the present life are great and certain,

Our view of Hamlet does not indeed clear away the difficulties and obscurities in the action of the piece; it leaves them standing just where they are, but it explains how they arose, how a poet, who elsewhere never leaves us in doubt of his intentions, and who is wont to paint with the brush of a Rubens, has given us here a production which creates an impression of intricacy and artificiality, and the consistency of which the after-world, in volumes of critical and hermeneutical essays, in vain endeavors to trace.

[Page 91.] The characters in *Hamlet* have a certain changeable coloring, which on the whole is not at all after Shakespeare's manner. It is not only the case with Hamlet himself, the most enigmatical and incomprehensible figure ever represented upon the boards of any stage, to such an extent that it is often very doubtful whether he is only playing the fool or is really a little crazed, but the other characters are also somewhat ambiguous. . . . .

Laertes is a fresh, brave, knightly figure; but when at the close he does not hesitate, in a sham conflict, to use a weapon with a sharpened and poisoned point, and thus to kill his unsuspicious opponent, this base, villainous trick, this most unknightly assassination, is in vain attempted to be made consistent with the character previously attributed to him. Here the old Northern idea of the duty of avenging blood, reckless of the means, plays as a foreign element into the action of the piece, which is otherwise based upon the laws of chivalry. Were it not so, the fact that Polonius had been killed unintentionally, and by the hand of a person mentally diseased, would have demanded some notice.

One is bound to infer, from the different representations that are given of it, that the poet has not drawn the character of Ophelia with any particular distinctness. . . . . But one thing we certainly do find, and that is, that the poet has not indicated with sufficient clearness the cause of her insanity.

It may be a subjective judgment, but we certainly do not stand alone when we advance a very strict theory in regard to the liberty of the poet, as to allowing his dramatis personæ to become insane, and to bring them in this condition upon the stage. We know, indeed, only one instance in which the finest use of this liberty has been made, and the most powerful effect produced. It is the dungeon scene in *Faust*. Gretchen's mind there appears not hopelessly overthrown; her despair mounts only to the borders of insanity, and passes lightly over them; her words still hint in intelligible visions at her position and state of mind, and their dreamlike symbolism is impressively beautiful. Otherwise is it when consciousness appears utterly and irrevocably gone, when the connection of ideas is no longer perceptible, and there is poured out upon us a multitude of senseless speeches. In this case the poet no longer discloses to us interior, mental processes, of which he himself has had experience, and which he is competent to make us feel with him. This is disease, and does not belong to the stage. As little does it become the poet to present us with cases of epilepsy and St Vitus's dance.

Shakespeare observes this limit most exquisitely in Lady Macbeth, and what has

---

and that what comes after death is uncertain, one would expect the conclusion, then the exchange is to be ventured. For, for the same reason that we prefer a certain good to an uncertain, one should choose rather the evil that is only questionable to one that is present and certain. Hamlet draws the opposite conclusion, and could in no more naïve way betray how the pleasure of living can with victorious sophistry delude even the worst pessimist. Still more simply and strikingly is this apparent in the brief and lovely close of these melancholy meditations: 'Soft you, now! The fair Ophelia!'

just been said about the psychological treatment of insanity by the poet does not prevent our admiration of those scenes. In King Lear it is the breadth and expansion given to the phenomenon of insanity that disturbs us; it is intolerable a whole piece through; the situation thus appears to be habitual, endless; death only can deliver Lear and the spectator, and we have to wait for it so long, and it cannot be brought about otherwise than by accident. Ophelia's madness comes before us as a natural consequence, the causes of which are not given, and which we have simply to receive as such. That a person should lose his wits upon receiving bad news is a very unusual case, and one dependent upon a combination of many attendant circumstances, and it seems, moreover, to be entirely removed from a dramatic treatment. In the previous scenes Ophelia is not so portrayed as to produce in us the impression that she will not be able to meet the blows of fate with the ordinary degree of human endurance. She appears to be affected not more than we should expect by the mental condition of Hamlet. The death of her father is certainly a new blow, but it is in the course of nature that parents should die before their children, and father Polonius is not so represented by the poet, that his daughter must think it impossible to live any longer without him. That he should have fallen by the hand of her lover is assuredly the heaviest blow of all, yet it was accidental and without design. That Hamlet, in case of his restoration, might not marry Ophelia is at least nowhere intimated by the poet, and, under the circumstances, by no means self-evident; it may even be said that he could make good what had mischanced in no better way, or more effectually console the orphan.

[Page 96.] There remains almost nothing further to be said than that a charming maiden, who, crazed by the heavy blows of fate, appears fantastically arrayed in weeds and flowers, singing loose songs, and dealing out her flowers with half-sensible speeches, is in itself a touching genre picture that cannot fail of its effect, although the dramatic How and Wherefore remain hidden in the dark.

Among the changes which Shakespeare has made of the material which he had in hand, the most important concerns the conclusion. In the legend, Hamlet, after killing the King, calls the people together, relates and justifies what he has done, is thereupon made king, and reigns long and gloriously. To such a destiny the Hamlet of Shakespeare was not called; he had to end tragically, like all the figures into which poets have infused their own morbid, spiritual affections, such as Werther, Clavigo, Faust, Eduard. They must, as it were, die as vicarious sacrifices, while the poet draws upon other registers of his genius, and plays new melodies. Thus the Hamlet-nature in Shakespeare was only a part of his inner life, although perhaps the ruling ground-tone of his personal temperament; but there were at his command yet other accords upon other strings of his genius, and in the same years in which he created Hamlet, he found the material for the *Midsummer-Night's Dream*, for *Henry IV*, and for the *Merchant of Venice*.

NO-PHILOSOPHER (1867)

(*Hamlet's Traits of Character*, by A No-Philosopher, Jahrbuch der deutschen Shakespeare-Gesellschaft, vol. ii, 1867, p. 16.)—In most of Shakespeare's pieces the characters are easy to be understood and true to life, although their outlines and salient points alone are prominent. But with Hamlet it is otherwise. The moving and retarding power, upon which the progress of the piece depends, resides in Hamlet's character; and hence the mirror which the poet holds up in his other dramas to the world and to men, but at a distance, he has to bring closer to a single individual, in order to delineate in detail his personal qualities and what passes within him; and with this, also, to show the motive of the piece. Only in portraying the subordinate characters does Shakespeare hold to his usual great manner; by the less minute way in which they are drawn, and by their inferior worth, they give us the idea that they are only added to adorn and illumine the otherwise strongly-marked character of the chief personage. Hence it is that Hamlet, who is described to us even to the most delicate recesses of his being, and is thus meant to be understood, notwithstanding an objective knowledge of man is so difficult, has become a subject of the most animated controversy. But further, to increase the difficulty, the direct path of inquiry has, it appears to me, been neglected, inasmuch as the general question as to the character of Hamlet has been merged in the question, why is Hamlet unable to act? and this point it has been sought to settle by some magical word, as one solves a riddle.

But suppose that all the instances in which Hamlet shows his inability to act are brought together, and suppose that for all these instances an explanation has been found in some peculiarity of character in Hamlet, a manifold incongruity will nevertheless be apparent when we put this one explanation to the test of all.

What quality is it which is held to be an exhaustive explanation of Hamlet's inaction? Is it his being too much given to thinking? He follows the Ghost quickly, bravely, recklessly. He stabs Polonius without a moment's hesitation. In the seafight he alone is the first to board the hostile vessel. These are not the acts of a man who from too much speculation cannot bring himself up to the point of action. Should not power to act and passion always agree, the one with the other? Even of quick, cool decision, Hamlet is not incapable. With what despatch, for instance, does he determine to send Rosencrantz and Guildenstern to their death! Whatever other quality of Hamlet's may be brought to view, there is no one that necessarily involves an inability in him to act, and no quality that purports to explain his inaction, which will so explain it as, at the same time, to throw a satisfactory light, as it should, upon his action.

It may happen rather that what is at one time a reason for not acting, at another will prompt to action; what operates negatively here will work reversely there. How then can it be said that here is a cause which acts only obstructively in a man's life, when elsewhere its influence goes directly the opposite way? A cause, moreover, which impedes activity is not itself always active; a passion, an impulse of feeling, or some other motive, will emerge from the deep, and a second, a third, suddenly or gradually rising, will in an instant neutralize the first, or combine with it. Who, proceeding systematically or in accordance with some theory, can select from the surging passions that impel a man to act some one particular quality, as explanatory of a certain failure to act, without hitting upon an intellectual defect rather than upon a personal quality? The ground of Hamlet's hesitation is to be found, not in selecting some one quality and inferring from that what takes place, but in Hamlet's whole character, in studying out the several elements of it as they manifest themselves. But, above all, his action and his inaction should not be separated; for in doing and in not doing combined is his character to be discerned. Separate the two, inquire for a special reason for his not doing, and you will come upon a fault, a moral defect, which stood in the way of his desire for revenge. But Shakespeare certainly would not have chosen a moral defect as the cardinal point upon which his whole piece is to move, or rather hang suspended. Rather to the will and the struggles of a

man, as Shakespeare here depicts him, the obstacle is a concatenation of peculiarities of mind and character, which in their extremes, mutually conditioning one
another, hold him captive as in a net; a single defect, as, for example, a tendency
to subtilizing, Hamlet, with his keen intellect, would soon have discovered and conquered. [He has discovered, but not conquered, it.—THE ED. *of the Yearbook.*]

It is not in *Hamlet*, as in other pieces of Shakespeare's, the history of a single
passion, the development of a few mental qualities, good or bad, that is set before
us. In this drama Shakespeare sets himself a greater task: to make clear and intelligible, from the whole structure of the piece, a human soul in its totality, in
its fluctuating action, and in the finest vibrations by which the nerves are thrilled.
This drama may not, indeed, be a mere portraiture of character, but yet a development, or rather a self-unfolding, of a character face to face with the misery of this
world. According to this design of the whole, Shakespeare does not mark single
defects, but, painting and adding, he unfolds, partly by action and partly by inaction,
the lineaments which combine to form a piquant and original portrait.

It is a peculiarity of Hamlet, which weakens his power of action, that the Real,
nearest to him, so often fades from his view. Excited by his imagination or by the
external world, he seizes upon a thought, which, once seized, he spins out, and
busies himself with to the utter forgetfulness of things around him. The instances
of his thus withdrawing into himself and into the subject of his musing are numerous.
On the platform, *e.g.*, he forgets that he is to see his father's ghost, in a digression
upon the drinking customs in Denmark. To the players whom he has summoned
as the instrument of his purpose, forgetful of that, he holds forth in a sound lecture
upon their art. In talking with Rosencrantz and Guildenstern, who wish to know
the cause of his melancholy, there stream from his lips wailings over the darkening
of all the joys of this world. Frequently he relieves himself in soliloquies, which
lead him from their special occasions away into generalities. The inner world is
even more to him than the outer world; it is the real world to him, into which he is
always retiring. It is natural, therefore, that the substance of his contemplations as
such should become for him a reality, the activity of mere thought his ultimate end.
He hovers from one subject to another; but the conclusion to which his meditations
lead him is not that which the law of an energetic action yields, but the result of his
thinking, in and for itself, contents him; it is equivalent to an act.

[Page 19.] Who can doubt that Hamlet is at home in the *intellectual* world?
He reigns royally there by insight, imagination, wit, and by the boldness with which
he confronts whatever is to be comprehended. That is to him the real world, his
home,—a world, indeed, very strictly bounded. In the outer world, lying far away
from him, he is a stranger, and as a stranger he wanders in it with uncertain step,
never finds his latitude, now going too much, now too little, to the right and to the
left. Thus clear and secure is Hamlet in himself, in his own ideal world; from the
foreign outer world comes bewilderment darkening his inner being. The more he
is thus disturbed from without, the more does the inner beauty disappear, and in its
place comes a mysterious darkness, which hides good and evil in wild confusion.

DR BENNO TSCHISCHWITZ (1868)

(*Shakespeare's Hamlet, vorzugsweise nach historischen Gesichtspuncten erläutert.*
Halle, 1868.)—TSCHISCHWITZ maintains that Shakespeare drew much of the philosophy in *Hamlet* from Giordano Bruno, a learned Italian, who lived in London

from 1583 to 1586, and was patronized by Sir Philip Sidney, Leicester, and by Queen Elizabeth. He finds a similarity even in phraseology between *Hamlet* and *Il Candelajo*, a comedy written by Bruno. To me this similarity of phrases, or of the principles of philosophy, is of the faintest. More importance might attach to it had Shakespeare written no play but *Hamlet;* and if we did not know that he was myriad-minded. The most striking of all the analogous passages that TSCHISCHWITZ adduces is perhaps the following: in *Candelajo*, Octavio asks the Pedant Manfurio, ' Che e la materia di vostri versi ?' Manfurio replies, ' Litteræ, syllabæ, dictio et oratio, partes propinquæ et remotæ.' Whereupon Octavio asks further, ' Io dico, quale è il suggetto et il proposito ?' It is needless to refer to the passage in *Hamlet* that recalls this; it will occur, I should suppose, quickly enough. According to Bruno's atomic theory there is no such thing as death, but merely a separation and combination of atoms : ' Seest thou not that what was seed becomes stalk, what was stalk becomes ear, what was ear becomes bread, what was bread becomes blood,' &c. TSCHISCHWITZ here finds a parallel with Hamlet's imaginary traces of the noble dust of Alexander. KLEIN states, in his admirable *History of the Drama*, (unfortunately I have not at hand my reference to the volume and page, and therefore quote from memory), that Giordano Bruno delivered lectures at Wittenberg during the very year that Hamlet was a student there, and that Hamlet might have attended them, supposing that Hamlet, like most of Shakespeare's characters, was a contemporary of the poet's.

Although TSCHISCHWITZ is evidently convinced of the genuineness of his discovery, he is moderate in his demands of those who are inclined to be skeptical, and (p. 59) says that he does not wish to maintain that Shakespeare went any deeper into Bruno's system than served his immediate purpose in *Hamlet;* but that such instances of parallelism, as he adduces, prove that when Shakespeare wrote *Hamlet*, he had ascended to the height of the consciousness that had been attained in those days (*Zeitbewusstsein*), and had become familiar with the most abstract of sciences.

W. OEHLMANN (1868)

(*Die Gemüthsseite des Hamlet-Charakters.* Jahrbuch der deutschen Shakespeare-Gesellschaft, 1868, vol. iii, p. 205.)—Whenever I observe how our German men of letters labor to distil fundamental ideas from dramatic works, I am reminded of Heine's witty words, ' Reason! When I hear this word, Dr Saul Ascher always comes up before me with his abstract legs, his tight, transcendental, gray body-coat, and with that hard, freezingly cold face of his, which might serve for a frontispiece to a manual of geometry. This man, far in the fifties, was a straight line personified. In striving after the positive, the poor man had philosophized all that is noble out of life, all the sunbeams, all the faiths, and all the flowers, and had nothing left but the cold, positive grave.' For ' the positive,' read ' fundamental idea,' and we have a portrait of the above-mentioned distillers at their dry, abstract labors. Shakespeare's *Midsummer-Night's Dream*, for example, they call: Imagination, the Creative Spirit = abstract leg. *The Comedy of Errors :* Critique on the Power of the Human Mind = transcendental body-coat. *Much Ado About Nothing :* Force of Temperament, raising man above his Finite and Individual Being = Dr Saul Ascher from top to toe!

A prince is said to have asked, when he found the frescoes of his court-painter full of ugly ladies, whether the man in all his life had ever seen beautiful women?

So I would ask, whether these profound thinkers have ever had feelings and passions? How little has the excellent dictum of our old Goethe to Eckermann been taken to heart: 'Ideas! The Germans are a strange people! What with their thoughts and ideas, which they are everywhere seeking and introducing, they burthen their life more than they need. Do pray have the courage, once for all, to give yourselves up to impressions, allow yourselves to be moved, to be delighted, to be elevated, yes, and to be taught, inflamed, and inspirited to something great; but do not be forever thinking that all is vanity, unless there is some abstract thought and idea everywhere! They come and ask me, "What idea I meant to embody in my *Faust?*" As if I knew and could tell! To depict- the region of love, of hatred, of hope, of despair, and whatever the states and passions of the soul may be, is native to the poet, and it is his success simply to represent them.' Must one seek for a fundamental idea in a drama? And not rather for a fundamental passion? And, moreover, such a practical stage-manager as Shakespeare, who knew he had among his spectators men from the army and navy, men hardened by fights with Spanish Armadas, and not only these rough fellows, but weather-beaten tars of all sorts, from the commonest sailor up to ships' captains, and mingled with these the honest London shopkeepers and a free and easy (*leichtlebig*), passionate *jeunesse dorée* of the high aristocracy,—surely he had to amuse these people with anything else rather than with a mere mess of literary Alexandrines, served up with perverted æsthetic principles. What to such a public was the caviare of fundamental ideas? They wanted to be pleased, delighted, moved, and for such purposes representations of passions, pieces full of blood and horrors, with highly-spiced plots, were indispensable. Even the better heads among the spectators were to be satisfied less by the material than by the form of the play. A stage-manager, even though he were no Montesquieu in intellect, certainly knew quite as well as the French philosopher, that *la raison ne produit jamais de grands effets sur l'esprit des hommes.* It is rather, as Goethe says, passions and feelings that are needed for that. This point of view is recommended not only by good sense, it is the true æsthetic standpoint. Indeed, like Luther's drunken boor, who, when he was helped up on one side of his horse, fell off on the other, German, and still more French, critics and poets, even when they undertake to ignore fundamental ideas, or, in fact, any ideas at all in dramas, tumble, by their abstractions of other sorts, into the second position of the drunken boor; thinking it is enough if a drama only shows passion, and if the persons of the drama 'rave and rant as if they had just escaped from bedlam.' It is evidently only another form of Strauss's well-known 'fruit in the abstract.' As there is no such thing as abstract fruit, but simply apples, pears, cherries, &c., so there are no passions in the abstract, but only ambition, pride, avarice, jealousy, and whatever passions there may be, single or complex. And because the Beautiful is heightened in proportion as it is expressed by an intense individuality, it follows that the dramatic poet (and the epic also) can only attain to the highest effects when selecting characters stamped with the most decided passions; in short, when he represents these passions as maintaining themselves, and effecting themselves in opposition to the deepest thinking, to the most comprehensive, sharpest, clearest understanding; then his characters, in spite of the sublimest reflections, in spite of situations the most significant, and in spite of the most manifest means of attaining the goal, are, nevertheless, true to their own individuality,—feeling like Medea: *video meliora proboque, deteriora sequor.*

[Page 208.] Are we then to look even in Hamlet for the passions that characterize him, Hamlet, who passes with so many for a person of mere intellect and abstract reflection, a genuine German, who has received and finished his education in a meagre university city? By all means, I say! I would rather ask, on the other hand, how can we help making this inquiry? What! a man with no passion! a man who denounces as vile the act of his mother in marrying again so quickly,—a man who wishes his heart may break, who is plunged into the deepest grief, for the death of his father, who would rather meet his dearest foe in heaven than see the funeral baked-meats so soon coldly furnishing forth the marriage-tables; a man who, at the communication made to him by the ghost of his father, well nigh goes mad, and cries out, ' O all you host of heaven! O earth! what else? And shall I couple hell?' &c.; a man who says of himself that he has the motive and the cue for passion not like a mere player; a man who reproaches himself for lack of gall, and pours out the most biting irony upon an egotistical court-circle seeking only its own advantage, and owning no law but external decorum; a man who knows how, with words like daggers, to pierce the conscience of his mother,—is such a man to be said to possess no passion! Truly, I think, for the sake of the pit, if even for no other reason, Stage-Manager Shakespeare would have had to lend a passion to his hero. But we will not waste another word upon such a question. Let us rather proceed at once to inquire: Of what kind was Hamlet's ruling passion, what was its special object, and to what class of feelings did it belong? Hamlet's chief and fundamental passion is that which, as Kreyssig says, is the sign of nobility in so many of the Shakespearian heroes, the sincerest truthfulness and conscientiousness, the feeling for the Befitting, the Right. He is through and through a genuine noble nature, conscientious and true, 'the glass of fashion and the mould of form;' and on this account it is that he is beside himself at the sudden marriage of his mother; this is the reason that the world seems to him out of joint, when he learns of his father's murder from the Ghost. . . . . It is this same feeling which makes him appear hard and indifferent in regard to the killing of the old hypocrite Polonius, and to the fate of Guildenstern and Rosencrantz, because he believes that he has discovered that they are contemptible ' vipers,' while the sterling honesty of Horatio has his heartiest sympathy.

But why does he not strive, above all things, to punish the capital crime, the murder of his father? Why, indeed, out of the Hamlet of the legend, who goes to work so systematically, why has the poet with evident purpose created this tardy procrastinator, this man who is without any plan, and who leaves everything to take care of itself? Is this lack of resolution inherent in the great, wonderful *understanding* with which Shakespeare has endowed his hero? I say, unconditionally, no! A brilliant understanding never makes a man a waverer! Were it otherwise, then all the greatest, most energetic heroes, a Cæsar, Frederick the Great, and, above all, Napoleon I, would have suffered from irresolution. Observation teaches us rather that there are characters that are unable to come to a decision, because it is in their temperament (*Gemüth*) to begin to deliberate when they ought to begin to act; not only had Fabius Cunctator and Field Marshal Daun this quality, or, if you please, this failing, but it is found in the most familiar conditions of life,—in ladies, who take so long to decide upon their purchases, that they are the despair of shopkeepers; in stupid boors, whose 'distrust,' after they have had the opinion of the village parson, who knows them thoroughly, is their only weapon against injury, since it is just their lack of understanding that affords them no means of seeing the whole matter in dispute; in that over-anxious official again, of whom Gall tells, who preseived whole heaps of documents because he thought, in every case that came up, he might possibly hit upon points in them which might affect his decision; in that over-zealous clergyman to whom Luther said, ' O thou good man, whilst thou wouldst fain make the church as pure as an angel, thou wilt make it as black as the devil;' in those members of the assembly who cannot sleep in their beds, unless to every ' amendment' they have moved ten more,—all these, and whosoever else resembles them, are only pendants to the crane in the fable, that, despising all the good fishes, had to take up at last with worms; they all preach the same lesson, that, with or without much understanding, a man may let slip the offered opportunity from mere deliberation, distrust, excessive caution, carefulness,—in short, from some bent of his nature which neutralizes the power of a strong understanding, or which, at all events, in many a character, forms an element quite independent of the understanding, and in regard to which one must comfort himself with the saying of Goethe's, ' The great secret of all our defaulting Is that we waver 'twixt running and halting !' At least every one suffers somewhat in this way, for almost every one knows how reluc-tantly matters are settled that have been long deferred, and how every postpone-ment makes the task harder, even when it is ever so urgent.

Now it is this excessive deliberation which is the second main ingredient of Hamlet's character, and upon which his first passionate abhorrence of shams and his love of right, honesty, and good morals, suffered such disastrous wreck ! He wills only *summum jus*, but, alas ! he does not know that he who clings too exactly to that runs into *summam injuriam;* he strives, indeed, for the Right, but without knowing that he, who undertakes to put it through, only too often must not shrink back, but be willing to cry, *Pereat mundus*, for an imperfect right. His is a nature that paralyzes all realization of the Right. Thus he has, as his second trait, only too easily united with his striving for purity, conscience, and right, a readiness to find objections to *every* decision, *every* plan which demands decisive action.

[Page 214.] But Shakespeare is never contented with one or two traits of cha-racter; he always shows us personalities true to life, and the more eminent they are, the more various the qualities with which he endows them. Therefore, with his quick conscientiousness and the sense of right resulting from it, Hamlet has, with a painful caution resulting in the greatest irresolution, the secretiveness and talent for mystifying so closely related to the above traits, and these qualities it is that render him so much interested in the players, and form a key to so much in his character. With his sense of justice is combined, also, a sense of honor. When Fortinbras passes by, he holds it right, where honor is concerned, to fight to the death for a straw. And these chief elements of his character are combined with and overshadowed by an astonishing intellect, which enables him (and here is the tragedy) to see through all and judge all rightly,—all, only not himself, only not his invincible propensity to hesitate, with its necessary consequences !

DR KARL ELZE (1869)

(*Introduction to Trans. of Hamlet.* Berlin, 1869, p. xii.)—*Hamlet* has exerted an incomparably greater influence upon the history of literary development in France and in Germany than in England. It stands alone in this respect among the dramas of Shakespeare, and it may be said, without exaggeration, that in both of the former countries the history of *Hamlet* is the history of the poetry of Shakespeare; in all cases, as his most original and peculiar work, it has been the pioneer, breaking the path to the poetry of its creator. In Germany especially it has produced an extensive literature of its own. In France there are evidences that the piece was known before Voltaire led to a more intimate acquaintance with it by translating passages of it (as, for example, the great soliloquy), and by various critical remarks thereupon. 'Voltaire,' as Boerne happily remarks, 'measured the mammoth bones of this to him unknown giant-spirit by the dainty *taille* of a French marquis, and, of course, found them ridiculous and unnatural.' Yet Voltaire admitted that pearls were to be found on this muck-heap, worthy of being worked up in accordance with the classic rules of French poetry. . . . . Various French translations have gradually led to a more correct understanding of the poet, which was furthered by the critical labors of the Sorbonne, and by the influence of the historical drama of the English upon the romantic school, until at last Victor Hugo, in his work upon Shakespeare, reached to a deification of Shakespeare no less unreasonable than was Voltaire's depreciation of the poet. The conspicuous rôle which *Hamlet* has played in all these phases is owing mainly to the attraction of the Mysterious and Incommensurable, for of all Shakespeare's dramas this piece it is which always strikes the French as the strangest and most unintelligible, and in spite of their present better understanding of the poet, they do not feel to this day quite at home with him.

It is far otherwise in Germany. GERVINUS with much acuteness distinguishes *Hamlet* as a poem, which has wrought upon our modern German life, and which has grown into it, as no work of the kind of our own times and nation has done, if we except *Faust*. . . . . The character of Hamlet, as is well known, has been in manifold ways regarded as the personification of that superabundance of thinking, that sickly irresoluteness, and that lack of power to act, which, in political affairs especially, disadvantageously distinguish the Germans; Hamlet has even come to be represented as a symbol of Germany, and Freiligrath has sharpened this idea to a point in the exclamation, ' Hamlet is Germany !'

[ELZE here speaks of the early *Hamlet* acted by the English comedians in Germany in 1626.]

It is certainly a proof of the greatness and immortality of this work, that, from such corruption and mutilation, it has, step by step, and hand in hand with advancing intelligence, been restored to its original purity; all the variations and changes of its form (even Shroeder's with its happy ending),—all have proved to be temporary, while the imperishable original survives them all. But it is the leading minds of our nation, Lessing, Schlegel, Tieck, and others, who have carried on this work of purification, and no less a person than Goethe was the first to throw open the doors of this mysterious temple. Hamlet has accompanied us, as of our own kith and kin, through all the stages of our intellectual development; and the knowledge of Shakespeare, especially promoted by him, is now reflected back from Germany to England, so that the present understanding and æsthetic criticism of Shakespeare in England is in no small degree based upon the German.

CARL KARPF (1869)

(Τὸ τί ἦν εἶναι. *Die Idee Shakespeare's und deren Verwirklichung.** Hamburg, 1869, p. 127.)—THE MYTHS. The Myths used by the poet as the foundation of

---

* [It is difficult, very difficult, to treat this volume of 166 pages charitably. And I have failed in the endeavor inasmuch as I have here given some extracts from it. The greatest charity would have been silence; the author, however is so thoroughly convinced of the truth and wisdom of his theory

Hamlet, we interpret in reference to the different activities personified in Hamlet and Laertes, the speculative and the active, the theoretic and the practical, the intensive and the extensive (Reason and Force). IN REFERENCE TO HAMLET. The First Myth, which may relate to the divine Thought, founded upon the One, the first Being.*

From the union of the god Odin and the giantess Jordh, the union of Spirit and of Matter, sprang Thor. ⌐hor carries Orvandill in a basket upon his back, wading through the floods, the wintry ice-streams, the Elivagar, which separates the kingdom of the giants from the world of gods and men. One of Orvandill's toes, sticking out of the basket, is frozen, and thrown by Thor at the heavens, where it is made a star, which is now called Orvandill's Toe. Some myths relate how Thor (the flash of lightning) waded through the sacred glowing water of heaven, the flaming clouds. In winter these became snow, frozen into ice, strange waves (Elivagar). But spring comes, and with it the faithful Thor bears the Lightning-spark Orvandill (*i. e.* the Beam) upon his shoulders through the icy streams, the seat of all wintry horror, to the earth, to the expectant wife of the same, Groa, *i. e.* to the vegetable green, which seeks to spread its covering over the rocks, to set loose the stones from the head of the building god. In the purified, clear heaven of spring shines Orvandill's Toe, which is in winter frozen; the lightning god gives again their brightness to the lights of the firmament, kindles it anew with the lightning-spark, and fixes the company of stars high above.

Orvandill (the Frozen Toe), the chilblain (*Frostbeule*), is, as the lightning-spark, the hypostasis of Thor. But Thor is the god of peasants, in reference to which the Myth says, the race of slaves (thralls), oppressed in this life by the burthen and trouble of labor, will find a resting-place after death with their friend Thor.

That the poet was acquainted with this myth, and had special reference to it, appears from the very significant remark of Hamlet, in the graveyard, in relation to the tragic singer, the first clown, and to his ambiguity and equivocation.

After recognizing the absolute, revealed in the tragic figure, and after emphasizing the equivocation (*Doppelsinnigkeit*), which points to annihilation, Hamlet says, ' By the Lord, Horatio, these three years I have taken note of it, the age is grown so picked † that the toe of the peasant comes so near the heel of the courtier, he galls his kibe' (*Frostbeule*).

---

that no criticism of mine can at all disturb him, and others can read and judge for themselves. I am willing to confess, in character, that an ' exposition of sleep' comes over me when I hear any discussion, conducted by men below Grote or Jowett, of Plato's τὸ τί ἦν εἶναι, or formal cause, but when it comes to reading it in German, I think I would prefer to meet my dearest foe in heaven. I therefore make no apologies for the above translation. If Germany has given us a KARPF, England has given us a MERCADE. ED.]

* In Bernardo's allusion [I, i] to the star in the west, which he connects with the appearance of the Ghost, as the clock strikes ' one,' and of which he says, that it makes its course, in order ' to illume the part of the heavens,'—not sky,—where now it shines, there lies a very significant image which is to be referred to the first myth of the star Orvandill (the father of the mythical Hamlet). At the words of Bernardo, ' the bell then beating *one*,' the free Ghost first steps forth before our eyes. Here is the One which the clock has announced. He is the Star in the West, the first reality (*Wesenheit*), which will run its course (ἡ ὑφηγημένη μέθοδος), in order to found the science of the creative essence, by means of the drama of *Hamlet*. That the striking of the clock at the first sight of the Ghost is designed to intimate something special is clear, otherwise the poet would have put the entrance of the Ghost, on the evening before, and Bernardo's remark, at the midnight hour, the appropriate time for ghosts to appear, and not have let them occur just after that hour had passed.

† Steevens here remarks that this word is taken from the preening of birds, and we think that there is here also an allusion to self-evolution for the purpose of purification (*Katharsis*, purgation).

In the relation which the star (the Frozen Toe, the chilblain) Orvandill stands to Thor as hypostasis, Hamlet may be regarded as standing to the time idea and destructive moment of the force immanent in matter, ' nature ' (comp. *Sonnet* 126) personified in the First Gravedigger (Chronos, or Æon), and Hamlet appears to intend to say that the tragical, personified activity, its own hypostasis, seeks to injure and annihilate himself.

[Page 129.] The poet may have referred his conflict with the passions, or rather the representation of them, by identification therewith, which was his ground for existence in purgatory, the thymosis and the thymopathic circumstance (see the image of the ' fretful porcupine,' used by the Ghost), this conflict the poet may [&c. &c. &c.]

HERMANN FREIHERR VON FRIESEN (1869)

(*Die Fechtscene im Hamlet.* Jahrbuch der deutschen Shakespeare-Gesellschaft, 1869, p. 376.)—How is it possible that Laertes and Hamlet could have exchanged rapiers?

There is only one way, I conceive, of solving this problem on the stage, and that is by reference to the Rules of the Fencing-school, and the lesson that relates to Disarming with the Left Hand.' The French translator possibly knew this lesson, as he paraphrases the stage-direction (' *They catch one another's rapiers, and both are wounded* ') with the following words, ' Laerte blesse Hamlet, et dans la chaleur de l'assaut ils se désarment et changent de fleuret, et Hamlet blesse Laerte.' The lesson upon disarming, if I may depend on the memory of my schooldays, is somewhat this : As soon as your opponent has made a pass, and is about to return to his guard, you strike the most powerful *battute* possible (*i. e.* a blow descending along the blade of your opponent), in order to throw your opponent's blade out of its position, if possible, with its point downwards, at the same instant you advance the left foot close to the outer side of the right foot of your opponent, seize with the left hand the guard of your opponent's rapier, and endeavor to wrest the weapon from his fist by a powerful pressure downwards; if this manœuvre succeeds, you put the point of your dagger to the breast of your opponent, and compel him to confess himself vanquished. When your opponent does not succeed in withstanding the *battute*, which makes it impossible for him to keep back his assailant with the point of his dagger, there is nothing for him to do but to meet the attack with the same manœuvre, and get his assailant's weapon in his hand in the same way. With persons of equal skill this is the usual result, whereby they change places, and the combat is continued without delay. It is obvious that in the execution of this manœuvre on the stage, the greatest skill is required, that the whole thing may not prove a mere scuffle, as Tieck says he has seen it in English theatres.

FRIEDRICH BODENSTEDT (1870)

(*Introduction to Trans. of Hamlet.* Leipzig, 1870, p. viii.)—Notwithstanding the wonderful manner in which Shakespeare has sublimated the material, the stuff of the old legend, there yet remains something of its original rudeness, and must always remain, because the fruit never can disown the soil out of which it has sprung.

As chief foes, and consequently as the chief representatives of the play and counter-play in the piece, stand opposed to each other Hamlet and King Claudius. Claudius is a bad man, but a monarch who understands how to rule, and in practical prudence and force of will far excels Hamlet. Arrived at the throne by a crime, he does not, like Macbeth, go from one murder to another, but seeks by intrigue to strengthen and establish his power. Against the pretensions of young Fortinbras he prepares for war, but avoids useless bloodshed, as the difficulty permits of being peacefully settled. He is identified with the interests of the country, for which Hamlet has neither eye nor ear, and accordingly, notwithstanding his superior culture, is not qualified to reign.

The courtiers, from their position, are all of the party of the King. They are neither better nor worse than the courtiers in the time of Elizabeth, or the average of the same class to-day. . . . .

[Page x.] Hamlet's first utterances in the drama are keen, cutting phrases. He is at this time about thirty years of age, and, while his country is in danger, he cherishes no wish but to go back to Wittenberg. . . . . He resolves to play before the King and the court the part of a madman. His talent for acting enables him to do this excellently well. Instead of exulting in his success in this particular, and taking advantage of it, he is vain enough to be offended, and indeed to fall into a passion, because he is thought to be really crazy. The scenes in which all this is represented are very effective on the stage; but, closely considered, they show the prince in no very favorable light, for a true man will never avail himself of a safe position to wound defenceless opponents. And besides it strikes us that the prince acts with very little prudence in betraying at every turn that he is not really crazy, but only making believe.

[Page xi.] Ophelia's eloquent praise of Hamlet is referred to by most of the commentators as a proof of what a combination of excellent qualities, as a statesman, soldier, and scholar, &c., he was possessed. We see in it only the natural expression of the enthusiasm of a young maiden to whom everything about a *Prince* appears glorified. Otherwise, her relation to him is to be regarded as perfectly pure. As a philosopher Hamlet loves to generalize, to establish a universal experience upon a particular case. Because his uncle has committed a murder, which he has to avenge, he looks upon the whole world as out of joint, and himself as born to set it right. Because his mother is a weak woman, he exclaims: 'Frailty, thy name is woman!' Because she was unfaithful to her first husband, he accounts the whole sex false, and misunderstands Ophelia even. It is in the nature of imaginative idealists, that they exalt the object of their love to such a height that the disillusion is all the more violent.

Old Polonius is befooled with the cloud; which, by the way, might have happened to a far wiser man at the hands of a prince supposed to be mad.

[Page xii.] Hamlet's behavior after the killing of Polonius evinces, almost as if he were proud of it, the deep-lying barbarian element which in weak, sensitive characters, so frequently crops out in connection with the highest intellectual culture. The madness of Ophelia, who was hardly of a nature to be thus powerfully affected, does not appear to us to be sufficiently accounted for and explained. After passing beyond the turning-point, the poet, we suppose, felt the need of a freshening up in the progress of the action.

The graveyard scene in Act V has been found much fault with, yet it is as necessary to the conclusion of the whole as the rafters are to the roof. The poet takes his hero through all possible situations to show that he was averse to all consistent, concerted modes of action With full consciousness Hamlet always takes a leap away from his object, which is often brought close before his eyes; and then vents his ill humor in soliloquies against himself, or in battles of bitter words with others. Even if he had not been supposed to be crazy, respect for his rank would have blunted the possible wit of the courtiers. Thus he has had easy encounters with Polonius, Guildenstern, and Osric, but in his fight of words with the hair-splitting old Gravedigger he gets rather the worst of it; the Gravedigger, not knowing who he is, of course gives free play to his tongue.

[Page xiv.] Up to the climax of the drama we are on the stretch to know how the task imposed on Hamlet is to be executed; after, our only curiosity is to see how it will always be evaded.

His misfortune is that his talents and inclinations demand a very different sphere from that in which he was born. This gives to his fate its tragic background and the motive of all the strange contrasts between his speech and his conduct. He has artistic tastes and philosophic endowments. Nevertheless, it is evident that neither as an artist nor as a philosopher would he ever have achieved any considerable work, because the energy required in both is wanting in him. From the clouds of his melancholy there flash out brilliant lightnings, but there burns not the steady fire which alone gives soul to great works and deeds. From his want of energy comes his want of character. Instead of being the master, he is the slave of his gifts, and in a false position; his talents are his ruin. At first he plays the part of a fool, which is offensive to all sound feeling, and he is soon in a fair way to become a fool in earnest, until fate severs his life-strings, and uses him, dying, as the instrument of its plans, permitting him to accomplish blindly the work, which he would never have accomplished with a clear eye and clear consciousness. But, by means of the long delay of punishment, the King is more severely punished than if he had been struck at once by the avenging steel, and herein lies the tragic expiation and justice of the piece.

W. OECHELHÄUSER (1870)

(*Introduction to Trans. of Hamlet.* Berlin, 1870, p. 5.)—I cannot accept as such those biographical hints, which, together with the *Sonnets*, are alleged to indicate in Hamlet the expression of Shakespeare's personal views of life. The poet lives unquestionably in his collective ideal figures; every one of them reflects a part, a side of his personality; from every one of them sounds one of the ground-tones of his being. But as every scion of the Germanic stock,—and only such,—is able to enter into Hamlet's thoughts, and perceive how near akin this character is to the Germanic archetype, without, therefore, necessarily manifesting in his own views of life any specific relationship to the character of Hamlet created by Shakespeare, so is this certainly true of the poet himself. I can, indeed, represent Shakespeare to myself, in his perfect insight into the Real and the Ideal, as the pure counterpart of Hamlet, but I have no faith in the bitterness and contempt for mankind ascribed to him.

But that which, of all the treasures it contains, has through all these centuries so extraordinarily enhanced the charm and attractiveness of this remarkable tragedy, is the mystery of the Insolvable, which still rests upon it, notwithstanding all the mountains of commentary that have been written. . . . Goethe's indication of the fundamental idea of the piece is, alas! no key, opening to us a correct view of the separate passages and characters. Shakespeare did not work out his characters after models, but for the most part lets them act from mixed motives. In respect of these very much is still obscure, and Ulrici is right in putting off the final conclusion of all controversy about Hamlet to an indefinite distance.

[Page 32.] According to my view, which corresponds substantially with Ulrici's, Hamlet is not at all of a melancholic or phlegmatic temperament, nor anything of the sort, but of a powerfully and healthily endowed nature, with the most brilliant gifts of mind and heart, and an instinctive abhorrence of lies, hypocrisies, and shams. [The various blows, that shatter his ideal,] fall upon him so heavily that the balance of his nature is lost, and then, in boundless exasperation and passionate pessimism, he plunges into errors the very opposite of his high personal qualities, not only wilfully, but, we may almost say, with a wild joy; his wit runs into sarcasm, his self-consciousness into self-torture, his good-will to men into contempt and recklessness, his love into indifference, his self-forgetfulness into self-seeking, his religious sensibility into apparent levity. . . . . But in death his character again appears in its original purity, which has never been wholly lost, but only overshadowed and darkened.

ROBERT ZIMMERMANN (1870)

(*Studien und Kritiken zur Philosophie und Æsthetik.* Wien, 1870, p. 96.)—Why should not Hamlet have caught something, externally at least, from the persons among whom he lived, while, in his inner character as a student, preserving his superiority? He is the Queen's own son, the King's own nephew; from childhood up he has lived and moved in this family, receiving impressions in this court atmosphere and making impressions, as we see in the case of Ophelia; it çannot be but the manner of life of those around him should be his manner of life; the views by which he saw them act should be those by which he also should be actuated. Hitherto almost all the commentators have committed the error of conceiving of Hamlet as isolated, as apart from his surroundings. They have overlooked the fact, that while his *talent* was trained in stillness, his *character* was formed in the current of the world, of course the Danish world. But one usually takes his ways of life from the influences that immediately act upon him, and these modes of living become unconsciously permanent traits of character. Family relationship appears plainly recognizable here. His weakness, his self-abandonment, Hamlet gets from his mother. By his foolhardy courage in boarding the pirate we are reminded of his father, who in an angry parle smote the sledded Polacks; his passion for crooked ways, intriguing, and undermining, hints to us of him whom he hated so mortally,—herein he bears only too close a resemblance to his uncle. They are alike, also, in that, while Hamlet is unable to execute the deed so long resolved upon, Claudius is just as unable to repent to any purpose of his crimes. The amusements and favorite pleasures of the court, —of which theatrical representations were one,—for whence, at the first hint, came the players, and how was it that Rosencrantz, when the question was how to pass the time, fell at once upon the idea of introducing a troop of actors?—the pleasures of the court, I say, are a speaking sign of Hamlet's acclimatization, the finer pleasures, at least, had become his, and it is wrong, so it seems to me, to treat his fondness for the stage, which he shared with the whole court, as peculiar to him. The idea of using the play to entrap the King,—that alone is Hamlet's; the proposal to have a theatrical entertainment comes from the courtiers.

H. A.. WERNER (1870)

(*Ueber das Dunkel in der Hamlet-Tragödie*, Jahrbuch der deutschen Shakespeare-Gesellschaft, 1870, vol. v, p. 40.)—In this drama the attempt has been made to study the hero exclusively, and to regard his character as the key to the whole tragedy. The reverse method would be the right one. It is an error, but an error arising from the fortunes of our nation and from the tendency of our time, to suppose that the hero creates and conditions his world and all his environment. He influences his century, but his century, with its loves and its hates, its virtues and its vices, its hopes and its trials, influences him, and has him in its leading-strings. And herein is Shakespeare the profoundest and the most faithful painter of nature, that he sees and depicts the mutual influence of the individual and of the masses.

[Page 43.] The relationship between Lear and Hamlet is striking even in form. Only compare the principal persons in their doing and being, their passive connection with the world around them; compare the respective groups of persons by whom they are surrounded, observe the like moving passions, the apparently hopeless results, upon which, however, a comforting beam of light is not wanting, and withal the soothing ending of each. A careful observer will be able to add to the number of points of resemblance even in particulars. It will be seen by him that these resemblances in situation and arrangement are due directly to the similar purposes of the poet in both these pieces. He will find that both these tragedies treat substantially the same theme, only with different applications. In both he will find pictures of the disturbance of social order, of the loosening of sacred ties, by which the whole collective life of human society is made impossible, sins which extend from the throne to the serf, and put in jeopardy all estates. From the first word of the age-bewildered Lear to his last breath over Cordelia's pale countenance, it is the corruption of domestic life, which is not only the key-note, but the impelling power, of the action of the piece, and just so is the corruption of the civil life of society in *Hamlet*. As in the former the poet breaks out in a mighty elegy over the grave of parental and filial love, so here in *Hamlet* we have the awful denunciation of a generation that has lost the conditions of a well-ordered society. Yes, like two members of one great whole, are these two songs of woe over humanity, whose whole suffering they take in, for between the State and the family springs up our whole collective life and being, and when both are diseased, then man is hurled back into the primeval chaos; where they are destroyed, there reigns eternal night.

Such are the mighty tasks which the poet set himself as the herald of a new epoch. Leaving all beaten paths far behind him, he created the tragedy of the masses, which, upon a newly born popular consciousness, has founded the sovereignty of society over the individual. But as the new law is yet struggling, even till now, not indeed for existence, but for exclusive jurisdiction, and therefore lives only in a broken, indistinct form, we cannot wonder if the prophetic revelations of the poet still sound as a dark word, whose import is doubtful and uncertain. His work comes to us like an oracle, which is first fully understood only when it is fulfilled.

[Page 81.] To us this tragedy, to state this *one* result, seems to be a question addressed to Fate. It is the first part of a work similar to the Arabian poem, the book of Job, an earnest, solemn setting in opposition, the one to the other, of the good and the evil in the world, neither coming off victorious; a true riddle without answer, so intended by the poet; and the longer he meditated it, the more distinctly did it take this shape. He paints a dark, mysterious side of man's being, a gloomy night-piece, putting into it everything that is dark in his otherwise clear soul. And, therefore, he chooses those mournful colors, the northern sky, the lonely sea, the sluggish, weedy brook, the sandy grave. Therefore he makes the dead awake, therefore he lets madness pass over the stage,—madness real, feigned, and doubtful. Where the Highest, the Holiest, is uncertain, confounded, out of place, where the cry for God and for Justice rings unanswered and unheard, there everything gathers that acts both on soul and body with a dark, weird effect, with the coldness of death. Over the misery of the shattered family of Lear the lightning flashes, the avenging thunder rolls; over the gloomy waste in which the state of Denmark is sunk [literally, *swamped*. Tr.] settles hyperborean night with clammy horror. Only beyond these graves glimmer the ruddy streaks of a new dawn.

G. F. STEDEFELD (1871)

(*Hamlet, ein Tendenzdrama Sheakspeare's* [sic*] *gegen die skeptische und kosmopolitische Weltanschauung des Michael de Montaigne.* Berlin, 1871, p. 9.)—Hamlet is, according to the intention of the poet, in his whole bearing a noble, manly, chivalrous presence, with moral and religious feeling; an intellectual hero, a Titan, who is far above his whole surroundings, rising thus above them by insight, learning, culture, wisdom, and knowledge of men and the world; there is lacking in him only the Christian godliness, faith, love, hope. He has no firm, positive faith, no love and no hope! Once they were his, but he lost them when his ideals melted away, and he discovered in his own family how evil reigns in the world. He has become a skeptic in regard to a righteous Providence, and has fallen out with himself, with God, and the world, although, together with his native truthfulness and manliness, with his hatred of everything base and false, and of the lies and hypocrisy which he sees busy at court, he still keeps his filial piety towards his mother and his devotion to his friend Horatio. This filial piety and this capacity of friendship and of recognizing the worth of others, this personal nobleness and knightly fashion of thinking, which never forsake him, even in his utter despair of the world, and in the deepest embitterment of his spirit, are certainly fine qualities adorning his character, but they are no longer hallowed by a *firm faith* in a just Providence. His love for Ophelia, which, as appears from his confession to his mother, in the churchyard scene, he has *felt;* but, unlike Laertes with his fraternal love, he makes no show of it at her grave, nor does he shriek it out to the world in big-sounding phrase,—yet is it no true passion, animated by virtue and religion, but only a sensual pleasure in the beautiful, finely cultured, charming maiden, a pleasure which ceases to be felt when he discovers by observation that her love is not for him *personally*, but is the offspring of design, and that she repels his advances under the instruction of her father and brother, who had directed

---

* It is altogether beneath the dignity of an editor to notice what might be a trivial misspelling on a title-page, most especially when it occurs in the name of Shakespeare. But in the present instance this spelling is maintained, with but a few exceptions, throughout Herr Kreisgerichtsrath Stedefeld's volume. I am therefore bound to believe it intentional. There is in my library a volume, sad monument of wasted time, containing the name of Shakespeare spelled in four thousand different ways. Herr Stedefeld's makes the four thousand and first. Ed.

her so to bear herself towards him, in order to draw him more surely into her net,
and win from him a promise of marriage, and thereby the prospect of the crown.

[Page 11.] Hamlet plays the part of a madman, because, doubting the moral order
of the world, he has lost faith, love, and hope, those saving sentiments, which, with
his deep moral sensibilities, and his ideal of life and the world, he urgently needed.
Here lies his tragical defect and the ethical reason for sympathy with his fate. He
must perish, because he will not see that evil, the passions of men, the tortures
of this life, are only instruments of divine Providence to stimulate the moral energy
of good. He will not see that every rational being is called upon to reconcile the
Ideal with the Real on this earth.

[Page 24.] One need not seek far for the reason why this drama, in all times
and in all nations, commands such a wondrously mysterious interest, whether when
acted or read. The contrast between the Christian view of God and the ideal *or*
materialistic pantheism which leads to skepticism, this opposition and this conflict,
of which every man has experience in his own soul, this great question, ' To be or
not to be,' the great riddle which the Sphinx puts to every man to guess, and for
which he and others are sacrificed, when he attempts to solve it without faith in a
higher power,—this pride of the old Adam, that would be like God and know all
things, would fain pluck the fruit of the tree of knowledge without putting forth
strength and resolution, without much spiritual and moral labor, to do the good
and to leave the evil, or when the evil presses upon us powerfully, with love and
merciful forbearance to render it innocuous;—this great Riddle it is which Shakespeare in *Hamlet* presents in the life of a man highly endowed with all intellectual and moral gifts, but he shows us also how that life was wrecked in the
attempt to solve it.

[Page 31.] It is, I think, extremely probable that Shakespeare sought by the
drama of *Hamlet* to free himself from the impressions left upon his mind by the
reading of the book of the French skeptic, Montaigne. It is known that a copy of
Florio's translation of this book was in the possession of Shakespeare.

If traces of Giordano Bruno's philosophy may be found in Hamlet's soliloquies,
with much more confidence may we suppose that the reading of Montaigne furnished
considerable material for the conception of the enigmatical Hamlet, or is it at all
improbable that the legend of Hamlet, the idea of the prince whose thoughts were
given to enigmas, and who acted the madman, may have shaped itself in the mind
of Shakespeare for the hero of a drama, who, as a skeptic, was consequently in-
efficient, hypochondriac, although intellectually gifted, and incapable of a *great act ?*

OTTO LUDWIG (1872)

(*Shakespeare-Studien.* Leipzig, 1872, p. 138.)—Shakespeare carefully avoids the
appearance of everything sketchy, rectilineal, hurried. The branch ramifies. The
situation is hollowed out. Here is an example: Hamlet appears, led by the Ghost
to a more lonely part of the terrace. He asks, ' Where wilt thou lead me ? Speak ;
I'll go no further.' The Ghost does not begin his story right off. He only says,
• Mark me.' Hamlet replies, ' I will.' And yet the Ghost does not begin ; he is
still preparing for the impression to be made : ' My hour is almost come, When I to
sulphurous and tormenting flames Must render up myself.' Hamlet says, ' Alas,
poor ghost !' Still the Ghost does not begin ; Hamlet does not even urge on the
communication. The Ghost says, ' Pity me not, but lend thy serious hearing To

what I shall unfold.' Hamlet replies, merely filling up the time, · Speak; I am bound to hear.' The Ghost adds, ' So art thou to revenge, when thou shalt hear.' Hamlet asks, ' What?' Even now the Ghost communicates nothing; he only tells who he is, which as a mere piece of intelligence would be unnecessary. All the while the due tone of feeling is in course of preparation, and is furthered when the Ghost describes his condition in Purgatory more strikingly by telling of the effect which a knowledge of it would have on Hamlet, did he dare unfold it to him. At the same time opportunity is given the Ghost for the employment of a style wondrously poetical. After a long period, his ' List, list, O, list!' makes an impression tending wonderfully to produce the due tone of mind. There are sighs at the same time. What must that be which the Ghost has to tell? A state of expectation is aroused, sweet, weird, in the spirit of the old popular ballads. But still the communication has not yet come. It is as if the Ghost himself purposely delays, that expectation may be still higher strung. But now comes only, ' If thou didst ever thy dear father love—.' Hamlet breaks in, ' O God!' and his excite-ment is betrayed thereby. How can the Ghost ask such a question? And now? How can Hamlet now declare how he loved his father, when the deepest, the most overwhelming sympathy and the burning impulse to avenge him kindle his love to a flame? He is to avenge his father, but it is not told even yet upon whom. The Ghost tells only the cause therefor: ' Revenge his foul and most unnatural murder!' Hamlet exclaims, ' Murder?' And then the murder is described merely in general terms: ' Murder most foul, as in the best it is, But this most foul, strange, and unnatu-ral.' Hamlet: ' Haste me to know't, that I, with wings as swift As meditation or the thoughts of love, May sweep to my revenge.' Observe how the question: Upon whom? that I may kill him!' is insinuated. The vehement impulse is here ex-pressed not in words swift and violently ejaculated. The swiftness is described. He says he will be quick, but he does not say it quickly. Even if the actor speaks this speech quickly, it will produce a greater effect than if the speech were short, and thereby directly expressive of swiftness. Not even yet does the Ghost say upon whom he is to be revenged. He says, ' I find thee apt; And duller shouldst thou be,' &c. Thus we have in anticipation the idea of Hamlet's character and of the whole piece. For Hamlet actually proves to be thus dull in his revenge. But once more: ' Now, Hamlet, hear.' Then the Ghost tells about his sudden death, and how the whole ear of the kingdom has been abused, and then at last he says upon whom he would be revenged. If of anything, it is of Beethoven's modula-tion that we are here reminded. But there still comes a delayed cadence; the Ghost does not speak out the name without further ado; he says, ' Know, The ser-pent that did sting thy father's life Now wears his crown.' Then Hamlet speaks out that he had suspected it: ' O my prophetic soul!' And at last, uttering the name, asks: ' My uncle?' ' Ay,' then finally says the Ghost, and begins his story. The heightening of the interest by keeping back the word is a high stroke of art in Shakespeare. After all this preparation the word thus has the greatest effect possible. While a mere bald narration is avoided, the impression is all the more artistic. The Ghost might have told it all right off; Hamlet knows it from the apparition alone and the demand for revenge. But the delay of both, deferring the horror, brings the spectator into full sympathy with the scene, producing, before the utterance of the word, the same state of terror which is felt at the beginning of the piece. Won-drously versatile is the genius of Shakespeare in devising these preliminary steps; one must anatomize almost every scene in order to perceive how firmly they are all constructed. Thus is the tone (*Stimmung*) of the separate scenes struck, and the impression of each scene completely secured, and stamped into the heart and memory of the hearer, which, in the wealth of his pieces, is necessary; were it otherwise, the impression of one scene would obliterate that of the others. And thus also, in the most important scenes, a due proportion of power is possible. A piece of Shakespeare's is a continuous preparation for the catastrophe, and every separate scene has its minor catastrophe, for which the previous dialogue is the preparation.

EDUARD AND OTTO DEVRIENT (1873)

(*Deutscher Bühnen und Familien Shakespeare.* Leipzig, 1873. Introd. p. 7.)— When Q_I is candidly and thoroughly studied in the interest of stage effect, (and, according to its title, it has had the test of the stage,) it will show, amidst all the abbreviations, absurdities, garblings, and whatever other faults there may be, an abundance of marks, which, apart from the fact that they follow much more exactly the even course of the original novel, cause the effective representation of the action, as well as of the characters themselves, to appear more distinct and logical.

[Page 9.] Taking Hamlet to be in his minority [on the authority of Q_I,], we have the fact explained that, gifted with no mean understanding, he has not yet at the beginning of the piece, with all his diligence, completed his studies, but resolves to return immediately to Wittenberg.

Upon this supposition of the minority of Hamlet is explained also the murderous scheme conceived by his uncle Claudius. If he wished to gratify his ambition, it behooved him to lose no time. While Hamlet is still a minor, the death of his father raises to the throne the widow whom Claudius had already won before his brother was put out of the way. With the consent of the nobles, she chose her husband co-regent. Claudius is compelled by Hamlet's reversionary right to the throne, which is unquestioned, to educate the young philosopher for political life. Hence he opposes his return to Wittenberg, and keeps him nearest to himself as the first person of his court. The character of guardian in which he meets the prince, and the sullen obedience which Hamlet renders to his uncle, are clearly significant of the relations between the two. Hamlet, as a full-grown man, silently submitting to such reproofs as he receives in the first scene at court, must at the outset forfeit our respect, while as a youthful enthusiast, under age, he wins all our sympathy.

But all those facts which go to show Hamlet's unripe youth first derive their full force from his inner qualities: this all-embracing pain (*Weltschmerz*), this pessimism, which springs from idealism, this blazing up of quickly-excited passion, this irresolute endurance of evil treatment, this yearning for the superlative and overlooking the positive, this continual carping and wanting everything better, this self-esteem with constant self-disparagement, and all the thousand little things which betray youth and excuse it, all show Hamlet as a very young prince, most lovable, unripe, enthusiastic, upon whom is imposed a man's task.

[Page 13.] According to the arrangement of Q_I, Hamlet, helplessly dispirited, and turned, after the command of the Ghost is laid upon him, from the half-wish to escape the task by suicide, and excited by the plottings of the King more and more to the thirst for revenge, finds at last in the players the means whereby he is not only enabled to see that his despair is wrong, but to have his uncle at the same time in his power; thus the dramatic interest goes increasing on and on to the catastrophe of the third act. According to the common arrangement, the passion drives on, breaks off, drives on, breaks off again, in order to appear again at the climax. A perfect impossibility has resulted for the actor from this alternating fashion of the play, which deprives the rôle of its original life, Passion. And what demands upon the intelligence of the public does not the common text make! Polonius tells the King that the cause of Hamlet's madness is love for Ophelia: ' How may we try it further?' Ophelia is to meet Hamlet in the gallery, and be overheard by the King; Hamlet comes, but the plan is not carried out. On the contrary, Hamlet charges Polonius with being a pander. How does he get that idea, when Polonius has just forbidden his daughter to have anything to do with Hamlet? The two courtiers come; Hamlet receives them with bitter scorn, and knows what they are sent for. From what source? The players come; Hamlet wakes at last out of his lethargy,—only again to appear immediately, wishing to escape his task by death. The whole court, having to retire without any reason, comes back again without any reason, in order to do at last what it purposed to do at the beginning of the act. Then, after Hamlet expresses the most complete distrust of Ophelia, and has declared her father interested in their intimacy, comes a scene which begins with the fullest confessions of love.

[Page 15.] Furthermore the text of Q_1 presents the rôle of the weak-minded Queen in a much softer light than in the ordinary reading, where it is only sketched. Her over-indulgent love for her son outweighs her love for her seducer. She is shocked at the suspicion of the fratricide, protests her ignorance of the crime, and shows abhorrence of the King when she learns from Horatio of the plots against Hamlet's life. Her rude behavior to the King, and the suspicion that she is poisoned, to which she gives instant expression in the last scene of the fifth act, are first fully explained in Q_1. How much the character of the Queen gains hereby with the public, and as a part for an actress, is evident.

[Page 18.] That Horatio has not prepared the prince for the sudden death of Ophelia is explained in Q_1 by the simple fact that he was ignorant of it himself whereas the common version represents him as attending the crazed Ophelia.

[Page 19.] If finally the poet should be hypercritically censured for a want of care in regard to the external accompaniments of this drama, we reply that Shakespeare never, in any one of his dramas, introduced to his public a new subject, a new plot, and as he thus dealt with knbwn materials, he did not need to put them together so carefully as a modern dramatist does, who has to make the public acquainted with the subject which he selects, and which lies far out of their knowledge. While Goethe and Schiller complain in their correspondence that the German public (it was so even in their day) desired nothing on the stage but the objective gratification of their curiosity, Shakespeare wrote to a public that, with a true artistic devotion, listened only for a new treatment of well-known subjects, and like the classic public of the Greeks, exalted in his lifetime, above all the great poets, the master who was able to set forth, in the loftiest form of art, events that were real and living in the popular heart.

JULIAN SCHMIDT (1873)

(*Neue Bilder aus dem geistigen Leben unserer Zeit.* Leipzig, 1873, p. 25.)—I believe that a critic who thoroughly and with the *understanding* studies and analyzes this piece, if he goes to work honestly, must come at last to the conclusion that it is, indeed, admirably thought out and designed, and in single scenes brilliantly executed, but that the composition and structure do not by any means correspond with the first plan, and that the poet, even like his hero, loses his way. Even allowing the value of the retarding moments, caused by the given characters of the persons represented, the critic will, nevertheless, mark many single scenes (the Gravediggers, &c.) as superfluous and retarding. He will conclude that the whole, as it now stands, must be tedious and wearisome.

The only thing is, that facts by no means bear out this conclusion. The piece *ought* not to have a tragic effect, but it *actually has* a tragic effect in the highest sense, which were impossible if the effect depended only upon single scenes. The feeling of the world has continued for a long time to distinguish whether it has here a fragment or a whole, although of the Why and the Wherefore it has taken no account. Among all Shakespeare's pieces there is no other that for three hundred years, both on the stage and in the closet, has made so profound an impression, and so occupied the feelings and thoughts of men. A transient influence of this kind may be a matter of chance, but an influence of three hundred years' duration is a fact which must have substantial grounds. And, furthermore, this effect is not confined to the blind multitude, but the first minds of all nations have been the most deeply impressed by it, and I venture to affirm that even the faithful critic, who, with pencil in hand, finds something to explain in almost every scene,—an obscure passage here, a contradiction there,—will, if he will lay down his pencil for a moment, and give himself up freely to the piece, come under the same influence with all the rest of the world.

Hence the idea is suggested that the supernatural element in the piece is not to be explained by the understanding. For the understanding can in this respect go no further than Goethe has gone. To analyze is the business of the understanding only. The question then is: Cannot the supernatural element at least be made manifest? I will endeavor indirectly to show it.

Every one is acquainted with the representation of the *Midsummer-Night's Dream* as arranged by Tieck with Mendelssohn's music, which obtained so much applause, and so long held command of the stage. With the exception of the tableaux at the beginning and end, which form, as it were, the outer frame, Tieck compressed the piece into one stage-scene, which remained unchanged throughout: it is a wood, seen by moonlight, in which the three groups, the fairies, the lovers, and the blockheads, appear first on the one side, then on the other. Fantastic chords, in the spirit of this green, moonlight night, mark the various changes: it is like a fugue, in which now one and now another voice rises above the rest. The tones and colors gracefully harmonize, we yield ourselves, idly dreaming, to be borne along by the serene melody of the piece with all its varied movements.

This effect would not be produced by the music and scenery alone, but the piece in itself is expressed with a heightened sensuousness by the arrangement; before we were acquainted with the representation, by the mere reading of the piece, we had the feeling of a green moonlit night, and heard the songs of the fairies. What passes in this night is a bright dream; the mortals are under the charm of the fairies, of Puck, of the moonlight, of the woodland solitudes. They dream or are dreamed about, it matters not which. A strong passion has driven them into the enchanted wood; they have forgotten it, another has taken its place, to vanish again in like manner; it is a mad chase after the impossible, and the more crazed they are, the more confident is their consciousness of being infinitely wise. The fairies make merry over the feelings which are sacred to these silly mortals, but they too suffer under the power of Venus; their queen fancies herself in love with a boor, on whom an ass's head has been set, and this dream of love is expressed as vividly as if it were real.

Leave out the coloring and pervading air of the piece, and the comedy would make only an ordinary impression. Indeed, whoever requires Tieck's scenery, in order to be sensible of the color and atmosphere of the play,—to him the scenery would be no help. One can no more appreciate Shakespeare than Murillo or Rubens by the understanding alone. The harmonious intermingling of the coloring tones (*Farbentöne*) is as important in a work of art as the firmness of the drawing.

It is true the color in a work of art would be inadequate without an intellectual background. The *Midsummer-Night's Dream* has a symbolical character, which wholly prevents it from being reduced to homely commonplaces. In order to understand the fun of this piece, one must have in mind the curse which, after the death of Adonis, Venus pronounces upon Love:

> ' It shall be fickle, false, and full of fraud,
> *Bud and be blasted in a breathing-while:*
> The bottom poison, and the top o'er-straw'd
> With sweets, that shall the truest sight beguile;
> The strongest body shall it make most weak,
> Strike a wise dumb and teach the fool to speak.'

Shakespeare meant not to say that love was altogether this and nothing else, nothing but a dream as Demetrius and Lysander dreamt it; but he meant that it is this besides; all love is this, although not merely this. He did not mean that life is only a dream, but that life is also a dream; it is indispensable to a full understanding of life that we should understand that whatever else it is, it is a dream.

[Page 28.] To return to *Hamlet.* Taking our stand at a distance, and in thought letting the scenes of the tragedy pass in swift succession before us, we perceive that there is something else going on besides the particular fable. As distinctly as in the *Midsummer-Night's Dream,* we are made aware of a certain expressive coloring. Again it is night, but no friendly moonlit night, no trace of green, no color that hints at life. It is a cold, gray, weird night, overcast and darkly shaded. No wonder that ghosts appear; the place is made for them. No wonder that we linger so long in the churchyard; the whole earth is a churchyard. The skulls which the Clown throws out are the only realities that survive of the living world, and as to those who still live,—what is true? what is real? Again we hear melodies ringing, but brokenly,—fragments vainly seeking to unite, as the Clown, as the crazed Ophelia, takes them up. Hamlet appears as a highly gifted man, intellectually far above the others around him, delicately strung; and now, as his eyes are opened, what are his feelings? what his thoughts? He has cherished a strong and earnest love for Ophelia; it has vanished,—he can be rude, and rough even, to the once beloved; he understands himself as little as he understands the world. Is this only this Danish prince, whose head has been somewhat turned by German philosophy in Wittenberg, and whom his mother's infidelity, as well as the crime of his uncle, has rendered quite distraught? There is something more behind.

As in the *Midsummer-Night's Dream,* the love-witchery is not explained merely by the peculiar natures of Lysander and Demetrius, Helena and Hermia, so in this tragedy, while the character of Hamlet is indeed a very significant representative of the universal tone (*Weltstimmung*), yet this is not wholly expressed by him. Under the green surface of life deep abysses lie hidden, to which at times a cleft opens: it is the realm of death and madness. Even to the clearest and firmest mind come moments when consciousness and will seem but a vanishing appearance, a self-illusion, and chaos the only reality. Then has it a sharp eye for characters like Polonius, who passes with people for a shrewd man,—and, in fact, he is not so bad as recent commentators would fain make him out,—when Hamlet quizzes him, Hamlet casts contempt upon himself also; thus it is, he thinks, with the world universally. A miserable wretch like the King leads it by secret strings and to chastise such poor creatures,—can that be a worthy task for a thinking and feeling man? 'I have no pleasure in man,—or woman either.' The Gravedigger, who plays at loggats with skulls,—he is the only realist, and even death,—is it a reality? Is he not perhaps the dupe of dreams that lead to madness even in the Beyond?

There have arisen in Germany in recent times philosophers who have, in simple earnest, declared this to be the final result of all human wisdom. The idea in itself is not void. It is the dark background of life, which the philosopher has to rise above, and which the poet may represent. How an individual man, how Shakespeare, could feel in himself with such power and express all those deeper movements of the soul (*Seelenstimmungen*), which at times pass over life and rule it, this no one may well be able to explain, but the fact remains unshaken: the world of *Hamlet* is as little the poet's whole world as is the world of the *Midsummer-Night's Dream*, but it is a part, a moment of his world; he had times when that which Schopenhauer names *Nirwana* vibrated through him to the inmost. It was at such a moment that he produced the traditional fable of Hamlet, and fashioned it to the shape which we know. At a similar moment he created *Lear* and *Timon*, and it is because something of this demon slumbers in every human breast, that these tragedies of the world's pain have everywhere made so powerful an impression, although no one has been able to interpret it. Let *Hamlet* be analyzed from this standpoint, namely, that the poet wished to turn out and make visible, as it were, every side and shade of this precise form of feeling, and then the scenes which appear most refractory to the logic of the drama will be the most clearly understood.

The world of *Hamlet* is a dream as truly as that of the *Midsummer-Night*, but it is a horrible, tormenting dream. In both pieces Shakespeare concludes with the awaking. As in the latter, Theseus comes at the break of day, with his attendants, for the hunt, and with the shrill summons of the horn awakens the sleepers, so also at the close of *Hamlet* the fanfare sounds, the drums beat, and Fortinbras appears at the head of his army, the man of a new world, in the freshness of youth, vigorous and resolute, inaccessible to the ghostly visions of the world of dreams. The dead are buried, the good as well as the bad, the simpletons and the knaves, the earth closes over them, the cock really crows, and the earth ceases to be the theatre for masks.

WILHELM KOENIG (1873)

(*Shakespeare als Dichter, Weltweiser, und Christ.* Leipzig, 1873, p. 33.)—Especial emphasis should be laid upon the fact, that nowhere in any of his numerous speeches does Hamlet intimate that he feels himself restricted by any definite consideration, by any external hindrance, or any moral scruple, and whatsoever can be understood elsewhere in the play as implying the contrary is to be regarded as erroneous. We are thus compelled, in our search for this hindrance, to return ever and again to Hamlet himself and to his own powers.

DR RODERICH BENEDIX (1873)

(*Die Shakespearomanie.* Stuttgart, 1873, p. 274.)—All these ingenious theories
of numberless critics for solving the mystery of Hamlet's character are wholly
superfluous; the inexplicable mystery is simply due to Shakespeare's having fallen
into a couple of gross faults of composition.

These faults of composition furnish us with the key by which we may explain
this mysterious unintelligibility of Hamlet. Take out these, and his character is as
plain and simple as any other.

These faults are pre-eminently a series of unusual, superfluous episodes, which
have not the slightest influence on the action of the tragedy, nay, have scarcely any
connection, or none, with it, and which must be pronounced, without qualification,
faults.

There is, first, the despatch of an embassy to Norway, and its return. Neither
the purpose nor the result of this proceeding has the slightest interest for us. But
weeks, perhaps months, pass before the return, which we have to wait for, of this
embassy.

The second episode is the journey of Laertes to Paris, with which the third is
connected, the sending of Reynaldo after Laertes. All the long-winded instructions
given by Polonius to Laertes and to Reynaldo are wholly devoid of any dramatic
character; they have not the remotest relation to the action of the piece, and accordingly they leave us perfectly indifferent. Until the return of Laertes, months
must pass away. And this return we have also to wait for.

The fourth episode is the journey of Fortinbras through Denmark to Poland. As
this is not possible without ships, months must go by before he returns. And this
return also we have to wait for.

The fifth episode is the embarking of Hamlet for England, which comes in just
when the action promises to be lively, and is tending towards a conclusion. This
departure of Hamlet is flung, like a drag-chain, right around the action. And we
have to wait for Hamlet's return also. We thus see four persons travel away out
of the piece, and not till late do they come back again. These journeys are wholly
superfluous episodes.

They cause the time of the action to be extended through many months, and to
these episodes, and to them alone, is it due that Hamlet's slowness becomes such a
mystery. When Hamlet, most urgently summoned as he is to avenge his father's
death, wanders about for months without doing anything, it is indeed unintelligible,
and, to speak politely, mysterious and profound. But strike out those five episodes,
which have not the least connection with the essential action of the piece, and all
becomes clear and simple. The action then takes only a few days, and of Hamlet's
mysterious irresolution there is no trace. It is true he proceeds only hesitatingly,
but for this there are very good reasons. . . . . In order to do away with all doubt,
Hamlet gets up the play. He obtains certainty, and immediately sets to work, stabbing Polonius, whom he mistakes for the King. Where now is the irresolution?
The Ghost appears to him again, and now we look for him to proceed against the
King, whereupon the poet shoves in the journey to England, and creates a new
delay. The whole fourth act looks like an interpolation, introduced to make out
five acts.

[Page 278.] Shakespeare is inconsequent in the delineation of character, and in *Hamlet* more than anywhere else. This inconsequence often appears strange enough, but as people do not venture to pronounce their idol inconsequent, they call his inconsequence, profundity. But let me mention some instances.

There is, in the first place, Hamlet's behavior to Ophelia. He has truly, ardently loved the maiden, but in his feigned madness he treats her shamefully. Here the poet has allowed himself to make a blunder. In the story from which this drama is fashioned, there is an intriguing lady of the court who endeavors, at the instance of the King, to act the spy upon Hamlet. This person is probably the prototype of Ophelia. The poet has added the incident of Hamlet's being in love with Ophelia, and thus comes the false stroke in the drawing. Hamlet's behavior would have been perfectly justifiable towards that court lady, but it was not justifiable towards Ophelia.

The second false stroke is Hamlet's rage at the way in which the courtiers treat him. The *Shakespearomaniacs* have not failed to find this rage very fine, and to applaud the poet for the surpassing skill with which he has delineated the pitiable behavior of the court people. But how is it? Hamlet represents himself as crazy, and they treat him accordingly. They do not contradict him, they flatter him, give in to his wildest conceits. But does not every sensible person do the same when he has to deal with a madman? Who would excite an insane person, and drive him to acts of violence by contradiction?* This groundless rage is most fully spoken out when he has killed Polonius. . . . . So is it also with Laertes. He first appears before us as a true and noble knight. In his demand of vengeance for his murdered father, he is seen in the finest light. And yet this noble person enters into a plot to allow, in a sham fight, the point of his rapier to be secretly sharpened, and even poisons the point. Horrible baseness! Here is the greatest inconsequence in character-drawing that can possibly be. The delineation of character is certainly not the strong side of the piece. There is not a person in it, save Hamlet, who knows how to awaken in us any interest. The King is an unmitigated rascal, and we can find no passion in him that renders his rascality intelligible.

The Queen is one of the—well, least agreeable of women. Polonius, with his pedantic garrulity, is one of the prettiest figures that the poet has drawn. Only his verbosity is somewhat wearisome. Ophelia is a maiden not so very agreeable, but her madness has made the rôle a favorite one. In representing insanity, an actress can make use of all the tones which she has in her power; she can utter any trifles, and draw upon all the registers. Thus some impression may be made, and it is not particularly difficult. Horatio is a thoroughly agreeable, graceful person, one of the best of Shakespeare's characters. Here we have done. The remaining persons of the piece belong to the supernumeraries, and are mostly very dull rôles. In them the actor must be every inch an artist, if he would awaken in us the slightest interest.

[Page 282.] I will grant that the death of Polonius serves a dramatic purpose, inasmuch as it is the cause of Ophelia's madness, although it is not a sufficient cause. No girl ever becomes insane because her father dies, least of all Ophelia, whose relation to her father we know was rather formal, lacking all heartiness. Besides, insanity

---

* The writer is unconsciously showing how *well* Shakespeare delineates the people about Hamlet, and how *naturally* they treated him.—TRANS.

is a physical evil. If we are to believe that it is due to psychological causes, they must be very strong and manifest. We can see how Gretchen, in *Faust*, becomes insane upon psychological grounds; but not Ophelia. Yet granting that it is so, why, I ask, does she become crazy and die? She is wholly guiltless. I ask still further, why does Hamlet die? What conceivable guilt has he incurred? The *Shakespearomaniacs* say, indeed, his weakness of will, his irresolution, was his fault, and he atones for it by dying. Without regard to the fact that weakness of will is a quality and no sin, I have shown that this is not in the character of Hamlet. In letting Hamlet perish, Shakespeare departs from the story upon which he constructed his drama. In that story Hamlet is a bold, energetic man, who comes back victorious from England, conquers the king and his party, and gains the throne. It is from this deviation from the original legend that the uncertainty, the inconsequence in Hamlet's character comes. It is one half the good, substantial hero of the old story, and the other half the creation of the poet. Shakespeare was not perfect master of his materials. That he lets Hamlet die without any necessity is simply unintelligible. No, there is not a syllable of poetic justice here. Fortinbras says at the conclusion: 'O proud Death! What feast is toward,' &c. This is the solution of the riddle. A banquet for death it was, suited to the steeled nerves of a public delighting in blood.

Notwithstanding all I have said, there is still much good in the piece. But as the *Shakespearomaniacs* seek out the good, and even endeavor to turn the bad into good, I seek, on the contrary, to set forth the bad. Of the poor economy of time, of the inconsequence of the characters, of the tediously long episodes, I have now spoken. But, apart from all these, the piece is badly constructed. The Ghost appears twice in the first act. Why? Once were enough. It has to speak to Hamlet only, therefore the first appearance of it, as it is described at length in the second scene, is all the more superfluous.

[Page 284.] Hamlet appears with the actors, and delivers a long lecture to them upon the art of speaking and acting. In this lecture Shakespeare, at all events, sets forth his own principles in regard to the player's art. But does this belong to a deep tragedy? And these very respectable principles Shakespeare has, as a poet, by his bombast and verbosity directly contradicted, for these characteristics of his must needs produce the very manner of delivery which he blames. . . . .

In Act IV, the King and the Queen, Rosencrantz and Guildenstern, are on the stage. The Queen says at the beginning to the two latter: 'Bestow this place on us a little while,' whereupon they retire. After eight-and-twenty verses they are again called in, receive a commission, and go off again without speaking a word. This is clumsy. Are the actors puppets, drawn hither and thither by wires?

[Page 287.] The result of the fight between Hamlet and Laertes is brought about in the strangest manner. *In the heat of the fight* the combatants exchange weapons. Is this a conceivable possibility? When a man knows how to handle a weapon, he never in a fight lets it go. And had it been possible, would not Laertes have stopped the fight under one pretext or another, since he knew that the slightest wound from the poisoned rapier in the hand of Hamlet would be certain death?

[Page 288.] After Hamlet is dead, there are fifty more lines spoken; persons altogether unknown appear. I find this conclusion as clumsy as that of *Romeo and Juliet*. What do we care, after Hamlet's death, for Rosencrantz and Guildenstern? What, for English ambassadors? for Fortinbras? What is to us the succession to the throne in Denmark? We have concerned ourselves only with Hamlet. With his

death our interest is at an end, entirely at an end. We do not want to know anything more.

[Page 289.] It is true this drama has been a stock-piece on the German stage for
a century. Its influence is easily explained. In the first place, the subject of it is
very interesting. It had already been used by others before Shakespeare. In the
second place, the chief character is a rôle unusually telling. Hamlet feigns mad
ness, and so makes many striking and acute speeches, which are the chief charm of
the piece, and have always given especial pleasure. This part pleases all the more.
because the poet has so portrayed the other parts, the court people particularly, that
they furnish food for Hamlet's satire. Furthermore, the piece has considerable
dramatic effects. I reckon Hamlet's feigned madness among them, although it is
too much spun out; Ophelia's insanity, on the other hand, is a mere theatrical effect.
Such purely theatrical effects are numerous in the piece, and have always charmed
play-goers. Among these effects belong the three appearances of a ghost with the
necessary, imposing accidents, a play upon the stage, a churchyard with graves and
a burial, a fight and half a dozen corpses, and an abundance of fustian phrases
withal.

That it is not the piece itself particularly which impresses the public is evident
from the fact, that for several decades the play has been given in different places in
different shapes. Every one who has undertaken to alter the piece has picked out
such parts as he considered especially effective, and left out other portions. . . . .
The fact that a piece has admitted of so many alterations shows how very loosely it
is constructed.

[Page 290.] The tragic issue of a drama must be in the drama itself, in its essential necessity; there must be no other possible. *Richard III* and *Macbeth* must
needs end tragically,—a reconciliation is in them not possible. In *Hamlet* no tragic
issue is necessary.

KARL WERDER (1875)

(*Vorlesungen über Shakespeare's Hamlet.* Berlin, 1875, p. 32.)—The critics one
and all, (with two exceptions,) Goethe at their head, have taken up the idea that,
personally from the beginning, throughout the piece, Hamlet is at fault, on account
of some subjective deficiency, failing or ill-desert. Were he not unfortunately for
his work and for himself just what he happens to be,—had he been by nature fitted
for what he had to do, then all would instantly, from the outset, have taken another,
and indeed, according to its nature and its spirit, a more direct course. Thus *he* is
the obstacle: he it is, who, through his natural disposition, drags everything out of
place, and gets everything in confusion by giving it a direction wrong in itself and
ruinous to himself and others.

Now from all this I must, for my part, utterly dissent.

One thing, I deny, first of all, the one point upon which all the rest depends, and
with which it all stands or falls, this one point, namely, that it is possible for Hamlet
to dare to do what all the critics, notwithstanding their *nuances*, almost unanimously
require of him. Whether or not he were naturally capable of doing it is a question
altogether impertinent. For it simply was not *possible*, and this for reasons entirely
objective. The situation of things, the force of circumstances, the nature of his task,
directly forbid it, and so imperatively, that he was compelled to respect the prohibi-

tion, if he were to keep his reason; above all, his poetic and dramatic, aye, and his human, reason. The critics have been so absorbed in the study of his character, that the *task* imposed upon him has been lost sight of. Here is the fundamental mistake.

What is it they require of him?

Why, that he should assault the King immediately, directly,—make short work with him, nay, the shorter the better; such has been the loudest and most unanimous demand. He is not to feign to be crazy. He is to draw out, not his tablets, but his dagger; not to cry, 'Farewell! remember me!' but, 'Death to the murderer!' He is to go right in and slay the King at once. *That* he can do the very first time he catches sight of him, in the very next hour; the opportunity is always at hand; there is nothing easier than this procedure. But after the dagger-stroke, what then? Why, then he is to call the court and the people together, and justify his deed, and take possession of the throne which belonged to him alone. But how is he to go to work to justify his deed? By telling what the ghost of his father had communicated to him? One must have a strange idea of Hamlet's public, of the community before which he was to conduct his case, of the people and nobility of Denmark, if one supposes that the people are going to believe him, that they will suffer themselves to be convinced, by evidence of this sort, of the justice of his action.

The critics are pleased to assume that he was the born sovereign judge in the land, and the legitimate heir to the throne, his right to which had been wrested from him by a usurper. But where stands it so written? Not in Shakespeare! It is a pure fiction. Hamlet himself breathes not a syllable of complaint ['Who stole the diadem?' ED.] of any wrong that he had suffered. But of that wrong, if such wrong there were, had there been a usurpation, Hamlet must needs have spoken, and not only he, and not only Horatio, but the King and others also. The courtiers, for example, when they were seeking to explain his madness, would certainly have hit upon this as the cause of it. And in the very first scene of the piece, where matters of State are mentioned in connection with the appearance of the Ghost, this fact, if it existed, would not have gone unnoticed.

[Professor WERDER here goes on at some length to prove that none of Hamlet's rights to the throne were infringed, and, misled through the translation of 'imperial jointress,' by the German word *Erbin*, asserts that the Queen was the legitimate heiress and successor to the crown, and that the most that Hamlet could hope for would have been his election as co-regent. And in a footnote the learned Professor proposes the following astonishing parallel: 'Suppose Queen Elizabeth had had a son, thirty years of age, by a former marriage, and had then taken a second husband, it never would have occurred either to her or to her subjects that her son must be King, and that she must descend from the throne.' To an English student, anxious to admire German criticism, few things are more discouraging than to note how frequently it ignores the labors of English scholars. Had Professor WERDER looked into any good annotated English edition of *Hamlet*, he would have found that, nigh a hundred years ago, STEEVENS called attention to the fact that Denmark was an elective monarchy, and he would have found, also, that a great legal authority, Mr Justice BLACKSTONE, had disproved the supposition that Claudius was a usurper. I should not have called attention to this slip of Professor WERDER'S were it not that his volume on *Hamlet* is one of the most noteworthy that has appeared in Germany, although its main idea is to be found in KLEIN, and in several minor details he has been anticipated. Since the foregoing sentences were written, and while these pages are going through the press, the news reaches us of the death of KLEIN. His *History of the Drama* must unfortunately remain a fragment. In the thirteenth volume, just published, the course is traced of the *English Drama* down to the time of Shakespeare. Whatever may be the estimate, by those most competent to judge, of the preceding volumes, no one who has read the last but will regret the loss of remarks keen and original which we had a right to expect from a writer whose style is never drowsy. ED.]

[Page 38.] But the mass of the people! Would they believe the prince's story? Perhaps; but perhaps not. Hamlet then,—this, too, has been suggested,—if it seemed to him the thing to be done, instantly to fall upon the King, should have employed the time, which he wasted in pretending to be crazy, in winning over the people. How? He should have spread among them a report of the communication made by the Ghost. For this proceeding he should have made use of Horatio, Marcellus, and Bernardo; they, too, had seen the Ghost,—they could, indeed, swear to that. But if after that the common people should ask further about what the Ghost disclosed, there was no one but Hamlet to answer,—he alone had received the disclosure from the mouth of the Ghost. His friends can only swear that they had seen the Ghost, and heard a voice from under the earth admonishing them to take the oath which Hamlet desired of them, not to blab about what they had seen, except, of course, with Hamlet's consent. So the hope of gaining the people is very doubtful; for they must be supposed to have enough sense to say to themselves: Hamlet, the only one personally interested, is party and judge at the same time,—judge in his own cause. It is an absolute impossibility, if he kills the King, that upon his testimony alone, for no other existed, the people could have a conviction, or the shadow of a conviction, of the justice of his act.

And now as to the rest, the nobility, the court, the collective dignitaries of the realm,—would they not all have risen at once against Hamlet as the most shameful and impudent of liars and criminals, who, to gratify his own ambition, had, wholly without proof, charged another, the King, with the worst of crimes, that he might commit the same crime himself? A man who sought to possess himself of power after such a fashion, they are to be ready to acknowledge as their king,—a notorious regicide! The shame alone that he put upon them, in holding them to be such fools as to believe his story, must have stirred up their wrath against him. As a worthless wretch must he appear to them, murdering the King, and covering his victim at the same time with a charge most shameful and incapable of being proved. The least they could do in the case would be to pronounce him a madman, and put him in confinement and in chains.

[Page 39.] His own position Shakespeare's Hamlet understands very well, and accordingly takes better care of his fame than the critics, by *not* stabbing the King; had he done that, such heroism would have proved him a most egregious simpleton.

Even the ghost of his father understands the state of things better than the critics. He requires his son to avenge his murder, but he by no means requires it with their hot bloodthirstiness. He is in no such haste, and manner and time he leaves to his son: '*Howsoever* thou pursuest this act,' says he. That merely the thrust of a dagger will suffice, the Ghost does not intimate; the Ghost is quite too judicious for that. Even when he comes the second time, his visit is only to whet the blunted purpose; but he does not blame his son, nor read him a lecture because he has done nothing, as the critics would have it, nor does he make a crime of his delay, as they do. Only Hamlet himself does that.

[Page 40.] Kreyssig has said quite truly, ' that, according to our feeling, Hamlet could, without further circumstance, make short work with the King.' 'According to our feeling,'—oh, yes! But according to poetic principle?—oh, no! According to our feeling, certainly; for *we* know, indeed,—although not with full certainty till Act III,—that Claudius is the murderer of his brother, and that the prince is perfectly in the right. *We* are in the secret, *we* sit, as the public, in the council of the gods. But the Danes do not know it, and are never to be convinced of it if Hamlet slays the King, and then appeals for his vindication to a private communication which a ghost has made to him. They, the Danes, in the intricate case before them, will never get at the right and the wrong of it in the way in which the critics would have matters decided; but all depends entirely upon the Danes finding out that, and not upon the right and wrong, what ought to be done or left undone, ' according to our feeling.' This is the great difference between the public before and the public behind the curtain; between us who see the play and those who act therein. These stand in the first line, and we in the second. What is right and wrong, truth and justice among them and for them,—the judgment of the stage,—this is the law for us, and to the supremacy of this judgment ours must submit.

Denmark is Hamlet's objective world. If that condemns him, and it must in justice condemn him, because it is impossible for him to justify himself before that, should he commit the murder which the critical spectators demand of him, if before that world he must needs appear as a brutal ruffian, as the most impudent and barefaced of liars, or as a maniac,—then are his honor and reason, dramatically and humanly considered, gone forever, even though his friend Horatio believed in him ten times over.

But what now has Hamlet in truth to do? What is his real task?

A very sharply defined duty, but a duty very different from that which the critics impose upon him. Not to crush the King at once,—he could commit no greater blunder,—but to bring him to confession, to unmask, and convict him: this is his first, nearest, inevitable duty.

As things stand, truth and justice can be known only from one mouth, the mouth of the crowned criminal, or at least from the King's party, or they remain hidden and buried till the last day.

This is the point! Herein lie the terrors of this tragedy,—its enigmatical horror, its inexorable misery! The encoffined secresy of the *unprovable* crime: this is the subterranean spring, whence flows its power to awaken fear and sympathy.

That this point, so simple, so humanly natural, that when once seen it is forever present,—that this point for a century long should *never* have been seen, is the most incomprehensible thing that has ever happened in æsthetic criticism from the very beginning of its existence.

[Page 47.] What Hamlet has nearest at heart, after the Ghost appeared to him, is not the *death*, but, on the contrary, the *life*, of the King,—henceforth as dear to him as *his own life!* These two lives are the only means whereby his task is to be accomplished. Now that he knows the crime, now that he is to punish it, nothing could happen to him worse than that the King should die, unexposed, and so escape justice! . . . . If by killing the King on the spot, he only deprived him of the fruits of his crime, or if he lost his own life in so doing, or if the Danes had been so insane as to set him on the throne after he had murdered Claudius,—would that be, in the tragical sense, the true revenge? Wherein would there be any essential differ-ence between such an ending and the accident of the King's dying a natural death, and thereby being deprived of the fruit of his crime? To a tragical revenge there is necessary, punishment, to punishment justice, and to justice the vindication of it before the world. And, therefore, Hamlet's aim is not the crown, nor is it his first duty to kill the King; but his task is justly to punish the murderer of his father, unassailable as that murderer is in the eye of the world, and to satisfy the Danes of the righteousness of this procedure. This is the point.

[Page 58.] Can we hear this interview between Hamlet and his mother, hear it only once, and not be satisfied that it is the voice of truth itself that here speaks? or do we misunderstand it, as if it were a particular that need not be, or indeed a mere negative that ought not to be? For both persons, considering their respective position and their fate, it is the indispensable, all-essential scene that must needs take place between them! And yet here come the gentlemen critics, and talk of the part full of genius, and the tragic scene that Hamlet plays with his mother, like a comedian to show himself off! Good God! Must Shakespeare be forever fixed upon to write schoolboys' compositions about? I should think there were others enough for that purpose!

[Page 70. ' O, that this too too solid flesh would melt,' &c.] What Hamlet,—I cannot say, *has a presentiment of*, but nevertheless what is *in* him, dark, voiceless, but yet *there*, wholly undefined, but not to be banished, and inborn, as it were, in his nature,—he does not understand, can form no idea of it, but *he feels* it! The atmo-sphere of murder which he inhales, which breathes upon him from the person of the murderer, the shuddering sense of the Ghost hovering near, all that awaits him, all that stands ready at the door, all that his friends have brought to his knowledge, all that the Ghost has upon its lips to say to him; the terror, terrible as Past and as Future,—all that is for him *here* and is his: all this is *in* him! *This* is the burthen which oppresses him, the immovable weight which he does not yet understand, but which he feels! Hence the tone and coloring of this soliloquy.

[Page 77. ' My tables! meet it is I set it down,' &c.] These words are an *avis* of the poet, *but*, with a view to the fundamental point of his piece as I understand it, not to the character, but to the *situation* of his hero. Instead of telling us what Hamlet can do first, he lets him do what he first can, namely, bring out, expose to view the character of the King. This is the symbolic act by which he, the poet, shows us the way to understand Hamlet,—the pantomime which is to give us to see the difficulty of Hamlet's task. These words, jotted down, are the expression of that which is at the first possible and impossible to him,—and not only subjectively, but objectively,—the possible and impossible not only to him, but in and for them-selves, under the circumstances. He can at the first only take passing note of the King, only point him out to himself: ' So, uncle, there you are!'—beyond this nothing else, absolutely nothing! Upon the one side, a well-defended fortress, and without, a single man, who is to take it, he alone. So stands Hamlet confronting his task!

[Page 80.] But will it not, however, be thought that he literally writes down the phrase? Must it still be said,—what even the poorest actor in *Hamlet* would not misunderstand in this fashion? Hamlet pulls out his tablets, and jabs the point of his pencil once or twice into the leaf,—because he cannot do the same to the King with his sword, as he would like to,—nothing further,—only such marks, such a sign does he make. That stands for ' So, uncle, there you are!' And although he says he must write it down for himself, he does not literally write,—that does not accord with his mood and situation.

[Page 89.] As soon as Hamlet has heard what the Ghost tells him, and is alone by himself, his clear head instantly takes in the whole dire pass to which Truth and Right, hopelessly beyond all human power, have come. The imminent agony, aye, the shudder of certainty that must seize him as to the impossibility, as things stand, of solving the difficulty; (for, let the case only be considered, it is such a task as exceeds the power of a single individual, exceeds every effort and every sacrifice that he, upon whom it devolves, can from his own resources bring and apply;) the horror and the crime, coming so close to him; his murdered father's cry for revenge; the triumphant murderer, who, if the task can be achieved, is certainly not to be reached by force, and hardly by cunning, with scarcely a glimmer of hope of success, so sagacious and artful is he;—all this forms a condition of things so dark and dread, a dilemma of so terrible and monstrous a nature, that for a man involved in it to break through it alone by his own unaided strength,—this is, indeed, a task which may well cost him the loss of his understanding!

This feeling, this sense of the situation! and Shakespeare *has* considered the task with this feeling, and has given it to his hero, so that the spectators also shall have it, and shall not, *without* it, look upon the prince from the outset as a shuffling, crackbrained fellow, who seeks to humbug himself and us, in order to hide his lack of energy,—this, too, is again, thoroughly positive and not negative, not a blamable personal defect, but the monstrous, real, objective, trouble and dilemma;—this feeling, this natural, immediate feeling, is the *inmost* impulse to his purpose of putting ' an antic disposition on.' This instinctive motive is the first original motive. His action is the direct outcome of this his full sense of the situation.

Thus, upon a sound nature is laid what is fitted to destroy it! And, in fact, it does destroy it, *all except the mind*, all except the knowledge and freedom of the mind.

Because he knows that all in him of happiness and peace is already destroyed by the situation in which, perfectly innocently on his part, he is placed,—for even were he to fulfil his task, how shall he ever again be glad?—and because he knows *at the same time* that the demon of his task is ceaselessly menacing the last thing which is left to him unshattered, his mind, ever helplessly imperilled also,—because this entire, utter suffering has come upon him, nothing being left in him which is not affected by it, and because it *wholly* possesses him, therefore he can do nothing else but give expression to this his condition, and this, too, out of the inmost core of his nature, and out of the strength and fineness of his understanding! . . . .

That from which he *actually* suffers, the *truth* of his position, he manifests; he moves in the element which his fate has made for him, and within which *alone* all that he may undertake is henceforth to go on. Others see this fact, viz: his blighted being and his clear head; but they do not understand it. And they are not to understand it. The appearance, the *simple fact*, fills them; the inner being, the suffering of the inner nature, the agony and the conflict of the free, strong mind, they do not understand.

But,—and this is the second point,—that instinctive motive *instantly* makes itself influential in him as an advantage. So it becomes effective as *design*.

The behavior, for which, as a matter that may chance to be serviceable to him, he prepares his friends, and the connection of which with the appearance of the Ghost they were not to tattle about, *is* in fact of the greatest possible service to him. Do not our practical gentlemen see now *how* practical it is? They would certainly see it, if only they did not think that the true practical way is to cut the King down at once. For this behavior enables him at least to give some vent to what is raging within him, and what he would fain shriek out, while at the same time it leads atten tion away from the true cause of his trouble, away from his secret, and secures it.

To behave in his natural manner in the circle that surrounds him, after the change wrought in him by the communication made by the Ghost, that,—putting wholly out of sight whether he could have done so or not,—that would be of no service, a very bad rôle. Besides, by the behavior he adopts, he has no need any longer to show respect for those whom he despises—despises? ay, indeed!

And possibly also, if he is supposed to be crazy, he can, under this cover, should any favorable opportunity offer itself, make use of it for more active operations against the enemy than would be permitted to a sane man; play a more active game, be perhaps foolhardy, and in case of failure still keep room, under the protection of his supposed imbecility, for a new attack. This also may occur to his mind when he finds himself suddenly caught in the clutch of his terrible fate,—*may* occur! but it is not such an inducement as is certainly included in his thoughts. No matter of detail can he take account of at the first. That would require a plan, and a plan he neither has, nor can have. He does what he must,—takes the step which is directly before him,—does what alone is actually at hand, does it without any other reflection; does what he in his situation must feel is to be done, and what he must recognize as most advantageous to his cause. And therefore, in thus acting, his thought must be that it will lead him the most surely and faithfully through the night of his task. Of the *How*, of the manner and preliminary steps of the work before him, he cannot by any means have an idea.

The third point, finally, the main point for a right understanding of the piece, is this: that it cannot be said, without qualification, that Hamlet plays the madman. Such play, in the primary sense of the word, actually feigning, belongs to the mere novel, but not to him, not to Shakespeare's Hamlet! The *degree* of feigning, the *kind* of play,—that is the nice and grand point to be considered.

Here again we have to do with Shakespeare's chief strength as a poet, which is to re-mould a given subject, and give it a finer shape, the best in spirit and in truth. Thus here he takes the fable from Saxo's chronicle and the novel of Belleforest. There Amleth really pretends to be crazy; he crows like a cock, flaps his wings, jumps upon the mattress under which the listener is concealed, and stabs him, and then hacks him into pieces, which he cooks and throws to the swine. He is the fellow to strike his foe dead at once,—the very man the critics want; they stand with him on the same level,—he actually does all that they require of Hamlet.

But it is by no means that history which Shakespeare's work represents. He uses it, and makes something entirely different out of it. *His* criminal, through his apparently impregnable position, bears a charmed life, and his Danes are not Saxo's Jutes. The subject, the problem, in his hands has become wholly different, something much deeper than a mere act of revenge, and consequently the character of the prince is another thing.

As we said, the behavior of Hamlet, which is the most natural for him in his situation, and which springs directly from it, is also the most serviceable for the accomplishment of his work. To foresee that when he gives himself out as insane, others will so regard him; and to *desire* that they should do so, and therefore to sustain the delusion, which they put upon themselves, by conduct which should tend to strengthen it,—seems to him to amount to the same thing. Therefore, to *this* degree, which is relatively slight, he makes believe, he *plays* the madman. But because it is essentially his truth, the effect of his real suffering, of his shattered being, to which his mind, still ever free, gives vent so far as it *dare*, without betraying his secret,— because it is *his* torture, his rage, his cry of woe, his agony, thus outwardly expressed, thus fully and entirely become known: therefore this play of his is not *merely* feigning, and because not *merely*, therefore not feigning at all, in the strict sense of the word.

[Page 95.] How loosely does he wear his mask! How transparent is it! He is always showing his true face. Not himself, only his secret, is hidden. And therefore is his mask so soon used up. For so soon as the first opportunity offers for action,—and how soon it comes through the court-play!—the King knows his secret; that the madness was no real madness, the King must naturally have seen even earlier. From the beginning his evil conscience scented under this madness a design against himself. He applies to Hamlet's behavior, even before he had clandestinely listened to him, the same word that Hamlet himself uses, 'puts on,'— 'why he puts on this confusion.' After he listens, his suspicion is certainty; but now, after the play, he sees, also, out of what knowledge and to what ultimate end the madness has been feigned. Hamlet knows very well, at the point which he has reached, that the old method is worn out. A new one must be found. But, first, *his mother is to be enlightened, and her conscience appealed to.* This is *now*, after he has convinced himself of the guilt of the King, her husband, the most important thing, the *actually urgent* duty which lies nearest to him, nearer than killing the King! But this, in fact, seems to have escaped all observation, viz: the inexorable necessity, according to the meaning and character of the piece, of just this action. That Shakespeare lets this action be introduced by the agency of others, and not by Hamlet, by the interest of Polonius, as a part of his machination against the prince and the Queen,—this action, which is in itself for both of them the most imperative necessity; and that, moreover, not merely notwithstanding this external agency, but rather for the sake of it, the *impersonal* Power (the Ghost) intervenes, as the power instantaneously helping all forward: this it is that impresses this scene so powerfully with the stamp of that unequalled power of invention which characterizes the work, and makes this scene the centre and turning-point of the whole.

Here, here comes in a circumstance which changes everything. Hamlet kills Polonius. He must now submit to be sent away. Thus, as the opportunity to adopt some new method of proceeding is cut off, the old one, although somewhat worn out, must be continued, because it suits both the King and the prince; it suits the King to consider the prince as really insane, and so to get rid of him, and it suits the prince to continue his peculiar behavior, although more carelessly than before, and without taking any special pains to dissemble, even wearily, because he has given the death-stroke. . . . .

It may be said, however, that Hamlet feigns only so far as is necessary to make the others show themselves. The real feigning is, in fact, always on their part; they all pretend to be honest, and play false comedy. He tells them only his truth and their lies, and makes them tell their lies. The case of Amleth in the novel does not necessitate the feeling that it was a case to lose one's understanding about: therefore he pretends to be mad. Hamlet, on the contrary, has that feeling, and therefore is his feigning so transparent, unreal, after an ideal fashion. The gravity of his fate is ever far more to him than his solicitude about his mask. It is only by the way, and is soon played. . . . .

[Page 119.] Hamlet, I have said, chooses the *best* means to his end. Ay, in-deed! For the court-play, by the vividness and transparency with which it repre-sents the deed,—this, rather than any other conceivable thing, this surprise at finding himself confronted with his secret in the full light of the lamps of the theatre,—this, if he committed the crime, must bring the King to confession, although at first only to Hamlet's eye and satisfaction. How much is thus hereby gained! The first indispensable step towards the solution of his task is actually taken; now, in deed, he first *knows* his way. And that Hamlet knows without doubt that confession is the point upon which all depends is seen *here,*—here at the close of this soliloquy he speaks out the *word,* 'That guilty creatures sitting at a play, ... have *pro-claimed* their malefactions!' Confessed,—and on the spot: *herein* is the effectiveness of this mode of proceeding.

[Page 121.] II, ii, 576–598, is said to mean, forsooth, that thus far Hamlet has mistaken and blundered about the whole thing. Pray, have people no ears for the agony of a human being, which is so intolerable that it drives him to the extremity of falling out with himself, no appreciation of a situation in which righteous indigna-tion, because it cannot reach its object, turns against itself, in order to give itself vent and to cool the heated sense of the impossibility of acting by self-reproach and all manner of self-depreciation? Is it his *will* then to be a dull and muddy-mettled rascal, and peak like John-a-dreams, unpregnant of his cause? Does he condemn himself thereto out of cowardice, incapacity, morbid scrupulousness, weakness of will, and all such-like fine motives? Is he not rather *forced* to be so? Is he not doomed thereto? I thought I had shown plainly enough the iron grasp in which he is held. That he can *say* nothing for a king upon whose property and most dear life a damned defeat has been made: that is the very horror of his position,—to be forced to speak not a syllable directly and to the point; if he had chosen to do only that, most assuredly and instantly he would have lost the game. And the critics insist upon condemning *him,* because he knows that and declares it, and *does* nothing! The actor, *he* can talk of Priam's death and Hecuba's grief—talk of them so movingly! Had he *his* (Hamlet's) motive, *his* cue for passion, he would drown the stage with tears, and make mad the guilty, &c., because he, in the freedom of the actor, of the objective, can act! But Hamlet cannot do that, *he* can act no play, but a real thing, directly, out of his own consciousness, and must suffer wreck, because he can adduce no proof of its *reality!* He must be silent, he can operate only indirectly, by means of a reflected image, must let play-actors speak and act for him, and can himself only *look on* and *observe!* . . . .

And when he says further, 'it cannot be But I am pigeon-livered, and lack gall To make oppression bitter,' &c.; *this* also is an outbreak of his wrath at not being permitted to follow the first impulse, the immediate prompting of the thirst for re-venge. He is thus enraged, because his reason is so strong as to restrain him, and, because he restrains himself, he has to suffer such pain. To smite down the King, to sacrifice his own life by the blow, in order to be quit of his task at once, instead of fulfilling it, that were the first, the easiest, the happiest thing for him; but he *wills* to fulfil it, wills to *fulfil* it faithfully, and not shamefully avoid it. His gall does not affect his head, his *will* tames his heart, the gnashing hunger for revenge, the storm of the blood; and that is the agony that makes the blood boil, from that nature revolts, every fibre quivers in rebellion and anguish: *so strong* is the will in him, whom people would make out to be a weakling, that he endures this torture in the fear and virtue of his duty. What he rails at as 'pigeon-livered,' when the mortal nature, impatient of pain, weary of suffering, cries out in him,—all this is enduring courage, the courage of reason, springing from reverence for a holy duty and from devotion thereto.

[Page 154.] On his way to his mother, Hamlet finds the King at prayer,—the King, who *here for the first time* makes verbal confession before us that he is the murderer, while confessing the crime to himself in soliloquy. So far have Hamlet and the *poet* brought him, by means of the play. Here is progress in the rôle of the *King*, and, from the negative side, in the *piece!!* There is a depth or power of invention here which has not its like! The wisdom in the *rhythm of the development*,—this it is which, if I may speak for myself, moves me the most deeply! the *tempo* of the onward movement in the piece, how measured is its step,—the course it takes, appearing to drag, and yet chased by the storm of God, Heaven, and Hell thundering together!

[Page 156.] Now, after the court-play, Hamlet knows, indeed, that he is discovered. As *he* knows his enemy, so after this attack his enemy knows *him*, and will strain every nerve to destroy him, to get clear of the pursuer, the avenger. This Hamlet knows, and must be prepared for, must expect, and,—trust to his righteous cause. Just this it is which is his motive, his absolute motive! his only support! And if, to the result just arrived at, nothing further should come to advance his aim, nay, even if the remoter consequence should prove injurious and outweigh the present advantage, and cause all to come to nothing, it must not be he himself through whose action it comes to naught. That would be the case should he now stab the King. He can never, by his own testimony alone, complete his work if he silences the guilty one forever.

Hamlet, it is true, does not himself say this,—no! But the state of the case says it instead. Perhaps Shakespeare meant not to take from us entirely the idea of the possibility of his yet saying something himself; has meant,—and not perhaps, but certainly, meant,—that we shall learn it from the piece itself, that our *judgment* should give heed to his *plot*, as well as our *ear* to the *words* of his characters! How if the poet should reserve the explanation of his plot for some other one of his dramatis personæ, who is to come forward at the end of the piece? How if his prince is not to be our interpreter of the plot beforehand, but rather is himself to be included in it?—the general idea, hidden in him, in the individual and the concrete, in the movement and the passion, in the *disjecta membra*, which do not yet recognize their master?

[Page 157.] Is it thought to be a mere subterfuge of Hamlet's irresolution, that he considers the moment when the King is praying as not the favorable moment for him to die? a refinement of Hamlet's subtle theorizing about revenge, by which he imposes on himself; that the avenging sword must know a more horrid hent? Are the critics struck with blindness? It is, I insist, the purpose of the poet, *his* determination the whole piece through, *his* decree, *his* judgment,—the object in view, to show how he himself understands it, and wishes it understood! instead of a lie, it is the truth which he wishes to make manifest,—it is *his* wisdom, *his* understanding, *his* idea of justice, that we are to receive! With this design upon us, he builds up his piece. [See, ' When he is drunk asleep, or in his rage,' &c., III, iii, 89–95.] Well,—and how then does the King fall at last? He so falls that we see that every other way would be more lenient, would be ' hire and salary,' *not* vengeance! not the vengeance to which he is doomed. Not in a sudden fit does he fall, not while drunk asleep, not while gaming, or swearing, &c.; then his fate would have been all too easy; but, *in fact*, at a moment, and when in the very act of doing what puts him so utterly beyond all hope of salvation, that even from the threatening words of Hamlet, terrible as they are, we neither can nor should, when he utters them, anticipate the catastrophe! *we*, even as little as *Hamlet himself*, have no premonition of the result! The King falls in perpetrating a crime, even greater than his first, at the moment when he is committing a *threefold* murder,—rather than be betrayed he suffers even his own wife to drink the poison which he had prepared for Hamlet,—in this moment, utterly hopeless of salvation, he falls: so 'that his soul may be as damned and black As hell, whereto it goes.'

Thus the *poet* fulfils the words of Hamlet! Thus do they express *his* idea, Shakespeare's idea to the letter, of vengeance, of punishment, of judgment, in such a case as this, *his* way of dealing justice to *this* transgressor. . . . .

And it must not be forgotten that Hamlet it is who brings the King to this end. *He alone does it*, by his hits *and* by his misses, by the play *and* by the killing of Polonius.

[Page 161.] Enraged, frantic, he rushes in wildly to his mother, and here, hearing the voice behind the tapestry, *here, now* supposing the King to be hidden there, he allows himself to be carried away by his hot blood, by rage; here, in this place and in this still hour, close by the bed where he himself was begotten, and which shall by his will be no couch for luxury and damned incest; here, where the worst personal dishonor which has been inflicted upon him, the living son, by the seducer of his mother, comes so near to him; here, where the whole air is full of it; here, the voice of the wretch (he is thinking only of the King, and therefore believes that it is the King whom he has heard), the voice of the wretch calls up all his shame, and, forgetting the strict obligation of his task, he gives full course to his thirst for vengeance (after the proof he has had by means of the play, he is, of course, morally free to kill the King), he is carried away into the grave error of plunging his sword through the tapestry. A grave error, indeed! For *here* his moral right and power are not at all concerned.

This is the *turning-point* of the piece, which includes in itself the second cardinal moment for the understanding of the whole. The first, that which I call the fundamental point, is the *conditio sine quâ non*, that guards the treasure, which can be exhumed only with the help and by the power of the second. . . . .

Only with this second point do we get an insight into the *tragic depth* of the piece, into the plot. To understand this turning-point is to understand Hamlet.

Something new is here before us, something surprising, for which we were not prepared. Hamlet commits an error! *And this error is Hamlet!*

But from now on, all hinges on this error, and only of this error shall we have to speak.

That Hamlet stabs at the tapestry is no proof forsooth that he was a coward, and would not have ventured the act face to face with the enemy (even this silliness has been suggested!); but it is the expression and the act of his blind passion. Without stopping to consider whether he hit or miss, he stabs, like lightning, blindly into the dark (the tapestry corresponding to the veil within, in which the storm of his blood wraps his reason for the moment); he looks neither to the right nor left,— only hears, and falsely! the foe without, and hears wrongly his own thirst for vengeance within, and is deaf to his duty.

He *has* made the thrust at last,—and what is the consequence? What has he accomplished? He has committed a murder! Instead of being freed from the old burthen, he has brought upon his soul a new one; instead of accomplishing what he is bound to do, he has become guilty. Thus the error punishes itself.

'But,' say the critics, ' if he had only slain the King before, which would have been no crime, he would have saved himself from this real crime now. *That* was his error, and for that error he commits this,—for *that* he is punished by *this !*' By no means! For then he would have committed a far greater error. Now there lies upon his soul a crime, a death-blow,—but an undesigned blow, more an unfortunate than a guilty act,—but, in the other case, had he killed the King, he would, indeed, have kept himself pure, morally pure, but his duty, the one great object or aim of his being, he would have ruined, shattered into atoms, and his father would have remained forever unavenged. It is for this, for this, his cause, he becomes a criminal; so wild, so narrow and precipitous, so fatal is the path in which his destined task urges him, that he has become a murderer in its service, because for once he has not kept in the course which it prescribed, because for once he has forgotten his true work. But he has not rendered himself wholly incapable of fulfilling its behests. He is still able to serve his cause, and is held in reserve.

Therefore is the opinion which GERVINUS expresses so false: 'This failure of vengeance must now compel him most powerfully to act at last in earnest.' Just the reverse is true. If anything could occur to bring him to his senses, to impress upon him the necessity of checking the pace of his task, it is this failure, this *mis-thrust*, precisely this! Instead of Polonius, had it been the King whom he had stabbed, what would he not have brought upon himself! What a disgraceful, wretched, irretrievable blow would he have struck! Fearfully near has he come, out of blind rage, to ruining his whole cause, ruining it in the most shameful and blundering manner. Accident alone, so to speak, has saved him. This consideration above all things must be brought home to him by the serious mistake which he has made, with overpowering and humiliating irony, warning him and bidding him beware how he comes any nearer to so fatal an end; more pressingly and emphatically than ever must he feel himself obliged to proceed gently, with redoubled foresight, with still more marked 'procrastination'; he must, in fact, proceed so carefully that he must feel himself, with a shudder, driven to a stand-still, since he has suffered himself by a senseless burst of passion to stumble over the abyss to which he had rolled down, driven to a full pause from the shock in his own mind, even though he perceives no circumstances forcing him thereto.

And yet forward all goes with him, rapidly forward! And therefore is the idea, that the error, which he has committed, must alone move him to fall at once upon the King, doubly wrong and false.

And thus he quietly submits,—as, indeed, he must,—to be sent off to England; still more passively than ever does he bear himself; ay, verily, he has become timid. He has, by a blunder, almost lost the game; has played into the hands of his opponent! He must begin anew, and from a worse position than before. The guilt of bloodshed lies upon him, which his madness, now become so transparent, does not conceal. In the eye of the world he is a dangerous character, to be confined, and watched, and kept from doing harm. In the power of the King is he! But the enemy, this he sees, will not aim directly at his life. He is to be got rid of by *cunning*. 'Hide fox, and all after,'—this is the game which is now offered him. His head may well be trusted to accept the game, against the heads of his opponents. The enemy means to attack him with snares and pitfalls, and *he* must try for his part to delve a yard below their mines.

[Page 172. 'How all occasions do inform against me,' &c., IV, iv, 32.] Weary is Hamlet, weary under his burden. Now, when he is shipped off to England, the charge of murder resting on him through his own fault,—comparing *his* lot, chained as he is to his task, with that of Fortinbras, who is so free in all his movements,—now comes the fear,—now at this passing moment, which puts him at a distance, and separates him from his foe and from the object and aim of his revenge, through *his* own fault,—now comes nearer to him than ever the fearful apprehension that, notwithstanding all his trouble, all his patient endurance, his task has at last become impossible. This horrible dread penetrates him to the quick, and weighs down his soul. Would it not be better to strike the blow at once, and ruin his cause, sacrifice it, become a traitor to it, than still to go on hoping and waiting, and yet not succeed after all, not *be able* to succeed, because success is impossible, because he himself, to all appearances, has already in part rendered it so by his bungling, and because no *help* comes to him *from above?* How,—considering the character of his task, which is unapproachable, not to be got at,—how he is to satisfy the *reason* of the thing, he cannot conceive, but he can at least content his blood, should he strike the decisive blow. And how it shrieks in his ear, how it surges over his soul! This horrible doubt, which is a very different thing from the cowardly complaining temper which is ascribed to him,—this horrible doubt, which has for its background the remorse which he feels for the error he has made, and which turns doubt into despair, the doubt whether he shall throw all the dictates of reason to the winds,— this is the demon that rules this soliloquy, and runs wild therein; and therefore I have said it is the shriek of Hamlet's agony which here relieves itself. And while he raves with this demon, and endures tortures, *his cause is already ripening towards its accomplishment!* ay, already is it as good as fulfilled, without any suspicion on his part or on ours, *through his error!*

[Page 176.] I should only like to know what they who criticise Hamlet would have done in his place? All intolerable torture does he endure for his cause, in order to accomplish it thoroughly and worthily. On his *life* depends the possibility of its success, the revelation of divine justice upon earth in this capital case. And now he is led to death! As surely as Rosencrantz and Guildenstern deliver their letter, his head falls. *That* letter, then, they *must not be allowed* to deliver, they *must* deliver a different one. That is clear, absolutely clear. If Hamlet suffers them to deliver that, he may well, with the strictest truth, say of himself, ' O what an ass am I!' But, do you say, he could have spared them? He could have written something that would endanger neither him nor them? Does he know, or can he discover from them so that he may depend upon their word, how far they are cognizant of the purport of their errand? whether they are not charged with some oral message? What if they should contradict what he might write of a harmless character? What if the king of England, being in doubt, should send back to Denmark for further directions, detain all three, and then, as surely was to be expected, put Hamlet to death? No, there is no expedient possible, no evasion, no choice between *thus* or otherwise, *no, not here, nor at any point in the whole destined course of Hamlet!* Just this is again the point upon which a right understanding of the piece depends! Rosencrantz and Guildenstern,—or he! Those two,—or that which weighs more with him the man himself, that which is most sacred to him, for which he endures a life full of torture; not for a moment does any but the one possible course lie between. He *must* sacrifice them, *and* even without allowing them time to confess,—*must* do this even! For if only they are allowed time for confession, after they are seized and made sensible of their position, there is no foreseeing what turn things may take for him;* any, the very least pause, the most insignificant delay, may have for its consequence an embassy to Denmark for instructions, and it might be thus, even if Rosencrantz and Guildenstern were disposed of, and only their confession, if it contained anything compromising the prince, came to the ears of the English king. We may pity Hamlet, then, for this act, if we will, but we must take care how we blame him.

[Page 179.] But are they guilty to a degree 'worthy of death?' This question need not be pressed. It is not at all necessary. They have done what puts them in peril of death, an act fatally thoughtless, such an act as may only too easily expose to death any one who commits it,—that is sufficient, amply sufficient. That the letter which they are to deliver contains nothing of advantage to Hamlet; that the journey is not for *his* welfare: so much it is certain, beyond all doubt; that Rosencrantz and Guildenstern knew. All that can be said in their vindication is that they may have believed that Hamlet, the assassin, deserved nothing good; it *cannot be said in their behalf* that their duty as subjects required them to render to the King the desired service, for this is not the motive which the poet represents them as determined by. Their willingness to do the business was the consequence of their nature, of their sort of character. . . . . Whoever, from his position, or from his zeal and officiousness, or whatever it may be, undertakes the office of carrying the letter and Hamlet to England must suffer whatever of harm to himself may be connected with such an errand. The business is dangerous; such affairs always are; here are 'the fell incensed points of mighty opposites,'—it has been made clear enough through the court-play what a conflict has been here enkindled; and if Rosencrantz and Guildenstern do not see or fear it, the fault is in their short-sightedness, or their levity; but they are only short-sighted and light-minded because they have minds and eyes only for the favor and gratitude of the King,—*such a King!* Because, out of the littleness of their nature, they court that, their baseness is their ruin; they promenade, so to speak, in the sphere of a fate which involves damnation, without scenting or wishing to scent the sulphur; instead of fleeing from it, they plunge into the baleful atmosphere as into their native element! And, only because of this same fate, Hamlet is compelled to sacrifice them; to this fate, and not to Hamlet, who is only its instrument, they fall victims. Where such a king bears rule, his servants are always exposed to the very worst that can befall, and, as is self-evident, at any moment their ruin may come through circumstances and causes, from which nothing may seem more remote than the catastrophe; for the main thing is overlooked, because it is *always* present, even the *ground* on which all concerned live and move, upon which all rests, and which is itself Destruction. Whoever serves such a king, and, without any misgiving of his crime, serves him with ready zeal; upon him Hell has a claim, and if that claim be made good, he has no right to complain. That he does not observe the seriousness and the peril of his position avails nothing, for of such a peril men ought to take note.

These are things in which Shakespeare knows no jesting, because he is so great an expounder of the Law, the Divine Law, and he holds to it as no second poet has done.

[Page 185.] But that stab through the tapestry,—as the death of Polonius was the disastrous consequence of that grave error, so also was the destruction of Rosen-

---

* Does not the letter of the King give him an example of such foresight?

crantz and Guildenstern. *Therefore*, on account of that error into which he allowed himself to fall, the original plot of the King is changed; *therefore*, instead of the commission to demand the arrears of tribute, the death-sentence of Hamlet is sent to England; *therefore*, Hamlet has to work against it, as he actually does; *therefore*, after an accident has rendered his counter-plotting useless, and made it impossible for him to nullify it, these two fall. *Therefore*, also, he falls himself. For that one error, which has, also, for its consequence, the madness of Ophelia, the poet lets him atone *with his life!* But not, I doubt, for the blood of these gentlemen; he has very little of that upon him, for that flows on the King's account, and serves to fill up *his* measure; but Hamlet atones for the offence committed against his cause, which can now be crowned with success only by *his blood's* being shed for it.

And now one question more in conclusion.

Why do not Rosencrantz and Guildenstern sail back to Denmark, after Hamlet has escaped from them? To take him to England is the purpose of their journey. To deliver the letter without *him*, what is the use of that? The same chance that favors Hamlet's return they might take advantage of also, yes, and they would do so if they knew what threatens them. What have the critics thought about this, or rather have they thought about it at all?

Their *fate* does not suffer Rosencrantz and Guildenstern to turn back,—the fate that, on account of their connection with *the King*, has them as well as him in its clutch, and drives them to their death.

From their quality, their nature, their habit, from their way of thinking, they keep on to England: from their servility and officiousness. For fear of being thought stupid, they do not desire to show themselves after the miscarriage of their errand; the *written* commission with which they are charged is a royal one, that they must deliver, they must discharge their function as ambassadors to a tributary court. All this one can imagine as passing through their minds; but the chief motive that governs them is yet another, one which is originated not in themselves, but for which their employer has given occasion. On this account, above all, they pursue their way, viz: because they *do not know* what is in the letter which the King has entrusted to them; therefore they have no choice; they *must* deliver it, because they are not initiated into the business. That is evident from their continuing on their voyage. Had they been made acquainted with the real object of their mission, they would not, perhaps (the King must at least have foreseen this possibility), have delivered the letter. Therefore he left them in the dark. *He* is thus accountable for their death, immediately so; because, designedly kept in ignorance by him, it is possible for them to conclude that, besides what relates to the prince, the letter makes mention of other matters,—there had been talk about demanding tribute,— which they are bound to attend to. The substituted letter does, indeed, cause their death, but only because the royal letter takes them to England, and because, after the escape of the prince, it could do so only by the writer's having kept them in ignorance of its contents, in order to make sure of their pliability. At the door of *this* writer, then, they must in truth lay their destruction.

[Page 230.] In what tragedy (I do not believe the very poorest could be guilty of such stupidity), in what tragedy, I ask, does there occur the assassination of the guilty, without proving their guilt for the truth of the piece and the satisfaction of the persons concerned?

But it is the difficulty of producing this evidence, this proof, the apparent impossibility of convicting the guilty person, that constitutes the cardinal point in *Hamlet!* And therefore killing the King *before* the proof is adduced would be, not killing the guilty, but killing the *proof;* it would be, not the murder of the criminal, but the murder of Justice! It would be Truth that would be struck dead, through such an annihilation of its only means of triumph; the tragic action would degenerate into the action of mere brutes; a strange, outrageous, brutal blow across the clear eyes of the understanding, would be this senseless stroke,—for which the critics are so importunate!

[Page 232.] It has been objected that the action of the tragedy pauses in the fourth act and in the beginning of the fifth; but it is precisely *here* that we find the *tragic* and *dramatic element.* For when Hamlet is made inactive, then *the King acts!* and thereby maintains himself as that which, for the sense and economy of the drama, he is, namely, *the second person in the piece.* *He* now seizes the offensive, the fatal rôle, so propitious for the avenger, and decisive of the result. The assailant has well nigh paralyzed himself; the first movement comes to a rest; at this rest the second movement takes fire and is kindled,—the second movement, no less important than the first, which unfolds the peculiar action of the criminal,—wherefore, the fourth act belongs to the King,—and it is these two movements of the persons, interchanging one with the other, which constitute the *action of the piece,* and which are united and concluded in each other, the persons making these movements neither understanding nor controlling the action.

This is the '*main action!*' To look for it, as SCHLEGEL does, only in what Hamlet does, proves that he had no understanding of the piece, and that he supposed that it must be here as it is elsewhere; *quod non!*

[Page 234.] Through Hamlet's action, fatal to himself, his cause is ripe for the final act. Hamlet is needed no more to conduct it. Only for the execution of the judgement is he to be further used: his arm and his life; only these are still required;—no longer is there need of his mind, his wit, his patience;—Another, who never errs, has stepped into his place and released him. He has *reached* the goal,—though he himself knows it not!

Hence the mood in which he appears in the churchyard, his repose, the tone of a man who has done all he can and has nothing more to do, the disgust at the finite nature of things, the melancholy, and sickening sense of mortality, which fill him. This feeling it is which finds expression in his meditation upon the skull, in his retorts, in his horribly witty, bitter-sweet talk. With this feeling he follows Alexander's dust until it stops a bunghole.

[Page 237.] And what are the circumstances by which the criminal is lured forth to judgement, and by which the higher Helper, in the form of accident, assists the avenger, and carries him forward, without his being able to see how surely and quickly the end is attained? By the players coming to Elsinore,—by the pirates meeting Hamlet, and conveying him back to Denmark,—and, above all, by the accident of Polonius's falling by his hand!—*that is the decisive thing! That* gives to Hamlet's cause the victory! To the Indian the gods are recognizable by their eyes, which never wink; thus out of this accident looks the eye of the goal,—the pure light of the Solution,—undazzled, without shadow, sure, eternally firm, not an eyelid quivering.

The *miss* that Hamlet makes, that it is which *hits;* but,—because it is his *miss,*—not *his* hit, but the hit of Fate! That is the secretest point in his fate-guided course, the most secret, the most completely hidden from him; that is the bright point in the *invention* of Shakespeare, and the turning-point of the piece, the thing *inwardly accomplished*, but only made visible outwardly in the *catastrophe.*

This blind death of Polonius is the death of *all; but* it also unmasks the criminal! Through that thrust, by which Hamlet in blind passion *tries* to hit the King and does *not* hit him; by this thrust the King *is* really hit! But *only* because Hamlet has *not* in downright reality hit him, is he *in truth* hit,—*so* hit that the *truth comes to light!* On this account, it is true, Hamlet himself falls,—but his task is fulfilled. . . . .

By the death of Polonius, Hamlet stirs up against himself a vengeance similar to that which he has to inflict; but *only similar*,—it has no righteous claim to his life, —and since, nevertheless, it is fulfilled, and he *suffers* death therefrom, it assists him to *do* what he is bound to do.

And it thus assists him : because the criminal whom he is to punish avails himself of it, and directs it, in order to secure *himself* and destroy *Hamlet.* . . . .

Such is the wonderful combination here before us. Hamlet stands involved in the Cause: *he* cannot choose his plan, for *it* strides on before him. And *this* it is that is described as 'the hero's having no plan!' *This* is the *positive* content of that negative proposition. He suffers himself to be led; for that, he is intelligent and passive enough,—passive in the large sense that he understands the difficulty of his task, understands in fear and agony; and thus he goes straight to the mark,— straight into the heart of the crime. And by no means *slowly !* This preposterous idea, that he goes slowly, has come to be a settled notion, only from the silly desire that he should slay the King right off. *The piece knows of no delay.** It drives ahead in storm! The fulfilment, the judgement,—and the death also of the King, come even quicker than Hamlet and we can foresee. With one stroke all is fulfilled,—in overwhelming surprise!

Now *may* Hamlet strike the King down, now at last when *he* himself is dying; now may he hearken to his blood when his blood is flowing! And now his thrust cannot injure the Cause; it seals and fulfils it. But never till now, only in *this* last moment, when Laertes and the Queen also have fallen.

And this is what is considered a needless blood-bath! Justice and her poet know better what blood she demands in expiation, and who is her debtor.

Indeed, even now the King makes no confession; even Death opens his mouth only for a lie, not for the confession of the truth; but his own confession is *no longer* indispensable. Laertes confesses for him, and the corpse of the Queen and the blood of the prince, all these victims proclaim aloud the murderer to all the world; now also Ophelia, and Polonius, and Rosencrantz, and Guildenstern, testify against him! All these dead now form the chorus to the solo of the Ghost; and when Horatio comes forward as the reporter to tell Hamlet's story, and to explain his cause to the unsatisfied, he will produce in all his hearers the conviction which he himself has and which we have, and the story which the Grave tells will be an unquestionable truth for the world,—now, when Hamlet himself exists no more or earth, and is no more a party to the scene.

When the piece is thus understood,—its foundation, its progress, its aim,—when the purpose of the action and its method,—when its meaning is thus conceived, *then*

---

* Let it only be considered how short the time occupied is : from the beginning of the second act, *only a few days !* This escapes notice, because the contents of the piece are so rich and deep, the subject so great, and the task of Hamlet so hard, and his suffering so intense. This interior infiniteness it is which makes it appear as if the process lasted long.

those significant passages ring out with the power of a refrain, with the clear tone of a catchword : ' Our wills and fates do so contrary run,' and ' That our devices still are overthrown,'—' Our indiscretion sometimes serves us well, When our deep plots do pall.'

HERMAN GRIMM (1875)

(*Hamlet.* Preussische Jahrbücher, April, 1875, p. 386.)—The labors which have, up to this time, been bestowed upon the play of *Hamlet*, so far as they are known to me, have had this in common, that they treat Hamlet as a self-included individual, whose nature is to be studied in connection with his actual life, even outside of what is represented on the stage. As Goethe's homunculus owes his origin to the creative effort of a bungler, who distilled an impossible individual from the noblest ingredients, Hamlet, on the other hand, represents the perfectly successful experiment. Shakespeare has introduced into the world a real human being, a sort of supplement to the divine Creation, for nowhere as yet has there been found a being run in the same mould with this Hamlet. There he is, living and moving. He is answerable for himself. He and his fellow-players are summoned directly before his judges. Whoever in this drama passes over the stage, and speaks only a couple of words, is regarded as one who knows, and is interrogated accordingly. Every one of these persons has, for the commentators, a life of his own, and an opinion of his own in regard to Hamlet, which must be brought out and elucidated. We thus have a view of an extended process, in which the various witnesses are of greater or less weight in the judgement of the different critics. Rosencrantz and Guildenstern, for example, are by some esteemed to be very important persons, whose secret is to be discovered, and whose final destruction is a very serious matter. Every critic constitutes himself presiding judge in an ideal court of justice, endeavoring according to his best conscience to examine and to render a righteous judgment.

But the truth is, the ships which were to take Hamlet to England sailed only in Shakespeare's imagination, and the echoes around Elsinore have never really answered back the thunders of the cannon, with which King Claudius accompanied his carousals. And the heavy trouble which oppressed Hamlet has, in truth, never moved any human heart, unless it were the heart of the playwright, Shakespeare, who, when he brought out Hamlet and the other *dramatis personæ* on the stage, knew, just as precisely as in his other dramas, what he was to represent and what his players were to represent. Shakespeare certainly knew his audience to the last fibre. The poor Danish prince appeared to him,—not in a night, as the ghost of his father appeared on the terrace to the prince himself,—whispered the secret of his sufferings in Shakespeare's ear, and made him his poetical historiographer and testamentary executor. But Shakespeare, from elements, of which no one will ever have any knowledge, gathered the stuff for the figure of Hamlet, began to model it, worked it out more and more fully, in hours, in nights, in days, of which again no one can ever know, and at last the work stood living there, just as he willed it. We conjecture not how this process went on. Goethe, here and there, has communicated to us how it went with his own labors; his work as a whole stood plainly before him from the very first; but afterwards, for ten years through, at long intervals, additional particulars were suggested, to be wrought into the work not without arduous and repeated labors. Shakespeare has not disclosed anything on this point. We know nothing of the way in which he worked. But we may conclude, not only from his other dramas, but also from the peculiar nature of the work of writing for the stage, that the poet looked very carefully to all the effects to be produced, and that, before this piece was brought out, his players received from him the most minute instructions. And for this reason his work contains contradictions which seem irreconcilable, but which are not accidental; Shakespeare *intended* that they should be there, and put them purposely into the scene. The poet knew how all hung together. It is not to be supposed that Shakespeare stood amazed at last before his own creation, as if it contained mysteries to which he himself possessed no key. To him the economy of the plot was entirely familiar. He knew the places where he was to allow things to be acted out visibly, and where they were only to be narrated. He knew how the action was to be gradually evolved, and he calculated what would be the immediate impression upon the spectator. He knew, also, that his public were not prepared with book in hand to call him to account, for his dramas were arranged not to be read, but to be acted directly on the stage. And therefore the best way to arrive at an understanding of the piece seems to be, to inquire, step by step, what Shakespeare intended in his *Hamlet,* how the situation of affairs, as seen on the stage, must have fashioned itself to the public.

[Herr GRIMM here traces the tragedy as it unfolds itself, scene by scene, before the spectator, and shows how surprises occur at every turn; nothing is to be guessed beforehand. At one time we are convinced that Hamlet is going to act with vigor, the next moment we are sure that he is insane, then again he appears most sane, and so on, first one way and then the other, until we give up conjectures and resign ourselves to Shakespeare's lead, content to await the result in his good time. ED.]

[Page 391.] Had Shakespeare wished us to perceive that Hamlet was playing the madman for the first time in his interview with Ophelia, as described by her to Polonius, he would, somehow or other, have given us a hint of it. When Shakespeare's characters have plots, upon the knowledge of which the understanding of the piece depends, he does not leave us a moment in doubt. Claudius lets us know in the most open-hearted manner what he thinks of himself, as well as his villainous plans to get Hamlet out of the way. From Ophelia's relation every spectator must feel that Hamlet acted thus strangely towards her from deep depression of spirits, not because he wished to give Ophelia the idea that he had lost his wits. But this view of things is immediately set aside by the poet himself; for in the following scene Polonius persuades the King and Queen that Hamlet has become crazed from his love to Ophelia. That this absurdity is an error, every spectator knows, and this better knowledge is so far productive, that our opinion, without our needing to know in what way it happens, must again turn in favor of Hamlet. Hamlet is, therefore, not yet insane,—he has his plans; the King and Queen are already aware of it!

People really reflect so little in the theatre. What has just passed is scarcely remembered, yet judgement is pronounced upon what is directly before their eyes; the public depends upon what it sees, and is so engrossed with that, that it is led without thought into the greatest violations of logic. To consider Hamlet insane, then again immediately to believe that it is mere feigning, and then to return to the first impression, and to continue changing thus backwards and forwards, is nothing that a poet like Shakespeare might not count upon in a susceptible public. He commands, and his audience follow him obediently like children, to whom he tells a story, making them laugh and cry by turns.

[Page 395.] The design of the poet is less, we think, to unfold the plot of the drama in due form than to prepare for us the highest enjoyment by the exhibition of a rare, and, intellectually, a highly gifted man. Hamlet deserves no reproaches, only study. But he is doomed. For when a man thus philosophizes, his energies become so corroded by excess of thought, that he lacks strength for action even under the simplest and most favorable circumstances.

And thus, independently of the crime of Hamlet's parents, of the appearance of the Ghost, and of Hamlet's plans of revenge, from quite another side the impression upon the mind of the spectator is renewed, that this figure is simply the embodiment of a spirit doomed to destruction from the first.

Surely it was the design of the poet to confirm this faith. Hamlet's dialogue with Ophelia, as well as his behavior during the court-play, are of that foolish, nay, repulsive, character, that we give up the idea of determining whether it were caused by real or pretended folly. Why make such cynical remarks to a maiden that he loves?

[Page 398.] In the fifth act the final effects are realized. Hamlet again appears. He philosophizes in the churchyard. We know that beforehand. Over Yorick's skull he forgets himself and the world around him. In a house on fire, instead of saving himself, he would have been absorbed in scientific observations upon the flames consuming the wood-work; in a sinking ship he would have calculated the time it would take in going down. The public have long before given up every hope of a favorable turn in outward circumstances, as well as every hope of such a character as this. King, Queen, Fortinbras, might all lie there dead, and Hamlet be called to be king; but, instead of mounting the steps to the throne, he would philosophize upon a fly buzzing about the golden circlet on his brows. It is true Fortinbras, at the conclusion of the piece, says that if Hamlet had ascended the throne, he would have reigned royally, but these verses belong as a last trump in that category of intended contradictions, by which the poet designed to render a final, decisive judgement impossible. In the mind of the spectator, since no decision between madness and sanity is to be permitted, there has been created a certainty, comprehending the one as well as the other, and supporting both possibilities, viz: ruined! A sorrowful riddle, that was not to be solved.

It is this riddle that the poet intended to present before his public. Thus was his task fulfilled. He had shown, symbolically, a process observed with especial frequency in England: first, over-excitement of the brain, then distrust, whether the mental equilibrium be preserved, next, diversion of this distrust to the surroundings; then come waiting, watching, violent means employed to ward off mischief; dissolution; and, at last, for survivors the feeling of a sad problem, of which the decisive final solution will never be found. Hamlet's fate concerns every one, because every man feels thankful that Fate has not placed him in the situation in which he is required to resort to the last, extreme, uncertain resources of his spiritual strength. Every one who goes deeply into the questions of his own spiritual existence must feel that he is wandering on the brink of the abyss into which Hamlet plunged; and how many are there who have not, once in their lives, looked down into that abyss with a shudder?

In no other piece has Shakespeare employed in such measure all the means of his art. The earlier acts are among the most powerful in all dramatic literature. The epic *ductus* of the last two must not be considered as a defect. We find the same mode of composition in his other dramas.

[Page 400.] A drama requires a crisis. A number of figures, every one of whom is recognizable as representative of one, or of several, of our human, spiritual forces, are, by a decree emanating from the upper powers, set one against another. A conflict arises, to be fought out to a decision. The public is satisfied when every single figure is absolutely qualified for the conflict, and when their several modes of action correspond at every moment to our highest demands.

These figures can have but little that is peculiar and individual; they are, as it were, principles clothed in human forms. What they do and suffer is far beyond anything which the spectator himself has ever been in a situation to experience. Antigone, Creon, Œdipus, &c., reveal to us the life of a soul, whose concentrated simplicity lies outside of all particular human experience. Without this simplicity the inexorably logical structure of a tragedy would not be possible; in a tragedy, as in a mathematical example, all must accord.

To produce dramas of this kind was to the Greeks, and, among modern nations, to the French, a necessity. The poets of these nations were in a position to produce such ideal conflicts with abstractions in human shape, and their audiences were inspired thereby. To the Germanic races, on the other hand, it is in general wholly impossible, when human beings are poetically represented, to fashion them otherwise than in the semblance of individuals. The spectator wants to see in the drama, not anything transcending his experience, but he requires that his experience shall furnish the measure for what he sees before his eyes on the stage; figures must appear, the very first condition of whose existence is, that they are human beings like ourselves; characters, individuals, although, it may be, in peculiar circumstances. We regard the ideal forms of Grecian art as more individual than the Grecian poets and sculptors themselves conceived of them. Not the simple, but the complex, is what we demand and understand.

But such figures, when they engage in conflict, do not bring about the catastrophe of their collective development in a single battle; they must carry on long wars, with alternations of fortune. And these wars are to be occasioned by some exciting problem, hurled down among them by a higher hand: a necessary revenge, an irresistible temptation (as in Macbeth), a fearful incitement to arrogance (as in Coriolanus), a political inducement to deadly ingratitude (as in Brutus); but the matter is not brought to an end by a single outbreak of the first cause of the conflict. In continued contest only does the character begin to unfold, and this unfolding the Germanic spectator requires to see before his eyes. The Greek was able to show it only in the epos. The development of Achilles step by step is the subject of the noblest epic poem which has ever been composed. Shakespeare, the only true Germanic man, who has labored as poet for a healthy national stage, sought to meet this want, and devised the union of the drama and the epos, which accomplished his purpose. Wherever he really makes the development of an extraordinary individuality the theme of his tragedy, he begins by giving us in the first three acts the urgent cause of the first great conflict, in which the character of his hero reveals, as it were, the deepest fundamental elements of his being; in the fourth and fifth acts the slow unfolding of the contest, to the fall of the one or the other of the parties, or to the destruction of both, is virtually only narrated, although put in the form of scenes dramatically constructed. To the dramas already mentioned, in which this is exemplified, we may add *Timon of Athens, Lear*, and *Richard III*. Of the imitators of Shakespeare, Goethe alone, in his *Goetz* and *Egmont*, has adopted this method, paying tribute in both pieces, as he himself says, to the great master.

[Page 402.] In the first three acts, Shakespeare lets the tragedy represent what

Goethe recognized as the inmost nature of Hamlet; but this was only the point at which he began. The prince falls into a vacillating condition not always to be distinguished from insanity,—the art consists in keeping the spectator in doubt whether it is the finest policy or mere folly that he sees before him. In the fourth and fifth acts the course of the piece is dramatically arranged; the character has passed the full bloom of its development, and is going to decay. Hamlet has received such a terrible shock that he is spiritually wasting away. The clockwork of his spirit, instead of counting twenty-four hours to the day, runs to ninety-six or more, and when occasionally, in this wild career, the hands point for a second to the true time, this correctness works only the more tragically. In the same way we see the arrogance of Coriolanus, the extreme political honesty of Brutus, the brutal ambition of Macbeth, Timon's grand liberality, becoming in each a consuming fire, which slowly turns to ashes the souls of these royally endowed characters. With them all, however, the reckoning at the end yields a clear sum-total. We have nothing more to ask of the poet that he has failed to let us know. His heroes take away with them no secret which was necessary to an understanding of their conduct. But Hamlet is an exception, and the poet intended he should be so. To the end and beyond, the spectator is to repeat the vain attempt to unite opposites, for which no union is possible. A complete contradiction has been embodied in Hamlet, and 'a perfect contradiction remains alike mysterious to the wise and to the foolish.' So surely as it is proved that such was the intention, so surely will this tragedy, as a work of art, forever have its effect, and, by the will of the poet, appear a riddle.

DR HEINRICH WOELFFEL (1853)*

(*Ueber Shakespeare's Hamlet.* Album des lit. Vereins. Nürnberg, 1853, p. 62.) —Dr Woelffel pronounces this the *tragedy of the moral ideal,* and believes that the critics of it have not given sufficient prominence to Hamlet's love for Ophelia. Her failure to respond to Hamlet's love in all its depth and ardor is the turning-point of the tragedy. When Hamlet, in the presence of the Ghost, does not set his life at a pin's fee, it is because, just before he came to watch for the Ghost, Ophelia has refused him admission to her presence, and has returned his letters unread (pp. 79, 80). Hamlet's revenge cannot be put in execution until he tests Ophelia's love for him,—if her love prove genuine, his faith in human nature is restored, and he can advance to his revenge. Ophelia does not stand the test, and the sigh that escapes from Hamlet does in truth shatter all his bulk.

Hamlet is not surprised that a company of children have forced the actors to travel; where his uncle reigns, sound taste must needs be perverted, and men prefer the false to the true.

Hamlet quietly submits to be sent to England, because he intends to enlist sympathy and an army there, and return to overthrow the usurper.

A CLERGYMAN (1864)

In the Evangelische Kirchen-Zeitung, Berlin, May, 1864, appeared a series of criticisms on *Hamlet* by A Clergyman, in which the tragedy is strongly recom-

---

* This, and the following criticism from the *Evangelical Church Gazette,* I obtained too late to insert in their chronological order. ED.

mended to all German pastors as a most improving study,—one that will enlarge their views of human life, freshen their minds, and aid them to the better discharge of their clerical duties, by supplying them with deep lessons of the Christian sanctity of marriage, of sin, of repentance, of judgement, and of grace. What though 'a sinner may have written the tragedy, a saint may learn from it.' An analysis is given of each act and scene, and all are shown to have been written in the interest of the loftiest Christian morality.

FREILIGRATH *

(Airil, 1844)

Yes, Germany is Hamlet! Lo!
   Upon her ramparts every night
There stalks in silence, grim and slow,
   Her buried Freedom's steel-clad sprite,
Beck'ning the warders watching there,
   And to the shrinking doubter saying:
'They've dropt fell poison in mine ear,
   Draw thou the sword! no more delaying!'

He listens, and his blood runs cold;
   The horrid truth, at length laid bare,
Drives him to be the avenger bold,—
   But will he ever really dare?
He ponders, dreams, but at his need
   No counsel comes, firm purpose granting,
Still for the prompt, courageous deed
   The prompt, courageous soul is wanting.

It comes from loitering overmuch,
   Lounging, and reading,—tired to death;
Sloth holds him in its iron clutch,
   He's grown too 'fat and scant of breath.'
His learning gives him little aid,
   His boldest act is only thinking;
Too long in Wittenberg he stayed
   Attending lectures,—may be, drinking.

---

* This translation, which it does not 'beseem me to praise, and which needs no praise of mine, was made for this edition by my sister, Mrs A. L. WISTER. ED

And so his resolution fails,
　Madness he feigns, thus gaining time.
Soliloquises too, and rails,
　Ana curses 'time' and 'spite' in rhyme.
A pantomime must help him, too,
　And when he does fight, somewhat later,
Why, then, Polonius Kotzebue
　Receives the stab, and not the traitor.

So he endures, thus dreamily,
　With secret self-contempt, his pain:
He lets them send him o'er the sea,
　And, sharp in speech, comes home again;
Jeers right and left,—his hints are dark,—
　Talks of a 'king of shreds and patches,'
But for a deed? God save the mark!
　No deed from all his talk he hatches.

At last he gets the courage lacked,
　He grasps the sword to keep his vow,—
But ah! 'tis in the final Act,
　And only serves to lay him low.
With those his hate has overcome,
　Scourging at last their black demerits,
He dies,—and then with tuck of drum
　Comes Fortinbras, and all inherits.

Thank God! we've not yet come to this,
　The first four Acts have been played through
See, lest the parallel there is
　Be in the Fifth Act borne out too.
Early and late we hope, we pray:
　O hero, come,—no more delaying,—
Gird up your loins, act while you may,
　The spectre's solemn call obeying.

Oh, seize the moment, strike to-day,
　There still is time,—fulfil your part
Ere with his poison'd rapier's play
　A French Laertes find your heart.

Let not a Northern army clutch
  Your rightful heritage beforehand.
Beware! And yet I doubt me much
  If next the foe will come from Norland

Resolve, and put fresh courage on!
  Enter the lists, make good your boast!
Think on the oath that you have sworn;
  Avenge, avenge your father's ghost!
Why thus for ever dilly-dally?
  Yet,—dare I scold?—a poor old dreamer,—
I'm, after all, 'a piece of thee,'
  Thou ever-loitering, lingering schemer'

PROF. DR KARL ELZE (1865)

(*Essays on Shakespeare. Hamlet in France*, 1865. Trans. by L. DORA SCHMITZ, London, 1874, p. 193.)—It is generally supposed that Voltaire first introduced Shakespeare into France; at least he has boasted loudly enough that this immortal service,—to his countrymen or to Shakespeare?—is due to him. If, however, Mons. de Voltaire be cross-examined, as has been done in Germany, particularly in Al. Schmidt's excellent treatise,* the popular proverb; 'Much cry and little wool,' will be found applicable to his case. Long before Voltaire's time we meet in France with various traces pointing to Shakespeare, and they might probably be multiplied by a careful searching of the Imperial Library at Paris. It may suffice to mention Cyrano de Bergerac's tragedy of *Agrippina*, in which reflections and even turns of language from *Cymbeline, The Merchant of Venice*, and *Hamlet* are to be found.†

This much in the mean time is correct, that it is only since Voltaire, and for the most part through him, that the general attention of the French literary world has been directed to England, and that since then the French drama, which during the seventeenth century had borrowed its material and suggestions from the Spanish, commenced to turn its attention to Shakespeare. Since that time there has arisen an intellectual struggle for conquest, in which the English have gradually acquired larger possessions in the domain of the French mind than they once actually possessed in the 'fair land of France.' What they have once been forced to surrender to the Maid of Orleans, Shakespeare has re-conquered for them in a higher sphere.

It is a curious fact that in this struggle *Hamlet*, the very play the subject of which came to England from, or at least through, France, is always found in the vanguard.

---

* Al. Schmidt, *Voltaire's Verdienst um die Einführung Shakespeare's in Frankreich*, 1864.

† According to Lacroix, *Histoire de l'Influence de Shakespeare sur le Théâtre Français*, 346, Rathery in the *Revue Contemporaine*, and Baron in the *Athenæum Français* (1855), have proved this in detail. Shakespeare seems to have been known, and perhaps even acted, at Paris as early as 1604. See *The Athenæum*, 1865, I, 96; *Notes and Queries*, 1865, No. 174, p. 335.

Whenever Shakespeare s spoken of, he is styled the author of *Hamlet, Hamlet* being to a certain extent regarded as the embodiment not only of Shakespeare, but of the English drama in general.

Whenever, in France, we meet with an investigation into the nature of Shakespeare's poetry, a criticism of its beauties or of its barbarous irregularities, it is always *Hamlet* from which the discussion proceeds, or to which it leads in the end. *Hamlet* has been, so to speak, the pioneer destined to break the ground for English taste in France, as well as elsewhere. The same, it is well known, was the case in Germany.* Doubtless, this historical part which *Hamlet* has had to play is by no means accidental. *Hamlet*, more than any other play, reveals the specific Germanic mind, which sets itself the task of solving the deepest problems of all existence. In no other of Shakespeare's plays do we see such a struggle to get at an understanding of the world and life, and for this very reason it lays hold of all minds with a mysterious force which charms them within its own magic circle. In English poetry in general, and especially in Shakespeare, characterization is the principal object, whereas in the French classic drama abstract generality predominates over concrete individuality. In no one of all Shakespeare's plays is this individuality so emphatically brought forward as in *Hamlet*, where the whole tragic conflict centres in it. In this respect *Hamlet* forms the culminating point of Shakespeare's poetry, and the most prominent representative of that Germanic element which is penetrating into France. Thus, *Hamlet* appears as the sharpest contrast to the classic drama of the French. In the latter, discreet moderation was considered as a fundamental law, whereas *Hamlet*, resisting every classification, exercised the attractive power of the Inscrutable and the Incommensurable; in substance as well as in form it was incomprehensible, and opposed to the French mind as one pole to the other. Instead of action, which, since Aristotle, has been considered the substance of every legitimate drama, non-action was here made the subject of tragedy. In regard to form, *Hamlet* was the very play that gave the greatest offence to the classic taste of the French, although from the very first they could not be insensible to some of its striking and overpowering beauties.

Nowhere were the sacred rules so trampled upon as here; nowhere were the three unities violated in so revolting a manner; nowhere did the subordinate personages taken from among the people,—who on the French stage were scarcely permitted to appear as dummies,—play such important and talkative parts as here; and nowhere were courtly manners more thoughtlessly disregarded. Nay, the French feeling of propriety is not even yet quite reconciled with the notorious *fossoyeurs*, great as is the change which has since taken place in the literary taste and criticism of the French.† In a word, the prevailing influence of *Hamlet* in France seems to us to rest principally upon the mysterious charm of contrast, as well as upon the charm of the Non-comprehended and the apparently Incomprehensible. It is said of the rattlesnake that it fascinates with its glance the birds which it has selected for its prey; in much the same manner *Hamlet* has fascinated the most eminent minds of the French nation, till step by step it has penetrated into wider and wider circles, and won them for itself.

At the time when Voltaire wielded the sceptre of the French Parnassus, the classical literature of the French resembled a garden laid out with hedges of yew, flower

---

* *Hamlet* is also the first of Shakespeare's plays which have been translated into Welsh.
† Lacroix.

parterres, statues, and basins, according to the strictest rules of Lenôtre. It was Voltaire who brought into the garden a pailful of the waters of English, especially of Shakespeare's, poetry, which were rushing past outside in the wilderness. He did this partially as a warning to his countrymen, to show them how wild and muddy this water was. *Hamlet* was uppermost in the pail. The wild water,—without Voltaire's either knowing or wishing it,—began to bubble as if by some magic power; it burst the pail, overflowed the marble basin, gradually formed a separate bed for itself, and refreshed the lawn and flower-beds in an almost marvellous manner. Shrubs, hedges, and avenues began to sprout and shoot forth so exuberantly that the scissors could no longer keep them in trim; enough, the wild water will not come to rest till it has transformed the stiff French garden into a natural and luxuriant English park.

[Page 251.] Voltaire, the representative of the French mind in the eighteenth century, threw dirt upon Shakespeare; Victor Hugo, a representative of the French mind in the nineteenth century, idolises him,—both in an equally senseless manner. The migration, however, has not yet come to an end, but is vigorously proceeding. . . . . Through *Hamlet* the Germanic mind has penetrated into French literature, which has already begun to modify its character. The influence is, however, a mutual one; the Germanic mind is already no longer like Hamlet, any more than the French mind is its opposite. . . . . In the way of mutual intermixing the French learn how to think like Germans, and the Germans how to enjoy themselves and to act like the Romance nations. May the mixture ever be a prosperous one, and may it result in genuine Corinthian metal!

[The foregoing extract from Dr ELZE's Essay, I have not put in its chronological sequence, but have reserved it to the last, that it may serve as the connecting link between the *German* and the *French Criticisms*, and as forming somewhat of an introduction to the latter. The volume of *Essays*, of which this *Hamlet in France* is one. is a highly valuable contribution to Shakespearian literature. ED.]

FRENCH CRITICISMS

VOLTAIRE (1768)

(*Theatre Complet*, ii, 201. Geneve, 1768.)—Englishmen believe in ghosts no more than the Romans did, yet they take pleasure in the tragedy of *Hamlet*, in which the ghost of a king appears on the stage. Far be it from me to justify every-thing in that tragedy; it is a vulgar and barbarous drama, which would not be tole-rated by the vilest populace of France, or Italy. Hamlet becomes crazy in the second act, and his mistress becomes crazy in the third; the prince slays the father of his mistress under the pretence of killing a rat, and the heroine throws herself into the river; a grave is dug on the stage, and the grave-diggers talk quodlibets worthy of themselves, while holding skulls in their hands; Hamlet responds to their nasty vulgarities in sillinesses no less disgusting. In the meanwhile another of the actors conquers Poland. Hamlet, his mother, and his father-in-law carouse on the stage; songs are sung at table; there is quarrelling, fighting, killing,—one would imagine this piece to be the work of a drunken savage. But amidst all these vulgar irregularities, which to this day make the English drama so absurd and so barbarous, there are to be found in *Hamlet*, by a *bizarrerie* still greater, some sublime passages, worthy of the greatest genius. It seems as though nature had mingled in the brain of Shakespeare the greatest conceivable strength and grandeur with whatsoever wit-less vulgarity can devise that is lowest and most detestable.

It must be confessed that, amid the beauties which sparkle through this horrible extravagance, the ghost of Hamlet's father has a most striking theatrical effect. It always has a great effect upon the English,—I mean upon those who are the most highly educated, and who see most clearly all the irregularity of their old drama.

VISCOUNT DE CHATEAUBRIAND (1837)

(*Sketches of English Literature*, &c. London, 1837, second edition, vol. II, p. 274.)—*Hamlet*: this tragedy of maniacs, this *Royal Bedlam*, in which every cha-racter is either crazy or criminal, in which feigned madness is added to real madness, and in which the grave itself furnishes the stage with the skull of a fool; in this Odeon of shadows and spectres, where we hear nothing but reveries, the challenge of sentinels, the screeching of the night-bird, and the roaring of the sea,—Gertrude thus relates the death of Ophelia, &c.

381

[Page 279.] To read Shakespeare from beginning to end is to fulfil a pious but wearisome duty to departed genius.

[Our estimate of the value of this criticism is lessened when we find its author asserting, as he does on p. 313, that Hamlet speaks of Yorick as of a woman, because Hamlet says: 'Here hung those lips that I have kissed I know not how oft!' CHA- TEAUBRIAND (whom on this occasion it seems scarcely disrespectful to call, after CHARLES LAMB, 'CHATTY BRYANT') adds: 'Hamlet speaks of Yorick as Margaret of Scotland did of Alan Chartier.' ED.]

PROF. PHILARÈTE CHASLES (1867)

(*Études Contemporaines.* Paris, 1867, p. 93.)—The Greek theatre has nothing analogous to this terrible dreamer, Hamlet! Follow him from his entrance on the scene; he is, says Shakespeare, very negligent in his dress; his 'stockings down gyved to his ancle,' and his doublet all unbraced; he dreams, waits, rests. The moment to act has not come, let him mourn and meditate; later he will act, be as sured, and when the hour shall strike, all scruples will disappear, blood will cover the path where you will see him march. There are two forces in him, and these two forces are in conflict: first, Passion which excites him to vengeance, which boils even to delirium, which fills his veins with feverish and tumultuous blood, which tears him from sleep, and makes him wander frenzied among the tombs of the dead; next, Thought which tortures him and stirs him to his inmost depths, phantom-thought, pale spectre (*the pale cast of thought*), which interposes itself in the moment of the catastrophe, which holds back his arm, and paralyzes action (*sicklied over*). He has to punish the murderer, and he will not hesitate; life is nothing to him; but he is a philosopher also, and he demands the solution of these problems, the answer of these enigmas: 'Why so many crimes? Why is Evil?—Why is Life?'

Such is the question; as he well says: *that is the question;* the question by which Pascal and St Augustin, by which the disciples of Jansen and of Buddha, have found themselves affronted. By a combination, the highest perhaps, or at least the most complex that the human mind has realized on the stage, this meditative person is a hero; this barbarian has studied at Wittenberg; this man who contrives nothing is a mystic. Such is the double Hamlet.

[Page 97.] Polonius! one of the most curious god-sends of the stage,—the petri faction of morality, the monument of commonplace, sententious drivel, discipline of sterility, the passion of formalism, the echo of ancient wisdom, the bit and the bridle upon a courser that does not go, the treasury of gabbling aphorisms, the sublime of stupidity! Polonius is not the little, old, dried-up graybeard that they would represent him to be. He is solemn, he speaks slowly, he steps squarely. He is dignified, he is official, he is sure of himself. The good Shakespeare had a pro-phetic idea of our M. Prudhomme, who is nothing but a *bourgeois* Polonius. For this beautiful invention alone I should be tempted to adore Shakespeare. Some of Molière's ideas appear in the insipid personages, Guildenstern, and Rosencrantz, and Osric, mannikin men, nullities of the court, instruments *de salon*, otherwise amiable, greatly resembling the *petit marquis* and pretty viscounts of Molière,—those of the *Misanthrope*, for example.

[Page 101.] *Hamlet*, which has never been fitly and perfectly played and never will be and never can be, *Hamlet* the intranslatable, *Hamlet* that twenty volumes of notes scarcely elucidate,—*Hamlet* is Shakespeare, as the *Misanthrope* is Molière.

There is in the work of every man of genius some special production which reproduces the distinct impress, and the inmost depth, of his thinking. Such is the *Misanthrope*, such is *Candide;* works of love, which are not always the most complete nor the most irreproachable, but the most personal. Racine reveals himself in *Bérénice* with less of grandeur and elegance, but with a more touching ingenuousness, than in *Athalie*. For those who are weary of the formula of art, there is always a great charm in these personal creations, which are the very cry and profound accent of the superior man, nay, his most secret inspiration.

PROF. A. MÉZIÈRES (1860)

(*Shakespeare, ses Œuvres et ses Critiques.* Deuxième édition, Paris, 1865, p. 317.) —The tragedy of *Hamlet,* which of all pieces, ancient and modern, has been most studied and commented upon, issued almost entirely from the brain of the poet. In his other dramas he follows the text of an Italian novel, or of some legend, with as much fidelity as if he were preparing an historical document. Here he found only a bare canvas, whereon there is no sign of Laertes nor of Ophelia. There were already, as is known, two *Hamlets* before that of Shakespeare,—one appeared in 1587, interlarded with sentences after the fashion of Seneca, the other in 1594; but it does not appear that the poet took anything from them for his work.

Evidently what attracted Shakespeare in this subject is the character, already marked out, of Hamlet. He seized this occasion to pour into a single rôle the philosophical ideas and the irony with which his own soul was filled; he draws with pleasure the portrait of this young man so irresolute, so sombre, so unhappy, but at the same time so generous and so tender; he retouched his work three several times, and every time added something to the soliloquies of Hamlet and to the conversations of the prince with Horatio.

The characters of Shakespeare are not drawn solely with a view to the dramatic action, for the heroes, whom he puts on the stage, do not concentrate upon it all their force, nor give it their whole attention. While, upon our theatre, the personages are presented only in their connection with the drama, upon the English stage they exhibit themselves in all the extent and complexity of their sentiments. They have an independent existence; they live outside of the tragedy. No character serves better to illustrate this than that of Hamlet. The prince of Denmark requires no events to drive him to think and to suffer. The evil which consumes him does not proceed from the circumstances in which he finds himself placed; whatever had been his fortune, he would have been filled with disgust at life and contempt for terrestrial joys. Before he had learned of the murder of his father,—listen to his first soliloquy; what bitterness! what sadness!

[Page 318.] Hamlet belongs to that class of unhappy spirits, who know only the dark side of human life, whom a melancholy temperament and a very keen penetration render more sensitive to the evils which afflict our nature than to the good things which are bestowed on us. These romantic heroes from the very first contemplate existence with an ironical contempt or with profound despair; wholly disenchanted, even before they have made acquaintance with misfortune, they bring to the battle of life the power to suffer, without the force to conquer the suffering.

[Page 320.] If Hamlet had never seen the terrible apparition that reveals to him a crime, and commands him to avenge it, he would have been neither happier nor more calm; he would not have desired any the less ardently to escape from earth and soar to loftier regions where shines a purer light; he would have carried thither none the fewer of those tempestuous doubts which try his courage and poison even his love. Incessant labor of thought, passionate reflection exhaust this morbid spirit. The pleasures of youth no longer bring him any enjoyment; the external world inspires him only with contempt and disgust. Had he no hard duty to fulfil, his career would not be less unhappy and brief. The ghost of his father does not decide his fate; it was decided long before; the apparition only gives a new direction to his meditations.

[Page 323.] Hamlet, in his quality as a Christian, must needs hesitate to stab his uncle, the husband of his mother, upon the faith of a vanished apparition, which, perhaps, was only the dream of a disordered imagination.

[Page 324.] It is demanded, why does not Hamlet act; why, when the crime is manifest, does he not punish it on the spot; why does he not seize his sword the moment he perceives the effect of the representation upon the countenance of the King? But think for an instant of the responsibility which falls upon him, and of the remorse which must follow his action, if he be mistaken! The feeling which he experiences is that of a jury about to condemn a criminal to death upon merely probable evidence. If all men hesitate then, if the firmest and most severe tremble, at the thought of striking the innocent, what must not a young prince feel who is charged with the execution of a sentence which he himself must pass, and who has to judge, not a stranger nor indifferent person, but the brother of his father, and the husband of his mother?

At this moment, doubtless, the hero is open to a reproach. Hamlet fails in good faith with himself; he does not avow to himself his secret pangs. In the soliloquy of Act III, while yet full of the rage which the strange agitation of his uncle before the players has excited in him, he finds his uncle alone and at prayer, when he might justly kill him; and when he has the desire to do so, he does not tell the true reason that arrests his arm. In still shrinking from the deed, it is not because he fears that he will send the soul of Claudius to heaven; no, the reasons of his hesitation are neither so specious nor so cruelly refined,—he does not strike, because he fears to commit a murder, and because his generous heart disdains an assassination.

[Page 326.] When Hamlet perishes, is it not the only *dénoûment* which fits his character? Death delivers him from all uncertainty. Had he survived his mother and his uncle, he would have killed himself immediately after. It is best that he should die, and by his death add to the tragic horror by staining with one crime more the memory of Claudius.

VICTOR HUGO (1864)

(*William Shakespeare.* Paris, 1864, p. 308.)—Hamlet. One knows not what fearful being,—complete in the incomplete. Everything in order to be nothing. He is prince and demagogue, sagacious and extravagant, profound and frivolous, masculine and neuter. He believes little in the sceptre, sneers at the throne, has a student for comrade, talks with the passers-by, argues with the first that comes, understands the people, despises the rabble, hates force, suspects success, interrogates obscurity, *thees* and *thous* mystery. He communicates to others maladies which he has not. His feigned madness inoculates his mistress with real madness. He is familiar with ghosts and players. He plays the jester, with the axe of Orestes in his hand. He talks literature, recites verses, composes a piece for the theatre, plays with bones in a graveyard, thunders at his mother, avenges his father, and terminates the redoubtable drama of life and death with a gigantesque mark of interrogation. He terrifies; then puts out of countenance. Nothing more overwhelming has ever been dreamed. It is the parricide saying, ' What do I know ?'

Parricide? Let us pause over this word. Is Hamlet a parricide? Yes, and no. He restricts himself to threatening his mother, but the menace is so savage that his mother quakes: ' Thy word is a dagger! What wilt thou do? Thou wilt not murder me? Help! help! holla!'—and when she dies, Hamlet, without mourning her, stabs Claudius with the tragic cry : ' Follow my mother!' Hamlet is this sinister thing, a possible parricide.

Instead of the North which he has in his brain, put some of the South, as in Orestes, in his veins, and he will kill his mother.

This drama is severe. Truth doubts in it. Sincerity lies in it. Nothing more vast, nothing more subtle. The man here is the world, and the world here is zero. In this tragedy, which is at the same time a philosophy, all is fluid, all hesitates, delays, wavers, is decomposed, scattered, dissipated, the thought is mist, the will is vapor, resolution is crepuscular, the action changes every instant, the compass rules the man. Work bewildering and vertiginous when of everything one sees the bottom, where there exists for the thought no other link but from the King killed to Yorick buried, and where that which is most real is royalty represented by a phantom, and gaiety by a death's head.

Hamlet is the *chef-d'œuvre* of tragedy dreaming.

[Page 311.] One of the probable causes of Hamlet's feigning madness has never yet been indicated by the critics. Hamlet, it is said, played the madman to hide his thought, like Brutus. In fact, it is easy to cover a great purpose under apparent imbecility; the supposed idiot carries out his designs at his leisure. But the case of Brutus is not that of Hamlet. Hamlet plays the madman for his safety. Brutus cloaks his project; Hamlet, his person. The manners of these tragic courts being understood, from the moment that Hamlet learns from the ghost of the crime of Claudius, Hamlet is in danger. The superior historian that is in the poet is here manifest, and we perceive in Shakespeare the profound penetration into the dark shades of ancient royalty. In the Middle Ages and in the later empire, and even more anciently, woe to him who discovered a murder or a poisoning committed by a king. Ovid, Voltaire conjectured, was exiled from Rome for having seen something shameful in the house of Augustus. To know that the king was an assassin was treason. When it pleased the prince to have no witness, one must be shrewd enough to know nothing. It was bad policy to have good eyes. A man suspected of suspicion was lost. He had only one refuge, insanity. Passing for an ' innocent,' he was despised, and all was said. Do you recollect the counsel which Oceanus gives to Prometheus, in Æschylus : *To pretend madness is the secret of the wise ?* When the chamberlain Hugolin found the iron spit with which Edric the ealdorman had impaled Edmund II, ' he made haste to appear stupid,' says the Saxon chronicle of 1016, and in this way saved himself. Heraclides of Nisibis having, by chance, discovered that Rhinometer was a fratricide, caused himself to be pronounced insane by the physicians, and succeeded in having himself shut up in a cloister for life. Thus he lived in peace, growing old, and awaiting death with an air of insensibility. Hamlet ran the same danger, and had recourse to the same means. He had himself pronounced mad like Heraclides, and he appeared stupid like Hugolin. This did not prevent the disquieted Claudius from making two attempts to get rid of him, in the middle of the drama, by the axe or the dagger, and at the close by poison.

The same thing is found in *King Lear:* Gloucester's son takes refuge in apparent madness. Here is the key to open and understand the thought of Shakespeare. In the eyes of the philosophy of art the pretended madness of Edgar explains the pretended madness of Hamlet.

H. TAINE (1866)

(*Histoire de la Littérature Anglaise.* Paris, 1866. Deuxième édition, vol. ii, p. 254. Trans. by H. VAN LAUN, Edinburgh, 1871, vol. i, p. 338.)—Do you understand that, as he says these words, ['Well said, old mole!' &c., I, v, 160,] his teeth chatter, and that he is 'pale as his shirt, his knees knocking each other'? His intense anguish ends in laughter akin to a spasm. Thenceforth Hamlet speaks as though he had a chronic nervous attack. I grant that his madness is feigned; but his mind, as a door whose hinges are twisted, swings and bangs to every wind with a mad precipitance and with a discordant noise. He has no need to search for strange ideas, apparent incoherences, exaggerations, nor for the deluge of sarcasm which he gathers. He finds them within him; he does himself no violence,—he simply gives himself up to them. During the court-play he gets up, he sits down, he asks to lay his head in Ophelia's lap, he talks to the actors, and criticises the play to the spectators; his nerves are strung, his excited thought is like a waving and crackling flame, and cannot find fuel enough in the multitude of objects around it, upon all of which it seizes. After the King is unmasked, Hamlet laughs terribly, for he is resolved on murder. It is clear that this state is disease, and that the man will not live. . . . . What Hamlet's imagination robs him of is the coolness and strength to go quietly, and, with premeditation, plunge a sword into a breast. He can only do the thing on a sudden suggestion; he must have a moment of enthusiasm; he must think the King is behind the arras, or else, seeing that he himself is poisoned, he must find his victim under his foil's point. He is not master of his acts; occasion dictates them; he cannot plan a murder, but must improvise it. A too lively imagination exhausts energy by the accumulation of images, and by the fury of intentness which absorbs it. You recognize in him a poet's soul, made not to act, but to dream, which is lost in contemplating the phantoms of its own creation, which sees the imaginary world too clearly to play a part in the real world; an artist whom evil chance has made a prince, whom worse chance has made an avenger of crime, and who, destined by nature for genius, is condemned by fortune to madness and unhappiness. Hamlet is Shakespeare, and at the close of a gallery of portraits, which have all some features of his own, Shakespeare has painted himself in the most striking of them all.

PROF. V. COURDAVEAUX (1867)

(*Caractères et Talents. Études sur la Littérature Ancienne et Moderne.* Paris, 1867, p. 305.)—Let us put aside altogether the idea that Hamlet, with his delays, was, in the mind of the poet, the type of the German race. In the first place, Hamlet is not German; he is a Dane, which is not the same thing; ask the Danes of the present day. Besides, are there not around him persons of the same race with him who do not, for their part, *delay* at all,—Claudius, for example, and Laertes also, and Fortinbras? By what right is he alone, in the piece, the representative of his race? And what, in fine, was there in the legend that could suggest to Shakespeare the idea of attributing these delays to him, in order to make him a type of his nation? If other personages created by the poet appear to reproduce the spirit of their respective countries; if Iago and Juliet, for example, resemble Italians, it is not because the poet was scientifically engrossed with the character of races, but it is simply because he drew his plot from an Italian novel, and because he restricted himself to raising to the third or fourth power the qualities and defects which the Italian story-teller has given to his personages. To talk of historical truth in Shakespeare, after *Cymbeline*, after the *Winter's Tale*, after *King Lear*, is to be very complaisant. If historical truth is found in Shakespeare, it is to be accounted for by his fidelity to the legend; it is merely an accident, and nothing else. The German GERVINUS, rebuking the torpor of his compatriots, may be permitted to cry out to them: ' Hamlet is you!' but to believe that the poet intended this resemblance, is to go contrary to all the facts.

Neither is it the interpretation which has prevailed in France. People here are more inclined to make a Werther out of Hamlet. And what a fine field is thus opened for moral amplifications! What a magnificent occasion to read young folks a lesson upon the seriousness of life, which has been given us for action, not dreaming! and what superb reproaches for effeminacy and idleness have been eloquently addressed to the poor Hamlet!

[Page 313.] 'Exactly so,' it is said, 'it is elasticity that Hamlet lacks; the courage is wanting in him to discharge his duty; he has not sufficient *daring* to strike Claudius; it is faint-heartedness that renders him unequal to the heroic act required of him. If any one deserves to be believed in regard to him, it is assuredly himself; just listen how he reproaches himself with cowardice after his interview with the players, and in the long soliloquy after meeting with the army of Fortinbras,—a soliloquy which is not in the First Quarto, and which the poet added in the Second, for the better elucidation of Hamlet's character.' But why, we reply, is Hamlet to have the privilege of being the best judge of himself? Why shall he have the gift, which no one else has, of appreciating himself exactly upon the impulse of the moment, without being deceived as to the good or the evil in himself? Hamlet is in a state of great excitement when he thus accuses himself of weakness and cowardice. After having learned of the murder of his father, there are in him two opposing currents, equally honorable to his nature: the filial sentiment, prompting him to strike Claudius, and repugnance to a murder. He speaks differently, as one or the other rules him. At a distance from the act to be done, it is the filial sentiment that is uppermost; he swears then to punish, and he thinks that, were the criminal there, he would kill him without hesitation. When the opportunity occurs, it is the repugnance to strike that overpowers him; he lets the chance go; when it is gone, then the filial sentiment again predominates, and he is vexed that he has not acted, he reproaches himself bitterly, he accuses himself of weakness and faint-heartedness, so culpable does he regard himself at that moment, but at the same moment also, he is deceived about himself: he sees himself with the eyes of passion, and he sees wrongly. We must not bring up his own words against him; we must not take him to the letter against himself; he must be judged by the rest of his conduct, and by what those say of him who have known him for a long time. Now does there fall from the lips of any one whomsoever, saving from his own, a word that accuses him of a want of courage? Observe how, in Q₂, Ophelia speaks of him when she no longer had any doubt of his madness: 'O what a noble mind is here o'erthrown! The courtier's, soldier's, scholar's, eye, tongue, sword; The expectancy and rose of the fair state, ... quite, quite down!' In Q₁ she restricts herself to saying: 'Great God of heaven, what a quicke change is this? The courtier, scholler, souldier, all in him, All dasht and splintered thence.'

What a difference between these two eulogies! And how does that in Q₂ show the settled purpose of the poet to exalt Hamlet!

[Page 315.] And what is there so noble in an assassination in cold blood, even though thereby a father's death is to be avenged, that it should be styled an *heroic* action, to which Hamlet, in default of courage, was not equal? No, it is not that, as is too often said, and as Goethe himself has wrongfully said,—it is not an heroic task, which Hamlet is not strong enough to accomplish: it is *a horrible obligation for which he is not made,* which is something very different, and against which, without his taking account of it, the honesty of his conscience, the instincts of his nature, all the habitudes of his education, all that, in other situations, would be his strength, revolt. A delicate soul, that education has still more refined,—it was utterly repugnant to him to devise an assassination long beforehand, and still worse to strike in cold blood. It is not the fear of danger that arrests him, and no per-sonal self-concern enters into his delays; but at the moment of throwing himself upon his victim, his arm, already raised, refuses to descend; for a murder delibe-rately planned, the steel remains suspended in his hand. Where is the cowardice here?

[Page 320.] To speak of the natural indecision of Hamlet and of the general in-constancy of his resolution may seem at first sight a convenient expedient, but it is an expedient that does not hold good in the presence of facts, any more than the alleged cowardice of our hero. Nowhere, it is true, does Hamlet say a word of this repugnance to strike in cold blood, by which we explain his hesitation and his delays. At first, he wishes to be sure that Claudius is really guilty. Afterwards, he will not strike him at prayer lest he should send his soul to heaven. On each occasion he gives no other motive for deferring action. There is a difficulty here, according to our way of understanding Hamlet, which we are the first to ac-knowledge. But no one takes in earnest the motive with which he satisfies him-self when he sees Claudius at prayer; every one sees that it is a mere pretext which he hastily accepts to dispense with acting at that moment, and every one is right, since among the new reproaches which he heaps upon himself immediately after, he makes not the slightest allusion to this excuse. At that moment there certainly passes in his inmost soul something of which he takes no account; an influence makes itself felt there, which he does not analyze nor distinguish, but to which he submits none the less. But it is not faint-heartedness, nor a natural inconstancy of will, since everything else, both in himself and in those around him, is opposed to these two interpretations. Why then may it not be what we suggest, namely, the secret voice of conscience, and the shrinking of a delicate soul from an assassination in cold blood?

Seek, outside of this explanation, one that explains everything, and you will seek in vain. The character of Hamlet must be accepted as we have represented it, or we have here only a work of bits and pieces, to which the poet contributed a scrap here and a scrap there, without troubling himself to fit together so many pieces of different manufacture, and to make of them a whole. Either our explanation is the true one, or the rôle which has engrossed the attention of mankind for three centuries is a work of chance and an indecipherable enigma. For ourselves the choice is not difficult.

[Page 323.] If Shakespeare were to return to life, and hear all the discussions to which the character of his hero has given rise, he could not suppress a smile, and he would say to us:

'To what purpose do you dispute thus to ascribe to me a profundity of thought which I never had? I am, perhaps, a great poet and an admirable arranger of tales for the stage, but I never was the profound philosopher that you make me out. Witness my life as an actor and the insufficiency of my early education. As to the subject which particularly occupies you, I found in the *Chronicles* of Belleforest a story which struck me as dramatic, and I endeavored to turn it to account for the theatre, just as I have done with so many others. As the public would not have tolerated the hero of my *Chronicle*, I had to modify him. In place of the savage, half sorcerer, with which the legend furnished me, I began by making out of Hamlet a gentleman of my own time, the flower of the courtiers of Queen Elizabeth, with all the intellectual culture of the sixteenth century; then, by a process sufficiently familiar to poets, I gave to this intelligent being, refined by education, sentiments which I myself entertained both by nature and by circumstances. Suffering from men and things, I have taken advantage of the situation of my hero to put into his mouth the troubles and disenchantments of my own heart, and feeling how I should recoil from a murder to be committed in cold blood, however obliged to enact it I might have felt myself, I have ascribed to him the hesitation which would have been mine in his case. Should I have been therefore a coward, or possessed of a mind fatally undecided? No more, I think, than I should have been a sick dreamer, fit only for suicide, because, at certain moments of my life, I have had the bitter sentiments which I ascribe to Hamlet.'

So, we believe, Shakespeare would speak. It is his life, in fact, which is the final explanation of the character of Hamlet, as it is that of the character of Timon, which was conceived at the same epoch.

[Page 326.] The drama of *Timon* was for a long time a problem, and for many of the critics at this day it is still a mere chaos, without cohesion or moral unity,— something resembling the dreams of a drunken man. But all this ceases, and the drama of *Timon* recovers its signification and its unity, if you understand it as the outburst of all the bitterness and disgust at life which had accumulated in the soul of Shakespeare. . . . . Between Timon and Hamlet there is only a difference in shading. Timon hates life; Hamlet finds it burthensome. Timon execrates society; Hamlet regards it with aversion and contempt. In Timon the misanthropy of the poet has reached its apogee; in Hamlet it has not yet gone so far. The former says *Raca!* to the world; the latter confines himself to *Alas!* The latter finds more echoes than the former, because the sentiment which he expresses, being less extreme, is in accord with the disposition of a much larger number. But both these two are of the same family, branches of the same trunk; both were born of the same sadness and of the same weariness of life from which Shakespeare appears to have suffered for some two-thirds of his career.

FRANÇOIS-VICTOR HUGO (1873)

(*Introduction to Trans.* Paris, 1873, p. 77.)—Erudite critics, while acknow-
ledging the fine wisdom of Hamlet's counsels to the players, have nevertheless
stoutly denied the dramatic propriety of introducing these counsels at all. The two
scenes, in which Hamlet makes the actors rehearse, have been regarded by these
critics as *hors-d'œuvre*, very magnificent, it is true, but none the less as *hors-d'œuvre*.
Herein lies, in my opinion, a very grave error. Hamlet wishes to have a piece
acted, the sight of which will force the guilty King to reveal his crime. It is
readily perceived that the manner in which this piece is to be interpreted is of
great importance to him. Hamlet has before him mere strolling players, buffoons
addicted to low clap-trap or grotesque contortions, decked out in ridiculous costume. Wherefore, if the scene to be acted before Claudius has not due decorum,
if one of the actors mouths it like a town crier, if another has his periwig be-
frouzled, if the clown, just at the most important point, cuts some of the wretched
jokes that clowns are so fond of, why then, forsooth, the whole effect that Hamlet
is aiming at is ruined. The terrible tragedy, whereof the last scene is to be acted
off the stage, will end like a farce in a market-place amid peals of laughter. But
if, on the other hand, the acting proceeds smoothly, the result is sure. The more
natural the actor, the deeper will be Claudius's emotion; the truer the acting of
the fictitious murderer, the more manifest will be the panic of the real one. It is,
therefore, essential that Hamlet should have the piece rehearsed with the greatest
care before it is performed in public.

[Page 97.] Hamlet is not, in my view, a courtier, he is a misanthrope; he is not
a prince, he is more than a prince, he is a thinker. What occupies his thoughts are
no beggarly matters, but eternal problems. 'To be or not to be, that is the question.' In his ceaseless dreaming, Hamlet has lost sight of the finite, and sees only
the infinite. He is forever contemplating this boundless Force which governs nature,
and which men sometimes call Providence, and sometimes Chance; and before this
Force he feels himself crushed,—he renounces his individuality, he abjures his will,
and declares himself a fatalist. . . . . Whenever he acts, he obeys an impulse which
drives him not from within, but from without.

[Page 98.] Hamlet believes himself to be no more master of his fate than is a
sparrow. And it is on this passive creature that the mission has devolved of overthrowing a tyrant. Hence all this wavering that we see, this uncertainty, these inner
struggles. Hamlet looks upon himself as powerless,—he has to overthrow a Power;
he does not look upon himself as free,—he has to make a whole nation free; he has no
faith in his own strength, and he has to force punishment on a royal assassin. Sublime
idea! Shakespeare has made Hamlet a fatalist avenger! This struggle between
Will and Fate belongs not alone to the history of Hamlet,—it belongs to the history
of us all. It is your life,—it is mine. It was that of our fathers,—it will be that
of our sons. And hence the work of Shakespeare is eternal.

PROF. DR HEINRICH VON STRUVE (1876)

(*Hamlet, Eine Charakterstudie*, Weimar, 1876, p. 52): How are we to regard the Ghost? It is self-evident that it can be regarded in no other light than as an hallucination.

Through the sudden death of his father, and its attendant circumstances, Hamlet was thrown into a state of excitement so intense, and dwelt upon his father's memory so tenderly, that it could not be but that his imagination, forever searching for the causes of the shocking event, should be in the highest degree liable to visions and hallucinations. At all events, it is much more natural to assume that the young Prince, excited and mentally tortured as he was, should have been the victim of an hallucination, at night, and in a retired spot, in which he saw his father's ghost, than that the canonized bones of his parent, hearsed in death, should really burst their cerements, and that the sepulchre in which they were quietly inurn'd should have oped his ponderous and marble jaws to permit them to visit the pale glimpses of the moon. Before the appearance of the Ghost, Hamlet had seen his father in imagination, and it needed but the trifling incitement from some superstitious soldiers to transform the figment of his fancy into the lively colors and plastic outline of reality.

We see, therefore, in the apparition of his father, nothing but the reflection of Hamlet's own mental exaltation, and the words addressed to him by the Ghost are merely the words which Hamlet, in the name of his father, says to himself. Hamlet's talk with his father is merely a soliloquy. If it were necessary, this could be proved down to the smallest particular, for everything that Hamlet's father says corresponds to a hair with the known traits of Hamlet's character; it contains nothing individual, nothing novel, nothing peculiar to a character of a different mould, but everything bears the stamp of Hamlet's inmost nature,—is the mere reflection of himself. Many an observation, made by chance and lost to memory, of his uncle's and his mother's conduct after his father's death; many a piece of gossip, which here and there reached his ears, and which by itself was insufficient to give his suspicions shape; many a significant shaking of the head by one or another of his father's faithful servants; many a fleeting observation which he had made unconsciously in connection with the numberless reports concerning the details of this mysterious event,—had worked night and day in Hamlet's mind, and struggled into shape not less effectively because unknown, or only half known, to himself; until at last all these separate items, insignificant in isolation suddenly took consistent shape in Hamlet's mind, and stood out before his consciousness as an external image, unmodified by any conscious mental exertion. And thus it follows that the apparition of Hamlet's father, with its precise and distinct accusation of Claudius and the Queen, is nothing else than the objective and personified result of a mental process in Hamlet, long antecedent and unconsciously carried on.

The Ghost appears. How does Hamlet act in its presence? Is he drawn by love to his father? is he rejoiced once more to behold the long-lost one? does he incline himself to him as a loving son assuredly would who actually saw his father bodily [sic, *leibhaftig*] before him? No, nothing of the kind! For all Hamlet was concerned, the apparition came to answer a flood of questions which have long agitated the son, and which he has long sought to answer for himself in vain. He seeks from the Ghost nothing else but that it inform him *why* it appears, what it requires of him, what he must do to allay its tormenting disquiet. At first he does not even know who it is; he himself first makes it his father, addresses it by this name to obtain more readily the answers to all his questions.

[Page 148.] Hamlet enters into life with the most beautiful ideals. The bitter experiences of life have shattered his ideals. He saw evil, murder, treason, falsehood, where he hoped to find good, self-sacrifice, love, and truth. He came upon meanness, where he sought nobleness; cunning hypocrisy and hidden treachery affronted him, where he looked to meet friendship and open-heartedness. This disillusion has taught him to regard life and mankind as of little worth. But his moral nature would not suffer him to be crushed by his experience. He lost not faith in the moral order of the world. He did not allow the germs which stirred down deep in his breast to be choked. With moral energy he devoted himself to a high mission, to the restoration of the disturbed order of the moral world, to the punishment of the bad, to the vindication and victory of the right. In firm faith in his mission, in the faith that he has to fulfil it in the name of Providence, he finds strength to engage in the conflict with evil, and he seeks above all things to keep himself pure. In the wild storm of passion his strong purpose is to keep firm hold of the helm, and keep his course straight towards the bright goal of his life.

DR H. BAUMGART (1877)*

(*Die Hamlet-Tragödie und ihre Kritik.* Königsberg i. Pr. 1877.) [The subject of this volume of 165 pages is a critique of the criticisms that have been passed on *Hamlet* by German Shakespeare scholars, but mainly of Werder, whose idea, as we have already seen, is that the tragic interest of the Play lies not in the character of Hamlet so much as in the nature of his task, which is, not to dispatch the King, but to unmask him, that justice and truth may be brought to light. Should he kill the King without doing this, he would strike like a simpleton, and kill his own cause. Such is the point affirmed by Werder. Thus Dr Baumgart:]

But what is the thought or purpose of an *avenger*, who by a monstrous act of violence has been wounded in his dearest, most sacred interests? If he be of a quick, fiery temper, disposed to revenge, he does not wait even for full proof of the wrong. He is often carried away to deeds of blood only upon strong suspicion. Is he of a cooler, more deliberate character, he waits, even if the strongest evidence lies before him, until he has an irresistible conviction of the injury. Then he acts with an energy only the more reckless, according to the force of his aroused will, whether others justify him or not, heedless even of his own destruction. When has a man, deeply wronged and thirsting for revenge, ever waited till he could lay his case before the great public? No, he keeps it hidden rather.

Revenge is a strictly personal affair, having nothing in common with *punishment*, which satisfies the simple sense of justice. And where does the Ghost or Hamlet speak of punishment merely, and of the necessity of a previous unmasking? It is

---

* This and the preceding volume, Dr Struve's, come to hand while these pages are going through the press. The printers are upon me, and I cannot stop to read the volumes through. From the former I have selected the most striking passage that has caught my eye; of the latter I have not had time even to cut the leaves. The few pages, however, that I have read here and there, give promise of an essay of unusual power, and of forebodings as to the soundness of Werder's theory. Probably under any circumstances but few extracts could have been made from Dr Baumgart's volume, so much of it is, professedly, criticism on criticism, which, as is stated in the Preface to Vol. I, has been excluded in the selection of extracts. Ed.

revenge alone that the Ghost calls for, and swift revenge that Hamlet promises. There is not a word about handing the King over to punishment, nor of punishment at all, but the first word with which Hamlet again recalls the warning of the Ghost. is a call upon himself, his own passion, that it may drive him at last to the vengeance which he has postponed.

Everything impels him to vengeance, his father's ghost, his own boundless excitement,—and yet there is something in him which checks him, *in him*, not *out of him*, —something that drives him to despair, to the bitterest self-reproaches, but, in spite of all, not to action. Thus, as he only *thinks* of what has befallen him, his soul rises in a storm, venting itself in the most violent expressions, and then immediately, aware of this empty rage, the more unsparing is his condemnation of himself for being so made as, in spite of all, to be unable to proceed to action. He should hold his tongue and act. He is not equal to the deed, and yet his sensibility, responsive to the slightest touch, breaks out into the wildest expressions, but yet he scolds himself for unpacking his heart with words, and then he resolves. But what does he resolve? To what does his thinking lead him? Does he seek how he shall discover the murder *to the world*, that at last, without another moment's delay, he may sweep to the act? Nothing of this sort! To secure certainty *for himself*, he resolves upon the court-play. What his 'prophetic soul' has told him from the very beginning, what the nightly apparition has stamped in fearful characters on his soul, that he will confirm by proof; which, indeed, is all very well *for a cool, deliberate judge*, but which would never be done in such a situation by one in any degree *disposed* to revenge. But *then*, when he has laid the *last* doubt, will he, without hesitation, proceed to act? That the conviction wrought by the play is to lead to any measure looking to the public arraignment of the King, there is *not a word* to intimate.

There is *nothing* in the whole piece which hints at any plan of Hamlet's, or at *any intention* to form one. His talk is of nothing but of taking immediate revenge, to which, however, he never makes up his mind until the hour of his death.

LIST OF EDITIONS COLLATED IN THE TEXTUAL NOTES

The Second Quarto (Ashbee's Fac-simile)	[Q₂] ..	..	..	.. **1604**
The Third Quarto (Ashbee's Fac-simile)	[Q₃] ..	..	..	.. 1605
The Fourth Quarto	[Q₄] ..	..	..	.. 1611
The Fifth Quarto	[Q₅] ..	..	..	no date.
The First Folio	[F₁] ..	..	..	.. 1623
The Second Folio	[F₂] ..	..	..	.. 1632
The Third Folio	[F₃] ..	..	..	.. 1664
Players' Quarto	[Q'76] ..	..	..	.. 1676
Players' Quarto	[Q'83] ..	..	..	.. 1683
The Fourth Folio	[F₄] ..	..	..	.. 1685
Players' Quarto	[Q'95] ..	..	..	.. 1695
Players' Quarto	[Q'03] ..	..	..	.. 1703
ROWE (First Edition)	[Rowe i] ..	..	..	.. 1709
ROWE (Second Edition)	[Rowe ii]	..	..	.. 1714
POPE (First Edition)	[Pope i] ..	..	..	.. 1723
POPE (Second Edition)	[Pope ii] ..	..	..	.. 1728
THEOBALD (First Edition) ..	[Theob. i]	..	..	.. 1733
THEOBALD (Second Edition) ..	[Theob. ii]	..	..	.. 1740
HANMER (First Edition) ..	[Han. i] ..	..	..	.. 1744
WARBURTON	[Warb.] ..	..	..	.. 1747
JOHNSON	[Johns.] ..	..	..	.. 1765
CAPELL	[Cap.] ..	..	..	.. 1768
HANMER (Second Edition) ..	[Han. ii] ..	..	..	.. 1770
JENNENS .. .. ., ..	[Jen.] ..	..	..	.. 1773
JOHNSON and STEEVENS	[Steev. '73]	..	..	.. 1773
JOHNSON and STEEVENS	[Steev. '78]	..	..	.. 1778
JOHNSON and STEEVENS	[Steev. '85]	..	..	.. 1785
MALONE	[Mal.] ..	..	..	.. 1790
STEEVENS	[Steev.] ..	..	..	.. 1793
RANN	[Rann] ..	..	..	(?) 1794
REED'S STEEVENS	[Reed '03]	..	..	.. 1803
REED'S STEEVENS	[Reed '13]	.	..	.. 1813
BOSWELL'S MALONE	[Var.] ..	..	..	.. 1821
SINGER (First Edition)	[Sing. i] ..	..	..	.. 1826
CALDECOTT	[Cald.] ..	..	..	.. 1832
KNIGHT (First Edition)	[Knt. i] ..	..	..	(?) 1841

Collier (First Edition) ..	..	[Coll. i] ..	..	..	.. 1843
Hudson (First Edition) ..	..	[Huds. i]..	..	..	.. 1856
Singer (Second Edition)	..	[Sing. ii] ..	..	..	.. 1856
Elze..	..	[El.]	..	..	.. 1857
Dyce (First Edition)	..	[Dyce i] ..	..	..	.. 1857
Collier (Second Edition)	,.	[Coll. ii] ..	..	..	.. 1858
Staunton	,.	[Sta.]	..	..	.. 1860
Richard Grant White	..	[White] ..	..	..	.. 1861
The Globe Edition (Clark and Wright)		[Glo.]	..	..	.. 1864
Charles and Mary Cowden Clarke		[Clarke] ..	..	..	(?) 1864
The Cambridge Edition (Clark and Wright)		[Cam.]	..	..	.. 1865
Delius		[Del.]	..	..	.. 1865
Halliwell (Folio Edition)	..	[Hal.]	..	..	.. 1865
Knight (Second Edition)	..	[Knt. ii] ..	..	..	.. 1865
Keightley..	..	[Ktly.]	..	..	.. 1865
Dyce (Second Edition) ..	..	[Dyce ii]..	..	..	.. 1866
Tschischwitz	..	[Tsch.]	..	..	.. 1869
Hudson (School Edition)	..	[Huds.] ..	..	..	.. 1870
Heussi	..	[Heus.] ..	..	..	.. 1872
The Clarendon Press Series (Clark and Wright).. ..		[Cla.]	..	..	.. 1872
The Rugby Edition (C. E. Moberly)	..	[Mob.]	..	..	.. 1873

The *First Quarto* having been reprinted in full, there is no collation of it recorded in the Textual Notes, except where an editor has adopted one of its readings.

The agreement of Q_2, Q_3, Q_4, and Q_5 is indicated by the symbol Qq.

In like manner, the accord of the four *Folios* is indicated in the Textual Notes by Ff. Manifest misspellings in both Qq and Ff are recorded, as an aid in estimating the value of these editions. I have referred to these early copies at some length in *The Date and the Text* at the beginning of this Volume, and on p. 36 to a peculiarity of the *Second Folio*, to which, by the way, Steevens, out of what I cannot but think was mere antagonism to Malone, imputed a value above that of the *First Folio*.

The *Players' Quartos* are recorded only in exceptional cases where it is well to have at hand all possible evidence. As a rule, the *Quarto* of 1676 includes them all; and even it is not noted when it agrees with the four earlier Quartos.

As in the former volumes of this edition, the agreement of Rowe, Pope, Theobald, Hanmer, Warburton, and Johnson is indicated by Rowe+. Occasionally, where they all agree with F_4, I have used, to save space, F_4+. Rowe did not print from F_4 in this tragedy, as he did in *Macbeth*.

When the Globe, the Cambridge, and Clarendon editions agree in the same reading, I have used the symbol Glo.+.

The abbreviation (subs.) indicates that trifling variations in spelling, in punctuation, or in stage-directions are not noted, but that one edition follows another substantially.

'Var.' stands for Boswell's edition of Malone, or, as it is usually called, the

Variorum of 1821, and for Malone's edition of 1790; where its editor, Boswell, here and there adopted his own text, it is indicated by Bos.; and so trifling is the difference between Singer's First Edition and the Variorum of 1821 that 'Var.' might stand for this edition also. Where Singer's readings are noted, they refer, as a rule, to his Second Edition.

The work of collation was well advanced before it was discovered that Caldecott's two editions of 1820 and 1832 differ somewhat from each other both in text and notes; there is no intimation on the title-page that the editions are not identical. To revise and change involved more labour and more time than it was thought worth while to bestow on it; 'Cald.' therefore refers generally to Caldecott's Second Edition of 1832.

'Coll. (MS)' refers to Mr Collier's annotated F_2.

'Quincy (MS)' refers to Mr Quincy's annotated F_4.

The abbreviation *et cet.* after any reading indicates that it is the reading of *all* editions *other* than those specified. Be it remembered that, to save space, the readings of some of the above enumerated editions are not recorded in every trifling instance, but only in obscure passages.

An Emendation or Conjecture which is discussed in the Commentary is not repeated in the Textual Notes; nor is 'conj.' added to any name in the Textual Notes unless it happens to be that of an editor, in which case its omission would be misleading.

In the matter of punctuation the colon is used, as it is in German, as equivalent to 'namely.' Only when thus used does it indicate any appreciable difference from the semicolon.

A dash at the close of a sentence indicates that the speaker changes his address from one person to another.

The Commentary, to be intelligible, must be read in connection with the Textual Notes. For instance, see I, iii, 74.

To save space in the Commentary, all phrases like 'I think,' 'it seems to me,' &c. have been omitted from the notes there cited.

In the preceding volumes of this edition I have given lists of 'Books quoted and consulted' in their preparation. Instead thereof, in the present volume will be found in the following pages what is almost the same: a *Bibliography of Hamlet*, as complete as may be. The number of books, essays, &c., there recorded, which have not been consulted for this edition, is comparatively small.

BIBLIOGRAPHY OF HAMLET

ENGLISH *

SEVENTEENTH CENTURY

The Tragicall Historie of Hamlet, Prince of Denmarke 1603

Reproductions :

The First Edition of the tragedy of Hamlet, by William Shakespeare. Reprinted at the Shakespeare Press by William Nicol for Payne and Foss. ['A remarkably accurate reprint of the first-discovered copy, in which even the broken letters are reproduced.'—*Timmins.*] .. 1825

Hamlet: First Edition (1603). The Last Leaf of the Lately Discovered Copy, carefully reprinted, with a Narrative of its Discovery, &c. by M. W. R [ooney], Dublin. ['Unfortunately, in one edition this "carefully reprinted" "last leaf" showed on collation no less than nineteen errors in twenty-five lines.'—*Timmins.* See *N. & Qu.*, 27 Sept. 1856; *The Athenæum*, 1856, p. 1168, 1537; p. 1191, letter from Rooney; p. 1220, from Collier; p. 1221, from Jones; p. 1303, from Halliwell.] [See also p. 13 of this Volume.—ED.] 1856

Fac-simile of the Last Page of the First Edition of Hamlet, 1603. [Only six copies of this were lithographed by Mr Ashbee. Two of these (one on India paper) occurred at Halliwell's sale, June, 1859. *N. & Qu.*, 2d Ser., vol. ix, p. 379.]

Photographic Fac-simile. [Forty copies for the Duke of Devonshire, under the supervision of Mr Collier.] 1858

Timmins's Reprints of Quartos 1603, 1604. *The Devonshire Hamlets.* [A very valuable contribution to Shakespearian study.] 1860

The Ashbee-Halliwell Fac-simile. [Thirty-one copies.] 1866

Reprinted in *The Cambridge Edition*, vol. viii, p. 197 1866

Reprinted in the present Volume, p. 37 1877

The Tragicall Historie of Hamlet, Prince of Denmarke 1604

Reproductions :

Photographic Fac-simile. [Forty copies for the Duke of Devonshire, under the supervision of Mr Collier] 1859

---

* This 'ENGLISH BIBLIOGRAPHY' has been most kindly prepared for this edition by my friend, Mr A. I. FISH. ED.

Timmins's Reprints of Quartos 1603, 1604. *The Devonshire Hamlets* .. 1860
The Ashbee-Halliwell Fac-simile. [Thirty-one copies.] [See p. 13 of
   this Volume.—ED.] 1867

The Tragicall Historie of Hamlet, Prince of Denmarke 1605

Reproductions
   Halliwell's Fac-simile. [Twenty-six copies, made under the superin-
   tendence of Mr Halliwell to show the identity of the two editions of
   1604 and 1605.—Bohn's *Lowndes*.] 1860
   The Ashbee-Halliwell Fac-simile. [Thirty-one copies. See Halliwell's
   Dictionary of Old English Plays, p. 113.] [See p. 33 of this Volume.—
   ED.] 1868

**The Hystorie of Hamblet. London. Imprinted by Richard Bra-
docke for Thomas Pauier.** 1608

Reproductions :
   Collier's Shakespeare's Library, vol. i. [Reprint of the 'Hystorie.'] .. 1843
   Halliwell's Folio Edition, vol. xiv, p. 122 1865
   Hazlitt : Shakespeare's Library, vol. ii, Pt. i, p. 212, 2d ed. [Reprint of
   Collier.] 1875

The Tragicall Historie of Hamlet, Prince of Denmarke. [This edition
is mentioned by Lowndes and Halliwell, *Shakespeareana*, p. 18 (1841), but
its existence is very doubtful. No fac-simile is found in the Ashbee-Halliwell Series, and no copy is known in any collection of Quartos.] 1609

The Tragedy of Hamlet, Prince of Denmarke 1611

Reproductions :
   Steevens's Reprint of Quarto 1611. Collated with Quarto 1605, 1607,
   1637. [Knight praises Steevens's Reprints of 1766, but the experience
   of the present writer is not so favorable; a careful collation of this particular play with Jennens's ed. and Halliwell's Fac-simile disclosed a
   number of discrepancies.—A. I. F.] 1766
   The Ashbee-Halliwell Fac-simile. [Thirty-one copies.] [See page 34
   of this volume.—ED.] 1870

The Tragedy of Hamlet, Prince of Denmarke. [See p. 34 of this
Volume.—ED.] . .. .n. d.

The First Folio. [Tragedies, p 152.] 1623
   Reproductions :
   Booth's Reprint of Hamlet from First Folio, 1623 1864
   Stratmann : Reprint of Hamlet from the First Folio, collated with Quar-
   tos 1603, 1604, 1605, 1607, 1611, 1637, and folios 1623, 1632 1869

The Second Folio. [Tragedies, p. 272.] 1632

The Tragedy of Hamlet. [The earliest Quarto known to Theobald when writing his *Shakespeare Restored*, and none earlier was known to Dr Johnson.] [See page 35 of this Volume.—ED.] 1637

The 'Grave-Makers,' from Shakespeare's Hamlet. [This is the 9th piece in the curious collection of drolls and farces, such as were presented in old times by strollers at Bartholomew and other fairs, edited by the bookseller Francis Kirkman, and entitled *The Wits, or Sport upon Sport*, 8vo, 1662. A second edition appeared in 1673 with frontispiece. See Baker and Jones's Biog. Dram., vol. iii, p. 414.] 1662

The Third Folio. [Tragedies, p. 730.] 1664

Players' Quarto. [See page 35 of this Volume.] 1676
Player's Quarto 1683

The Fourth Folio. [Tragedies, p. 59.] 1685

Players' Quarto 1695
Dr Ingleby in his 'Centurie of Prayse,' 1874, chronicles Hamlet allusions in—
Gabriel Harvey. [Ingleby, p. 8.] 1598
The Two Angry Women of Abington. [Rimbault's ed., 1841, pp. 73, 81. Ingleby, Postscript, p. 361.] 1599
Anthony Scoloker. [Ingleby, 46.] 1604
Sir Thomas Smithe's Voiage and Entertainment in Rushia 1605
Ratseis Ghost. [Ingleby, p. 48.] 1606
The Puritan. [Ingleby, p. 331.] 1607
Bel-man's Night Walkes. By Thomas Dekker. [Ingleby, p. 358.] .. 1612
The Night Raven, by Samuel Rowlands. [Ingleby, p. 358.] .. . 1620
Shakerley Marmion: Cupid and Psyche. [Singer's Ed., 1820, pp. 32, 33. Ingleby, Postscript, p. 362.] 1637
London Post. [Ingleby, p. 336.] 1644
John Evelyn. [Ingleby, p. 248.] Nov. 26, ... 1661
Samuel Pepys. [Ingleby, p. 247.] Aug. 31, ... 1668
Edward Phillips. [Ingleby, p. 281.] 1669
John Dryden. [Ingleby, p. 273.] 1679

EIGHTEENTH CENTURY

Players? Quarto. There are two editions of this date. [See p. 35 of this Volume.—ED.] 1703
Ditto, edited by the 'late accurate Mr John Hughs.' [See p. 35 of this Volume.—ED.] 1703
Rowe's First Edition 1709
Hamlet, Prince of Denmark 1710
Hamlet, an Opera, as it is performed at the Haymarket. [This piece, which is very rare, is founded rather on the old *Historie of Hamlet* than Shakespeare's tragedy. *N. & Q.* 2d Ser. vol. ix, p. 379.] 1712
Rowe's Second Edition 1714

Hamlet, Prince of Denmark. Lond., T. Johnson. 1720
Hamlet: Bettesworth. [Catalogued in the Birmingham *Shak. Mem. Lib.*; not
in Bohn's *Lowndes*.] 1723
Pope: First Edition 1725
Shakespeare Restored; or a specimen of the many errors, as well committed,
as unamended, by Mr Pope in his late edition of this poet. By Mr Theo-
bald. ['This, although the title does not say so, is entirely devoted to the
play of Hamlet.'—*Timmins*.] 1726
Pope: Second Edition 1728
Theobald: First Edition 1733
Hamlet, Prince of Denmark. 1734
The Dramatic Historiographer, or the British Theatre delineated. Contains
an account of *Hamlet*. 1735
Some Remarks on the Tragedy of Hamlet, Prince of Denmark, written by
William Shakespeare. [Reprinted in 1864. See p. 80 of this Volume.—
Ed.] 1736
Theobald: Second Edition 1740
Hanmer: First Edition 1744
Upton: Observations, &c. 1746
Warburton 1747
Hamlet. Collated with the best editions. Dublin. 1750
Miscellaneous Observations on the Tragedy of *Hamlet* 1752
Grey: Notes, &c. 1754
Hamlet. Players' Edition. 1754
Hamlet. Players' Edition. 1759
Johnson 1765
Steevens's Twenty Plays. *Hamlet*. Vol. iv. [See *ante*, 1611.] 1766
Capell 1767
Hanmer 1770
Hamlet altered by Garrick. [Not printed, *Lowndes*.] 1771
Jennens. Collated with Ancient and Modern editions. [This collation em-
braces Quartos 1604, 1611, 1637, the Four Folios, and Modern Editions
down to 1768.] 1773
Johnson and Steevens 1773
Richardson's Essays. Reprinted 1780, 1785, 1797, 1812. 1775
An Essay on the Character of Hamlet, as performed by Mr Henderson at the
Haymarket. Lond., n. d. (1777?), 8vo. [By Frederick Pilon, but as-
cribed to Thomas Davies in the Bodleian Catalogue. Second Edition, Lon-
don (1777?), 8vo.—*Bohn's Lowndes*.] 1777
Johnson and Steevens 1778
Capell: Notes and Various Readings 1779–81
Mackenzie: Criticism on the Tragedy of *Hamlet* 1780
Steevens 1785
Robertson: Essay on the Character of Hamlet. [Printed separately, from
Transactions of the Edinburgh Society, vol. ii.—*Lowndes*, by Bohn.] .. 1788
Hamlet. By W. Shakespeare, Esq. [Not in Lowndes, but in *Birm. Mem.
Lib.*, with qy.] 1788
Hamlet. [Manager's Book, Drury Lane.] 1789
Criticism on Mr Kemble's Hamlet 1789

NINETEENTH CENTURY.

Caldecott: First Edition. [Also in 1820.] 1819
Bicknell: Analysis of Hamlet. 1820
Barker: Players' Edition, regulated from the Prompt-Book. 1820
Boswell's Malone. 1821
Cumberland's British Theatre. Players' Edition. 1823
Mackenzie: Criticism on Hamlet. 1823
Oxberry's Drama. Players' Edition. 1823
Skottowe: Life of Shakespeare, &c., vol. ii, p. 1. 1824
Planchè: Costume of Hamlet. ,. 1825
Reprint of Quarto 1603. 1825
Graves: Essay on Genius of Shakespeare, with critical remarks on Romeo,
 Hamlet, Juliet, Ophelia, &c., p. 30, &c. 1826
Singer: First Edition. 1826
Oxberry's Drama. Players' Edition. 1827
Inchbald, Mrs: Players' Edition. 1827
Farren. [See 1833.] 1829
Caldecott: Second Edition. 1832
Mrs Jameson: Characteristics of Women. [Reprinted 1833, 1836, 1846, 1858,
 &c.] 1832
Hamlet in English and French, with a description of Costume. Paris. .. 1833
Farren: Essays on Mania. Including Hamlet and Ophelia. [First printed
 in 1826, and again in 1829.] 1833
Rush, James: Hamlet, a dramatic Prelude, in five acts, pp. 122. 1834
S. T. Coleridge: Literary Remains, vol. ii, p. 202. 1836
Burlesque: Hamlet. [Mentioned in Birmingham *Shak. Mem. Lib.*, Part I,
 Sec. ii, p. 106.] 1838
The Barrow-Diggers, a Dialogue in Imitation of the Grave-diggers in Ham-
 let, with Notes.' 4to. [Only a limited number printed. It contains many
 plates of articles found in tumuli in Dorsetshire. *N. & Q.* vol. ix, p. 379,
 2d Ser.] 1839
Hind's Acting Edition. 1839
Very, Jones: Essays on Epic Poetry, Shakespeare's Hamlet, &c., pp. 39–104. 1839
Douce: Illustrations, p. 438. [See 1807.] 1839
Wade: What does Hamlet mean? A Lecture, &c. [Printed at the office of
 The British Press, Jersey.] 1840
Knight: First Edition. 1841
Macdonell: An Essay, &c. 1843
Collier: First Edition. 1843
Collier: Shak. Library. [See 1608 and 1875.] 1843
Adams, John Q.: Hackett, James H. The character of Hamlet, pp. 7. [Re-
 printed in Griswold's *Prose Writers of America.*] 1844
Dyce: Remarks, p. 204. ,. 1844
Hunter: New Illustrations, vol. ii, p. 202. 1845
Adlard, Jones. [Mentioned in Birmingham *Shak. Mem. Lib.*, Part I, Sec. ii,
 p. 106.] 1846
French's Modern Standard Drama. Players' Edition. 1846
Ray: Shakespeare's Delineations of Insanity. Contributions to Mental Pathol-
 ogy. 1847
Strachey: An Attempt to find a Key to Hamlet. 1848

Hudson: Lectures, vol. ii, p. 86. 1848
Webster's Acting Edition. [Mentioned in Birmingham *Shak. Mem. Lib.*, Pt.
    I, Sec. ii, p. 106.] 1849
Travestie. [Mentioned in Birmingham *Shak. Mem. Lib.*, Pt. i, Sec. ii, p. 107.] 1849
Knight: Studies, pp. 57, 321. [Reprinted 1850, 1857, 1876.] 1849
Dawson: Two Lectures on Hamlet. [First published in *The Monthly Liter-
    ary and Scientific Lecturer*, vol. i.] 1850
Grinfield: Remarks, &c., with Illustrations from Hamlet. 1850
Webster: as performed at Windsor. 1850
Roffe: Essay on the Ghost-belief of Shakespeare. [Privately printed.] .. 1851
Coleridge, Hartley: Essays and Marginalia, vol. i, p. 151. [First appeared
    in *Blackwood's Mag.*, vol. ii, p. 504.] 1851
Causton: On 'Esile.' ['An able defence of the "River" reference, but very
    scarce, and apparently withdrawn soon after publication, on account of its
    libellous character.'—*Timmins*.] 1851
Rice, George Edward: An Old Play in a New Garb (Hamlet, Prince of Den-
    mark). In three acts. With Illus. Boston, 1852; 2d ed., 1853. 1852
Collier: Notes and Emendations. [Reprinted 1853.] 1852
Lacy: Players' Edition. 1853
Dyce: Few Notes, p. 134. 1853
White: Shakespeare's Scholar, p. 407. 1854
Walker, W. S.: Shakespeare's Versification. 1854
An Attempt to ascertain whether the Queen was an accessory, &c. 1856
Hudson: First Edition. 1856
Singer: Second Edition. 1856
Rooney. [See *ante*, Quarto, 1603.] 1856
H. Reed: Lectures, p. 241. 1856
Badham: Cambridge Essays, p. 261. 1856
Dyce: First Edition. 1857
Elze, Karl: The English Text, with an elaborate Commentary in German.
    [A careful study of this volume will show it to be a very valuable contribu-
    tion to Shakespearian scholarship. A. I. F.] 1857
Bathurst: Shakespeare's Versification. 1857
Lloyd: Essays. [Privately printed, also, in Singer's Second Edition of Shake-
    speare.] 1858
Collier: Photographic Fac-simile, 1603. [See *ante*, 1603.] 1858
Bucknill: Psychology. Hamlet, p. 40. 1859
Dyce: Strictures, p. 186. 1859
New Exegesis of Shakespeare, p. 66. 1859
Hamlet, Prince of Denmark, by W. Shakespeare, with notes Glossarial, Gram-
    matical, and Explanatory. Routledge & Co. 1859
Collier: Photographic Fac-simile of Quarto 1604. [See *ante*, 1604.] .. 1859
Halliwell: [Mentioned in *Shak. Mem. Lib.*, Part I, Sec. ii, p. 107.] .. 1860
Staunton. 1860
Bucknill: Medical Knowledge. 1860
Timmins's Reprints of Quarto 1603, 1604. [A very valuable contribution, in-
    cluding a bibliography, to which the present writer is indebted.] 1860
W. S. Walker: Critical Examination. 1860
Maginn: Shakespeare Papers, pp. 232, 275 1860

Lofft : Remarks on Hamlet... 1869
Hunter. 1869
French : Shakespeariana Genealogica, p. 299. 1869
Hunter. 1870
Ruggles : Method of Shakespeare, p. 52. 1870
Ashbee's Fac-simile of Quarto of 1611. 1870
Miles : A Review of Hamlet. [First printed in the *Southern Review* for April
    and July, 1870.] 1870
Rugby Edition, by Moberly. 1870
Wood : Hamlet from a Psychological View. 1870
Daniel : Notes, p. 73. 1870
Griffin : Studies in Shakespeare. Booth's Hamlet, p. 167. 1871
Hall : Shakespearian Fly-leaves, p. 35. 1871
Horne : Was Hamlet Mad? 1871
Hudson : Second Edition. 1871
Hudson : School Shakespeare, 2d Series, 12mo, Boston. 1871
Meadows : An Essay. 1871
Clark and Wright. Clarendon Press Series. 1872
Latham : Two Dissertations, 8vo, London. [From the *Transactions of the
    Royal Society of Lit.*, vol. x, New Series.] 1872
Rushton : Passages in Hamlet, &c. Illustrated from the Toxophilus of Ascham.
    Part I. 1872
Hudson : Life, Art, and Characters, vol. ii, p. 243. 1872
Durand : Contribution to Shakespearian Study. Hamlet. 1873
Moberly : Rugby Edition. 1873
Taylor : Acting Edition. 1873
Corson : On a Disputed Passage in II, ii, l. 180, 181. [Privately printed.] .. 1873
Ray : Shakespeare's Delineations of Insanity. [Reprinted from *The American
    Journal of Insanity*, April, 1847.] 1873
Woods : ' How Old was Hamlet?' Essays, &c. Boston, 12mo, pp. 399. .. 1873
Salvini : Acting Edition. 1873
Corson : Jottings on the Text. [200 copies privately printed.] 1874
Shakespeare Burlesque. Hamlet. [*Lond. Soc.* for Dec. 25, 1874.] 1874
Elze : Essays, 8vo, pp. 380. Hamlet, p. 193. 1874
Tyler : The Philosophy of Hamlet. 1874
Minto : Characteristics of English Poets, p. 403. 1874
Maudsley : Mind and Body. Hamlet, p. 123. 1874
Ingleby : Centurie of Prayse. 1874
Coleridge, S. T. : Notes and Lectures, p. 201. 1874
Collier : Trilogy, Part III, p. 53. [Privately printed.] 1874
Dyce : Third Edition. 1875
Collier : Fourth Edition. [Privately printed.] 1875
Mahony : Hamlet's Mission. A Critical Inquiry, &c. 1875
Lloyd : Critical Essays. 1875
Marshall : Study of Hamlet. 1875
Mercade : Shakespeare's Philosophy. 1875
Russell : Irving as Hamlet. 1875
Scott : Study of Hamlet. 1875

Study of Hamlet, by E. B. H. 1875
Dowden: Shakespeare, his Mind, &c., p. 125. 1875
Ingleby: Shakespeare Hermeneutics. 1875
Weiss, Wit, Humor, &c. Hamlet, p. 151. 1876

ILLUSTRATIONS IN ENGLISH AND AMERICAN PERIODICALS

[These are necessarily so numerous that a complete list can scarcely be hoped for.—*Timmins.*]

The Academy: Age of Hamlet, vol. viii, pp. 629, 651 ; vol. ix, p. 243.

Allusion in *Hamlet*, vol. vi, pp. 638, 658, 687.

Allusion to Hamlet, vol. vii, p. 481.

Anonymous article on Irving in Hamlet in *Macmillan's Magazine*, vol. vii, p. 25.

Article in *Kölnische Zeitung* on Irving in Hamlet, vol. vii, p. 102.

Cessation of Irving in Hamlet, vol. viii, p. 23.

Creswick in Hamlet, vol. vii, p. 360.

Graf on Hamlet, vol. ix, p. 309.

Irving in Hamlet, vol. vi, pp. 519, 546, 644.

Madame Sophie in Hamlet, vol. vi, p. 468.

Marshall's Study of Hamlet, vol. viii, p. 569.

Mercade's Hamlet, or Shakespeare's Philosophy of History, vol. viii, p. 569.

Passage in *Hamlet*, vol. vii, p. 16.

Rossi in Hamlet, vol. viii, p. 652.

Russell on Irving in Hamlet, vol. vii, p. 24.

'Some Dozen or Sixteene Lines,' vol. v, p. 13.

Werder's *Vorlesungen über Shakespeare's Hamlet*, vol. viii, p. 569.

Albion: The Stage-Hamlet. Dec. 24, p. 613. 1864
All the Year Round: Irving's Hamlet. Dec. 5, p. 179. 1874
Amer. Jour. of Insanity: Hamlet. April, ... 1847
Hamlet. April, p. 409. 1860
Athenæum: Review of Halford's Essays: Hamlet's Madness. P. 359. .. 1831
Mr Butler as Hamlet, p. 684. 1832
Mr George Jones as Hamlet, p. 788. 1835
Mr Charles Kean as Hamlet, pp. 35, 91. 1838
Mr Charles Kean as Hamlet, p. 438. 1839
Mr Morris's Hamlet, p. 58. 1840
Mr Macready as Hamlet, p. 238. 1840
Miss Horton as Ophelia, p. 238. 1840
Mr Charles Kean as Hamlet, p. 462. 1840
Master Webster as Hamlet, p. 19. 1842
Mr Gregory as Hamlet, p. 66. 1843
What does Hamlet mean? Review of Wade's Lecture, p. 713. 1844
Dumas's Translation, p. 78. 1848
Mr Brooke as Hamlet at Marylebone Theatre, p. 459. 1850
Schlegel's Hamlet at St James's, p. 683. 1852
Review of Dr Eckart's Dramaturgic Studies: A Course of Lectures on the Single Play of Hamlet, p. 1187. 1853

Athenæum (continued):

Hamlet Quarto, 1603; Letter from Rooney, p. 1191; Letter from J. Payne
Collier, p. 1220; Letter from I. Winter Jones, p. 1220; Letter from Henry
Foss, p. 1277; Letter from J. O. Halliwell, p. 1308; Letter from J. Payne
Collier, p. 1310. pp. 1168, 1404, 1537. 1856

V, ii, 369: 'Now cracks a noble heart,' p. 1221. 1856

Halliwell: V, ii, 407: ' Bear Hamlet like a soldier *to his grave*,' p. 1308. 1856

Mommsen: Hamlet Quarto 1603, p. 182. 1857

Hamlet Quarto 1611, found in Germany, p. 183. 1857

Review of Elze's Hamlet. Part I, p. 418. 1859

Review of New Exegesis. Part II, p. 808. 1859

Allen's Reprint of the Quartos of 1603, 1604. Part I, p. 137. 1860

Letter from J. O. Halliwell on the Hamlet of 1604. Part I, p. 272. .. 1860

Hamlet explained by Rohrback. Part I, p. 253. 1861

Review of Gerth's Hamlet. Part I, p. 529. 1862

Review of Conolly's Study of Hamlet; his madness. Part II, p. 104. .. 1863

Donbavand: I, ii, 65: 'A little more than kin,' &c. Part II, p. 683. .. 1863

Donbavand: II, ii, 397: 'I know a hawk from a handsaw.' Part II, p. 683. 1863

Atkinson: II, ii, 397: 'I know a hawk from a handsaw.' Part II, p. 722. 1863

Mitford: II, ii, 397: 'I know a hawk from a handsaw.' Part II, p. 884. 1863

Hausenbeth: II, ii, 397: 'I know a hawk from a handsaw.' Part II, p.
765, 766. 1863

Chatelain's French Translation of Hamlet. Part I, p. 298. 1864

II, ii, 397: 'I know a hawk from a handsaw.' Part II, p. 928. 1865

Elze: I, iv, 36: 'dram of eale.' Part II, p. 186. 1866

Elze: III, iv, 169: 'And either ... the devil or throw him out.' Part II,
p. 186. 1866

Elze: IV, v, 10: 'They aim at it,' &c. Part II, p. 186. 1866

Elze: V, ii, 42: 'And stand a comma 'tween their amities.' Part II, p. 186. 1866

I, iv, 36: 'dram of eale.' Part II, p. 217. 1866

III, iv, 169: 'And either .... the devil or throw him out.' Part II, p. 218. 1866

III, iv, 162: 'Of habits devil, is angel yet in this.' Part II, p. 218. .. 1866

I, iv, 36: 'The dram of eale.' Part II, p. 687. 1866

Street: V, i, 314: ' The cat will mew, and dog will have his day.' Part II,
p. 314. 1868

Forrest: V, i, 314: ' The cat will mew, and dog will have his day.' Part
II, p. 346. 1868

Elze: IV, vi, 21: 'Convert his gyves to graces.' Part I, p. 284. 1869

Elze: V, i, 108: 'tenures.' Part I, p. 284. 1869

Hall: IV, vii, 21: ' Convert his gyves to graces.' Part I, p. 318. 1869

Tschischwitz's Hamlet reviewed. Part II, p. 430. 1869

Wetherill: I, iv, 36: 'dram of eale.' Part II, p. 672. 1869

On Fortinbras. Part I, p. 114. 1872

Staunton: I, i, 94: 'And carriage of the article design*e*.' Confusion of
final *d* and *e* in old dramatists. Part I, p. 530. 1872

Staunton: III, iv, 121: 'Your bedded hair,' &c. Part I, p. 530. 1872

Staunton: V, ii, 7: 'And *praise* be rashness for it.' Confusion of final *d*
and *e* in old dramatists. Part I, p. 530. 1872

Staunton: II, ii, 421: 'for the law of *writ*.' Part I, p. 867. 1872

Blackwood's Magazine (continued):

Mr Young's acting of Hamlet. xxiv, 559.
Retzsch's illustrations of *Hamlet.* xxiv, 668.
John Kemble's acting in *Hamlet.* xxxi, 674.
Tragedy of *Hamlet.* xxxiii, 398.
Hamlet's love for Ophelia. xxxiii, 400.
Hamlet and Goethe's Faust. xxxvi, 236, 269.
Schrœder's version of *Hamlet.* xxxvii, 242.
German critics on Hamlet. xxxvii, 243.
Goethe on Hamlet. xxxvii, 246.
Tieck and Horn on Hamlet. xxxvii, 247.
Hamlet compared with *Romeo and Juliet.* xxxvii, 523.
Garrick's changes in Hamlet. xlv, 396.
Ducis's French version of *Hamlet.* xlvi, 339.
Feigned madness of Hamlet. xlvi, 449.
Play represented in *Hamlet.* xlvii, 146.
Passages in *Hamlet.* lxvi, 252; lxvii, 634-635.—[*Timmins.*]

Chicago Medical Journal: Hamlet's Insanity. Sept., p. 7. 1873
Christian World Magazine: Hamlet a Problem. April, ... 1875
Colburn's New Monthly Mag.: The Lost Hamlet. April, p. 279. 1873
Cornell Review: Antic Disposition. Dec., ... 1876
Cornhill Magazine: Hamlet. October, p. 452. 1869
Edinburgh Review: Garden at Elsineur in Hamlet. xiv, 171.
Character of Hamlet. xxviii, 483.
Goethe's Analysis of Hamlet. xlii, 433.
Le Tourneur's Translation of Hamlet. li, 230.
Closing Scene of Hamlet. lxxi, 490.
Texts of Hamlet. lxxi, 366-367, 370-371, 377-384.
Authorities of Saxo Grammaticus on Hamlet. lxxxii, 287.
Wailly's Translation of Hamlet. lxxxiii, 57-58.—[*Timmins.*]

Evangelical Quar. Review: April, p. 210. 1870
The Galaxy: Hamlet the Younger. April, p. 535. 1870
April, p. 507. 1873
Gentleman's Magazine: The Saga of Hamlet, from the Swedish. Oct., p. 369,
New Series. 1847
Philosophers and Jesters. March and June, ... 1873
Literary and Philosophical Society of Liverpool: 51st Session, on Hamlet and
Faust. 1861
London Magazine: Hamlet worn out. Aug., ... 1876
London Society: Hamlet the Hysterical. Dec., ... 1874
London University Magazine: Hamlet Criticism. 1858
Macmillan: On the extract from an Old Play in Hamlet, II, ii. Dec., p. 135. 1874
The New Hamlet and his Critics. Jan., p. 236. 1875
The Elder Hamlet. Aug., p. 351. 1876
The Nation: Mar. 29, ... 1866
Notes and Queries: I, i, 63: 'Sledded Polacks.' [Leo] .. 3d Ser. vi, 410
I, i, 63:   "   "   .. .. .. 3d " vii, 21
I, i, 113: 'Palmy state.' .. .. 1st " viii, 409
I, i, 117: 'As stars,' &c. .. .. 3d " viii, 126

Notes and Queries (continued):

I, iv, 36:	'the dram of eale.' [Leo]			.. ..	.. 5th Ser.	iii, 103
I, iv, 36:	" " " [Davies]			.. ..	.. 5th "	v, 201
I, v, 77:	'Unhousell'd, disappointed, unanel'd.'			..	.. 1st "	vii, 8
I, v, 80:	'Oh, horrible.' [Cornish] ..			.. ..	.. 1st "	viii, 195
I, v, 107:	'My tables.' [Brae]			.. ..	.. 1st "	v, 241
I, v, 108:	'That one may smile, and smile, and be a villain.'				1st "	v, 285
I v, 108:	" " " " "				1st "	vi, 270
I, v, 108:	" " " " "				1st "	vii, 449
I, v, 125:	'There needs no ghost.' ..			.. ..	.. 2d "	xi, 196
II, i, 65:	'Windlasses.' [Corney] ..			.. ..	.. 4th "	iv, 386
II, i, 181:	'For if the sun breed maggots,' &c. [Corson]			..	4th "	xii, 201
II, ii, 337:	'tickled o' the sere.' [Nicholson]			..	.. 4th "	viii, 62
II, ii, 397:	'I know a hawk from a handsaw.'			..	.. 3d "	xii, 3
II, ii, 397:	" " " "			..	.. 3d "	xii, 122
II, ii, 397:	" " " "			..	.. 4th "	ix, 189
II, ii, 397:	" " " "			..	.. 4th "	ix, 358
II, ii, 397:	" " " "		[Addis]	4th "	x, 57
II, ii, 397:	" " " "		[Chattock]	4th "	x, 135
II, ii, 397:	" " " "		[Addis]	4th "	x, 195
II, ii, 397:	" " " "		[Chattock]	4th "	x, 262
II, ii, 397:	" " " "		[Addis]	4th "	x, 375
II, ii, 397:	" " " "		[Pickton]	4th "	x, 425
II, ii, 451:	Parallel passage. [Addis] ..			.. ..	.. 5th "	ii, 303
II, ii, 525:	'the mobled queen.'			.. ..	.. 3d "	vi, 111
II, ii, 525:	" " "			.. ..	.. 3d "	vi, 66
II, ii, 529:	'With bisson rheum.'			.. ..	.. 4th "	xi, 320
II, ii, 632:	'Abuses me to damn me.' ..			.. ..	.. 3d "	v, 338
III, i, 59:	'a sea of troubles.' [Brae]			.. ..	.. 1st "	vi, 382
III, i, 59:	" " "		.. ..	.. ..	.. 5th "	iv, 366
III, i, 59:	" " "		.. ..	.. ..	.. 5th "	vi, 104
III, i, 67:	'this mortal coil.' [Ingleby]			.. ..	.. 1st "	i, 151
III, i, 67:	" " "		.. ..	.. ..	.. 2d "	i, 221
III, i, 67:	" " " [Ingleby]			.. ..	.. 2d "	ii, 207
III, i, 67:	" " "		.. ..	.. ..	.. 2d "	ii, 284
III, i, 67:	" " " [Ingleby]			.. ..	.. 2d "	ii, 368
III, i, 67:	" " " [Riley]			.. ..	.. 2d "	ii, 368
III, i, 67:	" " "		.. ..	.. ..	.. 2d "	ii, 368
III, i, 67:	" " "		.. ..	.. ..	.. 2d "	vi, 228
III, i, 76:	'These fardels,' reading of First Folio. ..			.. 2d "	iv, 263
III, i, 79:	'The undiscover'd country from whose bourn.'					
	[Addis] ..		.. ..	.. ..	.. 5th "	ii, 303
III, i, 175:	'for to prevent.'		.. ..	.. ..	.. 5th "	ii, 405
III, ii, 137:	'a suit of sables.' ..		.. ..	.. ..	.. 2d "	iii, 62
III, ii, 137:	" " [Warwick]			.. ..	.. 2d "	iv, 43
III, ii, 146:	'miching mallecho.'		.. ..	.. ..	.. 1st "	ii, 358
III, ii, 146:	" " [Collier]			.. ..	.. 1st "	iii, 3
III, ii, 146:	" "		.. ..	.. ..	.. 1st "	iii, 213
III, ii, 146:	" "		.. ..	.. ..	.. 4th "	iii, 386

Notes and Queries (continued):

Notes and Queries (continued):

V, i, 149: 'by the card.'				. 2d Ser.	i, 77
V, i, 149: " " [Easy]				. 3d "	ii, 503
V, i, 198: 'Yorick.'				. 2d "	xii, 264
V, i, 236: 'Imperious.'				. 4th "	x, 292
V, i, 236: " [Rule]				. 4th "	xi, 72
V, i, 236: "				. 4th "	xi, 106
V. i, 236: " [Nicholson]				.. 4th "	xi, 166
V, i, 255: 'crants.' [Charnock]				.. 5th "	vi, 345
V, i, 263: 'violets.' [Johnston]				.. 1st "	v, 492
V, i, 299: 'eisel.' [Singer]				.. 1st "	ii, 241
V, i, 299: " [Braybrooke]				.. 1st "	ii, 286
V,, i, 299: " [J. R. N.]				.. 1st "	ii, 315
V, i, 299: " [Hickson]				.. 1st "	ii, 329
V, i, 299: "				.. 1st "	iii, 66
V, i, 299: " [Hickson]				.. 1st "	iii, 119
V, i, 299: " [Singer]				.. 1st "	iii, 120
V, i, 299: " [Causton]				.. 1st "	iii, 210
V, i, 299: "				.. 1st "	iii, 225
V, i, 299: " [Rock]				.. 1st "	iii, 397
V, i, 299: "				.. 1st "	iii, 474
V, i, 299: "				.. 1st "	iii, 508
V, i, 299: "				.. 1st "	iii, 524
V, i, 299: " [Hickson]				.. 1st "	iv, 36
V, i, 299: " [Kamphin]				.. 1st "	iv, 648
V, i, 299: "				.. 1st "	iv, 155
V, i, 299: "				.. 1st "	iv, 193
V, i, 299: " [Bede]				.. 2d "	vii, 125
V, i, 299: " [De Soyres]				.. 4th "	x, 108
V, i, 299: " [Skipton]				.. 4th "	x, 150
V, i, 299: " [Williams]				.. 4th "	x, 151
V, i, 299: " [Williams]				.. 4th "	x, 229
V, i, 299: " [Kershaw]				.. 4th "	x, 282
V, i, 299: " [Hackwood]				.. 4th "	x, 292
V, ii, 11: 'Rough-hew them how we will.'				.. 5th "	i, 484
V, ii, 42: 'a comma.' [Cartwright]				.. 4th "	i, 576
V, ii, 42: " [Wetherill]				.. 4th "	i, 619
V, ii, 200: 'fond and winnowed opinions.' [Nicholson]				.. 3d "	v, 50
V, ii, 232: 'if it be not to come, it will be now.' [Warwick]			3d "	i, 266
V, ii, 298: 'He's fat, and scant of breath.' [Dixon]				.. 3d "	vii, 52
V, ii, 298: " " " [Kennedy]				.. 5th "	i, 484
V, ii, 298: " " " [Jaydee]				.. 5th "	ii, 64
V, ii, 298: " " "				.. 5th "	iii, 224
V, ii, 298: " " " [Wylie]				.. 5th "	iii, 273
V, ii, 317: 'as a woodcock to mine own springe.'				.. 5th "	i, 485
V, ii, 317: " " "				.. 5th "	ii, 103
V, ii, 353: 'Give me the cup.'				.. 3d "	ii, 502
Hamlet's madness in Saxo-Gram. [Buckton]				.. 1st "	xii, 238
Hamlet, Burbage first actor in.				2d Ser.	iii, 408, 490

GERMAN

TRANSLATIONS OF SHAKESPEARE'S COLLECTED WORKS*

Wieland: Shakespeare's theatralische Werke. Hamlet, vol. viii. Zürich, .. 1766
Eschenburg: Shakespeare's Schauspiele. Hamlet, vol. xii. Zürich, .. 1782
Schlegel, A. W.: Shakespeare's dramatische Werke. Hamlet, vol. iii. Berlin, 1798
Benda, J. O. W.: Shakespeare's dramatische Werke. Hamlet, vol. xiii.
Leipzig, ... 1826
Voss, J. H.: Shakespeare's Schauspiele. Hamlet, vol. viii. Stuttgart, .. 1827
Meyer, Joseph: Shakespeare's sämmtliche Schauspiele. Hamlet, vol. xxx.
Gotha, ... 1829
Schlegel und Tieck: Shakespeare's dramatische Werke. Hamlet, vol. vi.
Berlin, ... 1832.
Shakespeare's sämmtliche Werke, übersetzt von A. Böttger, &c. Hamlet von
Karl Simrock. Leipzig, ... 1836
Körner, Julius: Shakespeare's dramatische Werke. Hamlet, übersetzt von N.
Bärmann. Schneeberg, ... 1836
Fischer, A.: Shakespeare's dramatische Werke. Stuttgart, ... 1837
Ortlepp, E.: Shakespeare's dramatische Werke. Hamlet, vol. i. Stuttgart, 1838
Keller, A., und Rapp, M.: Shakespeare's Schauspiele. Hamlet, vol. vi.
Stuttgart, ... 1846
Wolff, O. L. B.: Familien Shakespeare. Leipzig, ... 1849
Sievers, E. W.: Shakespeare's Dramen für weitere Kreise bearbeitet. Leip-
zig [Thimm], ... 1851-52
Schlegel und Tieck. Hamlet, vol. iv. Fifth edition. Berlin, .. ' .. 1854
Jencken, Dr F.: Shakespeare's Dramen. [Zweite umgearbeitete Auflage, 1856.]
Mainz, ... 1853-55
Heinichen, C.: Shakespeare's Dramen. Bonn, ... 1859
Dingelstedtische Ausgabe: Hamlet, übersetzt von L. Seeger, vol. vii. Hild-
burghausen, ... 1867
Deutsche Shakespeare-Gesellschaft: Hamlet, übersetzt von A. W. Schlegel.
Durchgesehen, eingeleitet, und erläutert von K. Elze. Berlin, ... 1869
Bodenstedt, Fr.: Shakespeare's dramatische Werke. Hamlet, vol. xxv. Leip-
zig, ... 1870
Moltke, Max.: Shakespeare's sämmtliche Werke. Hamlet, vol. vi. Leip-
zig, ... no date.
Oechelhäuser, W.: Shakespeare's dramatische Werke für die deutsche Bühne
bearbeitet. Hamlet, vol. iii. Berlin, ... 1870
Devrient, Eduard und Otto: Deutscher Bühnen und Familien Shakespeare.
Hamlet, vol. i. Leipzig, ... 1873

---

* In this list, compiled mainly from the Editor's library, are to be found only those that assume
to be original and independent translations. The legion of republications is omitted. ED.

SEPARATE TRANSLATIONS OF HAMLET

Hamlet. [Die Bearbeitung von Heufeld. Gedruckt in: Neue Schauspiele, aufgeführt in den K. K. Theatern zu Wien.—Genée.] Pressburg, .. **1773**

Hamlet. Ein Trauerspiel in sechs Aufzügen. Zum Behuf des Hamburgischen Theaters. [Diese Bearbeitung wird in mehreren Recensionen, in Meusel's Schriftsteller-Lexicon (so sagt Genée), und selbst von Thimm in seiner Shakespeare Bibliographie dem J. C. Bock als Verfasser zugeschrieben, aber Genée (p. 238) ist überzeugt dass sie die Schroederische sei. ED.] Hamburg, ... **1777**

Hamlet. [Schroeders Zweite Umarbeitung. Andere Ausgaben sind in 1781, 1795, 1804, erschienen. Zuletzt in Schroeders dramatischen Werken, herausgegeben von Bülow mit einer Eintheilung von Tieck, Bd iv, S. 279. Berlin, 1831. ED.] **1778**

Hamlet. Zum Behuf des Frankfurter Theaters. [Genée sagt: In dieser Ausgabe, trotz des Verfassers Zurückweisung solchen Verdachtes, ist die Heufeld-Schroeder'sche Bearbeitung fast durchweg beibehalten. ED.] .. **1779**

Mauvillon: Der neue Hamlet, worin Pyramus und Thisbe als Zwischenspiel gespielt wird. [In ' Gesellschafts Theater,' Leipzig.—Genée.] **1790**

Schink, J. F.: Prinz Hamlet von Dänemark. Marionettenspiel. Berlin, .. **1799**

Schütz, K. J.: Hamlet, für das deutsche Theater bearbeitet. [Die ganze Schluss-scene dieser Bearbeitung ist, wie Genée sagt, folgendermassen umgewandelt: ' Laertes verwundet Hamlet, ohne zu wissen, dass die Degenspitze vergiftet war; dann stürzt Horatio herein und meldet, ein Page habe ihm so eben die Vergiftung der Waffe bekannt. Die Königin ist unterdessen durch die Wirkung des Trankes niedergesunken, und Hamlet ersticht den König. Im Sterben spricht Hamlet den Wunsch aus, die Wahl des Reiches möge sich auf Laertes lenken. Das Volk dringt herein, Horatio verkündet den letzten Willen Hamlet's und huldigt dem Laertes mit den Worten: " Hier steht der neue Herrscher Dänemarks." ' ED.] Leipzig, ... **1806**

Hamlet, Prinz in Dänemark, Karrikatur in 3 Acten. [Mit Gesang in Knittelreimen, von Joachim Perinet, Dichter, Schauspieler. Dem Andenken des 17 May, 1803, gewidmet.—Thimm.] Wien, ... **1807**

Sonnleithner, J.: Hamlet. Wien [Thimm], ... **1811**

Klingemann, Aug.: Hamlet. Trauerspiele in sechs Aufzügen. Nach Göthes Andeutungen in Wilhelm Meister und A. W. Schlegel's Uebersetzung für die deutsche Bühne bearbeitet. Leipzig und Altenburg, ... **1815**

Döring, H.: Hamlet. [—Thimm, von Genée nicht erwähnt.] Gotha, .. **1829**

Mannhart, Dr J. B.: Hamlet, übersetzt. Sulzbach, ... **1830**

Hamlet in deutscher Uebertragung. [Die Vorrede, datirt London, 1828, ist Ferdinand Jencken unterzeichnet.—Genée.] London und Hamburg, .. **1834**

Samson von Himmelstiern, R. J. L.: Hamlet, übersetzt. Dorpat, ... **1837**

Moltke, Max.: Hamlet, Englisch und Deutsch. Neu übersetzt und erläutert. Leipzig [Cohn], ... **1839**

Ruhe, A.: Die erste Ausgabe (1603) übersetzt. Inowraclaw, ... **1844**

Hagen, W.: Hamlet, übersetzt. .. .. **n. d.**

Köhler, Dr F.: Hamlet, Deutsch. Leipzig, ... **1856**

Lobedanz, H.: Hamlet, Deutsch. Leipzig, ... **1857**

Plehwe, Herman von: Hamlet, Deutsch. Hamburg, ... 1862
Hackh, C.: Hamlet. In Wort- und Sinngetreuer Prosa-Uebersetzung. Stuttgart, ... 1874

ENGLISH TEXT WITH GERMAN NOTES

Pierre, J. M.: The Plays of Shakespeare accurately printed from the text of
Mr Steevens's last edition, with Historical and Grammatical Explanatory
Notes in German. Hamlet, vol. iii. Frankfort-on-the-Main, ... 1833
Hoffa, Dr J.: Hamlet. Grammatisch und sachlich zum Schul- und Privatge-
brauch erläutert. Braunschweig, ... 1845
Francke, Dr Carl Ludwig Wilhelm: Hamlet, A Tragedy. Mit Sprache und
Sachen erläuternden Anmerkungen, fur Schüler, höhere Lehranstalten und
Freunde des Dichters. Leipzig, ... 1849
Delius, Prof. Dr N.: Shakspere's Werke. Herausgegeben und erklärt. Ham-
let, vol. i. Elberfeld, ... 1854
Elze, Prof. Dr: Shakespeare's Hamlet. Leipzig, ... 1857
Tschischwitz, Dr Benno: Shakespeare's sämmtliche Werke. Englisher Text,
berichtigt und erklärt. Hamlet, vol. i. Halle, ... 1869
Moltke, Max.: Shakespeare's Hamlet, Englisch und Deutsch. Text von 1603
und 1604. Quellen. Varianten. Noten. Excurse. Commentar. Literatur. Glossar. [Leider sind nur vier Hefte dieses Werkes, wovon man so
viel hoffen liess, erschienen. ED.] Leipzig, ... 1871
Heussi, Dr Jacob: Shakspeare's Hamlet, Erklärt. [2te Auflage.] Leipzig, 1872
Delius, Prof. Dr N.: Shakspere's Werke. Herausgegeben und erklärt. Dritte,
revidirte Auflage. Hamlet, vol. ii. Elberfeld, ... 1872

ENGLISH TEXT WITH ENGLISH NOTES

Fiebig, Dr Otto: Hamlet. With copious English Explanatory Notes. Leipsic, 1857
Stratmann, F. H.: The Tragicall Historie of Hamlet. Edited according to
the first printed copies, with various readings, and critical notes. London
and Krefeld, ... 1869

ESSAYS, CRITICISMS, &c.*

Lessing: Hamburgische Dramaturgie. 5 Junius, ... 1767
Wieland: Der Teutsche Merkur. Auszüge aus dem Hamlet, vol. iii. Weimar,
July, ... 1773
Schink, J. F.: Ueber Brockmann's Hamlet. Berlin [Cohn], ... 1778
Schink, J. F.: Shakespeare in der Klemme, oder Wir wollen doch auch den
Hamlet spielen. Wien, ... 1780

---

* This list, necessarily imperfect, is also made up almost exclusively from the Editor's library;
where a title is given at second-hand, I have endeavored in every case to give credit to the source
whence it is obtained. The number of a page following a title indicates the page on which the article
or chapter on *Hamlet* is to be found. ED.

Engel, J. J.: Ideen zu einer Mimik. Erster Theil, S. 130; Zweiter Theil, S. 62.
Berlin, ... **1785**
Warnekros, Dr Henrich E.: Der Geist Shakespear's. Zweiter Theil, S. 236.
Greifswald, ... **1786**
Lessing: Hamburgische Dramaturgie. Berlin, ... **1794**
Goethe: Wilhelm Meisters Lehrjahre. Berlin, ... **1795**
Garve, Christian: Ueber die Rollen der Wahnwitzigen in Shakspears Schau-
spielen und über den Charakter Hamlets ins besondere. Versuche u. s. w.
2ter Theil, S. 431. Breslau, ... **1796**
Gieseke, K. L.: Der travestirte Hamlet, in Knüttelversen mit Arien. Wien
[Cohn], ... **1798**
Henry, L., Balletmeister der Königl. Theater von Paris und Neapel: Hamlet.
Grosses Ballet in fünf Acten. Musick von Herrn Grafen W. Robert von
Gallenberg. Wien,* .. .. **n. d.**
Ziegler, F. W., K. K. Hofschauspieler: Hamlet's Charakter, &c. Wien, .. **1803**
Schmidt, F. L.: Sammlung der besten Urtheile über Hamlets Charakter.
Quedlinburg, ... **1808**
Schlegel, A. W. von: Ueber dramatische Kunst und Litteratur, vol. ii, part ii,
p. 146. Heidelberg, ... **1811**
Pries, Prof. J. F.: Ueber Shakespeare's Hamlet. Rostock, ... **1825**
Kries: Ueber Hamlet. Programm. Rostock. [Thimm, qy Pries?] .. **1825**
Horn, Franz: Shakespeare's Schauspiele erläutert. Hamlet. Zweiter Theil,
S. 1. Leipzig, ... **1825**
Hermes, K. H.: Ueber Shakespeare's Hamlet und seine Beurtheiler, Goethe,
Schlegel, und Tieck. Stuttgart und München, ... **1827**
Holtey, K. v.: Beiträge zur dram. Kunst und Literatur. Hamlet. May,
p. 126. [Thimm.] **1828**
Börne, Ludwig: Hamlet von Shakespeare. Gesammelte Schriften, 2ter
Theil, S. 172. [Der Aufsatz über Hamlet soll in 1816 geschrieben worden
sein. ED.] Hamburg, ... **1829**
Echtermeyer, Henschel und Simrock: Quellen des Shakspeare in Novellen,
&c., vol. i, S. 67. [Zweite Auflage, Bonn, 1870.] Berlin, ... **1831**
Trahndorff, Prof.: Ueber den Orestes der alten Tragödie und den Hamlet.
(Programm. des Freidrich Wilhems-Gymnasiums.) Berlin, ... **1833**
Gans, Eduard: Vermischte Schriften. Der Hamlet des Ducis und der des
Shakespeare. Vermischte Schriften, vol. ii, p. 269. Berlin, ... **1834**
Gutzkow, Karl: Gesammelte Werke. Hamlet in Wittenberg, 1832. [The
author prefaces this 'dramatische Phantasie' with the following note: Tieck
hatte die Hypothese aufgestellt, dass Hamlet bereits zu Ophelien im aller-
nächsten Verhältniss gestanden hätte, ehe er nach Wittenberg gegangen.
Ich wollte, ermuthigt durch meine Lectüre der Romantiker, eine Art geist-
iger Vertmählung mit Ophelien schildern. Goethe trat in dem erst nach
seinem Tode (1832) bekannt gewordenen zweiten Theil des Faust mit einer
solchen mystischen Ehe zwischen Faust und Helena heraus.] Vol. i, p. 369.
Jena, ... [no date. ?1838]
Heine, H.: Shakespeare's Mädchen und Frauen mit Erläuterungen. Ophelia.
Paris und Leipzig. [Vol. v, p. 315, Philadelphia, 1856.] **1839**

---

* As this has no date, for the credit of this century I have relegated it to the last. ED.

Marquard, F.: Ueber den Begriff des Hamlet. Berlin, ... 1839
Ulrici, Dr H.: Shakespeare's dramatische Kunst. [Second edition, 1847;
third edition, 1868; English translation. Second edition, 1876.] Halle, .. 1839
Schmidt, Dr Al.: Sacherklärende Anmerkungen zu Shakespeare's Dramen, p.
184. Danzig, ... 1842
Mönnich, Dr W. B.: Album des lit. Vereins. Ophelia, p. 75. Nürnberg, .. 1844
Rötscher, Dr H. Th.: Cyclus dramatischer Charaktere. Hamlet, p. 99. Ber-
lin, ... 1844
Delius, Dr N.: Die Tieck'sche Shakespearekritik beleuchtet, p. 62. Bonn, 1846
Carus, C. G.: Mnemosyne. Hamlet. Das Princip dieser Tragödie, 1827. S.
42. Pforzheim, ... 1848
Francke, C. L. W.: Probe eines Commentar zu Hamlet. Programm. Bern-
burg, ... 1848
Gervinus, G. G.: Shakespeare. [3te Auflage, 1862.] Leipzig, .. 1849–1850
Job: Beitrag zur Erklärung des Hamlet. Annaberg [Thimm], ... 1850
Sievers, Dr E. W.: Hamlet für weitere Kreise bearbeitet. Leipzig, .. 1851
Vehse, Dr Eduard: Shakespeare als Protestant, Politiker, Psycholog, und
Dichter. Hamlet, vol. i, p. 293; vol. ii, p. 141. Hamburg, ... 1851
Bräker, Ulrich: Etwas über Shakespeare, 1780. [In 'Der arme Mann im
Tockenburg,' herausgegeben von Eduard Bülow. S. 405.] Leipzig, .. 1852
Delius, N.: Shakespeare Lexicon. 2te Abth. Zur Textkritik und Erklärung
der einzelnen Dramen. S. 176. Bonn, ... 1852
Tieck: Dramaturgische Blätter. Zum ersten Male vollständig gesammelt.
Bemerkungen über einige Charaktere in Hamlet, &c. Erster Theil, S. 243.
Leipzig [first printed in 1826], ... 1852
Eckardt, Dr Ludwig: Vorlesungen über Hamlet. Aarau, ... 1853
Jänicke: Eine französische Abhandlung über Hamlet. Programm. Grau-
denz, ... 1853
Wölffel, Dr H.: Ueber Hamlet. Album des lit. Vereins, p. 62. Nürnberg, .. 1853
Levinstein, S.: Faust and Hamlet. Berlin [Thimm], ... 1855
Heintze, A.: Versuch einer Parallele zwischen dem sophocleischen Orestes und
dem shakspearischen Hamlet. Oster-Programm. Treptow a. d. R., .. 1856
Hülsmann, Eduard: Shakespeare. Sein Geist und seine Werke, p. 25. Leipzig, 1856
Noiré, Dr Louis: Hamlet. Mainz, ... 1856
Jänicke: Observations sur Hamlet. Potsdam [Cohn MS], ... 1858
Kreyssig, Fr.: Vorlesungen über Shakspeare, vol. ii, p. 215. Berlin [second
edition, 1862], ... 1858
Rohrbach, Carl: Shakespeare's Hamlet. Berlin, ... 1859
Storffrich, D. B.: Psychologische Aufschlüsse über Shakspeare's Hamlet. Bre-
men, ... 1859
Gerth, Prof. Dr A.: Der Hamlet von Shakspeare. Acht Vorlesungen. Leip-
zig, ... 1861
Vischer, Dr Friedr. Theod.: Kritische Gänge. Neue Folge. Hamlet, p. 63.
Zweites Heft. Stuttgart, ... 1861
Meissner, Alfred: Charaktermasken. Die Unschuld der Ophelia. [This is not
a Shakespearian disquisition, but a clever little story, in which the presumptive evidence of Ophelia's guilt comes uncomfortably home to a German
Professor (the father of a very pretty daughter), who was a strong advocate
of Tieck's theory. ED.] Vol. i, p. 149. Leipzig, ... 1862

Schipper, Dr L.: Hamlet. Aesthetische Erläuterung des Hamlet nebst Wider-
legung der Göthe'schen und Gervinus'schen Ansicht über die Idee und den
Haupthelden des Stückes. Münster, ... 1862

Flathe, Prof. Dr J. L. F.: Shakspeare in seiner Wirklichkeit. Erster Theil,
S. 279. Leipzig, ... 1863

Löffler, Dr Karl: Dramatische Charactere. I Hamlet. Leipzig [Thimm], 1863

Cohn, Albert: Shakespeare in Germany in the Sixteenth and Seventeenth Centuries. Berlin and London, ... 1864

Friesen, H. v.: Briefe über Hamlet. Leipzig, ... 1864

Döring, Dr August: Hamlet seinem Grundgedanken und Inhalte nach erläutert. Hamm, ... 1865

Flir, Alois: Briefe über Hamlet. Innsbruck, ... 1865

Hebler, Prof. C.: Aufsätze über Shakespeare, p. 83. [Zweite, beträchtlich
vermehrte, Ausgabe, 1874.] Bern, ... 1865

Klix, Dr G. A.: Andeutungen zum Verständniss von Hamlet. Programm.
Gross-Glogau, ... 1865

Neumann, Prof. Dr Heinrich: Ueber Lear und Ophelia. Breslau, ... 1866

Rümelin, Gustav: Shakespearestudien. [Zweite Auflage, 1874.] Stuttgart, 1866

Schindhelm: Ueber Hamlet. Programm. Coburg, ... 1866

Sievers, Dr E. W.: William Shakspeare. Sein Leben und Dichten, p. 438.
Gotha, ... 1866

Brachvogel, A. E.: Hamlet. Roman. 3 vols. Breslau, ... 1867

Lichtenberg, G. Chr.: Vermischte Schriften. Briefe aus England. [Es sind
dieselben zuerst im deutschen Museum, Jahrgang 1776 und 1778 gedruckt.]
Vol. iii, p. 199. Göttingen, ... 1867

Rodenberg: Hamlet's Grab (Vier Wochen in Helsingör). Berlin [Thimm], 1867

Schirmer, Adolph: Ein weiblicher Hamlet. Novelle. Wien und Leipzig, 1867

Petri, Moritz, Pastor: Zur Einführung Shakespeare's in die christliche Familie,
p. 7. Hannover, ... 1868

Schmalfeld, Prof. Dr: Einige Bemerkungen zur Elektra des Sophokles mit
einem Seitenblick auf Hamlet. Programm. Eisleben, ... 1868

Tschischwitz, Dr Benno: Shakspere-Forschungen. I Hamlet, vorzugsweise
nach historischen Gesichtspuncten erläutert. Halle, ... 1868

Tschischwitz, Dr Benno: Hamlet in sinem Verhältniss zur Gesammtbildung,
namentlich zur Theologie und Philosophie der Elizabeth-Zeit. Halle
[Thimm].

Saupe, Prof. Julius: Hamlet für obere Gymnasial-Classen erläutert. Programm.
Gera, ... 1868

Freymann, Julie: Kritik der Schiller-, Shakespeare-, und Göthe'schen Frauencharaktere, p. 117. Giessen, ... 1869

Goltz, Bogumil: Vorlesungen. Shakespeare's Genius und die Tragödie Hamlet. Berlin [2d edition, 1871], ... 1869

Heussi, Dr J. W.: Hamlet erklärt. Parchim, ... 1869

Karpf, Carl: Τὸ τί ἦν εἶναι. Die Idee Shakespeare's und deren Verwirklichung.
Sonnettenerklärung und Analyse des Hamlet. Hamburg, ... 1869

Genée, Rudolph: Geschichte der Shakespeare'schen Dramen in Deutschland.
Leipzig, ... 1870

Grabbe, Christ. Dietr.: Sämmtliche Werke. Hamlet, vol. ii, p. 429. Leipzig 1870

Zimmermann, Robert: Studien und Kritiken zur Philosophie und Aesthetik.
Hamlet und Vischer, p. 77. [Zuerst in d. Wiener Zeitung, No. 238, u. ff.
1861.—Cohn.] 1870
Zimmermann, W. F.: Die Hamlet-Tragödie, in philosophischer Beleuchtung
(2 Feuilletons der Berliner Brille). [Thimm], ... 1870
Kreyssig, Fr.: Shakespeare-Fragen, p. 112. Leipzig, ... 1871
Ludwig, Otto: Shakespeare-Studien, p. 138. Leipzig, ... 1871
Stedefeld, G. F.: Hamlet, ein Tendenzdrama Sheakspeare's gegen die skep-
tische und kosmopolitische Weltanschauung des Montaigne. Berlin, .. 1871
Benedix, Dr R.: Die Shakespearomanie. Zur Abwehr. p. 273. Stuttgart, 1873
König, Wilhelm: Shakespeare als Dichter, Weltweiser und Christ. Durch
Erläuterung von vier seiner Dramen und eine Vergleichung mit Dante, p. 1.
Leipzig, ... 1873
Schmidt, Julian: Neue Bilder aus dem Geistigen Leben unserer Zeit, p. 1.
Leipzig, ... 1873
Bodenstedt, Fr.: Shakespeare's Frauencharaktere. Ophelia, p. 91. Berlin, .. 1874
Marbach, Oswald: Hamlet. Tragödie nach Shakespeare. Leipzig, ... 1874
Schmidt, Dr Alexander: Plan und Probe eines Wörterbuchs zu Shakespeare.
(Programm der städtischen Realschule.) Königsberg i. Pr. 1871
Schmidt, Dr Alexander: Lexicon zu Shakespeare's Werken, vol. i, A–L.
Berlin, ... 1874
Schmidt, Dr Alexander: Vol. ii, M–Z. Berlin. [This work alone places all
of us under deep and lasting obligations to Germany.—ED.] 1875
Werder, Karl: Vorlesungen über Hamlet gehalten an der Universität zu Ber-
lin. (Zuerst im Wintersemester 1859–1860, zuletzt 1871–1872.) Berlin, .. 1875
Elze, Karl: William Shakespeare, p. 406. Halle, ... 1876
Friesen, Herm. von: Will. Shakspere's Dramen von 1601 bis zum Schlusse
seiner Laufbahn, p. 45. Wien, ... 1876
Liebau, Gustav: Erzählungen aus der Shakespeare-Welt, p. 81. Berlin, .. 1876
Struve, Dr Heinrich von: Hamlet, eine Charakterstudie. Weimar, ... 1876
Baumgart, Dr Hermann: Die Hamlet-Tragödie und ihre Kritik. Königs-
berg i. Pr. 1877

PERIODICALS, MAGAZINES, &c.

Archiv für das Studium der neueren Sprachen: Kritische Beleuchtung der
Ansicht Tieck's über den Monolog in Hamlet, Act III, sc. i, nebst Erör-
terungen über den Charakter Hamlets und die Tendenz der Tragödie,
von Dr A. L. Ziel. No. V, vol. ii, part i, page 1. Elberfeld, ... 1847
Studien zu Shakespeare's Hamlet, von Hoffmann. No. VI, vol. ii, part ii,
page 373. Zweiter Artikel, vol. iv, p. 56. Elberfeld, ... 1848
Noch ein Wort über Hamlets Monolog: Sein oder nicht sein! u. s. w., von
Dr Hüser. No. VIII, vol. iv, part ii, page 328, ... 1848
Zur Grundlegung einer neuen Auffassung des Hamlet, von Sievers in Gotha,
vol. vi, p. i. Braunschweig, ... 1849
Hamlet, &c., von Dr C. L. W. Francke. Eine Beurtheilung von V. F. L.
Petri, vol. vi, p. 89. Braunschweig, ... 1849
Jung, Albert: Hamlet. Eine Schicksalstragödie Herrig's Archiv, vol. xxvii.
[Thimm.]

Archiv für das Studium der neueren Sprachen (continued):
Ueber Hamlet, von Prof. Dr L. Eckardt, vol. xxxi, p. 93, ... 1862
Eine Beurtheilung über Gerth's Der Hamlet von Shakespeare, von (L.), vol.
xxxi, p. 323, ... 1862
Shakspeare hat behufs seines danischen Prinzen Hamlet die nordische
Geschichte des 16 Jahrhunderts studirt, von A. Gerth, vol. xxxvi, p. 53.
[Thimm.] 1864
Blätter für litterarische Unterhaltung: Ueber Hamlet und seine Beurtheiler:
Goethe, Schlegel und Tieck von K. H. Hermes, ... 1827
Ueber Hamlet. Von Immermann. No. 111, ... 1842
Hamlet in Paris, No. 16, ... 1868
Berliner Modenspiegel: Ueber Hamlet. Von J. L. Klein, ... 1846
Berlinische Zeitung: Hamlet in Deutschland. Sonntag's Beilage, Nos. 24,
25, ... 1870
Deutscher Jahrbücher: Die Beleuchtungston in Shakespeare's Dramen. Von
J. L. Klein, vol. ii, p. 457. Berlin, ... 1862
Deutscher Sprachwart: Hamlet's Monolog, ' To be, or not to be,' nach den
verschiedensten Lesarten und Uebersetzungen betrachtet und verglichen.
Max. Moltke. Vol. iii, No. 18, ... 1868
Deutsches Museum: Hamlet's Aufenthalt in Wittenberg. Von Kästner [Cohn.] 1777
Shakespeare-Studien: I, Hamlet. Von Gustav Hauff. No. 5. Februar, 1866
Shakespeare-Studien: VI, Hamlet. Von Karl Köstlin (3 Artikel, Nos. 29,
30, 31) [Thimm.] 1869
Dramaturgische Blätter: Hamlet. Prof. H. Th. Rötscher. First Year, 2
Heft. Dresden. [Cohn.] 1865
Worin liegt die Anziehungskraft zwischen Hamlet und Ophelia? Prof.
Rötscher. First Year, 2 Heft. [Cohn.] .. ..
Wie muss die Unterredung Hamlets mit Ophelien am Schluss des berühmten
Monologs, ' Sein oder nicht sein,' aufgefasst und behandelt werden? First
Year, First Part. [Cohn.] 1865
Worin liegt der Zauber, welchen Hamlet auf allen Klassen der Gesellschaft
ausübt? [Cohn.] 1867
Evangelische Kirchen-Zeitung: Hamlet eine pastorale Studie. Von M. P.
Nos. 40–43, ... 1864
Hamlet und Macbeth, 18 September, No. 75. Berlin, ... 1872
Die Gegenwart: Ein Paar Bemerkungen über Frl. v. Vestvali's und Herrn
Türschmann's Hamlet, No. 21. Berlin, ... 1873
Illustrirtes Familien Journal: Hamlet in der Eisenhütte, von Arnold Schloen-
bach. Nos. 9, 10, ... 1864
Internationale Revue: Faust und Hamlet, Eine ästhet. Parallele. Von C.
A. von Reichlin-Meldegg. No. 2 (August) [Cohn.] 1866
Jahrbücher der Deutschen Shakespeare-Gesellschaft: Hamlet in Frankreich.
Elze. i, 86, ... 1865
Die Charakterzüge Hamlets, nachgezeichnet von einem Nichtphilosophen.
ii, 16, ... 1867
Die realistische Shakespeare-Kritik und Hamlet. Friedr. Theod. Vischer.
ii, 132, ... 1867
Eine Charakteristik Hamlets fur Schauspieler. W. Rossmann. ii, 305, .. 1867
Hamlet's ' mortal coil.' Elze. ii, 362, ... 1867

Jahrbücher der Deutschen Shakespeare-Gesellschaft (continued) :
Die Gemüthsseite des Hamlet-Charakters. W. Oehlmann. iii, 205, .. 1868
Glosse zu III, ii, 18–23. H. von Friesen. iii, 229, ... 1868
Die Sh. Forschungen von Tschischwitz beurtheilt von Oehlmann. iii, 223, 1868
Literarische Uebersicht. Der Hamlet von Tschischwitz. iv, 369, .. 1869
Die Fechtscene in Hamlet. H. von Freisen. iv, 374, ... 1869
Zu Hamlet, I, ii, 187, 188. F. Lüders. iv, 385, ... 1869
Ueber das Dunkel in der Hamlet-Tragödie. H. A. Werner. v, 6, .. 1870
Literarische Besprechung : Carl Karpf, Tò τί ἦν εἶναι. H. Ulrici. v, 335, 1870
Miscellen : Zu Hamlet, I, ii, 187, 188. L. Schmitz. v, 364, ... 1870
Miscellen : Zu Hamlet, V, ii, 140. H. von Friesen. v, 365, ... 1870
Die Grundzüge der Hamlet-Tragödie. Wilhelm König. vi, 277, .. 1871
In dem Monolog, III, i, 59, statt ' a sea of troubles,' schlägt Dr Braunfels
  vor : ' a *set* of troubles.' H. Ulrici. vi, 354, ... 1871
Der Hamlet von Arthur Meadows, beurtheilt. vii, 362, ... 1872
Dr Latham's Two Dissertations, &c., beurtheilt. viii, 363, ... 1873
Chettle's Hoffmann und Shakespeare's Hamlet. Dr Delius. ix, 166, .. 1874
Der Hamlet von Marbach, beurtheilt. ix, 322, ... 1874
Hamlet in Spanien. Caroline Michaëlis. x, 311, ... 1875
Irving as Hamlet by Russell, reviewed. x, 376, ... 1875
Tyler's Philosophy of Hamlet reviewed. x, 377, ... 1875
Der Hamlet von Hackh, beurtheilt. x, 378, ... 1875
Elze's note on ' four hours,' II, ii, 159. xi, 288, ... 1876
  "   "   ' suit of sables,' III, ii, 122. xi, 294, ... 1876
  "   "   ' Convert his gyves to graces,' IV, vii, 21. xi, 295, .. 1876
  "   "   ' Vaughan,' V, i, 58. xi, 296, ... 1876
  "   "   ' dog will have his day,' V, i, 280. xi, 297, ... 1876
Jahrbücher für dramat. Kunst : Erklärung der Tragödie Prinz Hamlet von
  seinem Freunde Horatio. [Cohn MS.] 1848
Jahrbücher für Literatur : Ein Wort über Hamlet, vol. xxviii [Cohn], .. 1824
Journal für Theater, &c. : Etwas über Garves Abhandlung über d. Karakter
  Hamlets, vol. ii. Hamburg, ... 1797
Ein paar Worte über Einiges in Hamlet, vol. iii [Cohn], ... 1797
Leipziger Zeitung : Hamlet in Gera, von Dr W. Buchholz, 27 February, .. 1873
Literatur und Theater-Zeitung. [Enthaltend Nachrichten über die Aufführung
  Hamlets auf deutschen Bühnen.—Thimm.] Berlin, ... 1778–1779
Die Literatur : Hamlet in Rom. Von R. Vischer. Nos. 33, 34, 35, 36 [Cohn], 1874
Lit. Blätter : Der Hamlet des Ducis und der des Shakespeare. Von Ed.
  Gans. Stuttgart [Cohn], ... 1826
Literarische Kritische Blätter : Hamlet, ein literar-historisch kritischer Ver-
  such. Von W. Bernhardi [Cohn]. Hamburg, ... 1857
Magazin für die Literatur des Auslandes : Die Englischen Hamletdarsteller
  von der Zeit Shakespeares bis zur Zeit Lessings. 1. Burbage, Davenant,
  und Betterton. 2. David Garrick und J. P. Kemble. Nos. 29, 30 [Cohn], 1869
Morgenblatt : Briefe über Hamlet. Nos. 60–80 [Cohn], ... 1812
Dawison's Hamlet. No. 26,   " 1863
Shakespeare und Hamlet. Nos. 25 und 26,   " 1864
Hamlet. Von H. M. Zaubitz. Nos. 5, 6,   " 1859
Hamlet. Von Karl Silberschlag. Nos. 46, 47, ... 1860

Morgenblatt (continued):

Ueber Hamlet's Wahnsinn [Cohn], ... 1811
Hamlet auf der französischen Bühne. 1848
Nachtwachen: Briefe von Hamlet und Ophelia. Von Bonaventura (pseud.
    Schelling) [Cohn]. 1805
Neorama: Hamlet. Von F. W. Carové. Vol. i, p. 21. Leipzig, ... 1838
Neue Jahrb. f. Philologie und Pädagogie: Beurtheilung über den Delius'schen
    Hamlet von T. Mommsen, vol. lxxii, p. 57; p. 89; p. 139, ... 1854
Das neue Reich: Shakespeare als Kenner des Wahnsinns. Von M. Bernays,
    No. 29 [Cohn], ...: 1871
Olla Potrida: [See p. 117 of this Volume. Ed.]
Orion: Ist Hamlet toll? Studie von Karl Grun, p. 365. Mai, No. II, p. 440,
    June. Hamburg, ... 1863
Phöbus: Fragmente über Shakespeare. Hamlet und Lear, No. 9. Von A.
    Müller. Herausgegeben von Kleist u. Müller. [Cohn MS.] 1808
Preussische Jahrbücher: Ueber Hamlet. Von Karl Werder, Nov., Dec.
    [Cohn], ... 1873
    Hamlet, von Herman Grimm, vol. xxxv, part iv, p. 385, April. Berlin, .. 1875
Preussische Zeitung: Hamlet. Klein [Cohn MS.] 1859
Shakespeare-Museum: Hamlet in Leipzig, vol. i, 15, ... 1870
    Pole-axe oder Polacks, Ob Streitaxt oder Polacken. Max. Moltke, p. 23,
    37, 56.
    Ob Hamlet wahnsinnig war, p. 32.
    Anmerkung zu Hamlet, I, v, ' celestial bed.' Modlinger, p. 64.
    Herder's translation of IV, v, 1–195, p. 79.
    Amlethiana: 1. Das Urbild des Hamlet. 2. Hamlet auf der deutschen
    Bühne. 3. Friederich Haase als Hamlet. 4. Deutschland ist Hamlet
    von Freiligrath, p. 88.
Stimmen der Zeit: Recension über Hamlet, 17 Heft, p. 198. [Thimm.] .. 1861
Sibyllinische Blätter: aus der neuesten Zeit, 1 Heft. Tieck und Hamlet, von
    A. Beyfuss. Berlin [Cohn], ... 1826
Unterhaltungen am häuslichen Heerd: Ueber Hamlet. Eine Skizze. Von
    Prof. H. Hettner in Jena. [In a foot-note by the Editor, Karl Gutzkow,
    there is a comparison between Emil Devrient and Dawison in the part of
    Hamlet. Ed.] Vol. ii, p. 88. Leipzig, ... 1853–54
Urania: Ueber Shakespeare's Philosophie, Besonders in Hamlet, von E. A.
    H. Clodius, s. 275. Leipzig, ... 1820
Die Vossische Zeitung: Hamlet in Deutschland. Nos. 23 und 24.[—Thimm,] 1870
Westermann's Monatshefte: Hamlet. Friedr. Bodenstedt. October [Cohn], 1865
Zeitung f. d. elegante Welt: Ueber Hamlet (translated from the *Journal des
    Débats*) [Cohn], ... 1827

ANONYMOUS

Grundlinien zu einer Theorie der Schauspielkunst. Eine Analyse des Hamlet,
    p. 115. Leipzig [by F. H. von Einsiedel.—Thimm], ... 1797
Die Schauspielerschule. Quedlinburg, ... 1810

Scnerzius, Dr (pseud.): Prinz Hammelfett und Prinzessin Pumphelia. Eine Trauerposse für Polichinell- und Kasperltheater. Neu-Ruppin [Cohn], .. n. d.

TRANSLATIONS OF ENGLISH COMMENTATORS

Wagner, A.: Skottowe's Shakespeare's Leben, &c. Leipzig, ... 1824
Wagner, A.: Mrs Jameson's Shakespeare's Weibliche Karaktere. Leipzig [Thimm], ... 1834
Ortlepp, E.: Ditto. Stuttgart, ... 1840
Schücking, Levin: Ditto. Bielefeld [Thimm], ... 1840
Künzel, H.: Lamb's Erzählungen. Darmstadt [Thimm], ... ¸. 1842
Dralle, F. W.: Ditto. Stuttgart [Thimm], ... 1843
Frese, Dr Julius: Ergänzungsband zu allen englischen Ausgaben, und zur Schlegel-Tieckshen Uebersetzung. [Collier's *Notes and Emendations.*]
Berlin, ... 1853
Leo, F. A.: [Collier's *Notes and Emendations.*] Berlin, ... 1853
William Shakespeare. Von Sr. Eminenz Cardinal Wiseman. Köln, .. 1865

FRENCH TRANSLATIONS

COLLECTED WORKS

Le Tourneur: Shakespeare traduit de l'Anglais, vol. v, ... 1779
Guizot: Œuvres complètes de Shakspeare, vol. i. [Septième édition, 1868.] 1821
Avenel: Œuvres dramatiques, corrigées et enrichies de notes, &c. [Bohn.] 1822
Bruguière et Chénédollé: Chefs-d'œuvres; traduits conformément au tèxte original en vers blancs, en vers rimés et en prose, ... 1826
Havard, J. A.: Œuvres dramatiques, précédés des notices historiques et lit-téraires sur sa Vie, &c., Paris, ... 1834
Nisard, Lebas et Fouinet: Chefs-d'œuvre de Shakespeare, Othello, Hamlet et Macbeth, avec des*imitations en vers Français par MM. de Vigny, Des-champs, &c., et des notices critiques, &c. par D. O'Sullivan. [No date, but, according to Thimm], ... 1837
Michel, Francisque: Œuvres complètes, traduction entièrement revue sur le texte Anglais, vol. ii, Paris. [Deuxième éd. 1855; cinquième éd. 1869.] 1839
Laroche, Benjamin: Œuvres complètes. Traduction nouvelle, vol. ii. [Cinquième édition, 1869.] 1842
Hugo, Francois-Victor: Œuvres complètes. [This edition contains a transla-tion of the Q_1 and Q_2.] [Troisième éd. 1873.] 1862
Montégut, Émile: Œuvres complètes, ... 1867-70

SEPARATE TRANSLATIONS

De la Place : Hamlet traduit (Théâtre anglais) [Bohn], ... 1745–1748
Ducis : Hamlet. Tragédie imitée de l'Anglais en vers Français, ... 1769
Hamlet. Tragédie en cinq Actes, conformé aux Réprésentations donées à
  Paris [Bohn], ... 1827
Hamlet en Anglais et en Français, avec la description du costume, &c., .. 1833
Lainé, Jules : Une Scène d'Hamlet, traduite en vers [Bohn], ... 1836
O'Sullivan : Hamlet. Nouvelle édition, ... 1843
Dumas et Paul Meurice : Hamlet, drame en cinq Actes, en vers, ... 1848
Garal, Pierre : Traduit, ... 1862
Châtelain, Le Chevalier de : Hamlet traduit en vers Français. Londres, .. 1864
Brown, A. : Hamlet [in English, with a French translation of a few of the
  Variorum notes.] Truchy's edition, ... 1865
Cayrou, Alcide : Chefs-d'œuvre de Shakespeare. Traduction en vers. Avec
  une Introduction de M. Mézières, vol. i, ... 1876
Guillemot, Ernest : Hamlet par Shakespeare. Paris, .. -. .. .. n. d.

COMMENTARIES, ESSAYS, &c.

Voltaire : Théâtre complèt, vol. ii, p. 201. Geneve, ... 1768
Baretti, Joseph : Discours sur Shakespeare et sur Mons. de Voltaire. London,
  and Paris, ... 1777
Duval, A. : Shakespeare et Addison mis en comparaison, ou imitation en vers
  des Monologues de Hamlet et de Caton [Bohn], ... 1786
Barante, A. G : Sur Hamlet. [Mélanges, vol. iii, 1833—Bohn.] 1824
Duport, M. P. : Essais littéraires sur Shakespeare, &c., vol. i, p. 1. 1828
Villemain, A. E. : Cours de Littérature, ... 1829
Chateaubriand : Essai sur la Littérature anglaise. [Second edition, London,
  1837.] 1836
Girardin : Cours de la Littérature dramatique, vol. i, ... 1852
Guizot : Shakespeare et son Temps, ... 1852
Lacroix, A. : De l'Influence de Shakespeare sur le Théâtre française jusqu'a
  nos jours. Bruxelles, ... 1855
Mézières, A. : Shakespeare, ses Œuvres et ses Critiques. Paris, ... 1861
Hugo, Victor : William Shakespeare, ... 1864
Meurice : Théâtre. Hamlet, Falstaff, Parolles d'après Shakespeare. [Thimm.] 1864
Courdaveaux, V. : Caractères et Talents, p. 287. 1867
Dumas, A. : Étude sur Hamlet, ... 1867
Thomas, Ambroise : Hamlet. Opéra en cinq Actes, par Michel Carré et Jules
  Barbier ; musique de Amb. Thomas, ... 1868
Châtelain, Le Chevalier de : Shakespearian Gems in French and English Set-
  tings. London, ... 1869
Gomont, H. : Encore sur Hamlet, à propos d'Hamlet et à côté d'Hamlet, .. 1874
Mayow, M. : Hamlet. Revue des Cours littéraires de la France et de l'Étran-
  ger, 5me année. [Cohn.]

DUTCH TRANSLATIONS

Brunius, B.: William Shakespeare's Tooneelspeelen. [A Variorum edition, which is pronounced 'indifferent' in Bohn's *Lowndes*.] Vol. i, ... 1778
Kok, A. S.: Shakespeare's Dramatische Werken. Vertaald en toegelicht. Eerste Aflevering. Amsterdam, ... n. d. ? 1871

Separate Translations:
Brandt, G.: De veinzende Torquatus. [Imitation of Hamlet—Thimm.] Amsterdam, ... 1720
Cambon, M. G. de: Hamlet gevolgt naar het Franch, en naar het Engelsch. 1779
Zubli, Ambrosius Justus: Hamlet, Treurspel. Gevolgd naar het Fransche van den Heere Ducis. Amsteldam. [Tweede Druk, 1790; Zesde Druk, 1845.] 1786
Roorda van Eysinga, P. P.: Hamlet Treurspel uit het Engelsch in den vorm van het oorspronkelyke vertaald. Met Inleiding en Aanhangsel van J. Moulin. Kampen [Bohn], ... 1836
Susan, S.: Hamlet, Historisch Treurspel. Ten Gebruike der Gymnasia. [English text, with Dutch and English notes.—ED.] Deventer, .. 1849
Loffelt, A. C.: Hamlet. Uitgegeven en Verklaard. [English text, with Dutch notes.—ED.] Utrecht, ... 1867

Shakespeariana:
Van Hemert, Paulus: Lektuur bij het Ontbijt en de Thetafel, p. 45. Amsterdam. ['Reading for the Breakfast (!) and the Tea-Table.'—ED.] .. 1808
Van den Bergh, L., Ph. C.: Bloemlezing uit de dramatische Werken van Shakspeare in Nederduitsche Dichtmaat overgebracht, p. 98. Amsterdam, 1834
Sijbrandi, Klaas: Verhandeling over Vondel en Shakspeare als treurspel-dichters, p. 163. Haarlem, ... 1841
Moltzer, Mr H. E.: Het Drupje Boosheid. Groningen, ... 1870

Periodicals, Magazines, &c.:
De Nederlandsche Spectator: Het nieuwste over den Hamlet van Shakespeare, door J. d. W. v. C., 14 April. [Ook No. II, 12 Mei.] .. 1860
Het oordeel van Ed. Devrient over de rol van Hamlet. 8 October, .. 1864
Eene vernieuwde opvoering van den Hamlet, door A^a. 14 Juni, .. 1873
Rossi als Hamlet, door A. C. Loffelt. 8 April, ... 1876
De Gids: [Review of Loffelt's edition of Hamlet by] A. S. Kok, p. 568. Dec. Amsterdam, ... 1867
De Levensbode: Hamlet-Bespiegelingen, naar aanleiding der nieuwe Nederlandsche uitgave [Loffelt's] [door J. Van Vloten?]. Derde Deel. I, p. 51. Deventer, ... 1868
Dr Tijdspiegel: Shakespeare's Hamlet en Bara's *Herstelde Vorst.* Door A. C. Loffelt, p. 474–503. 1 Mei, ... 1869

ITALIAN

SWEDISH

SPANISH

Hamlet. Tragedia de Guillermo Shakespeare. Traducida é ilustrada con la vida del autor y notas críticas. Por Inarco Celenio. [Moratin—Bohn.] Madrid, ... 1798
Clark, Jaime: Obras de Shakspeare. Version Castellana, vol. v. Madrid, n. d.
Coello, Carlos: El Príncipe Hamlet, drama trágico-fantástico en tres Actos y en verso, inspirado por el Hamlet de Shakespeare. Madrid, ... 1872

BOHEMIAN

Musea Královstvi Českého. Dramatická díla Williama Shakespeara: Hamlet, princ Dánský. Přeložil Jos. Jiři Kolar. Díl i. Praze, ... 1856
Malý, Jakub: Kytice z dramatických spisů Williama Shakespeara. Praze, .. 1873

WELSH

Hamlet, Tywysog Denmarc. Gan W. Shakespeare. Cyfieithiad Buddugol yn Eisteddfod Llandudno, 1864. Wrexham, ... 1865

GREEK

ΑΜΛΕΤΟΣ, ΒΑΣΙΛΟΠΑΙΣ ΤΗΣ ΔΑΝΙΑΣ, ΤΡΑΓΩΔΙΑ ΤΟΥ ΑΓΓΛΟΥ ΣΑΙΞΠΗΡΟΥ. Ἐνστίχως μεταφρασθεῖσα, Ὑπὸ ΙΩΑΝΝΟΥ Η. ΠΕΡΒΑΝΟ-ΓΛΟΥ. ΔΡΟΣ, τῆς φιλοσοφίας. ΕΝ ΑΘΗΝΑΙΣ, ΤΥΠΟΙΣ Χ. ΝΙΚΟΛΑΙΔΟΥ ΦΙΛΑΔΕΛΦΕΩΣ. (Παρὰ τῇ Πύλῃ τῆς Ἀγορᾶς, ἀριθ. 420.) 1858

[I have also two Russian translations, which are beyond the resources of our printers; and Bohn mentions a Polish translation published in Warsaw, 1862. There is also a Hungarian translation, published in 1824. ED.]

FINIS

INDEX TO VOLUME II—APPENDIX

A CATALOG OF SELECTED
DOVER BOOKS
IN ALL FIELDS OF INTEREST

A CATALOG OF SELECTED DOVER
BOOKS IN ALL FIELDS OF INTEREST

CONCERNING THE SPIRITUAL IN ART, Wassily Kandinsky. Pioneering work by father of abstract art. Thoughts on color theory, nature of art. Analysis of earlier masters. 12 illustrations. 80pp. of text. 5⅜ x 8½.   23411-8 Pa. $4.95

ANIMALS: 1,419 Copyright-Free Illustrations of Mammals, Birds, Fish, Insects, etc., Jim Harter (ed.). Clear wood engravings present, in extremely lifelike poses, over 1,000 species of animals. One of the most extensive pictorial sourcebooks of its kind. Captions. Index. 284pp. 9 x 12.   23766-4 Pa. $14.95

CELTIC ART: The Methods of Construction, George Bain. Simple geometric techniques for making Celtic interlacements, spirals, Kells-type initials, animals, humans, etc. Over 500 illustrations. 160pp. 9 x 12. (USO)   22923-8 Pa. $9.95

AN ATLAS OF ANATOMY FOR ARTISTS, Fritz Schider. Most thorough reference work on art anatomy in the world. Hundreds of illustrations, including selections from works by Vesalius, Leonardo, Goya, Ingres, Michelangelo, others. 593 illustrations. 192pp. 7⅛ x 10¼.   20241-0 Pa. $9.95

CELTIC HAND STROKE-BY-STROKE (Irish Half-Uncial from "The Book of Kells"): An Arthur Baker Calligraphy Manual, Arthur Baker. Complete guide to creating each letter of the alphabet in distinctive Celtic manner. Covers hand position, strokes, pens, inks, paper, more. Illustrated. 48pp. 8¼ x 11.   24336-2 Pa. $3.95

EASY ORIGAMI, John Montroll. Charming collection of 32 projects (hat, cup, pelican, piano, swan, many more) specially designed for the novice origami hobbyist. Clearly illustrated easy-to-follow instructions insure that even beginning papercrafters will achieve successful results. 48pp. 8¼ x 11.   27298-2 Pa. $3.50

THE COMPLETE BOOK OF BIRDHOUSE CONSTRUCTION FOR WOODWORKERS, Scott D. Campbell. Detailed instructions, illustrations, tables. Also data on bird habitat and instinct patterns. Bibliography. 3 tables. 63 illustrations in 15 figures. 48pp. 5¼ x 8½.   24407-5 Pa. $2.50

BLOOMINGDALE'S ILLUSTRATED 1886 CATALOG: Fashions, Dry Goods and Housewares, Bloomingdale Brothers. Famed merchants' extremely rare catalog depicting about 1,700 products: clothing, housewares, firearms, dry goods, jewelry, more. Invaluable for dating, identifying vintage items. Also, copyright-free graphics for artists, designers. Co-published with Henry Ford Museum & Greenfield Village. 160pp. 8¼ x 11.   25780-0 Pa. $10.95

HISTORIC COSTUME IN PICTURES, Braun & Schneider. Over 1,450 costumed figures in clearly detailed engravings—from dawn of civilization to end of 19th century. Captions. Many folk costumes. 256pp. 8⅜ x 11¾.   23150-X Pa. $12.95

STICKLEY CRAFTSMAN FURNITURE CATALOGS, Gustav Stickley and L. & J. G. Stickley. Beautiful, functional furniture in two authentic catalogs from 1910. 594 illustrations, including 277 photos, show settles, rockers, armchairs, reclining chairs, bookcases, desks, tables. 183pp. 6½ x 9¼. 23838-5 Pa. $11.95

AMERICAN LOCOMOTIVES IN HISTORIC PHOTOGRAPHS: 1858 to 1949, Ron Ziel (ed.). A rare collection of 126 meticulously detailed official photographs, called "builder portraits," of American locomotives that majestically chronicle the rise of steam locomotive power in America. Introduction. Detailed captions. xi + 129pp. 9 x 12. 27393-8 Pa. $13.95

AMERICA'S LIGHTHOUSES: An Illustrated History, Francis Ross Holland, Jr. Delightfully written, profusely illustrated fact-filled survey of over 200 American lighthouses since 1716. History, anecdotes, technological advances, more. 240pp. 8 x 10¾. 25576-X Pa. $12.95

TOWARDS A NEW ARCHITECTURE, Le Corbusier. Pioneering manifesto by founder of "International School." Technical and aesthetic theories, views of industry, economics, relation of form to function, "mass-production split" and much more. Profusely illustrated. 320pp. 6⅛ x 9¼. (USO) 25023-7 Pa. $9.95

HOW THE OTHER HALF LIVES, Jacob Riis. Famous journalistic record, exposing poverty and degradation of New York slums around 1900, by major social reformer. 100 striking and influential photographs. 233pp. 10 x 7⅞. 22012-5 Pa. $11.95

FRUIT KEY AND TWIG KEY TO TREES AND SHRUBS, William M. Harlow. One of the handiest and most widely used identification aids. Fruit key covers 120 deciduous and evergreen species; twig key 160 deciduous species. Easily used. Over 300 photographs. 126pp. 5⅜ x 8½. 20511-8 Pa. $3.95

COMMON BIRD SONGS, Dr. Donald J. Borror. Songs of 60 most common U.S. birds: robins, sparrows, cardinals, bluejays, finches, more arranged in order of increasing complexity. Up to 9 variations of songs of each species. Cassette and manual 99911-4 $8.95

ORCHIDS AS HOUSE PLANTS, Rebecca Tyson Northen. Grow cattleyas and many other kinds of orchids—in a window, in a case, or under artificial light. 63 illustrations. 148pp. 5⅜ x 8½. 23261-1 Pa. $5.95

MONSTER MAZES, Dave Phillips. Masterful mazes at four levels of difficulty. Avoid deadly perils and evil creatures to find magical treasures. Solutions for all 32 exciting illustrated puzzles. 48pp. 8¼ x 11. 26005-4 Pa. $2.95

MOZART'S DON GIOVANNI (DOVER OPERA LIBRETTO SERIES), Wolfgang Amadeus Mozart. Introduced and translated by Ellen H. Bleiler. Standard Italian libretto, with complete English translation. Convenient and thoroughly portable—an ideal companion for reading along with a recording or the performance itself. Introduction. List of characters. Plot summary. 121pp. 5¼ x 8½. 24944-1 Pa. $3.95

TECHNICAL MANUAL AND DICTIONARY OF CLASSICAL BALLET, Gail Grant. Defines, explains, comments on steps, movements, poses and concepts. 15-page pictorial section. Basic book for student, viewer. 127pp. 5⅜ x 8½. 21843-0 Pa. $4.95

BRASS INSTRUMENTS: Their History and Development, Anthony Baines. Authoritative, updated survey of the evolution of trumpets, trombones, bugles, cornets, French horns, tubas and other brass wind instruments. Over 140 illustrations and 48 music examples. Corrected and updated by author. New preface. Bibliography. 320pp. 5⅜ x 8½. 27574-4 Pa. $9.95

HOLLYWOOD GLAMOR PORTRAITS, John Kobal (ed.). 145 photos from 1926-49. Harlow, Gable, Bogart, Bacall; 94 stars in all. Full background on photographers, technical aspects. 160pp. 8⅜ x 11¼. 23352-9 Pa. $12.95

MAX AND MORITZ, Wilhelm Busch. Great humor classic in both German and English. Also 10 other works: "Cat and Mouse," "Plisch and Plumm," etc. 216pp. 5⅜ x 8½. 20181-3 Pa. $6.95

THE RAVEN AND OTHER FAVORITE POEMS, Edgar Allan Poe. Over 40 of the author's most memorable poems: "The Bells," "Ulalume," "Israfel," "To Helen," "The Conqueror Worm," "Eldorado," "Annabel Lee," many more. Alphabetic lists of titles and first lines. 64pp. $5\frac{3}{16}$ x 8¼. 26685-0 Pa. $1.00

PERSONAL MEMOIRS OF U. S. GRANT, Ulysses Simpson Grant. Intelligent, deeply moving firsthand account of Civil War campaigns, considered by many the finest military memoirs ever written. Includes letters, historic photographs, maps and more. 528pp. 6⅛ x 9¼. 28587-1 Pa. $12.95

AMULETS AND SUPERSTITIONS, E. A. Wallis Budge. Comprehensive discourse on origin, powers of amulets in many ancient cultures: Arab, Persian Babylonian, Assyrian, Egyptian, Gnostic, Hebrew, Phoenician, Syriac, etc. Covers cross, swastika, crucifix, seals, rings, stones, etc. 584pp. 5⅜ x 8½. 23573-4 Pa. $15.95

RUSSIAN STORIES/PYCCKNE PACCKA3bl: A Dual-Language Book, edited by Gleb Struve. Twelve tales by such masters as Chekhov, Tolstoy, Dostoevsky, Pushkin, others. Excellent word-for-word English translations on facing pages, plus teaching and study aids, Russian/English vocabulary, biographical/critical introductions, more. 416pp. 5⅜ x 8½. 26244-8 Pa. $9.95

PHILADELPHIA THEN AND NOW: 60 Sites Photographed in the Past and Present, Kenneth Finkel and Susan Oyama. Rare photographs of City Hall, Logan Square, Independence Hall, Betsy Ross House, other landmarks juxtaposed with contemporary views. Captures changing face of historic city. Introduction. Captions. 128pp. 8¼ x 11. 25790-8 Pa. $9.95

AIA ARCHITECTURAL GUIDE TO NASSAU AND SUFFOLK COUNTIES, LONG ISLAND, The American Institute of Architects, Long Island Chapter, and the Society for the Preservation of Long Island Antiquities. Comprehensive, well-researched and generously illustrated volume brings to life over three centuries of Long Island's great architectural heritage. More than 240 photographs with authoritative, extensively detailed captions. 176pp. 8¼ x 11. 26946-9 Pa. $14.95

NORTH AMERICAN INDIAN LIFE: Customs and Traditions of 23 Tribes, Elsie Clews Parsons (ed.). 27 fictionalized essays by noted anthropologists examine religion, customs, government, additional facets of life among the Winnebago, Crow, Zuni, Eskimo, other tribes. 480pp. 6⅛ x 9¼. 27377-6 Pa. $10.95

FRANK LLOYD WRIGHT'S HOLLYHOCK HOUSE, Donald Hoffmann. Lavishly illustrated, carefully documented study of one of Wright's most controversial residential designs. Over 120 photographs, floor plans, elevations, etc. Detailed perceptive text by noted Wright scholar. Index. 128pp. 9¼ x 10¾. 27133-1 Pa. $11.95

THE MALE AND FEMALE FIGURE IN MOTION: 60 Classic Photographic Sequences, Eadweard Muybridge. 60 true-action photographs of men and women walking, running, climbing, bending, turning, etc., reproduced from rare 19th-century masterpiece. vi + 121pp. 9 x 12. 24745-7 Pa. $10.95

1001 QUESTIONS ANSWERED ABOUT THE SEASHORE, N. J. Berrill and Jacquelyn Berrill. Queries answered about dolphins, sea snails, sponges, starfish, fishes, shore birds, many others. Covers appearance, breeding, growth, feeding, much more. 305pp. 5¼ x 8¼. 23366-9 Pa. $9.95

GUIDE TO OWL WATCHING IN NORTH AMERICA, Donald S. Heintzelman. Superb guide offers complete data and descriptions of 19 species: barn owl, screech owl, snowy owl, many more. Expert coverage of owl-watching equipment, conservation, migrations and invasions, etc. Guide to observing sites. 84 illustrations. xiii + 193pp. 5⅜ x 8½. 27344-X Pa. $8.95

MEDICINAL AND OTHER USES OF NORTH AMERICAN PLANTS: A Historical Survey with Special Reference to the Eastern Indian Tribes, Charlotte Erichsen-Brown. Chronological historical citations document 500 years of usage of plants, trees, shrubs native to eastern Canada, northeastern U.S. Also complete identifying information. 343 illustrations. 544pp. 6½ x 9¼. 25951-X Pa. $12.95

STORYBOOK MAZES, Dave Phillips. 23 stories and mazes on two-page spreads: Wizard of Oz, Treasure Island, Robin Hood, etc. Solutions. 64pp. 8¼ x 11. 23628-5 Pa. $2.95

NEGRO FOLK MUSIC, U.S.A., Harold Courlander. Noted folklorist's scholarly yet readable analysis of rich and varied musical tradition. Includes authentic versions of over 40 folk songs. Valuable bibliography and discography. xi + 324pp. 5⅜ x 8½. 27350-4 Pa. $9.95

MOVIE-STAR PORTRAITS OF THE FORTIES, John Kobal (ed.). 163 glamor, studio photos of 106 stars of the 1940s: Rita Hayworth, Ava Gardner, Marlon Brando, Clark Gable, many more. 176pp. 8⅜ x 11¼. 23546-7 Pa. $14.95

BENCHLEY LOST AND FOUND, Robert Benchley. Finest humor from early 30s, about pet peeves, child psychologists, post office and others. Mostly unavailable elsewhere. 73 illustrations by Peter Arno and others. 183pp. 5⅜ x 8½. 22410-4 Pa. $6.95

YEKL and THE IMPORTED BRIDEGROOM AND OTHER STORIES OF YIDDISH NEW YORK, Abraham Cahan. Film Hester Street based on Yekl (1896). Novel, other stories among first about Jewish immigrants on N.Y.'s East Side. 240pp. 5⅜ x 8½. 22427-9 Pa. $6.95

SELECTED POEMS, Walt Whitman. Generous sampling from *Leaves of Grass*. Twenty-four poems include "I Hear America Singing," "Song of the Open Road," "I Sing the Body Electric," "When Lilacs Last in the Dooryard Bloom'd," "O Captain! My Captain!"–all reprinted from an authoritative edition. Lists of titles and first lines. 128pp. 5$\frac{5}{16}$ x 8¼. 26878-0 Pa. $1.00

THE BEST TALES OF HOFFMANN, E. T. A. Hoffmann. 10 of Hoffmann's most important stories: "Nutcracker and the King of Mice," "The Golden Flowerpot," etc. 458pp. 5⅜ x 8½.   21793-0 Pa. $9.95

FROM FETISH TO GOD IN ANCIENT EGYPT, E. A. Wallis Budge. Rich detailed survey of Egyptian conception of "God" and gods, magic, cult of animals, Osiris, more. Also, superb English translations of hymns and legends. 240 illustrations. 545pp. 5⅜ x 8½.   25803-3 Pa. $13.95

FRENCH STORIES/CONTES FRANÇAIS: A Dual-Language Book, Wallace Fowlie. Ten stories by French masters, Voltaire to Camus: "Micromegas" by Voltaire; "The Atheist's Mass" by Balzac; "Minuet" by de Maupassant; "The Guest" by Camus, six more. Excellent English translations on facing pages. Also French-English vocabulary list, exercises, more. 352pp. 5⅜ x 8½.   26443-2 Pa. $9.95

CHICAGO AT THE TURN OF THE CENTURY IN PHOTOGRAPHS: 122 Historic Views from the Collections of the Chicago Historical Society, Larry A. Viskochil. Rare large-format prints offer detailed views of City Hall, State Street, the Loop, Hull House, Union Station, many other landmarks, circa 1904-1913. Introduction. Captions. Maps. 144pp. 9⅜ x 12¼.   24656-6 Pa. $12.95

OLD BROOKLYN IN EARLY PHOTOGRAPHS, 1865-1929, William Lee Younger. Luna Park, Gravesend race track, construction of Grand Army Plaza, moving of Hotel Brighton, etc. 157 previously unpublished photographs. 165pp. 8⅞ x 11¾.   23587-4 Pa. $13.95

THE MYTHS OF THE NORTH AMERICAN INDIANS, Lewis Spence. Rich anthology of the myths and legends of the Algonquins, Iroquois, Pawnees and Sioux, prefaced by an extensive historical and ethnological commentary. 36 illustrations. 480pp. 5⅜ x 8½.   25967-6 Pa. $10.95

AN ENCYCLOPEDIA OF BATTLES: Accounts of Over 1,560 Battles from 1479 B.C. to the Present, David Eggenberger. Essential details of every major battle in recorded history from the first battle of Megiddo in 1479 B.C. to Grenada in 1984. List of Battle Maps. New Appendix covering the years 1967-1984. Index. 99 illustrations. 544pp. 6½ x 9¼.   24913-1 Pa. $16.95

SAILING ALONE AROUND THE WORLD, Captain Joshua Slocum. First man to sail around the world, alone, in small boat. One of great feats of seamanship told in delightful manner. 67 illustrations. 294pp. 5⅜ x 8½.   20326-3 Pa. $6.95

ANARCHISM AND OTHER ESSAYS, Emma Goldman. Powerful, penetrating, prophetic essays on direct action, role of minorities, prison reform, puritan hypocrisy, violence, etc. 271pp. 5⅜ x 8½.   22484-8 Pa. $7.95

MYTHS OF THE HINDUS AND BUDDHISTS, Ananda K. Coomaraswamy and Sister Nivedita. Great stories of the epics; deeds of Krishna, Shiva, taken from puranas, Vedas, folk tales; etc. 32 illustrations. 400pp. 5⅜ x 8½.   21759-0 Pa. $12.95

BEYOND PSYCHOLOGY, Otto Rank. Fear of death, desire of immortality, nature of sexuality, social organization, creativity, according to Rankian system. 291pp. 5⅜ x 8½.   20485-5 Pa. $8.95

A THEOLOGICO-POLITICAL TREATISE, Benedict Spinoza. Also contains unfinished Political Treatise. Great classic on religious liberty, theory of government on common consent. R. Elwes translation. Total of 421pp. 5⅜ x 8½. 20249-6 Pa. $9.95

CATALOG OF DOVER BOOKS

MY BONDAGE AND MY FREEDOM, Frederick Douglass. Born a slave, Douglass became outspoken force in antislavery movement. The best of Douglass' autobiographies. Graphic description of slave life. 464pp. 5⅜ x 8½. 22457-0 Pa. $8.95

FOLLOWING THE EQUATOR: A Journey Around the World, Mark Twain. Fascinating humorous account of 1897 voyage to Hawaii, Australia, India, New Zealand, etc. Ironic, bemused reports on peoples, customs, climate, flora and fauna, politics, much more. 197 illustrations. 720pp. 5⅜ x 8½. 26113-1 Pa. $15.95

THE PEOPLE CALLED SHAKERS, Edward D. Andrews. Definitive study of Shakers: origins, beliefs, practices, dances, social organization, furniture and crafts, etc. 33 illustrations. 351pp. 5⅜ x 8½. 21081-2 Pa. $8.95

THE MYTHS OF GREECE AND ROME, H. A. Guerber. A classic of mythology, generously illustrated, long prized for its simple, graphic, accurate retelling of the principal myths of Greece and Rome, and for its commentary on their origins and significance. With 64 illustrations by Michelangelo, Raphael, Titian, Rubens, Canova, Bernini and others. 480pp. 5⅜ x 8½. 27584-1 Pa. $9.95

PSYCHOLOGY OF MUSIC, Carl E. Seashore. Classic work discusses music as a medium from psychological viewpoint. Clear treatment of physical acoustics, auditory apparatus, sound perception, development of musical skills, nature of musical feeling, host of other topics. 88 figures. 408pp. 5⅜ x 8½. 21851-1 Pa. $11.95

THE PHILOSOPHY OF HISTORY, Georg W. Hegel. Great classic of Western thought develops concept that history is not chance but rational process, the evolution of freedom. 457pp. 5⅜ x 8½. 20112-0 Pa. $9.95

THE BOOK OF TEA, Kakuzo Okakura. Minor classic of the Orient: entertaining, charming explanation, interpretation of traditional Japanese culture in terms of tea ceremony. 94pp. 5⅜ x 8½. 20070-1 Pa. $3.95

LIFE IN ANCIENT EGYPT, Adolf Erman. Fullest, most thorough, detailed older account with much not in more recent books, domestic life, religion, magic, medicine, commerce, much more. Many illustrations reproduce tomb paintings, carvings, hieroglyphs, etc. 597pp. 5⅜ x 8½. 22632-8 Pa. $12.95

SUNDIALS, Their Theory and Construction, Albert Waugh. Far and away the best, most thorough coverage of ideas, mathematics concerned, types, construction, adjusting anywhere. Simple, nontechnical treatment allows even children to build several of these dials. Over 100 illustrations. 230pp. 5⅜ x 8½. 22947-5 Pa. $8.95

DYNAMICS OF FLUIDS IN POROUS MEDIA, Jacob Bear. For advanced students of ground water hydrology, soil mechanics and physics, drainage and irrigation engineering, and more. 335 illustrations. Exercises, with answers. 784pp. 6⅛ x 9¼. 65675-6 Pa. $19.95

SONGS OF EXPERIENCE: Facsimile Reproduction with 26 Plates in Full Color, William Blake. 26 full-color plates from a rare 1826 edition. Includes "TheTyger," "London," "Holy Thursday," and other poems. Printed text of poems. 48pp. 5¼ x 7. 24636-1 Pa. $4.95

OLD-TIME VIGNETTES IN FULL COLOR, Carol Belanger Grafton (ed.). Over 390 charming, often sentimental illustrations, selected from archives of Victorian graphics—pretty women posing, children playing, food, flowers, kittens and puppies, smiling cherubs, birds and butterflies, much more. All copyright-free. 48pp. 9¼ x 12¼. 27269-9 Pa. $7.95

PERSPECTIVE FOR ARTISTS, Rex Vicat Cole. Depth, perspective of sky and sea, shadows, much more, not usually covered. 391 diagrams, 81 reproductions of drawings and paintings. 279pp. 5⅜ x 8½. 22487-2 Pa. $7.95

DRAWING THE LIVING FIGURE, Joseph Sheppard. Innovative approach to artistic anatomy focuses on specifics of surface anatomy, rather than muscles and bones. Over 170 drawings of live models in front, back and side views, and in widely varying poses. Accompanying diagrams. 177 illustrations. Introduction. Index. 144pp. 8⅜ x11¼. 26723-7 Pa. $8.95

GOTHIC AND OLD ENGLISH ALPHABETS: 100 Complete Fonts, Dan X. Solo. Add power, elegance to posters, signs, other graphics with 100 stunning copyright-free alphabets: Blackstone, Dolbey, Germania, 97 more–including many lower-case, numerals, punctuation marks. 104pp. 8⅛ x 11. 24695-7 Pa. $8.95

HOW TO DO BEADWORK, Mary White. Fundamental book on craft from simple projects to five-bead chains and woven works. 106 illustrations. 142pp. 5⅜ x 8. 20697-1 Pa. $5.95

THE BOOK OF WOOD CARVING, Charles Marshall Sayers. Finest book for beginners discusses fundamentals and offers 34 designs. "Absolutely first rate . . . well thought out and well executed."–E. J. Tangerman. 118pp. 7¾ x 10⅝. 23654-4 Pa. $7.95

ILLUSTRATED CATALOG OF CIVIL WAR MILITARY GOODS: Union Army Weapons, Insignia, Uniform Accessories, and Other Equipment, Schuyler, Hartley, and Graham. Rare, profusely illustrated 1846 catalog includes Union Army uniform and dress regulations, arms and ammunition, coats, insignia, flags, swords, rifles, etc. 226 illustrations. 160pp. 9 x 12. 24939-5 Pa. $10.95

WOMEN'S FASHIONS OF THE EARLY 1900s: An Unabridged Republication of "New York Fashions, 1909," National Cloak & Suit Co. Rare catalog of mail-order fashions documents women's and children's clothing styles shortly after the turn of the century. Captions offer full descriptions, prices. Invaluable resource for fashion, costume historians. Approximately 725 illustrations. 128pp. 8⅜ x 11¼. 27276-1 Pa. $11.95

THE 1912 AND 1915 GUSTAV STICKLEY FURNITURE CATALOGS, Gustav Stickley. With over 200 detailed illustrations and descriptions, these two catalogs are essential reading and reference materials and identification guides for Stickley furniture. Captions cite materials, dimensions and prices. 112pp. 6½ x 9¼. 26676-1 Pa. $9.95

EARLY AMERICAN LOCOMOTIVES, John H. White, Jr. Finest locomotive engravings from early 19th century: historical (1804–74), main-line (after 1870), special, foreign, etc. 147 plates. 142pp. 11⅜ x 8¼. 22772-3 Pa. $10.95

THE TALL SHIPS OF TODAY IN PHOTOGRAPHS, Frank O. Braynard. Lavishly illustrated tribute to nearly 100 majestic contemporary sailing vessels: Amerigo Vespucci, Clearwater, Constitution, Eagle, Mayflower, Sea Cloud, Victory, many more. Authoritative captions provide statistics, background on each ship. 190 black-and-white photographs and illustrations. Introduction. 128pp. 8⅞ x 11¾. 27163-3 Pa. $14.95

THE INFLUENCE OF SEA POWER UPON HISTORY, 1660–1783, A. T. Mahan. Influential classic of naval history and tactics still used as text in war colleges. First paperback edition. 4 maps. 24 battle plans. 640pp. 5⅜ x 8½. 25509-3 Pa. $14.95

THE STORY OF THE TITANIC AS TOLD BY ITS SURVIVORS, Jack Winocour (ed.). What it was really like. Panic, despair, shocking inefficiency, and a little heroism. More thrilling than any fictional account. 26 illustrations. 320pp. 5⅜ x 8½. 20610-6 Pa. $8.95

FAIRY AND FOLK TALES OF THE IRISH PEASANTRY, William Butler Yeats (ed.). Treasury of 64 tales from the twilight world of Celtic myth and legend: "The Soul Cages," "The Kildare Pooka," "King O'Toole and his Goose," many more. Introduction and Notes by W. B. Yeats. 352pp. 5⅜ x 8½. 26941-8 Pa. $8.95

BUDDHIST MAHAYANA TEXTS, E. B. Cowell and Others (eds.). Superb, accurate translations of basic documents in Mahayana Buddhism, highly important in history of religions. The Buddha-karita of Asvaghosha, Larger Sukhavativyuha, more. 448pp. 5⅜ x 8½. 25552-2 Pa. $12.95

ONE TWO THREE . . . INFINITY: Facts and Speculations of Science, George Gamow. Great physicist's fascinating, readable overview of contemporary science: number theory, relativity, fourth dimension, entropy, genes, atomic structure, much more. 128 illustrations. Index. 352pp. 5⅜ x 8½. 25664-2 Pa. $8.95

ENGINEERING IN HISTORY, Richard Shelton Kirby, et al. Broad, nontechnical survey of history's major technological advances: birth of Greek science, industrial revolution, electricity and applied science, 20th-century automation, much more. 181 illustrations. ". . . excellent . . ."–*Isis.* Bibliography. vii + 530pp. 5⅜ x 8¼. 26412-2 Pa. $14.95

DALÍ ON MODERN ART: The Cuckolds of Antiquated Modern Art, Salvador Dalí. Influential painter skewers modern art and its practitioners. Outrageous evaluations of Picasso, Cézanne, Turner, more. 15 renderings of paintings discussed. 44 calligraphic decorations by Dalí. 96pp. 5⅜ x 8½. (USO) 29220-7 Pa. $4.95

ANTIQUE PLAYING CARDS: A Pictorial History, Henry René D'Allemagne. Over 900 elaborate, decorative images from rare playing cards (14th–20th centuries): Bacchus, death, dancing dogs, hunting scenes, royal coats of arms, players cheating, much more. 96pp. 9¼ x 12¼. 29265-7 Pa. $12.95

MAKING FURNITURE MASTERPIECES: 30 Projects with Measured Drawings, Franklin H. Gottshall. Step-by-step instructions, illustrations for constructing handsome, useful pieces, among them a Sheraton desk, Chippendale chair, Spanish desk, Queen Anne table and a William and Mary dressing mirror. 224pp. 8⅛ x 11¼. 29338-6 Pa. $13.95

THE FOSSIL BOOK: A Record of Prehistoric Life, Patricia V. Rich et al. Profusely illustrated definitive guide covers everything from single-celled organisms and dinosaurs to birds and mammals and the interplay between climate and man. Over 1,500 illustrations. 760pp. 7½ x 10⅛. 29371-8 Pa. $29.95

Prices subject to change without notice.